CONSCIOUS HISTORY

THE LITTMAN LIBRARY OF
JEWISH CIVILIZATION

*Life Patron*
Colette Littman

Dedicated to the memory of
Louis Thomas Sidney Littman
*who founded the Littman Library for the love of God
and as an act of charity in memory of his father*
Joseph Aaron Littman
*and to the memory of*
Robert Joseph Littman
*who continued what his father Louis had begun*
יהא זכרם ברוך

'*Get wisdom, get understanding:
Forsake her not and she shall preserve thee*'
prov. 4: 5

*The Littman Library of Jewish Civilization is a registered UK charity
Registered charity no. 1000784*

# CONSCIOUS HISTORY

*Polish Jewish Historians before the Holocaust*

NATALIA ALEKSIUN

London
**The Littman Library of Jewish Civilization**
in association with Liverpool University Press

The Littman Library of Jewish Civilization
Registered office: 14th floor, 33 Cavendish Square, London W1G 0PW

in association with Liverpool University Press
4 Cambridge Street, Liverpool L69 7ZU, UK
www.liverpooluniversitypress.co.uk/littman

Managing Editor: Connie Webber

Distributed in North America by Longleaf Services
116 S Boundary St, Chapel Hill, NC 27514, USA

First published in hardback 2021
First published in paperback 2025

© Natalia Aleksiun 2021

All rights reserved.
No part of this publication may be reproduced,
stored in a retrieval system, or transmitted, in any form or by
any means, without the prior permission in writing of
the Littman Library of Jewish Civilization

This book is sold subject to the condition that it shall not, by way
of trade or otherwise, be lent, re-sold, hired out or otherwise circulated
without the publisher's prior consent in any form of binding or cover
other than that in which it is published and without a similar condition
including this condition being imposed on the subsequent purchaser

Catalogue records for this book are available from the
British Library and the Library of Congress

ISBN 978–1–802072–00–6

Publishing co-ordinator: Janet Moth
Copy-editing: Laura Macy
Proof-reading: Mark Newby
Index: Sarah Ereira
Designed and typeset by Pete Russell, Faringdon, Oxon.

# Acknowledgements

THIS BOOK is about a cohort of historians struggling with the challenges of writing Polish Jewish history and trying to carve out a place for themselves and their work as Polish citizens and as Jews. It engages with the consequences of their conviction that history is indispensable for understanding the place of a minority and improving inter-ethnic relations in the Second Polish Republic. Their quest has remained relevant to the ongoing conversation about the contours of Polish history. Indeed, completing this book became an exercise in parallel realities as public discourse in Poland has increasingly borne troubling echoes of the atmosphere to which Jewish historians responded in the 1930s. Given these alarming developments, and the resurgence of nationalism more broadly, I wish this book felt less contemporary.

The book had its origins as a doctoral dissertation at New York University's Skirball Department of Hebrew and Judaic Studies. I am grateful to my teachers, who embraced the idea of a second doctoral degree with a great sense of humour. In particular I wish to thank my adviser, Professor David Engel, for suggesting that I attend his seminar on Jewish historiography when I first arrived at NYU on a Fulbright Fellowship. Nothing has been the same since. I am thankful for the patience and trust he has shown for this project, and for his thought-provoking and challenging discussions and suggestions. Deep thanks go to the members of my Dissertation Committee, Professors Hasia Diner, Samuel Kassow, Marion Kaplan, and Gennady Estraikh, as well as to Professor Antony Polonsky. Their scholarship has been a source of inspiration. Turning a very long dissertation into a book would not have been possible without my colleagues at the Touro College Graduate School of Jewish Studies in New York, and in particular without my dean, Professor Michael Shmidman, whose support and friendship I hope to emulate. I am also grateful to the late Professors Jerzy Tomaszewski, Feliks Tych, and Krystyna Kersten. Furthermore, interwar Poland came alive for me through my conversations with the late Professor Ezra Mendelsohn.

Writing this book took me across three continents as I chased after witnesses, libraries, and archives in Poland, Austria, Ukraine, Israel, and the United States. The process of seeking out personal accounts, institutional records, Jewish journals, and more reflected the rich and complex lives of Polish Jews who wrote and read Polish Jewish history before the Holocaust. This book was made possible by the help and expertise of an international army of archivists and librarians at the national libraries in Warsaw, Vienna, and Jerusalem; the university libraries in

Kraków, Warsaw, Tel Aviv, NYU, and the University of Pennsylvania in Philadelphia; the Ossolineum in Wrocław, the Stefanyk National Science Library in Lviv, the YIVO Institute for Jewish Research in New York, the Hoover Institution in Stanford, the Central Archives for the History of the Jewish People in Jerusalem, the library of the US Holocaust Memorial Museum in Washington DC, the Central Archives of Modern Records and the Archives of the Polish Academy of Sciences in Warsaw, the State Archive of Lviv Oblast, the Central State Historical Archive of Ukraine in Lviv, the university archives in Warsaw and Kraków, and the Diaspora Research Institute at Tel Aviv University in Israel. These men and women helped me find volumes and folders, patiently installed microfilms, and surprised me with scans of materials I could not access in person.

My teachers, mentors, and friends Professors Hasia Diner and Marion Kaplan shared with me their insights and supported me through the long process of revising this manuscript. Professor Szymon Rudnicki shared his material from the Library of the Polish Parliament; Professor Rachel Manekin made part of N. M. Gelber's collection available to me at the Central Archives for the History of the Jewish People; and Professor David Assaf gave me his file concerning the founding of the World Congress of Jewish Studies. Professor Gershon Bacon suggested I investigate the files of the military rabbinate, which led to my discovery of this fascinating collection. Professor David Roskies introduced me to Jewish folklore and supported my research. I am also grateful to Maria Cieśla, Kamil Kijek, Magdalena Kozłowska, Magdalena Matłoka, Adam Ostanek, and Taras Martynenko for their friendship and for helping me with research. I thank David N. Myers for a conversation about Jewish historiography more than a decade ago at the Center for Jewish History in New York. Karen Auerbach made me realize that I did not choose to write about Polish Jewish historians by accident.

This study would not have been possible without the generous doctoral fellowship and travel grants from the Skirball Department of Hebrew and Judaic Studies at New York University. The Aleksander and Alicja Hertz and Professor Bernard Choseed Memorial Fellowships at the YIVO Institute for Jewish Research helped me to carry out research in New York. The Ringelblum Fellowship of the American Society for Jewish Heritage in Poland gave me a chance to work at the Jewish Historical Institute in Warsaw. A research grant from the Touro Graduate School of Jewish Studies sent me to Lviv. A postdoctoral fellowship at the International Institute for Holocaust Research at Yad Vashem enabled me to further explore the experiences of Jewish students at Warsaw University. The spring semester of 2015 spent at the Herbert D. Katz Center for Advanced Judaic Studies at the University of Pennsylvania in Philadelphia and the countless discussions with my colleagues and fellows gave me a chance to fall in love with the project again. I would like to thank the Littman Library of Jewish Civilization, and especially Connie Webber, who took this book under her wing. I am grateful to Janet Moth for patiently guiding it to publication. My editor Laura Macy not only worked tirelessly on the manuscript but also offered generous and humorous advice as it took shape.

I would not have been able to complete this project without the help and encouragement of friends and colleagues who shared their knowledge and offered their support and good humour: Eliyana Adler, Laura Almagor, Gershon Bacon, Agnieszka Baumritter, Giles Bennett, David and Ayala Bigelajzen, Beata Bińko, Alisa Braun, Katerina Čapková, Robert Cherry, Batia Donner, Wika Dorosz, Havi Dreifuss (Ben-Sasson), Sofia Dyak, Katharina Friedla, Regina Fritz, Noga Gilad, Atina Grossmann, François Guesnet, Anna Hájková, Louise and Dieter Hecht, Asaf Kaniel, Eva Kovács, Ewa Koźmińska, Hana Kubátová, Marta Kurkowska-Budzan, Helise Lieberman, Olga Linkiewicz, Anna Lipphardt, Shari Lowin, Iryna Matsevko, Guy Miron, Ewa Nizińska, Wila and Michał Orbach, Annamaria Orla-Bukowska, Miri Paz, Monika and Krzysztof Persak, Eva Plach, Elżunia and Mietek Poran, Dorota and Michał Praszałowicz, Robert M. Shapiro, Bella Szwarcman-Czarnota, Elżbieta Sachs, Marcos Silber, Vincent Slatt, Judith Szapor, Karolina Szymaniak, Hava and Eli Tovel, Katja Vehlow, Tedd Weeks, Hana Wexler, Agnieszka Wierzcholska, Magda Wróbel, Raphael Utz, and Konrad Zieliński. Jerri Sherman especially has been a source of firm support and sound advice.

I am grateful to friends and colleagues who read various partial drafts, and patiently discussed Polish Jewish history with me: Ela Bauer, Elissa Bemporad, Anna Bikont, Jeffrey Blutinger, Michael Brenner, Cyndy Brown, Anna Cichopek-Gajraj, Eli Diner, Ofer Dynes, Glenn Dynner, Steven Feldman, Michal R. Friedman, Krysia Fisher, Harriet Freidenreich, Alexandra Garbarini, Emily Gioielli, Daniel Heller, Brian Horowitz, Agnieszka Ilwicka, Agnieszka Jagodzińska, Marion Kaplan, Kamil Kijek, Magdalena Kozłowska, Rachel Manekin, Sean Martin, Natan Meir, Katarzyna Person, Rebecca Schaeffer, Rivka Schiller, Naomi Seidman, Nancy Sinkoff, Joanna Śliwa, Lisa Silverman, Stephan Stach, Izabela Wagner, and Deborah Yalen. To those who braved the entire manuscript, I am profoundly thankful for their generosity: Imke Hansen, Arthur Kiron, Ilse Josepha Lazaroms, Anna Novikov, Antony Polonsky, and Sarah Zarrow. Writing this book has been an exercise in humility and brought me closer to my historians as I wrote in a language that was not my first. I am grateful to the late Lynn Gordon, who carefully read and reread every chapter and cheerfully encouraged me to instil more life into them.

Finally, I thank my husband and best friend, Shuki Ecker, for encouraging me to look for the people behind the articles and books published in the Second Polish Republic, for helping me to appreciate the intricacies of Galician Jewish history, and for patiently reading multiple drafts. I am grateful to my son Leon for telling me to 'finish the book already'. Finally, I thank my parents, Mira Żelechower and Jan Aleksiun, who supported all my choices, even when they took me far away from them.

*

Parts of this book first appeared in the following: *East European Jewish Affairs*; *Warsaw, the Jewish Metropolis: Essays in Honor of the 75th Birthday of Professor Antony Polonsky*, edited by Glenn Dynner and François Guesnet; *From Breslau to Jerusalem: Rabbinical Seminaries Past, Present and Future*, edited by Guy Miron; *TURIM: Studies in Jewish History and Literature Presented to Dr. Bernard Lander*, edited by Michael A. Shmidman; and the *Simon Dubnow Institute Yearbook and Anti-Semitism Worldwide, 2003–2004*. I am grateful to the publishers for granting permission to use these texts.

# Contents

| | |
|---|---|
| *List of Abbreviations* | x |
| *Note on Transliteration and Names* | xi |
| Introduction | 1 |
| **1.** Historical Beginnings | 13 |
| **2.** The Making of Professional Polish Jewish Historians | 63 |
| **3.** Becoming Polish Mainstream | 109 |
| **4.** Beyond the Ivory Tower | 162 |
| **5.** Themes and Trends of Historical Enquiry | 215 |
| Epilogue | 260 |
| *Bibliography* | 273 |
| *Index* | 313 |

# Abbreviations

| | |
|---|---|
| AAN | Archiwum Akt Nowych, Warsaw |
| AGAD | Archiwum Główne Akt Dawnych, Warsaw |
| APAN | Archiwum Polskiej Akademii Nauk, Warsaw |
| AUJ | Archiwum Uniwersytetu Jagiellońskiego, Kraków |
| AUW | Archiwum Uniwersytetu Warszawskiego, Warsaw |
| AŻIH | Archiwum Żydowskiego Instytutu Historycznego, Warsaw |
| BS | Bibliotecka Sejmowa, Warsaw |
| CAHJP | Central Archives for the History of the Jewish People, Jerusalem |
| CAW | Centralne Archiwum Wojskowe, Warsaw |
| CZA | Central Zionist Archives, Jerusalem |
| DALO | Derzhavnyi arkhiv L'vivs'koyi oblasti (State Archives of Lviv Oblast) |
| DRI | Diaspora Research Institute Archive, Tel Aviv University |
| IRRZ | Dr Zerah Warhaftig Institute for the Research on Religious Zionism, Bar-Ilan University |
| MSZ | Ministerstwo Spraw Zagranicznych |
| MWRiOP | Ministerstwo Wyznań Religijnych i Oświecenia Publicznego |
| PTH | Polskie Towarzystwo Historyczne |
| TsDIAL | Tsentralnyi derzhavnyi istorychnyi arkhiv, m. Lviv (Central State Historical Archive in Lviv) |
| USHMM | United States Holocaust Memorial Museum, Washington DC |

# Note on Transliteration and Names

THE transliteration of Hebrew in this book reflects consideration of the type of book it is, in terms of its content, purpose, and readership. The system adopted therefore reflects a broad approach to transcription, rather than the narrower approaches found in the *Encyclopaedia Judaica* or other systems developed for text-based or linguistic studies. The aim has been to reflect the pronunciation prescribed for modern Hebrew, rather than the spelling or Hebrew word structure, and to do so using conventions that are generally familiar to the English-speaking reader.

In accordance with this approach, no attempt is made to indicate the distinctions between *alef* and *ayin*, *tet* and *taf*, *kaf* and *kuf*, *sin* and *samekh*, since these are not relevant to pronunciation; likewise, the *dagesh* is not indicated except where it affects pronunciation. Following the principle of using conventions familiar to the majority of readers, however, transcriptions that are well established have been retained even when they are not fully consistent with the transliteration system adopted. On similar grounds, the *tsadi*, although generally 'ts', is rendered by 'tz' in such familiar words as barmitzvah. Likewise, the distinction between *ḥet* and *khaf* has been retained, using *ḥ* for the former and *kh* for the latter; the associated forms are generally familiar to readers, even if the distinction is not actually borne out in pronunciation, and for the same reason the final *heh* is indicated too. As in Hebrew, no capital letters are used, except that an initial capital has been retained in transliterating titles of published works (for example, Shulḥan arukh).

Since no distinction is made between *alef* and *ayin*, they are indicated by an apostrophe only in intervocalic positions where a failure to do so could lead an English-speaking reader to pronounce the vowel-cluster as a diphthong—as, for example, in *ha'ir*—or otherwise mispronounce the word. An apostrophe is also used, for the same reason, to disambiguate the pronunciation of other English vowel clusters, as for example in *mizbe'aḥ*.

The *sheva na* is indicated by an *e*—*perikat ol*, *reshut*—except, again, when established convention dictates otherwise.

The *yod* is represented by *i* when it occurs as a vowel (*bereshit*), by *y* when it occurs as a consonant (*yesodot*), and by *yi* when it occurs as both (*yisra'el*).

\*

The historians discussed in this book published in Polish, Hebrew, and Yiddish, and the spelling of their names varied accordingly. Rather than impose a rule that might suit some but not all, I have adopted the version of the name that appears most often in an author's writings.

# INTRODUCTION

IN THE COURSE of my history studies at the University of Warsaw, I asked Henryk Samsonowicz, a faculty member and one of the world's foremost Polish medievalists, for reading recommendations to help me prepare for an exam in the history of the Middle Ages. 'Have you read Bałaban's monograph on Jewish history in Kraków?', he asked. Intrigued, I scribbled down the name, which I had never heard before. A few days later, I searched the card catalogue at the Department of History's library—old entries handwritten with a fountain pen, housed in the drawers of an ageing wooden cabinet—and I discovered a rather impressive section for 'Bałaban, Majer'. Samsonowicz's recommendation proved transformative for me. When I first came to the programme, I had intended to work on nineteenth-century Polish political opposition to Russian rule, and in particular on my favourite failed Polish insurrection: the January uprising of 1863. But as I began reading the works of Majer Bałaban, I was instantly attracted to his colourful, slightly old-fashioned tales of daily life in the Jewish communities in the Polish–Lithuanian Commonwealth, their institutions, merchants, artisans, and rabbis. I found myself drawn to his biography as well, and, gradually, I shifted my focus to Polish Jewish history.

The reading room at the university library in Warsaw, where I subsequently spent countless hours working on my dissertation, was adorned with a black and white photograph of Marceli Handelsman, a formidable scholar and long-time Dean of Humanities at my *alma mater*. An acculturated, Polonized Jew, Handelsman had taught many of the future leading historians enrolled at the university in the late 1930s. As dean, he encouraged scholarship on the history of Jews in the Polish lands and made possible the creation of an academic chair for the study of Polish Jewish history, which was held by Bałaban for over a decade before the outbreak of the Second World War. In Poland, Handelsman's work remains a significant point of departure for students of early modern history and the philosophy and methodology of the field. Although I was not aware of this at the time, in the mid-1980s Bałaban's work also began to appear in Polish bookstores in new editions, and it was being cited with greater frequency by contemporary scholars of Polish and east European Jewish history.[1] Only years later, in the course of my own

---

[1] For example, volume i of *Dzieje Żydów w Krakowie i na Kazimierzu (1304–1868)* was reprinted in Kraków in 1985, and *Historja i literatura żydowska ze szczególnem uwzględnieniem historji Żydów w Polsce* was reprinted in Warsaw in 1982–8. In the 1990s some of Bałaban's work was translated into Hebrew,

research on interwar Polish Jewish historical writing, did I learn that in the 1920s and 1930s there had been a group of Jewish men and women who wrote their dissertations on Polish Jewish history under the guidance of Bałaban, Handelsman, and a few other members of the faculty. For these Jewish students, the personal would become professional: they were Polish Jews who believed academic history could not only help them understand where they came from, but also prove their right as Jews to call Poland 'home'.

In this book I explore the cohort of university-educated Polish Jewish historians active before the Holocaust: their lives and their self-conscious deployment of historical writing. As a collective biography, the book situates the academic and popular work of these historians in the context of the time in which they lived, while resisting the impulse to understand and explain their experiences in the light of the tragic fate that befell many of them and their communities. The interwar period presented its own personal, professional, and communal obstacles to Jewish citizens: the rise of exclusionary nationalism in the new Polish Republic, the frailty of parliamentary democracy, the effects of the economic crisis, and growing threats to Poland's independence. Nonetheless, in 1938 Majer Bałaban, who had entered the profession in the early twentieth century, looked back on his life and his accomplishments with deep and earnest satisfaction:

Some thirty-five years ago, when I began my research on the history of Jews in Poland, I was one of very few, and maybe even in some ways the only [scholar] who dealt with this subject matter. Today we can no longer complain about the lack of people working in the field of Jewish history in Poland, especially among young scholars.[2]

By this time Bałaban had become one of the leading Jewish scholars who had turned to history in order to write a place for their community into the narrative of the new Polish Republic that emerged from the havoc of the First World War. In researching, publishing, and teaching about the past, Polish Jewish historians laboured not only for their own professional standing but also for the future of Polish Jewry—at that time the largest Jewish community in Europe. Within a mere six years of Bałaban's assessment of the development of Polish Jewish history, most of his colleagues and students had perished in the Holocaust. Bałaban himself died in the Warsaw ghetto in 1942. After the war, with the destruction of the Jewish community and the Soviet subjugation of the Polish state, most of those few Polish Jewish historians who had survived abandoned their previous scholarship. They left the academy or worked on other subjects. In the aftermath

including his two-volume *Historja Żydów w Krakowie i na Kazimierzu 1304–1868*, originally published in 1931 and 1936.

[2] Bałaban, 'Najnowsze rozprawy z historii Żydów w Polsce', 1 Jan. 1938, 9.

of the Holocaust, the project of writing the history of Polish Jewry seemingly lost its urgency and relevance. In Poland, it may also have seemed politically unsafe.[3]

The fate of the Second Polish Republic (1918–39) and its Jewish population is well known. In the following chapters I reconstruct the professional trajectories of Jewish scholars, university students, teachers, rabbis, and journalists in the period before the catastrophe. I examine their academic and communal projects, which were founded on the idea that understanding the place that Jews had occupied over many centuries of Polish history would foster legitimacy and acceptance for them in contemporary Poland. I trace the hopes, battles, achievements, and disappointments of this group of young Jewish historians as they struggled to translate their academic work for a broader audience and to promote a political agenda of minority rights and understanding across ethnic and religious lines among citizens of the Second Polish Republic.

The issue of national minorities and their integration into the Polish state was one of the most difficult political questions of the time. Polish Jewish historians believed that the study of history could both help Jewish citizens of the Second Polish Republic feel at home in Poland and promote a genuine acceptance of Jews as part of Polish society and as loyal Polish nationals. Viewing history as a tool in fighting long-held misconceptions and stereotypes about Jews, these historians brought to their study of the Jewish past a sense of political, social, and cultural urgency. In the debate between two visions of Poland—one, a nation state of Catholic Poles (a view championed by Roman Dmowski, ideologue of the rightwing National Democracy movement), the other a multi-ethnic, multinational, and religiously diverse country (the approach advocated by the Polish statesman Józef Piłsudski)—Jewish historians had no choice but to side with Piłsudski's principle of the modernized Polish commonwealth.

Although focusing on this intellectual enterprise, my study extends beyond the academy and the world of historical scholarship to examine both scholarly and popular expressions of the importance of history to Polish Jewish culture in the 1920s and 1930s. It tells the story of how, over the course of twenty years, a group of historians positioned themselves as politically engaged actors and turned their writing into a form of political engagement. Their story begins in 1918, with the collapse of the three empires that had partitioned the Polish–Lithuanian Commonwealth at the end of the eighteenth century and the emergence of an independent Poland from the devastation of the First World War. But we must begin with the background in the late nineteenth century, when Polish statesmen and intellectuals first turned to history in search of an understanding of contemporary Polish–Jewish relations.

[3] See Goldberg, 'Artur Eisenbach'; Nalewajko-Kulikov, 'Three Colors: Grey', 216–26.

This book traces the political and intellectual project of Polish Jewish historians up to its abrupt and tragic end with the outbreak of the Second World War and the Holocaust. I describe the processes through which Jews living in the territory of the Second Polish Republic became Polish Jews in the context of a modern nation state. The book thus engages in a conversation with a growing body of scholarship on the transformation of regional Jewish identities in the new political contexts that emerged in the late nineteenth century and extended to the Second World War.[4] Faced with their minority status, antisemitism, the lack of professional outlets, and their country's own backwardness, these Jewish historians used historical scholarship to make public their Polishness in a republic that was creating itself anew. By analysing this project of community-building on the eve of the Holocaust, I bring a new perspective to interwar Polish Jewish history. For this was a time of high hopes for many Jews, as a system for minority protection was inscribed into Poland's constitution. In addition, this era witnessed Jews' experimentation with their own identities and cultures. Rather than focusing on Jewish politics, I seek to retrieve the lost contours of a Jewish communal consciousness—one forged across numerous divisions.[5] The history studied and written by Jewish men and women became a 'usable Jewish past' for all Polish Jews, regardless of ideology or political affiliation,[6] and available in all the languages Jewish citizens of Poland read, depending on their age, education, gender, class, politics, and region: Polish, Yiddish, Hebrew, German, and Russian. While many of these historians had close ties to secular Yiddishist culture, their work—both academic and popular—was not merely a matter of writing history in Yiddish.[7] They perceived historical scholarship as an essential tool in creating modern Jewish identities, by showing Jewish citizens of the Second Polish Republic to be a community that had been living in the Polish lands throughout the ages.[8]

The rise of nationalism, which had begun decades earlier, and the collapse of the multi-ethnic empires in the First World War, played a significant role in shaping Jewish intellectual aspirations. In the aftermath of the First World War—and without ever moving from their homes—Jews as well as non-Jews who had lived in Galicia, the Pale of Settlement, Congress Poland, and Prussia under the three partitioning powers of the Russian, Austro-Hungarian, and German empires,

[4] See Rechter, *Becoming Habsburg*; Silverman, *Becoming Austrians*; Bemporad, *Becoming Soviet Jews*; Cohen, *Becoming Ottomans*.

[5] Studies on Jewish politics in the Second Polish Republic, both classic and more recent, include Mendelsohn, *Zionism in Poland*; Melzer, *No Way Out*; Rudnicki, *Żydzi w parlamencie II Rzeczypospolitej*.     [6] Roskies, *The Jewish Search for a Usable Past*.

[7] For excellent studies that focus on the importance of Yiddish in Jewish culture and politics in eastern Europe, see Trachtenberg, *The Revolutionary Roots of Modern Yiddish, 1903–1917*; Moss, *Jewish Renaissance in the Russian Revolution*; Weiser, *Jewish People, Yiddish Nation*.

[8] See Anderson, *Imagined Communities*.

found themselves citizens of a new state: the resurrected Polish Republic. In this new political context, Jews would turn to their own history in order to understand their place in the Jewish diaspora. Yet the rise of the nation state and its attendant national identity made the Jewish cultural identity difficult to sustain.

For some Jewish observers, the collapse of the old order was a sign of crisis. Leading Zionist activist Nahum Goldmann bemoaned the loss of a unified east European Jewry, which before the war had constituted 'a reservoir of strength from which emanated the greatest part of Jewish creative energy'. He feared that the politically atomized Jewry of the former Russian empire lacked energy and creative possibilities: 'Instead of a community of five million Jews centred in one territory, new Jewish communities live today in several territories, separated from one another, and therefore deprived of one of the sources of its strength.'[9] Other intellectuals, however, welcomed the very conditions that Goldmann decried. Abraham Ozjasz Thon, a Jewish communal leader and rabbi in Kraków and a Zionist politician and scholar, celebrated what he saw as an opportunity for Polish Jews to make the Polish Republic a new centre of Jewish cultural creativity—in contrast to the thorny fate of assimilation he foresaw for both Russian and American Jews. He argued that Polish Jews were 'destined—both quantitatively and qualitatively—to lead world Jewry' and that they would soon be called to the task.[10] In his eyes, the promising future of Polish Jewry grew out of the community's deep historical roots.

Many Jewish scholars in interwar Poland shared Thon's view, and they strove to inspire in their Jewish audiences a sense of belonging and an appreciation of their distinctiveness as Polish Jews. Theirs was a perspective founded in optimism—in both Polish and Jewish terms. For example, Jewish historians insisted that Poland was unique in that it had seen the development of Jewish political autonomy and separate Jewish institutions during the early modern period, before the partitions of the Polish–Lithuanian Commonwealth in the late eighteenth century. Now, in the post-partition period, they believed that Polish Jewry had surpassed German Jewry in vitality, reflecting notions of communal authenticity that German Jewish intellectuals themselves had begun to articulate.[11] More broadly, Polish Jews also thought of themselves as different and superior to assimilated Jews in other communities. They favourably noted the existence of Poland's autonomous Jewish institutions, presenting the country's Jewish cultural legacy as equal to, or even surpassing, Polish (Catholic) culture. Hence, the development of Polish Jewish historiography was part of a larger, non-Jewish discourse about Poland's exceptionalism that stated that Polish history would furnish a model of

[9] Goldmann, 'Naród żydowski w dobie kryzysu światowego', 171.
[10] Thon, 'Wstęp', in Schiper, Tartakower, and Hafftka (eds.), *Żydzi w Polsce Odrodzonej*, i. 17.
[11] Sinkoff, *Out of the Shtetl*, 168–202; Efron, *German Jewry and the Allure of the Sephardic*, 231–7.

political moderation and cultural efflorescence for the citizens of the Second Polish Republic.

The biographies of the Jewish men and women who pursued the study of Polish Jewish history reflect to a great extent the time and place in which they grew up, studied, wrote, and taught. As Czesław Miłosz cautions us, 'Biographies are like seashells; not much can be learned from them about the mollusk that once lived inside them ... The value of biographies, then, is solely that they allow one to more or less re-create the era in which a given life was lived.'[12] Working with the traces of that turbulent era of Jewish history, I delve into the biographies of Polish Jews who were engaged in an exploration of their communal past. I discuss the hopes and ambitions of several renowned historians—Majer Bałaban, Ignacy Schiper, Mojżesz Schorr, Raphael Mahler, Filip Friedman, and Emanuel Ringelblum—and draw on the work of others, such as Bela Mandelsberg and Dawid Wurm, who perished at a young age in the Holocaust and whose research has until now remained unknown beyond a small circle of specialists. Rather than as individual historians, I analyse these figures as a group, a perspective that facilitates a nuanced examination of their collective enterprise: the development of a new conceptual framework for the history of Polish Jewry. How did these historians, who were products both of traditional Jewish communities and of modern universities, define their mission? How did they hope to practise their craft and turn it to the service of the quest for civil rights? How did they use history to reach both Jewish and non-Jewish audiences? The effort to write conscious Jewish history is a European Jewish phenomenon tied contextually to the state's 'modernization'. Building on the intellectual efforts of the earlier projects of studying Judaism by German Jews committed to the study of Judaism (Wissenschaft des Judentums) and east European authors who engaged in examining Jewish texts from a more traditional perspective (ḥokhmat yisra'el),[13] these men and women raised questions as Polish Jews and engaged with the fragile republicanism of the new state.[14]

The Jewish men and women who are portrayed in this book found personal and collective redemption in the writing of history. They were born and raised in different parts of eastern Europe, some in traditional Yiddish-speaking homes and some in middle-class Polish-speaking ones. Most of them attended Polish universities having come from diverse backgrounds. Driven by the promises of modernity, these east European Jews believed in progress, enlightenment, and rationality. They took advantage of a university education in Warsaw, Kraków, Wilno, Lwów, and Vienna. At these universities, they adopted history as their

---

[12] Miłosz, *Miłosz's ABC's*, 60.

[13] See Brenner, *Prophets of the Past*, 21–4; Feiner, 'Nineteenth-Century Jewish Historiography'.

[14] See Myers, 'The Ideology of *Wissenschaft des Judentums*'; Feiner, 'Nineteenth-Century Jewish Historiography'.

scholarly field, and despite obstacles that made it difficult for them as Jews to pursue their studies, they formulated their own research agendas and created their own venues for presenting the results of their work. With graduate degrees in hand, they faced fresh obstacles in the pursuit of academic careers, many finding employment as teachers, journalists, or communal activists rather than within university walls. They drew on a model of historical scholarship created in Galicia—a province in the south-eastern part of the former Polish–Lithuanian Commonwealth—before the First World War, which focused on writing the history of Polish Jewry based on both Jewish and general sources. To meet the exigencies of the newly established Polish state, these historians built on the Galician model to fashion some of the core elements of interwar Polish Jewish public culture, including a pantheon of historical heroes to celebrate and anniversaries to commemorate. Their range of topics included local history, cultural studies, and the examination of encounters between Jews and non-Jews. As public intellectuals, they sought to create a Jewish community acutely aware of its past, its cultural heritage, and its achievements, while working to safeguard the rights of that community in the face of increasing hostility towards Jews in public discourse.

What did they hope to accomplish? Bałaban's colleagues, students, and rivals pursued two related projects: to convince Jews that they were *Polish* Jews rather than merely Jews who happened to live in the newly resurrected Poland, and to make non-Jewish Poles see Jews as an integral part of the new political and social reality. Jewish historians hoped they could change both Jews and Poland through scholarship and rational argument. With their books and articles describing the long and venerable past of Polish Jews, which stretched back to the beginnings of Jewish settlement in the country in the Middle Ages, they believed they could give a voice and a sense of pride to their Jewish audiences, as well as improve Polish–Jewish relations. Combining an apologetic urge and professional standards of scholarship, these historians emphasized the origins of the Jewish presence in Poland, the long relationship between Jews and the Polish state, the history of Polish–Jewish relations, and Jewish attitudes towards the Polish struggle for independence following the partitions.

Significantly, these shared intellectual and socio-political projects of the 1920s did not emerge out of a single ideological framework. The intellectuals, activists, and patrons of the Yiddish Scientific Institute (YIVO) in Wilno, the Institute of Jewish Studies in Warsaw, and the Department of History at the University of Warsaw brought to the study of Polish Jewish history a wide range of ideological commitments. The majority were Zionists of diverse and competing perspectives—from members of the left wing of the Po'alei Zion (Workers of Zion) and General Zionists to the religious Zionist Mizrachi—while others were closely associated with the Jewish socialist party Bund or the Folkist Party. Yet even the

Zionists among these historians, with the understanding of Zionism as a form of diaspora nationalism, employed the past to envision a future in which Jews would be at home in Poland while maintaining a strong Jewish national identity and culture.

The first project—giving a voice and a sense of pride to Polish Jews—succeeded to a remarkable degree. The second—improving Polish–Jewish relations—grew more difficult as the situation of the Jews in Poland deteriorated, especially in the 1930s, when public debate became increasingly permeated by antisemitism. Nevertheless, amid these worsening conditions students continued to pursue research on Polish Jewish history, Polish historical journals published articles and reviewed work by Jewish historians, and liberal intellectuals continued to argue that Jewish intellectual life formed part of Polish scholarship, even if it was carried out in Yiddish.[15] Jewish historians clung tenaciously to history as a source of hope and solace, using their scholarship to argue that Jews had a rightful place in Polish society—that, in essence, they were native to Poland.

Not all Jewish scholars chose to study Polish or general Jewish history, but Polish Jewish history remained a field studied almost exclusively by Jews. As well as addressing their work to both Jews and non-Jews in Poland itself, they also engaged in a transnational dialogue. Researchers investigating Polish Jewish history in Poland formed part of a broad network of Jewish scholars emerging across Europe from different national seedbeds. Their activities illuminate the development of a particular construction of Jewish identity based on a vision of the Jewish past closely intertwined with both the transnational history of diaspora Jewry and Poland's cultural and political heritage. This entailed both innovation and continuity with an earlier nineteenth-century European Jewish historiography that reflected on the history of Jewish religion, which still flourished on the eve of the First World War in both western and eastern Europe.

Compared with existing scholarship on German and Russian Jewish historiography, contemporary historians have neglected the major concerns and practices of their counterparts in interwar Europe's largest Jewish community. Previous research on interwar Polish Jewish historians has focused on reconstructing biographical details, without paying attention to the place these scholars occupied—in general or in Jewish circles of professional historians—in the Second Polish Republic. Moreover, current scholarship has discussed the lives of leading Polish Jewish historians in isolation, often with a hagiographical tone. It has focused on the older generation of scholars, including Bałaban, Schorr, and Schiper, while writing on Ringelblum has dealt primarily with his stunning achievements in the Warsaw ghetto.[16] Scholars and students of east European

---

[15] See Hirschberg, 'Kulturalny ruch żydowski w Wilnie', 2.
[16] On Ringelblum see Kassow, *Who Will Write Our History?*

Jewish history have discussed the emergence of modern historical scholarship in Yiddish, and in particular the significance of YIVO, highlighting those members of the Jewish intelligentsia who supported Jewish national autonomy in Poland while neglecting those who were fluent in Polish and intimately familiar with Polish culture. My study demonstrates the existence of a broader historiographical school that emerged despite the linguistic diversity, a school that, while ideologically diverse, focused specifically on the Polish context. While Polish scholars have recently turned their attention to the question of how Polish historiography treated the subject of Jews in general, and Polish Jews in particular, they have not addressed the question of a separate Polish Jewish historiographical school.[17] This book traces that history.

The first chapter, 'Historical Beginnings', focuses on the foundations of the study of Polish Jewish history in the second half of the nineteenth century. It discusses the emergence of scholarly writing on the history of Jews in the Polish lands and the ideas that drove the development of this new field. It traces the ways in which non-Jewish Polish writers such as Tadeusz Czacki, Wacław Aleksander Maciejowski, and Władysław Smoleński engaged with the subject of the Jewish past in the Polish lands. It shows how their programmes, questions, and biases spurred Polish Jewish authors, such as Aleksander Kraushar and Ludwik Gumplowicz, to bring a historical dimension to their public discussions about the place of the Jews in the Polish lands and to their agenda for recasting Jewish relations with the surrounding society.

The second chapter analyses the academic agenda of professional Jewish historians who received their training before 1918, in the imperial context of Austria–Hungary, at the universities of Lwów, Kraków, and Vienna, and the social and political contexts in which they were active. In the early works of Schorr, Schiper, and Bałaban in the first decade of the twentieth century, a more substantial and critical scholarship on the history of the Jews of Poland emerged. I argue that their understanding of Polish Jewish history was shaped by their immersion in Polish historical writing and by their responses to political developments in Galicia, such as the emergence of the Jewish national movement and the increasingly complex position of the Jewish community in the region in relation to the Polish and Ukrainian national narratives.

The major breakthrough in Polish Jewish historical scholarship, however, came with the rebirth of the sovereign Polish state in 1918 when the Jews were able to create a vibrant and newly diverse modern cultural life. In the third chapter, 'Becoming Polish Mainstream', I trace the trajectories of Jewish scholars in the aftermath of the First World War. In the Second Polish Republic, scholarship by Bałaban, Schiper, Schorr, Mahler, and Ringelblum, among others, crafted a Polish

[17] See Makowski, *Siła mitu*.

Jewish communal narrative that offered the approximately three million Jewish citizens in the new Polish state a unified sense of their past in the Polish lands. Much of their work focused on the history of the relationship between Jewish and non-Jewish cultures across eastern Europe. They delineated the deep roots of the Jewish community in the Polish lands and emphasized the contribution of the Jews to Poland's prosperity. They strove to correct a biased historiography that had been shaped by ignorance of Jewish sources, nationalism, and anti-Jewish prejudice. These Jewish historians shared the belief that history was a crucial tool for the work of answering questions arising in the current situation, as well as for achieving the aspirations of the Jews in the new Polish nation. History provided a model for Jewish cultural autonomy as well as for inter-ethnic relations.[18] Finally, this chapter analyses the struggle of these Jewish historians to get their scholarship included in the broader Polish historiography and examines the difficulties they encountered as Jews in their professional lives. It asks whether Jewish students who entered the universities became part of the country's historical guild, or whether they were forced to create a parallel system of academic institutions.

The fourth chapter, 'Beyond the Ivory Tower', explores the tensions between popular and scholarly writing on Polish Jewish history. It traces the channels through which Polish Jewish historical scholarship reached a broader public in Poland. Although ideologically animated, this historical discourse often served practical political purposes. Polish Jewish historians worked in close relationship with Jewish communities, and they believed that by pursuing a scholarly course they were fulfilling an important social, cultural, and political mission. In particular, a new generation of university-educated rabbis delivered sermons for Jewish schoolchildren and soldiers and participated in public ceremonies commemorating events of Polish Jewish history. These public historians frequently published popular articles (in Yiddish, Polish, or Hebrew) in the Jewish press. Private and state schools for Jewish children commemorated national Polish holidays, taught Polish and Polish Jewish history, and took students on historical tours. Time and again, Jewish representatives at both the local and national level referred to history to strengthen their political claims.

When depicting Jewish history in their textbooks, sermons, popular articles, and public speeches, historians focused on several aspects of the Polish Jewish past. In particular, they detailed the Jewish contribution to Poland's culture and economy throughout the centuries and discussed Jewish loyalty to the Polish

---

[18] In public discussions, various aspects of the situation of the Jewish community, including questions around the economic role, legal status, and political aspirations of Polish Jews, were lumped together under the phrase 'The Jewish Question'. Although the term was used by Polish and Jewish scholars alike, growing antisemitism, especially in the 1930s, gave it an increasingly darker shading, with 'Jewish Question' being used to mean 'Jewish Problem'.

state.[19] The approach taken in these popular historical narratives was not radically different from that of the authors' academic work, relying on similar symbols and commemorating the same heroes of the Jewish past. Yet this engaged scholarship reveals a tension between the objectivity demanded by the historical discipline and the sense of national mission in their civic activism.

The final chapter explores the broad topics and genres of Polish Jewish historiography addressed by historians in the 1920s and 1930s. Among the most important topics repeated in academic and popular contexts were Polish–Jewish relations in the past, with particular attention to the Jewish contribution to the country's economic prosperity and to Poland's struggle for independence, and the internal life of individual Jewish communities, their leaders, and their institutions. When writing about Polish–Jewish relations in previous centuries, and particularly in their accounts of conflict and coexistence, Jewish historians in interwar Poland paid close attention to mutual cultural influences between Jews and non-Jews, attempting to account for instances of friction and anti-Jewish violence. This chapter focuses on the ways in which Jewish historians presented Polish Jewry as a social, cultural, and political entity closely linked with the history of Poland. They raised such issues as historical precedents for Jewish cultural autonomy in the Polish–Lithuanian Commonwealth and Jewish support for the Polish struggle for independence during the partitions as counter-arguments to the calls for limiting Jewish participation in public life during the Second Polish Republic. Polish Jewish historical writing took on a direct political meaning as a response to the treatment of these subjects by contemporaneous Polish historiography.

*

Without a doubt, Polish Jewish historians considered themselves part of the wider historical profession in Poland. They attended Polish universities, participated in conferences for Polish historians, and published in Polish academic journals. Their visions of history, their paths to professionalization, and their academic foci were shaped by the Polish historiographical context. In their understanding of Poland as a historical community, these historians argued that Jews had played an indispensable role and made a crucial contribution to the cultural élan of its capital. Conversely, they believed that the security Jews had enjoyed throughout the centuries was a testament to the country's benevolence and tolerance.

This book engages with the questions raised by historian Yosef Hayim Yerushalmi in *Zakhor: Jewish History and Jewish Memory*, probing within the Polish context his idea that in modern times a secularizing and consciously Jewish

[19] This discourse resembled the German Jewish post-emancipatory use of history. See Sorkin, *The Berlin Haskalah and German Jewish Religious Thought*. But Polish Jewish historians carried it out in the context of the fragile inclusionary project of Poland's non-ethnically Polish minorities in the Second Republic.

intelligentsia takes on history-writing as a profoundly Jewish act.[20] While academic interest in east European Jewish history may shed new light on the broad themes of modernization and secularization, I argue that Polish Jewish historians in the interwar period strove to integrate an academic study of the Jewish past into a community that remained largely traditional or at least intuitively Jewish; the majority of Poland's Jews in the interwar period still lived their lives according to the Jewish calendar, provided their children with a Jewish education, remained concentrated in traditional Jewish professions, and spoke Yiddish at home. Polish Jewish historians of the interwar period did not see their historical work as being in tension with the identity and perspectives of this largely traditional community. Moreover, I contend that they perceived the relationship between the academic study of Jewish history and Jewish communal memory as a challenge rather than a rift.[21]

Polish Jewish historians played a significant role in shaping the consciousness of the largest Jewish community in Europe on the eve of the Holocaust. Examining their contributions to the construction of a Polish Jewish historical narrative sheds new light on the role of the Jewish intelligentsia in interwar Poland, located as it was 'between tradition and assimilation', and provides new insights into questions of assimilation and acculturation on the Continent from the late eighteenth century until the mid-twentieth.[22] And beyond the experiences of the Jewish intellectual elite and their audience, their ideas, tropes, and research methods relate to those of other minority communities in modern nation states.

Polish Jewish historiography was an expression of communal identity. In this way it resembled the role of Jewish historiography in Germany in the nineteenth century. But the political context of the Second Polish Republic gave rise to a distinctive conception of Jewish historiography. Rather than debating the question of secularism, or advocating new approaches to Jewish religious practices, Polish Jewish historians focused on forming new articulations of multi-ethnic Polish national life and Jewish communal existence that continued to reinforce Jewish ethnic identity. Their historical project illuminates the diversity of approaches to the writing of Jewish history. Their dream was not realized, but they made an impact on the generation raised in the Second Polish Republic and on the Polish historiographical tradition. When they dreamt about Poland, they were dreaming as Jews.

[20] Yerushalmi, *Zakhor*, 81–103.

[21] Yet in her review of Yerushalmi's *Zakhor*, Lucy Dawidowicz argued that 'all our great historians have evolved a modern equivalent to prompt collective Jewish consciousness. Driven by a commitment to Jewish survival, they have animated their work with commitment' (Dawidowicz, '*Zakhor*', 115). I am grateful to Nancy Sinkoff for bringing this review to my attention.

[22] See Agnieszka Jagodzińska's brilliant study of the complex cultural project of the Warsaw Jewish intelligentsia, *Pomiędzy*.

## ONE
# HISTORICAL BEGINNINGS

MODERN INTEREST in Jewish history in Poland emerged at a time of acute political crisis, as members of the Polish elite studied the rise of Poland as a regional power in the early modern period and its subsequent collapse at the end of the eighteenth century. They valiantly prepared to fight the battle for Poland's future using the only tools they had: pens and ink. Their approach was inevitably political, and the Jewish community in Polish lands loomed particularly large in their discussions of the country's economic and political reforms. In 1807 Tadeusz Czacki published his *Rosprawa o Żydach* (Treatise on the Jews), the first study of the social and economic aspects of Jewish history in Poland. That same year saw the establishment of the short-lived Duchy of Warsaw, which ushered in new hopes for national revival and presented an opportunity to reflect on the glories and failures of the old Polish state. The status of Jews in the past would now merit renewed consideration, especially given the background of Napoleonic reforms, the prospects of a new constitution, and the question of equality and political rights for the Jewish population.[1]

Czacki considered Jewish history to be important to any broader understanding of the history of the Polish–Lithuanian state. *Rosprawa o Żydach* includes a brief survey of ancient Jewish history, but the main focus is on the origins and legal status of Polish Jewry.[2] In contemporary discussions about the status of the Jewish population, Czacki supported the Enlightenment idea of transforming Jewish subjects into citizens in exchange for their embrace of Polish culture and language and their abandonment of separateness.[3] His interest in the Jewish inhabitants of the Commonwealth was an integral part of his interest in the country's past and his commitment to political, economic, and educational reforms. As Polish Jews were becoming subjects of the Russian, Prussian, and Austrian monarchs, Czacki's treatise raised questions concerning the history of Jewish participation in the

---

[1] Czacki, *Rosprawa o Żydach*. On Czacki, see Knot, 'Tadeusz Czacki'. See also Stanley, 'The Politics of the Jewish Question in the Duchy of Warsaw, 1807–1813'.

[2] For his treatment of Jewish history before the settlement in Poland, see Czacki, *Rosprawa o Żydach*, 2–66.

[3] See Eisenbach, *Z dziejów ludności żydowskiej w Polsce XVIII i XIX wieku*, 52–3. Regarding Czacki's opinion on the 'Jewish Question', see Danowska, 'Poglądy Tadeusza Czackiego na kwestię żydowską'. On Czacki's project of Jewish reform, see Dąbkowski, 'Tadeusz Czacki jako prawnik'.

economic and urban life of the Polish–Lithuanian Commonwealth. His exploration of the Jewish past in the Polish lands was thoroughly rooted in a contemporary project of social and political reform and the search for answers to the collapse of the Commonwealth. Czacki's Polish-language treatise was republished in Poznań, Kraków, and Lwów, and it became an essential textbook on Polish Jewry, frequently cited by both Polish and foreign authors.[4]

It was not until the early 1860s, several decades after Czacki's pioneering text first appeared, that a handful of Polish and Polish Jewish authors began to compile comprehensive histories of the Jews.[5] This generation of intellectuals set out to discuss the role of the Jews in the country's economy, the policies of the kings, the attitude of the nobility, Jewish–Christian relations in Polish lands, and plans for the reform of the status of the Jews. For them, Czacki's work was a seminal reference point.[6]

The establishment of Polish Jewish history as a field of enquiry, also owes a debt to the rise of the Haskalah (Jewish Enlightenment).[7] The advent of the Haskalah in late eighteenth-century western Europe led to a radical change in Jewish intellectual attitudes towards history. Proponents of the Haskalah, the maskilim (sing. maskil), believed that Jews needed to study and reflect on their past as history rather than concentrating on a set of religious beliefs and practices. This shift from a theological approach to a critical one played an essential role in the emergence of Wissenschaft des Judentums in Germany as early as the second decade of the nineteenth century, with its calls for a scholarly approach to Judaism and its historical sources.[8] The emergence of a critical literature on the Jewish past

---

[4] For the various nineteenth-century editions of *Rosprawa* see the bibliography. In 1820, the journal *Pszczoła* issued a call for a history of the Jewish people in Poland. On the reception of Czacki's treatise in the work of Zygmunt Krasiński, see Jerkiewicz, '"Kwestia żydowska" w Królestwie Polskim w latach 1815–1830', 165–9.

[5] See Opalski and Bartal, *Poles and Jews*. See also Pisulińska, *Żydzi w polskiej myśli historycznej doby porozbiorowej (1795–1914)*, 69–93. There is a vast literature on the origins and role of the Polish intelligentsia in the nineteenth century. See Czepulis-Rastenis, 'Klassa umysłowa', 5–24; Jedlicki, *Błędne koło, 1832–1864* and *Jakiej cywilizacji Polacy potrzebują*; Janowski, *Narodziny inteligencji, 1750–1831*; Micińska, *Inteligencja na rozdrożach, 1864–1918*.

[6] See for example Löwensohn, *A Call in Israel* (Heb.), 34, 46, 111. See also the list of Polish and Jewish authors who were using Czacki in studies published between 1818 and 1866 in Harkavy, *Jews and the Language of the Slavs* (Heb.), 12–13. Listed are Krasinski (1818), Malte-Brun and Chodzko (1830), Lubliner (1839), Carmoly (1841), Hollaenderski (1846), Chajes (1847), Weil (1848), Zunz (1859), Sternberg (1860), and Kraushar (1864–6). Graetz also used Czacki in the ninth volume of his *Geschichte der Juden* (1866), referring to Czacki's work in the text (p. 68), and citing Czacki many times (see pp. 66–71, 461–83).

[7] See Feiner, *Haskalah and History* and *The Jewish Enlightenment*.

[8] The Wissenschaft des Judentums movement began its formal activities with the founding of the Verein für Kultur und Wissenschaft der Juden in Berlin in 1819. See Schorsch, *From Text to Context*;

in the diaspora corresponded closely to the debate about the status of the Jews in contemporary European societies and the struggle for their emancipation.[9] In eastern Europe, the maskilim engaged with philosophy, ethics, science, and Hebrew grammar. They envisioned the continued existence of separate Jewish society, but, while advocating Jewish cultural and intellectual rejuvenation, they also discussed a measure of acculturation.

Modernizing Jewish circles in Congress Poland and Galicia, with their close ideological ties to Polish liberal elites, debated the merits of embracing the Polish language and culture and studying Polish history.[10] A new Jewish intelligentsia formed, which supported cultural frameworks and institutions in Warsaw such as the Polish-language newspapers published there—*Jutrzenka* (The Dawn) and *Izraelita*—and the Rabbinical School, which became a centre for the study of the history of Polish Jewry.[11]

Jewish interest in the history of Jewish communal institutions in Poland and the Polish–Lithuanian Commonwealth was not limited to studies invested in promoting Jewish integration. Appearing first in the second half of the nineteenth century, monographs written in Hebrew addressed different aspects of the history of Jewish institutions in local settings in eastern Europe. Written by maskilim, who relied mainly on Jewish sources and appealed to a traditional Jewish reading public, these works blended a critical historical approach with more traditional forms of Jewish religious literature to create a new genre. While studies published in the Polish language for Polish and acculturated Jewish audiences delved into the policies of the kings, the legal status of the Jews, and Jewish–Gentile relations in the past, works in Hebrew focused on internal Jewish affairs. Although Polish Jewish historical writing built explicitly on the model of Wissenschaft des Judentums, it was in dialogue with the history of the Polish lands and Polish historiographical themes. Together with the Hebrew monographs, Jewish histories written in

---

Meyer, 'Two Persistent Tensions within Wissenschaft des Judentums'; Brenner, *Prophets of the Past*, 17–50.

[9] See Feiner, *Haskalah and History*, 9–70; Yerushalmi, *Zakhor*, 81–103.

[10] In the nineteenth century, Warsaw and Kraków emerged as important centres of the Polish Jewish intelligentsia. For an in-depth discussion of the intelligentsia's ideas about Jewish culture and religious practice, see Cała, *Asymilacja Żydów w Królestwie Polskim (1864–1897)*; Datner, *Ta i tamta strona*; Jagodzińska, *Pomiędzy*; Bauer, 'The Ideological Roots of the Polish Jewish Intelligentsia'; Hońdo, 'Das Verhältnis der Juden in Westgalizien'; Galas (ed.), *Synagoga Tempel i środowisko krakowskich Żydów postępowych*; Galas, *Rabbi Marcus Jastrow*; Maślak-Maciejewska, *Rabin Szymon Dankowicz (1834–1910)*.

[11] On *Jutrzenka*, published in Warsaw from 1861 until 1863 and edited by Daniel Neufeld, see Daniłowicz, '*Jutrzenka*—tygodnik Izraelitów polskich'. On *Izraelita*, see Jagodzińska and Wodziński (eds.), '*Izraelita*' *1866–1915*. On the Rabbinical School in Warsaw, see Polonsky, 'Warszawska Szkoła Rabinów'.

Polish constituted—to use historian Shmuel Feiner's distinction—'the second track of nineteenth-century east European Jewish historiography'.[12]

At the same time, the burgeoning Polish intelligentsia, driven by a strong sense of patriotism, began to organize institutional frameworks for scholarly activism. Warsaw and Kraków emerged as prominent centres for the project of safeguarding the Polish historical tradition through scholarship. Following the period of Polish–Jewish rapprochement on the eve of the failed January 1863 uprising against Russia, the Polish Jewish past attracted the attention of a variety of authors, both in and out of the academy, including non-Jewish Poles, observant Jews—including those who began to define themselves as Jews only in terms of their denomination—and authors who identified themselves as Poles with Jewish roots. With a background in the European and Jewish Enlightenment this amorphous group differed in methodological approaches to and scholarly practices of writing the history of Polish Jews. However, most of the Jewish authors who took up the subject did so outside academia or outside their primary fields of research and work: as communal leaders, lawyers, or as scholars of general Polish history. While they saw history as an important part of Jewish collective memory, they saw Polish Jewish history as intimately tied to the contemporary dilemmas faced by their communities.[13]

## Agendas and Methodologies

Social, political, and cultural agendas, as well as current questions and biases, spurred both writers who regarded themselves as Poles of the Mosaic faith (*Polacy wyznania mojżeszowego*) and those who saw themselves as Poles of Jewish heritage to consider Polish Jewish history. The subject served as their *entrée* into public discussions about the place of Jews in the Polish lands and the future of Polish–Jewish relations. Although nineteenth-century authors publishing on Polish Jewish topics in the Polish language have traditionally been divided into 'Polish historians' and the 'Jewish assimilationist school', these two groups shared a belief in the need for Jewish integration, as well as an ambivalent attitude towards the autonomous Jewish institutions in the Polish–Lithuanian Commonwealth.[14]

---

[12] The term 'second track' used by Shmuel Feiner points to the contrasts between the academic writings of members of the Wissenschaft des Judentums movement and the maskilic literature produced in eastern and central Europe. See Feiner, 'Nineteenth-Century Jewish Historiography'; Blutinger, 'Writing for the Masses', 28.

[13] See Jagodzińska and Wodziński (eds.), *'Izraelita' 1866–1915*, 227–32.

[14] Ludwik Gumplowicz and Kraushar both considered themselves primarily Polish scholars, with Polish academia as their main point of reference, although in the case of Gumplowicz his hopes were disappointed. See Biderman, *Mayer Bałaban*, 12–17, 20–7. See also Kraushar, 'Ludwik Gumplowicz', 63; Żebrowski, *Mojżesz Schorr*, 96.

Discussions about the legal status of the Jews, their relations with non-Jews, and the autonomous Jewish institutions of the Polish past dominated early surveys; but with a growing number and variety of authors writing the history of Jews in the Polish lands, and with increasing methodological sophistication, the new field gradually moved away from legal history, broadening into an examination of social, economic, cultural, and religious phenomena.

While pioneering Jewish authors of Polish Jewish history hardly constituted a cohesive group, they shared the conviction that knowledge of the past would promote Polish–Jewish rapprochement and mitigate antisemitism. To this end, this first generation of Jewish historians stressed the need to build a professional field through scholarly enquiry. Writing in Polish, in 1863, Daniel Neufeld quoted the Talmud in the opening of his proposal to create a new umbrella organization of Polish Jews. He reminded his readers: 'The ancient history of the Israelites presents the scholars of history [with] an extensive field for reasoning.'[15] A member of the Polish Jewish intelligentsia in Warsaw, and the editor of the weekly *Jutrzenka* and the Jewish section of a general Polish encyclopaedia, Neufeld argued that since the beginning of the diaspora, learning had played a particularly important role for Jews, who were deprived of political and religious leadership. While praising the development of Jewish scholarship in his own time, Neufeld criticized the state of Jewish research in the Polish lands, complaining that 'the knowledge of Hebrew archaeology [history] here is foreign to the scholars'. He lamented the fact that Czacki's study remained the only such work.[16]

In 1916 a well-respected Polish Jewish historian, Aleksander Kraushar, who had begun his career some fifty years earlier writing for *Jutrzenka*, recalled with satisfaction the gradual recognition of the importance of the field by leading Polish scholars.[17] In his two-volume *Historya Żydów w Polsce* (History of the Jews in Poland), published in 1865–6, Kraushar had expressed the hope that his study would 'awaken deeper interest in exploring the path I have attempted to point

---

[15] Neufeld, *Urządzenie konsystorza żydowskiego*. He also published the book of Genesis, with both the Hebrew text and his Polish translation, under the title *Pięcioksiąg Mojżesza dla Żydów-Polaków*, as well as a translation of the Hebrew prayer book *Modły starożytne Izraelitów*, and a translation of *Pirkei avot*. See Neufeld, *Syfse Jeszenim* and *Pirke Aboth*. See Landau, 'Neufeld Daniel'; Shatzky, 'A Contribution to the Biography of Daniel Neufeld' (Yid.). [16] Neufeld, *Syfse Jeszenim*, pt. 1, p. 3.

[17] Kraushar, 'Ludwik Gumplowicz', 60–2. Kraushar was steeped in Polish literature and history; involved in the uprising of 1863, he increasingly defined himself as a Polish scholar, eventually sealing his identity with a conversion to Christianity in 1903. Like several other emerging scholars of his generation, Kraushar studied law at the Department of Law and Administration in Warsaw; he subsequently became a respected advocate, publishing his own literary work as well as historical articles. In October 1916, in the introduction to a collection of essays (published in 1917), Kraushar restated his commitment to 'the love for the past of the native [*rodzimy*] society and the desire to express the beautiful, humanitarian qualities of its customs' (Kraushar, *Echa przeszłości*, p. x).

out'.[18] Attempting to bring together all the existing data on the Jews in the Polish lands, Kraushar aspired to lay the foundation for future scholars of Polish Jewish history while making the case for a more inclusive understanding of Polish history in general.[19] In order to fully conceptualize Polish history, he suggested it was necessary to examine both peasants and Jews. He believed that all elements within a society deserved to become subjects of historical analysis, and he defended the idea of studying those groups that were ostensibly devoid of political existence. According to Kraushar, social history offered a more nuanced perspective than did an exclusively political focus.[20] Examining the legislative history of the legal status of Polish Jews was important, but Kraushar aspired to '[present] in a precise framework a picture of the historical life of the Jewish tribe in Poland from the *purely social* point of view, capturing the facts relating to the inner, religious life of this element in its external expression'.[21] From this social and intellectual perspective on history, Kraushar criticized the literature of the first half of the nineteenth century for its simplistic methodology and divisions between subjects.[22] His was a vision for an integrated history of the Polish lands.[23]

Like Kraushar, many members of the Jewish integrationist group in Warsaw in the second half of the nineteenth century were committed to communal service through education, in which history was a key to understanding contemporary relations.[24] While working as a merchant, Hilary Nussbaum taught at an elemen-

[18] Kraushar, *Historya Żydów w Polsce*, ii, p. ii.

[19] Ibid. ii, pp. xii and ii–iii. Critical of his own work, Kraushar referred to it as a survey of facts about the epoch, comprising 'everything that has been written so far here and there about Jews of the Piast [epoch]', and as an introduction to the study of other epochs (ibid. ii, p. ii). An anonymous reviewer criticized Kraushar for not using Jewish sources and for writing legal history, rather than the history of Jewish institutions and community. See *Gazeta Polska*, 3 Apr. 1865, 1–2. See also Kraushar, *Historya Żydów w Polsce*, ii, p. iii.

[20] Kraushar, *Historya Żydów w Polsce*, ii, pp. v–vi. In response to a similar dilemma of writing Jewish history as a history of a non-political entity, Dubnow defined Jewish history in national terms. See Nathans, 'On Russian-Jewish Historiography'.

[21] Kraushar, *Historya Żydów w Polsce*, ii, p. xi; Kraushar, 'Ludwik Gumplowicz', 62.

[22] Kraushar, *Historya Żydów w Polsce*, p. i. Kraushar found the fault in 'internal and external difficulties, in the lack of appropriate sources and in the spirit of the time, made such an enterprise impossible'. The writing of Jewish history needed to be 'precise and animated by the newer ideas of the history of the Jews in Poland' (ibid.).

[23] Kraushar contributed to the founding of two associations central to the development of the Polish historical profession, Towarzystwo Naukowe Warszawskie (Warsaw Scientific Association) and Towarzystwo Miłośników Historii (Association of History Lovers), and he belonged to the first editorial board of *Przegląd Historyczny*. See Maternicki, 'Kraushar Aleksander, pseud. Alkar'. In 1895, his two-volume *Frank i Frankiści polscy 1726–1816* appeared in Kraków. See also Shatzky, 'Alexander Kraushar and His Road to Total Assimilation'.

[24] See Peltyn, 'Żydzi ze stanowiska ekonomii publicznej uważani', 83.

tary school and remained active in community work. A graduate of the Rabbinical School in Warsaw and a columnist for *Jutrzenka*, he published a study of the Jewish community in Warsaw and authored five volumes of Jewish history in Polish that began with Moses and ended with the Polish–Lithuanian Commonwealth.[25] Supportive of the Jewish involvement in the Polish uprising of 1863, Nussbaum promoted Jewish integration into Polish society, including the adoption of the Polish language. Sketching the history of the Jews in Warsaw, he listed a number of issues worthy of scholarly attention, including 'the excessive concentration of the Jews in this city, their great influx into the capital, their internal struggle with the supporters of ignorance, excess, and superstition, external conflicts with the local elements about material existence, the continuous state of temporariness in their social life, [and] continuously changing forms of government'.[26] If the list seems coloured by Nussbaum's ideological commitments, it nonetheless demonstrates his attention to both political and social aspects of Polish Jewish history, examined from the vantage points of internal developments and Jewish–non-Jewish relations. But his ambition went beyond sketching the life of the Warsaw Jewish community. 'Would the history of Jews in Warsaw be only an echo of the Jewish history in Poland?' he asked.[27] Nussbaum questioned the relationship between the local and general history of Polish Jewry and understood that the Jews in Warsaw had brought their customs and habits to the capital from other Polish cities and hamlets. His overall ambitious and multifaceted project was to elucidate 'the individual character of Israelites, their religious system, their social isolation, and their attitude towards the society that surrounded them'.[28]

Nussbaum's survey of Jewish history stopped short of examining the policies of Polish kings, the contours of the legal status of the Jews, and their relations with non-Jewish society. He aspired to a better understanding of 'what stopped the Jews, despite their benefiting from tolerant laws and privileges, from merging with the local population'.[29] He hoped his work would have an impact in Poland, comparable to that of the circle of Wissenschaft des Judentums in Germany:

I express an ardent wish that the general history of the Jews that I have prepared for the first time here, will be capable of leading to such a turn in the general public and in the notions of my co-religionists, as caused once by the first history published in German by Dr Jost, and I will consider myself sufficiently rewarded for my arduous work of several years.[30]

[25] See Nussbaum, *Historyja Żydów od Mojżesza do epoki obecnej*.

[26] Nussbaum, *Szkice historyczne z życia Żydów w Warszawie*, pp. i–ii.

[27] Ibid., p. i. Local history of the Jews also drew the attention of the integrationist circles. *Izraelita* published a series of articles delving into the history of the Jewish presence in Warsaw (Jakób K-t [Kirszrot], 'Żydzi w Warszawie').    [28] Nussbaum, *Szkice historyczne z życia Żydów w Warszawie*, p. ii.

[29] Nussbaum, *Historyja Żydów od Mojżesza do epoki obecnej*, v. 2.    [30] Ibid. v. 449.

This perspective mirrored larger developments in Polish historiography, which ascribed a great importance to history in the political education of society. In these writers' views, historical arguments served as a tool for shaping national political consciousness.[31]

How was one to study the history of Polish Jewry? What sources would be needed to write this new kind of critical history? In order to anchor the new field and move past myths and legends, Jewish authors increasingly turned to archives in search of materials documenting the legal status of the Jews in Old Poland, Jewish economic activity, and Jewish–non-Jewish relations in the past. While recognizing the importance of 'the history of the internal life of the Jewish tribe in Poland' for understanding Polish Jewry, Kraushar complained about the lack of such internal Jewish documents for earlier periods of Polish Jewish history.[32] Indispensable for any significant historical narrative, such traces could only be found for later periods, and the overall enterprise 'required not the efforts of one person but a shared [effort] of many [people], driven by the thought of a civic duty for learning and practical use'.[33] In his monograph on the Frankist movement, Kraushar elaborated on a variety of archival sources that he consulted, including images and oral accounts.[34] He described his own role as that of an 'impartial scholar' who sought out new sources and investigated all available material.[35] Nussbaum collected historical material in the archives of the Warsaw City Council (Magistrat) and the local Jewish community. He mined Polish chronicles and collected accounts from Jewish elders whose parents had moved to Warsaw after the collapse of Poland in the aftermath of the third partition in 1795.[36]

Jewish communal activists and scholars devoted their attention to collecting material that would strengthen the sense of rootedness of Jews in the Polish lands. Kraushar's father-in-law, Mathias Bersohn, spent several years working on the publication of primary documents pertaining to the history of Polish Jewry, a collection that appeared posthumously in 1910.[37] Committed to the idea of awakening 'a sense of Polishness among the Jews in Poland', he collected both Judaica and Polish art, wrote articles on Jewish history and culture for *Jutrzenka*, and authored

---

[31] Maternicki, 'Historyk sługą narodu'.
[32] See Kraushar, *Historya Żydów w Polsce*, ii, p. iii.
[33] Ibid. ii, p. v.
[34] Kraushar, *Frank i Frankiści polscy 1726–1816*, i. 16–23.
[35] Ibid. i. 23. In a letter to Abraham Duker, Gershon Scholem noted that Kraushar took little interest in the history of the group or their conversion: 'It is evident that Kraushar did so out of considerations for the Frankist families who gave him some material, but obviously did not want the history of their group after their conversion to be discussed in detail' (DRI, P 65, file 174: typed copy of a letter, dated in Jerusalem 17 Jan. 1965).
[36] Nussbaum, *Szkice historyczne z życia Żydów w Warszawie*, p. ii.
[37] Bersohn, *Dyplomataryusz dotyczący Żydów*. He donated his collections to museums in Poznań, Kraków, and Warsaw. Moreover, his collections formed the basis for the Museum of Jewish Antiquities, named after him and founded in 1904 by the Warsaw Jewish community. Critical of Kraushar,

the first study on wooden synagogues and a review of Jewish scholarship in the Polish lands.³⁸ Bersohn explained that the work of Czacki and other Polish historians relied on a limited number of documents. The thirteenth-century privileges or charters issued in the region of Greater Poland, which offered Jews protective legislation and broad autonomy, served as the basis for many of Polish scholars' generalizations. The paucity of primary sources resulted in the lack of a 'thorough and critically elaborated history of the Jewish population in Old Poland–Lithuania, beginning with its arrival here in the twelfth and thirteenth centuries and until our time'. Bersohn resolved to bring together all the privileges, legal documents, and local anti-Jewish legislation.³⁹

Neither the tension between political and social history nor the choice of archival materials were purely academic issues. The commitment to Jewish integration and the promotion of the Polish patriotic cause of both Polish and Polish Jewish scholars shaped Jewish historians' views on the purpose of writing history. In the spirit of the Enlightenment, they believed that legal status shaped and affected individuals and groups. Therefore, studying Polish Jewry in the past would help better to understand contemporary Jewish institutions, culture, and mentality, and would point to possible solutions and much needed reforms.⁴⁰ Already in 1807, in line with Enlightenment dogma, Czacki had declared that the study of the Jews in Poland was important for 'a man, a citizen, and a sage', suggesting that such knowledge could serve all the inhabitants of the Polish lands in the wake of the partitions.⁴¹ 'Today', he wrote, 'there are new rulers in our land but the Jews remain the same.'⁴² Seeking to assess the economic and social contribution of Polish Jews in past centuries, on the basis of Polish legal and historical sources, Czacki set out to explain the origin of Polish Jews, a question that was central to understanding their occupational structure and cultural characteristics. He wrote his treatise in order to educate the public about Polish Jewry and thereby promote his project of reform.⁴³

Smoleński, and Gumplowicz, Maciejowski praised Bersohn for his collection of documents pertaining to the history of Polish Jews that he put at Maciejowski's disposal (Maciejowski, *Żydzi w Polsce, na Rusi i Litwie*, 109).

³⁸ Bersohn, *Kilka słów o dawnych bóżnicach drewnianych w Polsce*; id., *Słownik biograficzny uczonych Żydów Polskich XVI, XVII i XVIII wieku*. Regarding Bersohn's public activism, see Rabska, 'Bersohn Mathias'; Shatzky, *History of the Jews in Warsaw*; Guesnet, 'Bersohn, Mathias (1824–1908)', in Hundert (ed.), *The YIVO Encyclopedia of Jews in Eastern Europe*, i. 169–70.

³⁹ Bersohn, 'Słowo wstępne', in id., *Dyplomataryusz dotyczący Żydów*. Bersohn collected material while working on wooden synagogues (L-t, 'Z piśmiennictwa: "O dawniejszych bóżnicach drewnianych w Polsce"').   ⁴⁰ Veidlinger, *Jewish Public Culture*, 232.   ⁴¹ Czacki, *Rosprawa o Żydach*, 1.

⁴² Ibid. 215–16. On the projects for reform concerning the Jews, see Eisenbach, *Z dziejów ludności żydowskiej w Polsce XVIII I XIX wieku*, 31–40.

⁴³ Czacki considered his ideas to be better than the projects discussed at the time in St Petersburg.

Later scholars shared Czacki's confidence that the past held the key to introducing the necessary changes in the status of Jews in the Polish lands and improving contemporary Polish–Jewish relations. In Daniel Neufeld's view, the lack of appropriate original research in 'Jewish archaeology' in eastern Europe, meant that Polish society remained uninformed about Polish Jews. As a result, biases and exaggerations persisted, affecting not only popular opinion but also regulations concerning Jews. Although Polish legislators read about Jewish history, argued Neufeld, they had to rely on new literature from abroad, which often described Jewish–non-Jewish relations in other countries.[44] He contrasted the status of Jewish scholarship in western Europe with the drastically different situation in the Polish lands, where 'the knowledge of Jewish archaeology is necessary for the evaluation of the relations of Judaism, because the Jews in Poland and in the majority of other Slavic countries continue living a completely ancient life, shaped as well by . . . a range of medieval concepts, and formed under the influence of the religious persecution they have experienced'.[45] Any substantial change in the legal and social status of the Jews required the support of both Polish and Jewish public opinion. Therefore, in his project of organizing Jewish institutions, Neufeld discussed the communal and regional organizations of Jews in Poland–Lithuania throughout the centuries.[46] Neufeld reminded his readers that the situation of the Jews in the Polish lands needed to be evaluated in a different spirit than that in western Europe, where an immense literature had been published since the late eighteenth century. In western Europe, he wrote, 'the Jew today is no longer this mysterious and unappreciated person he was for Europe a hundred and twenty years ago'.[47]

Making a distinction between policy and scholarship, Neufeld argued for an open, multifaceted discussion about ancient Jewish customs rather than a set of possibly biased individual expert opinions. Both popular and scholarly publications as well as the press offered the best forums for such discussion. Neufeld's own study of the past also strengthened his conviction about the value of Jewish integration into the general community. He predicted a bright future for relations between Jews and non-Jews in the Polish lands, envisioning religious tolerance, the emancipation of estates and denominations, and the progress of Jewish studies, which he believed would in turn end the suspicion and mistrust that arose from ignorance about Judaism.[48]

Hilary Nussbaum used information concerning the general history of the

As Danowska rightly pointed out, the treatise was both a historical and a legal work. See Danowska, 'Poglądy Tadeusza Czackiego na kwestię żydowską', 162.

[44] Neufeld, *Syfse Jeszenim*, pt. 1, p. 4.       [45] Ibid., pt. 1, p. 5.
[46] See Neufeld, *Urządzenie konsystorza żydowskiego*, ch. 4.       [47] Neufeld, *Syfse Jeszenim*, pt. 1, p. 5.
[48] See Neufeld, *Urządzenie konsystorza żydowskiego*, 83, 100.

Jews in Poland to contextualize Jewish history in Warsaw and make it accessible to a wide audience, especially Jewish youth, because, he said, the 'majority of the educated [among the] young generation of the Mosaic faith, who have lived by the general social ideal, are less familiar with the affairs of their [own] co-religionists'.[49] Although he was addressing both Jews and non-Jews, young Jews were the primary audience for his historical accounts. Nussbaum hoped to motivate the younger generation to learn historical facts and 'to arouse in them a civic feeling [so] that their enlightened ideas, healthy notions, and a mind enriched with the acquisitions of knowledge return to that part of the local population, which needs to become enlightened, elevated and nationalized for the best interest of the country'.[50] Imbued with trust in the transformative power of historical knowledge, Mathias Bersohn explained that he chose simply to present the past rather than indulge in 'sword-play', or 'the useless polemics that always vex without ever convincing a party; instead of justifying mutual complaints and charges, faults and weaknesses, inseparable from human nature whenever prejudices and infatuations play a role as factors'.[51] With the publication of primary documents, Bersohn hoped to strengthen the historical connection between the legal existence of the Jewish population in the former commonwealth, the royal decrees in the past, and the contemporary government of the country.[52] For Czacki, Nussbaum, Neufeld, and Bersohn, studying the past provided ideas without which the current state of Polish–Jewish relations in Congress Poland could only lead to mutual antagonism or bloodshed—or so they thought.[53]

Other authors who explored the history of Polish Jewry shared the conviction that historiography not only added to knowledge about the past, but also held solutions to contemporary relations. Aleksander Kraushar listed instances in which Polish Jewish history provided relevant circumstances and useful data for those who wanted to understand the current Jewish community: economists, philosophers of history, theologians, and philanthropists.[54] For the pioneering sociologist Ludwik Gumplowicz, the history of Polish Jewry and Polish legal history were interconnected, and therefore deserved the attention of Polish historians, who had not thus far studied the privileges given to the Jews by Polish kings.[55] Legal history, he believed, held the key to understanding the contemporary situation of the Jewish community and Jewish–non-Jewish relations—

---

[49] Nussbaum, *Szkice historyczne z życia Żydów w Warszawie*, p. iii.     [50] Ibid., pp. iii–iv.
[51] Bersohn, *Dyplomataryusz dotyczący Żydów*, 12.
[52] Ibid. 5.     [53] Ibid. 12.     [54] Kraushar, *Historya Żydów w Polsce*, ii, p. vi.
[55] See Gumplowicz, *Prawodawstwo polskie względem Żydów*, 130. On the implications of the privileges for general Polish legal history, see ibid. 133–5. See also Kozińska-Witt, 'Ludwig Gumplowicz's Programme for the Improvement of the Jewish Situation'. On Gumplowicz, see Surman and Mozetič (eds.), *Dwa życia Ludwika Gumplowicza*.

a theme on which Gumplowicz elaborated in his *Prawodawstwo polskie względem Żydów* (Polish Legislation Concerning the Jews), published in Kraków in 1867. Trained at the Jagiellonian University in Kraków, Gumplowicz wrote about history in Polish and Polish Jewish journals, including *Jutrzenka*.[56] He made his agenda quite clear: to see Poland united and Jews included seamlessly into the population. When discussing Kazimierz the Great (1310–70), the last monarch of the Piast dynasty, who was credited with issuing a general privilege for the Jews living in his realm, Gumplowicz pointed to the role this legal document continued to play: 'Jews remain a separate caste—this issue, after five centuries, has barely moved forward.'[57]

In 1876, the Polish non-Jewish historian Władysław Smoleński published *Stan i sprawa Żydów polskich w XVIII wieku* (The State and the Question of Polish Jews in the Eighteenth Century), presenting a broad picture of the economic functions of the Jews in Poland and their influence on the country.[58] To understand the issue in depth and to ensure the means for assimilation of the Jews—Smoleński's ultimate goal—he elaborated on their status, their role in the country's economy, and the attitudes of both the government and the educated elites in the eighteenth century.[59] Though he strove for objectivity in reconstructing the past, he did see it as closely connected to the contemporary state of affairs. Relying primarily on published source material and diaries, Smoleński stressed the revolutionary attempts to forge a new social order in the eighteenth century. While the work of the previous century was unfinished, Smoleński hoped to see it completed in his own time, a project that required his contemporaries to have their 'eyes constantly set on the past'.[60] In fact, the solutions put forth in the past remained relevant: Smoleński compared them to 'the architecture of the edifice' which required only new building material 'on the ready founding block cast by the forefathers'.[61]

---

[56] Kraushar, 'Ludwik Gumplowicz'. Having worked in the legal profession, journalism, and publishing, Gumplowicz attempted to have his published research recognized by the Department of Law in Kraków as a basis for the *Habilitation* (tenured status) he needed for a future university appointment. Following its rejection, he continued his scholarly career in Graz, where he converted to Protestantism and focused his research on the theory of law and sociology. See Bieńkowski, 'Gumplowicz Ludwik'. See also Żebrowski, 'Trzy pokolenia rodu Gumplowiczów' in *Mojżesz Schorr*.

[57] Gumplowicz, *Prawodawstwo polskie względem Żydów*, 17–18.

[58] Yet Polish Jewish history remained marginal in his work, as the bulk of his publications pertained to the social history of the petty nobility and its mentality, and the social and intellectual history of Polish society during the eighteenth century, with particular attention to the Four Year Diet, Warsaw, and the region of Mazovia. See Michalski, 'Smoleński Władysław'; Wierzbicka, *Władysław Smoleński*.

[59] Smoleński, *Stan i sprawa Żydów polskich w XVIII wieku*, 4.

[60] Ibid. This tension between objectivism and influencing society has been expressed by Polish historians such as Tadeusz Korzon. See Maternicki, 'Historyk sługą narodu', 62.

[61] Smoleński, *Stan i sprawa Żydów polskich w XVIII wieku*, 3.

Therefore, linking past and contemporary attempts to change the status of Jews in the Polish lands, Smoleński concluded that the 'Jewish question' 'could only be understood and solved with the co-operation of history'.[62] Given this link between past and present, Smoleński's own work would aid the cause of Jewish integration, since 'the spiritual revival of Jewry still requires a reform, and one based on the ideas of the eighteenth century, which, while breaking down the separatism of the Jews, intended to transform them and incorporate them into the nation's body'.[63]

The connection between past reform projects and the perceived contemporary need for remaking Polish Jews inspired the work of the Polish legal historian Wacław Aleksander Maciejowski, who, in 1878, published *Żydzi w Polsce, na Rusi i Litwie* (The Jews in Poland, Ruthenia, and Lithuania). Like Czacki's, Maciejowski's study of Jewish history complemented his earlier work on the peasants and his future study of cities, artisans, and commerce in the Russian empire.[64] Plans for possible reform enticed him to elucidate the historical origins of the contemporary Jewish question. Trained at the Jagiellonian University in Kraków, as well as in Berlin, Breslau, and Göttingen, Maciejowski settled in Warsaw, where he lectured at the Department of Law. After the closure of Warsaw University in 1869, he taught at the Theological Seminary (Akademia Duchowna) and for professional legal courses offered in the city.[65] In his study of the Jews, he discussed reform projects of the Polish–Lithuanian state that had been brought forward starting in the last decades of the eighteenth century and continuing until the partitions of Poland.[66] Maciejowski's book had explicit contemporary overtones, not only because of the calls for a shift in the patterns of Jewish economic activities, but also in his stated opposition to hasidism and his support for transforming 'fanatical Judaism into rational and European style civilization'.[67] The language Maciejowski used shows the cleft between the way Jews saw themselves and the way they were perceived by non-Jewish Poles.

Authors of historical studies shared archival resources and notes, and read and reviewed publications pertaining to the history of Jews in the Polish lands.[68] The emerging body of historical scholarship relied on the expectation of the transformative power of knowledge, which could help transform the Jews in a way that

[62] Ibid.     [63] Ibid.
[64] Maciejowski, *Żydzi w Polsce, na Rusi i Litwie*, pp. v–vi. On Maciejowski, see Bardach, *Wacław Aleksander Maciejowski i jego współcześni* and Borowski, *Maciejowskiana*.
[65] Maciejowski, *Żydzi w Polsce, na Rusi i Litwie*, 4–5.
[66] Ibid. 82–94. Maciejowski claimed that the Four Year Diet aimed at ending the exploitation of the masses by the Jews through new laws (ibid. 96).     [67] Ibid. 105, 108.
[68] For example, Kraushar thanked Bersohn for allowing him to use Bersohn's notes relating to *Dyplomataryusz dotyczący Żydów*, and shared important archival details concerning the period of King Zygmunt the Old. He also thanked the Polish scholars Julian Bartoszewicz, Maciejowski, and K. Łaski for sharing materials with him. Kraushar, *Historya Żydów w Polsce*, ii, pp. xii–xiii.

would put an end to tensions between Jews and non-Jews. Despite these high hopes for the ability of historical accounts to educate and remake society by bringing different religious communities in the partitioned Polish lands closer to one another, pioneering Polish and Polish Jewish authors increasingly expressed concern for striking a balance between present-day considerations and objective scholarship. Bersohn felt driven not only by social concerns but also by scientific-historical ones, publishing primary documents on Polish Jewish history 'in the name of truth, public good, and science'.[69] Kraushar described the dangers of connecting the history of the Jews in Poland too closely with present-day conditions, rather than evaluating the facts 'from the historical point of view'.[70] He compared the role of a historian to 'a judge free of bias who examines the facts but does not choose them; evaluates them but does not transform them'.[71] While deeply involved in contemporary Polish and Polish Jewish affairs, Kraushar also assured his readers that he began his research without a priori assumptions, with a firm belief that facts 'faithfully presented and skilfully arranged will speak for themselves and will explain their meaning better than any even the most noble biased descriptions the author could add to accompany them'.[72]

## The Legal Status of Jews in Old Poland

Hoping for a change in the status of the Jewish community, and seeking to hasten the integration of Polish Jewry, Polish and Polish Jewish authors of historical studies based in Warsaw and Kraków concentrated on analysing the legal status of the Jews and the relationship between Jews and non-Jews in the past. With their formal training in law, many of the scholars were uniquely qualified for research that delved into those general and local privileges and decrees that defined the position of Jewish communities in the Polish lands.[73] Some—among them Czacki, Gumplowicz, Smoleński, and Maciejowski—sought to evaluate the policies of

---

[69] Bersohn, *Dyplomataryusz dotyczący Żydów*, 13.

[70] Kraushar, *Historya Żydów w Polsce*, ii, p. xi. The discussion centred on the importance of the contemporary 'Jewish Question' and its influence on attempts to analyse the past (ibid., pp. vi, viii).

[71] Ibid., pp. ix–x.

[72] Ibid., p. x. In his monograph on Frank and the Frankist movement, Kraushar made a case for the impartial (*bezstronny*) scholar who studies the subject using newly discovered sources (Kraushar, *Frank i Frankiści polscy*, i. 23).

[73] Brian Horowitz pointed out a similar connection between emerging Russian Jewish historiography and the government's policies, given that 'Jewish historians linked their historical views to political concerns. In fact, historians played important roles in the struggle for Jewish emancipation' (Horowitz, *Russian Idea–Jewish Presence*, 88). Progressive circles were also interested in Jewish law in general. See Cohn, *Rzut oka na prawo i prawodawstwo mojżeszowe podług źródeł najnowszych*; id., 'Prawa żydów'; Kirszrot, *Prawa Żydów w Królestwie Polskiem*.

Polish monarchs and the effect royal and private Jewish privileges had on the economic role played by the Jews, on internal Jewish autonomy, on Jewish–non-Jewish relations, and on the emergence of the social distance that continued to separate Polish Jewry from the rest of Polish society.[74] Czacki discussed the rights of Jews in Poland, where Jews 'had multiplied from time immemorial' (though his starting point is the beginning of Jewish immigration from German and Ruthenian lands between the eleventh and thirteenth centuries), and where royal privileges were based on Czech and Austrian precedents.[75] He reminded his readers of the roles the Jews played in the scarcely populated country, and of their contribution to trade and finance. Only following the death of Kazimierz the Great did the legal status of the Jews worsen, due to the general weakening of royal authority.[76] Like Czacki, Neufeld underlined the contribution of the early Jewish settlement to the budding Polish state. He reminded his readers that Poland 'had at the time no autochthonous middle class. The nation strove to fill in this shortage by bringing in foreigners, Germans and Jews for the most part.'[77]

When addressing the legal status of Polish Jewry, integrationist historians applied two frameworks: a comparison with the situation in western Europe, and internal economic and political developments in the Polish realm. Both pointed to an unmatched level of protection and religious liberty that Polish Jews had enjoyed, and both helped to explain the motives behind the Polish exception. Polish non-Jewish historians Maciejowski and Smoleński criticized the government's policies over the centuries with regards to Jews settling in Polish lands. In particular, in their interpretation of the privileges bestowed on the Jewish population these authors alluded to an undue excess of Jewish influence. According to Maciejowski, Jews who came to Poland from Germany at the dawn of Poland's statehood between the eighth and tenth centuries had fared well, and had engaged in commerce thanks to the support of the Polish monarchs, the bishops, and the

---

[74] Czacki had a long-lasting interest in legal history. Kraushar, Maciejowski, Smoleński, and Ludwik and Maksymilian Gumplowicz all graduated from departments of law. According to Veidlinger, 'A modern Russian Jewish historiography that used archival and primary sources emerged chiefly as a means of ascertaining the legal status of Jews in Russia. A similar process occurred in Poland, where the Four-Year Sejm necessitated the first systematic surveys of the legal status of Polish Jews.' Veidlinger concludes that 'The juridical training of early East European historians of the Jews led them to think in terms of individual legal rights rather than collective cultural rights' (Veidlinger, *Jewish Public Culture*, 231–2).

[75] Czacki, *Rosprawa o Żydach*, 66–7. For Czacki's discussion of the early Jewish settlement in Poland, see ibid. 67–71.

[76] Ibid. 74. Czacki devoted one chapter of his treatise to the analysis of the first privilege issued by Bolesław and confirmed by Kazimierz the Great and Witold (ibid. 107–19). He presented several instances of anti-Jewish legislation and violence under the reign of kings of the Jagiellonian dynasty and the elected kings (ibid. 76–103).    [77] Neufeld, *Urządzenie konsystorza żydowskiego*, 19.

nobility.[78] Although critical of the generous policies, and especially of the attitudes of the nobility, Smoleński pointed to the country's merits in its treatment of the Jews as 'gentler than in the west, where in the eighteenth century harsh, intolerant legislation and protectionist privileges persisted, combined with the most severe treatment of this tribe'.[79] Examining legal sources in order to analyse the social and political status of the Jewish communities and their relations with non-Jews, Ludwik Gumplowicz concluded that Old Poland was both progressive and civilized. His evidence came from the first privilege given to Jews by Prince Bolesław V the Chaste (1226–79), which he compared to earlier documents from Germany.[80] With this favourable comparison in mind, Gumplowicz praised the attitudes of Polish monarchs towards the Jews, who had received a more favourable treatment in Poland than at the hands of other European kings. In contrast to the German lands, for instance, in Poland Jews 'constituted a class of the nation and belonged to it as an integral part, as much as the nobility, the peasants and the burghers'; their status was equal to the burghers and in some ways even higher.[81]

Such auspicious policies implemented by the Polish kings required explanation. Striving to elucidate the economic motives and political vision behind the granting of royal privileges, these historians stressed the policies of the kings, whom they saw as having actively pursued the inclusion of Jews into the dominant society.[82] Maciejowski pointed out that the privileges Jews enjoyed in the Polish lands reached their peak in the mid-fourteenth century, with the charter granted in 1334 by Kazimierz the Great. Their status would vastly improve again with the reforms planned in 1792.[83] Indeed, no other king was praised quite as highly as was Kazimierz the Great, for his support of Jewish settlement in Poland, his granting of a generous general privilege in anticipation of financial and economic profits for the country and the royal coffer, and his protection of the Jews from

---

[78] He rejected the idea that Jews had ever engaged in working the land or in crafts, but instead focused from the beginning of their settlement in Poland on commerce with the support of the monarchs and the bishops. See Maciejowski, *Żydzi w Polsce, na Rusi i Litwie*, 10–15, 34–5, 42–3.

[79] Smoleński, *Stan i sprawa Żydów polskich w XVIII wieku*, 40. Smoleński compiled a list of places where the Jews were worse off than in Poland, which included Prussia, Bavaria, Silesia, and Austria, among others.

[80] See Gumplowicz, *Prawodawstwo polskie względem Żydów*, 124–7.    [81] Ibid. 109.

[82] See Nussbaum, *Historyja Żydów od Mojżesza do epoki obecnej*, v. 47. There is a rich literature on medieval charters and privileges granted to European Jewish communities, and on the 'vertical alliance' between monarchs and the Jewish communities. See Yerushalmi, *The Lisbon Massacre of 1506*, 35–66; Myers and Kaye (eds.), *The Faith of Fallen Jews*, 245–76.

[83] Maciejowski, *Żydzi w Polsce, na Rusi i Litwie*, 14–15. Even during the less fortunate period, claimed Maciejowski, Jews were better off in Poland than anywhere else, due to the tolerance of the Poles (ibid. 4–5, 8–9, 104–5).

anti-Jewish superstitions by bestowing upon them judicial privileges.[84] Gumplowicz described Kazimierz the Great as 'a genius legislator' who wanted to '*bring them* [the Jews] *closer to other classes of the nation and unite them with the nation in one political body*'.[85] His legislation 'breathed tolerance and free-thinking', expressing 'the tendency of unifying the Jews into one with the nation' and testifying to 'the great mind and legislative genius of the king'.[86] Gumplowicz insisted that for the last Piast king, the 'so-called Jewish question was a social question' and thus he sought to solve it within the social context.[87]

Examining Jewish legal status in Polish lands led these Polish and Polish Jewish authors to conceptualize their general vision of the country's history and its periodization. Moreover, delving into the legal status of the Jews helped trace general political and social patterns of the Polish Kingdom and later the Polish–Lithuanian Commonwealth. Kraushar divided the history of Polish Jewry into three distinctive periods, according to the shifts in privileges issued to them. He associated the first period with the general privileges that lasted until the end of the Piast dynasty, the second with the statutes until the end of the Jagiellonian dynasty, and the third with the parliamentary constitutions during the era of elected kings.[88] Comparing three independent and often contradictory sources of legislation in the Polish Kingdom—the kings, the nobility, and the Catholic clergy—Gumplowicz examined how each shaped both the law and its practice in relation to the Jews in each period.[89] In particular, he contrasted the 'liberal laws' of Kazimierz the Great with the 'fanatical church regulations', while the diets of the nobility took a middle ground, protecting nobles' material interests.[90] In a more general sense, he juxtaposed the 'national' policies of the monarchs with the attitudes of the Church.[91] The latter, slowly but surely, influenced the nobility, the diets, and the monarchs of the Jagiellonian dynasty, who were increasingly driven by religious prejudices rather than by economic considerations in their policies towards the Jews.[92] The elected kings, who for the most part lacked the vision of their predecessors in crafting policies concerning the Jews, upheld Jewish rights as

---

[84] Nussbaum, *Historyja Żydów od Mojżesza do epoki obecnej*, v. 49–50, 53. In his quest for justice, Kazimierz the Great issued a special edict against the blood libel (ibid. 58).

[85] Gumplowicz, *Prawodawstwo polskie względem Żydów*, 17, emphasis original.

[86] Ibid. 26. The king's influence remained limited, as the Catholic Church continued to exert its influence (ibid. 27). Gumplowicz singled out the policies of the last king of the Jagiellonian dynasty, Zygmunt August, who considered the Jews in his kingdom part of the nation, believing his royal obligation was to maintain privileges they had previously received, and whose policies were 'liberal and freethinking' (ibid. 41–5).

[87] See Gumplowicz's comments regarding various social interactions between Jews and non-Jews (ibid. 21–2). [88] Kraushar, *Historya Żydów w Polsce*, ii. 11–12.

[89] See Gumplowicz, *Prawodawstwo polskie względem Żydów*, 1–3.

[90] Ibid. 28. [91] Ibid. 53. [92] Ibid. 55–61.

part of their legal obligations, but the moral decline of the nobility increasingly allowed the Catholic clergy and the Jesuits to shape the laws of the country.[93] Kraushar stressed the contrast between the tradition of religious tolerance and the involvement of the Church in matters of Jewish ritual, epitomized by the forced participation of the rabbis in the public religious disputation in Kamieniec Podolski in 1757.[94] Nussbaum, too, considered the Church and its influence on Polish kings to be crucial in determining attitudes and policies towards the Jews. Clerical dignitaries encouraged the kings to issue canonical limitations and to turn the masses against the Jews.[95] But in Nussbaum's interpretations, they also caused the 'lower Christian strata' to riot 'by reminding them about the host desecrations and murder of Christian children by Jews'. This led to many instances of persecution and violence.[96]

Historians struggled with the tension between the notion of the unique legal status of the Jews and the treatment of various other religious and ethnic communities in the multi-ethnic Polish–Lithuanian Commonwealth. Jewish legal status needed to be evaluated in relation to other groups of newcomers settling in the Polish lands. Neufeld proposed to compare the status of the Jews to that of the burghers: newcomers who also enjoyed their own legal system and self-government.[97] In so doing, he linked the German burghers, who had brought their own German legislative systems, to the Jews, who governed themselves according to their own traditional laws and institutions, including communal courts.[98] According to Nussbaum, the granting of privileges to the Jews arose from the same policies that motivated Polish kings to invite and support German colonization, namely, improving economic conditions in Poland and bringing culture to the peasants.[99] Similarly, Kraushar believed that the status of the Jews in Poland during the Middle Ages was only part of a broader context of foreign colonists settling in the country, especially Germans, who, like Jews, were allowed to govern themselves with their own laws.[100] Non-Catholic subjects of the Polish kings provided an important framework for evaluating the legal status

---

[93] See Gumplowicz, *Prawodawstwo polskie względem Żydów*, 87–100. Still, most of the Polish kings, in particular Stefan Batory (1533–1586) and Jan III Sobieski (1629–1696), took a kind, lenient approach to the Jews and lacked fanaticism (Gumplowicz, *Prawodawstwo polskie względem Żydów*, 63–6, 79, 81–4, 93).

[94] Kraushar, *Frank i Frankiści polscy*, i. 82–3. In 1757 the local bishop Mikołaj Dembowski forced a public disputation between Jews and the followers of Jacob Frank, a leader of a Jewish religious movement and a self-proclaimed reincarnation of Shabetai Tsevi.

[95] Nussbaum, *Historyja Żydów od Mojżesza do epoki obecnej*, v. 65–74.   [96] Ibid. v. 70.

[97] See Neufeld, *Urządzenie konsystorza żydowskiego*, 23. See also the publication that Neufeld mentioned: Rosenblatt, 'Dokument prawodawczy Czterech Ziemstw kraju Polskiego'.

[98] See Neufeld, *Urządzenie konsystorza żydowskiego*, 19–20.

[99] Nussbaum, *Historyja Żydów od Mojżesza do epoki obecnej*, v. 42–3.

[100] Kraushar, *Historya Żydów w Polsce*, ii, p. vii.

of the Jews. In Kraushar's view, under the rule of Zygmunt I (1467–1548), during Poland's Golden Age, the Jews benefited from the same religious tolerance as did other dissenters.[101] The Church initiated the majority of intolerant decrees, but, as Smoleński noted, it did not treat non-Catholic Christians any better. Moreover, the Jews found ways to circumvent many of these strict laws.[102]

Writing about the history of Jews in Polish lands, historians struggled with the tension between their hope for Jewish integration in the present or near future and the patterns of Jewish life in the past. As proponents of the Enlightenment and of the integration of Jews into general Polish society, these historians were also critical of long-term effects of policies that encouraged a chasm between the general Polish society and the Jews. These qualms led Kraushar to argue that the Polish–Lithuanian Commonwealth erred in allowing Jewish 'indifference to the matters of the general public, particularism, and a concern for personal gain alone which does not benefit the nation'.[103] According to Nussbaum, the privileges became a double-edged sword for Polish Jewry, proving Poland's tolerance and hospitality on the one hand, and reinforcing the Jewish community's isolation from the rest of the society on the other.[104] He pointed to the negative impact the failure of integration had on both the country and the Jews. In particular, the separate Jewish courts, having weakened the Jews' interest in Polish culture, contributed to the excessive authority enjoyed by rabbis.[105] The Polish government deprived the Jews of any political influence, bringing them to economic ruin, while maintaining their spiritual isolation. The Polish historian Smoleński was the most extreme in his views, likening Jewish separatism to 'a monstrous growth and a cancer eating [Poland] from within'.[106] In his interpretation, the generous tolerance towards Jews in the past created conditions that made future Polish–Jewish rapprochement difficult. The legal status of the Jews served as a barometer for political strength, economic well-being, and the moral authority of the Polish Kingdom and the Polish–Lithuanian Commonwealth. For some authors, criticizing the privileges Jews enjoyed in Poland dovetailed with a denunciation of their economic roles. The privileges led to what Maciejowski decried as excessive Jewish dominance in trade in Poland and Lithuania, which ultimately bore conflicts and violence. His list of Jewish economic vices included their participation in the slave trade in the wake of the Polish Kingdom, their competition with Christian city dwellers, their failure to become peasants, and their role in distilling and selling alcohol.[107] Gumplowicz singled out the Charter of Privileges, granted in 1264,

[101] Ibid. ii. 152.　　　　　　　　　　[102] Smoleński, *Stan i sprawa Żydów polskich w XVIII wieku*, 42–4.
[103] Kraushar, *Historya Żydów w Polsce*, ii. 120.
[104] Nussbaum, *Historyja Żydów od Mojżesza do epoki obecnej*, v. 42–3.
[105] Ibid. v. 45.　　　　　　　　　　[106] Smoleński, *Stan i sprawa Żydów polskich w XVIII wieku*, 41.
[107] See Maciejowski, *Żydzi w Polsce, na Rusi i Litwie*, 14–15, 22, 53–9, 62, 67–8, 94–5.

decrying the separation of Jews from the rest of the nation, which forced them to become a social class engaged in lending money.[108] On the other hand, the inclusive and liberal treatment of the Jews went hand in hand with the vitality of Polish society and with aspirations for a strong state. Smoleński argued that whenever legal decrees marginalized the Jews and limited their economic roles, it resulted in a deepening crisis in the social and economic realms for Polish Jewry and in their physical and spiritual persecution, while the Jewish communities sank further and further into debt. Ultimately, injustices experienced by Polish Jews negatively affected the entire social body and crippled it.[109]

For historians making a case for political integration, changes to the legal status of Polish Jewry discussed during the last decade of Poland's independence, and, in particular, the reforms considered during the Four Year Diet (1788–92) but never enacted, represented a return to the country's best traditions of liberty and toleration. Smoleński believed that in the second half of the eighteenth century, the sheer size and dire situation of the Jewish community necessitated its integration into the nation and into Polish society.[110] He recognized that the traditionally minded Jewish community saw the plans for reform of the status of Jews in the country as a threat, especially because 'Jewish pioneers of progress', having themselves become 'good Poles and enlightened citizens', proved even more radical in their demands than the Poles, and often spoke of the Jewish masses with distaste.[111] Despite the noble intentions of the reformist camp, the question of the place of Jews in Polish society remained unresolved.[112] Given the emancipation of the Jews in 1862 and 1864, historians continued to express high hopes for future integration.[113] They believed that their work had contributed to the positive decrees and would help them in the fight against what they saw as Jewish obscurantism.

[108] Gumplowicz, *Prawodawstwo polskie względem Żydów*, 11.

[109] Smoleński, *Stan i sprawa Żydów polskich w XVIII wieku*, 39–40. Note that Smoleński alleged that traditional Jewry were Poland's ailment, rather than that a lack of progress endangered the Jews, as some Jewish authors suggested.

[110] See ibid. 45–56, 66–9, 70–1. Smoleński praised the idea of making general education for Jews mandatory, even when other groups in Polish society were not included in that measure, as proof that the luminaries supported the philosophy of progress (ibid. 62).

[111] See ibid. 88–9. No wonder, Smoleński argued, that 'superstitious inn-keepers, having no access to the spring of the country's education, who drew their knowledge from the stinking puddle of the Talmud, could not be the pioneers of reform; the Jewish elders, who lived at the expense of the superstitious masses, desired no change, since they did not want to lose the hen laying golden eggs' (ibid. 90). [112] See ibid. 72–6, 83, 87.

[113] With regard to the growing and expanding Jewish population in Warsaw in the second half of the nineteenth century one author commented, 'Since that time other neighbourhoods in the city have been slowly settled by Jews, who through elegant lifestyle and good manners try to come closer to the inhabitants of other denominations' ([Kirszrot], 'Żydzi w Warszawie').

## Jewish–Non-Jewish Relations

Integrationist Polish and Polish Jewish scholars took a keen interest in elucidating historical relations between non-Jews and Jews in the Polish lands, painting a rather cheerful picture. Not only did the country profit from the presence of the Jews, Czacki argued, but Jewish immigration caused no social friction: 'A Christian merchant did not grumble against an Israelite, and when commerce flourished in the shadow of freedom, a Christian in church and a Jew in *shul* blessed the heavens for one motherland and for equal justice.'[114] Others presented an equally harmonious picture of Jewish–non-Jewish relations in distant centuries of Polish history. Moments of crisis—euphemistically called 'sad incidents'—constituted exceptions to the rule and as such were 'written down in the annals of our motherland's history as a special symptom of the population temporarily going insane'.[115]

Instances of friction, persecution, and violence occurred only sporadically and were limited in scope, according to these historians. Moreover, the situation of the Jews varied from town to town, and therefore Jews could always find a new hospitable place somewhere in the Polish lands.[116] The dire situation of the peasants and the persecution of the Jews in western Europe provided a further perspective for the incidents of violence against Jews in the Polish lands, who were generally better off and enjoyed greater religious freedom.[117] This idealized vision of Jewish–non-Jewish relations in the Polish Kingdom and the Polish–Lithuanian Commonwealth served a didactic function: 'since it happened like that in the past, nothing prevents returning to the same honourable tradition in the nineteenth century'.[118]

Historical accounts of Polish Jewish history suggest three explanations for

[114] Czacki, *Rosprawa o Żydach*, 76.

[115] Kraushar, *Historya Żydów w Polsce*, ii. 52–3. Kraushar gave a few examples of such instances from the first decade of the fifteenth century: Poznań, Głogów, and Kraków (ibid. 52–5). As the rumours about Jewish allegiance with the devil spread, 'higher minds looked with terror upon this strange notion of the folk and tried to influence them and calm down their passions with their writings' (ibid. 277).

[116] The larger the community, the more problematic was its relationship with the local burghers (ibid. 56–7).

[117] Ibid. 55. An unattributed article published in *Izraelita* described sixteenth-century Poland as 'a true refuge for all who were hunted and persecuted elsewhere. [In Poland] there was no uncontrolled penchant for wiping out all those who believed differently which we find in other countries... Poland became a new Babylon for the Jews, here they lived safe from bloody persecution of barbarians, some reached high offices and in general nobody prohibited them from being themselves' ('Z historji żydów w Polsce', 44–5).

[118] Analysing the vision of Polish Jewish history published on the pages of *Izraelita*, Zuzanna Kołodziejska suggested that the narrative according to which Jews had found in Poland refuge from persecution in other lands was either a nod to Polish readers who 'cherished the myth of their tolerant

episodes of conflict, hatred, and violence: foreign influence, the Church, and economic competition. In the view of many of these historians writing in Congress Poland, foreign ideas or foreign settlers had threatened to spoil the good relations. Neufeld stressed the initial Jewish encounter with old Polish hospitality and the warm reception they had enjoyed due to the high culture of the country's ruling class. With the influx of foreign burghers from western and central Europe, and the increasing power of the Jesuits, however, anti-Jewish prejudices snuck into Poland.[119] In Kraushar's interpretation, hatred of the Jews was essentially imported into Poland, and when the Jews had suffered persecution, it was 'always incited from the outside and a copy of what was happening at this time in the West on a grander scale'.[120]

A prime example of the disastrous effects of anti-Jewish propaganda brought into Poland was the case of Jan de Capistrano (1386–1456), a Franciscan monk and preacher whose sermons incited a wave of violence and ended the quiet existence of Polish Jews. In Nussbaum's words, the preacher 'pushed Polish Jewry, almost the only [Jewish community] in all of Europe who had lived in peace, into the same abyss of misery and humiliation in which their brethren lived in [other] countries, where his Jew-baiting sermons sowed the poison of hatred and persecution'.[121] Gumplowicz alluded time and again to the Germans as the elements of society most hostile to the Jews.[122] According to Maciejowski, only when 'ignorance took over reason' did Jews become victims of anti-Jewish violence.[123] Like Gumplowicz, he considered the Germans to be 'the second worst enemies of Israel after the Romans'. Germans followed Jews to the Polish towns, competed with them, limited their rights, and eventually tried to remove them from the towns.[124] Awareness of foreign influence helped to clarify the anti-Jewish attitudes and policies of the clergy. Commenting on the canonical laws imposed in 1420 circumscribing relations between Jews and Christians, Nussbaum wrote about a 'barbaric trend, blowing from the Christian countries of western and southern Europe which took over the clergy in Poland ... which broke off relations between Jews and Christians that had been based on the feeling of mutual dependence and need since the era of the Piast dynasty'.[125]

The Church, too, bore responsibility for inciting anti-Jewish prejudice, and

motherland' or a rhetorical tool, since the articles did not shy away from writing about problems (Kołodziejska, 'Izraelita' (1866–1915), 139.)

[119] Neufeld, Urządzenie konsystorza żydowskiego, 67.
[120] Kraushar, Historya Żydów w Polsce, ii. 48–51.
[121] Nussbaum, Historyja Żydów od Mojżesza do epoki obecnej, v. 91.
[122] Gumplowicz, Prawodawstwo polskie względem Żydów, 130–3.
[123] Maciejowski, Żydzi w Polsce, na Rusi i Litwie, 75. Maciejowski mentioned only two religiously motivated anti-Jewish incidents in Kraków, and few all over the country (ibid. 47).
[124] Ibid. 95.    [125] Nussbaum, Historyja Żydów od Mojżesza do epoki obecnej, v. 73–4.

therefore preventing Jewish integration. Blood libel accusations served as the most striking example of religious fanaticism.[126] Gumplowicz argued that the Church continued to play an antagonistic role, opposing new ideas and 'preaching the same regulations it had spread for eight hundred years in sovereign Poland'.[127] Historians stopped short of implicating the Church directly in igniting and legitimizing irrational anti-Jewish practices.[128] Commenting on the disputations between the rabbis and the supporters of Jacob Frank, which tackled the question of the blood libels, Kraushar decried 'an accusation hatched in the darkness, condemned by the more enlightened, and renewed always with a similar horror, whenever passion takes over reason'.[129] The conflict between the traditional Jewish communities and the Frankist movement worsened because the Church stood to gain from it.[130]

Historians of Polish Jewry rejected the notion that anti-Jewish prejudice in the Polish Kingdom and the Polish–Lithuanian Commonwealth, either domestic or imported, was based exclusively on religious difference. Instead, they suggested that conflicts also arose as a result of economic competition, friction described by some authors as 'natural'. Gumplowicz marvelled at the 'simple, common sense and the practical sense' evident in the decisions of the diets seeking to protect the material interests of the Polish gentry.[131] Discussing the influence of the Reformation, Kraushar insisted that clashes and conflicts between non-Jews and Jews stemmed from the 'natural antagonism, with the personal interest of the parties in the narrow field of commercial competition' rather than from religious hatred.[132] The Jewish ability to rely on business networks abroad, and their success in retail, put non-Jewish merchants at a disadvantage. This superiority caused constant friction and incited attempts to limit Jewish economic activities.[133] Competition with non-Jewish townspeople created tension, exacerbated by the nobility's support for the Jews, which led, in turn, to clashes.[134] Thus, historians looked at structural

[126] Nussbaum mentioned blood libel accusations in Poznań in 1399, in Głogów in 1401, and in Kraków in 1407 (Nussbaum, Historyja Żydów od Mojżesza do epoki obecnej, v. 70–2).

[127] Gumplowicz, Prawodawstwo polskie względem Żydów, 106. He argued that, as a result of the pernicious influence of the Jesuits, who controlled the schools in Poland, the nobility radically changed its approach to faith and people of other religions, and hatred of the Jews permeated the resolutions of the diets. The nobility regained its tolerant and generous approach only in the last decades of Poland's independence (ibid. 86–7, 95, 97, 101).

[128] Maciejowski suggested that blood libel accusations resulted from the activities of 'bad people', who placed corpses of Christian children in Jewish homes to incite riots. These acts, he argued, had been perpetrated for centuries, until recent times (Maciejowski, Żydzi w Polsce, na Rusi i Litwie, 18).

[129] Kraushar, Frank i Frankiści polscy, i. 152. Describing instances of religious persecution following the rise of Frankism, Kraushar called the blood libel a 'medieval superstition' (ibid. 111).

[130] Ibid. 107.  [131] Gumplowicz, Prawodawstwo polskie względem Żydów, 31.
[132] Kraushar, Historya Żydów w Polsce, ii. 192, 212–15.  [133] Ibid. ii. 193–4.
[134] Some towns attempted to create coalitions to exert pressure on the king—for example, in 1521 in

aspects of the economic roles played by the Jews to explain prejudice and violence. In Nussbaum's view, the oppression of the poor in Lithuania and the Jewish monopoly on distilling alcohol led to the Cossack uprisings of the mid-seventeenth century.[135] An article in *Izraelita* argued that Jews had been craftsmen from time immemorial and that they engaged in trade only because they were banned from the guilds. Neither the Jewish nor the general society knew enough about Jewish craftsmen, whose history needed to be studied further.[136] By asserting positive Jewish–non-Jewish relations in Old Poland and in the Polish–Lithuanian Commonwealth, and attributing the episodic tensions to competition, these historians attempted to shed light on the role played by Jews in the Polish economy. The primary concern of these discussions was the role Jews played in trade, attempting to explain the reasons for the Jewish occupational structure.

The privileges of Warsaw burghers were issued and confirmed for the last time by Stanisław August.[137] The burghers' relations with the Jews, who poured into the city in the late eighteenth century, proved volatile, with several eruptions of anti-Jewish violence.[138] In his study of the Frankist movement, Kraushar mentioned the bloody persecutions of Zelezniak and Gonta in Ukraine, which 'renewed the scenes of the Chmielnicki era', as the context for Frank's activities and his desire to serve 'in the role of a prophet'.[139] Historical assessments, however, remained optimistic: despite occasional clashes, Jews in Poland enjoyed unparalleled religious freedom, and they had good relations with peasants, the nobility, and the lords. Protected by the kings and the diets, they did not need to worry about conflict with burghers and magistrates.[140] As Zuzanna Kołodziejska has emphasized, the argument was that the history of Polish Jews demonstrated 'the absurdity of antisemitic ideas'.[141]

While explaining the 'natural' causes of prejudice and violence, some Polish

---

Lwów, Poznań, and Kraków—with unknown results (ibid. 186). In 1527, requests from the magistrates caused the king to expel the Jews from Warsaw and its suburbs, prohibiting them from living or trading there. Likewise, at the request of the magistrates, Jewish freedom of living, purchasing, and trading was revoked for Radziejów (ibid. 190).

[135] Nussbaum, *Historyja Żydów od Mojżesza do epoki obecnej*, v. 71–2. In this context, the author mentioned *Yeven metsulah*, which he translates as 'deep puddle' (*głęboka kałuża*) and ascribes to 'Matias Berson'.     [136] L. W-w, 'Słów kilka o rzemieślnikach żydach'.
[137] Nussbaum, *Szkice historyczne z życia Żydów w Warszawie*, 1–7.
[138] Ibid. 18–27.     [139] Kraushar, *Frank i Frankiści polscy*, i. 279.
[140] Kraushar, *Historya Żydów w Polsce*, ii. 196–8. He also referred to accusations of Jews smuggling converts to Turkey via Hungary and pointed to the roots of these accusations in Russia. He expressed doubt that the Jews, with their traditions and awareness of being tolerated, would want to risk their status by engaging in proselytizing activities, which the clergy watched closely. These rumours negatively affected the status of the Jews (ibid. 199–204).     [141] Kołodziejska, '*Izraelita*' (1866–1915), 138.

historians discussed the so-called moral shortcomings of the Jews. Maciejowski portrayed the characters of the peoples among whom the Jews had settled—Poles, Russians, and Lithuanians—as lacking Jewish thriftiness, cunning, and shrewdness, and the ability to build on small profits, which contributed to Jewish prosperity in Poland–Lithuania.[142] He portrayed Jews as impatient, greedy, and ignorant of the political and economic situation in Poland.[143] Maciejowski contextualized Jewish vice in history, but also tied it to the Talmud.[144] Smoleński constructed a similarly ambivalent argument. While paying close attention to the historic economic roles of Polish Jews, he showed ambivalence, if not bias, in attributing Jewish prominence in trade to their 'cunning' and 'ruthless means'. According to Smoleński, Jews who left Polish towns at the beginning of the seventeenth century to settle in villages in Ukraine, and later in Ruthenia and Lithuania, harmed the local population while serving greedy landowners.[145] The Jews took to the occupations of leaseholding and innkeeping, which Smoleński believed corrupted them more easily because 'they have long been inclined to take the twisted path of fraud, encouraged even to take such a path'.[146]

However, Smoleński did not put all the blame on the Jews for the demoralization and ruin of the peasants in the villages and the downfall of the towns. Behind the immoral economic practices of the Jews lay the pressure put on them by the greedy and spoiled nobility over the course of three centuries.[147] Combined with the influence of the Catholic clergy, he argued, these factors pushed Polish Jews into unethical practices and professions. Smoleński criticized the abuse of the Jews by their lords, and the contempt for Jews exhibited by the enlightened elites, pointing out that on the eve of the country's collapse much misdirected intellectual effort went into ridiculing and blaming all evils on the Jews. He admitted that the Jews proved indispensable to the country's economy, even in their much-criticized traditional roles, and that they failed to embrace agriculture due

[142] Maciejowski, *Żydzi w Polsce, na Rusi i Litwie*, 28.   [143] Ibid. 42–3, 110–11.

[144] See his examples of unethical economic strategies employed by Jews in *Żydzi w Polsce, na Rusi i Litwie*, 23, 65. In accordance with the Enlightenment discourse about the need for 'improvement' of the Jews, Maciejowski linked Jewish 'flaws' not only with the Talmud but also with the persecution the Jews had suffered in Christian lands (ibid. 32–3). Smoleński both condemned the attitudes of the Catholic Church in Poland and pinpointed Jewish moral shortcomings. He argued that 'pushing the Jews away from the springs of education forced them to pollute themselves with the mud of the Talmud' (Smoleński, *Stan i sprawa Żydów polskich w XVIII wieku*, 21).

[145] See Smoleński, *Stan i sprawa Żydów polskich w XVIII wieku*, 7–15.

[146] Ibid. 12. Moreover, Smoleński argued that through their shrewd operations in tax collecting, brewing, and distributing liquors, Jews exploited the simple folk and destroyed the peasants. They manipulated their local lords, always finding moral justification in the Talmud, and they preyed on people's weaknesses and mistakes (ibid. 13–15).

[147] Ibid. 15–18. In the eighteenth century, no productive lines of work were offered to the Jews, who lived for the most part in poverty.

to the lack of appropriate legislation encouraging them to do so. But in contrast to his quest for a just and balanced picture of the situation of the Jews in the eighteenth century, and his emphasis on mistaken government policies in the past, Smoleński summarized the impact of hundreds of years of Jewish presence in Poland in harsh terms. He accused Jews of inducing alcohol consumption among peasants, flooding the country with false coins, and having a disastrous effect on agriculture and trade. In his view, in the eighteenth century the Jews caused only damage, contributing to the moral decay and material collapse of the country.[148]

## The Jewish Community and Its Institutions

Despite their idealized accounts of Jews and non-Jews living together peacefully at the dawn of Jewish settlement in the Polish lands, with only occasional crises in the course of Polish Jewish history, integrationist historians recognized that Jews had lived apart from the rest of Polish society over the centuries.[149] Internal relations were regulated by religious law, and this made the difference between the Jews and the other inhabitants an impenetrable obstacle to rapprochement.[150] Jewish self-government in the Polish Kingdom and in the Polish–Lithuanian Commonwealth reinforced the separation. It is no wonder that most historians discussed the institutions of Jewish autonomy in ambivalent terms. Neufeld seems to have taken the most moderate position among Polish Jewish historians.[151] He reminded his readers of the high standing and authority of the Council of Four Lands—the central Jewish governing body in Poland and beyond—and of the progressive laws it passed, at times surpassing the scope of Napoleonic legislation.[152] On the other hand, he judged the role played by communal councils of individual communities (*kehalim*) in harsh terms. Calling them a 'people's plague', he described these bodies as despotic and accused them of exploiting their authority and ruling by fear.[153] Until the last king, Stanisław August, stripped them of their civil and criminal jurisdiction, these institutions separated the Jews from the nation. For Neufeld the limits Stanisław August imposed on these councils, and other sweeping reforms of religious institutions proposed by the Four Year Diet,

---

[148] Smoleński, *Stan i sprawa Żydów polskich w XVIII wieku*, 21–37.

[149] Reflecting on the social, cultural, and political divide between Jews and non-Jews, they criticized the fact that the Jews were 'forced to live separately, [and] led life within their limits, without going beyond the drawn confines' (Kraushar, *Historya Żydów w Polsce*, ii. 64).

[150] Ibid. ii. 121. See the footnote on pp. 121–2 about the Jews beginning to leave 'the narrow tribal circle [*ciasne koło plemienności*]'.

[151] It closely resembled his take on hasidism. See Wodziński, *Haskalah and Hasidism*.

[152] See Neufeld, *Urządzenie konsystorza żydowskiego*, 23. See also the publication that Neufeld mentioned: Rosenblatt, 'Dokument prawodawczy Czterech Ziemstw kraju Polskiego'.

[153] Neufeld, *Urządzenie konsystorza żydowskiego*, 23–4.

signalled hopes for a thorough reform of Jewish institutions.[154] Still, he associated the old communal Jewish councils with abuse, humiliating punishments, extortion, and even 'religious terrorism', calling them 'the Jewish inquisition'.[155] Believing in a synthesis of Jewish and Polish cultures, combining Polish patriotism and the Jewish religion, Neufeld singled out for criticism hasidic leaders, accusing them of keeping their flock in ignorance.[156]

For Kraushar, Jewish autonomy appeared anachronistic and harmful, as Jews 'showed insufficient desire for worldly matters, which in their opinion could deprive them of the biblical character and religious quality which tradition, origin, and events of the past gave [them]'.[157] He blamed their excessive numbers in towns, and the influence of rabbis grounded in their own system of education, for hindering 'progress' among Polish Jews under the Jagiellonian dynasty and the elected kings.[158] Ultimately, he argued, Jewish autonomy prevented the integration of Polish Jews with 'the rest of the nation'. In the introductory chapter to his second volume, Kraushar stressed the 'completely different life that Polish Jews developed in the course of the centuries, separated from that of their western tribe members; but this life relied at first on institutions taken from elsewhere and conditions to which they have become accustomed for centuries'. Old Polish law took a neutral position regarding the Jews, regulating only their external relations with the other inhabitants of the land and setting some limits on them. Polish law left the entire field of internal relations untouched, so that Jews observed their customs in autonomous communities and enjoyed freedoms they had not always had before. These facts, and the Jews' standing in other European societies, Kraushar declared, helped explain their external contemporary conservatism, 'so contrary to the general progress'.[159]

Unlike most integrationist historians, who elaborated on Jewish institutions in the past in order to address the issue of what they perceived as Jewish separatism, Kraushar researched the workings of internal Jewish life, in addition to the legal status of the Jews and the attitudes of Polish monarchs, nobles, and the Catholic Church. He praised the richness of Jewish intellectual life in the period of the Reformation. However, he noted that their lack of knowledge of the Polish language hampered closer encounters with Christians, and Christian scholars did not familiarize themselves with the achievements of Jewish learning. The situation was better in Lithuania, where the Karaites were familiar with Polish-Latin literature.[160] Discussing the status of Jewish education during the reign of Zygmunt I, Kraushar argued that 'Poland was the only country where the scattered vestiges of

---

[154] See ibid. 23–4. These hopes failed to materialize, and the communal councils continued to function until 1821, when at last Dozory Bóżnicze (new synagogue boards) replaced them.
[155] See ibid. 25, 84.   [156] See ibid. 54.   [157] Kraushar, *Historya Żydów w Polsce*, ii. 122.
[158] Ibid. ii. 123–4, 240–6.   [159] Ibid. ii. 1–2.   [160] Ibid. ii. 264–5.

the once great nation could unite its spiritual activity for preserving and propagating its rich rabbinical literature'.[161] In his book on the Frankist movement, he described the attempts to free the Jews 'from age-old misery' by seeking 'new truth in another faith'.[162] While this historian was all too happy to point out the ignorance and internal contradictions in Frank's teachings, he also appreciated 'the glimmer of philosophical thought not inferior to many pagan ideas'.[163] Kraushar attributed the rabbis' response to Frank to their 'fanaticism', intensified by 'the intellectual level of contemporary [Polish] Jews', which was inferior to that in western Europe and conditioned by settlement patterns in the villages and towns of the Polish–Lithuanian Commonwealth that were virtually unknown in Germany.[164]

Nussbaum went even further, comparing Jewish autonomy to 'the seed of the cancer eating, to this very day, the body of Polish Judaism . . . Respect and submissiveness of the Jewish masses, shown to their religious guides, taught them to follow the decrees [of their leaders] in the same measure as religious laws.'[165] The Jewish judicial system set up by Kazimierz the Great strengthened internal Jewish autonomy, making it dependent on rabbis and elders who sought to continue isolation from the outside world.[166] Nussbaum bemoaned the fact that Polish Jews did not appreciate secular knowledge, but focused on trade and industry instead. As a result, while contributing to the development of the cities and general prosperity, Jews failed to participate in public activities other than commerce. Ultimately, 'The governments erred, the Jews erred, and the fatal results fell on the entire country!'[167]

Although he was mostly concerned with its legal basis in the privilege of Kazimierz the Great, rather than the social reality, Gumplowicz also analysed the organization of the Jews in Poland. It stemmed from two factors, he claimed: their legal status as defined by royal privileges and the legislation of the *voivode*—which Gumplowicz described as 'the bureaucratic' part of the picture—and the autonomous Jewish legal structure. Gumplowicz divided the institutions of Jewish autonomy into national and local organizations.[168] He described the *kehalim*

---

[161] Kraushar, *Historya Żydów w Polsce*, ii. 217.

[162] Kraushar, *Frank i Frankiści polscy*, i. 10. See the critical review of the book by Korzon, 'Kraushar Aleksander: Frank i Frankiści polscy 1726–1816'.

[163] Kraushar, *Frank i Frankiści polscy*, i. 291. See also ibid. i. 64–5, 112. Kraushar saw the movement as yet another expression of the 'continued evolution of reformist attempts of Jewish dreamers who wished to wrest Judaism from age-old backwardness and sought in the mystical books of the East the key to knowledge [of] the religious truth' (ibid. i. 23).    [164] Ibid. i. 212.

[165] Nussbaum, *Historyja Żydów od Mojżesza do epoki obecnej*, v. 56.    [166] Ibid. v. 52.

[167] Ibid. v. 56. Nussbaum complained bitterly that 'neither the government nor the communities worried about educating enlightened rabbis'. As a result of this neglect, he argued, 'the study of Talmud flourished at a remove from independent thinking and logical conclusions'.

[168] See Gumplowicz, *Prawodawstwo polskie względem Żydów*, 115–17.

with their rabbis as 'small republics with elected presidents', arguing that 'if one looked at their self-governing with their own law, the laws of Moses and the Talmud, if one was led blindfolded through these numerous small towns, from one *kahal* to another, without being shown the rest of the country, one would think he was not in Poland, but in Palestine'.[169]

Over and over again, historians denounced what Gumplowicz described as a 'chasm' separating the Jews from the Christian population; they called for the chasm to be bridged, following the example of western Europe, by 'education and civilization'.[170] For Gumplowicz, the privilege granted to the Jews in 1264 distanced them from Poland's affairs, eventually harming them morally. For Nussbaum, the same phenomenon was epitomized by the Council of Four Lands.[171] Smoleński harshly criticized the scope of Jewish autonomy in Poland. The traditional community centralized all religious and social affairs, as well as a substantial portion of judicial affairs. The selfish elders of Jewish communities controlled the lives of simple Jews through the threat of ostracism (*ḥerem*), and carefully guarded their separation in all realms of social interaction and spiritual life.[172] Smoleński decried the despotism of the rabbis, the high cost of supporting Jewish communal organizations, and the Jewish religious lifestyle, all of which contributed to what he saw as the wretched state of Polish Jewry.[173] Still, the responsibility did not rest exclusively with the Jews, as non-Jews, too, encouraged separation.[174] Ultimately, Smoleński argued, Poland needed the Jews, their skills, and their money, and therefore treated their economic activities with restraint. He acknowledged that Jews 'at times of need opened for [the country] their hearts and their pockets'. Moreover, he conceded that the anti-Jewish resentment of the Warsaw burghers led to anti-Jewish violence during the Diet, forcing those responsible for keeping order to remove Jews from the city.[175]

Closely linked to the subject of the legal status of Jews was the interest in Jewish internal institutions and communal life. Polish integrationist historians discussed Jewish educational institutions and intellectual interests in the Polish–Lithuanian Commonwealth with ambivalence. Kraushar praised the fact that every Jewish child received a traditional Jewish education, with instruction in reading and writing. However, he criticized its one-sidedness, which 'has a bad effect on the social standing of contemporary Jews, who became easy victims of

---

[169] See ibid. 118.  [170] Ibid. 11.

[171] Nussbaum, *Szkice historyczne z życia Żydów w Warszawie*, 36–7. Nussbaum castigated the council as the institution that 'for a century and a half hindered any independence in Polish Jews, any aspiration for general education, any sense for a state prosperity, getting them used to blind obedience and slavish submission to those among them who appeared superior in the smallest measure in their religious practice and rabbinic learning' (ibid. 39–40).

[172] Smoleński, *Stan i sprawa Żydów polskich w XVIII wieku*, 6, 21, 83–6.

[173] Ibid. 20.   [174] Ibid. 5–6.   [175] Ibid. 78–83. Quotation from p. 80.

metaphysical and kabbalistic dreams'.[176] While Kraushar found fault in the narrowness of Polish Jewry's intellectual pursuits, he also understood it in light of the centuries-long Jewish tradition, which had fulfilled spiritual needs. Jewish intellectual pursuits had shaped the Jewish character, which Kraushar saw as ridden with 'duality'—between the contemporary pursuits of income and material goods and the passion for rabbinical literature and metaphysical enquiries. Kraushar did not blame the lack of intellectual interaction with non-Jews on the Jews, as the clergy had made it difficult for Jewish children to attend Polish schools, and therefore to acquire the Polish language. The second explanation for intellectual isolation, however, was related to the prevalence of the 'German language' (Yiddish) among Polish Jews and its negative influence.[177] Due to the protests of the Polish clergy, as early as the sixteenth century Jewish children were not allowed to study together with Christians.[178] Adolf Jakub Cohn, a graduate of the Rabbinical School in Warsaw, a lawyer, and a member of the Warsaw progressive circle, bemoaned the far-reaching negative effect of separate Jewish schools: 'The fate of the Jewish people in Poland would without a doubt be different, and would have taken a better direction, if the youth could from the earliest childhood receive an education in the same institutions together with their compatriots of other denominations.'[179] Maciejowski blamed hasidic leaders for keeping Jews and Poles apart. In contrast, he wrote in very positive terms about Jacob Frank, as a leader who tried to bring the two groups closer to each other.[180] They concluded that religious fanaticism blocked the path that would have led to harmonious cohabitation.

While arguing for a fair judgement of the role the Jews played in Poland's economy, Smoleński expressed unequivocal contempt for most aspects of internal Jewish social and religious life. Like Maciejowski, he criticized the emergence of hasidism, which he felt the government should have opposed, describing it as one of 'the various sects proving its [Jewry's] moral gangrene. They [the hasidim] negatively affected the economic situation of the Jews, increased hatred towards them by the simple folk, and tore down their exemplary solidarity, dividing them into factions fighting intensely with each other.'[181] Driven by his conviction that the only solution to the Jewish question was their radical integration into Gentile society, Smoleński also argued that the Frankist movement 'augured the turning

---

[176] Kraushar, *Historya Żydów w Polsce*, ii. 219–24.

[177] Ibid. 218–25. Kraushar referred to the problematic linguistic situation of contemporary Jewish communities: 'In Russia, Jews spoke good Russian, while here [*u nas*] the jargon [Yiddish] was hard to uproot' (p. 225).

[178] See Cohn, 'Wstęp: Wiadomości historyczne o szkołach dla żydów w Polsce', 1–2.

[179] Ibid. 1.   [180] Maciejowski, *Żydzi w Polsce, na Rusi i Litwie*, 77–80.

[181] Smoleński, *Stan i sprawa Żydów polskich w XVIII wieku*, 33.

away of Jewry from the path of isolation and their merging into the national body—a change even more fortunate because it came from within Jewry'.[182]

In the work of Jewish historians one finds palpable ambivalence about traditional Jewish society and its institutions. Nussbaum described the excommunication of those evading taxes on kosher food in 1817 as an example of 'stupidity, lack of common sense, and superstition' and an 'embryo hatched in the brains of the religious leaders, Polish rabbis—the children of the past era of the Synods... who did not contribute a single book to general secular knowledge and progress, but rather kept the Jews away from logic, rationalism, and real science'.[183] He contrasted this 'reactionary heritage' prevailing in Congress Poland with the progressive Jewish circles in Warsaw, especially those associated with the Rabbinical School (Szkoła Rabinów).[184]

Despite their critical views of the past, these historians drew hope from the study of Polish Jewish history. For Czacki, this hope stemmed from the fact that, although in the past Polish Jews had focused on religious studies, they demonstrated their devotion to the motherland by participating in the failed 1794 Polish insurrection against Russian imperial domination.[185] Nussbaum concluded his book with a discussion of the Jews' emancipation. He assured his readers that society's expectation that Jews should prove their attachment to the country was just: 'We have an obligation to prove ourselves worthy of the rights that have been bestowed upon us and to earn through our behaviour more and more trust, so that we can serve all the branches of the civil service and in each field of work.'[186] Was scholarship thus simply a tool for demonstrating Jews' worthiness while transforming and improving them at the same time?

Following the period of emancipation, as Nussbaum argued, the attitudes of non-Jews towards Jews became increasingly negative and the conflict grew deeper.[187] He described the phenomenon of antisemitism as 'hatched in Germany' and 'brought to Poland'. He bemoaned the negative impact of anti-Jewish slander on 'reactionary Jews', because it discouraged their assimilation and their

---

[182] Ibid. 34.

[183] Nussbaum, *Szkice historyczne z życia Żydów w Warszawie*, 48. Nussbaum translated and published the text of the *ḥerem* (ban) of 1817, which he found in the local archive. See ibid. 44–8.

[184] Ibid. 56–75.

[185] Czacki wrote his treatise on the Jews in Poland in the context of the Polish state, its economic and social agendas, and the interests and relations between its non-Jewish and Jewish inhabitants. He only briefly concerned himself with phenomena affecting mainly the Jewish community in Poland and beyond, such as the Shabatean movement, or the emergence of Jacob Frank and hasidism (Czacki, *Rosprawa o Żydach*, 99, 102, 104–7). On the focus of Jewish education in Poland on religious learning with rudiments of philosophy, see ibid. 214–15.

[186] Nussbaum, *Szkice historyczne z życia Żydów w Warszawie*, 262.

[187] Nussbaum, *Historyja Żydów od Mojżesza do epoki obecnej*, v. 446–7.

embrace of the Polish language, pushing them back into isolation, as they 'lost their enthusiasm for anything concerning the country in which they have been living for hundreds of years, and as Palestinian inspirations began to prevail'.[188] Linguistic dissimilation became so prevalent that the Jewish intelligentsia had to use Yiddish to address the masses 'in order to serve them healthy spiritual food in a filthy vessel'. Nevertheless, Nussbaum praised his own social circle, full of hope for the inevitable triumph of 'progress and nurturing general human ideals', while also proving Jews worthy of equal rights.[189]

These ideas met with a critical response. In 1901, Adolf Jakub Cohn published an article in *Izraelita* offering a survey of Polish Jewish literature, broadly defined, which also included the work of historians. Cohn found the body of work deficient compared to the German and Russian Jewish writing.[190] He focused for the most part on work dealing with 'the life, scholarship, and religion of their tribe'.[191] Although Cohn had a favourable opinion of Nussbaum's brochure on the history of the Jews in Warsaw and his five-volume survey of Jewish history, as well as Kraushar's work, he complained about the 'unparalleled poverty' (*bezprzykładne ubóstwo*) of Polish Jewish literature. He lamented the Jewish intelligentsia's hesitation to take on Jewish subjects—either for fear of being attacked by antisemites or because they lacked sufficient knowledge and familiarity with the Jewish tradition, despite being raised in nominally Jewish families.[192]

Meanwhile, the study of internal Jewish life gained importance as a subject in its own right.[193] A host of Jewish authors began delving into individual communities in major cities of the Polish–Lithuanian Commonwealth, focusing on local rabbinical elites. Wilno became the first community of the Polish–Lithuanian Commonwealth whose past served as a subject of historical investigation by a maskil and scholar. In 1860, Samuel Joseph Finn published *Kiryah ne'emanah: korot adat yisra'el ba'ir vilna vetsiyunim linefashot ge'oneiha, ḥakhameiha, sofreiha unediveiha* (Faithful City: History of the Wilno Jewish Community and Memorials to Its Sages, Writers, and Benefactors).[194] In the introduction, he claimed he had come to Lithuania to pursue historical research and collect material about its Jewish communities, but the material on Wilno was so rich that he decided to devote a separate volume to the city.[195] He explained his reasons for taking up the historical enterprise: 'I have seen that in our generation, a generation that wakes

---

[188] Nussbaum, *Historyja Żydów od Mojżesza do epoki obecnej*, v. 447.
[189] Ibid. v. 448–9.   [190] Cohn, 'Nasz dorobek literacki'.   [191] Ibid. 110–11.
[192] Ibid. 111. Cohn raised several solutions: creating an association to support Polish Jewish literature, expressing support for the authors of such works, explaining to those who were fearful that they could continue to write about general subjects, as well as competitions and a reform of child-rearing practices (ibid. 112). See Kołodziejska, '*Izraelita*' *(1866–1915)*, 141.
[193] Horowitz, *Russian Idea–Jewish Presence*, 91.
[194] Wilno, 1860; 2nd edn. 1915.   [195] Finn, *Faithful City* (Heb.), p. v.

the slumbering and rouses the dormant, there arose many men of wisdom who cherished the memories of their people and published the inscriptions found in the cemeteries of their cities.'[196] Finn hoped to write a volume about the leading figures in Poland–Lithuania as part of a study on the Jewish diaspora.[197] Inspired by Samuel David Luzzatto, Yitshak Ber Levinzohn, and Koppelman Lieben and their works on illustrious Jewish communities in Germany, Italy, and the Czech lands, Finn consulted *matsevot* (gravestones), communal records, books, old letters and stories collected from the Jewish elders of the city (*sipurim miziknei ha'ir*). He also relied on his personal connections with people in the city, referring to books he had seen in the hands of his acquaintances, and on references from Matitiahu Straszun, a prominent maskil and communal leader in Wilno. Finn complained that he lacked materials to write a complete history of the Jewish community there.[198] Although interested in the history of the Jewish community, he discussed it in the general context of the city of Wilno from the time of Giedymin (r. 1316–41) to that of Alexander I (r. 1492–1506). Drawing on secondary sources in Polish and Russian, he mentioned the legal status of the Jews, the taxes they paid, and the persecution they suffered. The second part of the book dealt with Wilno's rabbis, from 1640 to 'the last generation'. Consulting both Jewish and non-Jewish sources, Finn did not limit himself to rabbinical figures, but included other members of the elite, such as communal leaders.[199]

In 1886, Arie Leib Feinstein, a traditional scholar and communal leader, published his volume on Brześć Litewski (Brisk) entitled *Ir tehilah* (City of Praise), of which the first part discussed the history of the community, while the second part portrayed its last hundred years, covering its regulations, charity, synagogues, and rabbis.[200] Personalizing Brisk, Feinstein pointed to books on other Jewish communities as a motivation for his work: 'Our city is ashamed in front of other, younger towns, which have their chronicles (*pinkasim*).'[201] He found his task particularly difficult, since the material that 'everybody uses'—the old communal records—had disappeared, and the old cemetery of Brisk had been destroyed. For information, he turned to rabbinical sources, but also to non-Jewish published primary and secondary sources.[202] He listed events important in the community's history and institutions, such as the establishment of a cemetery, laws issued

---

[196] Ibid. Translation as quoted in Biderman, *Mayer Balaban*, 37.
[197] Finn, *Faithful City* (Heb.), pp. vii–viii.
[198] He was motivated by research on gravestones in Trieste, Toledo, Worms, and Prague. At the same time, he complained of destroyed gravestones, especially during the Franco-Russian war of 1812, and communal records lost during wars and conflicts in the Rabbinical Court. See Finn (Heb.), *Faithful City*, pp. vi–vii. [199] Ibid. 1–37. [200] Feinstein, *City of Praise* (Heb.). [201] Ibid. 7.
[202] Ibid. 5–8. Among others, Feinstein relied on the fifteen-volume *Słownik geograficzny Królestwa Polskiego i innych krajów słowiańskich*, Harkavy's *Jews and the Language of the Slavs* (Heb.), the Russian periodical *Voskhod*, and the works of Czacki and Kraushar (ibid. 21). In this volume, Feinstein included

by the kings, and the regulations of the Council of the Land of Lithuania (Va'ad Medinat Lita) pertaining to Brisk, and he named Brisk's representatives, as well as books relating to Brisk. In addition to the rabbinical elite, Feinstein discussed Jewish occupations and local customs, and included information about recent developments, such as the new town, Kobryn, and new cemeteries and synagogues.[203]

The author of one of these monographs on local Jewish communities, Chaym Nathan Dembitzer, had devoted himself since the 1870s to collecting manuscripts and studying the past, especially the rabbinical elite of the major Jewish communities in Poland. An Orthodox communal leader, religious court judge, and preacher in Kraków, in 1888 Dembitzer published a small volume in Hebrew, *Kelilat yofi* (The Perfection of Beauty), on the history of Lwów rabbis.[204] The core of the book consisted of chronologically arranged biographical articles about the rabbis. Dembitzer listed the requirements for writing such a book: in addition to access to printed books, to have the manuscripts of the community records of the city available at all times and the time 'to investigate every detail'. Of all these precious commodities, Dembitzer claimed to have had only the books.[205] Ultimately, he was not discouraged by the fact that he had never been to Lwów and did not have access to the material; he claimed to have written accurately from memory of material he had seen in the past.[206] He relied on Jewish sources, collecting books and old manuscripts to write his history of the rabbinical elite, and sending letters to people asking about family connections. Praising the rabbis of Lwów from both the distant and more immediate past, Dembitzer assured his readers that, although he was interested in rabbis, the various unhappy events afflicting the city—the loss of life, the destruction of the city in the seventeenth-century wars, and plagues—did not escape his attention.[207] Finally, Dembitzer expressed hope that 'the lovers of antiquities' (*alizei kadmoniyot*) would like his work.[208]

Dembitzer described the period predating the earliest available documents of 1500 as 'chaos', because Jews who came from France and the German lands could not support rabbis in the same way as they did in western Europe, lacking adequate resources until the mid-seventeenth century. The situation improved under King Zygmunt I, who granted the Jews privileges. At this time, a *beit midrash* (Jewish study hall) was established in Lwów.[209] Dembitzer divided the rabbis into

letters from Harkavy with his comments and historical references. He referred to existing literature, correcting, for example, mistakes made by Tadeusz Czacki (ibid. 63).

[203] Feinstein, *City of Praise* (Heb.), 207.
[204] 2 vols. (Kraków, 1888–93).                    [205] Dembitzer, *Kelilat yofi*, i, pp. i–ii.
[206] Ibid. i, pp. ii–iii. However, Dembitzer advised Salomon Buber to add data from communal records and manuscripts available to him to complete the research (ibid. i, p. x).
[207] Ibid. i, pp. v–vi.          [208] Ibid. i, p. x.          [209] Ibid. i. 2.

four generations of students of the great rabbis, and he praised the Council of the Four Lands.[210] He presented a picture of Poland as a centre of learning and coexistence, superior to Germany and Italy 'where religious hatred grew. Only in the lands of Poland did they find a place to study Torah.'[211]

Another important author of Hebrew monographs, Salomon Buber, a Galician Jewish scholar and editor of Midrash and medieval Hebrew texts, published a work on the Lwów rabbis entitled *Anshei shem* (Men of Renown). Buber located and used communal records, and took note of the meetings of the Council of Four Lands in the city, the city's yeshivas, and many leaders of the talmudic academies. But he also consulted non-Jewish sources at the Bernardine Archives in Lwów.[212] Buber explained that writing history proved quite difficult, if not impossible, when important sources disappeared. He stressed that the city was ancient, but the earliest sources dated back only to the beginning of the sixteenth century.[213] He expressed astonishment that no one before him had bothered to record the names of 'all the rabbis of the great city for their eternal memory [*mazkeret olamim*]'.[214] Drawing on the *pinkasim*, books, and inscriptions on gravestones, and applying as critical an eye as possible, Buber organized his material and composed stories about the lives and works of the rabbis and, more generally, about 'the situation of our people at the time'.[215] He saw his own work as a useful contribution to the future scholarship on the history of the town's rabbis. With that vision in mind, Buber closed his introduction with an appeal to the leaders of the community to put the *matsevot* in their places, clean the stones, and seek out and copy the inscriptions of the gravestones of great scholars.[216]

In 1903, Buber published a monograph on the rabbis of Żółkiew, *Kiryah nisgabah hi ha'ir zolkva* (The Exalted Town of Żółkiew), with the biographies of 307 rabbis based on the inscriptions of gravestones, books, and *haskamot*

---

[210] Ibid. i. 12, 17.

[211] Ibid. i. 17. Dembitzer admitted, however, that learning was common among rabbis but not among the simple Jews (ibid. i. 18). He briefly considered the distinctions between the scholars who ran the yeshivas, the rabbis, and the members of rabbinical courts (ibid. i. 26).

[212] Buber, 'Introductory Remarks', to *Men of Renown* (Heb.), pp. vi–vii, xi–xiii. He published examples from the *pinkas* at the end of the volume. Buber relied on inaccurate notes from the communal records of the Jewish council in the city of Lwów, lost in 1860 after Gabryel Suchystaw copied from them for his publication *Matsevet kodesh* (Sacred Monument). He chose scholars from among 240 names appearing in the *pinkas*, supplementing them with the names of rabbis appearing in *matsevot* and in books. A respected banker in Lwów, Buber served as president of the Lwów Chamber of Commerce and board member of the Lwów Jewish Community Council from 1870.

[213] Ibid., pp. x–xi.    [214] Ibid., p. v.

[215] Ibid., p. vi. Buber was particularly aware of the difficulty with the inscriptions on gravestones: Suchystaw had made mistakes, and many gravestones had fallen over and there was no way of determining the exact original inscription. Buber also mentioned the crises of war, plague, and persecution (ibid., p. xxii).    [216] Ibid., pp. vii–viii.

(approbations) in old books and communal records (*pinkas hakehilah*).²¹⁷ In his introduction, Buber expressed his hope that 'these few words will quench the thirst of those longing to know the whereabouts of our people in the city of Żółkiew. The reader will find more about it inside the book and in the appendices.' He concluded modestly, 'I know, however, that I have not fulfilled my duty by all of this, but the lack of sources on the subject will justify my actions to those readers who know about these things, and it is not for me to finish the job'.²¹⁸ He strove to reconstruct the areas of the town in which Jews first lived, and the changes in the Jewish neighbourhood, especially the construction of the synagogues. He traced the history of Jewish institutions in the city, such as the rabbinical court, and mixed in anecdotes about the relations between Jews and non-Jews.²¹⁹ Buber was also interested in the social life of the community, but here too he limited himself to several anecdotes, in chronological order, without connecting them to a larger historical narrative.²²⁰ He demonstrated the strength of the local Jewish community by giving occasional data on the number of Jewish houses and the size of the population in the second half of the seventeenth century. However, the book focused mainly on the rabbis and scholars who turned Żółkiew into 'the city and the mother in Israel'—an important centre of Jewish learning.²²¹ As was the case with other Hebrew communal chronicles, Buber relied almost exclusively on Jewish religious sources.

A growing interest in recording and celebrating the history of Jewish communities and their rabbis brought together authors—Haim Gertner calls them 'chroniclers'—who corresponded with one another, exchanging materials and historical references and offering feedback and encouragement for ongoing projects.²²² This budding network of researchers included both autodidacts and

---

²¹⁷ Buber, *The Exalted Town of Żółkiew* (Heb.).                       ²¹⁸ Ibid. 5.

²¹⁹ Ibid. 1–5. For example, Buber mentioned that in 1649 a Christian who had killed a Jew was executed. He also touched on the Chmielnicki uprising and quoted from Jewish sources, such as from the chronicle of Natan Hanover and others, about the pogroms that accompanied it.

²²⁰ Buber mentioned that in 1691 a fire consumed all the privileges of the town, and as a result, in 1693, new privileges were issued, including for the Jews, outlining their equal rights with and obligations to the rest of the population (ibid. 3).

²²¹ Not all of the figures covered served as role models. For example: 'From this city came a Shabatean Mojsze Meir Kaminker who was sent in 1725 all around Europe to collect money and to do evil' (ibid. 2–4).

²²² Gertner, 'Dembitzer Hayim Natan', in Hundert (ed.), *The YIVO Encyclopedia of Jews in Eastern Europe*, i. 401. As an introduction to the first volume of his *Kelilat yofi*, Dembitzer published a letter to Salomon Buber, dated 1886, in which he responded to Buber's enquiry. Dembitzer congratulated him on his intention to write about the rabbis of Buber's home town, Lwów, and confessed that he yearned to finish 'the little book I began to write: *Kiryat melekh rav* about my home town Kraków and the town of the graves of my ancestors for generations and generations until our Rabbi Isserles. I have stopped in the middle' (Dembitzer, *Kelilat yofi*, i, p. ii). Elsewhere in the book, Dembitzer wrote of his monograph

university-trained scholars. The authors of Hebrew chronicles were inspired by historical investigations carried out in the Russian empire, Germany, and Italy.[223] In a letter from 1899, Avraham Harkavy, a Russian Jewish philologist and orientalist working at the Imperial Public Library, described to Shlomo Baruch Nissenbaum the rapid development of the field of Jewish scholarship and the growing interest of the Jewish public in the history of eastern European Jewry, reminding Nissenbaum of his appeals in 1878 for the importance of history and 'the need to collect all the pieces of information and remnants of the past from all the important communities in these places'.[224]

## New Influences and Agendas

During the last decades of the nineteenth century, the developments in Polish historiography echoed in the works of Polish Jewish historians, who also responded to works published in German and Russian. Driven by their conviction that Jewish identity in modern times should be grounded in historical consciousness, historians of Polish Jewry read and discussed the works of Graetz and Dubnow, in particular.[225] Scholars in Galicia and Congress Poland referred to the body of literature pertaining to Jewish history amassed by their colleagues in the Posen region, a territory of the Polish Crown within the borders of the former Polish–Lithuanian Commonwealth, and by historians discussing various aspects of the Jewish past in the Pale of Settlement. Studies in German and Russian often focused on the legal status of Jews and Jewish communal institutions.[226] The Russian publications of Sergei Bershadski, Avraham Harkavy, and Simon Dubnow discussed the Jewish past in the Polish Kingdom and Polish–Lithuanian Commonwealth in the broader context of east European Jewish history. Similarly, the writings of Heinrich Graetz were widely read by Jewish audiences in eastern Europe, while his presentation of the east European Jewish past drew the critical attention of Polish Jewish historians.

Graetz's eleven-volume *Geschichte der Juden: Von den ältesten Zeiten bis auf die Gegenwart* (History of the Jews from the Oldest Times to the Present), published

of the community in Kraków as an existing text: 'I put together *Kiryat melekh rav* on Kraków, here [I include] just chapter headings' (ibid. i. 2).

[223] Biderman, *Mayer Balaban*, 37.

[224] Nissenbaum, *History of the Jews of Lublin* (Heb.), 159. See also Harkavy, *Compendium or Rare Sources*, part A, number 6. Harkavy reminded Nissenbaum that, in 1877–8, the only studies available dealt with the history of Jewish communities in Wilno and Kraków (in Hebrew), and Poznań (in German). Studies of Grodno, Brisk, Lwów, Minsk, Kiev, Warsaw, and other towns followed. Harkavy celebrated the work that was carried out by Buber about the community of Żółkiew (Nissenbaum, *History of the Jews of Lublin* (Heb.), 160).

[225] Soifer, 'The Bespectacled Cossack: S. A. Bershadskii (1850–1896)'.

[226] Bloch, 'Die General-Privilegien der polnischen Judenschaft'.

between 1853 and 1876, profoundly influenced Jewish scholars in eastern Europe. It had bearing on both the subject matter and methodology of writing Jewish history.[227] Graetz popularized the idea that the Jewish nation, rather than Judaism, constituted the subject of Jewish history, and that historical narrative strengthened the Jewish identity of his readers. He also suggested an approach that historian Jeffrey Blutinger has called 'National Judaism', which proved to be an important stage in the development of Jewish nationalism.[228]

A Jewish reading public interested in the Jewish past had access to Graetz's work in both the original and in Hebrew, Russian, Polish, and Yiddish translations.[229] In eastern Europe, Hebrew, German, and Polish Jewish journals reviewed his books and, beginning in the 1860s, Hebrew periodicals published various translations of Graetz's work.[230] One scholar of Russian Jewish history has described it as 'probably the most widely read work of Hebrew historiography ever produced in Russia... already... adapted to the new currents of Russian Jewish historiography'.[231] Rabinovich's translation, with commentaries by Harkavy, was published in Warsaw in 1907/8, 1911, and 1912. In 1905, it was published in Warsaw in Nachum Sokołów's Hebrew translation, which he offered to the subscribers of *Hatsefirah*. Finally, Kalman Shulman translated it into Hebrew, while omitting 'those parts of the book that he feared might offend orthodox sensibilities. By offering a selective translation he hoped to reach as many readers as possible.'[232]

In addition to the Hebrew translations of Graetz's *History of the Jews*, the Polish Jewish intelligentsia had Stanisław Szenhak's 1902 Polish translation at their disposal.[233] The Polish translation offered a chance to familiarize a younger

---

[227] Graetz, *Geschichte der Juden*. See the bibliography for some of the translations of this work.

[228] Blutinger, 'Writing for the Masses'.

[229] For bibliographical citations of the major translations discussed here, see the bibliography under Graetz.

[230] Blutinger, 'Writing for the Masses', 152–64. On east European Jewish historians reading Graetz, see Wodziński, *Haskalah and Hasidism*, 221–2, 235–6, and Schedrin, *Jewish Souls, Bureaucratic Minds*, 194–6.

[231] Nathans, 'On Russian-Jewish Historiography', 417. As Nathans observed, 'Rabinovitch's translation, in fact, was virtually a new version of Graetz, with substantial additions and footnotes, particularly in sections relating to the history of Russian and Polish Jewry by Rabinovich, Abraham Harkavi, and other Russian Jewish historians'. On the translation, see Blutinger, 'Writing for the Masses', 273–91. On other translations into Hebrew, see Feiner, *Haskalah and History*, 226, and Blutinger, 'Writing for the Masses', 153–5. On chapters added by the translator, see Blutinger, 'Writing for the Masses', 285–8.

[232] Bauer, *Between Poles and Jews*, 43. According to Bauer, 'Shulman not only had the right to tailor the book to his readers' tastes but ... also had an obligation to prevent them from identifying the haskala movement with Lilienblum's radical circle'. In Sokołów's view, only material that had been selected and filtered would accomplish this purpose of bringing ever-greater numbers of Jews closer to the Haskalah and to modern opinions (ibid. 44).

[233] Several editions of the work translated into Polish by Szenhak appeared between 1929 and 1939.

generation of the Jewish intelligentsia, immersed in Polish culture and ignorant of the basic tenets of the Jewish faith and the biblical past, with Jewish history. As *Izraelita* argued in 1903, in the wake of the publication of the Polish edition, the public gained access to 'appropriate scholarly textbooks for this purpose in the Polish language. The publication of the so-called "smaller" *History of the Jews* by the eminent scholar Professor Dr H. Graetz will remedy this severe absence.'[234] Praising the book's rich material, erudition, and literary style, *Izraelita* expressed confidence that the translation 'will greatly serve the general reading public, will be purchased appropriately, and thus will contribute to prompt publication of the further volumes'.[235]

Although the price of his books limited the spread of Graetz's work in eastern Europe, and this prevented his becoming 'a writer of the people', he was certainly read by the Jewish intelligentsia, especially those with an interest in the Jewish past. Finally, Jewish journals *Moment* and *Hatsefirah* also offered editions of Graetz's books to their subscribers.[236]

Though they were inspired by Graetz's presentation of Jewish history, Polish Jewish historians criticized him for his skewed treatment of east European Jewry and what they saw as his ignorance and contempt. Kraushar, for instance, charged Graetz with baseless accusations against the Frankist movement, which lacked grounding in the source material, and for his ignorance of the Polish context and of the language of the sources.[237] *Izraelita* published a number of historical texts, with a view to enabling its readers to learn more about and better understand the hasidic movement. A lengthy article on the origins of the movement, entirely based on Graetz's *History of the Jews*, was prefaced by Samuel Peltyn, editor of *Jutrzenka* and *Izraelita*, who wrote: 'Bearing in mind that pathological historical phenomena develop and progress normally, and are deserving at times of reflection, we believe that our readers will not complain when we present them here with a more or less comprehensive history of this association [hasidism].'[238] Graetz's critical history of hasidism influenced the editors of *Izraelita*'s views on the subject.[239] Nussbaum, however, while reproducing the historical facts described by Graetz, provided his own interpretation, attempting to explain the mechanisms of hasidic expansion, an understanding of which was crucial to developing an effective plan to reform the hasidim. Unlike Graetz, Nussbaum

---

[234] '"Historja Żydów" prof. H. Graetza'. [235] Ibid.
[236] See Blutinger, 'Writing for the Masses', 160–2. Thus 'these Yiddish translations, combined with the Hebrew, Russian, and later Polish ensured that Graetz's texts had as wide a distribution in Eastern Europe as they had in Western Europe and the United States'.
[237] Kraushar, *Frank i Frankiści polscy*, i. 6.
[238] 'Głośni a nieznani: Szkic historyczny'; see Wodziński, *Haskalah and Hasidism*, 208.
[239] Wodziński, *Haskalah and Hasidism*, 219.

believed that solving the hasidic issue was not a historiographical problem, but a crucial and current social issue.²⁴⁰

By contrast, modern historical consciousness came to Russian Jews comparatively late.²⁴¹ Calls for a new historiography, underscoring the social and national aspects of Jewish life, appeared only in the 1860s, with the influx of Russian Jews into Russian gymnasia and universities. In his survey of Russian Jewish historiography, Benjamin Nathans noted the change in the world-view of the Russian Jewish intelligentsia by the late 1870s, when 'contemporaries were already noting a fundamental realignment of the Jewish intelligentsia, bringing it for the first time within the orbit of its Russian counterpart'.²⁴² In the 1880s, the Russian Jewish intelligentsia became interested in the literature of Wissenschaft des Judentums, while at the same time offering criticism of it. Russian Jews began exploring their past 'in a manner shaped to a considerable degree by conditions in Russia itself', as Nathans has argued.²⁴³

Nineteenth-century Russian Jewish historiography shared several key characteristics with its Polish counterpart. Both emerged within the context of intense public debate about the so-called 'Jewish question'. Like their colleagues in Poland, who showed an increasing interest in Polish culture and a desire to speak to a general Polish audience in Congress Poland and Galicia, in the last decades of the nineteenth century the Jewish intelligentsia within and beyond the Pale of Settlement increasingly immersed themselves in Russian culture, wanting to present their case to non-Jewish society. Therefore, most Russian Jewish historiography between the 1880s and 1920s appeared in Russian. As in Congress Poland, historians interested in exploring the Russian Jewish past wrote outside the academy.

As in the case of Polish Jewish historiography in the second half of the nineteenth century, Russian Jewish historiography focused on questions of the legal status of Jews in the Russian empire. In the struggle for Jewish emancipation, legal scholars wished to give practical guidance to Jews as well as to tsarist bureaucrats attempting to understand legislation and court rulings concerning Jews and Jewish issues, and to present the Jews' legal standing in the broader imperial context.²⁴⁴ They strove to demonstrate the Jews' rightful place in, and allegiance to, the Russian motherland, refuting charges of disloyalty and separatism while critiquing official policies regarding the Jews. This research proved influential

---

²⁴⁰ Wodziński, *Haskalah and Hasidism*, 221. See also Nussbaum, *Szkice historyczne z życia Żydów w Warszawie*. ²⁴¹ Nathans, *Beyond the Pale*, 315.
²⁴² Nathans, 'On Russian-Jewish Historiography', 401; Nathans, *Beyond the Pale*, 23–4.
²⁴³ Nathans, 'On Russian-Jewish Historiography', 400.
²⁴⁴ Benjamin Nathans pointed to factors responsible for the dominance of the legal standing of the Jews as the central aspect of Russian Jewish historiography. In particular, he notes that 'emancipation,

among Polish Jewish historians, who took an interest in Russian-language research, especially editions of primary sources.[245] In Russia as in Poland, non-Jewish scholars participated in these early endeavours, which included legal history and the publication of primary materials. Sergei Bershadski, a non-Jewish Russian historian, produced a series of studies on the history of the legal status of Jews in the Polish–Lithuanian Commonwealth and served as professor of law at the Saint Petersburg Imperial University. He was the guiding spirit behind the publication of several important collections of archival documents, and his work was published in Polish translation in *Izraelita*.[246] Dubnow's work appeared in the pages of *Izraelita* in Alfred Lor's Polish translation.[247] And in his short study of Jewish educational institutions in the Polish lands, Cohn relied heavily on Dubnow.[248]

In the case of Russian Jewish institutions, the lawyers who embraced Dubnow's platform of historical scholarship, and who gathered to study history, customs, and legislation, constituted its core. By the turn of the century, this group had attached itself to the Society for the Spread of Enlightenment under the name of the Historical-Ethnographic Commission.[249] In 1908, it became the independent Jewish Historical-Ethnographic Society, with headquarters in St Petersburg, sponsoring public lectures, research projects, a Jewish ethnographic museum, and a scholarly journal devoted to Russian Jewish history, *Evreiskaya starina* (Jewish

the guiding issue in the pan-European relationship between Jews and the societies in whose midst they lived, was understood across the nineteenth century largely in terms of legal rights and restrictions' (Nathans, *Beyond the Pale*, 315–16). See also Veidlinger, *Jewish Public Culture*, 232–4, and Nathans, 'On Russian-Jewish Historiography', 404–7.

[245] In particular, the work of Harkavy played a significant role, with his focus on the Hebraic influence on early Slavic chronicles, the allegedly Slavic dialect spoken by Jews on the shores of the Black Sea in late antiquity, and the contacts between Kievan Rus' and the Khazar kingdom (whose leaders converted to Judaism in the eighth century) (Nathans, 'On Russian-Jewish Historiography', 408–11).

[246] See Bershadski, 'Pierwsze Jeszyboty w Polsce'.

[247] See Dubnow, 'Społeczne i duchowe życie żydów w Polsce' and 'Szkice historyczno-obyczajowe'.

[248] See Cohn, 'Wstęp: Wiadomości historyczne o szkołach dla żydów w Polsce', 6–10.

[249] The prototype, the Society for Jewish Culture and Learning, was founded in 1819 by Eduard Gans, Heinrich Heine, Isaac Jost, and Leopold Zunz. The establishment of the Jewish Theological Seminary of Breslau followed in 1854. In 1880, in Paris, the Society of Jewish Studies was founded, with the journal the *Revue des études juives*. In 1892, the American Jewish Historical Society was founded. In England, the *Jewish Quarterly Review* was founded in 1888, and the Jewish Historical Society of England in 1893. In 1891, the Society for Jewish History and Literature was established in Berlin. For a discussion of the role of the Society for the Promotion of Culture among the Jews (Obshchestva dlia Rasprostraneniia Prosveshcheniia Mezhdu Evreiami v Rossii; OPE) and the commission in developing Russian Jewish historiography, see Horowitz, *Jewish Philanthropy and Enlightenment in Late-Tsarist Russia*, 161–9; Nathans, 'On Russian-Jewish Historiography', 417–19; Armborst, 'Wegbereiter der Geschichtsforschung'.

Antiquity).²⁵⁰ The Society for Jewish Scholarly Publications, founded in 1907 in St Petersburg, sponsored the publication of the monumental sixteen-volume *Evreiskaya entsiklopediia* (Jewish Encyclopedia). On the eve of the First World War, the society initiated the writing of a five-volume narrative history of the Jews in Russia, of which only the first volume, about the Jews of the Polish–Lithuanian Commonwealth, was completed. Polish Jewish historians participated in the activities of these institutions.

In the twentieth century historians who came to play a central role in the development and gradual professionalization of the field often referred to this existing nineteenth-century scholarship in their own scholarship. Writing with a keen sense of the importance of Polish Jewish history for contemporary discussions about Jews in the Polish lands, they addressed both Polish and Jewish audiences. They continued exploring subjects central to the development of the field before 1918, including the legal status of the Jews in Poland, Jewish–non-Jewish relations, and the rise of Jewish institutions and self-government. Indeed, history continued to show that Jews had long been part of the Polish landscape. Although historical studies did not directly contradict the claims that contemporary Jews may have required economic, social, and religious improvement, they provided the Jewish community with the sense of belonging and an awareness of its long-standing legal settlement and its economic usefulness. In raising these arguments, the scholarship engaged with contemporary Polish and Polish Jewish discourse. The function of history varied depending on the intended readers and the broader political context, as well as on internal Jewish developments.²⁵¹

## Collecting Jewish Antiquities: Ideal and Practice

Whatever the many differences among integrationist historians and Hebrew chroniclers, they shared a belief that their work required searching for historical sources. They appealed to the Jewish public in eastern Europe to collect documents, and they asserted the importance of this task in mapping out the communal and national pasts. These calls signified a turn to history as a wider social project beyond a small circle of scholars. The earliest appeal came out of Galicia

---

²⁵⁰ Nathans, 'On Russian-Jewish Historiography', 417–18. Veidlinger points to the broader movement in Russian middle-class and intellectual circles to engage in educational projects as part of their 'civic obligation' to turn 'subjects into citizens' (Veidlinger, *Jewish Public Culture*, 230).

²⁵¹ Kołodziejska argues that articles about the history of Polish Jews in *Izraelita* showed 'the way the integrationist programme used history. It was to help counter allegations about Jews being strangers and almost genetically bound to trade and lacking care for the country in which they lived, in a scientific and factual manner' (Kołodziejska, '*Izraelita*' (1866–1915), 142). She suggests that the decline in the number of historical articles published by *Izraelita* can be linked to the rise of antisemitism and ambivalence towards assimilation in Western Europe (ibid. 143).

in 1881, penned by Izydor Bernfeld.[252] Entitled 'Rise up, Rise up, Prepare the Way', it appeared in *Hamazkir*, the Hebrew supplement to the Lwów Polish-language newspaper *Ojczyzna*. This was the official organ of the Agudas Achim (Przymierze Braci), an association committed to opposing antisemitism and disseminating among Galician Jews a pro-Polish, rather than pro-German, orientation. It provided a forum for collaboration between young maskilim and young Polonized Jews, 'out of the firm conviction that Jews must integrate within Polish language and culture'. In the appeal, Bernfeld stressed the importance of Polish Jews writing Polish Jewish history. This could not be done without a proper understanding of Polish Jewry, and therefore it needed to be carried out by Jews. He also asked his readers to submit articles on Polish Jewish history and to collect historical sources, such as community registries (*pinkasim*) and the epitaphs from the tombstones of rabbis.[253]

A decade later, in the different political context of the Russian empire, Simon Dubnow published an article sharing several important characteristics with Bernfeld's shorter and less elaborate piece. In November 1891, Dubnow's programmatic essay 'On the Study of the History of Russian Jews and the Establishment of a Russian Jewish Historical Society' appeared in the Russian journal *Voskhod* (Dawn) in St Petersburg.[254] In the spring of the following year, he published it in Hebrew in *Hapardes* in Odessa. Dubnow directed his appeal to a wide Jewish audience in the Pale of Settlement, both the acculturated Jewish intelligentsia and the rabbis and yeshiva youth reading in Hebrew. In the wake of the failure of Russian Jewish integration, Dubnow envisioned a historiography that took Jews as the subject, not the object, of history.[255] No longer focused on legislation, he saw the Jewish collective as the new focal point of a historical narrative. Because history

[252] Izydor Bernfeld published a Polish-language textbook for Jews (*Nauka języka polskiego dla Izraelitów*) and a Hebrew–Polish dictionary (*Zupełny słownik języka hebrajskiego i polskiego*). He was the brother of the scholar and writer Szymon Bernfeld, who published studies about the German Haskalah, the Reform movement, Jewish philosophy, and the Crusades. For an in-depth analysis of the appeal, see Manekin, 'Constructing Polish Jewry's "Shrine of History"'.

[253] Manekin, 'The Galician Roots of the Historiography of Polish Jewry' (Heb.), 319–20. On the German orientation represented by the Shomer Israel Society, see Shanes, *Diaspora Nationalism and Jewish Identity*, 41–5. See also Mendelsohn, 'Jewish Assimilation in L'viv: The Case of Wilhelm Feldman'.

[254] Dubnow, 'Iz izucheniia istorii russkikh evreev i uchrezhdenii istoricheskogo obshchestva', *Voskhod*, November 1891. In the same year, the essay appeared as a separate booklet: *Ob izuchenii istorii russkikh evreev i ob uchrezhdenii russko-evreiskogo istoricheskogo obshchestva* (On the Study of the History of Russian Jews and on the Institution of a Russian–Jewish Historical Society). See also Dubnow, 'Let Us Seek and Investigate'. In order to ensure a widespread reception of his appeal, Dubnow published it again as a separate pamphlet, which he mailed free of charge to communities throughout the Pale. See Jockusch, 'Introductory Remarks on Simon Dubnow's "Let Us Seek and Investigate"'.

[255] Nathans, 'On Russian-Jewish Historiography', 411–12.

was to serve the people while recounting their past, it could not be a guild discipline: 'Its place is not under the academic cap, but in the open forum. We work for the people's self-recognition and not for the sake of our own intellectual sport.'[256]

Dubnow pioneered the understanding of Jewish history from the inside, based on Jewish sources, with Jews as central actors of the past.[257] Though he was building on the work of Heinrich Graetz, his focus shifted to Russian and Polish Jewry.[258] He ascertained with dismay that east European Jews did not know their own history, and he appealed to his readers to recognize the national significance of historical research by participating in the mission. Writing about the Jewish experience in eastern Europe required sources that were either neglected or inaccessible.

Not every literate person or one who writes can become a true author of history, but each of you can become a collector of material, can help in the building of history... Let us set to work, gather the scattered fragments from wherever they have been dispersed, arrange them and reveal them to the public, and then build upon them the temple of history.[259]

Dubnow described Jews as a unique nation, whose survival depended on historical consciousness rather than on religious beliefs and customs.[260] Accordingly, he deemed historical research and Jewish historiography necessary for strengthening national cohesion, a task for scholars and laypeople alike.[261] Jewish historiography needed to focus on the Jewish nation as the chief subject of the past, and especially on the social, political, cultural, and intellectual developments of Jewish society throughout the ages, rather than on religion and the governments under which the Jews lived.[262] Dubnow held up as a model the efforts of the Jews in western Europe, who had already established the field of modern Jewish history, while their brethren in Poland and Russia lagged behind as 'savages' in need of higher cultural development.[263] He appealed to his compatriots 'to take bricks and

---

[256] Dubnow, *Kniga zhizni*, 282, as quoted in Nathans, 'On Russian-Jewish Historiography', 415.

[257] Nathans, 'On Russian-Jewish Historiography', 413.

[258] See Jockusch, 'Introductory Remarks on Simon Dubnow's "Let Us Seek and Investigate"', 344–5.      [259] Dubnow, 'Let Us Seek and Investigate', 382.

[260] Ibid. 353–6. According to Dubnow, three elements contributed to the continued existence of the Jews: a sense of family (*regesh mishpaḥah*) based on an awareness of blood relations linking all Jews together; shared religious beliefs and customs (*regesh ha'emunah*); and the strongest factor, common historical consciousness (*regesh hahistoryah*). Dubnow identified 'a sense of history' as 'the inner awareness that for thousands of years we have been connected and bonded one to the other, that we have experienced joy and despair together' (ibid. 354).      [261] Ibid. 362.      [262] Ibid. 360.

[263] Dubnow explained: 'Among the groupings of peoples you will find nations without any history whatsoever (the savages and the unenlightened on the plains of Asia and Africa and the island of Australia), nations that have already departed the stage of history and ceased to exist (the Egyptians, the

mortar to build history'.²⁶⁴ Ahead of them lay the task of exploring their 800-year history and revealing 'what we have been, how we have arrived at our present situation, and how our forefathers have lived for eight hundred years since Jews first settled in Poland'.²⁶⁵ Since gathering and preserving historical material was a precondition for history-writing, Dubnow examined different types of historical source—in particular Hebrew sources, such as community registers—which served as the basis for the new field of Jewish historiography.²⁶⁶ In his programmatic essay about research into the past of east European Jews, Dubnow divided their history into six periods, from the First Crusade through Dubnow's own time, as a rudimentary 'map' to guide the new field of research.²⁶⁷ With his theory of 'hegemonic centres', which dominated the other Jewish communities at any given time in the past, he placed east European Jewish history in the context of general Jewish history. Following ancient Israel, Babylonia, and medieval Spain, the centre shifted to eastern Europe, where Jews preserved an 'authentic' communal organization and spiritual life.²⁶⁸ He situated Russian Jewry 'in two larger contexts: vertically, with respect to the 4,000-year trajectory of Jewish history, and horizontally, with the specifically nineteenth-century east European landscape of stateless nationalities for various forms of self-government'.²⁶⁹

Dubnow proposed a radical re-evaluation of Jewish institutions in Poland and the Polish–Lithuanian Commonwealth. He considered these institutions the basis for writing about the Jews as a collective, in view of their lack of political sovereignty. In the Russian imperial context, the shift proved radical. As Benjamin Nathans has noted, 'The boldness of this claim can be appreciated only when one recalls that the spectre of a Jewish "state within the state," of the *kahal* as a kind of collective Jewish conspiracy against the rest of society, was nothing less than the mantra of Russian anti-Semitism.'²⁷⁰ Polish Jewish historiography, however, repeated a similar mantra, referring to the *kehalim*, the rabbinical courts, the regional councils, and the national council of Va'ad Arba Aratsot with suspicion and ambivalence. Dubnow's perspective on Jewish autonomous institutions suggested that the Jews could not be reduced to a religious community in exchange for political and civil rights. On the contrary, 'despite shifting borders

Greeks and Romans, and suchlike), and nations that have only recently became part of history (the contemporary peoples of Europe and America)' (ibid. 354).

²⁶⁴ Ibid. 363.

²⁶⁵ Ibid. 361–2. As Nathans has noted, Dubnow was not referring only to Russian Jews. See 'On Russian-Jewish Historiography', 398.   ²⁶⁶ Dubnow, 'Let Us Seek and Investigate', 368–76.

²⁶⁷ Ibid. 363–7. During the Period of Rights, following the privileges of 1364, Jews enjoyed a peaceful life, with only a short period of confusion due to religious fanaticism coming from the West under Kazimierz IV Jagiellon in Poland and under Duke Aleksander Jagiellon in Lithuania in the second half of the fifteenth century.   ²⁶⁸ Nathans, 'On Russian-Jewish Historiography', 413.

²⁶⁹ Ibid. 411.   ²⁷⁰ Ibid. 413. On 'state within a state' see also Katz, *From Prejudice to Destruction*, 60.

and sovereignties, the Jews of the present-day Russian empire could look back on a continuous national development that originated with the first Jewish migrations from western to eastern Europe in the late eleventh century, brought on the atrocities of the Crusades'.[271] Jewish historiography as envisioned by Dubnow could not only strengthen national historical consciousness among the Jews, but could also become 'the cornerstone of a modern, secular, Jewish identity'.[272] Dubnow's ideas about the past shaped his vision of the future for east European Jewry when he proposed that the *kahal* should become fundamental to Jewish secular institutional life, formulating a programme of diaspora nationalism and autonomy.[273] *Izraelita* introduced Dubnow as 'one of the best known and most objective historians of Polish and Russian Jews',[274] and expressed confidence that 'our readers will read excerpts from the work of the great scholar who knowing the past, often with a word of encouragement or condemnation speaks about all the currents pervading the Jewish masses at present'.[275] Dubnow's essay marked the turning point for east European Jewish historiography as a field with its own subject matter, periodization, and methodology. As part of this influence, 'historians have increasingly referred to this text as the origin of certain proto-professional traditions of Jewish history-writing that became especially widespread among the Jews of eastern Europe'.[276] Dubnow shifted the interest in writing Jewish history from the religious sages celebrated by Wissenschaft des Judentums and the external legal status of Jewish communities to the Jewish masses. He also championed writing history for the Jewish masses.

Dubnow's essay influenced the institutional map of east European Jewish historiography. He put forth a plan for creating the Association of Scholars of Jewish History in Russia to work in all towns of Jewish settlement, with the mission to assemble manuscripts, books, and memories, and to place them in the custody of five eminent scholars who would assess the materials, publish them, and urge other scholars to use them in writing history. He appealed to rabbis and community leaders in possession of most of the old registers and other manuscripts, as well as to scholars and wealthy individuals in possession of old books, imploring them to publish the material.[277] The essay encouraged the work of the Jewish

[271] Nathans, 'On Russian-Jewish Historiography', 414.

[272] Ibid. 411. Nathans continues, 'In Dubnov, Russian Jewry found its own version of the nineteenth-century European ideal: the historian as nation builder and culture-hero. How he arrived at this remarkable position is worth a closer look.'

[273] Ibid. 415–16. See also Jockusch, 'Introductory Remarks on Simon Dubnow's "Let Us Seek and Investigate"', 348–52.

[274] Dubnow, 'Społeczne i duchowe życie Żydów w Polsce', no. 27, p. 319.    [275] Ibid. no. 27, p. 319.

[276] Jockusch, 'Introductory Remarks on Simon Dubnow's "Let Us Seek and Investigate"', 343–4.

[277] Dubnow, 'Let Us Seek and Investigate', 376–7. Dubnow appealed to the young, especially the scholars, among them: 'Why should you spend your time composing vacuous rhetoric which

ethnographer and writer S. An-sky (Solomon Zainwil Rappoport), who between 1912 and 1914 conducted an ethnographic expedition to small towns in Volhynia and Podolia to record folksongs and stories, collect manuscripts and ritual objects, and take photographs on behalf of the society.[278]

Similar calls for collecting and preserving Jewish historical records came out of Congress Poland. Dr Samuel Poznański, assistant preacher at the Warsaw Great Synagogue from 1897 to 1908 and chief preacher from 1908 onward, envisioned a rabbinate steeped in Jewish tradition, but also having knowledge of Jewish history, philosophy, and religion.[279] He participated in the activities of the Historical Commission in the Delegation for the Affairs of the Library of the Great Synagogue in Warsaw (Delegacja do Spraw Biblioteki Wielkiej Synagogi na Tłomackiem w Warszawie). In the 1880s and 1890s, the Commission began collecting primary sources and copies, especially *pinkasim*, of the provincial communities and Jewish associations. He issued appeals to the public in the press.[280] In June 1899, on the pages of *Izraelita*, Nachum Sokołów, a Zionist activist and pioneer Hebrew journalist, elaborated on the appeal of the committee of the Tłomackie Synagogue with regard to collecting Hebrew manuscripts related to Jewish history. He reminded his readers that it was not relevant only to scholars. On the contrary, it was 'a matter of the highest importance for our general public. As our history is the basis for our intellectual existence, our spiritual essence, a testimony to our dignity and a source of our inspirations, a link connecting us with the past, our shield and armour, the soul of our community and a torch on the path of our life.'[281] History covered the entire experience of the Jewish people in the diaspora, including those of local Jews (*Żydzi krajowi*). He argued that only by researching Jewish history in individual countries of the diaspora could the long and rich history of the Jews be systematized. 'On the one hand', he wrote, 'history . . . gives us, the Jews, spiritual legitimacy and a possibility for understanding the issues of our own existence, while on the other hand it enlightens us as local Jews.'[282]

Sokołów maintained that a strong bond with the country was a natural phenomenon and did not contradict Jewish identity:

you send to the editorial offices of journals to be used to fill the baskets destined for burning, when you could be furthering a great and valuable objective and not be prevented from so doing, since this is only a matter of will?' (ibid. 381).

[278] See Kuznitz, 'An-sky's Legacy'.

[279] Bałaban, 'Doktor Samuel Poznański (1864–1921)', pp. xviii–xx. Poznański followed this vision while building the library of the Great Synagogue, where historical books constituted its integral part. He formed and taught courses for teachers of the Mosaic faith, which led to the creation of the State Seminary in 1918, where he taught Jewish history, Bible, and ethics. See also IRRZ, Oral Testimonies 20, 11 June 1973.     [280] See Żebrowski, *Mojżesz Schorr*, 20. See also 'Odezwa Komitetu Synagogi'.

[281] Sokołów, 'Dla postępu wiedzy judaistycznej'. On Nachum Sokołów, see Bauer, *Between Poles and Jews*.     [282] Sokołów, 'Dla postępu wiedzy judaistycznej'.

There are historical, ancestral, universal ideals connecting all Jews, for thousands of years, and besides them there are some categories of aspirations, traditions, and even interests which have formed in the course of centuries among many Jewish communities of various countries. We reject neither, since we are dealing here with moral elements which do not collide with one another.[283]

Indeed, Jewish history constituted a treasure trove of both local and national memories, which belonged both to Jewish history and to the history of the country. Given the importance of local history, the mission of purchasing and examining *pinkasim* had tremendous importance for the Jewish community in the country.[284] Therefore, the communities, rabbis, and private individuals were to be approached in order to salvage these invaluable materials.

The appeal to gather historical material came from a circle of Jewish scholars on a committee overseeing the Judaica Library at the Tłomackie Synagogue. Sokołów described the library in 1879 as 'the most fitting institution for keeping the manuscripts, and enabling the scholarly and literary spheres to use the collections'.[285] Supportive of the appeal, *Izraelita* celebrated the influx of manuscripts, questions, and comments, and the article called on readers to continue spreading the word among those unaware of the importance of historical material. In this project, the involvement of the Jewish intelligentsia was seen as critical. People who maintained contacts with the provinces could, while visiting small towns and meeting local people with little understanding of scientific, literary, and historical matters—what *Izraelita* called 'small town half-intelligentsia', especially Jewish youth—convince them to collect old chronicles and copy inscriptions.[286] *Izraelita* expressed confidence that all these activities would lead to the library acquiring 'a very interesting and educational historical collection'.[287] The idea of collecting historical documents was also supported by Sokołów in the pages of *Hatsefirah*, a Warsaw Hebrew journal. Here we see similarities in the public appeals by Dubnow, Bernfeld, and Sokołów, who wrote about the historical project as a mission shared with the people, and therefore as a Jewish national endeavour. They wrote with a sense of urgency, employing the language of redemption in their respective appeals.[288] Like Bernfeld and Dubnow, the Jewish intelligentsia of *Izraelita* appealed to the public in the hope of making it aware of the value of Jewish historical texts and the need to preserve the remnants of the past from oblivion.

---

[283] Sokołów, 'Dla postępu wiedzy judaistycznej'. [284] Ibid. [285] Ibid.
[286] 'Odezwa Komitetu Synagogi'. Among those considered particularly promising for this enterprise were university students, though not the radicals detached from Jewish affairs and without any knowledge of Jewish matters. [287] Ibid. 299.
[288] Manekin, 'The Galician Roots of the Historiography of Polish Jewry' (Heb.), 319–21.

## Conclusion

In the nineteenth century, the task of studying and writing the history of Polish Jewry appealed to authors of diverse backgrounds in several geographical centres. Without formal historical training, they embraced history as an important political and cultural tool for improving the status of the Jews and for strengthening communal self-awareness. The Jewish intelligentsia in Congress Poland and Galicia, who envisioned the integration of the Jews in the Polish lands, pointed to historical parallels to make the case for political reforms and for the cultural transformation of the Jewish community. Daniel Neufeld, Aleksander Kraushar, Hilary Nussbaum, Mathias Bersohn, and Ludwik Gumplowicz contributed to contemporary political debates through their books, brochures, and articles, hoping to create historical consciousness among Jews and to educate the non-Jewish reading public. For this political project, legal history paved the way. The seminal works of Polish Jewish historiography in the nineteenth century were penned by amateur historians or chroniclers.[289] For these Jewish scholars, journalists, and community leaders, the history of Polish Jews remained a marginal aspect of their work. Similarly, the Polish authors Władysław Smoleński and Aleksander Maciejowski wrote primarily about other topics. Nevertheless, their publications constituted the core library of Polish Jewish history at the beginning of the twentieth century. This body of literature was not only connected to contemporary political concerns, but was embedded in scholarly debates within Polish historiography and emerging modern Jewish scholarship.

In the second half of the nineteenth century, Jewish history-writing in and about east European Jewry became increasingly influenced by the idea of writing a national Jewish history, as formulated by Heinrich Graetz and Simon Dubnow. Literature on the history of Polish Jewry became a multilingual field, with authors trying to balance contemporary concerns with academic objectivity and new sources. Emerging scholars of Polish Jewish history shifted their focus away from Polish kings and their policies and towards the Jewish communities, their culture, economy, and institutions. They increasingly voiced the need to broaden their archival source base and research agendas. Informal networks of scholars of east European and Polish Jewish history gave rise to institutions, as historians sought to establish forums for their research.[290] These forums included Jewish journals for the publication of research articles and historical documents, and associations commissioned with promoting east European Jewish scholarship. The initiative of

---

[289] Wodziński called Nussbaum an 'amateur historian'. Wodziński, *Haskalah and Hasidism*, 220.

[290] Scholars pursuing Jewish history in and of the Prussian partition of the former Polish–Lithuanian Commonwealth belonged to the German scholarly network, not only in terms of the language of their writing but also beyond it.

the Jewish intelligentsia followed the pattern of Jewish academic societies acting as surrogates to academia, given the limited access Jews had to universities.[291] In the case of Congress Poland and Galicia, informal and formal societies devoted themselves to the study of Polish history, in which some Polish Jewish historians actively participated. As the nineteenth century turned to the twentieth, the modes of writing Jewish history were changing, but the literature created by amateur historians, legal scholars, and Hebrew chroniclers raised questions with which the university-trained historians who followed them would continue to engage.

[291] Veidlinger, *Jewish Public Culture*, 229–60.

TWO

# THE MAKING OF PROFESSIONAL POLISH JEWISH HISTORIANS

POLISH JEWISH historiography emerged as a field of interest among the Polish intelligentsia and the enlightened Jewish elite throughout partitioned Polish lands in the early to mid-nineteenth century. Ignoring the political borders between the Prussian, Russian, and Austro-Hungarian empires in the aftermath of the Commonwealth's demise, pioneering amateur historians and chroniclers investigated a wide range of subjects, from legal history and Jewish–non-Jewish relations to Jewish communal institutions and individual Jewish communities in Poland–Lithuania. By the late nineteenth century, members of the Jewish intelligentsia were increasingly calling for the collection of Jewish manuscripts and antiquities in all three partitioned territories.[1] They perceived as inadequate both the Polish-language research by Polish and Jewish scholars and the local studies penned mostly in Hebrew by maskilic Jewish authors.

Unlike the authors discussed in the previous chapter, this new cohort boasted professional university training and saw themselves as part of the guild. For these scholars, archival research and a critical analysis of documents were a given, and so was a sense of history as both a profession and a public calling. They envisioned their work as a contribution to critical historiography of Polish Jewry, and they sought both recognition and comprehensive development of their field. Rejecting an overtly apologetic approach to the past, they called for the creation of a national Jewish historiography in accordance with the academic standards of critical scholarship. They sought to write east European Jewish history for the benefit of both the diverse Jewish audiences living under the Austrian, Russian, or Prussian rule and non-Jewish audiences in the region.

Most Jewish historians had received their formal secondary education and university training at a time of rapid Polonization of the gymnasia and universities, and were intimately familiar with Polish language, culture, and history.

---

[1] Manekin, 'The Galician Roots of the Historiography of Polish Jewry' (Heb.). Manekin points to the prominent role of amateur historians in Galicia in the second half of the nineteenth century in leading the way to the professionalization of Polish Jewish history.

In fact, already by the mid-nineteenth century, a Polish orientation affected the cultural identity of the modernizing Jewish elite in western Galicia. After 1867, eastern Galicia also underwent a process of energetic Polonization. A series of imperial decrees between 1867 and 1871 gave Poles virtual autonomy in the entire province. Jews were dependent on a Polish-dominated society and embraced Polish culture either out of conviction or in pursuit of professional careers.[2] Not surprisingly, 'by the end of the century the secular Jewish intelligentsia, relatively stronger and more influential here [in Galicia] than anywhere else in the Polish lands, saw itself as part of the Polish cultural world'.[3] Jewish graduates of university-level history departments combined their professional training with a knowledge of traditional Jewish texts. This dual intellectual background and expertise allowed them to utilize a broad spectrum of sources and broaden their research questions.

The story of the professionalization of historians active in Galicia in the last decades of the Austro-Hungarian empire, at a time when they were formulating new ideas about history and their own roles as professional historians, demonstrates the transition from the historical practices of the nineteenth century to the historical profession that would later arise in Warsaw. Although these scholars sought to define and strengthen Jewish national identity by writing a broader east European Jewish history, they did not abandon the concept of Polish Jewish identity championed by Polish and Polonizing Jewish intelligentsia during the nineteenth century. While they wrote for and about Polish Jews, they also remained preoccupied with non-Jewish readers in academia and beyond, and they hoped for a wide reception of their work among the Polish reading public. Their scholarship grew out of tensions between Polish historiography and Jewish nationalism, and between academia and the profoundly political mission of writing Jewish history as a national enterprise.

In the early twentieth century, both the institutional framework and the content of the history of Polish Jewry began to change. And Galicia, located on the easternmost edges of the Austro-Hungarian empire, where most of the scholars in the field of Polish Jewish history had been born or received their university training, emerged as a centre of the Polish Jewish historical enterprise. This younger generation of university-trained scholars developed a complex relationship with the integrationist, maskilic, and Dubnowian traditions of writing east European Jewish history. Intimately involved in the political, social, and cultural debates of their time, they self-consciously reflected on the specific directions that academic research on the history of Polish Jews should take. Although they built on the

---

[2] On the political context of Galician Jewry from the first partition until 1883, see Shanes, *Diaspora Nationalism and Jewish Identity*, 16–45, and Shedel, 'Austria and Its Polish Subjects, 1866–1914'.

[3] Mendelsohn, 'A Note on Jewish Assimilation in the Polish Lands', 142–3.

experiences and paradigms of integrationist Polish Jewish historians, on material amassed in Hebrew monographs, and on Dubnow's programme of national Jewish historiography in eastern Europe, these scholars combined the various models to create a national Jewish historiography rooted in the Polish academic tradition.

## Szymon Askenazy and the Academic Training of Polish Jewish Historians in Galicia

In October 1919 Szymon Askenazy bid an emotional farewell to the Department of Philosophy at the University of Lwów, where he had lectured on early modern Polish history and trained young scholars in the field. Having graduated from the Department of Law at the Imperial University of Warsaw, Askenazy studied history at the University of Göttingen, receiving a doctorate in 1893 for his thesis, *Die letzte polnische Königswahl* (The Last Polish Royal Election). In this study and numerous others, Askenazy focused on diplomatic history and international relations.[4] He was unable to teach Polish history at a Russified university in Warsaw. He considered offering classes in Polish history as his national duty. 'It is not up to me to pass a verdict about my work as a teacher', he wrote in a letter to his colleagues. 'If the fruit it bore has proven more modest than I had hoped for, one should also consider difficult circumstances.'[5] His innovative use of methodologies, and his discovery of previously unknown archival sources, served as the basis for a new romantic school of Polish history.[6] From his arrival at the University of Lwów in 1898, he became a popular lecturer with both students and the general public.[7] After two decades in Lwów it was time to return to Warsaw, which Askenazy described as a fitting place for a Polish historian, especially one writing about

---

[4] In 1897 the History Department of the University of Lwów accepted Askenazy's study of the Polish–Prussian Alliance (Askenazy, *Przymierze polsko–pruskie*) as his *Habilitationsschrift*. See Wróbel, 'Szymon Askenazy', 221–4.

[5] DALO, fond 26, opis 5, sprava 35, p. 152, a handwritten letter from Askenazy to the University of Lwów, 11 Oct. 1919, Warsaw.

[6] Nurowski, *Szymon Askenazy*, 221. Moreover, the Jewish intelligentsia respected him as a Polish historian, as is testified in articles in the Jewish press following his death. Bałaban and Schiper stressed the Jewish elements of Askenazy's funeral. While Bałaban emphasized the fact that the procession stopped at the Tłomackie Synagogue and Kaddish, for Schiper the lonely Kaddish in the Polish context of the funeral underlined the tragedy of Askenazy's life. See Bałaban, 'Profesor Szymon Askenazy (1867–1935)', 4; Schiper, 'Prof. Szymon Askenazy z˝l' (Yid.), 4.

[7] Askenazy mentored an entire generation of Polish historians, many of whom went on to play important roles in political life—in the national democratic or socialist and communist movements. See Nurowski, *Szymon Askenazy*, 29–32. For a discussion of the school of Polish history created by Askenazy, see Dzwonkowski, 'Szymon Askenazy 1866–1935', 1; Nurowski, *Szymon Askenazy*, 42–59; Szczerbakiewicz, 'Sprytny dostawca optymizmu narodowego', 336; Barycz, *Na przełomie dwóch stuleci*, 272.

the period after the partitions.⁸ His departure marked the end of the period in which Lwów was a centre of Polish historical scholarship as well as Polish Jewish historiography.

Although in his own work Askenazy paid limited attention to the history of Jews in Polish lands, he recognized the importance of Jewish history for Polish historiography. He belonged to the academic milieu in Lwów that played a pivotal role in structuring the field of Polish Jewish history. In the second half of the nineteenth century, universities in Kraków and Lwów emerged as bastions of Polish historiography in both the history and law departments. Unlike universities in western Europe, where legal training was becoming increasingly professionalized and pragmatic and the history of law gradually marginalized, the Jagiellonian University and the University of Lwów sustained the traditional format, giving students a broad education across disciplines. In 1875, following the reform of the Galician Diet (Sejm Krajowy), the history of law in Poland and Polish as the language of instruction both returned to university programmes; the university became 'not only a school of professionalism but also of patriotism'.⁹ Numerous Polish historians at both the Jagiellonian University and the University of Lwów 'looked favorably on works on Jewish history because they explored new sources and integrated the results into Polish history . . . The interpretation of unknown Hebrew documents was regarded as a scholarly attainment.'¹⁰

In this intellectual climate Askenazy shepherded young Polish Jewish historians seeking university training and encouraged the inclusion of Jewish history as part of Polish history. This prominent Polish Jewish historian was instrumental in establishing a competition for scholarly works in the history of Polish Jewry through the Department of Philosophy at his university in Lwów. Endowed by Hipolit Wawelberg, a prominent banker, Jewish communal leader, and philanthropist, in June 1900 the contest rewarded the two best scholarly works in the field with publication.¹¹ In January 1906 Askenazy reported to Ludwik Finkel that he had arranged, together with Wawelberg's son, the first instalment of the funds for the competition to be transferred to the rector of the University of Lwów.¹² Samuel Adalberg, a historian and scholar of Polish folklore and a prominent member of the Polonized Jewish intelligentsia in Warsaw, administered the fund, while Askenazy may have written the prospectus defining the goals of the competition,

---

⁸ See DALO, fond 26, opis 5, sprava 35, p. 152. In his letter, Askenazy celebrates the revival of free chairs of Polish history; alongside Kraków and Lwów, there were Warsaw, Wilno, Poznań, and Lublin: 'Happy that I have lived to see it, I return where I came from. Lwów does not need me anymore' (ibid.).

⁹ See Wierzbicki, 'Oswald Balzer (1858–1933)'.

¹⁰ Dold, 'A Matter of National and Civic Honor', 59; See also Pisulińska, 'Problematyka żydowska w pracach historyków tzw. lwowskiej szkoły historycznej'.

¹¹ See the description of the contest in 'Konkurs naukowy z ofiary p. Hipolita Wawelberga'.

¹² Letter 8 in Hoszowska, *Szymon Askenazy i jego korespondencja z Ludwikiem Finklem*, 203–4.

which appeared in *Izraelita*.[13] The competition encouraged the submission of scholarly editions of primary sources or scholarship based on primary sources, especially monographs focusing on one particular period or one aspect of the legal, political, or economic history of Polish Jews in a given province or community.[14] Despite its apparent openness, the competition had a built-in political agenda: the organizers actively encouraged writers to focus on

> the attitude of the Polish–Lithuanian Commonwealth with regard to the Jewish population, namely bringing out these exceptionally favourable conditions—in comparison with other countries—of higher religious and political tolerance in Poland, which resulted in an extraordinary concentration of the Jewish population within Poland's borders, and at the same time elucidating both positive and negative effects of such a concentration, both on the country and on the aforementioned population.[15]

The competition closely followed the intellectual and political lines of nineteenth-century integrationist Polish Jewish historiography. But it also advanced a new agenda, in that it sought to advance studies that examined

> the internal development of the Jewish population in Poland with respect to its denominational, administrative, judicial, and tax organization etc., its distribution and concentration in various parts of the country, its work and occupations, schools, religious, and social notions: above all elucidating its attitude to the Polish nation as a whole and various strata and classes, to economic and political matters of the country and the influence on it exerted by Polish culture of the country in customs, traditions, language, attire, etc.[16]

Finally, the competition encouraged research into more contemporary Jewish history by examining 'the mutual relations between the country and the Jewish population in the modern period'.[17] The committee also hoped that the competition would spur research on the policies of the three partitioning powers with respect to the Jews.[18]

Though the competition was aimed at Galician universities, the call ignored the political borders of the partitions, inviting 'Polish academic youth studying at other universities' and 'all scholars of Polish nationality who had graduated from universities since 1895' to submit material in Polish.[19] In addition to Askenazy, the committee included highly respected medievalists such as Bronisław Dembiński, Władysław Abraham, Tadeusz Wojciechowski, and Ludwik Finkel, who focused

---

[13] See Shatzky, 'Balance Sheet of a Jewish Historian', 267.
[14] See 'Konkurs naukowy z ofiary p. Hipolita Wawelberga'.   [15] Ibid.   [16] Ibid.
[17] Ibid. It defined the modern period as 'the attitude to it of the government, legislation, and Polish public opinion in the era of the Four Year Diet, the Duchy of Warsaw, and Congress Poland until and including Wielopolski reforms; the relationship of this population vis-à-vis certain crises of the country, and its role between these crises'.   [18] Ibid.   [19] Ibid.

on political and diplomatic history, as well as Oswald Balzer, an authority on the medieval Church and legislation in Poland. None of these luminaries conducted research on Jewish history themselves; but their support was important, as their leading roles in university governance at the University of Lwów signalled that the endeavour enjoyed the support of the Polish academic establishment.[20] The prize encouraged Polish Jewish scholarship that closely followed the paradigms of nineteenth-century integrationist history and was designed explicitly to 'counter the Dubnowian model' of writing east European Jewish history.[21] As Askenazy explained to one of the prize recipients, Polish Jewish history was the task of 'Polish historians of the Jews', implying the significance of a Polish patriotic lens. He believed that Jews who studied the history of Polish Jewry, even those who were native to the country and published in Polish, 'wrote about the partitions of Poland in a neutral spirit, without any feel for the "tragic end" of the Polish state'. Thus, he claimed, they could hardly be regarded as 'Polish historians of the Jews'. He criticized the adoption of an imperial Russian perspective, according to which 'Jews had it bad in Poland because it was a kingdom of the nobility, and their political and economic situation improved greatly after Poland's fall, especially in the regions taken by Russia'. In contrast, Askenazy maintained that the task of a historian of the Polish Jews was 'to show that, in Poland, Jews had always had it good, and things only became worse after Russia helped bury [the Polish–Lithuanian Commonwealth]'.[22]

The vision of Polish Jewish history evident in the Wawelberg competition elicited mild criticism in *Izraelita*. The editors drew the Jewish public's attention to the competition's political agenda and the detachment of its patrons from the Jewish community, simultaneously comparing the rapid growth of Jewish studies and literature over the course of the nineteenth century to a plant that 'derives its vital juices from below and not from above'.[23] Contributors to this literature, *Izraelita* reminded its readers, were motivated by

> a desire to bring to light the monuments of life, suffering, and creativity of the Jews ... a noble desire for the truth, and the hope that the light flowing from the results of the scientific research of the past would brighten the present, elucidate the path towards the future, and ... contribute to an improvement in the moral and material existence of the masses [*lud*].[24]

[20] Błachowska, 'Ludwik Finkel (1858–1930)', 287. Dembiński was to become entangled in a bitter conflict with Askenazy, first on the pages of *Kwartalnik Historyczny* and then in the heated discussion over the appointment to the chair of Polish history in Lwów, in which he raised the question of Askenazy's Jewish roots as an argument against the appointment.

[21] Engel, 'On Reconciling the Histories of Two Chosen Peoples', 918. Engel brings as evidence the testimony of Shatzky, *History of the Jews in Warsaw* (Yid.), iii (New York, 1953), 93.

[22] Shatzky, 'My Memories' (Yid.), 130–1.   [23] B.W.S., 'Nauka na obstalunek', 277.   [24] Ibid.

Furthermore, *Izraelita* explained that, until relatively recently, the work of Jewish scholars had enjoyed very little support from governments, universities, or even wealthy Jews, who should have seen it as their duty to help and encourage the development of Jewish studies. Instead, Jewish scholarship relied on wide popular support. Only at the beginning of the twentieth century, 'as if from the horn of plenty', did wealthy Jews set out to support Jewish studies through the funding of academic competitions, including the Wawelberg prize.[25] *Izraelita* argued that the establishment of the prize did not augur a new era in research on the history of Polish Jewry, as research should not be tailored to the desires of a wealthy patron. In fact, despite the initial excitement and high hopes of the committee, no submissions for the Wawelberg prize arrived during the first year of the competition. *Izraelita* argued that the lack of response should not have surprised anyone, and doubted that the competition would bear any fruit in the future.[26] The journal also questioned the modest monetary value of the prize, which did not ensure further development of the field.[27]

The most problematic aspect of the competition, however, stemmed from its polonocentric framework, since the committee did not include

> a single member who knew Hebrew or had any notion of institutions or religious life of the Jews, while one who aspires to investigating more deeply the history of the Jewish population in Poland can by no means do so without thorough information on this subject. After all, it is known that all documents pertaining to the inner life of Polish Jews, in manuscript and in print, are written in Hebrew.[28]

Such criticism not only reflected the writer's investment in research that would transcend the history of the legal status of Jews in Polish lands, but also suggested that future historians of Polish Jews required a particular set of professional and linguistic skills. Ironically, the committee included eminent scholars of merit, but they had no knowledge of Jewish judicature, Jewish tradition, or Jewish customs, and they could not properly evaluate scholarly editions of primary sources, especially communal records.[29] *Izraelita* thought the committee, though driven by the best intentions, was incompetent to carry out its tasks, since its members 'obviously have never researched particularly the history of the Jews in Poland. No one among them is capable of deciphering and judging an old document in

---

[25] The other competitions mentioned in the article were based in Geneva and Berlin. See ibid.

[26] See ibid. 277 and 279.

[27] In order to encourage work in a field that had lain fallow due to the lack of material support, sufficient funding was necessary. Meanwhile 'the maintenance of a favourite Doberman pinscher probably cost more' than the amount awarded for years of demanding research necessary for producing a submission (ibid. 278). There were two prizes established, of 600 crones and 400 crones. See 'Konkurs naukowy z ofiary p. Hipolita Wawelberga'. [28] B.W.S., 'Nauka na obstalunek', 278. [29] Ibid.

Hebrew.'[30] *Izraelita* concluded that wealthy Jewish patrons needed to channel their efforts into traditional philanthropic activity and allow the field of Jewish studies and literature to develop independently of their agenda.[31]

The competition was nevertheless influential. Over the course of a decade, young Polish and Jewish scholars submitted entries, and volumes that were published thanks to the prize include the doctoral dissertations of three leading historians of Polish Jewish history in the Second Polish Republic—Mojżesz Schorr, Majer Bałaban, and Ignacy Schiper—as well as a study by Zbigniew Pazdro, a legal scholar and historian of Polish law.[32] More than providing for publication, for Schorr, Bałaban, and Schiper the prize signified the inclusion of their work in the annals of Polish historiography and the recognition of their status as university-trained historians of Polish Jewry. Yet this inclusion came with a price. Askenazy made repeated efforts to censor Bałaban's submission to the Wawelberg competition, crossing out entire passages. When Bałaban restored the original text, Askenazy and Pazdro excised them from the forthcoming book.[33] Askenazy criticized Schorr, Bałaban, and Schiper for what he perceived as tendentiousness, and he called for 'rigorously examining these rascals [*gałgani*]'.[34]

## Bałaban and Schorr: Galician Academic Historians

Schorr, Bałaban, and other historians received their academic training at Polish academic institutions in Galicia and forged close relationships with leading Polish scholars. They linked themselves to the integrationist school; and not only were they aware—if critical—of previous research, they also had personal ties to senior scholars. Schorr befriended Maksymilian Gumplowicz and sustained a correspondence with his father, Ludwik, who advised the budding scholar,

---

[30] B.W.S., 'Nauka na obstalunek', 278–9.     [31] Ibid. 279.

[32] The winning dissertations were Schorr, *Żydzi w Przemyślu do końca XVIII wieku*; Bałaban, *Żydzi lwowscy na przełomie XVI i XVII wieku*; and Schiper, *Studya nad stosunkami gospodarczymi Żydów w Polsce*. Pazdro's winning contribution was *Organizacya i praktyka żydowskich sądów podwojewodzińskich w okresie 1740–1772 r.*; Pazdro did not seem to continue with any significant research pertaining to the history of Polish Jews. See Pazdro, *Przyczynek do historyi morderstw rytualnych*, offprint from *Teka* (Lwów, 1899). See Schorr, Letter 36, Berlin, 10 Feb. 1903, in Żebrowski, *Mojżesz Schorr*, 173. Finally, Maksymilian Weissberg won the prize for his study of Hebrew literature in Galicia, 'Literatura nowohebrajska w Galicyi (1786–1850)'. According to Żebrowski, in the first round of the competition Mojżesz Schorr won, against Pazdro (*Mojżesz Schorr*, 173).

[33] DALO, fond 254, opis 1, sprawa 295, p. 57, Warsaw, 9 Oct. 1912. Also published as Letter 38 in Hoszowska, *Szymon Askenazy i jego korespondencja z Ludwikiem Finklem*, 259–60. Askenazy expressed suspicion that Schiper may be 'the same kind of rascal'; he sent an article to the Jewish Kwartalnik from which I personally removed two thirds (two thirds!), as it was literally steeped in virulent tendentiousness' (ibid. 260). By 'Jewish Kwartalnik' Askenazy means *Kwartalnik poświęcony badaniu przeszłości Żydów w Polsce*.     [34] Ibid.

sharing both materials and knowledge with him.³⁵ In particular, Gumplowicz made materials pertaining to the history of the Jews in Poland available to him, especially the records of the Jewish community in Kraków.³⁶ Gumplowicz also put Schorr in touch with Aleksander Kraushar, who offered his assistance in conducting research in archives in Warsaw.³⁷ Another senior scholar, Tadeusz Wojciechowski, shepherded Schorr through the early stages of his academic career, possibly upon the recommendation of his personal friend Ludwik Gumplowicz, and he insisted that Schorr consult archives in Kraków, Poznań, and Warsaw.³⁸

Born in Przemyśl in 1874, Schorr graduated from a gymnasium (secondary school) in his home town in 1893, and soon afterward moved to Vienna to enrol both at the Rabbinical Seminary (Israelitisch-Theologische Lehranstalt) and at the Department of Philosophy at the University of Vienna. He concentrated on Semitic philology, medieval history, and early modern history. In the summer of 1897 he studied Polish and Austrian history in Lwów, attending the seminars of Wojciechowski, Bronisław Dembiński, Izydor Szaraniewicz, and Ludwik Finkel. Although torn between careers in the rabbinate, education, and scholarship, by the autumn of 1897 Schorr had decided to devote himself to the study of Jewish history in Polish lands.³⁹ Having prepared his doctoral dissertation, *Organizacya Żydów w Polsce (od najdawniejszych czasów aż do r. 1772)* (The Organization of the Jews in Poland from the Earliest Times until 1772), Schorr received his Ph.D. in 1898. The following year, *Kwartalnik Historyczny* published his thesis, praised by both Polish historians and leading Jewish scholars Simon Dubnow and Marcus Brann.⁴⁰ By 1901 he was increasingly feeling drawn to Assyriology, and eventually, as he confessed over three decades later, he 'betrayed this scholarly field [*niwa naukowa*]'.⁴¹ More accurately, Schorr never quite abandoned his scholarship on

---

³⁵ Żebrowski, *Mojżesz Schorr*, 96.

³⁶ Schorr, Letter 2, Vienna, 27 Nov. 1897, in Żebrowski, *Mojżesz Schorr*, 102–3. See also Letter 6, Vienna, 19 May 1898, ibid. 110.

³⁷ Schorr, Letter 7, Przemyśl, 9 Aug. 1898, in Żebrowski, *Mojżesz Schorr*, 111–12.

³⁸ Żebrowski suggested that Ludwik Gumplowicz recommended Mojżesz Schorr to Tadeusz Wojciechowski (Żebrowski, *Mojżesz Schorr*, 103). Schorr intended to carry out archival research in Warsaw, understanding that it had 'true treasures for the history of Jews in Poland', but he was unable to do so due to financial difficulties (Schorr, Letter 7, Przemyśl, 9 Aug. 1898, in Żebrowski, *Mojżesz Schorr*, 112).

³⁹ In Letter 7 to Ludwik Gumplowicz, dated 9 Aug. 1898, Schorr mentioned his 'plan to devote myself to philology'. See Żebrowski, *Mojżesz Schorr*, 111, and Schorr, Letter 2, Vienna, 27 Nov. 1897, ibid. 104; see also pp. 13–58.

⁴⁰ See Schorr's curriculum vitae, submitted to the Imperial Ministry of Religion and Education in Vienna, AGAD, CK Ministerstwo Oświaty, sygn. 121 u. Mojżesz Schorr, 20 June 1907, Lwów, 305–7; Schorr, Letter 2, Vienna, 27 Nov. 1897, in Żebrowski, *Mojżesz Schorr*, 103. In 1900, his dissertation was published in Russian in the journal *Voskhod*; See Letter 22, Vienna, 8 Mar. 1900, in *Mojżesz Schorr*, 147–8.

⁴¹ AAN, B'nai B'rith, file 3, p. 269: protocol of a closed meeting chaired by M. Tauber with fifty-eight brothers present, 11 Mar. 1933.

Polish Jewish history, but he did not produce another extensive work after 1903.[42] Following his *Habilitation* in 1910 at the University of Lwów, Schorr taught there as an untenured professor.[43] The Department of Philosophy at the university granted Schorr *Venia Legendi* in Semitic philology, but also underscored his work in the history of Jews in Poland, in which he 'showed that he understood how to utilize the source material and [that] he was a methodically trained historian'.[44]

In 1904 Schorr befriended Bałaban, who at the time was working at the Teachers' Seminary in Lwów and preparing a conference for teachers of the Mosaic faith. Although only three years his senior, Schorr mentored Bałaban, encouraging his younger colleague, who was already completing bibliographical reviews on Jewish history, to carry out research on the history of Polish Jewry.[45] Born in 1877 to a family with strong roots in Lwów, Bałaban graduated from the IV Polish Gymnasium in 1895, and studied law at the University of Lwów. After financial difficulties forced him to interrupt his studies, Bałaban taught in Jewish schools in Galicia, before returning to Lwów and re-entering the university.[46] Driven by his 'fondness for Polish history and indirectly for the history of the Jews in Poland', Bałaban decided to continue his university studies in history rather than in law.[47] In 1906, he submitted a work entitled *Żydzi lwowscy na przełomie XVI i XVII wieku* (Lwów Jews at the Turn of the Sixteenth and Seventeenth Centuries) to the dean of the Department of Philosophy at the University of Lwów, requesting that it be recognized as a doctoral dissertation.[48] Bałaban's application—submitted by a student who worked as an assistant teacher of the Mosaic faith in one of Lwów's gymnasia—epitomizes the shift that took place at the turn of the nineteenth century

---

[42] Żebrowki, *Mojżesz Schorr*, 25–6.

[43] See Toczek, 'Środowisko historyków lwowskich w latach 1860–1918', 144.

[44] See the copy of a recommendation signed by J. Nussbaum and sent to the Imperial Ministry of Religion and Education in Vienna recognizing Schorr's academic status in the field of Semitic philology, AGAD, CK Ministerstwo Oświaty, sygn. 121 u. Mojżesz Schorr, 22 Jan. 1910, Lwów, 304: 'Dr Moses Schorr, Erteilung der Venia legendi fur Semitologie, KK Ministerium fur Kultus und Unterricht'.

[45] AAN, B'nai B'rith, file 4, p. 185: plenary session chaired by R. Szereszewski, 22 Feb. 1937; Biderman, *Mayer Balaban*, 57. In 1933 Bałaban referred to Schorr as his 'teacher', while Schorr would describe Bałaban as his 'brother by profession' and a 'student who had outdone his mentor' (AAN, B'nai B'rith, file 3, pp. 269–70).

[46] See Bałaban's curriculum vitae attached to his application for accepting his doctoral dissertation, DALO, fond 26, opis 5, sprava 54, p. 5. This curriculum vitae gives the date 1899 for his gymnasium graduation. For more detailed information about his secondary education and his initial university training, see Wierzbieniec, 'Z badań nad lwowskim okresem życia i działalności Majera Bałabana', 298–300, and Biderman, *Mayer Balaban*, 53–4, 59–61. On his teaching career see Chapter 4. For a discussion of Bałaban's education see Gotzen-Dold, *Mojżesz Schorr und Majer Bałaban*, 49–67.

[47] Jolles (ed.), *Księga jubileuszowa Bałabana*, 37–8.

[48] DALO, fond 26, opis 5, sprava 54, p. 4, 24 Feb. 1906 in Lwów, Majer Samuel Bałaban. His dissertation was published in 1906.

in the status of Polish Jewish historiography and its practitioners. His university experience signalled Polish academia's readiness to welcome Polish Jewish history as a contribution to a decidedly *inclusive* Polish history.[49] Seemingly, his in-depth study of a local Jewish community perpetuated both the tradition established by integrationist historians writing in Polish, such as Daniel Neufeld and Aleksander Kraushar, and authors who published in Hebrew, such as Samuel Joseph Finn and Salomon Buber.

The doctoral degrees that the University of Lwów conferred on Schorr and Bałaban, and the early publications by these scholars, were emblematic of the trajectory of Jewish historians writing Polish Jewish history. Both Bałaban and Schorr, as well as the great majority of Jewish historians in the field of Polish Jewish history, came from Galicia or had received their training there. Others included Nathan Michael Gelber from Lwów, Ignacy Schiper and Salo Baron from Tarnów, and Jakub Schall from Romanówka, near Trembowla. However, they shared more than their Galician origins. As Rachel Manekin has shown, these emerging Polish Jewish historians belonged to an intellectual milieu shaped by the educational opportunities in the Austro-Hungarian empire, where Jews enjoyed unlimited access to secular education at the gymnasium and university levels, and often combined a traditional Jewish education with a university degree.[50] In addition to Schorr's and Bałaban's doctoral degrees from Lwów, the academic trajectories of other scholars who took advantage of educational opportunities in Galicia suggest the role of these institutions in the development of modern Jewish historiography. Schiper studied at the Jagiellonian University in Kraków before transferring to Vienna in 1905. Schall was educated in Lwów and Vienna. Gelber attended a gymnasium in Brody, and eventually studied at universities in Vienna and Berlin.[51] Mark Wischnitzer grew up in Wołyń, but completed his secondary education in Brody, while Jacob Shatzky left Warsaw to study in Kraków and Lwów.[52]

[49] Finkel played a role in granting Bałaban a generous scholarship, enabling him to carry out archival research in Poznań, Leszno, Radzyn, Berlin, and Vienna during the academic year 1912/13 (Jolles (ed.), *Księga jubileuszowa Bałabana*, 38–9). Similarly, the support of Finkel and Askenazy made Schorr's appointment at the University of Lwów possible (Schorr, Letter 45, Swiatzk, 24 July 1907, in Żebrowski, *Mojżesz Schorr*, 189). Influenced by Finkel and Askenazy, Bałaban also pursued research in bibliography, and he ended up defending his doctoral dissertation at the University of Lwów in 1906 (Eisenbach, 'Jewish Historiography in Interwar Poland', 457). For the curriculum vitae Bałaban composed as part of his application for an appointment as a professor at the Warsaw University and dated 16 Dec. 1935, see AAN, MWRiOP, 1614.

[50] See Manekin, 'The Galician Roots of the Historiography of Polish Jewry' (Heb.) and Manekin, 'Constructing Polish Jewry's "Shrine of History"'.

[51] See Biderman, *Mayer Balaban*, p. xxv; Mieses, 'Udział Żydów Polskich w nauce', 49–50; Goldberg, 'Majer Bałaban—czołowy historyk polskich Żydów'; Żebrowski, *Mojżesz Schorr*, 13–58.

[52] See Manekin, 'The Galician Roots of the Historiography of Polish Jewry' (Heb.).

## Jacob Shatzky—from Warsaw to Galicia

Jacob Shatzky went to Galicia to become a historian of Polish Jews with the support of Askenazy, who attached great importance to the opportunities Galicia offered for educating historians of Polish Jewish history. Yet none of Askenazy's students made a significant contribution to the field, and only two of them, Dawid Kandel and Rafał Kempner, were Jewish.[53] Believing in the urgent need to train professional historians of Polish Jewry, Askenazy made Shatzky his protégé.[54] Shatzky seemed an unlikely candidate for a historian of Polish Jewry as envisioned by his patrons, Askenazy and Bernard Lauer, a Jewish manufacturer and banker in Warsaw.[55] Born in Warsaw to a Yiddish-speaking family from the Pale of Settlement, Shatzky received a traditional Jewish education, both in a ḥeder and with private teachers, while studying Polish language and literature, especially historical works, on his own.[56] Shatzky's father, who provided food for the Russian army, supported the ideas of the Haskalah and took his son to the Jewish cemetery to observe the funerals of Chaim Zelig Słonimski in 1904 and Mathias Bersohn in 1908. During Bersohn's funeral Shatzky met Aleksander Kraushar, who gave the boy the second volume of his *Historia Żydów w Polsce* (The History of Jews in Poland) with the author's inscription: 'To the boy who under auspicious circumstances will grow into the kind of man that the author of this book wanted to be when he was his age. But life decreed otherwise.'[57] At the library of the Tłomackie Street Synagogue, where he carried out independent studies, Shatzky met Bernard Lauer. A close associate of Askenazy, Lauer argued that only Polish Jews could explain their situation and their relations with the Poles; neither German nor Russian Jews could do so because of their different backgrounds and world-views. While Russian Jews never enjoyed civic equality, even

---

[53] Nurowski lists them both as Askenazy's students (*Szymon Askenazy*, 53). However, according to another account, Kempner studied at Warsaw University, where he belonged to socialist circles and to the Koło Młodzieży Studenckiej. See Rzymkowski, 'Siedziba Kempnerów'. Kempner was appointed to the position of secretary of the Jewish community in Warsaw. He came from a wealthy family in Płock who owned a large book-trading store in the city and a printing house. The family was for the most part Polonized, and Kempner's sister Cecylia married one of the leaders of the Polish Socialist Party (PPS), Ignacy Daszyński, in 1935. See ibid. and Rozen, 'A Bunch of Memories from the Days of the Past' (Heb.), 140.

[54] See *Biographical Dictionary of Modern Yiddish Literature* (Yid.), viii. 546–8; Shapiro, 'Jacob Shatzky', in Hundert (ed.), *The YIVO Encyclopedia of Jews in Eastern Europe*, ii. 1704–5; Shapiro, 'Jacob Shatzky, Historian of Warsaw Jewry'; Shatzky, 'Balance Sheet of a Jewish Historian'; Żebrowski, 'Jakuba Szackiego żywot paradoksalny'. [55] Shatzky, 'Balance Sheet of a Jewish Historian', 266.

[56] Hafftka, 'Życie i twórczość dr. Jakóba Szackiego', 13–14.

[57] Shatzky, 'Balance Sheet of a Jewish Historian', 265. His father also encouraged Shatzky to decipher Hebrew dates and copy the inscriptions on the old gravestones at the Jewish cemetery in Warsaw (ibid.).

on paper, Polish Jews knew their rights. Moreover, Russian Jews had no emotional ties to the state.[58] For Askenazy, Jews from Russian-partitioned Poland felt more Polish than Galician Jews, and therefore were better suited to become historians of Polish Jewish history.[59]

In 1912 Lauer's funds, and the support of Askenazy, Adalberg, and Rabbi Samuel Poznański, sent Shatzky to Kraków to become a historian and to write from the perspective of Polish tradition about the Polish struggle for independence. Shatzky recalled Adalberg's instructions upon his leaving for Kraków:

> There you will inhale the spirit of free Polish culture. There, in Kraków, you will understand not only the spirit of Poland, but also the spirit of historical Jewry in Poland. In Warsaw, one cannot be as Polish as in Kraków. You will complete the Gymnasium and then study at the ancient Jagiellonian University. Only then, when you return to Warsaw, will you be able to write a history of Jews in Warsaw.[60]

According to Shatzky, both Adalberg and Askenazy believed that 'a true Jewish Polish historian must be a Warsaw Jew. The geographic factor had enormous psychological significance. It meant more than being merely a historian of Jews in Poland.'[61] Shatzky took classes with private instructors in Kraków, studied informally with Askenazy at the University of Lwów, and joined the Jewish Historical-Ethnographic Society in St Petersburg. In 1917 he graduated as an extern from the V Kraków Classical Gymnasium and received two scholarships to attend the Jagiellonian University.

The integrationist vision of Polish Jewish history shaped both Shatzky's early work and his personal trajectory. Starting in 1913, he published historical reviews in the Polish and Polish Jewish press: *Izraelita*, *Nowa Gazeta*, *Głos Związkowy*, *Nasz Kurier* in Warsaw, *Krytyka* in Kraków, and *Nasz Kraj* in Wilno. In 1914, he began publishing in *Evreiskaya starina*.[62] During the First World War he served as a lieutenant in Piłsudski's Legions, and he was twice wounded and thrice decorated for courage. In 1915 he participated in a failed attempt to organize a Jewish military unit and co-edited a call to support the Polish national cause, 'To Jewish Youth', in Polish and Yiddish. Shortly after the war, Askenazy helped him gain access to the archives in Warsaw, and, as Shatzky remembered it, he 'became the first Jew in Warsaw to work on a Jewish theme in Polish government archives'.[63]

---

[58] Lauer, 'Zum Polnisch–Jüdischen Problem', 282–3.

[59] Shatzky, 'Balance Sheet of a Jewish Historian', 267.

[60] Ibid. 266–7. See Askenazy's critical review of the state of university education in Warsaw, where he attributes its failure to meet the needs of Polish society to the Russification of the university after 1869 (Askenazy, *Uniwersytet Warszawski*).     [61] Shatzky, 'Balance Sheet of a Jewish Historian', 267.

[62] Shatzky's first publication was a review of Bałaban's works, in *Izraelita* 1913. See Hafftka, 'Życie i twórczość dr. Jakóba Szackiego', 20.     [63] Shatzky, 'Balance Sheet of a Jewish Historian', 269.

## The Polish Scholarly Journal: *A Quarterly Devoted to the Jewish Past in Poland*

The impulses that informed the competition sponsored by Wawelberg, and the assistance afforded to young Polish Jewish historians, also shaped the journal *Kwartalnik Poświęcony Badaniu Przeszłości Żydów w Polsce* (KPBPŻwP; A Quarterly Devoted to the Jewish Past in Poland), published in Warsaw for a brief two-year run in 1912 and 1913.[64] Founded by Askenazy, who envisioned it as a forum for discussing the history of Polish Jews but also a tool in promoting the model of a Pole of the Mosaic faith, the journal featured a combination of academic and political agendas.[65] Having appointed Kempner and Kandel as editors, Askenazy worked on the *KPBPŻwP* himself, seeking to acquire scholarly contributions by young historians.[66] The journal brought together university-trained historians, both Poles and Polish Jews. Explaining the need for a special organ to tackle the research on Polish Jewish history, the editors proposed a vision of Polish Jewish scholarship as a subject 'of the first rank for the general inner history of Poland, and, at the same time, particularly close to the hearts and thoughts of Polish Jews'.[67] The editorial board formulated the urgent need for a Polish periodical 'which could deal systematically and strictly academically with the pursuit of historical issues, belonging... to the realm of Polish historiography'.[68] This acute need was for a proper journal not only to delineate a field, but also to serve as a response to such journals as *Voskhod*, *Evreiskaya starina*, and *Perezhitoe*, 'devoted in principle to the past of Russian Jews, [but which] actually in large, if not decisive, part treat the history of the Jews either in the Crown and Lithuania of the time of the former Polish–Lithuanian Commonwealth or of Congress Poland of today'.[69]

It is no wonder that *KPBPŻwP* included primary sources, mainly of Polish archival provenance, and was concerned with various aspects of Polish–Jewish relations, such as Polish Jewish political, economic, and cultural history, as well as

[64] According to Tadeusz Wojciechowski, the initiative's short life was the result of increasing Zionist influence. See Nurowski, *Szymon Askenazy*, 137 and 142, which quotes a letter from Wojciechowski to Askenazy. See also Askenazy, *Szkice i portrety*, 312.

[65] Barycz, *Na przełomie dwóch stuleci*, 252. Ewa Guściora-Szeloch argued that Askenazy tried to link his ideas about Polish–Jewish rapprochement to certain conditions that the Jews needed to meet, but the failure of the journal proved his 'enlightened project' unrealistic (Guściora-Szeloch, 'Żydzi i ich rola w dziejach Polski w pracach Szymona Askenazego', 263). It seems that quarterly issues signified a scholarly journal, as opposed to monthly or weekly periodicals, which were aimed at a broader readership. [66] Bałaban, 'Profesor Szymon Askenazy (1867–1935)'.

[67] Editors' introduction to *Kwartalnik Poświęcony Badaniu Przeszłości Żydów w Polsce* (KPBPŻwP), 1/1 (1912). [68] Ibid. [69] Ibid.

Hebrew literature.⁷⁰ With articles discussing, for instance, the legal status of the Jews, their institutions, and their culture, as well as Polish–Jewish relations shortly before and during the partitions of Poland, the journal continued some of the central themes characteristic of the nineteenth-century integrationist school. The editors gave clear preference to sources pertaining to Jewish figures who symbolized Polish–Jewish brotherhood, and Jewish contributions to Poland's struggle for independence or Polish–Jewish co-operation: Berek Joselewicz (1764–1809), who fought as a colonel in the Polish army in the Kościuszko uprising; Rabbi Dov Ber Meisels (1798–1878), an Orthodox chief rabbi in Kraków and Warsaw; Michał Landy (1844–61), a Jewish student killed in the Polish patriotic demonstration in 1861; and the maskil Jakub Tugenhold.⁷¹ In addition, the journal published documents about Jewish patriotism, such as a chorus of praise sung at the celebrations of 3 May 1792, proving the gratitude and attachment of Polish Jews to the last king of Poland and their solidarity with the general national cause.⁷² A smaller number of articles touched on medieval Jewish history or contemporary issues such as the emergence of the Zionist movement.⁷³ The political agenda of the new journal appeared particularly striking in the context of the tensions and embitterment in Polish–Jewish relations in 1912, connected with the elections to the legislative assembly—the Fourth Duma of the Russian empire—in the summer of that year, in which the socialist candidate Eugeniusz Jagiełło won a seat with Jewish and Polish workers' votes.⁷⁴

The journal constituted a short-lived but important forum for discussions of the Polish Jewish past from a distinctively Polish point of view. Not all the articles followed in the footsteps of the nineteenth-century integrationist school of Polish Jewish history, but it focused on Polish and Polish Jewish historical references and expressed Polish objectives and hopes under Russian rule. It is no surprise that, according to one account, the journal did not find favour with

---

⁷⁰ The journal strove to make available to its readers examples of historical documents pertaining to Jewish history in Polish lands: Turowski, 'Polska rajem dla żydów', for example, discussed a 1760 manuscript by Józef Andrzej Załuski. A Hebrew deed of gift was included with an unattributed Polish translation in 'Akt darowizny bóźnicy przez Berka', and Dawid Kandel provided a short introduction to a letter of 1831 in 'Żydzi w wojsku polskiem w r. 1831'. Among articles discussing Jewish history in Polish lands in the nineteenth century, see Askenazy, 'Z dziejów Żydów polskich w dobie Księstwa Warszawskiego', and id., 'Ze spraw żydowskich w dobie kongresowej'.

⁷¹ On Joselewicz, see Askenazy, 'O Berku'; on Meisels, see Kandel, 'Z korespondencyi rabina Meiselsa'; on Landy, see the letter from his father, Henryk Landy, 'Zapiska o Michale Landym'; and on Tugenhold, see Kandel, 'Z papierów Jakóba Tugendholda'.

⁷² D[awid] K[andel], 'Hymn przy obchodzie uroczystości dnia 3 Maja 1792 roku', esp. 166.

⁷³ See e.g. Weissberg, 'Język literacki Żydów w Galicyi', 1/2 (1912), 11–12. On medieval history see Warchał, 'Żydzi polscy na Uniwersytecie padewskim'; Schiper, 'Żydzi neofici i prozelici w Polsce do r. 1569'. On contemporary history see K. Horowicz and R. Kempner, 'Podatek gminny w Warszawie, 1903–1912'. ⁷⁴ See Weeks, *From Assimilation to Antisemitism*, 163–9.

Russian Jewish historians: 'St. Petersburg did not like its tone; Dubnow did not like its Polishness.'⁷⁵ Despite the only partial success of some of these initiatives, through his involvement in training young historians of Polish Jewry and his involvement with the Wawelberg prize and the founding of *KPBPŻwP*, Askenazy emerged as a somewhat ambivalent organizer of Polish Jewish history.

## Apologetics and the Writing of Polish Jewish History

Throughout his career, Askenazy emphasized Poland's greatness, maintaining that the end of the eighteenth century had been a moment of political and economic progress, and the struggles for independence in the nineteenth century a glorious cause. He differed rather dramatically from the pessimistic Kraków school of Polish history in his attitude towards the past, especially in his interpretation of the reasons for Poland's partitions.⁷⁶ The same patriotic sensibility informed the areas of research that he encouraged in Polish Jewish history and in the work of his students. They contrasted the flourishing of Jewish culture and community and the planned reforms of the last years of the Polish–Lithuanian Commonwealth with the discrimination and decline ushered in by the rule of the partitioning powers. In particular, Askenazy and his students adopted an anti-Russian stance, juxtaposing the good fortunes of Jews under the rule of Polish kings with the Jews' misery in the aftermath of the state's demise. In their interpretation, the project of writing Polish Jewish history stemmed from the concerns of Polish history. Embracing a polonocentric research agenda, they investigated internal Jewish affairs to learn why Jews behaved in certain ways in relation to the Poles and the Polish cause. The study of Polish Jewish history served as an indispensable tool for understanding the dynamics of Polish–Jewish relations, and for proving the Jews worthy of civil rights.⁷⁷ Askenazy and those in his milieu singled out topics such as 'the attitude of the Jews to Napoleon, to the Duchy of Warsaw in general, and to the 1812 war', in order to evaluate Jewish attitudes towards the Polish national cause in the aftermath of the partitions.⁷⁸ They perceived no tension between strictly academic and patriotic or apologetic intentions.

In 1912 Askenazy published a lengthy article in which he discussed the history of Polish Jews during the time of the Duchy of Warsaw (1807–15). He reminded his readers that the partitions of Poland resulted in the deterioration of the status of Polish Jews, with numerous limitations placed on their activities by the parti-

---

⁷⁵ Shatzky, 'Balance Sheet of a Jewish Historian', 268. Shatzky continued, 'It did not occur to either side that there could be a third party, a Jewish one, unassociated with either Polishness or Russianness—Jewish not necessarily in language, but in the internal rhythm of the Jewish historical process, played out, it is true, against a background of political reality but not always closely intricated in it' (ibid.). ⁷⁶ See Maternicki, 'Historyk sługą narodu', 71–7.

⁷⁷ See Kandel's reflections on Jewish traditional attitudes towards military service and their response to Napoleonic campaigns, Kandel, 'Żydzi w roku 1812', 158–9. ⁷⁸ Ibid. 157.

tioning powers and thorough and severe administrative police control.[79] Only during the Napoleonic Wars, with the creation of the Duchy of Warsaw and the return of the sovereign Polish government, did the situation of the Jews improve.[80] Askenazy believed that the Jews in Lithuania and Ruthenia, especially those influenced by hasidic leaders, were easily manipulated by the Russian empire, and they turned against France and thus against Polish political aspirations.[81] Unlike in western Europe, truly patriotic Jews were rare in Polish lands.[82] Askenazy described Jewish leaders as 'ignorant', 'fanatical', 'narrow-minded', and 'backward', saying they enviously guarded their control over the Jewish masses. They selfishly resisted the idea of equal rights and equal obligations, since equal rights would become an effective 'battering ram to break the Chinese wall of age-old talmudic orthodoxy and the more recent, even worse, hasidic one'.[83] These themes of the Jewish leadership's backwardness, Russian political manipulations in Polish–Jewish relations, and unease about the perceived shortcomings of Jewish patriotism informed the historical work of Askenazy and his students.

A similar outlook informed Askenazy's examination of the policies of Nikolay Novosiltzev (1761–1836), who had been head of the Russian administration in Warsaw. Askenazy insisted that this ardent supporter of Russification protected the Jews because it suited his political intentions, and that in doing so he was 'sticking a mighty Jewish wedge into the very core of the system of the Duchy, a new vast Russian conquest'.[84] According to Askenazy, Novosiltzev played the Jewish card rather than let the Poles decide, even though they were the only ones competent to do so, while some Jews tried to circumvent the Poles in their quest for favourable policies.[85] Askenazy criticized Jews for what he called 'extraterritorial action' —that is, viewing themselves as outside the society of their country (*społeczeństwo krajowe*).[86] Here again, the historian contrasted the patriotism of German Jews with that of Polish Jews.[87] Instead of growing, the number of patriotic Polish Jews had declined, since, according to Askenazy, when 'progressive Warsaw Jews' converted to Christianity, they

impoverished spiritually and rendered sterile the wide masses of Polish Jewry, binding them even closer to the passionate and fanatical tie to the faith of their forefathers, and

---

[79] Askenazy, 'Z dziejów Żydów polskich w dobie Księstwa Warszawskiego'. The worsening of the situation resulted from the partitioning powers' desire for social and state assimilation of the conquered Polish land, with more severe taxes (ibid. 1). Discussing the status of Jews in the early years of the Russian conquest, Henryk Mościcki contrasted 'the enlightened reform projects of the Four Year Diet, plans of Kołłątaj, Czacki, or Butrymowicz' with the policies of Catherine II, which left the 'Jewish masses in their old time ignorance, closed in the outdated communal organization and burdened with taxes' (See Mościcki, 'Żydzi polscy pod berłem Katarzyny II', 60).
[80] Askenazy, 'Z dziejów Żydów polskich w dobie Księstwa Warszawskiego', 2.   [81] Ibid. 7.
[82] Ibid. 9.   [83] Ibid. 10–11.   [84] Askenazy, 'Ze spraw żydowskich w dobie kongresowej', 3.
[85] Ibid. 15, 22.   [86] Ibid. 11.   [87] Ibid. 14–15.

alienating them from Polishness by equating the notion of Jew-Pole with a religious treason [*zaprzaństwo*], and in this way in the end, deprived the country of... cultural and political influence of these masses.[88]

While pointing out these challenges to Jewish patriotism, Askenazy was eager to present to his readers certain model Polish Jews who had been committed to and involved in Poland's struggle for independence. In particular, he praised those Polish Jews who took up arms of their own free will and fought for Poland's independence. Among these was Berek Joselewicz, 'once a soldier in the Kościuszko uprising and an eminent officer in the army of the Duchy'.[89] He also published an article, 'U grobu Żyda-Polaka' (At the Grave of a Jew-Pole'), discussing the life of Henryk Wohl, who served in the National Government during the January 1863 Polish uprising against Russia.[90] For Askenazy, Wohl personified the ideal of 'an upright Polish Jew [who] became an upright Pole, giving the purest and most generous model of patriotic virtue'. Praising Wohl, Askenazy reminded his readers that 'Polish virtue can and should flourish in the heart of any Pole, without any difference of background or faith'.[91] Such a tradition promoted mutual love and cooperation and offered hope for rebuilding Polish–Jewish relations, predicated on the premise of a Jewish embrace of Polish culture and the Polish national cause.[92]

The issue of patriotism animated much of the discussion of Jewish history in the Polish lands. Like Askenazy, his student Dawid Kandel celebrated Joselewicz as a reformer who had found a solution to the so-called 'Jewish question' in Poland, and had pursued the path of assimilation through the armed struggle against Poland's enemies rather than through baptism.[93] He went as far as turning Joselewicz into a prototype of the Pole of the Mosaic faith. Motivated by a 'passionate love' of his brethren and a 'true love of Poland whose good and faithful son he was', Joselewicz sought to solve the 'Jewish question' in a 'logical and realistic manner'. Rejecting religious reform, Joselewicz believed that 'religious separateness did not hinder being as good a citizen of the country as others'.[94] To deserve civic equality and 'to safeguard their future in the country that had adopted Jews as its sons', Joselewicz joined Poland's struggle against its enemies, providing an example to thousands of Jews who followed a similar line of thought and awaking the 'spirit of the Maccabees'.[95]

Askenazy's students found more examples of Jewish patriotism and Polish–Jewish rapprochement. A 'thought-provoking and pleasing' eulogy by Warsaw

[88] Askenazy, 'Ze spraw żydowskich w dobie kongresowej', 27.
[89] Askenazy, 'Z dziejów Żydów polskich w dobie Księstwa Warszawskiego', 11–12.
[90] Askenazy, 'U grobu Żyda-Polaka'. [91] Ibid. 921. [92] Ibid. 921–2.
[93] Kandel, 'Berek Joselewicz', 295–6. Following Askenazy's example, another of his students, Emil Kipa, took an interest in Joselewicz as well. See Kipa, 'Berka Joselewicza projekt legionu ochotniczego dla Austryi w r. 1796'. [94] Kandel, 'Berek Joselewicz', 296. [95] See ibid. 297.

Jews, written upon the death of Prince Józef Poniatowski in 1813 and printed in *KPBPŻwP*, testified to 'the positive spiritual mood of Warsaw Jews in the last years of the Duchy of Warsaw, who should otherwise be harshly criticized'.[96] Despite the fact that they had left the ranks of the insurgents and sought the support of the Russians at the time of Napoleon's downfall, 'it turns out that they still harboured not fully extinct heartfelt feelings for the country since at this disastrous time, without a concern for the military power of the Russian enemy in the conquered paradise, they tenderly mourned the death of the chief Polish commander.'[97] Other examples of Jewish patriotism included Jewish youth enlisting for the Polish war effort in 1831, a poem to the Jews of Poland calling for national unity and co-operation in 1848, the support of Rabbi Meisels for Polish struggles for independence, and positive attitudes towards Jews within Polish society on the eve of the January 1863 uprising.[98] In 1917 Shatzky published a book on Kościuszko and the Jews, in which he explained why Polish Jews should feel gratitude to Kościuszko: 'By calling on the Jews to sacrifice [their] blood on the altar of the Motherland, he elevated them ... to the same status as in Poland only nobility had enjoyed.' Thus Joselewicz and Bartosz Głowacki, a peasant who joined Kościuszko's army and distinguished himself in the battle of Racławice, were 'two symbolic names representing the democratic ideas, fulfilling the rule and the right of winning freedom with one's own blood'.[99]

In the same year, Shatzky composed a short study, 'Rok 1863 a Żydzi' (The Year 1863 and the Jews), as a part of a planned larger monograph on the role of the Jews in the January 1863 uprising, the completion of which required extensive archival research abroad.[100] This text serves as a good example of an attempt to inscribe Polish Jews into the annals of Poland's struggles for independence. He hoped that their sacrifice would not be forgotten and that 'the glory of their recent martyrdom and sacrifice [would] guide the current generation'.[101] Shatzky

---

[96] See Kandel, 'Elegia na śmierć księcia Józefa', which includes the original eulogy.  [97] Ibid.

[98] Dawid Kandel, 'Żydzi w wojsku polskiem w r. 1831'; a photograph of a Jewish banner from the campaign appeared in *KPBPŻwP*, 1/2 (1912), 135, along with a description signed only D., but probably by Kandel. The poem can be found in Emil Kipa, 'Z r. 1848'. According to Kandel, even the townspeople who were 'usually presented as the blindfolded and sworn [*ślepy i zajadły*] enemy of Polish Jews, governed by their passionate economic competition, in reality were able to transcend these competitive issues at the moment of historical importance for the nation' (Kandel, 'Z korespondencyi rabina Meiselsa', 1/3 (1913), 185).

[99] Shatzky [Szacki], *Kościuszko a Żydzi*, 11. On the Polish celebrations of anniversaries connected to Kościuszko see Micińska, *Gołąb i Orzeł*.

[100] CAHJP, P 9, file 15: Shatzky [Szacki], 'Rok 1863 a Żydzi'. Shatzky used extensive archival material, interviewed veterans of the uprising, including Dr Bolesław Limanowski, and consulted Hebrew and Yiddish sources, the latter of which he described as 'jargon' (ibid. 5).

[101] Ibid. 5–6. The chapter prepared for publication included a list of Polish Jews from all Polish

reminded his readers of the Jews who participated in the patriotic demonstrations in the years leading up to the uprising, and who propagated 'the idea of brotherhood and the necessity of sacrifice and offerings on the altar of the Motherland'.[102] Responding to this Jewish involvement in the patriotic movement, Poles started 'to pull down this medieval battering ram of religious prejudices, the walls of bias and mistrust'.[103] Shatzky recalled the death of Michał Landy as a powerful symbol of Polish Jewish brotherhood, which had threatened Russian rule to such an extent that the Jews received from the Russians a bill of emancipation.[104] Shatzky declared that the names of Jewish heroes needed 'to be immortalized by native history'.[105] He compiled a list of some participants who responded to the calls of the insurgent National Government, including Aleksander Kraushar, a member of the government's press department; Jakób Rotwand, who upon his return from Siberia became secretary of the Jewish community in Warsaw; and Ignacy Gumplowicz, the brother of Ludwik Gumplowicz.[106] Shatzky also used moving examples of Jews who fought in the uprising, distinguishing themselves with courage and patriotic heroism. Some remained 'anonymous martyrs' of the Polish national cause: 'Jews who died for Poland'.[107] According to Shatzky, the uprising constituted the triumph of the idea of Poles and Jews working together for the welfare of the country; therefore, it was close to the hearts of even the 'ignorant mass' supportive of the Polish struggle for independence.[108] He concluded that Jews flocked to the banners of the 1863 uprising 'driven by the watchword: free with the free, equal with the equal'.[109]

Askenazy's students repeatedly examined the cunning of the Russian government and the ways in which it tried to use the Jews as a destabilizing factor in society and to win their loyalty in exchange for certain concessions, especially in Lithuania during the Kościuszko uprising.[110] In their collaboration with the Russians, Jewish leaders 'had renounced any memory of the declining Polish–Lithuanian Commonwealth, a safe haven for the Jews for many long centuries, and served the new power in hope of gaining an ample prize for their co-religionists'.[111] Despite signs of Polish–Jewish rapprochement, Kandel reported on the numerous accounts in military sources of Jewish spies during the last years of the Duchy of Warsaw and the 1812 war. According to Kandel, these spies served the Russians 'not only for the monetary reward but as if under some special moral obligation'. Moreover, contemporary sources 'declare[d] a certain essential prevailing unfriendliness of the Jews for the Polish cause and their dedication to the Russian cause'.[112]

lands who participated in the national movement from 1860 to 1863; they 'suffered and gave their lives for their attachment to the country' (Shatzky, 'Rok 1863 a Żydzi', 4).

[102] Ibid. 7 and 9.    [103] Ibid. 8.    [104] Ibid.    [105] Ibid. 11.    [106] Ibid. 14–36.    [107] Ibid. 37–46.
[108] Ibid. 48.    [109] Ibid. 49.    [110] See Mościcki, 'Żydzi polscy pod berłem Katarzyny II', 61, 64.
[111] Ibid. 66.    [112] Kandel, 'Żydzi w roku 1812', 159.

While confirming that in 1812 Jews in Lithuania provided services to the Russian army, Kandel dismissed previous interpretations of the phenomenon as lacking knowledge of the Jews' true motives.[113] The explanation required analysis of 'internal Jewish relations' and the policies of the Russian government, which used the Jews for its own benefit.[114] In an article about Moses Montefiore's visit to Warsaw, Kandel discussed the polices of Ivan Paskiewicz (1782–1856), the commander of the Russian troops in Congress Poland that crushed the Polish uprising of November 1830, who was responsible for the economic repression and forced Russification in its aftermath. His harsh policies, 'particularly severe as far as the Jews were concerned, [were] economic, social-legal, and educational'.[115] Polish Jews educated in the public schools and universities of the Duchy of Warsaw and Congress Poland experienced the 'iron hand of Paskiewicz'.[116] They owed their emancipation to Aleksander Wielopolski (1803–77), who emancipated Polish Jews 'out of his own Polish inspiration and without any external initiative coming from abroad'.[117] Shatzky described the regime of Tsar Nicholas I (1796–1855) as a time of poverty, misery, and persecution for the Jews, as the government attempted to reform educational institutions, making civil rights contingent on the success of these plans.[118]

Kandel's articles included several other tropes characteristic of his mentor's treatment of Polish Jewry. He portrayed Poland as a safe haven where Jewish wanderers escaped from persecution and found refuge.[119] Kandel called it

a blessed site, which the Jews call their new motherland. Astute [*przenikliwi*] Jews, who had come into contact with almost all nations of the world in the course of sixteen centuries [of Jewish history], immediately recognized that the Poles, who are not always able to be consistent in relation to them, are nevertheless in fact good and honest. The Jews understood it immediately, and their happiness was great, when they felt a more solid ground under their feet on which they would be able to remain for a long time.[120]

Kandel repeated a basic tenet of integrationist historiography: the exceptional treatment of the Jews in Poland and the essential hospitality of the Poles. Granted royal protection and autonomy as well as separate institutions, synagogues, and schools, Jews flourished spiritually, transforming Poland 'into the new Zion'

---

[113] Ibid. 160.
[114] According to Kandel, the behaviour of Polish Jews could only be explained and properly understood by getting to know the activities of 'strange, holy', dark Lithuanian Jewish 'tzaddik' Shneur Zalman of Lyady. While critical of Polish historical scholarship that ignored internal Jewish relations, he made an exception for his mentor Szymon Askenazy's 'Pierwszy "syonista" polski', discussed later in this chapter. See Kandel, 'Żydzi w roku 1812'.
[115] Kandel, 'Montefiore w Warszawie', 74. [116] Ibid. 75. [117] Ibid. 84.
[118] See CAHJP, P 9, file 4: Shatzky, *Szkolnictwo żydowskie w dobie paskiewiczowskiej 1832–1855*, 36.
[119] Kandel, 'Berek Joselewicz', 291. [120] Ibid. 292.

and making it a magnet for Jews from around the world.¹²¹ Until the 1648 Chmielnicki uprising and the devastation that followed in its wake, Polish Jews enjoyed their own spiritual world and autonomous government, constituting what Kandel called 'a nation'.¹²² In the wake of the massacres, however, and especially after the demise of the centralized communal autonomy in 1764, Kandel argued that Polish Jews ceased to be a nation. From that moment onward, they ought to have reformed their religious practices and embraced assimilation.¹²³

Critical views of Jewish institutions and organizations played an important role in the apologetic vision of Polish Jewish history. Askenazy criticized Jewish leadership at the time of the Duchy of Warsaw, while Kandel condemned the outdated Jewish communal organizations at the time of the creation of Congress Poland, which he said had contributed to the poverty of the Jewish masses and had been led by irresponsible leaders who were hardly devoted to the Jewish cause.¹²⁴ The communal structures controlled every aspect of Jewish life, but 'in their content did not rise up to the level of the old *kehalim* in the Old Commonwealth'.¹²⁵ The cultural conditions of Polish Jews were described as deplorable because they lacked primary schools providing instruction in secular subjects. Even the study of the Talmud deteriorated in comparison with how it had been during the Polish–Lithuanian Commonwealth; instead, hasidism spread among Polish Jews.¹²⁶ Kandel admitted to the virtues of a hasidic leader, Israel Ben Shabbetai, known as the Kozienice Maggid (c.1737–1813): his devotion to the motherland and the Polish cause, his rejection of Jewish separatism—telling his followers to stick with the Poles—and his use of Polish proverbs.¹²⁷ Rafał Kempner discussed the decline of autonomous Jewish communal institutions, praising the *kehalim* of the Commonwealth, which, 'based on the principles of broad and full autonomy, constituted almost a separate form of Jewish state government. Jews living in Poland in fact were not familiar with another form of government.'¹²⁸ But the power of

---

¹²¹ Kandel, 'Berek Joselewicz', 293. Kandel wrote a series of three articles about ancient Polish synagogues, as they marked the strong roots of the Jewish settlement in Polish lands and the prosperity of Jewish communities. The series was titled *Bóżnice starożytne w Polsce* and the articles were 'Bóżnica w Sandomierzu', 'Bóżnica w Pinczowie', and 'Bóżnica w Stepaniu'.

¹²² See Kandel, 'Berek Joselewicz', 292–4.

¹²³ He argued that Jewish leaders such as Shabetai Tsevi and Jacob Frank had embraced assimilation, putting forward ideas for reforming religious practices. Frank, in particular, acted out of an honest desire to save his brethren through conversion to Catholicism. See Kandel, 'Berek Joselewicz', 294–5.

¹²⁴ Askenazy, 'Z dziejów Żydów polskich w dobie Księstwa Warszawskiego'; Kandel, 'Żydzi w dobie utworzenia Królestwa Kongresowego', 96–7.

¹²⁵ Kandel, 'Żydzi w dobie utworzenia Królestwa Kongresowego', 97.     ¹²⁶ Ibid. 99.

¹²⁷ Ibid. 106. See also Kirszenbaum, 'Bractwo Pogrzebowe na Pradze', 133–46, an article on Hevra Kadisha, the traditional Jewish burial society, in Praga (a district of Warsaw).

¹²⁸ Kempner, 'Agonia Kahału', 67.

the communal authorities depended on the government of the Polish–Lithuanian Commonwealth, and with the latter's decline, the former was gradually abolished.[129] Although the *kehalim*, which 'had ruled the Jewish population in Poland over three centuries', left behind a mixed legacy, Kempner also recognized 'beautiful pages in their history', as their existence coincided with the golden era of Polish Jews.[130]

Like his mentor Askenazy, Kandel wrote about hasidism in utterly negative terms, as an expression of 'dark religious fanaticism' to which the overwhelming majority of the Jews of Congress Poland had succumbed, especially in provincial towns and hamlets.[131] It brought ignorance, vanity, and demoralization, contributing to poverty and destitution.[132] In Warsaw, the Jewish intelligentsia failed in their struggle for Jewish education, and after 1814 hasidism spread, attracting many marginal elements in Jewish society.[133] Kandel held Shneur Zalman of Lyady (1749–1812), the founder and first leader of Chabad hasidism, responsible for bringing the upper strata of Jewish society to the movement. An ambitious and power-hungry leader, argued Kandel, Shneur Zalman had tried to achieve his goals by suppressing the irrational elements of hasidic practice.[134] While trying to gain absolute power over the Jews—not only for himself but also for his offspring—Shneur Zalman had relentlessly separated the Jews from European culture, introducing a principle profoundly paradoxical and harmful to vital Jewish interests but indispensable to his own personal dynastic ambitions: that Jews should not aspire to emancipation, but rather should resist it with all their might as something dangerous.[135]

For all his nostalgia about the place of Jews in the Old Poland, Kandel wrote critically about the attempts to reform the status of Jews in Congress Poland.[136]

---

[129] Ibid. 69.

[130] Ibid. 70. Kempner focused on the short-lived Warsaw *kahal*, following the partitions of Poland, which was replaced by the new organization in Congress Poland (ibid. 73).

[131] Kandel, 'Komitet starozakonnych', 88.

[132] Kandel, 'Żydzi w dobie utworzenia Królestwa Kongresowego', 107. Kandel praised his native Płock's relatively large group of 'progressive Jews, the so-called maskilim'; in the Płock area, in contrast to the rest of Congress Poland, hasidism remained weak. Kandel, 'Komitet starozakonnych', 93.

[133] Kandel, 'Żydzi w dobie utworzenia Królestwa Kongresowego', 112–13; id., 'Żydzi w roku 1812', 175.

[134] Kandel, 'Żydzi w roku 1812', 170–1. Kandel argued that only by understanding the role of this hasidic leader could one understand both history and a large section of contemporary Jewish society. According to Kandel, analysis of Shneur Zalman's life allowed the historians to see 'in what hands the poor and ignorant Polish Jewry used to be and to a large extent finds itself until this very day' and 'what leaders and for what personal motives has been used and moved to either considerable monetary contributions or Palestinian wanderings' (ibid. 160).

[135] Ibid. 172. [136] Kandel, 'Komitet starozakonnych', 101–2.

He also noted new and disturbing phenomena in attitudes towards Jews in the Polish lands. Discussing the influence of the Reverend Luigi Chiarini (1789–1832), who had occupied the chair of the history of the church at Warsaw University and prepared the translation of the Talmud into French as a path to reforming the Jews, Kandel deplored the awakening of a 'strong antisemitic movement in certain circles in the country'.[137]

Indeed, the picture of Polish–Jewish relations, while directly influenced by a political agenda, was ambivalent. Bernard Lauer observed that neighbourly relations between the city of Kraków and the Jews of Kazimierz were not always agreeable. On the contrary,

over the course of many centuries, we encounter in the chronicles descriptions of various fights and clashes between the townsmen of Kraków, for the most part German, and the elders of the Jews of Kazimierz. The matter was the privileges of free trade in the capital of Kraków, which the local Jews received from the kings themselves or the mighty lords in exchange for expensive ransoms, temporary and permanent.[138]

The king and other powerful protectors and monasteries often supported the Jews to extract taxes or get business partners.[139] Lauer reminded his readers of the Polish landscapes that were saturated with Jewish historical presence: 'The ashes of their ancestors lie in Polish cemeteries and the books of rabbis published in Polish printing houses spin their sayings of learned ones and miracle workers. They have their *shuls*, yeshivas, and synagogues.' Polish Jews could rely on a history that, Lauer claimed, 'told them about the royal decrees and the peaceful coexistence of their ancestors with the Poles at a time when murder and horrible persecution drove the Jews out of Spain, England, France, and Germany'.[140] Commenting on contemporary conflicts, Lauer argued that the Polish Jewish intelligentsia, raised in Polish culture, were inclined towards Poland both in Congress Poland and in autonomous Galicia, and that Jews should assimilate linguistically as well.[141] Historical evidence in Lauer's argument included Jews who had served the 1863 uprising with goods and blood, including Rabbi Meisels.[142] Lauer figuratively called for bringing down the walls of the ghetto, so that Poles and Jews could work together on rebuilding the country after the destruction of the First World War.[143]

Askenazy considered the demand for civil rights for all Jews and political rights for Jews of merit well justified, unless formulated 'in the fog of abstract, absolute claims'.[144] He reminded his readers of the literary character Jankiel—a

---

[137] Kandel, 'Komitet starozakonnych', 103.
[138] Lauer, 'Przyczynek do historyi żydów krakowskich', 117.    [139] Ibid. 118.
[140] Lauer, 'Zum Polnisch–Jüdischen Problem', 283.    [141] Ibid. 283–4.
[142] Ibid. 293. Lauer himself drew on stereotypical images of Jews. He discussed the danger posed by Russified Jews who came to Poland in the 1880s (ibid. 294–5).
[143] Ibid. 299.    [144] Askenazy, 'Ze spraw żydowskich w dobie kongresowej', 31.

patriotic Orthodox Jew featured in Adam Mickiewicz's epic poem *Pan Tadeusz*—arguing that the only basis for a claim for civil rights was not dress, profession, religious observance, or cultural refinement, but 'unconditional unification with the power of sacrificial feeling and deeds with the general national cause'.[145] In line with the nineteenth-century notion of Poles of the Mosaic faith, Kandel defined Jews as a religious community, preserved over the course of centuries by laws designed by 'the Talmudists ... who had chained the hands of the Jews in unbreakable links and blocked their path with a Chinese wall [the Great Wall], ordered them to create for themselves a separate world ... in order to isolate them completely, which was to provide the safest guarantee for the eternal existence of the Jews'.[146] Returning to the metaphor of the Great Wall, Kandel bemoaned the divide 'between the local population and the Jews, which began before the November 1830 uprising and influenced the political orientation of the Jews as well as internal relations after the revolution in the Polish Kingdom'.[147]

But these historical claims also had strong contemporary undertones. Askenazy and his students rejected ideas of a 'separatist' Jewish identity, which they considered harmful for both Polish society and Polish Jewry. Instead, Askenazy hoped for a return to what he perceived as the tradition of 'the age-old unifying power and assimilating quality of the Polish spirit and national culture, this heritage of the past and the crucial warrant for the future'.[148] He shared concerns about more recent developments in the relations between Jews and non-Jews. No wonder that contemporary Polish historians portrayed Askenazy as a representative of the generation that still believed in the ultimate triumph of assimilation, despite being attacked both by Polish nationalists and by Zionists, and a noble intellectual who tried to disseminate his 'enlightened project' about Polish–Jewish rapprochement.[149]

One article by Askenazy, published in 1908 in the prestigious Polish journal *Biblioteka Warszawska*, helps to understand his grappling with the dangers of modern Jewish nationalism. 'Pierwszy "syonista" polski' (The First Polish 'Zionist') seemingly offered a close reading of a handful of Hebrew letters that had triggered a Russian police investigation in 1821. The article not only mocked the absurdities of Russian political oppression, but also attacked Zionism. Askenazy contrasted the 'Zionism' of the vast majority of Polish Jews, 'the understandable and agreeable purely confessional tradition, rooted exclusively in the passionate religiosity of the Jewish masses in Poland', with the dangerous contemporary

[145] Ibid. 32–3.
[146] Kandel, 'Berek Joselewicz', 291.
[147] Kandel, 'Komitet starozakonnych', 103. See Marcinkowski, 'Luigi Chiarini (1789–1832)'.
[148] Askenazy, 'U grobu Żyda-Polaka', 921. See also Kandel, 'Berek Joselewicz', 297.
[149] See Szczerbakiewicz, 'Sprytny dostawca optymizmu narodowego', 339; Guściora-Szeloch, 'Żydzi i ich rola w dziejach Polski w pracach Szymona Askenazego', 263.

ideology of 'material, geographical, and nationalistic Zionism', threatening to harm Polish Jews and Poland. That ideology was—he suggested—born in the unholy alliance between German Jews and the Russian secret police, transplanted to Polish lands from western Europe. It was the work of 'politicking cosmopolitan German Jews of large cities, the least Jewish of all and not belonging to any nation, freed from any connection with the Jewish religion, devoid of any feeling for a historical development, notions and needs of Polish Jewish masses'.[150] 'It is noteworthy,' warned Askenazy, 'that this fatal fiction, before it had been elevated to the level of a political rallying call by its contemporary Jewish apologists, had been previously expressed in the denunciatory creativity of Novosiltzev, and before it had been used to turn many unwary Jews mad, it led to the persecution of the first alleged Polish "Zionist" [Salomon Płoński]'.[151] Despite his clear personal vision of how and by whom the history of Polish Jews should be written, Askenazy played a role in the academic careers of Jewish historians whose work on Jewish Polish history departed from their patron's original vision.

## The National Jewish History School in Poland

At the time when Askenazy and his students were envisioning a Polish Jewish history written from within the contemporary Polish historiographical context, nationalist ideas were increasingly shaping the terms of political discourse in Galicia, and Jews came more and more to see themselves as members of a Jewish national community. Deeply affected by the Polonization campaign, but facing exclusivist Polish nationalist claims, the Jewish intelligentsia 'began to perceive themselves as constituting a distinct Jewish nation deserving the same national rights as everyone else'.[152] While graduating from Polish gymnasia and attending Polish universities at the beginning of the twentieth century, the Galician Jewish intelligentsia combined an immersion in Polish culture with a strong national Jewish identity. In Samuel Kassow's words: 'Although young Jews received a Polish education, they did not become young Poles.'[153] As a result, university-

---

[150] Askenazy, 'Pierwszy "syonista" polski', 469.   [151] Ibid.

[152] Shanes, *Diaspora Nationalism and Jewish Identity*, 40. See also Porter, *When Nationalism Began to Hate*.

[153] Kassow, *Who Will Write Our History?*, 19. According to Shanes, Jewish nationalism 'drew support from two disparate groups: acculturated integrationists, propelled by an inhospitable Gentile world, and modernising ethnicists seeking a secular, Jewish identity able to compete with rival national ideologies' (*Diaspora Nationalism and Jewish Identity*, 49). Discussing the situation in Tarnów at the beginning of the twentieth century, Litman claimed that 'The main and hardest struggle of the Zionists was with the local assimilationist trend, deeply rooted among the wealthy and educated' (Litman, *The Economic Role of Jews in Medieval Poland*, 13–14).

educated Galician Jews retained a complex tripartite identity: 'Austrian by political loyalty, Polish by cultural affiliation, and Jewish in an ethnic sense.'[154]

As was usual in their generation in Galicia during the last decades of the nineteenth century, Bałaban, Schorr, and Schiper joined Zionist youth groups. As a student in Lwów, Bałaban joined the Zionist association Mikra Kodesh, and he continued to be active in the organization—which later changed its name to Syjon (Zion)—when he was teaching in Gliniany, south-east of Lwów.[155] Bałaban published in the group's bi-weekly journal, *Przyszłość* (Future), launched in 1897,[156] and he participated in the annual Hanukah and Bar Kochba festivals organized by young Jewish intellectuals concerned with the need for a national rebirth. In 1899, Ludwik Gumplowicz mentioned Schorr as an enthusiastic Zionist in a letter to Theodor Herzl.[157] That same year, Abraham Weiss described his colleague Schorr as a founding member of the Zionist movement in Galicia.[158] Discussing his affinity with Zionism, Schorr noted the positive take Polish scholars had on the Jewish national movement and the affinity of Jewish history with the Polish past. He reassured his adviser that he 'acknowledged Zionism in theory', but did not get involved in the practical matters.[159] Nevertheless, in 1905, Schorr participated in the Seventh Zionist Congress in Basel, where he favoured the general Zionist idea of unifying all Jews, rather than identifying himself with any of the political and ideological divisions within the movement.[160] Both Schorr and Bałaban participated in Zionist activities, primarily within the realm of culture and education.[161] As Bałaban's biographer concluded, 'The political and organizational activities into which the Zionist movement in Galicia was drawn from its earlier days apparently did not much interest Bałaban.'[162]

Young Jewish historians walked a fine line in public expressions of their political alliances to avoid jeopardizing the support of Polish academic institutions. Schorr needed to submit a statement about his continued 'exclusive commitment to scholarly work, with eyes always fixed on the welfare and knowledge of the country'.[163] The classical philologist and dean of the Faculty of Humanities at the University of Lwów, Stanisław Józef Witkowski, held a seemingly informal conversation with him in March 1909. In the course of that conversation, Schorr

---

[154] Rozenblit, *Reconstructing a National Identity*. Their multiple cultural affiliation resembled that of the Russian Jewish intelligentsia with 'local, national and Imperial identities superimposed' (Nathans, 'On Russian-Jewish Historiography').

[155] See Wierzbieniec, 'Z badań nad lwowskim okresem życia i działalności Majera Bałabana', 301.

[156] Biderman, *Mayer Balaban*, 56.

[157] Cahnman, 'Scholar and Visionary'. [158] See Weiss, 'Moses Schorr' (Heb.), p. x.

[159] Schorr, Letter 11, Vienna, 11 Apr. 1899, in Żebrowski, *Mojżesz Schorr*, 119–20.

[160] Schorr, Letter 40, Basel, 24 July 1905, in Żebrowski, *Mojżesz Schorr*, 181.

[161] Gelber, *History of the Zionist Movement in Galicia* (Heb.), 644–5.

[162] Biderman, *Mayer Balaban*, 57. [163] DALO, fond 26, opis 5, sprava 2143, p. 33, 20 June 1907.

again declared that 'he [had] no intention of engaging actively in politics, that he [was] well disposed towards Polishness and that he consider[ed] himself a Polish Jew'.[164]

While their public affiliation with the Zionist movement was scrutinized, it also sparked tensions with historians concerned about driving Polish Jewish history away from the Polish political agenda. Asked to elaborate on his take on Jewish identity and its relationship to Poland and Polish culture, Schorr did not reject limited assimilation:

> Even the most ardent Zionists are to some extent assimilated in the world of ideals [*ideowo zasymilowani*]. Not only are the Polish writing skills of many of them excellent, but they encounter Polish culture beginning in their school years and [continuing] throughout their lives, and it affects them in all aspects of their spirit, in the sciences, art, and literature.[165]

And yet his scholarly agenda differed from the work of nineteenth-century integrationist authors and the apologetic vision of Askenazy and his students.

Bałaban grappled explicitly with the concept of Jewish identity, taking issue with the statements made by Dawid Kandel, especially his rejection of the continued existence of the Jewish people as a national entity.[166] This difference was indeed at the heart of a clash of research agendas between the young Polish Jewish historians from Galicia and the apologetic historiography of Polish Jewry. Bałaban rejected Kandel's conclusion that the Jews had ceased to be a separate nation in the destruction and chaos that followed the 1648 Chmielnicki uprising. Their autonomous institutions continued until 1764, and their collapse was part of the crisis of the Polish–Lithuanian Commonwealth, argued Bałaban, and, in fact, the communal institutions continued to exist even after the partitions. Likewise, he mocked the idea that Shabetai Tsevi, Jacob Frank, or Berek Joselewicz could be considered as forerunners of assimilation,[167] although he acknowledged the sacrifice of Joselewicz in the struggle for the safety and well-being of his motherland and the well-being of its Jews.[168]

This rebuttal of Kandel points to another subject that separated the young generation of Polish Jewish historians in Galicia from the apologetics of Askenazy and the integrationist model of the past. While not denying close ties between Poland and its Jews, the young historians allowed for different interpretations

[164] DALO, fond 26, opis 5, sprava 2143, p. 39, a handwritten note signed by Witkowski.

[165] Schorr, 'Przemówienie Prof. Uniw. dra Mojżesza Schorra', 95.

[166] Kandel had been praised for 'a new and original treatment of the subject matter in our literature' (Kandel, 'Berek Joselewicz', 290, introductory footnote).

[167] Bałaban, 'Obzor literatury po istorii evreev v Pol'she (1907–1909)', *Evreiskaya starina*, 3 (1910), 312–14. See Veidlinger, *Jewish Public Culture*, 267–8.

[168] Bałaban, 'Obzor literatury po istorii evreev v Pol'she (1907–1908)', 313.

of subjects such as Jewish autonomous institutions and Jewish–non-Jewish relations. Turning Jews into the subjects rather than objects of scholarly enquiry, Galician historians published articles devoted to various aspects of Jewish institutional life and culture. In the pages of *KPBPŻwP*, *Evreiskaya starina*, and other forums Jewish historians from Galicia pointed to important differences between their work and integrationist historiography.

Although Askenazy's hope of training historians of Polish Jewry from Congress Poland who were educated in the Polish institutions of Galicia proved short-lived, academic scholarship in the field flourished at the turn of the century and in the first decade of the twentieth century, when Bałaban, Schiper, and Schorr started to publish. These scholars celebrated the development of modern Jewish historiography that had begun with the achievements of the Wissenschaft des Judentums movement and continued with the writings of Heinrich Graetz. Schorr read Graetz with Harkavy's introduction and recommended it to Ludwik Gumplowicz,[169] and Bałaban used Graetz's books when preparing his lectures on Jewish history at the Syjon association in Gliniany.[170] Schiper declared Graetz 'the first modern historian of great stature [*wielkiego pokroju*] who articulated the depth of Jewish tribal sentiment [*plemienne poczucie żydowskie*]'.[171] Despite new research in Jewish historiography that corrected his mistakes and used additional primary sources as well as new methods and concepts, Graetz's work remained relevant, argued Schiper.[172] He appreciated the details amassed by the German Jewish historian, his intuition, and his ability to mesmerize his readers.[172] While paying tribute to Graetz's unmatched literary skills, 'his enthusiasm and pathos', Schiper argued that Graetz's lasting influence and importance stemmed from his 'inner vision'.[174] He insisted that Graetz promulgated the vision of an eternal Jewish people, in contrast to the scholars of Wissenschaft des Judentums, and despite persecution, criticism, and accusations of charlatanism.[175] Although not a Jewish nationalist, Graetz was 'in touch with the feelings and notions which awoke in the hearts and minds of the Jewish people'.[176] Graetz's work resonated so powerfully, according to Schiper, because it referred to centuries-old ideas of eternal Jewish peoplehood, its suffering, and its relationship with Erets Yisra'el (the Land of Israel). Graetz's impact would continue, argued Schiper, 'due to the popular character [*folks-karakter*] of his work'.[177]

---

[169] See Schorr, Letter 9, Lwów, 2 Sept. 1898, in Żebrowski, *Mojżesz Schorr*, 115.
[170] Wierzbieniec, 'Z badań nad lwowskim okresem życia i działalności Majera Bałabana', 301.
[171] Schiper, 'Graetz "W setną rocznicę urodzin historyka żydowskiego"', 56.
[172] Schipper [Schiper], 'Graetz and his Monumental Work' (Yid.), pp. xxxiv–xxxv.
[173] Schiper, 'Dr. Josef Meisl: Heinrich Graetz', 74.
[174] Schiper, 'Graetz and his Monumental Work' (Yid.), p. xl.
[175] Ibid., p. xxxix.  [176] Ibid., p. xxxvii.  [177] Ibid., pp. xli–xlii.

Schiper praised Graetz's work for being personal and embedded in the present. According to Schiper, 'history was for Graetz a preparation for life, public activism [and] politics'.[178] Graetz's vision of eternal Jewish peoplehood and the sense of responsibility it imposed had 'created a broad ideological basis for Jewish activism', bringing the historians close to the Jewish national camp.[179] As Graetz 'has been and remains our first great historian of the people [folks-historiker]', Schiper asserted that he strengthened the sense of the Jews' continued existence in the past and future: 'We have been and we will be!'[180]

But although Graetz's historical writing remained an essential reference point for contemporary Jews on their national existence, Schiper believed that the need to develop a national Jewish historiography—close to but not the same as his *folksgeshikhte*—continued.[181] For Schiper, the work of Simon Dubnow, whom he described as Graetz's 'worthy [*virdiger*] successor', represented an important step in building a Jewish national historiography.[182] The historians from Galicia adhered to the national perspective on Polish Jewish history and made it their goal to develop research on the history of the Jews in eastern Europe. Thus, Schiper criticized Graetz for his 'unjust anathemas cast against *kabbalah* and *hasidism*' and 'cursory knowledge of Polish-Lithuanian Jews'.[183] Galician historians perceived east European Jewry as a distinct group, with a different mentality from the Jews of western Europe. In a lecture celebrating Dubnow's seventieth birthday, Bałaban said of the distinguished historian, 'In the Western understanding, Dubnow is an autodidact. However, we—east European Jews—know how many geniuses arrived at European [secular] knowledge by this very path.'[184] And yet

the more Dubnow explored our history the more he came to the conclusion that there is a difference between him—an eastern Jew—and his western masters that ought to be explained and justified. And once he reached this conclusion, he understood that all of Jewish history has to be reworked '*in capite et in membris*' [both as a whole and in its parts].[185]

---

[178] Schiper, 'Dr. Josef Meisl: Heinrich Graetz', 74.
[179] Schiper, 'Graetz and his Monumental Work' (Yid.), p. xlii.
[180] Ibid.     [181] Ibid., p. xliii.     [182] Ibid., p. xxxiv.
[183] Schipper [Schiper], 'Graetz "W setną rocznicę urodzin historyka żydowskiego"', 56. In his introductory article to the Yiddish edition of Graetz's work, Schiper pointed to Graetz's mistakes and shortcomings in methodology and interpretation; he specifically noted Graetz's superficial treatment of east European Jews, his neglect of such important aspects of Jewish life as economic history, and his treatment of the modern period. However, Schiper also explained these shortcomings as arising from Graetz's adherence to the ideal of Jewish eternal existence, making Graetz pass harsh judgement on phenomena he believed to be a danger to this uniform existence: kabbalah, karaism, hasidism, the Jewish language (Yiddish), and even the modern civilization. See Schiper, 'Graetz and his Monumental Work' (Yid.), pp. xxxvi–xxxvii, xl–xli.
[184] Bałaban, 'Szymon Dubnow', 78.     [185] Ibid. 83.

While recognizing the contributions of previous scholars, and participating in the initiatives of Poles of the Mosaic faith and Jewish national historians in Russian, Galician scholars considered their own work exceptional and groundbreaking. Bałaban contrasted Polish Jewish scholarship with the German Wissenschaft des Judentums, focusing on German Jewish historians of the nineteenth century, Jost, Geiger, and Graetz. For example, he argued that in trying to understand the Shabatean movement in Poland, 'they spent much time and effort explaining the essence of this movement, but none was able to do it and to objectively evaluate it, since all of them laid down a historical monument for a nation breathing its last breath or already dead'.[186] He also criticized what he perceived as their negative assessment of pre-modern Jewish life. In contrast, Bałaban saw some advantages in a separate Jewish existence within the metaphorical ghetto.[187] According to Bałaban, 'there was no scholarly history of the Jews in Poland before [Schorr]'.[188] With a sense of not simply building a body of literature but also of articulating an influential point of view, Bałaban noted, 'In the past, one considered Jewish history a small and secondary subject of scholarship, and looked upon those who wanted to devote themselves to it as eccentrics. There was no understanding of this matter at all.'[189] Schorr described Dubnow as 'one of the best specialists [znawcy] on the history of the Jews in Poland', celebrating Dubnow's positive response to his own work. Dubnow not only considered Schorr's research the most thorough and scholarly since Gumplowicz's, but also promised to review it in *Voskhod*.[190]

The organizational framework created by Askenazy provided a locus for the scholarship of Jewish historians from Galicia. In addition, both Bałaban and Schiper belonged to the St Petersburg-based Jewish Historical-Ethnographic Society and contributed to its journal, *Evreiskaya starina*, which combined academic scholarship with a nationalist agenda.[191] The journal, where Bałaban and Schiper appeared alongside such leading Russian Jewish scholars as Simon Dubnow, Iulii Gessen, Maksim Vinaver, and S. An-sky, 'became an important forum for delimiting, articulating, and propagating Jewish public history in the Russian empire'.[192] In addition to news about the Jewish Historical-Ethnographic Society, *Evreiskaya starina* published new research, primary source material and documents, reviews, and bibliographies.[193] Bałaban acknowledged the influence

---

[186] Bałaban, 'Sabataizm w Polsce', in *Księga jubileuszowa Schorra*, 47–8.

[187] Ibid.; see also Seidman, 'Meir Bałaban' (Heb.), 258–9; Bałaban, *Dziesięciolecie 'Braterstwa'*, 7.

[188] AAN, B'nai B'rith, file 3, p. 240: protocol of a closed meeting chaired by M. Tauber, 1 Mar. 1933.

[189] Ibid.    [190] Schorr, Letter 22, Vienna, 8 Mar. 1900, in Żebrowski, *Mojżesz Schorr*, 147.

[191] Veidlinger, *Jewish Public Culture*, 247.

[192] Ibid. 282. For a list of Bałaban's publications in Russian, see Biderman, *Mayer Balaban*, 315–16.

[193] See Dubnow's discussion of the journal's goals in its first edition (1909). See also Veidlinger, *Jewish Public Culture*, 246.

of Dubnow on his own work and appreciated his relationship with leading Russian Jewish historians.[194] Galician Polish Jewish historians also contributed the eleventh volume of the *Istoriya evreiskogo naroda* (History of the Jewish Nation), a monumental Russian-language collective history of the Jews in Poland to 1795.[195]

Although Bałaban has been described as 'one of Dubnow's allies in promoting a liberal vision of Jewish public culture through the study of Jewish communal life', he criticized Dubnow's methodological approach and political frame of reference.[196] In contrast to grand narratives of Jewish history in Russia, Bałaban emphasized the importance of writing local history. According to Jeffrey Veidlinger, this focus on local history 'implicitly challenged the grand imperial narratives of the J[ewish] H[istorical] E[thnographic] S[ociety]'.[197] Schorr and Schiper may have engaged in local studies for similar reasons.[198] In 1908, Schorr praised Bałaban for preparing a study of the Jewish community in Lwów as a way of building the field of Polish Jewish history, which had been on a new path for several years:

Instead of going out of his way [*silić się*] in a dilettantish manner to embrace the whole of Jewish history in Poland, he [Bałaban] has decided to limit himself to a given city, or period, or issue, in order to thoroughly study, publish and elaborate on archival material, and in this manner create a basis for general, deeper conclusions.[199]

Although Schorr's notion of building Polish Jewish historiography echoed the nineteenth-century German scholarly idea of gradually building the edifice with detailed studies, it also resembled the contemporary programme of Polish historical scholarship.[200]

Schorr, Bałaban, and Schiper entered the historical profession driven by a sense of urgency and opportunity. Aware of how little had yet been done in this field, Schorr hoped he 'would be capable of thorough systematic work to achieve much in the field of the history of Polish Jews'.[201] More than thirty years later, speaking at the celebration of his own jubilee in 1934, Schorr pointed out that 'nowadays the scholarship of Judaism is not a luxury [*zbytek*] in Jewish intellectual life, but should be an integral part of every member of Jewish intelligentsia, in

[194] Jolles (ed.), *Księga jubileuszowa Bałabana*, 38–9.
[195] The volume also included studies by Dubnow, Stanisław Kutrzeba, J. Hessen, P. S. Marek, M. Wischnitzer, S. L. Zinberg, S.M. Ginsburg, E. N. Frenk, and others. The publication of this encyclopedia was interrupted by the First World War, and only volumes i and xi were published, both in 1914.    [196] Veidlinger, *Jewish Public Culture*, 268.    [197] Ibid. 282.    [198] See Chapter 3.
[199] Schorr, 'Bałaban Majer: Żydzi lwowscy na przełomie XVI i XVII w.'. Schorr contrasted Bałaban's work with the study by Jecheskiel Caro, *Geschichte der Juden in Lemberg*.
[200] See Żebrowski, *Mojżesz Schorr*.
[201] Schorr, Letter 23, Wiedeń, 10 Mar. 1900, in Żebrowski, *Mojżesz Schorr*, 150. In 1900, while preparing for his rabbinical exams, Schorr informed Gumplowicz of his plans to edit the privilege of Stanisław August.

order to become aware of his Jewishness'.²⁰² Adolf Stand, a Zionist leader in Galicia, said that although he encouraged Bałaban to explore Jewish history in 1897, 'Balaban's interest in history... had started earlier... part of the rich and intense cultural atmosphere in which he grew up... [and] his personal way of expressing his Zionist beliefs'.²⁰³ Schiper declared that his literary, journalistic, and scholarly pursuits inspired and fed into each other. He explored Jewish economic history and statistics 'to create historical economic fundaments of the Po'alei Zionist idea'.²⁰⁴ Moreover, he complained that historical work from Jost and Graetz to Kayserling, Steinschneider, Harkavy, and Dubnow limited its perspective to presenting a 'pleasing historical picture of the spiritual leaders of Jews in the diaspora. We lack, however, the history of the hundreds of thousands who left [traces of] themselves... not of the riches of the spirit, but by the work of their hands and their speculative talents'.²⁰⁵

The Galician historians' sense of national Jewish identity was not rooted to the same degree in 'a strong and vibrant Yiddish-speaking folk culture nourished in many places by deep-rooted hasidic traditions'.²⁰⁶ Schiper declared that his 'historical work resulted from a protest against existing Jewish historiography, created first of all by Graetz'.²⁰⁷ Schiper criticized this historiography as 'romantic' and 'too celebratory', whereas he, under the influence of the ideas of Po'alei Zion, had decided to write a history of a 'grey Jewish day' and of the Jewish masses, instead of outstanding individuals. Ultimately, he explained, the secret of Jewish survival could be explained in more prosaic and realistic terms, through economic history. And so he took on the project of writing economic history in countries of the Jewish diaspora, starting with Poland, the 'least researched and known'.²⁰⁸ In February 1919, Schorr participated in the hearings of the special commission 'for the investigation of our attitude to the Jews and to find the path to Polish–Jewish reconciliation' formed by the Tymczasowy Komitet Rządzący (Temporary Governing Committee) in Lwów in November 1918 to administer Eastern Galicia.²⁰⁹ Asked to define the Jewish collective, Schorr stressed the importance of

---

²⁰² AAN, B'nai B'rith, file 4, 'Protokóły zebrań zamkniętych Stow. Humanitarnego Braterstwo B'nai-Brith w Warszawie, Posiedzeniu B'nai B'rith z okazji Schorra Jubileuszu', 67, 28 May 1934.
²⁰³ Biderman, *Mayer Balaban*, 56–7.
²⁰⁴ Brandstaetter, 'Ignis Ardens, Rozmowa z d-rem Ignacym Schiperem'.
²⁰⁵ Schiper, *Studya nad stosunkami gospodarczymi Żydów w Polsce*, 1.
²⁰⁶ Kassow, *Who Will Write Our History?*, 19.
²⁰⁷ Brandstaetter, 'Ignis Ardens, Rozmowa z d-rem Ignacym Schiperem'.   ²⁰⁸ Ibid.
²⁰⁹ In the aftermath of the pogrom in Lwów, the commission invited Polish and Jewish politicians and communal leaders to answer questions about their attitude to the Polish state, nation, and other nations living in Poland and to suggest laws and policies that would best serve their suggestions. Leonard Stahl chaired the sessions. See *W sprawie polsko-żydowskiej: Przebieg ankiety odbytej w dniach 2, 3, 4, 9 i 16 lutego 1919 we Lwowie*, 3–4.

two intertwined elements—the national and the religious—because in the Jewish case 'religion and nationality . . . are two inseparable sisters'.[210] Bałaban avoided defining 'true Jewishness', as opinions on the matter varied:

Everyone can be a Jew in his own way [*na swoją modłę*]. In a nation like ours assimilation must exist, as we have borders with all the nations and as there are no borders without assimilation, this cannot be avoided. Let us bring Jews together and try to keep Jewishness alive [*utrzymać żydostwo*], but let us not define this notion precisely.[211]

What was the relationship of the national Jewish historians in Galicia to Polish historiographical tradition? They understood Polish history as being defined by the political borders that existed before the partitions. Despite the political divisions created by the partitions, excluding Galicia from the Russian empire and annexing the Posen region to Prussia, Galician historians continued writing about Polish Jewry as a single unit.[212] The positive figures presented in the work of Galician Jewish scholars of Polish Jewish history included people—like the pantheon of the Jewish Historical-Ethnographic Society—'extolled for actively partaking in general society while retaining their own autonomous values and culture. One of the models for this type of relationship was the leader of Tadeusz Kościuszko's Jewish regiment, Berek Joselewicz.'[213] Galician historians tapped into the integrationist tradition, portraying Jewish heroes of the past as Polish patriots. Their pantheon of historical heroes thus reflected both the Jewish national agenda and the Polish historical tradition.

For their part, Dubnow and the Russian Jewish historians of the Jewish Historical-Ethnographic Society 'sought to embrace the geographic area of the Russian empire as it stood in their own time at the beginning of the twentieth century as a legitimate framework for envisioning the extent of Russian Jewry',[214] and thus 'implicitly imposed Russian imperialist notions of nationality upon its subject communities'.[215] While endorsing the imperial project, Galician Polish Jewish historians resisted using it for their work. Schorr, Bałaban, and Schiper operated, for the most part, within the political borders before the partitions. For Russian Jewish historians, their approach solidified the awareness of a Russian Jewish identity within the world Jewish community, which found itself in a relationship

---

[210] Schorr, 'Przemówienie Prof. Uniw. dra Mojżesza Schorra', 93.
[211] AAN, B'nai B'rith, file 3, p. 286: closed meeting chaired by M. Tauber.
[212] On a very different approach, taken by Russian Jewish historians, see Veidlinger, *Jewish Public Culture*, 274.      [213] Ibid. 266.
[214] Ibid. 272. A Russian imperial perspective is evident in Dubnow's conception of Russian Jewish history as expressed in his introduction to the first issue of *Evreiskaya starina*: 'We intend to embrace all epochs—from the development of Jewish settlements in ancient Rus and Poland to the present times, as well as the bright prospects of modern times and the recent past, through which our generation is living' (ibid.).      [215] Ibid. 273.

with Russian society and the tsarist government. In contrast, Galician Jewish historians continued to apply categories of Polish historical narrative and borders, referring to the place the Jews occupied in the Polish–Lithuanian Commonwealth. Within these categories, they demanded greater rights for Jews and recognition of Jewish national rights within the Austro-Hungarian empire, communicating their programme to the Polish majority. While Russian Jewish historians 'constructed an imagined proto-nation that embraced all Jewish groups in the Russian empire while at the same time differentiating it from non-Jews within the same geographic area and from other Jews outside its borders', Schiper, Schorr, and Bałaban preserved and identified with the historical categories of Polish and Lithuanian Jewries.[216] Russian Jewish historians published pro-Russian materials on 1812 and the attitude and suffering of the Jews, while Galician historians focused on Jews who were Polish patriots.[217] In the pages of *Evreiskaya starina*, Jews and Russians suffered together, but in the publications of Bałaban, Schorr, and Schiper, the Polish–Jewish connection remained an important paradigm.

As intellectuals, Galician scholars presented academic interpretations of history. However, they also hoped to construct a popular historical narrative, well aware of its importance as a tool for cultivating a cohesive national identity in an area where Poles were either a majority (Western Galicia) or dominant minority (Eastern Galicia). Instead of a gulf between popular history and academic writing, national Jewish historians envisioned a dialogue.[218] Scholars who participated in the activities of the Jewish Historical-Ethnographic Society sought to disseminate their own research and encouraged similar endeavours 'in essence engaging the broad population in the project of creating a usable past', and Bałaban modelled his writing of Polish Jewish history on romantic historiography.[219] Blutinger's characterization of Graetz fits Bałaban's style as well: 'His text recounted the history of a nation, the Jews; the story was to be told dramatically and emotionally, like a romantic novel, with heroes and villains; and his ultimate goal was the strengthening of a Jewish collective identity.'[220]

For Polish historians in Galicia and Warsaw, Polish Jewish history was part of mainstream Polish scholarship. Veidlinger has noted the difficult position of Jewish scholars: 'Unable to establish themselves in formalized academic environments, many Jews throughout Europe turned to informal journals and societies as surrogates for the ivory tower.'[221] This was not the situation in Galicia, where Jewish historians participated in the Polish academic milieu. Ludwik Finkel's

---

[216] Ibid.    [217] Ibid. 255–6.
[218] See Veidlinger's comparison between the popular and the academic understanding of Jewish history (ibid. 252).    [219] Ibid. 249.
[220] Blutinger, 'Writing for the Masses', 29–30.    [221] Veidlinger, *Jewish Public Culture*, 230.

bibliography of Polish history, which began to appear in Kraków in 1891, listed scholarship on Polish Jewish history, but did not include literature in Hebrew.[222] In 1900, Finkel invited Schorr to lecture at the Congress of Polish Historians in Kraków on the history of the Jews in Poland, discussing the state of research in the field, to be published in the proceedings of the Congress.[223] Between 1903 and 1912, Bałaban covered the literature since 1899 in a survey published in the prestigious *Kwartalnik Historyczny*, based in Lwów, and *Przegląd Historyczny*, founded in Warsaw.[224] Thus, Galician Jewish historians participated in Polish academic institutions and contributed to the discourse.

Galician historians complained about underdevelopment in the field of Polish Jewish history and reviewed critically most of the scholarly literature pertaining to the history of Polish Jewry. They argued for the need of scholarship on the history of Jewish institutions. As early as 1897, in his review of Salomon Buber's, *Anshei shem* (Men of Renown), Schorr distinguished between a history of internal Jewish life and the external aspects Jewish life such as legal status of relations with the non-Jewish community in Poland. He noted, 'While the *external* history of the Jews in Poland has been described at least in a general outline (Kraushar, Nussbaum), *internal* [Jewish history], its development, customs, traditions, and organizations is an almost untouched subject today.'[225] He pointed to the rich material in city and country archives, and public and private libraries. No less important were Hebrew chronicles, religious-scholarly writings by Polish Jews, especially the so-called *responsa*, interwoven with historical episodes, inscriptions on gravestones, and genealogical documents. In particular, Schorr considered Hebrew sources to be central for anyone researching the lives of Polish Jews and their cultural activities. Thus, he expressed his gratitude to Buber for publishing Hebrew sources that were otherwise not easily accessible.[226] Likewise, he praised the books of Hebrew documents pertaining to the history of the Jews in Poland, in particular, the collection on the Jews of Kraków, edited by P. H. Wettstein and published in 1902.[227] According to Schorr, the documents included details that

---

[222] Finkel, *Bibliografia historii polskiej*. See also CAHJP, P 9, file 6, Polonica Judaica 1: 'Materiały bibliograficzne literatury historycznej o Żydach w Polsce za rok 1913', 1.

[223] Schorr, Letter 20, Vienna, 31 Jan. 1900, in Żebrowski, *Mojżesz Schorr*, 143.

[224] *Kwartalnik Historyczny* was published by the Towarzystwo Historyczne (Historical Association), founded in Lwów in 1886, while *Przegląd Historyczny* appeared in Warsaw in 1905, and in 1906 became the official organ of the Towarzystwo Miłośników Historii (Association of the Lovers of History). Both of these prestigious Polish historical journals published historiographical surveys of material pertaining to the history of Jews in Poland, prepared by Bałaban. Instalments of the survey appeared in volumes 17 (1903), 18 (1904), and 22 (1908) of *Kwartlnik Historyczny* and volume 15 of *Przeglad Historyczny*. The survey also appeared in *Evreiskaya starina*, in 1909 and 1910.

[225] Schorr, 'Buber Salomon: Ansche-Schem', 585.

[226] Ibid.

[227] See Schorr, 'Wettstein P.H.: Diwre chefec'.

would serve the scholar as important material for portraying the culture of Polish Jews. Schorr considered this Hebrew publication so important that he refrained from making any critical remarks.[228] At the same time, Polish Jewish historians in Galicia viewed history written by rabbis living in the Prussian partition and in Imperial Russia with a degree of reserve or suspicion, and they assumed towards these works a tone similar to that adopted by Askenazy.[229]

Seeking to explain the state of their field, Galician historians framed the underdevelopment of Polish Jewish history in both political and cultural contexts, namely as a product of the distinct political status and conservative character of east European Jews. In 1900, Schorr reminded his readers of 'the difference in the civilizational progress between the Jews in eastern and western Europe' and of 'specific conditions related to Poland's partitions' which thwarted the development of Polish Jewish historiography. Thus in a familiar trope, he pointed to Germany, which had witnessed 'an unprecedented rise and development of Judaic-historical knowledge, in which Jewish historians such as Jost, Herzfeld, and Graetz have not only described the fortunes of the Jewish people at large, but also made special studies of the history of the Jews in Germany'. In contrast, Schorr argued, the study of Jewish history in Poland lagged behind; it 'progressed at a snail's pace and only in recent years—thanks to several outstanding historians—has it picked up more speed'.[230] In the introduction to his dissertation on Jewish economic history, Schiper pointed out that for the lands of the Polish Crown even 'a general history has hardly been written in Jewish historiography'.[231]

Exploring complexities of Jewish culture, these historians discussed examples of Jews participating in the societies where they lived while retaining their Jewish identity and values. They stressed the creativity of Jewish institutions in the past and their continued vibrancy in the present. Departing from a historiography centred on the legal status of the Jews and on Jewish–non-Jewish relations, in 1912 Bałaban published an article on the internal government of Polish Jews in the sixteenth to eighteenth centuries.[232] He argued that the authority of the *kahal* depended on state law, but sometimes arose not from intentional legislation, but from the lack of it, filling the void of authority.[233] Jews settled according to the general practice of groups living in Polish towns, because of their status as subjects to the king, the Church's demands that Jews should live separately, and economic concerns.[234] Jewish autonomy in Poland was rooted in the legal standing of Polish towns, based on the Magdeburg law and settled by townsmen from the German

---

[228] Ibid. 487.
[229] Shatzky, 'Balance Sheet of a Jewish Historian', 267.   [230] Schorr, 'Historya żydów w Polsce', 1.
[231] Schiper, *Studya nad stosunkami gospodarczymi Żydów w Polsce*, 2.
[232] Bałaban, 'Ustrój kahału w Polsce XVI–XVIII wieku', 17. He had also published on this topic in *Evreiskaya starina* in 1910–11.
[233] Bałaban, 'Ustrój kahału w Polsce XVI–XVIII wieku', 17.   [234] Ibid. 19–20.

lands. Jews sought communal offices as their only opportunity for careers in public service and political activism, but also as a response to the surplus of people qualified for rabbinical posts.[235] Bałaban wrote critically of the attempts of *voivode* (*wojewoda*; the king's representative in a province) and other great lords to influence and control the choice of rabbis, especially in private towns, where everything depended on the whims of the lord.[236] Since the end of the fifteenth century, each community in the crown cities fought with the magistrate for the right to trade and manufacture. As Bałaban explained, 'Jews could not give up, as they did not want to starve to death, and the cities did not want to put up with them as competitors. This background mixed with religious intolerance led to large-scale pogroms against the Jews... Smaller scale assaults took place every year.' Thus, the situation of Jewish communities deteriorated due to economic crises, wars, and anti-Jewish violence.[237] Schiper argued that the hostile attitude of German-Polish townspeople stemmed for the most part 'not from religious rancour against Jews, but from economic factors, a result of competition in the fields of manufacturing and trade'.[238] Bałaban published studies of Jewish communal organizations on the local, regional, and national levels and the Jewish judiciary.[239]

In addition to delineating basic demographic information about Jews in Poland and Lithuania, Schiper addressed the issue of the Jewish taxes.[240] He also analysed the status of Jewish converts in Poland and concluded that Polish Jews who enjoyed the royal privileges and were protected by the nobility were hardly tempted to convert.[241] According to Schiper, the most characteristic feature of conversion among Jews in medieval Poland was its occurrence almost exclusively in connection with pogroms, that is, under duress. Otherwise, the most generous favours from the highest authorities proved ineffective to convert the Jews.[242] Normally, he argued, Polish society remained for the most part indifferent towards converted Jews.[243]

The research of these historians focused mainly on Polish Jewry, particularly on the history of the Jews in pre-partition Poland. Polish Jewish historians shared distinctive interests. They had a sense of mission towards both Jewish and Polish audiences. In his introduction to the history of the Jews in Galicia, published in

[235] Bałaban, 'Ustrój kahału w Polsce XVI–XVIII wieku', 30, 33.   [236] Ibid. 34.
[237] Ibid. 40–4, quotation on p. 41.   [238] Schiper, 'Żydzi neofici i prozelici w Polsce do r. 1569', 70.
[239] Bałaban, 'Kagal', in Braudo et al. (eds.), *Istoriya evreiskogo naroda*, xi. 132–60; 'Tsentral'noe samoupravlenie pol'sko-litovskikh evreev' (ibid. 161–80); 'Sud (organizatsiya evreiskogo suda)' (ibid. 211–32). In the same volume Marek Wischnitzer published a study of the Lithuanian Va'ad, 'Litovskii vaad' (ibid. 180–205).
[240] See Schiper, 'Rasselenie evreev v Pol'she i Litve (Ot drievnieshikh vremen do kontsa XVIII veka)', in Braudo et al. (eds.), *Istoriya evreiskogo naroda*, xi. 105–31; 'Podatnoe oblozhenie evreev' (ibid. 300–19).   [241] Schiper, 'Żydzi neofici i prozelici w Polsce do r. 1569', 66, 69.
[242] Ibid. 71.   [243] Ibid. 77.

1914, Bałaban declared that its purpose was 'to elaborate on one hundred years of Jewish history on this soil . . . and to acquaint the Polish reading public with this history. Therefore, I had to take into account Austrian and Polish history [as well as] Jewish history and literature.'[244] On numerous occasions, in their early publications on the history of the Jews in the Polish–Lithuanian Commonwealth, both Bałaban and Schorr expressed their belief in a close link between the fate of Jews and non-Jews in the region. They aimed, like the apologists, to persuade Poles that Polish Jews had shared their historic burden, and thereby to improve contemporary Polish–Jewish relations. In a monograph on the history of the Jewish community in Lwów, Bałaban stressed misfortune as the common denominator. 'Lwów . . . suffered a great deal', he wrote. 'It was besieged numerous times, paying exorbitant ransoms. Together with the [other residents] of the town, the Jews experience economic crises; bankruptcies multiply, merchant credit disappears, trade with the East almost ceases. One misfortune after another.'[245] Thus, Polish Jewish historians tried to teach Poles how much they shared with Polish Jews. Analysing the genesis of Jewish institutions in the Polish–Lithuanian Commonwealth, Schorr emphasized a common institutional and legal tradition:

The autonomous institutions of the Jews in Poland . . . were a product of several factors —legal, social, and religious—which to varying degrees contributed to their inception, development, and glorious realization. It is beyond doubt that the basis of these institutions was the Polish legal system in its application to the Jews; on this basis in the course of centuries Jewish autonomy was formed, which was a product worthy of admiration.[246]

Discussing Poland's partitions, Bałaban noted that, after 1772, 'Polish Jews became Galician Jews and underwent various developments according to the plans and policies of the Viennese government'.[247] At the same time, he stressed the durability of the connection between the Jews of Galicia and those of the Russian partition, suggesting that Polish Jewry as a cultural community continued to function, despite the demise of the Polish state. In his book on the history of the Jews of Galicia and the Kraków Commonwealth between 1772 and 1868, Bałaban described the hopes of the Jews in Galicia during the Napoleonic wars and the Spring of Nations. He devoted several paragraphs to the January uprising of 1863, stressing the enthusiasm of the Jews' response, particularly those of the Russian partition.[248] Concerning the Jews of Galicia, he wrote, 'The patriotic

[244] Bałaban, *Dzieje Żydów w Galicyi i w Rzeczypospolitej Krakowskiej*.
[245] Bałaban, *Żydzi lwowscy na przełomie XVI i XVII wieku*, p. xviii.
[246] Schorr, *Organizacya Żydów w Polsce*, 2.
[247] Bałaban, *Dzieje Żydów w Galicyi i w Rzeczypospolitej Krakowskiej*, 1.
[248] Ibid. 196. See also his description of patriotic enthusiasm of the Jews in 1809 and their support of the French (ibid. 84).

proclamations and the fever of the Polish youth in Galicia also affected Jewish youth, and behold—despite the military cordon at the border they crossed secretly along with others to stand together in the lines of those who fought for Poland's freedom and independence.'[249] Here was yet another dimension of Polish–Jewish commonality: the feeling of belonging to Poland, which was displayed by Jews even after the partitions.

Galician historians studied the intersections between Jewish and non-Jewish neighbours in the Polish Kingdom and the Polish–Lithuanian Commonwealth at both the local and the state level. Despite their occasional forays into the partition period to demonstrate Polish Jews' continuing sense of Polishness, Schiper, Schorr, Bałaban, and other Jewish historians of their generation devoted most of their scholarly attention to the pre-partition years. This concentration reflected the emphases and concerns of their non-Jewish colleagues in the Polish academy. Their scholarship reflected the larger developments in Polish historiography, preoccupied with a 'glorious' Polish past and the need to explain Poland's collapse at the end of the eighteenth century. Early twentieth-century Jewish historians in Galicia presented a picture of the Jewish past in Poland within a vision of the splendour of the Polish–Lithuanian Commonwealth. Certainly, theirs was not the 'lachrymose conception' of Jewish history criticized by Salo Baron in his *Social and Religious History of the Jews*. Baron chastised Jewish historiography for 'viewing the destinies of the Jews in the Diaspora as a sheer succession of miseries and persecutions'.[250] In fact, the early work of Schorr, Bałaban, and Schiper agreed with Baron's admonition: 'It would be a mistake . . . to believe that hatred was the constant keynote of Judeo-Christian relations, even in Germany or Italy . . . Normal relations between Jews and Christians were generally amicable or at worst characterized by mild mutual suspicion.'[251] This perspective on Jewish history, adopted by Polish Jewish historians and developed before Baron's work appeared, constituted yet another distinctive characteristic of the Polish Jewish historiographical school.

Similarly, Schorr opposed the notion of a hermetically sealed Jewish ghetto in Old Poland. Describing the organization of Polish Jews, he emphasized that

many of [the ghetto's] qualities were at the same time characteristic of the general society in which it was conceived and developed. This development could not have taken any other path. The influence of constant contacts with the urban middle class and nobility on the internal lives of the Jews was bound to find its expression in the character of their institutions.[252]

[249] Bałaban, *Dzieje Żydów w Galicyi i w Rzeczypospolitej Krakowskiej*, 201. He added: 'The registers of the insurgents included many Jewish names; however it is hard distinguishing the names of the Galician Jews among them.'   [250] Baron, *A Social and Religious History of the Jews*, ii. 31.
[251] Ibid. ii. 40.   [252] Schorr, *Organizacya Żydów w Polsce*, 4.

Schorr elaborated on the nature of this influence: '[It] is most visible in the era of religious reformation. The literary movement of that time, and even more so the religious movement, resonated strongly with the Jews, whose fondness for education and particularly for philosophical studies enabled some outstanding individuals to polemicize in a lively fashion with the leaders of the reformation.'[253] Bałaban argued that analyses of relations between Jews and non-Jews in Old Poland that were based on standard legal documents lacked complexity.[254] Interested in the daily social interactions, he stressed the many links that had bound the Jewish population to the fate of the towns in which they lived, as well as to those towns' other inhabitants.[255]

At the same time, Polish–Jewish relations encompassed conflicts, even violence. '[G]enerally speaking', Bałaban wrote, 'in Poland . . . at the time, [Jews] enjoyed complete security. [Nonetheless] there were two opposing groups with a different worldviews, conflicting economic interests, and different goals and aspirations.'[256] Characteristically, in writing about tensions and conflicts, Bałaban interpreted them as the unavoidable and natural consequences of economic competition in which the Jews were hardly passive:

[Economically] Jews in Poland belonged to the middle class . . . and as such their aspirations conflicted with those of the [Gentile] bourgeoisie [*mieszczaństwo*]. The latter tried to defend their rights and prerogatives, refusing to grant the Jews any share in their commercial privileges. Guilds opposed Jewish craftsmen as much as they could, and the Jews struggled in every way possible.[257]

The early works of Bałaban and Schorr were not univocal in their evaluations of Jewish separateness. Apart from the hostility Jews aroused because of the functions they fulfilled in the economy of Old Poland, Bałaban saw in 'the separateness of life [*odrębność życia*]' one cause of the 'strengthening of race antagonism', ultimately fuelled by the decrees of the Church synods.[258] In a similar vein, as Schorr noted in a review, Bałaban emphasized the role of 'religious motives' that

contributed to the nature of mutual relations between Jews and Christians. These motives were the same throughout Old Poland; they triggered similar phenomena as well. The Lwów chronicle for that time often takes note of bloody tumults like those in other towns. These incidents were stirred up by students from the cathedral schools, despite the fact that the Jews paid a tribute in order to avoid such disturbances.[259]

[253] Ibid.     [254] Biderman, *Mayer Balaban*, p. xxiv.
[255] Bałaban, *Żydzi lwowscy na przełomie XVI i XVII wieku*, p. xvi.     [256] Ibid.
[257] Ibid., p. xvii. See also Bałaban, *Dzieje Żydów w Galicyi i w Rzeczypospolitej Krakowskiej*, 6; id., *Życie prywatne Żydów lwowskich na przełomie XVI i XVII wieku*, 18–19.
[258] Bałaban, *Żydzi lwowscy na przełomie XVI i XVII wieku*, p. xviii.
[259] Schorr, 'Bałaban Majer: Żydzi lwowscy na przełomie XVI i XVII w.', 552–3.

At the same time, Bałaban suggested that the high degree of Jewish separateness in pre-partition Poland resulted from 'all the measures undertaken against them'. Against these measures 'Polish Jewry stood adequately armed. The Jewish *kehilah* [community] constituted a well-organized body that was fully entrenched. Jewish communities and regional Jewish councils [*ziemstwa*] would deliberate, through their delegates at Jewish councils, about the welfare of all the Jews of the Polish crown and Lithuania.'[260] Maksymilian Weissberg pointed to the positive aspects of traditional education in *ḥeder*s, which had turned into a 'pedagogical ghetto due to the oppression of the Jews in the Middle Ages and bore the signs of the economic situation of Galician Jews'. The culture of the Jews and their *ḥeder*s flourished in the Old Polish Commonwealth.[261] His study identified the shortcomings that the Haskalah shared with hasidism: 'Both sides excluded women and shared a mutual hatred and fanaticism, not shrinking from violence and murder on the side of the hasidim and ignoble denunciation on the part of the maskilim.'[262] Maskilic criticism of the rabbis, he argued, rightly pointed to their 'pride, greed, lack of forbearance and desire to pore over dead books', but generalized these accusations against all rabbis.[263] Simple Jews could not see in the 'clean shaven, elegant, German' chaplains of the progressive synagogue their co-religionist, and therefore rejected them as their spiritual guide.[264]

Separateness enabled the Jews to build autonomous institutions: 'The *kahal* was for the Jews the highest legal authority in matters of the law, treasury, and education. This was possible because the Jews lived separately, often cut off from the other inhabitants of a given town by a wall or rampart.'[265] Nonetheless, Bałaban criticized the degree of linguistic separatism among Polish Jews of the eighteenth century. Writing about the relatively low cultural level of Galician Jews, he stressed, 'One cannot even talk about acquiring the culture of the country or mastering of the Polish language among the Jewish townspeople. Merchants or factors would murder this language when forced [to speak it], but almost no Jew was able to [speak it well].'[266] Jewish historians described Jewish autonomy in the Polish–Lithuanian Commonwealth as particularly advantageous for the development of Jewish culture and literature. Writing about a later period, however, Bałaban supported liberal integration and acculturation. Commenting on equal legal standing of all Austrian citizens, regardless of their national allegiance or creed, Bałaban noted enthusiastically, 'At once the shackles that had tied the Jews for thousands

---

[260] Bałaban, *Żydzi lwowscy na przełomie XVI i XVII wieku*, p. xviii. On the cultural achievements of Polish Jewry, see Bałaban, *Dzieje Żydów w Galicyi i w Rzeczypospolitej Krakowskiej*, 10–11.
[261] Weissberg, 'Język literacki Żydów w Galicyi', *KPBPŻwP*, 1/3 (1913), 103–4.
[262] Ibid. 132.     [263] Ibid. 109.     [264] Ibid. 111–12.
[265] Bałaban, *Dzieje Żydów w Galicyi i w Rzeczypospolitej Krakowskiej*, 5. On the cultural divide that separated Polish Jewry from non-Jews, see ibid. 3.     [266] Ibid. 10.

of years broke, all the privileges of towns and guilds and all limitations were abolished; the walls of the ghettos, both spiritual and physical, fell down.'[267] With the Austrian constitution of 1867 and the law of 25 May 1868, regulating the relationship between church and state, he noted, the Jewish struggle for emancipation ended, and a normal life under normal conditions began.[268] Bałaban and other historians subscribed to a complex view of Jewish history that was closely connected with non-Jewish history while at the same time autonomous, a view that pointed simultaneously to emancipation and to the flourishing of Jewish national identity in Polish lands.

Weissberg's articles devoted to the language and literature of Galician Jews give us an insight into complex issues that touched on the questions of continuity, cultural integration, and linguistic assimilation.[269] He stressed the cultural change among Polish Jews in Galicia in the aftermath of the partitions: 'Polish Jews in the course of centuries gained a characteristic original culture not without points of contact with the original Polish culture . . . They did not avoid, even in the old times, secular studies.'[270] Weissberg called maskilim 'the indirect product of the partitions of Poland [and] . . . a thin layer of Jewish-Czech newcomers, who enjoyed at first the protection of the officials who had come—as we know—also from the Czech lands.'[271] While discussing Hebrew literature in Galicia, he emphasized its patriotic tone following the seventeenth-century massacres by the Cossacks, proving that Jews of that time truly considered Poland their motherland.[272] And while discussing the literature in Galicia, Weissberg insisted that Hebrew was a living language that linked the Jews with generations of authors and the sages of the distant past, but that it also influenced daily life in the present and the daily language of the Jews. Moreover, 'Only Hebrew was a literary language of all spheres of the Jewish population in Galicia in the period of Haskalah.'[273] Weissberg bemoaned the fact that 'Jews, who once so easily assimilated . . . here in Poland, to this very day, have retained both literary Hebrew and jargon saturated with Hebrew.'[274] Recalling Harkavy's 1867 study of Jews and the Slavic languages, Weissberg noted,

In Poland, local Jews at the beginning of the Middle Ages spoke only Polish and Russian; Jews from Germany brought with them the German dialect, which—despite

---

[267] Ibid. 205.

[268] Ibid. 210. However, Bałaban, who was supportive of cultural integration in general, criticized Jewish German schools in Galicia introduced after 1787 because of what he labelled the 'low ethical level' of teachers who lacked the understanding of local Jewish society and culture (ibid. 55).

[269] Weissberg, 'Język literacki Żydów w Galicyi'.

[270] Weissberg, 'Literatura nowohebrajska w Galicyi (1786–1850)', 46.   [271] Ibid. 51.

[272] Weissberg, 'Język literacki Żydów w Galicyi', 1/1 (1912), 7.   [273] Ibid. 1–2.

[274] Ibid. 2–3. By 'jargon saturated with Hebrew' Weissberg is referring to Yiddish.

Hebrew elements—retained until the seventeenth century an unusual linguistic purity and was very similar to the so-called *Mittelhochdeutsch*. This dialect slowly pushed away the local language previously used by the Jews and led to this situation where Jews have retained neither the Slavic literary language nor the spoken one.[275]

The chances of Jews embracing the Polish language diminished because of their autonomy and the lack of a social class willing to absorb Polish Jewry.[276] But alongside his implicit criticism, Weissberg dwelled on the parallel between the Golden Age in Polish literature and education, in the sixteenth century, and Jewish writings in Poland: 'This third fatherland of Jews surpassed previous centres in Babylon, Spain, northern France, and Germany as far as the spread and intensity of Torah studies was concerned. At that time, almost each and every adult Jew was capable of holding office as a rabbi.'[277]

## Conclusions

The emergence of a cohort of Galician university-trained historians pursuing research on Polish Jewish history marked an important change in the status of the field before the First World War. This group of professional Polish Jewish scholars, which began to form in the last decade of the nineteenth century, enjoyed explicit and implicit patronage of Polish academic networks, encouraging their quest as a welcome part of Polish historiography. Their early career trajectories and body of work demonstrate the transition from earlier practices to the historical profession later imported to Warsaw. Indeed, the studies published by Bałaban, Schorr, and Schiper in Polish, Russian, German, and Yiddish included a full academic apparatus, referred to a wide variety of sources of diverse provenance, and discussed the existing state of research. With both rigour and vigour, they created a scholarly milieu of established professional Jewish historians writing on the Polish Jewish past, with educational backgrounds and credentials from academic Polish institutions.

Jewish historians in Galicia viewed themselves as Polish Jews, reaching professional maturity when the need for a Polish Jewish history had already been discussed and recognized, and when some work had been done, albeit by autodidacts or by scholars who often viewed Jewish history as marginal to their work. Broader concepts of 'Ashkenaz' or east European Jewry remained relevant in both the academic and popular work of Schorr, Bałaban, and Schiper, but their primary reference remained Old Poland, its political and social contexts, and its Jewish institutions. Despite their interest in local conditions of the province, Galician Jewish historians saw themselves as historians of Polish Jewry. Among others, Bałaban's book on the history of Jews from Galicia, published in 1914, offers a dual

[275] Weissberg, 'Język literacki Żydów w Galicyi', 1/1 (1912), 3.   [276] Ibid. 3–4.   [277] Ibid. 6–7.

perspective: that Jews in Galicia after the partitions remained Polish Jews. In 1916, Schorr wrote a letter to the dean of the Department of Humanities in Lwów, describing the deep emotional effect that the November 1916 declaration of the Central Powers to re-establish an independent Polish state had on him, calling it 'the happiest day of [his] life' and wishing to be younger and able 'to fight with a gun for Poland's independence'.[278]

What inspired emerging scholars in Galicia to pursue Polish Jewish history? They chose history as a field that was key for the community of which they were part. In their research and writing they undertook a complex project of building a conscious Jewish community, encompassing both a strong sense of Jewish identity and a close affinity with the Polish past. Among the first to use systematic and methodological tools in research on the history of Polish Jews, Jewish historians from Galicia based their research on both Jewish and Polish sources. The writings of Polish Jewish historians in Galicia reflected the dichotomies between popularization and their scholarly ambitions, reverence for the academy—especially Polish scholarship—and the national calling, and the desire to speak both to Polish and Jewish audiences. Indeed, for Bałaban, Schiper, and Schorr it was history that was needed for their scholarly community and for both broader Jewish and general audiences.[279] This programme of national Jewish identity accompanied by full participation in Polish intellectual, social, and political life also appealed to a handful of Polish intellectuals.

Jewish historians from Galicia built on themes laid out by previous Jewish scholarship, while also positioning themselves in opposition to some of these antecedents. At the root of Polish Jewish history was a debate over what kind of story Jewish history should tell and how it should be told. Galician scholars struggled to balance academic apparatus with the polemical outlook of political debates. On the eve of the rebirth of the Polish Republic, the experiences and ideas of Galician historians were useful both to the Jewish community within the new borders and to the Poles. Moreover, these scholars moved to Warsaw, gaining important access to the development of Polish historical scholarship and the means to disseminate elements of popular historical culture. They built new relationships with Polish academia and focused on three topics: local history, internal Jewish history, and Polish–Jewish relations. Historians of Polish Jewry with their intellectual roots in Galicia referred to interpretive traditions of integrationist writing, but they also sharpened their position as Jewish historians of Polish Jews. Their focus on the history of Jews in Polish lands proved most useful in the nation state of Poland after the First World War.

[278] See Pawlak (ed.), *Księgi życia profesora Mojżesza Schorra*, 39.
[279] History was not the only field pursued by Jewish scholars from Galicia with close ties to the Zionist movement. Among others, Ozjasz Thon studied philosophy.

Decades before the rebirth of the independent Polish state, Galicia became the centre for training aspiring Jewish historians, offering possible political, communal, and, to a limited degree, academic careers to aspiring Jewish academics and historians, even those from outside Galicia. Galicia serves also as the point of departure in national Polish Jewish historiography practised in the Second Polish Republic, because it emerged as the birthplace of the Warsaw 'school' of Jewish historians. Their early availability enabled them to capitalize on this and, by moving to Warsaw, to disseminate their ideas to a wider audience of Jewish readers in Polish and later, often via translations, in Yiddish. It also enabled them to attract and professionally train young historians from all over the Polish state, not only those following them from Galicia. On the eve of Poland's rebirth, no comparable group of professional Jewish historians writing in the Polish language and trained by Polish historians was available. Before the Second Polish Republic emerged in 1918, these historians created a vision of the Jewish past and a Polish Jewish national identity in which the liberal values of the Austro-Hungarian constitutional monarchy played a significant role. Their work was crucial in helping the next generation of Polish Jewish historians grapple with the issues of Polish–Jewish relations and the development of Jewish institutions from local, regional, countrywide, and international perspectives. These writers would remain leading figures in Jewish historical scholarship in the interwar period in Poland.

# THREE
# BECOMING POLISH MAINSTREAM

IN DECEMBER 1935 the Historical Commission at Warsaw University recommended bestowing the title of professor on Dr Majer Bałaban, in recognition of his valuable scholarship on the history of Polish Jews and his contribution to the creation of 'a substantial centre of interest in the history of Jews' at the university. The commission praised him for 'having dealt with a student body that is not always cultured, and requires a tremendous effort' and for 'guiding a relatively large percentage of students, who rise to serious academic standards'.[1] This acknowledgement of Bałaban's work as a historian of Polish Jews and as a mentor of Jewish students at the Polish state university demonstrated the shift of his field into the mainstream of Polish academia. Now, under the scrutiny of their peers, Bałaban and his cohort proved themselves capable of applying the scholarly tools and standards of their profession.[2] The growing recognition of their field of study made it possible for Bałaban and other historians of Polish Jewish history to claim coveted professional status in the eyes of their non-Jewish counterparts. Did the academic community in the Second Polish Republic genuinely see Polish Jewish scholars and their field of study as part of the 'academic community of historians'? In what ways and for what purpose did Polish Jewish historians seek such a recognition?

The foundations of the new centre in Warsaw had been laid at the turn of the century by Bałaban, Mojżesz Schorr, and Ignacy Schiper, who had the interests and agenda of integrationist historians but nevertheless sought to follow the calls for research from a national Jewish perspective. The small cadre of university-trained historians maintained close contact, engaging in scholarly discussions, publishing in the same journals and newspapers, and reviewing each other's work in both the Polish and the Jewish press. Their career paths and scholarly interests dovetailed closely with their intellectual roots in Galicia, which, due to the

---

[1] Quoted from a report of the historical commission, Warsaw, 20 Dec. 1935, signed by Marceli Handelsman (AAN, MWRiOP, 1614, Akta osobowe: Majer Bałaban, Referat komisji historycznej w spr. mianowania docenta dra Majera Bałabana profesorem tytularnym, 12).

[2] Torstendahl, *The Rise and Propagation of Historical Professionalism*, 16.

political reforms in the Austro-Hungarian empire, also accounted for their immersion in Polish culture. In Galicia, they had enjoyed the support of prominent scholars of Polish history, who encouraged them to write about the history of Polish Jewry. Moreover, Jewish historians at the local centres of historical research in Galicia benefited from scholarly opportunities in the imperial capital, Vienna.

In 1918 Warsaw replaced Vienna as the political reference point for Galicia, offering numerous professional opportunities for the Jews educated at Polish gymnasia and universities. Members of the Galician intelligentsia took positions in Jewish educational and communal institutions in the cities of the former Congress Poland, often assuming key roles in the intellectual and cultural life of the emerging Polish Jewish community.[3] Thanks to their facility in the Polish language and their formal education, they secured appointments as teachers in Jewish secondary schools and various Jewish institutions as well as in state schools established for Jewish children. Historians working on Jewish themes flocked to the capital of the independent Polish state and became the spearheads and facilitators of new initiatives within professional Polish Jewish historiography. Schiper moved to Warsaw around 1919 to carry out his political and academic activities. A leading member of Po'alei Zion Left, he served as a representative in the Polish parliament until 1927.[4] Schorr, who had taught at the University of Lwów (renamed Jan Kazimierz University in November 1919) from 1896 to 1922, moved from Lwów to Warsaw permanently in 1922, where he became a preacher at the Tłomackie Street Synagogue.[5] In 1925 he was invited to teach at Warsaw University.[6] Bałaban moved first to Częstochowa, to head its Jewish gymnasium, and then to Warsaw in 1922 to run the new rabbinical school, Tachkemoni, which was associated with the Mizrachi religious Zionist movement.[7] Yet he yearned to con-

---

[3] See Rawicz, untitled article, and Kassow, *Who Will Write Our History?*, 19. Among many examples is Dawid Geier, who came to Włocławek in 1922 to teach history in the Jewish Gymnasium. See Biderman, 'The Jewish Press', 95; Korzen, 'The Jewish Gymnasium' (Heb.), 391, 394. Sławomir Maguński recalled that all his teachers in the Jewish gymnasium in Mława came from Galicia (DRI, A 7, file 14).

[4] A reference book on the members of the Polish parliament issued in 1923 listed Schiper as an attorney living in Warsaw at Tłomackie 6–8 Apt. 10. See Rzepecki and Rzepecki, *Sejm i Senat 1922–1927*, 227. See also AAN, Ministerstwo Spraw Wewnętrznych, 1056: Organizacja Poale-Sjon na ziemiach polskich, 7.

[5] Schorr's appointment as a preacher reflected the expansion of the role of traditional sermons in the nineteenth and early twentieth centuries. Such sermons also reflected new ideological trends and developments. See Saperstein, '*Your Voice Like a Ram's Horn*'.

[6] In December 1923 Schorr asked for a leave of absence from his position in the Philosophical Department of the University in Lwów due to his rabbinical appointment in Warsaw. But he also requested a confirmation of his academic career for Warsaw University, where he 'intended to continue my scholarly work' (DALO, fond 26, opis 5, sprava 1721, p. 135, a handwritten letter dated 5 (or 4) Dec. 1923). [7] On Tachkemoni, see Chapter 4.

tinue his scholarly work in the field of Polish Jewish scholarship and to find a position at an academic institution.

Jewish men and women from Galicia who were interested in pursuing academic Jewish studies continued to enrol at the University of Vienna. Upon completion of their degrees, however, many moved to large urban centres in former Congress Poland to take advantage of employment opportunities in Jewish secondary schools. Coming from Nowy Sącz in western Galicia, Raphael Mahler received his secondary secular education in Kraków. In 1922 he earned a doctorate from the University of Vienna and a certificate for teaching in secondary schools. Upon his return to Poland in the autumn of that same year he first taught history and geography at the Hebrew gymnasium 'Jabne' in Łódź; from September 1924 he was at the Ascola boys' gymnasium in Warsaw, where he taught Polish history, Jewish history, geography, Bible, and Hebrew and Jewish religion.[8] Lwów-born Filip Friedman received both his teacher's diploma and, in 1925, his doctoral degree in Vienna; he formally confirmed (nostrified) the latter at Warsaw University in 1932.[9] After his graduation, Friedman returned to Lwów, teaching briefly in a gymnasium there, and then moved to Łódź, where he took a position at the prestigious Polish-Hebrew gymnasium of the Association of Jewish Middle Schools (Towarzystwo Żydowskich Szkół Średnich), thereby joining the ranks of the Jewish intelligentsia.[10] He later taught at YIVO and the Institute of Jewish Studies in Warsaw.

Galician Jewish historiography continued to influence Polish Jewish historiography, as a new cadre of historians referred to the published work of Schorr and the ongoing work of Bałaban and Schiper. The Galician context remained essential to their understanding of Polish–Jewish relations in the past.[11] In addition to Friedman and Mahler, other new historians with roots in Galicia who began their careers in independent Poland included Emanuel Ringelblum, Artur Eisenbach, Nachman Blumental, and Dawid Wurm. Together they strove to make Polish Jewish history an acceptable, legitimate, and useful professional field of academic enquiry. Newly established institutions and organizations devoted to training historians of Polish Jewry struggled for professional recognition in the Polish academy and faced both external and internal constraints, limited resources, political pressures, and ideological tensions.

The field expanded rapidly, and by the 1920s Warsaw had emerged as the

---

[8] See DRI, P 66, file 3: certification (zaświadczenie) issued 18 Apr. 1922, Tłomackie 11; Gimnazjum hebrajskie 'Jabne' Łódź Cegielna NR 75, Zaświadczenie, dated 1 Sept. 1924, number 4207 13/6 924.

[9] Friedman, *Die galizischen Juden*. See Friedman's student file at Warsaw University (AUW, RP 24591).

[10] See Orenstein, *The Life and Work of Dr Filip Friedman*, 8; Spodenkiewicz, *The Missing District*, 46.

[11] For the discussion of the lasting Galician mentality see Wolff, *The Idea of Galicia*.

centre of Polish Jewish historiography.[12] A parallel shift occurred among leading Polish historians. Since the second half of the nineteenth century the universities in Kraków and Lwów had produced Polish intellectuals and served as centres of Polish historical scholarship, while Warsaw lacked a formal Polish academic infrastructure. Poland's newly regained independence created the opportunity—indeed, the necessity—to rebuild the university in the capital. Establishment of new university-level history seminars led to the recruitment of scholars from among faculty of the Jagiellonian University in Kraków and the University of Lwów,[13] most notably a medievalist, Jan Karol Kochanowski, who studied history in Kraków and Breslau and became a professor of history at Warsaw University in 1919, and Bronisław Dembiński,[14] who taught in Warsaw from 1916 to 1923.

In 1923 the young graduate student Ringelblum, joined by Mahler and Bela Mandelsberg, organized an informal seminar for Jewish history in Warsaw. Enthusiastically supported by Schiper and Bałaban, the seminar was intended 'to encourage Jewish students of history to embark upon subjects connected with the history of the Jews of Poland and to acquaint them with the appropriate source materials, scientific bibliography, and methodology'.[15] This pioneering group of men and women, many of whom had studied history at Warsaw University and who attached great importance to academic scholarship in Yiddish, came under the auspices of the newly founded YIVO Institute as its Warsaw Historical Commission. During its existence, the seminar attracted over thirty enthusiasts, who interacted with leading scholars at its monthly meetings. In 1928 more concerted efforts to form a recognized institution of Jewish studies culminated in the establishment of a seminar in Polish Jewish history, directed by Bałaban, at both the Institute of Jewish Studies and Warsaw University. Bałaban's dual appointment created a formal scholarly setting of great consequence, enabling him to train over sixty male and female students of Polish Jewish history who would receive formal university diplomas. Many of them strove to participate in the scholarly exchange on the subject of Polish Jewish history and published regularly in journals in Poland and abroad. The interwar period marked a broadening of popular interest in Jewish history and the emergence of a growing cohort of professional historians

---

[12] Eisenbach, 'Jewish Historiography in Interwar Poland', 453.

[13] The Szkoła Główna (Main School) had opened in 1863 in Warsaw and went through a process of Russification in the aftermath of the January 1863 uprising; in 1869 it was replaced with the Russian Imperial Warsaw University. Already under the German occupation of Warsaw during the First World War, Polish intellectuals strove to build the Philological-Philosophical Department of the Polish University in the future capital of Poland, with seminars in Polish and general modern and ancient history. See Garlicki (ed.), *Dzieje Uniwersytetu Warszawskiego 1915–1939*, 13–52; Manteuffel, *Uniwersytet Warszawski w latach 1915/16–1934/35*.      [14] Pawelec, 'Bronisław Dembiński (1858–1939)', 275.

[15] Eisenbach, 'Jewish Historiography in Interwar Poland', 466–7; see also Kassow, *Who Will Write Our History?*, 413–14.

of Polish Jewry. Despite ideological and political differences, Jewish historians in the Second Polish Republic contributed to the continuing discourse about the nature of Polish–Jewish relations in the past and the impact of the Jewish presence on the Polish economy and Polish culture. They struggled to combine standards of intellectual integrity with an engagement in communal needs and contemporary issues, while facing constant material constraints.

## Academic Frameworks and University Faculty

In the independent Polish Republic, Jewish students continued to enrol in the departments of history at the University of Lwów, the Jagiellonian University in Kraków, and Stefan Batory University in Wilno. These departments, however, produced only a handful of theses and dissertations on the history of Polish Jewry. Although Lwów remained an important centre of Polish historiography, it ceased to attract young scholars of Polish Jewish history. Two main supporters of research into the history of Polish Jewry, Szymon Askenazy and Ludwik Finkel, no longer played an active role at Lwów: Askenazy left for Warsaw and then for a position in the League of Nations in 1920, and Finkel retired in 1918.[16] Of the 149 doctoral dissertations defended at Jan Kazimierz University (formerly the University of Lwów) between 1918 and 1939, only six dealt explicitly with Jewish history, all devoted to ancient history and written in the seminar of Professor Konstanty Chyliński, who specialized in ancient history.[17] Similarly, only a handful of Jewish students at the Jagiellonian University wrote theses and dissertations on the history of Polish Jewry, and its Institute of History offered no courses on the subject.[18]

The shift from Lwów and Kraków to Warsaw in the Second Polish Republic arose, to some extent, from the focus of the former on political rather than social history, as evidenced by the doctoral dissertations defended at the Jan Kazimierz University and Jagiellonian University.[19] Even more influential were attitudes about Jewish history held by some leading members of the faculties of these two universities. The most striking case in point was the highly successful and influential seminar run by Franciszek Bujak, who left his position at the Jagiellonian University and taught briefly in Warsaw from 1919 until 1920, before moving to Lwów.

[16] See Błachowska, 'Ludwik Finkel (1858–1930)', 303.
[17] See Pisulińska, 'Doktoraty historyczne na Uniwersytecie Jana Kazimierza'.
[18] See Kraków, AUJ: 'Księga Dyplomów Magisterskich UJ'. On the Jewish students at the Jagiellonian University, see Kulczykowski, *Żydzi—studenci Uniwersytetu Jagiellońskiego w Drugiej Rzeczypospolitej, 1918–1939*.
[19] See Pisulińska, 'Doktoraty historyczne na Uniwersytecie Jana Kazimierza'; Kliś and Majorek, 'Doktoraty historyczne w Uniwersytecie Jagiellońskim', 157–9.

There he created a centre of social and economic history at Jan Kazimierz University, with a cutting-edge focus on local studies and social and economic history.[20] But local history, for Bujak, was exclusively Polish. His students showed no interest in the Jewish aspects of Polish social and economic history, and this most likely reflected Bujak's own attitudes. For Bujak, the Jews constituted an alien, criminal, and harmful element in Poland's history, often conspiring against the interests of the country that had granted them refuge and unprecedented freedom. In 1919 he portrayed Jews as a dangerous world-wide web, playing a role in international politics, finance, and the press, and trying to achieve a position of power in the emerging Polish state against the interests of the state and the host society: 'Taking advantage of the circumstances arising from the organization of the state of things in the whole of central and eastern Europe, they endeavour to assure themselves the best possible conditions of existence in the future on Polish territories, from an economic as well as a political point of view.'[21] Such a perspective on Polish–Jewish relations hardly encouraged research about Jews in Polish history, nor did it make his seminar a welcoming place for young Jewish historians.[22]

In Warsaw, Marceli Handelsman played a crucial role in envisioning and building the Department of Humanities and especially the Institute of History. Handelsman had received a degree in law at the Russian Imperial University in Warsaw in 1904, and had continued his studies in Berlin and Zurich (where he completed a doctorate in 1908), as well as in France. Upon his return to Warsaw in 1912, he participated in the activities of the Warsaw Learned Society (Towarzystwo Naukowe Warszawskie; TNW), and in 1913 he organized under its umbrella a historical section (Gabinet Nauk Historycznych). In 1915, he joined the faculty of the newly established Warsaw University, shaping the faculty and influencing research agendas in the Department of Humanities. Handelsman remained one of the country's most prominent historians, thanks to his patriotic record and close personal ties with the Piłsudski camp.[23] While engaged in his own research and

[20] See Budzyński, 'Franciszek Bujak (1875–1953)'; Budzyński, 'Szkoła historii społeczno-gospodarczej Franciszka Bujaka na Uniwersytecie Jana Kazimierza we Lwowie'. For more on Bujak see Shelton, 'Franciszek Bujak (1875–1953)'. [21] Bujak, *The Jewish Question in Poland*, 4.

[22] Shelton's characterization of Bujak seems quite apologetic, describing his seminar in the 1930s as 'a haven for students of all types, including those out of favour with the regime of the "Colonels" after 1935: peasants, Ukrainians, Jews, and communists all found academic and personal refuge there' (Shelton, 'Franciszek Bujak (1875–1953)', 292). Not only did Bujak exclude Jews from Polish society, but his students, among them Stefan Inglot, completely ignored Jews or wrote about them as a foreign, harmful element. Despite testimonies about openness of his seminar, only one student, Adolf Hirszberg (Hirschberg, Józef Sieradzki), was identified as 'a Jew' by Bujak's biographer.

[23] Gieysztor, 'Środowisko historyczne Warszawy w okresie międzywojennym'. Among other achievements, Handelsman headed the Archives of Premodern History (Archiwym Akt Dawnych) from 1916 to 1919, when he became a full professor at Warsaw University and the editor of the second most prestigious Polish historical journal *Przegląd Historyczny*; he founded a new journal, *Rozprawy*

academic service, he also trained a group of historians that included many future deans of Polish historiography. Handelsman mentored his male and female students and developed affectionate relationships with them that lasted long after the completion of their graduate training. Ringelblum compared it to a relationship between a father and his children, an image evoked in several other accounts.[24]

Handelsman himself was distanced from the Jewish community and from writing about Jewish history. Reminiscing about his former teacher, Ringelblum stressed that Handelsman 'cut off all his ties with the Jewish community. He did not even belong to the assimilationist camp, which fought for some principles and ideals from within the Jewish community.'[25] And though he published essays on the development of the modern nation, Handelsman took little interest in Jewish history.[26] And yet, motivated by liberal concepts of an open Polish identity based on the traditions of the multi-ethnic Polish–Lithuanian Commonwealth, he encouraged his Jewish students to carry out research about Polish Jewish history.

Handelsman's role at Warsaw was comparable to that played by Szymon Askenazy at the University of Lwów at the beginning of the century.[27] But now historians who subscribed fully to traditions of integrationist historical writing found themselves marginalized and increasingly disillusioned. Tolerated before the First World War, even by some intellectuals associated with the nationalist Endecja, in the Second Polish Republic Askenazy was attacked for his Jewish roots and increasingly sidelined.[28] The professional paths of Askenazy and his student Jacob Shatzky reflect the difficult position of Jewish scholars in the new Polish state. Their heartbreak was the result of the political climate in the newly independent Poland, where attitudes towards Jews ranged from ambivalence to hostility, with calls for the boycott of Jewish stores and a wave of anti-Jewish violence. Shatzky's career in the immediate post-war years exemplified several shifts from Galicia to Warsaw and from Askenazy to Handelsman. In 1918–19,

*Historyczne*, in 1921. For a discussion of Handelsman's biography and work, see Biskupski, 'Marceli Handelsman (1882–1945)'.

[24] Ringelblum, 'Profesor Marceli Handelsman', 541. See the correspondence sent to Handelsman by Raphael Mahler from New York, in APAN, III-10: Materiały Marcelego Handelsmana, 333, Mahler R., 1 list Vancouver, 1938. Tadeusz Manteuffel compared the close relations between Handelsman and his students to a family in which friendship and respect continued, despite ideological and scholarly differences, long after the students graduated from the University (Manteuffel, 'Marceli Handelsman jako nauczyciel'). [25] Ringelblum, 'Profesor Marceli Handelsman', 541.

[26] See Handelsman, 'Problem narodowości współczesnej'. For Handelsman's ideas about teaching history at a university see his 'O nauce i nauczaniu historji nowożytnej w szkole wyższej'.

[27] Dutkiewicz compared Handelsman's seminar to the way Askenazy worked with his students at the University of Lwów. See Dutkiewicz, 'Seminarium Marcelego Handelsmana', 135.

[28] Although he hoped to receive a professorship at Warsaw University, Askenazy remained without a teaching position and outside the academic milieu, ceasing to carry out new research. See Wróbel, 'Szymon Askenazy', 234–6; Kipa, 'Prawda o Askenazym'.

thanks to the Mianowski Fellowship for collecting documentation pertaining to the history of Polish Jewry, Shatzky conducted research in Lwów, Vienna, Berlin, and Dresden.[29] Upon his return, he worked in the Division of Jewish Affairs in the press department of the Ministry of Foreign Affairs and participated in the work of a commission looking into anti-Jewish pogroms in Wilno and Minsk in April 1919. He resigned from his post when the commission's report got no response from the government. Before leaving Poland for New York, in 1922 Shatzky defended his doctoral dissertation, sponsored by Handelsman, on the Jewish question in Congress Poland under Russian viceroy Prince Paskiewicz.[30]

Ringelblum and Mahler also carried out research in Handelsman's seminar. Handelsman supported Mahler in his archival research in 1926 and in the formal confirmation of his Viennese diploma in 1927.[31] Ringelblum attended a variety of Handelsman's lectures and seminars throughout his student years at Warsaw University and earned his doctoral degree in 1927.[32] Thanks to Handelsman and Kochanowski, the History Seminar offered a relatively hospitable place for students interested in researching the past of the Jewish community in the Polish lands. Handelsman created and preserved a liberal atmosphere in the History Department, attracting many Jewish students to Warsaw, and he also took under his wing Jewish students interested in carrying out projects on the history of Polish Jews.[33] During his tenure, the History Department at Warsaw University emerged as a leading centre for students interested in pursuing Jewish history and seeking opportunities to research and write on the subject.

## New Academic Frameworks: Student Seminar in Jewish History

In 1923, a group of Jewish students led by Emanuel Ringelblum organized the Jewish History Seminar (Seminar far Yidisher Geshikhte; Akademickie Seminarium Historii Żydów) at the Jewish Academic Centre in Warsaw (Żydowska Strzecha Akademicka w Warszawie). This university-level seminar provided a venue for the

---

[29] Hafftka, 'Życie i twórczość dr. Jakóba Szackiego', 15.

[30] Hafftka identified it as *Kwestja żydowska w Królestwie Polskim za czasów Paskiewicza, 1831–1861* (Hafftka, 'Życie i twórczość dr. Jakóba Szackiego', 16). On Shatzky see Kuznitz, *YIVO and the Making of Modern Jewish Culture*, 69.

[31] Handelsman wrote letters of recommendation and underwrote the confirmation of Mahler's doctoral diploma. See Handelsman's letter, dated 5 Dec. 1926 to the director of the Main Archives (Archiwum Główne) asking permission for Mahler to use the archives for his work on the the economic relations of Jews in Masovia in the sixteenth century (DRI, P 66, file 3). See also a certification of the nostrification of Mahler's diploma by Warsaw University, 13 Dec. 1927, in the letter from the dean of the Department of Humanities, M. Handelsman, dated 15 Dec. 1927 (DRI, P 66, file 4).

[32] See Ringelblum's student file (AUW, RP 9070).

[33] Biskupski, 'Marceli Handelsman (1882–1945)', 355.

exchange of ideas and presentation of their work on Polish Jewish history.[34] Mahler stressed Ringelblum's central role in the organization of the seminar, saying that he put his 'heart and soul into the mission of furthering Yiddish culture in general and scholarship in Yiddish in particular', making the work of the group possible.[35] Following the establishment of the YIVO Institute in Wilno in 1925, with the Historical Section (Historishe Sektzye) run by Elias Tcherikower in Berlin, the group of young male and female Jewish historians in Warsaw came to form a historical branch focused on Polish Jewish history; this was to become YIVO's Warsaw Historical Commission, mentioned earlier.[36] In the autumn of 1926 YIVO's leadership created a historical commission in Wilno, where Ringelblum temporarily settled.[37] The seminar ceased to meet for discussions from around 1929 until 1933, when it convened again under the new name of the Young Historians Circle (Yunger Historiker Krayz).[38] On the eve of the Second World War, at least a third of the Young Historians Circle members held doctoral degrees, and the majority had written their dissertations on Jewish subjects, attesting to the opportunities available at Warsaw University.[39] They raised the bar for the professional training required of a historian of Polish Jewry, and they envisioned Jewish history in general—and Polish Jewish history in particular—as a field of scholarly pursuit and a profession in its own right, requiring rigorous university-style training. These young historians created a Yiddish journal to publish their research: *Yunger historiker* (Young Historian), renamed *Bleter far*

[34] In his account of the first three years of activities of the seminar in Polish Jewish history, Ringelblum mentioned earlier, short-lived attempts to organize a group with similar goals. See Ringelblum, 'Three Years of a Jewish History Seminar' (Yid.), 7.

[35] Mahler, *Historians and Guides* (Yid.), 304, quoted in Kassow, *Who Will Write Our History?*, 413–14.

[36] Mahler, 'The Circle of Young Historians in Warsaw' (Heb.), 32. On the mentoring role of Elias Tcherikover, see Leff, *The Archive Thief*.

[37] YIVO Archives, RG 82, folder 2401: Ringelblum to Historical Section, 1 Mar. 1926. See Kuznitz, *YIVO and the Making of Modern Jewish Culture*, 88.

[38] Mahler, 'The Circle of Young Historians in Warsaw' (Heb.), 32. The Historians Circle and Historical Commission were formally run as two different bodies, although their memberships overlapped. A report on the Circle's activity presented at a meeting of the Commission's Presidium in April 1938, for example, lists the Circle's activities for April and May as consisting of three lectures, including one by Bałaban on his pet project, the bibliography for the history of the Jews in Poland. See the protocol of the meeting of the Presidium of the Historical Commission, Warsaw, in *YIVO Bleter*, 46 (1980), 302–3, document 11.

[39] Mahler and Friedman held doctoral degrees from Vienna University. Ringelblum, Ostersetzer, Mandelsberg, Lota Wegmeister, Celina Mendelsohn, Lipman Comber, Szmuel Szymkiewicz, Mojżesz (Moses) Krämer, and Kermisz graduated from Warsaw University. Kermisz received his Ph.D. in 1937 for a dissertation on Lublin and the surrounding district in 1788–1794, written under Handelsman. Szymkiewicz, who was Arnold's student, received his Ph.D. from Warsaw University in 1938; it was published in 1959.

*geshikhte* (Pages of History) after two issues. In the first volume in July 1926, the editors expressed hope for a periodical journal devoted to 'Jewish history in the Jewish language'.⁴⁰

The importance of such scholarship went beyond writing for a Jewish audience that was not fluent in Polish. Rather it was a declaration of the importance of publishing in Yiddish, the language of secular Jewish culture in eastern Europe. Although they took an interest in all aspects of Jewish history, authors in this journal focused on Jewish history in the Polish lands. As the editors explained in 1934, their concentration resulted from both practical and scholarly matters: on the practical level, the archives available to them in Poland held materials linked to Poland, and as the field of Polish Jewish history had been less studied than others, there were also scholarly reasons for the emphasis.⁴¹

Despite the lack of an organized, authoritative body to lead Jewish scholarship in Poland, Ringelblum considered systematic, collective work carried out under the auspices of the seminar an indispensable addition to a formal university training. He encouraged students to undertake research projects on Jewish, and especially Polish Jewish, history.⁴² In a letter to Abraham Duker in December 1936, Ringelblum reported that the work of the seminar continued normally, and that members 'presented interesting lectures, proving that our young people do not fall behind'.⁴³ The seminar served as a non-partisan venue of intellectual discourse, while at the same time seeking to defend the rights of Polish Jewry in independent Poland. Although the majority of participants leaned to the political left, the membership remained open. Several members of the seminar belonged to the Po'alei Zion Left party, but it also included a prominent Bundist, Lipman Comber; Eliezer Feldman, who in his university records declared Hebrew to be his mother tongue; the observant Israel Ostersetzer, who taught Talmud at the Institute of Jewish Studies in Warsaw; and Falik Hafner, who studied at Warsaw University and the Institute of Jewish Studies. A few members, Hava-Joheved Warszawska, Ester (Emilia) Tenenbaum, and Jakub Berman, at first active in Po'alei Zion Left, eventually joined the Communist Party. In addition to bringing together members of political parties competing against one another on the Jewish street, the seminar became a meeting ground for Jews from all parts of recently reborn Poland. About one-third of those who attended the seminar were women.⁴⁴

⁴⁰ 'From the Editors' (Yid.), *Yunger historiker*, 1 (1926), 6.
⁴¹ 'From the Editors' (Yid.), *Bleter far geshikhte*, 1 (1934), 4.
⁴² Ringelblum, 'Three Years of a Jewish History Seminar' (Yid.), 9–10. See also Berman, 'The Tasks of the Historical Section' (Yid.), 19.
⁴³ DRI, P 65, file 169: copy of a Yiddish typed letter dated 6 Dec. 1936.
⁴⁴ On the role of women among the young Jewish historians in Poland, see Aleksiun, 'Female, Jewish, Educated, and Writing Polish Jewish History'.

Most importantly, the research carried out under the auspices of the seminar bore great relevance for the Jewish community in Poland, inserting a real political purpose into Polish Jewish history. Its founders hoped to promote a national Jewish agenda by struggling against 'inertia' and 'passivity' among Jewish university students. Ringelblum envisioned discussions about Jewish history entering university classrooms as a chance to dispel misrepresentations and lies about contemporary Jewish society and the Jewish past. In such a way, he hoped, Polish–Jewish relations would eventually improve.[45] The members of the seminar believed that they 'perform[ed] a task of immense social significance [*gezelshaftlekhe arbet*], a task whose goal [was] not just to know the Jewish past, but also to lay the foundation for the struggle that the Jewish nation in Poland [was] waging for its national and social liberation'.[46] For Schorr, Bałaban, and Schiper, teaching a Polish audience about the Jews was only implicitly a political statement; the young members of the seminar took it to a new level of political engagement, describing their profession as a tool in the fight for Jewish rights in Poland. Only when maintaining contacts with future Polish gymnasium teachers, publishing in professional Polish journals, and speaking at seminars and conferences could the young historians have an opportunity to carry out their mission to influence the Polish audience. This generational shift marked a move towards the use of history as an explicitly political tool. They strove to accomplish this with no compromise of academic standards of research—an inevitable source of tension for young scholars who practised their profession as a minority in a nation state.[47]

The relationship between the Warsaw seminar and the Berlin-based Historical Section of YIVO was complex. Although members of the Warsaw seminar greeted the founding of the YIVO Institute warmly, the background and research agendas of the Historical Section and Ringelblum's group's differed.[48] The group in Berlin relied on a cohort of self-taught scholars, while the seminar in Warsaw relied on university students and graduates.[49] Moreover, the Historical Section envisioned the focus of its work in broad terms,[50] while the Young Historians Circle in Warsaw

[45] Ringelblum, 'Three Years of a Jewish History Seminar' (Yid.), 10.

[46] Ibid., as quoted in Kassow, *Who Will Write Our History?*, 60.

[47] See Michlic, *Poland's Threatening Other*.

[48] See Mahler, 'The Circle of Young Historians in Warsaw' (Heb.), 31; Kuznitz, *YIVO and the Making of Modern Jewish Culture*, 87–90.

[49] In her work on YIVO, Kuznitz acknowledged the differences between the founders of the Institute and the Warsaw Historical Commission, explaining them in generational terms and in terms of differences in formal education. However, the difference lay also in the largely Galician roots of the Warsaw cohort and in the different professional trajectories between those at the YIVO Institute and the university-trained Ringelblum, Mahler, Schiper, and Bałaban (Kuznitz, *YIVO and the Making of Modern Jewish Culture*, 88–9). See also the discussion in Fishman, *The Rise of Modern Yiddish Culture*, 127–8.

[50] At its founding meeting, in October 1925, Tcherikower sketched out its future activities, which

concentrated primarily on Polish Jewish history. In December 1926, Ringelblum proposed creating an autonomous body to deal solely with Polish Jewish history. YIVO's Organizational Committee recognized these different approaches, agreeing to create a Wilno-based commission for Polish Jewish history, while the Historical Section retained responsibility for work on all other countries. YIVO spoke in the name of the entire Jewish people, while the Warsaw historians affiliated with it concerned themselves with the affairs of the Polish Jewish community. For historians writing Polish Jewish history, all Polish Jewish history proved relevant.[51] And although the four volumes of *Yunger historiker/Bleter far geshikhte*, published by the Warsaw historians in 1926, 1929, 1933, and 1938, contained only a handful of articles discussing general issues of Jewish history, the editors argued that the history of Polish Jewry was relevant not only for the Jewish community in Poland, but also for the Jewish people in general, since 'the majority of Jews in the entire world stem from the lands of Old Poland'.[52]

## Academic Appointments in Jewish Studies and the Influence of Majer Bałaban

While Jewish students of history formed an informal group with loose membership, the Jewish intelligentsia discussed the need to make formal academic training available to Jewish historians by including Jewish history in the university curriculum. As early as 1919, Schorr argued that, although Jews in Poland did not demand their own institutions of higher education, given the size of the Jewish community and the number of Jewish students 'it is only fair that Jews could insist that special chairs of Hebrew language and literature be created at already existing universities and separately for Jewish history'.[53] In 1921, the first anniversary of Poznański's death, Bałaban criticized Jewish society in Poland,

> which did not create for such a man a scholarly work place, where he could be active in the sphere which befitted him and educate a generation of students who would continue the work begun by the master. Poznański dreamed of establishing a *Judaic Univer-*

---

included surveying and describing archival sources, publishing a volume on Jewish history with original sources and archival material, compiling bibliographies, and holding public lectures. He singled out research on such topics as Jews in revolutionary and workers' movements in Europe. See 'The First Founding Meeting of the Historical Section of the Jewish Scientific Institute, Saturday, 31 October [1925] in the Evening' (Yid.) in *YIVO Bleter*, 46 (1980), 291–3, document 4. See also Kuznitz, *YIVO and the Making of Modern Jewish Culture*, 85–6.

[51] YIVO Archives, RG 1.1, folder 2: minutes of meeting of the Organizational Committee, 22 Dec. 1926. See Kuznitz, *YIVO and the Making of Modern Jewish Culture*, 88–90.

[52] 'From the Editors' (Yid.), *Bleter far geshikhte*, 1 (1934), 4.

[53] Schorr, 'Przemówienie Prof. Uniw. dra Mojżesza Schorra', 102.

*sity* [*Uniwersytet judaistyczny*] in Warsaw [emphasis in original]; in the last years of his life he began working in this direction, sent an application to the authorities and looked for funds.... Jewish society, if it cares for sustaining and broadening Jewish knowledge among future generations should undertake this plan, develop it, and strengthen it.

Bałaban considered the establishment of a Judaic university, a 'Centre for Jewish Studies [*placówka dla nauki żydowskiej*]', 'a national necessity, if we want to stand with dignity among cultured nations and not lag behind forever'.[54] He envisioned this institute in terms comparable to the Hebrew University in Jerusalem:

On the Mount of Olives in Jerusalem a part of the grand Jewish university destined for world Jewry already stands, but in Warsaw, in the heart of the greatest concentration of the diaspora an echo of lectures from the Mount should sound, a loud and harmonized echo, and above all an echo of the true melody in response to all the lies about us spread in various so-called scientific journals by so-called scientists.[55]

Ignacy Schwarzbart, a prominent Zionist leader from western Galicia and an editor of the Polish-language Jewish newspaper *Nowy Dziennik* (New Daily), argued the need for a Jewish university in the diaspora, while insisting that the support and planning for a Hebrew University in Jerusalem (the cornerstone was laid in the summer of 1918) remained valid. A diaspora Jewish university was necessary because the *numerus clausus* (quota system) hindered student enrolments, while the economy and anti-Jewish sentiment created a dearth of stable positions available to Jewish professors for carrying out research; related to this was the absence of any existing university programmes that included a course of Hebrew and Jewish literature and history.[56]

The idea of including Polish Jewish history in the university programme came to fruition with the establishment in Warsaw of the Institute of Jewish Studies (Instytut Nauk Judaistycznych), an independent institution of Jewish learning with a formal link to a university, which enjoyed official state recognition. The Institute was founded in 1927 with the help of Bałaban and Schorr, support from the Society for the Advancement of Judaic Studies in Poland (Towarzystwo Krzewienia Nauk Judaistycznych w Polsce),[57] and financial backing from B'nai B'rith.[58] The Institute claimed to represent the entire Polish Jewish community, as a non-partisan, apolitical institution where Polish Jews with different political

---

[54] Bałaban, 'Rabin Dr. Samuel Poznański'. See Poznański, 'Widoki nauki judaistycznej w nowotworzącej się Polsce'. [55] Bałaban, 'Rabin Dr. Samuel Poznański'.

[56] Ignacy Schwarzbart in *Nowy Dziennik*, 1 May 1924, cited in Bałaban, 'Kronika: O uniwersytet żydowski', 120. By Jewish literature, Schwarzbart presumably means Yiddish.

[57] See Biderman, *Mayer Balaban*, 76; Eden, 'The Institute of Jewish Studies' (Heb.). Founded in 1927, the Institute opened officially on 19 Feb. 1928.

[58] See the budgets in AAN, B'nai B'rith, files 8 and 9.

affiliations came together to engage in research.⁵⁹ The founders described it as an important development 'for the glory of Polish Jewry',⁶⁰ which needed its own centre of scholarship as 'a matter of national and civic honour'.⁶¹ The new institution strove to achieve a status comparable to a university and to educate Jewish communal leaders, rabbis, and teachers to serve the Polish Jewish community.

Bałaban's was among the Institute's first faculty appointments, and it fulfilled his lifelong dream of working in an institution of higher education; he began teaching classes in Jewish and Polish Jewish history and served as the Institute's second rector, following in Schorr's footsteps. The Institute offered a broad range of topics in Jewish studies, with a faculty that also included Schorr, who lectured in the Bible and Semitic philology; Israel Ostersetzer and Abraham Weiss, who taught Talmud; Menachem (Edmund) Stein, teaching Midrash and Jewish literature in the Hellenistic period; Markus Braude, who taught homiletics; Mojżesz Goliger, responsible for Hebrew grammar; Majer Tauber, lecturer on the pedagogy of Jewish studies; and Arie Tartakower, in charge of Jewish social work. Abraham Joshua Heschel joined the faculty shortly before his emigration to England to teach Jewish philosophy.⁶² The Institute offered teaching and research opportunities to leading scholars in Jewish studies in Poland. Among a wide range of subjects, Jewish political, cultural, and economic history formed the core of the Institute's programme, with lectures and seminars delivered by Bałaban, Schiper, and Friedman. The Institute sought to prepare teachers to teach Hebrew language and literature in secondary schools, and to train rabbis in the methods of modern research. But the founders also saw it as an institution for preparing a number of young men and women to become scholars of Polish Jewish history, since, as Bałaban wrote, 'the history of Jews in Poland awaits its researchers; in our archives there are sources never touched and histories of Jewish communities have not been properly elaborated; the same is true about other subjects in the field of Jewish history in this land'.⁶³

---

⁵⁹ Schorr, 'Jewish Scholarship and the Jewish Book in Poland'.

⁶⁰ Schorr, 'Stan i potrzeby wiedzy żydowskiej w dobie dzisiejszej', an inaugural lecture given at the opening of the Institute on 19 Feb. 1928, p. xxi.

⁶¹ Inaugural speech by Dr Markus Braude given at the opening of the Institute on 19 Feb. 1928, quoted in *Sprawozdanie Instytutu Nauk Judaistycznych w Warszawie*, p. ix. Braude described creating Polish Jewry's own Institute of Judaic Studies as an act 'of national and civic honour' (ibid.).

⁶² Fial, 'Alma Mater Judaica', 11; Kaplan and Dresner, *Abraham Joshua Heschel*. In a letter dated 30 Jan. 1939, Schorr enquired whether Dr Jacob Teicher might be interested in taking over the chair in the philosophy of religion and ethics of Judaism at the Institute. At the same time, Schorr advised Teicher to remain in England if such a possibility opened up. I am grateful to his daughter, Anna Teicher, for sharing this letter with me.

⁶³ Bałaban, 'Wiedza żydowska i jej uczelnie w Polsce', 32–3. See also the assessment of the field of Polish Jewish history in the inaugural lecture delivered by Schorr on 19 Feb. 1928: Mojżesz Schorr,

The Institute's close link to Warsaw University reinforced its academic agenda.[64] The university's rector, Antoni Szlagowski, dean of the Theology Department, participated in the Institute's opening and emphasized the close relationship between the two institutions: 'Judaic subjects, which at our institutions are being taught as an integral part of the Semitic languages and the history of the ancient East, here, at the Institute will be supplemented and comprehensively illuminated'.[65] The Institute required that all students attend classes at the university, and formal graduation from the Institute required a master's degree from the university.

During Handelsman's tenure as Warsaw University's dean of the Department of Humanities, the he sought to include minority histories as a part of Polish historical narratives. In the autumn of 1928, Bałaban obtained a lectureship in Jewish history at Warsaw University's History Department,[66] and a year later a leading Ukrainian historian, Myron Korduba, received an invitation to take a position in Ukrainian history at Warsaw University.[67] With the appointment of Korduba and Bałaban, both focusing on Polish lands, Handelsman championed the inclusive multi-ethnic vision of Polish history, and, by extension, of a Polish culture and identity not based on religion or ethnicity.

Bałaban's joint appointments at the university and Institute carried tremendous significance, enabling Jewish students to receive academic training in Jewish history, and potentially ensuring the recognition of Polish Jewish history within Polish academia.[68] The Warsaw branch of B'nai B'rith celebrated the university appointment,[69] and Schorr praised the fact that Bałaban 'aroused respect for our past among non-Jews'.[70] Interestingly, Bałaban's students recognized the implicitly political character of his seminar; according to Marek Bosak, the sheer fact of his appointment bore 'national significance'. At Warsaw University, he continued, 'new adepts of the [field] of the history of Jews in Poland have the opportunity to set their passion for historicizing freely in the Jewish-scholarly atmosphere,

'Stan i potrzeby wiedzy żydowskiej w dobie obecnej', p. xx. On other goals of the Institute, see also the speech delivered by Dr Markus Braude at the opening of the Institute, in *Sprawozdanie Instytutu Nauk Judaistycznych w Warszawie*, pp. viii–x.

[64] Biderman, *Mayer Balaban*, 77.

[65] Speech by Professor Antoni Szlagowski quoted in *Sprawozdanie Instytutu Nauk Judaistycznych w Warszawie*, p. xi.

[66] AAN, MWRiOP, 1614: Bałaban, curriculum vitae, 13. Dold suggests that 'Bałaban's advancement appears to have been connected to his prominent position at the Institute of Jewish Studies, even in years of vehement anti-Jewish campaigns in the higher educational system'; see Dold, 'A Matter of National and Civic Honor', 56.

[67] See Pedycz, 'Myron Korduba (1876–1947)', 462.   [68] See Friedman, 'Prof. Majer Bałaban', 345.

[69] See AAN, B'nai B'rith, file 3, p. 4: protocol from the closed meeting on 17 Sept. 1928.

[70] AAN, B'nai B'rith, file 3, p. 270: protocol from the closed meeting on 11 Mar. 1933.

in harmony with their national attitude'.⁷¹ The academic context, it seems, was taken for granted, but the fact that Jews could engage in studying their past under the roof of the university drew particular attention. Even Ringelblum, who disapproved of the Warsaw Institute as a 'reactionary institution' because it ignored Yiddish language and literature and did not take a critical approach to the Bible, admitted that it was the only institution of higher education where young scholars could pursue Jewish studies.⁷²

Indeed, Bałaban's appointments were exceptional not only in the context of Polish academia, but also worldwide. His position can be compared only to Salo Baron's Chair in the History and Literature of the Jewish People at Columbia University, in December 1928, and to the Institute of Jewish Studies in Jerusalem, which was inaugurated in 1924 and became part of the newly established Faculty of Humanities at the Hebrew University four years later.⁷³ In Europe, only the University of Madrid had a chair in Jewish studies.⁷⁴ And Bałaban's position teaching Polish Jewish history and his cohort of Jewish students were unique. Bałaban saw his success as the first opening for academic positions in Jewish history. Speaking at the Congress of Polish Historians in 1930, he argued that Polish Jewish history was a branch of Polish scholarship and needed centralized management to train scholars in Poland and abroad. He envisioned the creation of chairs in Jewish history or Polish Jewish history in at least two centres with rich archives, where a new cadre of scholars could be trained. Alternatively, he thought the task should be assigned to the Institute of Jewish Studies itself, either by securing substantial financial assistance from the Polish state or by nationalizing it.⁷⁵

The number of students enrolled in Bałaban's seminars and attending his lectures at the Institute grew steadily.⁷⁶ At the Institute of Jewish Studies the numbers more than tripled: from twenty-three during the first academic year 1927/8, to seventy-one in the 1933/4 academic year, though firm numbers of those who participated in Bałaban's seminars are lacking.⁷⁷ Still, the majority of both male and female students chose to study history at Warsaw University, where they also

---

⁷¹ Meir Bosak, 'Prof. Dr. Majer Bałaban (*Nowy Dziennik* z dnia 20 II 1937)', in Jolles (ed.), *Księga jubileuszowa Bałabana*, 76–9: 77.

⁷² Ringelblum, *Kronika getta warszawskiego*, 557.

⁷³ Liberles, *Salo Wittmayer Baron*, 58, 81; Engel, 'A Book Is Born' (Heb.), 141.

⁷⁴ In 1914, Jerusalem-born scholar Abraham Shalom Yahuda was appointed to a chair in Jewish studies in the University of Madrid, Spain. See Michal Friedman, 'Reconstructing "Jewish Spain"'. See also the discussion of the initiative in Wilno, in Weiser, 'The Jewel in the Yiddish Crown'.

⁷⁵ Bałaban, 'Zadania i potrzeby historjografji Żydów w Polsce', i. 118.

⁷⁶ Aleksiun, 'Training a New Generation of Jewish Historians'.

⁷⁷ See *Sprawozdanie Instytutu Nauk Judaistycznych w Warszawie*, p. xxxi; 'Sprawozdanie Instytutu Nauk Judaistycznych w Warszawie', , in *Księga jubileuszowa Braudego*, 22; and 'Statystyka słuchaczy w latach akad. 1931/32–1933/34', in *Księga jubileuszowa Schorra*, p. xix.

attended Bałaban's classes.[78] In 1935, Bałaban claimed that 'almost always over fifty students' attended his seminar at Warsaw University.[79] Bałaban's Festschrift, published in 1938 to celebrate his sixtieth birthday, listed sixty theses written by students in his seminars at the Institute of Jewish Studies and Warsaw University —almost half of them by women—but the actual number was probably higher, as the list did not include incomplete projects.[80]

Bałaban attracted a large following by capturing students' attention and finding ways to make subjects relevant to them on a personal level. Hillel Seidman, Bałaban's student and the secretary of the Agudat Israel representatives in parliament, recalled that during the first meeting, Bałaban routinely asked students about their family names and home towns, beginning his lectures by telling stories about relevant historical figures or communities.[81] For example, Clara Minskberg remembered being asked to prepare a family tree as her graduation assignment at the Institute of Jewish Studies.[82] His seminars also stood out due to the collegial atmosphere and passionate discussions which 'he never dominated. Instead, he chaired the debate, expressing his opinions in a moderate and cautious manner at the very end without imposing them, as [was] often done in other seminars.'[83] He forged a bond with and among his students that continued after their graduation.[84] Ostersetzer praised Bałaban as an educator devoted to his students:

the spirit of truth permeates his activities as a teacher: love of his profession, of Jewry and its spiritual values and sympathy for his student, working together with him in the field of Jewish history in Poland. This relationship of mutual love would not stop the moment they left the walls of the university and began independent work in the scholarly and pedagogical field.[85]

Bałaban lectured at the university on topics that concerned his own work; but he also designed classes that would give students the basis for carrying out their

[78] Seidman, 'Meir Bałaban' (Heb.), 228.   [79] AAN, MWRiOP, 1614: Bałaban, curriculum vitae, 13.

[80] See 'Prace Magisterskie pisane w seminarium hist. żyd. Profesora Bałabana', in Jolles (ed.), *Księga jubileuszowa Bałabana*, 102–4. Bałaban likely worked with over a hundred students of Jewish history. See Krämer, 'Prof. M. Bałaban—Jubilatem', ibid. 87. See also Biderman, *Mayer Bałaban*, 77.

[81] According to Seidman, Bałaban instilled in his students 'not only knowledge but also curiosity and enthusiasm': Seidman, 'Meir Bałaban' (Heb.), 243–5.

[82] Oral history interview with Clara Ma'ayan (USHMM, RG-50.120*0096, tape 1: 1.00.59). Born to a Zionist family in Rzeszów in 1915, Clara recalled a crucial role Jewish history played in her education, both at home and at the Institute of Jewish Studies in Warsaw. Her father insisted that she recognize the importance of Jewish history—that it was as worthy of study as Polish history or the French Revolution.

[83] Falik Hafner, 'Przemawia w imieniu uczniów', in Jolles (ed.), *Księga jubileuszowa Bałabana*, 30–5: 33.   [84] See ibid. 32–3.

[85] Ostersetzer, 'Majer Bałaban—historiograf żydostwa polskiego', in Jolles (ed.), *Księga jubileuszowa Bałabana*, 59–65: 65.

independent assignments. For example, in the autumn semester of 1928 he taught 'Introduction to the General History of the Jews', 'A Survey of Jewish History', and 'History of the Jewish Organization in Poland'.[86] He also taught the more advanced group at the university, while students who required more attention met with their mentor at the Institute of Jewish Studies.[87] In addition, he advised students writing on Polish Jewish history at other Polish universities, and he became, as Falik Hafner put it, 'an honorary mentor of all Jewish students in the country who devote themselves to the study of our history'.[88] His position, which was made possible thanks to the generally liberal atmosphere among the faculty's senior and junior members, gained particular importance in the late 1930s, when Jewish students at Polish universities faced persistent ostracism and violence.[89]

In March 1937 Bałaban addressed an audience at the Main Judaic Library in Warsaw to celebrate his birthday, expressing his 'gratitude to God for having been given the opportunity to educate a generation of historians of Polish Jewry [that] will continue the golden chain of Jewish studies'.[90] The diverse social and geographical backgrounds and motivations of Bałaban's students suggest the wide appeal of the study of Polish Jewish history. Their writings and career paths were inspired by a combination of a sense of being rooted in Polish culture and a commitment to Jewish nationalism. Both their scholarship and their social activism in the field of education demonstrate Bałaban's influence on this emerging school of Polish Jewish historians. These students of Polish Jewish history came from diverse social backgrounds and political cultures, but they shared important characteristics, and they belonged to what historians have described retrospectively as the generation with 'no future' or 'the last generation'.

### Graduate Training at YIVO

Mirroring Ringelblum's and Bałaban's solutions in Warsaw, the YIVO Institute in Wilno offered aspects of Jewish history that the university lacked. YIVO's significant contribution lay in collecting and cataloguing on the one hand, and publishing and popularizing on the other: aspects encouraged by the Warsaw commission. Despite its wide popular appeal, YIVO was late in implementing a programme for training a younger generation of scholars. Before the Aspirantur graduate programme was founded in 1935, YIVO had mostly served as a centre for established scholars, offering short-term courses and conferences. It also trained

---

[86] See Szaja Friszman, student file, *Wykaz wykładów i ćwiczeń* (AUW, RP 28145).

[87] See *Sprawozdanie z działalności Wydziału Humanistycznego Uniwersytetu J. Piłsudskiego za rok akademicki 1935–1936*, 72.   [88] Hafner, 'Księga ku czci prof. dr. Majera Bałabana', 11.

[89] Ibid. See also Gieysztor, 'Środowisko historyczne Warszawy w okresie międzywojennym', 97–101.

[90] Bałaban, 'Praca mojego życia', in Jolles (ed.), *Księga jubileuszowa Bałabana*, 35–40: 39–40.

teachers in a variety of topics, including the challenges of teaching Jewish history. It relied on the co-operation of many lay Jews in both fundraising and scholarly efforts, building a wide network of collectors (*zamlers*) across Poland and beyond, who collected information on Jewish life. These were mostly untrained volunteers, and few received any training from YIVO.[91]

The Aspirantur programme ran for four years before the outbreak of the war, and the number of applications grew every year. Isaiah Trunk estimates the total number of 'aspirantn', or graduate fellows, during the four years at more than sixty students.[92] Aspirantur's focus was on areas such as economy, folklore, and pedagogy, rather than on historical topics per se. Lucy Dawidowicz, an aspirant for one year, lists only four people specializing in history. These four profiles present some of the characteristics of the aspirants in general and the history aspirants specifically. Three had been students of history at Stefan Batory University: Rachel Golinkin, from Wilno, worked on the Wilno *kahal* records from 1808 to 1845; Chana Smuczkewicz, from a town near Wilno, worked on Jewish guilds in Wilno in the first half of the nineteenth century; and Pinchas Tikoczinski, from Białystok, a fellow for the third time, focused on east European Jews during the First World War. The fourth, Chaim Munitz, from Braslaw near Wilno, who had studied at the Wilno Teachers' Seminary, prepared a project in social history: a lexicon of Jewish clothing in the first half of the nineteenth century.[93]

An academic degree was usually required for participation in the Aspirantur programme, though not always. At least seven fellows in Dawidowicz's year had studied at Stefan Batory University. The programme was not affiliated with the local university, but it evidently attracted current and past students of that institution, who were expected to reside in Wilno and work on material held at the YIVO archives. Pinchas Kon, a historian affiliated with the Historical Commission in Warsaw, reported the finding of the Wilno *kahal* records in 1937, and the fellows' efforts were directed towards exploiting this newly identified source.[94] Out of a

---

[91] See Gottesman, *Defining the Yiddish Nation*, 138–46, 169–70; Kuznitz, *YIVO and the Making of Modern Jewish Culture*, 73–6. See also the list of collecting circles in 163 towns in 1929, in *YIVO Bleter*, 46 (1980), 321–3, document 25. According to this document a total of 139 of these circles were in Poland, of which only about fifteen were in Galicia (interestingly, Galicia was considered 'an undercollected area'; see Gottesman, *Defining the Yiddish Nation*, 149). For the same year, Dawidowicz identifies some 500 circles of *zamlers* throughout Poland (*From that Place and Time*, 87). A publication in 1938 listed 138 points of origin of the folklore material and 311 *zamlers* who had contributed to the work (Gottesman, *Defining the Yiddish Nation*, 162).

[92] For general surveys of the Aspirantur programme see Gottesman, *Defining the Yiddish Nation*, ch. 6; Kuznitz, *YIVO and the Making of Modern Jewish Culture*, 153–5. Numbers taken from ibid. 153 n. 115; Trunk, 'On the History of Polish Historiography' (Heb.), 251–2.

[93] See Dawidowicz, *From that Place and Time*, 94–5.

[94] Kon, 'The Recently Found Portions of the Wilno Kehilah Archives' (Yid.). Kon, who studied

total of sixty-eight seminar papers from the Aspirantur, Trunk counted nineteen with historical themes, and concluded that a considerable number of fellows wrote on such themes, especially in eastern Europe. He also asserted that the papers selected for publication in *YIVO Bleter*, founded in 1931 as a forum for all fields of scholarship in which the institute engaged, demonstrated the positive results of the history studies in the programme. Of the aspirants presenting their work at the end of the first year, Daniel Lerner reported on Jewish businesses in Wilno in 1905, which could be considered contemporary history, and Yosef-Dovid Derevianski presented his work, later published in *YIVO Bleter*, on the Rabbinical School in Wilno, 1847–73.[95] These local history themes reflected the requirement of one year's work at the YIVO Institute itself.[96]

The aspiring researchers were trained and supervised mainly by YIVO directors Max Weinreich, Zalman Reisen, and Zelig Kalmanowicz, whose own research focused on Yiddish linguistics, philology, and literature. However, recognizing the shortcomings of the resident staff regarding professional historical training and methodology, they also relied on the affiliated university-trained Warsaw historians. As many aspirants in the historical section seem to have graduated from the History Department in Stefan Batory University, the YIVO programme began to address the needs of emerging standard Polish university training with regard to the field of Jewish studies, precisely what the Young Historians Circle had advocated from the outset. The need for 'outsourcing' seems to have been accentuated by the fact that YIVO's 'own' historians, especially Tcherikower, head of the historical section, lived elsewhere (Berlin and Paris). A branch of the Warsaw-based Jewish historians thus provided training, bringing with them their own interpretations and methods, not always in line with the official policy of YIVO. Earlier, in the training YIVO offered its Jewish teachers, it turned to the same group of historians for additional lectures and introductions; this dependence was therefore an established procedure.[97]

---

at Stefan Batory University and conducted research in the local archives and libraries, discovered seventy-three volumes for the years 1808–45 in the state and municipal archives.

[95] Derevianski, 'The Attitude of the Society and the Government Circles to the Rabbinical School' (Yid.).

[96] See the description in Dawidowicz, *From that Place and Time*, ch. 4, esp. 89–99. See also Kuznitz, *YIVO and the Making of Modern Jewish Culture*, 157. The records of the Aspirantur programme housed at YIVO archives deserve a separate study of their own. As this was not a history programme per se, and most aspirants were not historians, further exploration of this programme is beyond the scope of this book.

[97] On training, see Gottesman, *Defining the Yiddish Nation*, 146. On courses given by leading historians of Polish Jews, see Trunk, 'On the History of Polish Historiography' (Heb.), 252. See also the content of classes given by Mahler in the third year of the programme, September 1937: *YIVO Bleter*, 46 (1980), 319–20, document 23. Teachers and lecturers at YIVO included Max Weinreich, Zelig

Ringelblum took part in shaping the training offered by the Aspirantur programme as a whole; and in October 1937 he successfully limited their number, even though applications multiplied, arguing they would find no employment as full-time scholars and none could be offered to them within YIVO, as its own resources were limited.[98] The shrinking of the scope of YIVO fellowship programmes indicates the problems inherent in the lack of the kind of official recognition that would have offered the fellows additional venues of employment in Poland. At the same time, the programme experimented with widening its geographical coverage, in recognition of archival materials available elsewhere. The Historical Commission in Warsaw was inclined to advocate acceptance of research done on Warsaw records by an aspirant working in Warsaw, instead of limiting YIVO research exclusively to Wilno as stipulated in the original terms of the fellowships. Hence in April 1938 Eisenbach, Hafner, Trunk, Linder, Comber, and Ringelblum discussed the candidacy of Azriel Reichzeig, requiring a detailed research plan to verify that his was a suitable case to promulgate a change in the Aspirantur programme.[99]

The work that resulted from the Aspirantur fellowships reflected the interdisciplinary nature of YIVO's training and its aim to include aspects of Jewish life in both the past and the present. For example, fellows wrote historical surveys of linguistic and literary subjects, and many projects had historical aspects, even when grounded in different disciplines. This can be seen in Elias Schulman's project, *A History of Yiddish Literature in the United States, 1879–1900*, which was favourably reviewed.[100] However, the most significant work, at least in the eyes of the resident instructors, dealt with contemporary economic and social problems. In the interwar period, YIVO's initiative had not yet made a considerable mark in the field of Jewish history, and the number of its history fellows could not be compared with the much larger number of students emerging from the Warsaw institutions. YIVO lacked both Warsaw's focus on historical training and methods

---

Kalmanowicz, Zalman Reisen, Jacob Lestschinsky, Simon Dubnow, Rudolf Glanz, and Pesakh Libman Hersh, alongside Mahler, Friedman, and Schiper.

[98] Kuznitz, *YIVO and the Making of Modern Jewish Culture*, 155–8. Kuznitz concludes that the additional programme created in 1937, known as pro-Aspirantur and originally intended for training students without an academic background, changed its focus, preparing students for careers in social work and teaching in Yiddish schools, practically replacing the Wilno Teachers' Seminary, which had closed in 1931. [99] *YIVO Bleter*, 46 (1980), 301–2, document 11.

[100] A. A. Roback, 'A History of Yiddish Literature in the United States, 1879–1900 by Elias Schulman'. The reviewer praised it as the work of 'an American aspirant (research fellow) of the Yiddish Scientific Institute in Wilno during the years 1935–36 ... If this book is a sample of what the YIVO's aspirants produce, we may well conclude that the training they receive is of high quality. There is many a doctoral dissertation which contains less substance than this limited History' (p. 313).

and its diversity of topics, but it did have the greatest appeal to Jewish history students graduating from Stefan Batory University.

## Bringing Together Jewish Historians Worldwide

Both YIVO and the Warsaw historians considered themselves part of a greater community of scholars beyond the political confines of interwar Poland. YIVO was established in Polish territory only out of convenience and the availability of funds, and it promoted itself as the new centre for Jewish scholarship. It built on discussions pertaining not only to the location of the future academic centre, but also to the language to be used and the role of Yiddish before the First World War.[101] Stressing Yiddish as the common language of the Jewish people and the research community limited its audience, but it still had a considerable appeal. With growing branches in other cities, YIVO advanced its own agenda, holding conferences in Wilno, publishing research, building a network of popular support and co-operation, and collecting artefacts and documents to be stored in its central branch. The historians in Warsaw focused on Polish Jewish history, but they saw their focus as relevant beyond Poland. And they aimed to combine efforts with other schools and other research agendas to form a working academic research community involved in all aspects of Jewish history and culture. While focusing on research in Polish Jewish history, scholars in Poland put forth competing blueprints for establishing a centralized organization for Jewish studies in Poland and abroad.

With their strong convictions about the importance of academic training for Jewish historians, the Jewish intelligentsia in Poland discussed the creation of a separate institution to provide such training in an organized way. They aspired, for instance, to found a Jewish university in Europe and to promote the inclusion of special programmes within existing universities. They asked whether their aim should be to help developing Jewish culture and knowledge or to produce diplomas—or whether they should strive for both.[102] Those opposed to the idea of founding a Jewish university in Europe pointed to practical and ideological problems. Since building a university required resources and time, they argued, a European university could not soon play a role in developing Jewish culture and knowledge, but it might instead produce worthless diplomas and serve to justify more limitations on Jewish students. Furthermore, the university would not be able to take in all those kept out of regular universities. Yiddish would not answer the needs of scientific terminology, and not enough academicians were fluent in

---

[101] Kuznitz, *YIVO and the Making of Modern Jewish Culture*, 20–3.
[102] See L.H., 'Kronika: O uniwersytet żydowski'.

Hebrew. A new university founded away from large Jewish centres would also distance the Jewish intelligentsia from the Jewish masses. Last but not least, a new university would split limited resources that needed to be channelled into the nascent Hebrew University in Jerusalem.[103]

While discussions about the role of a potential Jewish university in Europe took into consideration the overall role of higher education and the needs of a Jewish intelligentsia, historians also expressed views about the importance of creating an organizational framework for Jewish studies and Jewish history in particular. Bałaban, Schorr, and Schiper actively supported the Hebrew University in Jerusalem, which had its official opening ceremony in April 1925. They worked on behalf of the Association of the Friends of the Hebrew University (Towarzystwo Przyjaciół Uniwersytetu Hebrajskiego), operating in Poland as early as 1922. Bałaban and Schorr also represented Poland on the Board of the Institute of Jewish Studies of the Hebrew University in Jerusalem, created in 1924. Furthermore, Schiper managed the enterprise of collecting books on the history of Polish Jews and purchasing printed matter and copying archival documents for the National Library in Jerusalem.[104] In 1924, Bałaban addressed the plans for a Jewish university in Europe in the pages of the journal *Nasze życie*, which he helped found and edit.[105] Discussing the plan put forward by Henryk Doktorowicz to establish a Jewish university in Danzig or Klaipeda, he disparaged it as a 'spectacle' (*impreza*), quoting extensively from a critical article by a 'serious Warsaw attorney', Borys Stawski, who had argued that 'such a university would sanction the *numerus clausus* and weaken the efforts of creating a Hebrew University in Jerusalem'.[106]

The differences of opinion between supporters and opponents of a European-based Jewish university did not necessarily follow the Zionist/diaspora nationalist divide.[107] Despite tension between YIVO and some Warsaw historians of Polish Jewry, especially those associated with the Institute of Jewish Studies, they all agreed on the need to create an organization that would centralize research in the field of Jewish history and Jewish studies. Though they were members of Zionist parties, Schiper, Ringelblum, Mahler, and Friedman collaborated closely with the YIVO Institute, which was implicitly in competition with the Hebrew University in Jerusalem. While informed by their Zionist sympathies, Jewish historians'

---

[103] Ibid. 273–4.
[104] *Sprawozdanie z działalności 'Towarzystwa Przyjaciół Uniwersytetu Hebrajskiego w Jerozolimie' w roku 1927*. See Szulkin, 'Projekt utworzenia Katedry Historii Żydów w Polsce'.
[105] See Bałaban, 'Kronika: O uniwersytet żydowski'. [106] Ibid. 119.
[107] In an article quoted extensively by Bałaban, Ignacy Schwarzbart argued in favour of the continued campaign against *numerus clausus*, calling it an anti-democratic institution that was in opposition to the freedom of science and harmed the interests of the state by marginalizing and embittering a number of its citizens (Schwarzbart in *Nowy Dziennik*, 1 May 1924, cited in Bałaban, 'Kronika: O uniwersytet żydowski', 119).

debates about the need for creating new professional opportunities for the young, and their investment in the Hebrew University in Jerusalem, had much to do with the external realities of Jewish students' situation entering Polish universities. Already in the 1920s they faced repeated calls by non-Jewish students and faculty for limiting Polish Jews' access to universities in general and to medical and legal faculties in particular.[108]

Historians envisioned creating not only alternative academic centres but also international frameworks for Jewish studies. Schorr's and Bałaban's positions as members of the Governing Council of the Institute of Jewish Studies at the Hebrew University, representing the Polish Committee, offered them the opportunity to discuss the necessity of creating an organization uniting all aspects of Jewish studies. On behalf of the council, Schorr took the initial steps in proposing a World Congress of Jewish Studies, and he circulated his ideas among leading Jewish intellectuals worldwide.[109] At the meeting of the Governing Council of the Institute of Jewish Studies held in August 1928 in Basel, both Schorr and Bałaban argued in favour of the initiative, urging its immediate implementation.[110] Schorr stressed that a World Congress of Jewish Studies had become necessary due to the rapid growth of the field and as part of a spiritual renaissance of the Jewish people. He pointed out that 'such a congress will also convince the non-Jewish world of scholars about the existence of Jewish studies as an independent field of scholarship [*der wissenschaftliche Organismus*]'.[111] Schorr believed that a congress of Jewish studies would prove 'the unity and liveliness of Jewish civilization'.[112] He lobbied with Cyrus Adler for the support of this vision. Adler did not share Schorr's vision, and he responded with a list of practical reservations:

I think we have to admit that these international gatherings have not made for peace or friendship that they have also not brought out notable or important discoveries. They are largely taken up in the reading of general papers, in entertainment, they are expensive, they are troublesome, and I do not believe, in the present condition of the Jews and

---

[108] Mahler, 'Jews in Public Service and the Liberal Professions in Poland, 1918–39'.

[109] See CZA A354/45: Protokoll der 5. Sitzung des Verwaltungsrates der Judaistischen Instituts der Hebraeischen Universitaet in Jerusalem, Maintz, 27–28 Dec. 1927, p. 9. See also letters sent to Schorr by Martin Buber, J. Elbogen, Ussishkin, Cyrus Adler, A. Freimann, and I. Levi between May 1928 and January 1929, in response to his proposal for the congress, in CZA L12/32, 1–5: Gutachten ueber den vorgeschlagenen weltkongress fuer die Wissenschaft des Judentums.

[110] Bałaban, 'Historycy Żydzi i historycy żydowscy'; CZA A354/45: Protokoll der 6. Sitzung des Verwaltungsrates des Judaistischen Instituts an der Hebraischen Universitaet in Jerusalem, Basel, 21/22 Aug. 1928, pp. 6–8.

[111] CZA A354/45: Protokoll der 6. Sitzung des Verwaltungsrates des Judaistischen Instituts an der Hebraischen Universitaet in Jerusalem, Basel, 21/22 Aug. 1928, p. 6.

[112] See AAN, B'nai B'rith, file 3, p. 6: protocol of Schorr's lecture 'Organizacja nauk judaistycznych' given at a closed meeting of the Warsaw branch of B'nai B'rith, 1 Oct. 1928.

of Jewish scholarship such a Congress would repay either the energy or the expenditure of money. Moreover, these International Congresses get a good deal of their standing through Government patronage and official delegates which we could not expect or even want. What I have urged for a number of years is the formation in each country, where there is a group of Jewish scholars, of a local academy and when these academies become strong enough then I think there should be an Association of Academies.[113]

Schorr continued to discuss this matter at the seventy-fifth jubilee celebration of the Theological Seminary in Breslau in 1929, but, complained Bałaban, 'we have never been able to go beyond the framework of theories and ideas'.[114]

Jewish historians hoped the Congress would serve as a springboard for organizing a body to co-ordinate individual projects of scattered Jewish scholars, who complained about the lack of a structure to organize their individual efforts worldwide. Bałaban considered scholarly journals and institutions as the only arena that could bring scholars together; but these could only partially answer the need for an institution that would allow for personal scholarly exchange. He bemoaned that 'all the scholars have experienced for years ... [the] lack of personal communication and exchange of thoughts in a direct way and therefore many times the idea of calling a scholarly congress of Judaic studies was raised'.[115] Friedman enquired about holding a Jewish historians' conference in the autumn of 1929, in London, and his enquiry may reflect broader discussions about such an endeavour.[116] He also supported the idea of an international organization as an indispensable tool in co-ordinating historical research to avoid the neglect of certain issues in Jewish history. He wanted to ensure that all epochs and all issues were studied, lest they be taken over by non-Jews (*w ręku obcych*), leading to misconceptions about Jewish history among Jews and non-Jews.[117] He envisioned local chapters of a society of lovers of Jewish history (Towarzystwo Krzewienia Nauk Historycznych, or Towarzystwo Miłośników Historji Żydowskiej), bringing together the Jewish intelligentsia, in a similar way to existing non-Jewish historical associations, such as the Polish Historical Association (Polskie Towarzystwo Historyczne; PTH).[118] In 1933, he set up a scholarly historical seminar in Łódź, modelled on the Warsaw seminar, with the hope that these two together with a similar initiative in

---

[113] See copy of Adler's letter to Schorr, 9 Jan. 1929 (Philadelphia, University of Pennsylvania Libraries Special Collections, Arc MS 26 Cyrus Adler, box 96, f. 5). See also Schorr's Hebrew letter to Adler, dated 12 July 1928, and a letter of 22 Aug. 1928 to Adler from Louis Finkelstein, to whom Schorr had handed his memorandum in the summer of 1928, while in New York.

[114] Bałaban, 'Historycy Żydzi i historycy żydowscy'. The first World Congress of Jewish Studies was held at Hebrew University in Jerusalem in 1947.   [115] Ibid.

[116] In his letter to Salo Baron, Friedman expressed interest in coming to London to participate in the conference of 'Hebrew historians [*historyonim ivrim*]' in the autumn of 1929 (Engel, 'A Book Is Born' (Heb.), 156).   [117] Friedman, 'O zjazd historyków'.   [118] Ibid. 282.

Częstochowa would lead to creating a country-wide network of study groups, which would eventually join a world organization of Jewish studies.[119]

Friedman called on Jewish scholars to take advantage of the opportunity of gathering together at the Seventh International Congress of Historical Studies scheduled to meet in Warsaw in the summer of 1933.[120] Representatives of both the YIVO Institute and the Institute of Jewish Studies successfully negotiated an independent, though informal, status for the Jewish delegation from each institution. Handelsman's support must have played a crucial role in including two special sessions devoted to Jewish history at the Congress in Warsaw, as he was among its chief organizers.[121] Historians of Polish Jewry celebrated the presence of the small Jewish delegation at the Congress as a groundbreaking precedent for recognition of Jewish history as a separate field. Bałaban applauded the fact that the papers on Jewish history sparked great interest among participants of the Congress.[122] Yet the sessions reflected the ambiguous status of Jewish history in the academy. Only Jewish scholars from Poland and abroad participated in the discussion following all the 'Jewish' papers, with the notable exception of Hilarion Święcicki, a Ukrainian scholar from Lwów.[123] The discussions revealed differences in the ways Jewish scholars envisioned their professional organization. Arguing against the ghettoization of Jewish scholarship, Schorr opposed creating a separate section at the International Committee of Historical Studies, but sought rather to have Jewish history included in various national histories.[124] Schorr and Bałaban wanted to include scholars of broadly defined Jewish studies, while Mahler and Ringelblum opted for a 'strictly secular character of the association and thus uniting historians only'.[125] The discussions during the international historical congress in Warsaw led to the formation of a committee, including Bałaban, Schorr, Schiper, and Friedman, to co-operate with YIVO and the Hebrew University in creating an international organization of Jewish studies.[126]

[119] DRI, P 65, file 149: handwritten Hebrew letter from Filip Friedman to Abraham Duker in New York, dated in Łódź, 1 Jan. (?) 1934.

[120] Friedman, 'O zjazd historyków żydowskich', 283. In his letter to Abraham Duker, who was Salo Baron's doctoral student, Jacob Shatzky regretted that he was unable to participate in the congress as a result of financial constraints. See DRI, P 65, file 182: New York, 30 Aug. 1933.

[121] Ringelblum, 'Profesor Marceli Handelsman', 541; Bałaban, 'Historycy Żydzi i historycy żydowscy'. Ringelblum credited the Historical Section of YIVO with negotiating the inclusion of Jewish representation at the International Congress in Warsaw and its organizing committee in August 1933. R[ingelblum], 'Historja Żydów na VII Międzynarodowym Zjeździe', 258.

[122] Bałaban, 'Po 7 kongresie historyków w Warszawie'.

[123] See R[ingelblum], 'Historja Żydów na VII Międzynarodowym Zjeździe', 259. Although Ringelblum mentioned 'prof. M. Swiecicki', he most probably meant Hilarion Święcicki, a Ukrainian philologist, museum manager, and art historian.

[124] R[ingelblum], 'Historja Żydów na VII Międzynarodowym Zjeździe', 260.   [125] Ibid.
[126] Ibid.

## Research and Publishing on Polish Jewish History: Sources and Archives

Polish Jewish historians bemoaned the sorry state of Jewish historical relics and the lack of appreciation for the importance of Jewish documents.[127] Throughout the 1920s and 1930s, they appealed to scholars to undertake systematic searches in various archives and to catalogue the available materials. Bałaban repeatedly appealed for the organization of the Central Archives of Polish Jews in Warsaw, to ensure the safety of the most valuable historical materials, especially Jewish communal archives and records. He also argued for the establishment of a library, a museum, and workshops to create a complete infrastructure for advanced scholarship in Jewish history. Bałaban hoped to secure future historical research on the private lives of Polish Jewish individuals and their communities.[128] In May 1929, on Bałaban's initiative, the Warsaw branch of B'nai B'rith discussed organizing an exhibition of Jewish antiquities. Schorr supported the idea, pointing to the political importance of such an exhibition, 'which will show clearly that we are not strangers in Poland but that we have been living in this land since the dawn of its history, and for many generations we have been sharing the fate of this country'. The meeting also discussed organizing an association to care for Jewish monuments, or, as suggested by Schorr, using the template of such an organization already existing in Lwów, but broadening its scope to the whole country.[129] This apologetic impetus would only intensify in the 1930s. In 1930, Bałaban envisioned creating a Central Archives of Polish Jewry at the Institute of Jewish Studies and a Museum of Jewish Monuments at the National Museum or Jewish Museum in Warsaw.[130] These initiatives sought to demonstrate the creativity and longevity of the Jewish communities in the Polish lands.

The new cohort of professional Jewish historians followed up on these ideas, envisioning institutions necessary for the preservation of Jewish historical documents and monuments, which would ensure future historical research.[131] Seidman took an interest in the communal archives in Tarnopol and Warsaw, as well as in private libraries containing rare manuscripts. Following his graduation in 1937, Seidman worked in the archives of the Jewish community in Warsaw, drafting blueprints for its modernization and for 'rationally organized Jewish archives', as the condition for any further development of Jewish historical research. He argued that the treasures of the Warsaw community archives should become

---

[127] See Seidman, 'Archiwum Gminy Żydowskiej w Warszawie', 70–2.
[128] Bałaban, 'Wiedza żydowska i jej uczelnie w Polsce' and *Zabytki historyczne Żydów w Polsce*.
[129] AAN, B'nai B'rith, file 3, pp. 38–9: protocol of a closed meeting on 13 May 1929.
[130] Bałaban, 'Zadania i potrzeby historjografji Żydów w Polsce', i. 119.
[131] See Berman, 'The Tasks of the Historical Section' (Yid.), 19.

accessible to historians, scholars, statisticians, and politicians. Ultimately, Seidman hoped Warsaw's Jewish communal archives would become the basis for a future Central Jewish Archives in Poland. This new institution, located in the country's capital, would be charged with acquiring and storing valuable documents from Warsaw and from communities lacking proper space to accommodate them, writing inventories, registers, and extracts, and also summarizing the documents in general Polish archives.[132] In Seidman's vision, the Central Archives '[would] become a scholarly hotbed for a host of historians especially of the young generation and the practitioners of scholarship, who will find here a convenient place of work and sometimes a field which has lain fallow'.[133]

Professional historians recognized the obstacles to gaining access to state, institutional, and private archives. Regulations and the need for letters of recommendation and formal authorization limited access to university libraries and state and municipal archives. Academic recognition, university appointments, and personal reputation played an essential role in making these sources available to Jewish historians.[134] Thus, the new affiliation of Jewish research with established universities opened new possibilities for research. Yet in order to become part of the scholarly discourse, new scholarship on Polish Jewish history needed a platform.

## Academic Publishing

Jewish historians created journals as platforms for scholarly discussion and for sharing the results of their research. The border between scholarly publication and popular presentation of historical material was sometimes porous. The choice of language reflected not only the ideological agenda of the editors, but also the audience they wanted to address. Bałaban participated in several initiatives to set up scholarly journals in Polish, most notably, *Nowe Życie*, in 1924, which he edited,

---

[132] See Seidman, 'Archiwum Gminy Żydowskiej w Warszawie', 70–5.

[133] Ibid. 75. Aside from Warsaw, B'nai B'rith took an interest in the exhibition of Jewish books and monuments in Lwów. See 'Ze sprawozdania Stowarzyszenia "Leopolis" B'nai B'rith we Lwowie', 29. See also Zarrow, 'Object Lessons'.

[134] Hillel Seidman received letters of recommendation from his teachers at Warsaw University, among others. A letter of recommendation by Wałek Czarnecki, dated 22 Feb. 1933, describes Seidman as a member of his seminar who specializes in the Jews' attitude to the Graeco-Roman world, and confirms his skills. There are also two letters of recommendation written for Seidman as a recent graduate of Warsaw University in support of his application for the position of archivist in the archives of the Jewish community in Warsaw (Archiwum oraz Muzeum Gminy Żydowskiej): from Schorr, dated 6 June 1937, and from Zmigryder-Konopka, dated 1 June 1937. Seidman's certificate, written by Rabbi Professor Dr S. A. Taubeles and dated in Tarnopol on 20 May 1933, stating that he had worked for quite some time in the local Jewish archives founded and named after J. Perl, also survives. All these documents have been made available to me by Mrs Sarah Seidman.

and *Miesięcznik Żydowski*, published from 1930 until 1935 and edited by Zygmunt Ellenberg,[135] which served as a forum for established and younger scholars, but also aimed at educating a broader reading public.

The most notable of the journals in Yiddish were the four volumes—two each of *Yunger historiker* and *Bleter far geshikhte*—published by the Young Historians Circle in Warsaw.[136] These volumes were devoted to lengthy studies, which limited the number of authors they could accommodate. Among those who did publish here were Feldman, Krämer, and Rosenblatt, participants in the activities of the Young Historians Circle. They had searched for an opportunity to publish in Yiddish, allowing them to reach a segment of the Jewish audience different from those who read *Miesięcznik Żydowski*. The Jewish student self-help organization funded the first volume.[137] In 1934, at the time of the economic crisis, it took a great effort to collect the money to cover the cost of printing and paper. The third volume of *Yunger historiker* (now the first volume of *Bleter far geshikhte*) was financed by individual subscribers from Poland and abroad along with a subsidy from the board of the Jewish community of Kutno.[138] But the journal continued to struggle with the lack of funding. In December 1936, Ringelblum wrote to Abraham Duker complaining that the journal 'does not come out. There is no money for publishing.'[139]

Ellenberg introduced *Miesięcznik Żydowski* as 'a serious Jewish monthly ... representative of Polish Jewry comparable to the American *Menora* or the German *Der Jude*'.[140] This ambitious vision expressed a transnational perspective on Polish Jewish history by the Polish Jewish intelligentsia. Indeed, Eugenia Prokop-Janiec has lauded the journal as 'one of the most valuable and ambitious Polish-Jewish periodicals'.[141] The publication of *Miesięcznik Żydowski* was a response to the lack of periodicals exclusively 'devoted to the substantial and universal examination of the issues of Jewish life and culture ... [bringing] together academics and critics, literary figures, and Jewish artists'.[142] The journal aspired to offer a non-partisan platform and describe all aspects of Jewish life objectively as a general Jewish journal. Apart from contemporary issues, the editors paid close attention to the Jewish

---

[135] See Fuks, *Prasa żydowska w Warszawie*, 285–9.
[136] For the new journal's agendas see 'From the Editors' (Yid.), *Yunger historiker*, 1 (1926), 6.
[137] 'From the Editors' (Yid.), *Yunger historiker*, 1 (1926), 6.
[138] 'From the Editors' (Yid.), *Bleter far geshikhte*, 1 (1934), 4.
[139] DRI, P 65, file 169: copy of a typed Yiddish letter dated 6 Dec. 1936.
[140] Stanford University Libraries, Special Collections and University Archives, M0580, box 1, folder 5, a letter from Ellenberg to Salo Baron, dated from Zawoja, 25 July 1930. I would like to thank Professor David Engel for making this document available to me.
[141] Prokop-Janiec, *Polish-Jewish Literature in the Interwar Years*, 11.
[142] *Miesięcznik Żydowski*, 'Prospekt', undated, 2, as cited in Borzymińska, '*Miesięcznik Żydowski*: w 50 rocznicę wydania pierwszego numeru', 63–4.

past in Poland.¹⁴³ The journal promised to present academic research in an 'independent spirit,'¹⁴⁴ and drew together writers who shared the desire to address both the Polish and Jewish intelligentsia. Wilhelm (Ze'ev) Berkelhammer of the contemporary *Nowy Dziennik* asserted that the editors understood that their audience consisted of 'Jewish classes which [are] limited to just the language of the country, as well as . . . non-Jewish society with which we must maintain a constant and comprehensive contact'.¹⁴⁵ The journal worked to fulfil a crucial need for Jews who felt comfortable in Polish, by providing them with information about the Jewish past and present, as well as materials for intellectual reflection on their Jewish identity and culture. The editors sought to provide an 'objective scholarly critique', making the journal a venue for discussing general and Polish Jewish history,¹⁴⁶ and including articles by leading historians as well as Bałaban's students.

The editors of *Miesięcznik Żydowski* also hoped to serve 'Polish society and all people of good will, giving them the chance to get acquainted with the problems of [Jewish] life and [Jewish] culture'.¹⁴⁷ Bałaban argued that 'the monthly was assigned the apologetic task of properly informing the Polish-Christian intelligentsia about issues of [Jewish] life of which it usually knew nothing'.¹⁴⁸ They welcomed the participation of the most enlightened Poles who would also potentially submit articles for publication in the new journal.¹⁴⁹ *Miesięcznik Żydowski* was to become a tool in overcoming misunderstandings between Poles and Jews, and it represented the hope of building 'two kinds of "bridges"'.¹⁵⁰ Funding for the journal came mainly from the Warsaw and other chapters of B'nai B'rith, true to that organization's obligation to support Jewish scholarship in Poland, as well as from individual donations.¹⁵¹ Despite the financial backing, *Miesięcznik Żydowski* struggled throughout its existence, as its subscribers remained limited almost entirely to the members of B'nai B'rith.¹⁵² The journal never reached Bałaban's

---

¹⁴³ AAN, B'nai B'rith, file 3, p. 96: the protocol from the closed meeting of the members of 'Braterstwo-B'nai Brith', 24 Nov. 1930.      ¹⁴⁴ *Miesięcznik Żydowski*, 'Prospekt', undated, 3.

¹⁴⁵ Wilhelm Berkelhammer, 'Pierwszy tom Miesięcznika Żydowskiego', quoted in Prokop-Janiec, *Polish-Jewish Literature in the Interwar Years*, 11.

¹⁴⁶ See the exchange between Grossfeld, Schorr, and Bałaban, AAN, B'nai B'rith, file 3, 'Protokół zebrania zamkniętego członków Stowarzyszenia Humanitarnego "Braterstwo-B'nai Brith"', 96–9, 24 Nov. 1930.      ¹⁴⁷ *Miesięcznik Żydowski*, 'Prospekt', undated, 4.

¹⁴⁸ Bałaban, '"Miesięcznik Żydowski": Na marginesie dwóch roczników', quoted in Prokop-Janiec, *Polish-Jewish Literature in the Interwar Years*, 11.      ¹⁴⁹ *Miesięcznik Żydowski*, 'Prospekt', undated, 4.

¹⁵⁰ Steinlauf, 'The Polish-Jewish Daily Press', 229. See also Chapter 4 below.

¹⁵¹ See AAN, B'nai B'rith, file 4, p. 42: protocol from the meeting chaired by M. Tauber on 3 Mar. 1934.

¹⁵² In 1929 B'nai B'rith had 927 members. See 'Sprawozdanie z V Posiedzenia Komitetu Generalnego Związku Żydowskich Stowarzyszeń Humanitarnych B'nai B'rith w Rzeczypospolitej Polskiej w Krakowie, odbytego w Warszawie dnia 6 maja 1929 r.', 17.

minimum goal of 1,000 subscribers,[153] and in 1935 it ceased publication due to financial difficulties. Filip Friedman summed it up concisely in his letter to Abraham Duker in New York, 'There is no money. Too bad.'[154] After the journal's demise, leaders of B'nai B'rith repeatedly discussed the need for creating a similar annual publication.[155]

Bałaban's students and members of the Young Historians Circle who began their professional careers in the 1930s struggled to have their work published, since Jewish publishers could not afford to invest in books on Jewish history.[156] A growing number of university-trained historians who carried out research on the history of Polish Jewry saw publishing in Yiddish, Polish, Hebrew, and German—and less frequently in other European languages—as an essential part of building and contributing to their field. The young Jewish scholars lacked the opportunity that the Wawelberg Prize at the University of Lwów had offered to Schorr, Bałaban, and Schiper before the First World War. In general, as Eliezer Feldman remarked, 'it is almost impossible to dream about publishing work dealing with Jews and written by a Jew, by non-Jewish factors'.[157] YIVO and the Institute of Jewish Studies offered limited opportunities for publishing, even as both struggled with economic difficulties threatening their existence. The Institute began publishing a Hebrew and Polish series entitled *Pisma Instytutu Nauk Judaistycznych*, with lengthy historical studies by Bałaban and Schiper. Hopes for an ambitious multi-volume edition of communal monographs and archival sources under the auspices of the Institute's Scholarship Commission (Komisja Naukowa), with the participation of Jewish students in all university centres in Poland, never materialized.[158] YIVO published historical research in its Library series. In a sense, the Institute and YIVO aspired to the same goal, with the Institute building a strong student body and YIVO building a series of periodical publications and only then developing its training element.

Despite these efforts, Feldman observed, 'Conditions in Jewish society in Poland result in the situation that publishing "Jewish" research in general and

---

[153] AAN, B'nai B'rith, file 3, pp. 162–3: protocol from the closed session chaired by Mayzel on 5 Oct. 1931.  [154] DRI, P 65: file 149, 11 Nov. 1936.
[155] See AAN, B'nai B'rith, file 4, pp. 190–1: protocol of a meeting on 27 Feb. 1937. See also Tauber's recommendation, expressed at a closed meeting chaired by Seidenman on 25 Nov. 1937, ibid. 212. For comparison see Kruk's comments about the circulation of the YIVO scholarly publications: 1,755 subscribers in 210 cities and towns. 'The actual number of subscribers is much larger because these figures don't include such cultural centers as Warsaw, Łódź, Kraków, and Białystok, which have undertaken to enlist larger numbers of subscribers. Warsaw alone distributed 100 copies of the third volume of *Historishe shriftn*. In fact, we must count more than 2,000 subscribers to YIVO publications' (Kruk, *The Last Days of the Jerusalem of Lithuania*, 41).
[156] Blumental, 'A Profile of Bela' (Heb.), 27.   [157] Feldman, 'Dzieje Żydów w Warszawie'.
[158] See Schorr, 'Stan i potrzeby wiedzy żydowskiej w dobie dzisiejszej', p. xx.

especially in the field of history, is very rare. Poland lacks a Jewish scholarly and publishing institution which would centralize and subsidize research and research work.'[159] Schorr published his doctoral dissertation as an offprint of *Kwartalnik Historyczny*, the most prestigious Polish historical journal at the time, and Bałaban's doctoral dissertation was published through the aforementioned Wawelberg prize. Only thanks to a fellowship received through Salo Baron from the Dr S. A. Bettelheim Memorial Foundation in the United States could Filip Friedman eventually publish his dissertation in Germany, in 1929.[160]

Two genres had the best chance of getting subvention support from the Jewish community: projects focusing on a local Jewish community or institution, and publications devoted to the Jewish role in Poland's struggles for independence. In 1936, the board of the Progressive Synagogue in Stanisławów published a modest brochure celebrating its history.[161] In the second half of the 1930s, the board of the liberal synagogue (Templum) in Bałaban's native Lwów commissioned him to write a study of its history. Their choice was based not only on Bałaban's familiarity with the synagogue of his youth, but also on his prestige. Indeed, the chairman of the Templum expressed the conviction that scientific work by a historian was the most fitting way of celebrating the hundredth anniversary of the synagogue's founding, hoping that the book would 'find its place in the home of each and every member of the synagogue's board as well as in wide circles of our society in Lwów'.[162] Bałaban realized that historians could reach out to liberal Jewish communities for funding for historical writing, and he suggested continuing the work he started with the study of the liberal synagogue in Lwów: 'Publishing this book should become an example for the Warsaw synagogue, with the sixty years that have passed now since its founding at Tłomackie [Street].'[163] On the eve of the Second World War, on 3 July 1939, Bałaban signed a contract with the Jewish community in Lwów for a monograph under the working title *Historia Żydów lwowskich od najdawniejszych czasów (XIV wiek) do czasów najnowszych* (History of Lwów Jewry from the Oldest until the Latest Times).[164]

---

[159] Feldman, 'Dzieje Żydów w Warszawie', 521.

[160] Friedman, *Die galizischen Juden*. On Friedman's difficulties and the circumstances of the publication see Engel, 'A Book Is Born' (Heb.), 141–2, and the letters, 144–56.

[161] Streit, *Dzieje Wielkiej Miejskiej Synagogi w Stanisławowie*.

[162] Wasser, 'Słowo wstępne', in Bałaban, *Historia lwowskiej synagogi postępowej*, pp. iii–iv, quotation from p. iv.

[163] See AAN, B'nai B'rith, file 4, p. 222: closed meeting chaired by Seidenman on 25 Nov. 1937.

[164] On the basis of the agreement between the author and the Jewish community, represented by Michał Ringel, Bałaban promised to prepare the manuscript of the book by 1 May 1940. See Central State Historical Archives of Ukraine, L'viv (Tsentalnyi derzhavnyi istorychnyi akkhiv Ukraiiny m. L'viv), fond 701, opis 4, sprava 237, 1; see also Chonigsman and Wierzbieniec, 'Z badań nad lwowskim okresem działalności naukowej, dydaktycznej i społecznej Mojżesza Schorra', 233. The Lwów com-

Other historians also recognized the potential for writing local studies with the support of local Jewish communities. In fact, the only thesis written in Bałaban's seminar to appear as a book before the Second World War was another local study, published thanks to the financial support from leaders of the local Jewish community: Dawid Wurm's monograph on the Jews of Brody.[165] The Jewish community of Łódź also funded a monograph on the old Jewish cemetery in the city, edited by Friedman. In the introduction to the volume, Jakub Lejb Mincberg, the chairman of the Jewish community, member of the city council in Łódź on behalf of Agudat Israel, and Jewish representative in the Polish parliament, expressed the idea that the best way to celebrate the 125 years since the founding of the first Jewish communal institution in the city was to fund a history of the Jewish community. Mincberg hoped that 'this modest contribution to the history of Jewish culture in Poland will not be without meaning for a future scholar of the history of Polish Jewry'.[166] In 1939, the Jewish community in Żółkiew published Jakub Schall's monograph on the history of the town's Jewish inhabitants.[167]

Jewish cultural associations, especially the Jewish Tourist Association in Poland (Landkentnish or Żydowskie Towarzystwo Krajoznawcze), also had a vested interest in sponsoring regional and local studies.[168] Despite limited financial resources, in 1935 the Jewish Tourist Association published Friedman's study of the history of the Jews in Łódź.[169] All these publications appeared in Polish, probably the language of choice of the organizations and institutions supplying the funding. B'nai B'rith also commissioned works of history, aspiring to represent an apolitical stance and promising to stay away from religious controversy.[170] Thanks to his association with B'nai B'rith in Poland, Bałaban received grants

munity appointed a special historical committee to oversee the publication of a monograph about the Jews in Lwów, which set the requirements and probably searched for the appropriate candidate. This was reported at the meeting of the 'historical committee' of YIVO/Historians Circle of April 1938. See *YIVO Bleter*, 46 (1980), 302, document 11.

[165] Wurm, *Z dziejów żydostwa brodzkiego*, pp. iii–ix.
[166] J. L. Mincberg, introduction to Friedman, *Stary cmentarz żydowski w Łodzi*, 11–12.
[167] Schall, *Dawna Żółkiew i jej Żydzi*.
[168] See Kassow, 'Travel and Local History as a National Mission'.
[169] Friedman, *Dzieje Żydów w Łodzi*, 8.
[170] Mateusz Mieses belonged to the 'Humanitas' chapter of B'nai B'rith in Przemyślu. As part of the work in the cultural-educational field, B'nai B'rith published his booklet *Hellenizm a Judaizim*: 'the first serious and scholarly negative response to the book of Zieliński'. The chapter also provided funds for the Institute of Judaic Studies and its own library in Przemyśl. See 'Ze sprawozdania Stow. "Humanitas" w Przemyślu', 31. Its Kraków chapter turned to Bałaban as 'the most eminent specialist of that subject' requesting that he write a guide to Jewish antiquities in Kraków. See the foreword, signed by 'Stowarzyszenie "Solidarność-B'nai B'rith" w Krakowie', to Bałaban, *Przewodnik po żydowskich zabytkach Krakowa*, p. viii.

and commissions for his publications. At a meeting in May 1929, the General Committee decided to fund Bałaban's study of Jews in Kraków.[171] In this climate of difficulty in getting published, Bałaban's successes were the cause of some resentment. The art historian Zofia Ameisen referred to this work when she bitterly complained about the difficulties of publishing her own work: 'In Poland one does not receive an author's fee unless one is Bałaban. His *History of Kraków Jews* ... has been subsidized by the lodges [of B'nai B'rith] and it is only thanks to this that it was published at all.'[172] When Bałaban's sixtieth birthday was approaching, the Warsaw lodge of B'nai B'rith, 'Braterstwo', decided to raise money and cover the expenses of a book of Bałaban's choice.[173]

Jewish professional organizations also took an interest in historical scholarship. Schiper published his volume on the history of Jewish commerce in Polish lands with the financial assistance of the Central Merchants' Association (Centrala Związku Kupców w Warszawie). With the upcoming thirtieth anniversary of the association's founding in 1906, the organization turned to Schiper in mid-1934, commissioning him to write a study on the history of Jewish trade in Poland, with a focus on contemporary history, especially the history of Centrala.[174] Schall's monograph on the history of the Jewish community in Żółkiew, published by the town's Jewish community, also received subsidy from the local guild of Jewish shoemakers.[175] This funding came with expectations of historical publications documenting the achievements and the role of the organization. A laudatory tone was an inevitable price to be paid for their support.

Although Jewish charitable and professional organizations tended to support well-established scholars like Bałaban and Schiper, their willingness to fund authors of Jewish history and the publication of their books suggest a potential alliance between Jewish scholarship and communal activists. Such an alliance would of course create tensions, due to differences of opinion and expectations about the nature of historical work. In some cases, historians steered popular initiatives in a more scholarly direction. Schiper persuaded his benefactors at

---

[171] Ultimately published in two volumes as *Historja Żydów w Krakowie i na Kazimierzu 1304–1868*. See 'Sprawozdanie z V Posiedzenia Komitetu Generalnego Związku Żydowskich Stowarzyszeń Humanitarnych B'nai B'rith w Rzeczypospolitej Polskiej w Krakowie', 15–16.

[172] CAHJP, P 9, file 97: letter from Zofia Ameisen, dated 3 May 1934, Kraków.

[173] See AAN, B'nai B'rith, file 4, p. 188: protocol from the meeting chaired by Tauber in February 1933, p. 42.    [174] Schiper, 'Słowo wstępne', in id., *Dzieje handlu żydowskiego*, p. v.

[175] In the introduction to his book, Schall thanked several individuals and organizations for making the publication possible: the Jewish Furriers' Guild (Cech Kuśnierzy żydowskich) in Żółkiew and its senior member (Józef Meister), The Jewish Association of the Lovers of Culture and Art in Żółkiew (Żydowskie Towarzystwo Miłośników Kultury i Sztuki w Żółkwi) and its chairman (pharmacist Adolf Friedman), the president of the Jewish community (Dr Febus Rubinfeld) and its board, and Lwów rabbi Jehezkiel Lewin. See Schall, 'Przedmowa', in id., *Dawna Żółkiew i jej Żydzi*, 3–4.

Centrala to sponsor a large survey on the history of Jewish trade.[176] Such was also the case with Bałaban's commemorative album devoted to Berek Joselewicz.[177]

Historical anniversaries offered opportunities for both individual studies and collective efforts. These attempts were not always successful; even with an impressive committee of backers, funding remained a challenge.[178] It was not only the historians trained in the 1920s and 1930s but even Schiper and Bałaban who struggled to find financial resources for scholarly publications such as critical editions of sources. In 1936, having been commissioned by Leon Tenenbaum, the president of the Jewish community in Drohobycz, Schiper produced a manuscript about the history of the Jews in that town. Although the community paid his honorarium of 400 zloty, it could not afford the cost of publishing the book. Depositing the manuscript in the communal archives, the community decided to postpone publication.[179]

In *Miesięcznik Żydowski*, Feldman described the riches of the work originating in the Young Historians Circle but hinted that it might not find publishers: 'Dr Ringelblum and a whole Pleiad of other young scholars have a plethora of works ready for print, such as a monograph on the Jews in Mazovia, in Lublin, Poznań, Kalisz, works of statistics about Jews in Poland in the sixteenth to eighteenth centuries and more.' Feldman hoped to encourage the establishment of a publishing house for Jewish scholarship in Poland.[180] The second volume of Bałaban's Festschrift, as envisioned by his students, was to encompass excerpts from their theses.[181] Speaking on behalf of Bałaban's students, Samuel Jolles declared that 'making these studies available to a wide circle of scholars became over the years one of [Bałaban's] most pressing concerns'.[182] Other publications by his students appeared in journals and the daily press.

The authors of local studies also sometimes failed to find a publisher and funding. The first volume of Ringelblum's monograph on the history of the Warsaw Jewish community was published thanks to a grant from the city council, rather than the Jewish community; but the second volume—despite explicit

---

[176] Schiper, 'Słowo wstępne', p. v.     [177] Bałaban, 'Przedmowa', in id., *Album Pamiątkowy*, 6.

[178] An example is the attempt to publish a study of the work of Shmuel Lehman. Lehman was the most prolific collector of Yiddish folklore between the wars. Leading Jewish scholars, including Ringelblum and Schiper, celebrated his thirty years of fieldwork in 1932. They printed a collection of his materials in book form to help raise money for the publication of a full-length study of his work, which never materialized. See Gottesman, *Defining the Yiddish Nation*, 11–28.

[179] The manuscript was lost when Dr Tenenbaum took it with him to the ghetto in the attempt to protect it. Hirschaut, 'Dr I. Schiper—His Life and Work (1884–1943)' (Yid.), 248–9.

[180] Feldman, 'Dzieje Żydów w Warszawie', 522.

[181] 'Prace Magisterskie pisane w seminarium hist. żyd. Profesora Bałabana, które będą drukowane w części drugiej Księgi Jubileuszowej', in Jolles (ed.), *Księga jubileuszowa Bałabana*, 102–4.

[182] See 'Od redakcji', in Jolles (ed.), *Księga jubileuszowa Bałabana*, 5.

appeals in the Jewish press by Schiper and Feldman—remained in manuscript form. It was buried and preserved in the Oyneg Shabes Archives of the Warsaw ghetto.[183] Bela Mandelsberg's monograph on the Jewish community in Lublin, which she struggled to complete and publish due to financial constraints, was eventually lost, together with the material she had collected.[184] Ultimately, the growing numbers of professional Jewish historians in interwar Poland relied on journals and newspapers to publish both archival sources and their research. Friedman published fragments of his work on Łódź in Polish and Jewish journals, never expecting to see his work in book form due to the financial situation in the publishing market.[185] Publishing in newspapers was not only the result of technical and financial constraints, but to a certain extent also a matter of preference, reflecting the conviction that scholarly work by trained historians was of relevance to the broader Jewish community of Poland. For instance, Bałaban's study of Jewish historical monuments, published by the Institute of Jewish Studies, had appeared almost a decade earlier in Polish and Yiddish newspapers.[186] However, the dependence of the burgeoning field on private and institutional funding raised the crucial question of how to maintain scholarly objectivity in historical research supported by private monies.

## Jewish Historians and the Polish Academy

Apart from formal and informal Jewish scholarly networks and institutions, the field of Polish Jewish history functioned inside Polish academia. Bałaban's formal appointments at Warsaw University, and at Wolna Wszechnica from 1933, and Schorr's professorship at Warsaw University, placed them at the very heart of the country's historical milieu. Moreover, Jewish students received training with a number of distinguished historians. As the Jewish academic infrastructure in Poland created a forum for discussing research questions and methodology, it also safeguarded the future of the field by training Jews to write as professional historians.

Why did the writing of the history of Polish Jewry require an academic mantle? The status of Jewish historians within the Polish academy gave them authority when addressing both Polish and Jewish audiences, especially professional ones, allowing them to discuss the Jewish past in Poland on equal terms with their Polish counterparts, to correct mistakes, and to fight omissions and misrepresen-

---

[183] The manuscript was found 1950 (Kassow, *Who Will Write Our History?*, 66). See Schiper, 'The Earliest History of the Warsaw Jews'; Feldman, 'Dzieje Żydów w Warszawie', 528.

[184] Blumental, 'A Profile of Bela' (Heb.), 26.    [185] Friedman, *Dzieje Żydów w Łodzi*, 8.

[186] See Bałaban, 'Wstęp', in id., *Zabytki historyczne Żydów w Polsce*, 3. The work had appeared in the Polish *Tygodnik Żydowski* and the Yiddish *Nayer haynt*.

tations. With their training, Jewish historians hoped to enter the general historical discourse, inform Polish scholars, and encourage research into Polish Jewish history. Opinions expressed by Polish historians mattered beyond the confines of academia. In the Second Polish Republic, historians occupied official positions and helped shape political decisions for the country. They served as ministers (Franciszek Bujak), managed departments in ministries (Bronisław Dembiński), held seats in the Diet (Władysław Konopczyński), and trained the Polish military elite (Marian Kukiel). The academic context gave the historians of the Jews the tools and the opportunity to argue for the inclusion of Jews in Polish history.

Jewish scholars strove for recognition in the academy, emphasizing the inclusion of Jewish history in Poland as a part of Polish history. Ultimately, the inclusion or exclusion of professional Jewish historians from Polish academia went beyond an intellectual project, becoming a national mission. Once Jewish historians' work became a legitimate part of Polish history and historiography, it would arguably signify contemporary Jews becoming a part of the Polish Republic. The line between the academic and the popular, therefore, remained constantly blurred. What was at stake went beyond the academy, but the path to achieving it led through academic inclusion and recognition.

Jewish historians scored some successes in their pursuit of academic inclusion. Several professional historians of Polish Jewry, like Bałaban and Schorr, joined national and local Polish historical associations. The two participated in the activities of the PTH, founded in 1886 in Lwów, whose main goal was 'uniting all Polish historians and lovers of history in Poland'. Friedman belonged to the chapter of the association in Łódź, while Mahler, Ringelblum, and Feldman joined the Association of History Lovers (Towarzystwo Miłośników Historii; TMH), founded in Warsaw in 1906, which functioned as a Warsaw chapter of the PTH.[187] Ringelblum also belonged to the Polish Commission for the History of Social Movements, part of an international research effort to collect bibliography and archival material, and prepare scholarly publications. His colleagues on the committee included leading Polish historians and sociologists known for their

---

[187] The first post-war volume of *Kwartalnik Historyczny* published obituaries of several members of Polskie Towarzystwo Historyczne and scholars who had died during the war years ('Wspomnienia o pracownikach naukowych i członkach PTH zmarłych w latach 1939–1945'). These included articles on Bałaban and Schorr. See Pieradzka, 'Majer Bałaban', and Patkaniowski 'Mojżesz Schorr'. The first post-war issue of *Przegląd Historyczny* published the list of the members who lost their lives during the years 1939–1945, including Ringelblum and Mahler. See 'Lista zmarłych członków w latach 1939–1945', *Przegląd Historyczny*, 36 (1946), 196. See also 'Członkowie Towarzystwa Miłośników Historii w 1946 r' in the same issue (pp. 198–9), which included Eleazar Feldman. Thus Jewish professional historians participated in general Polish associations. For more on the PTH see Rachuba and Rutkowski (eds.), *Towarzystwo Miłośników Historii: Stulecie 1906–2006*; Bujak, 'Kilka uwag w sprawie dalszego rozwoju Polskiego Towarzystwa Historycznego'.

liberal or left-wing political leanings.[188] Jewish historians were also active in local historical associations. Along with others, Bałaban was among the core members of Association of the Lovers of Lwów's History (Towarzystwo Miłośników Przeszłości Lwowa), created in 1906.[189]

Jewish scholars depended on Polish historians who occupied leading positions in the country's professional associations to include their field in discussions on Polish historiography. A few Jewish historians participated in conventions organized by the Polish Historical Association. While their presence at these conventions constituted a statement about the status of Polish Jewish history, participation was limited to just a few; and of those who participated, even fewer spoke as historians of Polish Jewry. In June 1900 Bersohn, Kraushar, and Schorr took part in the Third Congress of Polish Historians in Kraków, where the latter presented a paper about the state of research on Polish Jewish history, commissioned by Fink.[190] Bałaban, Schorr, and Kraushar participated in the Fourth Congress of Polish Historians in December 1925, bringing together historians for the first time in the newly re-established Polish state. Although none of the papers in Poznań addressed Polish Jewish historiography, Bałaban participated in the discussions and reminded his colleagues about Jewish aspects of Polish economic and cultural history.[191] Five years later, at the Fifth Congress of Polish Historians in Warsaw, probably with Handelsman's support, Bałaban spoke about the goals and needs of the historiography of Polish Jewry.[192] At the last Congress of the Second Polish Republic, convened in Wilno in September 1935, neither Bałaban nor Schorr was present and no discussion of Polish Jewish history took place.[193]

Academic credentials helped to secure academic recognition of the research that Jewish historians carried out, without obliterating their national identity as Jews. At a meeting of the executive board of the Organizational Committee of the

---

[188] See APAN, PTH, I-3, j. [folder] 143, pp. 48–9: 'Protokół zebrania organizacyjnego Polskiej Komisji Historii Ruchów Społecznych 18 i 19 stuleci', 1 Dec. 1933, w lokalu Tow. Miłośników Historii.

[189] Bałaban joined the association together with such leading Polish historians as Władysław Abraham, Oswald Balzer, and Ludwik Finkel. See Charewiczowa, 'Towarzystwo Miłośników Przeszłości Lwowa', pp. ix–x. Bałaban published his study on Lwów as part of the association's series Biblioteka Lwowska, published from 1907, which was distributed in the schools as an annual prize (see ibid., p. xi). The association was revived in the Second Polish Republic. See *Statut Towarzystwa Miłośników Przeszłości Lwowa*.      [190] Schorr, 'Historya Żydów w Polsce', 1–3.

[191] Following a lecture by Mieczysław Gębarowicz, 'W sprawie badań nad historją sztuki i kultury wczesnego średniowiecza polskiego', at the first session of Section V, on 6 Dec. 1925, Bałaban reminded Gębarowicz of the close link between Jewish monuments and Polish cultural monuments (*Pamiętnik IV*, ii. 108).      [192] Bałaban, 'Zadania i potrzeby historjografji Żydów w Polsce', i. 115–21.

[193] Menachem (Edmund) Stein spoke at the Congress, but his subject was ancient history. See *Pamiętnik VI*. The next congress was planned to convene in Lwów in 1940, though I have not been able to locate the list of invited speakers. See APAN, PTH, I-3, j. [folder] 143, p. 4a: 'Projekt organizacji VII Powszechnego Zjazdu Historyków Polskich we Lwowie 1940' (typed, undated, unsigned).

International Congress of Historical Studies in June 1933, on Handelsman's initiative the committee decided to allow 'faculty members of a Polish university of non-Polish nationality' (Bałaban, Schorr, Korduba, and Święcicki) to publish their lectures in the Polish proceedings from the Congress.[194] The existence of the field of Polish Jewish history as part of a larger project on Polish culture was acknowledged when the Polish Ministry of Foreign Affairs discussed the possibility of supporting a chair of Polish Jewish history at the Hebrew University in Jerusalem in 1934–5. It also proposed three candidates for the prestigious position: Bałaban, Schiper, and Gelber.[195] However, Polish diplomats in Palestine reported not only the high cost of such an enterprise but also an ambivalent response from the Hebrew University. Thus, in the summer of 1935, the political department of the Polish Ministry supported the idea of a lectureship in Polish language and literature, pending the solution of how to finance it.[196]

Since the beginning of their academic careers, Schorr, Bałaban, and Schiper had published their work in leading Polish scholarly journals, especially the Lwów-based *Kwartalnik Historyczny* and the Warsaw-based *Przegląd Historyczny*. In this way they made an unambiguous statement about the place of Jewish history within a broader Polish historical narrative and shared their findings with non-Jewish Polish historians. However, only a handful of articles on Polish Jewish history appeared in the pages of these prestigious journals between the two world

[194] See APAN, PTH, I-3, j. [folder] 142, pp. 29–35: 'Protokół zebrania Wydziału Wykonawczego Komitetu Organizacyjnego Międzynarodowego Kongresu Nauk Historycznych odbytego w Warszawie w Dziekanacie Wydziału Historycznego', 29 June 1933. Oskar Halecki was to be responsible for passing on the actual invitation, and Dembiński chaired the meeting. The participation of the Jewish historians meant that their subjects in Jewish history were approved by the leadership of the Polish Historical Association and the leadership of the Polish delegation. See APAN, PTH, I-3, j. [folder] 142, pp. 9–10: 'Instrukcja'.

[195] See Szulkin, 'Projekt utworzenia Katedry Historii Żydów w Polsce'. Szulkin mentioned Bałaban as the only candidate for the position. The correspondence in the file, however, contains a discussion about the possibility of creating a Polish chair that makes no mention of Bałaban's name. See AAN, Ministerstwo Spraw Zagranicznych (Ministry of Foreign Affairs), 6288, pp. 1–16. Gelber, however, mentioned himself, Bałaban, and Schiper. See CAHJP, P 83: Gelber's calendars, with notes in uncatalogued collection. I would like to thank Professor Rachel Manekin for making this material available to me.

[196] See the letter from the General Consul in Jerusalem, Dr Z. Kurnikowski to the Consular Department of the Ministry of Foreign Affairs, Nr 298/Pl/7/T, dated 31 Dec. 1934, referring to a number of concerns about creating a Polish chair at the Hebrew University (AAN, Ministerstwo Spraw Zagranicznych (Ministry of Foreign Affairs), 6288, pp. 1–11). See also a note signed by the vice director of the Political Department T. Kobylański, August 1925 (AAN, Ministerstwo Spraw Zagranicznych (Ministry of Foreign Affairs), 6288, p. 16). Bałaban visited Palestine in the autumn of 1935 and delivered a lecture at the Hebrew University: 'The Migration of Hebrew Cultural Values between the Rhine and the Vistula, from the Twelfth to the Seventeenth Centuries'. See 'Beyn ha-baim', *Davar*, 6 Oct. 1935, p. 1; 'Social and Personal', *Palestine Post*, 24 Oct. 1935, p. 5.

wars: two in *Przegląd Historyczny*, with a third promised for the forthcoming 1939 issue.[197]

Polish and Jewish historians collaborated on a few publication projects, especially on local and regional history and Jewish participation in Poland's struggles for independence. Although rare, these projects made possible a meeting ground and mutual professional recognition. In 1932, the Polish Academy of Letters (Polska Akademia Nauk) published a volume entitled *Kultura staropolska* (The Culture of Old Poland), a reference work for future scholars interested in various cultural aspects of the golden age of the Polish–Lithuanian Commonwealth in the sixteenth century. In addition to contributions from established Polish scholars, it included Bałaban's article on the intellectual and moral life of Polish Jewry.[198] Another example is the volume published by a joint committee of the 'most eminent representatives of the Polish and Jewish society in Wilno, in 1927, under the patronage of the founder of the reborn Commonwealth's army, Józef Piłsudski'.[199] In 1932 Bałaban accepted an invitation to edit the volume, to which the leading Polish historians Marian Kukiel, Emil Kipa, and Ernest Łuniński contributed,[200] as well as Bałaban and Pinchas Kon.[201]

The support of the Polish historical establishment created opportunities for funding. For the most part, however, funding came from Jewish organizations and institutions. Only in a few instances were works of Jewish historians pertaining to the history of Polish Jewry published with the financial assistance of general Polish scholarly institutions. Handelsman in particular used his position in TNW and his editorship of *Przegląd Historyczny* to help his students get their work published.[202] A grant from the Warsaw city council for Ringelblum's book brought Jan Józef Siemieński—the influential historian of law, archivist, and publicist, and the head of the Archiwum Główne Akt Dawnych in Warsaw—to complain in his critical review that it was published with public funding. He suggested that at an open meeting of TMH not only had the book itself been criticized but also the fact that it was published at all.[203] Ringelblum believed that the attack on his book was an attempt to undermine Handelsman's position.[204] In any case, this response

---

[197] The two articles published are Ringelblum, 'Ze studjów nad dziejami Żydów na Mazowszu', in 1927, and Bałaban, 'Żydzi w powstaniu 1863 r.', in 1937–8.

[198] Bałaban, 'Umysłowość i moralność żydostwa polskiego XVI w.'.

[199] Bałaban, 'Przedmowa', in id., *Album Pamiątkowy*, 7.

[200] Ernest Łuniński was a Polish historian, with degrees from the Jagiellonian University. Born Ernest Arnold Deiches, he converted to Catholicism. In the Second Polish Republic he lectured in history at the School of Political Studies (Szkoła Nauk Politycznych) in Warsaw.

[201] Bałaban, 'Przedmowa', in id., *Album Pamiątkowy*, 8.

[202] See Dutkiewicz, 'Seminarium Marcelego Handelsmana', 136.

[203] Siemieński, 'Ringelblum Emanuel: Żydzi w Warszawie', 646.

[204] Ringelblum, 'Profesor Marceli Handelsman', 542.

exemplifies the challenges Polish Jewish historians faced. When their work was funded at all, that funding was criticized and the work was devalued by non-Jewish critics.

Although the viciousness of antisemitic Polish discourse was toned down in the academy, Jewish historians noticed a decline in the way their Polish colleagues related to them. Already in 1924, on the occasion of the death of Regina Liliental, a researcher of Polish and Jewish folklore, Bałaban remarked nostalgically that when she first began scholarly research on Jewish rituals and customs, Polish journals had received her articles eagerly. This he referred to as the '"pre-revolutionary period" . . . when liberalism reigned in scholarship and Polish scholars were pleased that someone [was] building and deepening Jewish scholarship and especially historical and folkloristic knowledge of the life of Polish Jewry'.[205] However, in the 1920s and the early 1930s their work was not entirely ignored. Polish historians reviewed the work of their Jewish colleagues, and a number of Polish historians seemed to have accepted Polish Jewish history as an interesting contribution to general historical knowledge and, more specifically, to Polish historiography. Jewish historians continued publishing in existing general Polish scholarly journals.[206] In addition, they utilized several new academic outlets, such as the local and regional *Ateneum Wileńskie* and *Roczniki Łódzkie*. In the second half of the 1930s the situation would worsen, and Polish Jewish history experienced a process of marginalization parallel to the status of the Jewish community in the country.

The very presence of Jewish scholars at meetings—including the Congresses of Polish Historians—served as a reminder of their part in the Polish historical profession. They spoke about Jewish history's place in the field and argued that care for Jewish monuments and documents should be of concern to Polish scholarship and the Polish state.[207] In 1925 Kon located part of the Jewish communal records in the municipal archives of Wilno, presenting his findings at a meeting of the An-ski Historical-Ethnographic Association in Wilno. In 1928, he published a report on these materials in *Ateneum Wileńskie* 'for the broader community of scholars [*szerszy ogół naukowców*]', and especially 'colleagues— students at the Stefan Batory University working on subjects from the past of Wilno Jews'.[208] Only in a few instances did Polish scholarly journals review or refer to historical publications in Yiddish and Hebrew pertaining to the history of Polish Jews.

---

[205] Bałaban, 'Regina Lilientalowa', in id., *Studja historyczne*, 194.
[206] See Ringelblum, 'Ze studjów nad dziejami Żydów na Mazowszu'.
[207] Bałaban, 'Zadania i potrzeby historjografji Żydów w Polsce', ii. 225–7.
[208] Kon, 'Odnaleziona część Archiwum dawnego Kahału Wileńskiego'. He later published a version in Yiddish.

Chana Szmuszkowiczówna described the second volume of *Historishe shriftn* as a 'valuable contribution of Jewish historians'.[209] A review in *Ateneum Wileńskie*, of Izrael Klauzner's book on the old Jewish cemetery in Wilno, expressed astonishment that Polish historiography 'and stranger yet, Jewish historiography, does not yet have an in-depth [*wyczerpująca*] monograph about the history of the Jews in Wilno'. The author contrasted this state of affairs with work done in other cities, praising the achievements of Kraków and Lwów Jews as personified in monographs by Bałaban, and the Jews of Warsaw and Łódź in the works of Ringelblum and Friedman. The author welcomed initiatives to publish Klauzner's book in Hebrew, with the subvention of the Jewish community.[210] And he praised Klauzner, a graduate of Stefan Batory University, for basing his work on primary sources and their critical interpretation, for his 'scholarly scrupulousness', and 'skilful application of scholarly apparatus'.[211]

Jewish historians used Polish scholarly journals to review one another's work. In this way, they marked Polish Jewish history as part of the general Polish professional discourse. In many instances, Jewish scholars reviewed works on Polish Jewish history for both professional historians and interested readers.[212] Rather than a sign of professional ghettoization (in the sense of Jews reviewing Jews), discussing Jewish themes in Polish journals proved that Jewish historians had entered the mainstream historical profession and that Polish Jewish history appeared relevant for general audiences.

The reviews published by Polish historians revealed a more complex picture and the changing dynamic for Jewish scholars in Polish academia. Polish historians referred to the work of Jewish scholars, consulted them, and used their help with sources otherwise unavailable to them.[213] They described Jewish history as relevant to general Polish historiography, adding to the body of knowledge and

---

[209] See Smuszkowiczówna, 'Historyše Šriftn fun Jiwo: Prace historyczne JIWO, pod redakcją E. Tscherikowera'. The review also summarizes the content of the 1929 volume of YIVO's *Historishe shriftn*.

[210] W.M. [Wilhelm Mermelstein], 'Klauzner, Izrael Mgr. "Dzieje starego cmentarza żydowskiego w Wilnie", Wilno 1935', 630. The author erroneously gives Ringelblum's first initial as J.

[211] Ibid. 631.

[212] See Roth, 'Dr. N. M. Gelber: *Aus zwei Jahrhunderten*'; Schall, 'Friedman Filip: Dzieje Żydów w Łodzi'; Gerber, 'Ringelblum Emanuel: Żydzi w powstaniu kościuszkowskiem'.

[213] For example, in *Ateneum Wileńskie* Stefan Rosiak discussed the alleged privilege of Jan Sapieha issued for the Jews in Lubcz. It was Kon who drew his attention to the 1690 privilege when Rosiak was working on his monograph on the small town. He was able to familiarize himself with the text published in *YIVO Bleter* by Kon. Rosiak concluded that the privilege was false, and he felt compelled to publish his findings, since the document had been published as authentic in a scholarly journal. See Rosiak, 'Rzekomy przywilej Kazimierza Jana Sapiehy', and Kon, 'Przyczynki do historji Żydów w Lubczy'.

filling in important gaps.[214] Some scholars of Polish history expressed interest in the further development of Jewish scholarship. According to Jan Adamus, Ringelblum's article on the reform projects regarding the Jews in the last decades of the Polish–Lithuanian Commonwealth contributed 'many unknown details to this important issue'.[215] Tadeusz Lutman, a Polish historian and librarian, described Schiper as a 'well-known scholar of merit in the field of Jewish history', who showed full understanding of economic issues and discussed in detail Jewish contributions to domestic and international trade.[216] He pointed to some shortcomings in the literature, including works by such authors as Antoni Kalina, Łucja Charewiczowa, and Dawid Wurm. Lutman aptly described Schiper's political agenda: 'The author wants to stress the role of Jews in Poland's economic life and their importance for the economic development of our state. He tries also to defend his nation against accusations from Christian society.'[217] On the whole, however, Lutman took a negative view of Schiper's work: 'One cannot deny that in the overwhelming majority of cases Jewish merchants acted only for their own benefit; their selfish policies harmed Polish societies in many instances.'[218] Lutman dismissed Schiper's portrait of Christian burghers, who had the most contacts with Jews and competed with them, as mean-spirited. Schiper, concluded Lutman, was unwilling to accept any charges against the Jews.[219] Still, he characterized Schiper's work as 'valuable and serious because of its synthesizing character' and thus relevant for economic historians and especially historians of commerce, culture, and those interested in the 'Jewish question'.[220] Lutman parroted economic antisemitism—a particularly virulent anti-Jewish trope in interwar Poland—even as he found Schiper's work useful.

The main journal of economic history, *Roczniki dziejów społecznych i gospodarczych*, published in Lwów from 1931 and edited by Franciszek Bujak of Lwów and Jan Rutkowski of Poznań University, published numerous reviews of the work of Polish Jewish historians, but not a single article by them. It briefly reviewed Bałaban's 'Zadania i potrzeby historjografji Żydów w Polsce' (Functions and Needs of Jewish Historiography in Poland), summarizing the stages of organizing and systematizing Jewish research in Poland, and concluding that 'this issue has also an important meaning for the economic historian'.[221] It also published a somewhat

---

[214] Henryk Mościcki noted the work N. M. Gelber, as well as Shatzky's work in *Historishe shriftn*. See Mościcki, 'Historiografia powstania styczniowego ostatnich lat piętnastu', 400.

[215] See Adamus's response to Ringelblum's article, 'Ringelblum Dr. E.: Projekty i próby przewarstwowienia Żydów w epoce stanisławowskiej'. The only critical remark concerned the title and the neologism 'przewarstwowienie'.

[216] Lutman, 'Schiper Ignacy: Dzieje handlu żydowskiego w Polsce'.

[217] Ibid. 189–90.     [218] Ibid. 190.     [219] Ibid.     [220] Ibid. 190–1.

[221] A.G., 'Bałaban Majer: Zadania i potrzeby historjografji Żydów w Polsce', 184.

critical review of Mark Wischnitzer's *Die Stellung der Brodyer Juden im internationalen Handel in der zweiten Hälfte des XVIII Jahrhunderts* (The Role of Brody Jews in International Trade in the Second Half of the Eighteenth Century), written by Lutman, who nevertheless admitted that the discussion of the Jewish role was important by itself.[222] Adolf Hirschberg, a historian of medieval and modern history who taught in Wilno secondary schools, criticized Schall's *Historja Żydów w Polsce na Litwie i Rusi* (The History of Jews in Lithuania and Ruthenia) for the author's inability to use sources and his incomplete review of secondary literature. Hirschberg concluded that the history of the Jews in Polish lands remained to be written, following Schall's failed attempt.[223] Natalia Gąsiorowska praised Friedman as one of the few Jewish historians with training in economic history, but suggested that he should work on his style and language.[224] In a much more critical tone, Artur Wagner described Steinberg's book on the Jewish community of Jarosław as a work of an amateur, useless for a historian of urban history, and even for the Jewish community, due to its numerous mistakes. He alleged that Steinberg did not properly use communal records or the information about the history of Jarosław Jews available in the earlier publications of Bałaban.[225] More importantly, the motivation for writing the review was to 'bring to attention of those interested that Steinberg's thesis has no scholarly value and that the subject remains to be elaborated, especially since the city played such a great role in the history of the Old Polish Commonwealth'.[226]

Even Polish historians whom Jewish scholars described as free of antisemitism seem to have been unwilling to discuss the subject of Polish–Jewish relations. Some reviewers debated the status and limits for Jewish practitioners of Polish Jewish history. Tadeusz Lutman published a lengthy review of Dawid Wurm's monograph on the Jewish community of Brody,[227] in which he rejected

---

[222] Lutman, 'Marek Wischnitzer's *Die Stellung der Brodyer Juden*'.

[223] Hirschberg, 'Schall Jakób: Historja Żydów w Polsce, na Litwie i Rusi', 451. Hirschberg, who wrote a doctoral dissertation, *Stosunki osadnicze w dobrach klasztoru tymienieckiego w początkach jego istnienia*, in Bujak's seminar, also reviewed Schiper's work on the Jews in Congress Poland at the time of the November 1830 uprising. See Hirschberg, 'Schipper Ignacy: Żydzi Królestwa Polskiego w dobie Powstania Listopadowego'.

[224] Gąsiorowska reviewed three articles that appeared in *Rocznik Łódzki*, 3 (1933): Friedman's 'Początki przemysłu w Łodzi 1823–1830' and two other studies on the industrial history of Łódź published in the same volume by Robert Rembieliński and Mieczysław Komar. Her review appeared in *Roczniki Dziejów Społecznych i Gospodarczych*, 3 (1934), 516–19.

[225] Wagner, 'Steinberg Mojżesz: Żydzi w Jarosławiu'. See also Steinberg, *Żydzi w Jarosławiu od czasów najdawniejszych do połowy XIX wieku*.

[226] Wagner, 'Steinberg Mojżesz: Żydzi w Jarosławiu', 451.

[227] Lutman, 'Wurm Dawid: Z dziejów żydostwa brodzkiego za czasów dawnej Rzeczypospolitej Polskiej'.

Wurm's and Bałaban's criticism of Polish historians for their insufficient or unfair treatment of Jewish history in the context of Polish urban history. Lutman admitted that Polish historians might have a biased attitude towards Jews, but he asserted that Bałaban's remark 'surprises because it does not recognize the correct accusations brought against the Jews, and one gets an impression that Jews are simply untouchable and cannot be criticized. He was alarmed that Bałaban's introduction did not even spare Prof. Ptaśnik, who was known for his thoroughness, fairness [*bezstronność*] and progressive world-view.'[228]

Numerous Polish historians encouraged research in Polish Jewish history, but they wanted to see Polish–Jewish relations portrayed in a light flattering to the Poles. They had a vision of tolerance and generosity towards the Jews in Polish lands over the course of centuries, and they mocked Jewish historians who dared to discuss Jewish persecution in Poland. The response to Ringelblum's monograph *Żydzi w Warszawie: Od czasów najdawniejszych do ostatniego wygnania w roku 1527* (Jews in Warsaw: From the Earliest Times until the Last Expulsion in 1527), published in Warsaw in 1932, reflected the precarious position of Jewish scholarship in Poland. Józef Siemieński and Jadwiga Karwasińska, members of the TMH, which published the book, criticized it harshly and dismissed its value for the reading public.[229] Siemieński claimed to have written the review unwillingly, after repeated requests by colleagues, to put an end to discussions about it, as the book deserved to be 'rebuked' (*skarcenie*) in the small circle of historians rather than to be reviewed.[230] A year later, Karwasińska—Polish medievalist and archivist—reviewed Ringelblum's book. Like Siemieński she accused Ringelblum of numerous formal mistakes: sloppiness in translations, transliterations, and bibliographical references.[231] In addition, Siemieński questioned Ringelblum's knowledge of Latin and legal history and accused him of misinterpreting legal sources.[232] These specific accusations could not be dismissed entirely as driven by antisemitic bias, especially since Jewish historians criticized the book for the same problems.[233] Yet the non-Jewish reviewers' dislike of Ringelblum's style revealed

---

[228] Ibid. 418.

[229] Siemieński, 'Ringelblum Emanuel: Żydzi w Warszawie', and Karwasińska, 'Ringelblum Emanuel: Żydzi w Warszawie', 581. Siemieński admitted that the field of Polish Jewish history deserved to be cultivated, but said that it was 'cluttered up by dilettantes and people with political agendas' (ibid. 646).

[230] Siemieński, 'Ringelblum Emanuel: Żydzi w Warszawie', 646–7. Ringelblum's book reminded Siemieński of Russian historiography during the partitions, which suggests that he had doubts about the Jewish historian's loyalty to the Polish national cause (p. 647).

[231] Ibid. 648–9; Karwasińska, 'Ringelblum Emanuel: Żydzi w Warszawie', 581.

[232] Siemieński, 'Ringelblum Emanuel: Żydzi w Warszawie', 649–50.

[233] See Feldman, 'Dzieje Żydów w Warszawie'. In his review of the literature, Filip Friedman also described Ringelblum's other studies in the social and cultural history of the Jews in eighteenth-

their sense of his having stepped out of line by voicing critical opinions about Poland in the past. Thus Siemieński compared Ringelblum to Iłowajski, a Russian historian writing with an unfriendly bias against Poland.[234] Karwasińska claimed Ringelblum used an 'improper tone and bold and naive tendentiousness and one-sidedness and wrong suggestions'.[235] She considered subtitles such as 'the last of the Mohicans' and 'the twilight of the Warsaw [Jewish] community' inappropriate. She further objected to Ringelblum's use of the word 'pogrom' to describe the events of 1454 or 1455, instigated by the Bernardines, calling it 'very flashy' and unjustified. She accused Ringelblum of failing to 'familiarize himself with the general legal system within which Polish Jewry must have arranged its existence or with Polish law, especially the court law [*prawo sądowe*], for the sorry victims as he [Ringelblum] constantly considers them [the Jews]'.[236] Siemieński, for his part, not only argued that Ringelblum had no basis for his theories about the pogrom in 1454 or 1455 and the expulsion of the Jewish community from Warsaw in 1483, but also implied that Ringelblum's conclusions were driven by 'moods' or political needs.[237] Both Siemieński and Karwasińska rejected Ringelblum's claims about the greediness of Mazovian princes and Polish kings, the ruthless brutality of the Gentile burghers, and the role of Christian clergy in inciting anti-Jewish violence. In essence, they refused to discuss any possible maltreatment of the Jewish community in the past. According to Ringelblum, antisemites could not bear the fact that his book 'shattered the myth about the hospitality of Polish kings and idyllic relations which allegedly prevailed between Jews and Poles'.[238]

Jan Warężak, a Polish historian and archivist who specialized in social and economic history, expressed similar suspicions about alleged Jewish persecution and suffering in the more recent past, in his review of Friedman's *Dzieje Żydów w Łodzi*.[239] Warężak confirmed that the Jews played an important role in Łódź's economy, and he praised Friedman for his skilful use of rich archival material, which resulted in 'an extensive work on the history of Jews in Łódź . . . filling in a gap in bibliography on this subject'. He anticipated a second, more thorough volume.[240] However, Warężak noted that Friedman undermined the 'serious results of his work by tendentious treatment of almost all more serious issues'.[241] Instead of realizing that the accusations of the townspeople against Jewish tailors were just, argued Warężak, Friedman exaggerated anti-Jewish laws and policies in the

---

century Warsaw as 'much better'. Friedman, 'Polish Jewish Historiography between the Two Wars (1918–1939)', 398.

[234] Siemieński, 'Ringelblum Emanuel: Żydzi w Warszawie', 647.
[235] Karwasińska, 'Ringelblum Emanuel: Żydzi w Warszawie', 581.
[236] Ibid. 579–80.    [237] Siemieński, 'Ringelblum Emanuel: Żydzi w Warszawie'.
[238] Ringelblum, 'Profesor Marceli Handelsman', 542.
[239] Warężak, 'Friedman Filip: Dzieje Żydów w Łodzi'.    [240] Ibid. 280.    [241] Ibid. 281.

old city of Łódź, deviating from an objective and scholarly approach. Thus, Warężak noted ironically,

It seems that Jews who followed the rules and the country's laws did not experience limitations on settling in Łódź and were not condemned to the martyrdom to which the author [Friedman] dooms them [in the years before] 1862. The mass emigration of the Jews to the New City before 1862, i.e. before [the] removal of the limitation on settling, proves it.[242]

Warężak concluded his review by suggesting that Friedman's view of Jewish suffering was out of proportion: 'Having confirmed the constant influx of the Jews to Łódź and the rising standard of living of the Jewish population, what was the nature of this martyrdom that the Jews of Łódź patiently endured for such a long time, [evidently] exaggerated by the author?'[243]

Jewish historians writing about Polish Jewish history were part of the academic discourse in the Polish academy. Yet the attitudes to their work were at times ambivalent and even dismissive. Moreover, some scholars of Polish history suggested an essential divide between Jewish and 'our' historians, whom they defended against any criticism voiced by Bałaban, Schiper, Ringelblum, and others. Not only did they mock translations of Latin documents published by Bałaban and Ringelblum, but some authors also alluded to Jewish authors' weak Polish, and compared them to Russian historians who were enemies of Poland.[244] Leon Koczy, a Polish historian based at the University of Poznań, devoted several chapters of his *Handel Poznania do połowy wieku XVI* to the contribution of Jews and Italians to the trade of the city,[245] referring to Jewish historians as 'Semites', listing among more recent studies the work of Dubnow, Bałaban, and Meisl.[246] In anticipation of 'possible accusations from the Jewish side', Koczy clarified that he 'did not use the Hebrew sources in the Jewish Archives in Berlin that are known to me and accessible.'[247] He thus suggested that a non-Jewish Polish historian could not be expected to read historical sources in Hebrew. Touching on one of the tropes in discussing the economic role of the Jews, Koczy debated with Schiper, who argued that Jews did engage in trade in the early stages of their settlement in Polish lands, rather than solely being moneylenders until the sixteenth century, as Koczy insisted.[248]

[242] Ibid. 282.
[243] Ibid. 283. See also Warężak, 'Friedman Filip: Rozwój gospodarczy Łodzi do roku 1914'. Here Warężak offered a balanced review, critical but recognizing Friedman's contribution.
[244] See e.g. Koczy, 'Studja nad dziejami gospodarczemi Żydów poznańskich przed połową wieku XVII', *Kronika Miasta Poznania*, 3 (1934), 263 n. 9.   [245] Koczy, *Handel Poznania do połowy wieku XVI*.
[246] Koczy, 'Studja nad dziejami gospodarczemi Żydów poznańskich przed połową wieku XVII', 3 (1934), 258.   [247] Ibid. 259–60.
[248] Ibid. 261. See Schiper, *Studya nad stosunkami gospodarczymi Żydów w Polsce*, 69–72.

## Insiders, Outsiders, and the Limits of Academic Inclusion

Bałaban seems to have been the most successful at carving for himself a place in the Polish academic landscape. In addition to his university appointments, he received a nomination to the Education Committee of the Polish Academy of Letters (Komitet Oświatowy Polskiej Akademii Umiejętności) in Kraków,[249] and was invited to join the Institute of National Studies (Instytut Badań Spraw Narodowościowych). Polish scholars often quoted and referred to his work.[250] He sustained close relations with some of his Polish colleagues, as evidenced by his article in the Festschrift for a distinguished historian of law at Jan Kazimierz University, Przemysław Dąbkowski, as well as by the public congratulations he received on the occasion of his own sixtieth birthday in March 1937.[251]

Handelsman, who played a key role in the professional recognition that Jewish historians of Polish Jewry received, was a supporter of Bałaban.[252] But despite Handelsman's help, and his own relations with the eminent Lwów historians Dąbkowski and Łucja Charewiczowa, Bałaban did not escape professional marginalization of the field of Polish Jewish history. In the 1937 volume of *Kwartalnik Historyczny*, reviewing the state of Polish historiography, specifically on the study of Polish urban history, Stefan Inglot recommended the work of Franciszek Bujak, Stanisław Kutrzeba, Jan Ptaśnik, and Wojciech Wasiutyński—scholars with a strong bias against Jews. As for the work of Jewish historians, Inglot added just one dismissive sentence: 'In addition there are quite a number of works on local and general Jewish history written by Jews: Schorr, Schiper, Bałaban, Friedman, and others.'[253]

In the 1930s Bałaban experienced both increasing professional marginalization and actual physical violence at the university. In 1932 a group of students

---

[249] AAN, B'nai B'rith, file 3, p. 99: protocol from the closed meeting of the members of 'Braterstwo-B'nai Brith', 24 Nov. 1930.

[250] See Kutrzeba, *Sprawa żydowska w Polsce*, 7, 12, and Charewiczowa, *Dzieje miasta Złoczowa*, 23. See also Dold, 'Die Wahrnehmung Majer Bałabans im polnischen Kontext'.

[251] See Bałaban, 'Ze studjów nad ustrojem prawnym Żydów w Polsce'. He received letters of congratulation both from Jewish organizations and institutions and from representatives of the Polish academy, including the rector of Warsaw University, Włodzimierz Antoniewicz, Przemysław Dąbkowski, Tadeusz Kotarbiński, and Marceli Handelsman. See 'Gratulacje', in Jolles (ed.), *Księga jubileuszowa Bałabana*, 41–50.

[252] Handelsman's considerable influence in this area can be seen in the fact that, in 1928, when his students published a Festschrift for their teacher on the occasion of twenty-five years of scholarly activities, they insisted on inviting Jacob Shatzky, already in New York, both to contribute financially and to submit an article. See YIVO Archives, RG 356, folder 18: handwritten postcard signed by Stefan Pomarański, post-stamped in Warsaw 19 Sept. 1928. See also *Księga pamiątkowa ku uczczeniu dwudziestopięcioletniej działalności naukowej prof. Marcelego Handelsmana*.

[253] Inglot, 'Rozwój historii społecznej i gospodarczej'.

attacked him after his lecture.²⁵⁴ Although he was not hurt, the incident made a deep impression on Bałaban's students, undermining their trust in university education for young Jews in Poland.²⁵⁵ In November 1938 Bałaban and his students were assaulted again; this time several of them were injured and classes were temporarily suspended.²⁵⁶ The deteriorating status of Jewish academia reflected a broader phenomenon in which liberal intellectuals gradually found themselves marginalized and physically threatened.²⁵⁷ Handelsman came under attack at the university, and his students began escorting him to and from lecture halls. When Stefan Czarnowski passed away in 1937, Bałaban eulogized him at a special meeting of the Warsaw branch of B'nai B'rith. Describing the late sociologist as a 'man of progress' and 'a friend of Jewish youth', he bemoaned the fact that Czarnowski died a lonely man; only one member of the Theological Department, a Protestant pastor in his capacity as a university professor, attended his funeral.²⁵⁸

Thus, in the second half of the 1930s, signs of erosion appeared in the formal recognition of the field, and Polish Jewish historians became what Samuel Kassow termed 'a counter profession'. As Kassow argues in his path-breaking book on Emanuel Ringelblum and the Oyneg Shabes Archives in the Warsaw ghetto, young historians in the Second Polish Republic had to create this unofficial *modus operandi* as Jews and as scholars, because they found themselves doubly marginalized:

Largely ignored by their Polish colleagues and hampered by serious financial constraints as well as hostility and indifference both from Poles and within the Jewish community . . . They needed journals that would publish their work and seminars where they could discuss research with colleagues, and also the satisfaction of knowing that they were having an impact on the intense but fractious cultural life of interwar Polish Jewry.²⁵⁹

Yet this marginalization was neither a given nor complete. Professional acceptance of Polish Jewish historians and Polish Jewish history hung in the political balance, tenuous and qualified.

---

²⁵⁴ See the testimony of Czesława Erlich, born 25 Sept. 1912 in Siedlce, who graduated from a gymnasium and enrolled at the Department of Humanities at Warsaw University (Yad Vashem Archives, O 3/1589, p. 1). Following the incident, which for Erlich 'became a symbol of our humiliation', she left the university and studied to become a nurse.     ²⁵⁵ Bosak, *Shadows of the City* (Heb.), 31–2.

²⁵⁶ See 'In Poland: The Attack on the Seminar of Prof. Bałaban' (Yid.), *Davar*, 29 Nov. 1938, 5.

²⁵⁷ See Stach, 'The Institute for Nationality Research (1921–1939)'.

²⁵⁸ See AAN, B'nai B'rith, file 4, pp. 222–3: protocol of a closed meeting chaired by Seidenman on 25 Nov. 1937. According to Bałaban, Czarnowski surrounded himself with Jewish students and assistants, whom he supported to the best of his abilities, and fought against the ghetto benches.

²⁵⁹ Kassow, *Who Will Write Our History?*, 49.

Samuel Margulies's 1936 attempts to pursue research on a Jewish topic at Jan Kazimierz University in Lwów reflect the reality of shrinking opportunities for Jews to study Jewish history within Polish academia. A graduate in law, he detailed in his application to the Aspirantur programme failed attempts to pursue a Jewish topic of research at Jan Kazimierz University. He turned to his mentor Dąbkowski, asking for a topic for his doctoral dissertation in the field of Polish Jewish history or institutions of Polish Jewry. The historian of Polish law, whom Margulies described as a 'very liberal person indeed', advised decidedly against it, claiming that 'given the antisemitic moods prevailing in the Senate of the Jan Kazimierz University, such a dissertation, even if expertly written, has no chance of approval'.[260] In his letter, Margulies sought suggestions for topics in the history of law, guidelines for possible future applications, and library privileges.

One of many unsuccessful applicants hoping for an affiliation with the Aspirantur programme, Seweryn Brüh, explained his motives, constructing a brief intellectual autobiography. Initially interested in economics, he had focused his university work in that field, and later participated in a seminar in criminal law. In the process, he became interested in criminal psychology and sociology: 'Currently, I work in the field of library studies, running a library that serves over 2,000 subscribers, and I have taken to [the fields of] extracurricular education, psychology of reading, and reading in general.' Seeking a forum for the exchange of ideas, he approached the Polish Union of Librarians, but as a Jew he was denied membership. Applying to Aspirantur in 1939, he promised to improve his Yiddish and to carry out research in the field of library studies and readership.[261] The applications of Polish Jews seeking a chance to study as fellows at the YIVO Institute may indicate their growing perception that Polish academia was no longer welcoming to them.

Was the hope of engaging in dialogue with Polish historians and becoming part of Polish academia futile for Jews? Not entirely. In the second half of the 1930s, positive reviews of the work of Jewish historians still appeared in the pages of professional journals. In January 1938, Bałaban delivered a lecture at a conference commemorating the uprising of 1863, which was later published in *Przegląd Historyczny*.[262] His presentation at a prestigious conference signalled inclusion. The programme of the conference suggested that its organizers saw Jews as part of Polish society.[263] And Bałaban's article on Jewish autonomy was scheduled to be

---

[260] YIVO Archives, RG 1.3 Aspirantur, Box 13, file 4063 a, p. 165531.

[261] YIVO Archives, RG 1.3 Aspirantur, Box 13, file 4063 a, p. 165427.

[262] See Bałaban, 'Żydzi w powstaniu 1863 r.'. Following Bałaban's lecture, Rafał Gerber, Zdzierski, Kulczycki, and Handelsman all participated in the discussion.

[263] See the list of conference participants, 'Protokoły konferencji', *Przegląd Historyczny*, 34/2 (1937–8), 739–59. Included in the programme, and also published in this issue of the journal, were

published in *Kwartalnik Historyczny* in 1940.[264] Liberal circles, usually politically linked to the left and in opposition to growing right-wing polity, continued to view the Jews, their history, and their historians as an indispensable part of the Polish cultural landscape. Such inclusion notwithstanding, on the eve of the Second World War, many Polish scholars rejected the work of Jewish historians or discarded any interpretation of the past not simply praising Poland's treatment of the Jews.

## Conclusion

In the Second Polish Republic the history of Polish Jewry became a well-defined professional field, with scholarly literature, journals, research questions, and methodological and ideological debates. With the assistance of some Polish historians and the building of formal and informal institutional frameworks, a generation of professional historians of Polish Jewish history emerged from Polish universities, especially Warsaw University, the leading centre for graduate students of Jewish history in Poland. While Bałaban ran the only university seminar devoted to the history of Polish Jews in Europe at the time, Handelsman, Arnold, and several other scholars in the History Department encouraged students to prepare theses and dissertations on various aspects of Polish Jewish history. Jewish students also had at their disposal the informal group, the Young Historians Circle.

The academic field of Polish Jewish history flourished in the Second Polish Republic despite considerable constraints. Jewish historians in Poland saw the field of Polish Jewish history as part of mainstream intellectual culture, both Polish and Jewish. They envisioned their expanding field and its institutions as participating in general Polish historical scholarship. For Jewish scholars who needed access to state and private libraries and archives, letters of recommendation, funding, and opportunities to publish their work, becoming part of Polish academic discourse was a professional necessity. But inclusion was also a matter of intellectual and ideological conviction. As Jewish history constituted an indispensable part of Polish history, according to these scholars, it belonged in Polish universities, professional organizations of Polish historians, and Polish scholarly journals. They believed such inclusion could have a significant impact on Polish

---

Gąsiorowska, 'Mieszczaństwo w powstaniu styczniowym'; Żywczyński, 'Kościół i duchowieństwo w powstaniu styczniowym'; Wrona, 'Chłopi w powstaniu styczniowym'. Thus, the journal discussed Jews among other segments of society at the time of the uprising.

[264] A note in the 1939 volume of *Kwartalnik Historyczny* announced articles scheduled to appear in forthcoming issues of the journal, including Bałaban, 'Autonomia Żydów w Polsce: jej analogie w krajach sąsiednich: Przegląd literatury z lat ostatnich'. With the outbreak of the war, these projected articles never appeared. See 'W następnych zeszytach Kwartalnika Historycznego znajdą się następujące artykuły', in the table of contents for *Kwartalnik Historyczny*, 53/2 (1939).

historiography and, at least as a discursive model, it would help them explore and improve the status of the contemporary Jewish community.

At the same time, a growing number of professional Jewish historians strove to develop autonomous Jewish academic institutions and networks, discussing the Jewish past with other Jewish scholars and creating a historical literature for the consumption of the Jewish public in Poland. The need to build a seemingly parallel scholarly infrastructure revealed the difficulties in gaining full access to Polish academic resources and full recognition of the work of Jewish historians. While all professional historians faced limited opportunities for employment and funding, Jewish scholars encountered additional, ideologically motivated obstacles in which antisemitic bias often played a role. Even Bałaban, the only scholar to hold a university position teaching Polish Jewish history, encountered difficulties in finding publishers and carrying out his research. Despite these limitations, Jewish scholars, communal leaders, and activists created considerable resources for university-trained historians.

While Bałaban and Schiper continued to pursue their research, they, as well as Schorr, became deeply involved in assisting and facilitating the training of the new group of scholars.[265] On the occasion of his sixtieth birthday, Bałaban even complained that he could never engage solely in research, but only in addition to carrying out other obligations as a teacher and educator. He had to interrupt his research without finishing many of the projects.[266] In 1937, Schorr assured Bałaban that his students would 'add bricks to the edifice of the general synthesis of history and culture of the Jews in Poland, the finishing of which is nobody else's calling more than Prof. Bałaban's himself'.[267] Indeed, he witnessed the flourishing of Polish Jewish historiography and the emergence of a cohort engaged in studying Jewish–non-Jewish relations and various aspects of Jewish social, cultural, and religious history in Polish lands. Students of Polish Jewish history began their professional careers in the 1930s with no prospects of achieving academic positions or rising in the university ranks. Although lacking the prospect of a university appointment and research funding for their work, Jewish historians continued writing about the history of Polish Jewry while teaching in Jewish schools and publishing in the daily Jewish press. These venues provided opportunities to transmit their ideas about Jewish history well beyond narrow academic circles.

The writing of Jewish history in interwar Poland was a creative experiment in which university-trained Jewish historians created a body of scholarly literature

[265] According to Seidman, 'Meir Bałaban' (Heb.), 228.
[266] See AAN, B'nai B'rith, file 4, p. 187: plenary session chaired by R. Szereszewski, 22 Feb. 1937.
[267] Schorr, 'Prof. Dr. Majer Bałaban (Z powodu 60-lecia Jego urodzin, 20 lutego 1878)', *Nasz Przegląd*, 21 Feb. 1937, printed in Jolles (ed.), *Księga jubileuszowa Bałabana*, 56–7.

devoted to the history of Polish Jewry. At the time this was meant to mark the birth of a new school of historiography. The significance of their research stemmed from the scope of the collective study of the Polish Jewish past, carried out by members of formal and informal seminars and from a wide range of methodological approaches. Schorr, Bałaban, Schiper, and younger Jewish historians also defined their profession in terms of a national mission, combining their academic interests with political and communal activism. They felt responsible not only for an academic and intellectual field, but also for shaping and improving the status of Polish Jewry. True to the diversity of interwar Polish Jewry, they represented not one community but several: Jewries from Galicia, Congress Poland, and the eastern borderlands.[268] When working in Galicia, they searched for a common collective identity for the Jewish community in the province. During the interwar years, they took part in crafting Jewish identity for the Jewish citizens of the newly resurrected country. The Galician historians' vision of Polish Jewish history, articulated before the First World War and further developed in the Second Polish Republic, played a seminal role in the formation of a national identity among Jewish citizens of the Polish state and contributed to the emergence of the sense of a Polish Jewish community on the eve of the Second World War.

[268] Mendelsohn, *The Jews of East Central Europe*, 17, 18.

FOUR

# BEYOND THE IVORY TOWER

IN THE 1930s Aron Sawicki served as a teacher of the Mosaic faith, lecturing to Jewish students on Jewish religion, history, and literature at the State Gymnasium of Kujawy in Włocławek, as well as at the Jewish secondary school there. Having received his master's degree in history at Warsaw University in 1931, he not only taught Jewish studies, but also wrote articles for the local Yiddish weekly *Vlotslavker shtime*. 'He often published articles on historical subjects', recalled fellow teacher and journalist Israel M. Biderman fondly. 'In these articles he emphasised the Jews' share in Poland's struggles for freedom and, whenever he could, he laid special stress on the part played in them by the Jews of Włocławek.'[1]

Sawicki's career was typical of the young Polish Jewish historians who received graduate university training but held no illusions about securing academic appointments. Instead, like Sawicki, they juggled positions as educators, rabbis, public speakers, and journalists. In these professional capacities, they fostered an interest in history among Polish Jews and disseminated historical knowledge, often based on their own forays into archives and libraries. These men and women wanted the public to learn not only about Jewry's contribution to Poland's economy and culture, but also about conflicts and persecution. They supplied material for debates about the community's historical heritage in the Polish lands for Jewish representatives and for lay Jews in their everyday lives. According to Jacob Shatzky, 'The arguments and evidence that historian[s] uncovered in the dark and dusty cellars of the archives were intended for academic interpretation only when published in books. In everyday life, [this material] was used in the fight for rights [of the Jews] in the Polish parliament, in speeches delivered by political and national activists, and in passionate polemics in the press.'[2]

Although Poland had regained its political independence in 1918, history continued to matter beyond the academic ivory tower. During the Second Polish Republic, interest in Polish history and the histories of Poland's minorities never faded away, nor was it an academic activity carried out by detached historians indifferent to the opinions of the general public. Historians from minority groups in Poland sought to highlight their people's contribution, and Jewish historians

[1] Biderman, 'The Jewish Press', 99. See Sawicki's student file (AUW, RP 28441).
[2] Shatzky, Introduction to id., *In the Shadow of the Past* (Yid.), 7.

were no exception.³ The key role played by history in shaping collective identities, and the political involvement of historians, were hardly unique to Poland. History served to justify claims of national independence and unification throughout the nineteenth century, and took centre stage in the nation states that emerged from the First World War, employed by various movements as tools in justifying political and territorial claims across east and central Europe.⁴

The entry of Jewish historians into careers outside academia was thus not simply the result of the limited professional opportunities for young scholars in general and Jewish ones in particular. Majer Bałaban, Ignacy Schiper, Mojżesz Schorr, Filip Friedman, Emanuel Ringelblum, Bela Mandelsberg, and others intentionally sought ways to popularize historical writing in their efforts to effect the inclusion of Jews in the general Polish historical narrative. How did stories about the Polish Jewish past circulate beyond academia? To popularize history, these figures published a plethora of articles in the Jewish press and lectured to diverse Jewish audiences. They also participated in Jewish politics and represented Jewish parties in the country's general political life, speaking in the Polish parliament on their own behalf and on behalf of Polish Jewry. Last, but not least, they penned textbooks and involved themselves with training rabbis and teachers. In their deliberations at B'nai B'rith meetings and in the Jewish press, Schorr and Bałaban reiterated the need to reach wide circles of Polish Jews and to arm them with appropriate historical knowledge. They envisioned ways to get new material into print, for example by creating new journals, and to reach ordinary Jews throughout the country, such as by training rabbis who recognized the importance of history. As a result of these efforts, the discipline of Jewish and Polish Jewish history played a critical role in educating the generation of young Jews growing up in the 1920s and 1930s, providing them with tools to explore their identities both as Jews and as Poles. Increasingly, Polish Jews encountered historical narratives in the press, at the synagogue, and during army service. Both in primary schools and gymnasia (secondary schools with a strong emphasis on academic learning), Jewish students read the textbooks and visited local archives and cemeteries guided by university-trained teachers.

## Jewish History in the Polish Parliament

During the interwar period, Jewish political leaders with competing programmes—the traditionalists from Agudat Israel, the Zionists, the *Folkists*, and the acculturated communal activists—spoke on behalf of Polish Jewry in parliament.⁵ The Polish parliament, with its Jewish caucus, constituted a crucial space

---

³ See Wendland, *Trzy czoła proroków z matki obcej*; Adamski, *Nacjonalista postępowy*; Zaszkilniak, 'Historia Ukrainy'.          ⁴ Geary, *The Myth of Nations*, 15.

⁵ On the attempt to create joint political representation, see Silber, 'The Development of a Joint

for discussing the place of the Jewish minority, defending the rights of the Jews when they came under attack and evoking Polish Jewish history in doing so.[6] Jewish historians provided political representatives with arguments in their struggle to defend Jewish rights, and some personally represented their voting public. Schiper was elected to the Polish Constituent Assembly (Sejm Ustawodawczy) in 1919. He worked in the Constitutional Commission and the Investigative Commission, investigating anti-Jewish pogroms, where he encountered Polish attempts to cover up what had happened. He spoke against the Sunday Rest legislation and in favour of passing social welfare laws. In the first Polish parliament—from 1922 until 1927—he continued to speak in defence of Jewish rights.[7] Schorr served as a senator in the fourth Polish parliament, from 1935 to 1938. From 1938 to 1939, in the Senate of the fifth and last Polish parliament of the Second Republic, the Jewish population was represented by Zdzisław Zmigryder-Konopka, a historian and vice president of the Union of Jewish Participants in the Struggles for Poland's Independence (Związek Żydów Uczestników Walk o Niepodległość Polski), who did not join the Jewish Parliamentary Caucus.

Professional historians serving as Jewish representatives, rabbis, lawyers, and communal leaders used history and historical arguments in contemporary political debates in defence of the Jews. Although they referred to Polish historians as authoritative sources of information, they clearly drew both directly and indirectly from Jewish historiography.[8] In 1938 the YIVO Institute prepared information for Jewish politicians on ritual slaughter, which the Polish government planned to restrict.[9] Bałaban, Schorr, and Schiper participated in the work of the Institute of National Studies (Instytut Badań Spraw Narodowościowych), which sought to inform and shape Polish policies with regard to minorities and was closely connected to the government. Bałaban, Tartakower, and Ringelblum also published in the Institute's journal *Sprawy Narodowościowe* (National Affairs), which promoted knowledge about national minorities among policy makers and the broader public.[10]

Despite differences in Jewish political parties' views on social, religious, and

Political Program'. For a discussion of modern Jewish politics in interwar Poland see Mendelsohn, *The Jews of East Central Europe*, 43–63, and Engel, 'Damaging Traditions' (Heb.).

[6] For a comprehensive discussion of the Jewish caucus in the Polish parliament during the interwar period see Rudnicki, *Żydzi w parlamencie II Rzeczypospolitej*.

[7] See Hirschaut, 'Dr. I. Schiper—His Life and Work (1884–1943)' (Yid.), 205–14.

[8] See the speech at the 10th session of the Senate, 14 Mar. 1939, made by Zmigryder-Konopka, in which, 'as a historian', he brought 'some arguments of this kind' (BS, Sejm 1919–1939, Stenogramy Senatu, RPII/5/10, no. 000023084, p. 76).

[9] YIVO, RG 1.1, folder 15, minutes of meeting of the Central Board, 8–10 Oct. 1938. See Kuznitz, *YIVO and the Making of Modern Jewish Culture*, 174.

[10] See Stach, 'The Institute for Nationality Research (1921–1939)'.

linguistic issues—to name just a few—Jewish parliamentarians drew upon the common historical past when addressing their Polish colleagues and demanding full civil rights, cultural autonomy, and religious tolerance. Speaking in parliament, Jewish representatives—some of them professional historians—who served as members of the Jewish caucus and worked as communal leaders invoked history while pleading with the government to provide Jews with basic physical security and dignity and to follow the provisions of the Constitution.[11] They reminded the officials of the long and peaceful Polish–Jewish coexistence embedded in the legitimate tradition of the Polish state and nation, and the underestimated but considerable Jewish contributions to Poland's economic development. The new Constitution, and the Minorities Treaty that created a formal legal basis for Jewish demands, were justified by Jewish contributions evident in Poland's own national heritage. Their right to feel at home in Poland and to enjoy equality as Polish citizens, they argued, was founded upon a centuries-long history of tolerance.[12]

Time and again, Jewish representatives in the Sejm and the Senate stated that Jews had been part of Polish society through the centuries. Because of their stake in the Polish state, Jews had fought and suffered together with the rest of society under the partitions.[13] A prominent attorney in Lwów and vice president of the Zionist Organization in eastern Galicia, Emil Sommerstein, called on Polish members of parliament to read history books rather than relying on antisemitic propaganda: 'It was said that Poland had no moral obligation towards us, since we are an alien population. But we ascertain—referring to the most prominent Polish historians—that we arrived before Poland adopted Christianity, as early as in the ninth and tenth centuries, at the time of Mieszko I, and we lived here for many centuries.'[14] To those who considered Jews a foreign element, Sommerstein suggested that they themselves might be in fact more foreign, having ancestors who immigrated to Poland long after Jews settled there. Sommerstein and others argued that their long history in Poland entitled the Jews to equal and irrevocable civil rights in the Second Polish Republic.

History figured in the charged political debates about driving Jewish citizens out of Poland. In 1935 Izaak Rubinstein, chief rabbi of Wilno and a chair of the

[11] See for example interpellations against government disinformation about violence against Jews, signed by Schiper, 25 Nov. 1920 (BS, Sejm 1919–1939, RPII/0/157, no. 000011916).

[12] On the legal status of the Jews in Poland, see Żyndul, *Państwo w państwie?*, 63–156; Fink, *Defending the Rights of Others*.

[13] See the statement made by the senator Zmigryder-Konopka in the 7th session of the Senate, 10 Mar. 1939, in the context of mobilization of Poland's society for the Fundusz Obrony Narodowej (National Defence Fund), about the 'bloody line of underground struggle against the tsar' in which the Jews participated (BS, Sejm 1919–1939, Stenogramy Senatu, RPII/5/7, no. 000023081, 14).

[14] The 41st Session of the Sejm, 18 Feb. 1937 (BS, Sejm 1919–1939, Stenogramy Sejmu, RPII/4/41, no. 000021917, pp. 46–7).

Zionist religious Mizrachi in the eastern borderlands (*kresy*), reminded the Sejm that forced emigration would not solve the so-called Jewish question in Poland. 'We have lived in some parts of the Republic for a thousand years. In the east, in Wilno, we have evidence [*pamiątki*], proving that we lived there before the [1569] Union of Lublin. We are autochthons in Poland and this land must feed us just like all its other inhabitants.'[15] In a heated budgetary discussion he complained about the grim prospects for Jewish youth, drawing a parallel between exclusionary practices in contemporary Poland and the policies of the Russian authorities during the partitions.[16] In 1938 he again rejected the notion of Jews being 'foreign' in the country, where 'we are citizens, have been living [here] for about a thousand years, and have all the rights not only based on the Constitution but also according to ethics'.[17] Therefore, Jewish representatives explained, even expulsion would not put an end to the so-called Jewish question. Despite ever more vicious attacks, Jews would inevitably stay in Poland. In the words of Jakub Lejb Mincberg, a member of the municipal council in Łódź and the Jewish *kehilah*, and co-founder of Agudat Israel in the city: 'For centuries, Jews have created deep roots in the life of this land, they are not some kind of rubbish to be thrown out the window. We have the right to full civic equality and ... development.'[18] In the same discussion, over the budget of the Treasury, he suggested that the current government's treatment of Jewish citizens stood in contrast to the models set by Kazimierz the Great and Józef Piłsudski.[19] In 1937, when a Polish member of the Sejm interrupted Sommerstein during a discussion on the state's investment of funds with a loud remark 'To Palestine!' [*Do Palestyny*], Sommerstein, a staunch Zionist, assured fellow parliamentarian Michał Wymysłowski:

We will go and we are going [there] but we will also stay here. . . . The population which has lived [here] for nine or ten centuries, will not allow itself to be expelled and will not give up, but it will fulfil all its obligations and will contribute in equal or even larger measure than you to creating all the conditions which introduce a new economic life.[20]

Two years later, Jakub Trockenheim, cofounder of Agudat Israel, member of the Warsaw city council, and president of the Warsaw *kehilah*, used a very similar historical argument to defend the right of Polish Jews to continue living in Poland:

[15] The 4th session of the Sejm, 5 and 6 Dec. 1935 (BS, Sejm 1919–1939, Stenogramy Sejmu, RPII/4/4, no. 000021880, p. 90). [16] Ibid.
[17] The 66th Session of the Sejm, 10 Feb. 1938 (BS, Sejm 1919–1939, Stenogramy Sejmu, RPII/4/66, no. 000021942, p. 80).
[18] The 18th Session of the Sejm, 26 Feb. 1936 (BS, Sejm 1919–1939, Stenogramy Sejmu, RPII/4/18, no. 000021894, p. 42). [19] Ibid.
[20] The 36th Session of the Sejm, 9 Feb. 1937 (BS, Sejm 1919–1939, Stenogramy Sejmu, RPII/4/36, no. 000021912, p. 74).

'One must not tell Jewish citizens who have lived in Polish lands for over eight hundred years: you must leave, because you are Jews.'[21]

Responding to antisemitic language and the rise of anti-Jewish violence in the 1930s, Jewish delegates to the Polish parliament argued that Poland had long benefited from the Jewish presence. While Jews featured prominently in the speeches of numerous Polish politicians as a detriment to Poland's economic development past and present, Jewish representatives countered those accusations with contemporary statistics and historical claims. In 1936 Schorr, serving as a Jewish representative in the Senate, described the effects of the economic marginalization of the Jews in the struggle to remove them from the Polish economy, asking, 'will this calamity of ours be a victory for the State?' He referred to history, arguing that the considerable number of economic privileges that Jews in the Crown Lands and in Lithuania had received from the sixteenth to the eighteenth centuries allowed them 'to trade in all parts of the Crown lands' and that 'granting them the same commercial rights as Christian merchants, confirms, beyond the shadow of a doubt, the positive and from a certain point of view meritorious role of the Jews in Polish history'.[22] At stake was the situation of the Jews in the Second Polish Republic. If Jews had contributed to Poland's economy in the past, contemporary policies aimed at limiting Jewish economic activities harmed the country.

Sommerstein reminded the Polish parliament of the Jewish contribution to the Polish economy, particularly to the development of its cities and trade. In 1936 he invoked history to address 'economic antisemitism' and claims about Jewish domination in commerce and the free professions. In order to explain the complex reasons behind Jewish prominence in these fields, he reminded his listeners that Jews were barred from other pursuits. Hardworking and patriotic, Polish Jews had been 'brought to Poland to break the hegemony of Germans in Polish cities. And they did. Their commercial talents served the Polish state and served it well.'[23] In discussions about the budget for 1938–9 of the Internal Ministry, Sommerstein assured the Prime Minister that 'we have never stopped improving and

---

[21] See Trockenheim's speech at the 11th session of the Sejm, 16 Feb. 1939, against the idea of depriving Polish Jews of Polish citizenship. He declared willingness to cooperate with the government in searching for a territory suitable for colonization for impoverished Jews, unemployed workers, and landless peasants (BS, Sejm 1919–1939, Stenogramy Sejmu, RPII/5/11, no. 000021977, p. 62).

[22] The 16th Session of the Senate, 24 June 1936 (BS, Sejm 1919–1939, Stenogramy Senatu, RPII/4/16, no. 000023002, p. 87).

[23] The 10th session of the Sejm, 17 Feb. 1936 (BS, Sejm 1919–1939, Stenogramy Sejmu, Sejm RPII/4/10, no. 000021886, p. 97). Sommerstein returned to this theme in several of his speeches, arguing that Jews had defended Polish trade against German influence. See also the 41st session of the Sejm, 18 Feb. 1937 (RPII/4/41, no. 000021917, p. 47); the 71st session of the Sejm, 17 Feb. 1938 (RPII/4/71, no. 000021947, p. 152); and the 88th session of the Sejm, 9 July 1938 (RPII/4/88, no. 000021964, p. 3).

creating new economic values in Poland in the lands that are now a part of the new sovereign Polish State'. Jews wanted to move to other professions, including physical labour and agriculture, but 'we were given a mission of creating a middle class, we were ordered to stay in commerce and industry. We stayed, gave [and] created higher economic values.'[24] Sommerstein asked rhetorically: 'Who created the sugar industry and metallurgy in the Congress [Poland] lands?' He answered with the names of pioneering industrialists Toeplitz, Epstein, and Kronenberg, and added Natansohn in the field of chemical and paper industry and Loewenstein in mechanical industry. In the discussion about the proposed budget for 1936, Rubinstein reminded the Sejm that, when given the opportunity, Jews also founded and developed the production of tobacco, matches, and alcohol—the very industries that, when they became the monopoly of the Polish state, then barred Jews.[25] To Zmigryder-Konopka, history offered a useful perspective on contemporary attacks against the Jews in Poland and their economic role: 'There were in various periods various opinions about the development of Polish towns. There was a period when Jewish commerce opposed the taking over of these positions in towns by foreign capital and in this way—although it goes unappreciated—played its role.'[26]

Vitally important for the community seeking an organizational model, the past provided Jewish representatives with arguments in favour of Jewish cultural autonomy based on the model of the *kehilah* (Jewish community) in the Polish lands. In 1924 Jewish senator Markus Braude, a rabbi of the liberal synagogue in Łódź since 1909 and a member of the Central Committee of the Zionist Organization, affirmed the wide definition of the *kehilah* prerogatives: 'Such an understanding of the Jewish *kehilah* [*gmina żydowska*] is in fact in harmony with the tradition of the Polish State. Independent Poland never saw it only as a religious community, but treated it always as a basic organizational form of Polish Jewry.'[27] The notion of limiting the *kehilah* to fulfilling only religious needs, argued Braude, was new and had been imported from western Europe.

Jewish parliamentarians sought solutions to contemporary crises in history. Schiper added his name to a petition demanding justice for the Jewish community in Beresteczko and for two Jews tortured by Polish soldiers in May 1920, during the Polish–Bolshevik war: 'Means applied by the soldiers . . . in order to force the con-

---

[24] The 69th session of the Sejm, 15 Feb. 1938 (BS, Sejm 1919–1939, Stenogramy Sejmu, RPII/4/69, no. 000021945, pp. 79–80).

[25] See Rubinstein's speech at the 4th session of the Sejm, 5 and 6 Dec. 1935 (BS, Sejm 1919–1939, Stenogramy Sejmu, RPII/4/4, no. 000021880, p. 89).

[26] The 10th Session of the Senate, 14 Mar. 1939 (BS, Sejm 1919–1939, Stenogramy Senatu, RPII/5/10, no. 000023084, p. 76).

[27] The 70th session of the Senate, 28 July 1924 (BS, Sejm 1919–1939, Stenogramy Senatu, RPII/1/70, no. 000007742, p. 2).

fession from the accused can only be compared with the refined methods of medieval Inquisition.'[28] But historical precedents went further. In parliament, Jewish representatives analysed contemporary antisemitism, violence, propaganda, and legal discrimination, referring to Jewish history in general and Polish Jewish history in particular. They insisted that these antisemitic behaviours were in contrast to Polish culture and politics in the past. Sommerstein evoked a 'noble tradition of tolerance and coexistence', based on the idealistic historical heritage of a 'knightly spirit', in which there was no shedding of Jewish blood, and no expulsions or Jewish yellow badges.[29] This knightly spirit implied generous hospitality towards those in need of protection. More generally, Jewish parliamentarians claimed that it was 'Poland's beautiful historical tradition' to grant religious tolerance to the Jews.[30] In February 1936 Sommerstein referred to the violence against the Jews and especially Jewish students as a 'scandalous, chronic disease' to which the new elements of racist antisemitism imported from Germany were now added. He contrasted it with the Poland of Konopnicka's *Rota*, which— he insisted—exemplified Poland's tradition of not following foreign examples blindly.[31] Discussing anti-Jewish propaganda and violence, especially a recent pogrom in Przytyk in March 1936, Schorr also contrasted an idealized past with the worrisome current situation of Polish Jews: 'The great traditions of the Polish nation, traditions of religious tolerance and respect for the rights of national minorities, were not lost during the partitions of Poland. They do exist, [but they] are being suppressed and fouled by those who instigate the lowest instincts in the name of their immediate goals in the struggle for power.'[32]

Jewish parlamentarians repeatedly referred to historical figures representing these Polish traditions: King Kazimierz the Great, who granted the Jews their rights, the bard Adam Mickiewicz, and the statesman Józef Piłsudski, who championed the equality of all citizens of Poland.[33] Mincberg argued that violence

---

[28] 'Interpelacja posła Schipera i tow. Do Pana Ministra Spraw Wojskowych i Pana Ministra Skarbu w sprawie torturowania Barucha Fuhrera, aptekarza, oraz Icka Bergera, obu z Beresteczka, przez ułanów z VI-tej dywizji z rozkazu nieznanego z nazwiska porucznika i podporucznika tej samej dywizji oraz wynagrodzenia wyrządzonej im szkody', Warsaw, 14 Dec. 1920 (BS, Sejm 1919–1939, RPII/0/1632, no. 000011975).

[29] The 16th session of the Sejm, 24 Feb. 1936 (BS, Sejm 1919–1939, Stenogramy Sejmu, RPII/4/16, no. 000021892, pp. 36–7). Moreover, he noted, the current waves of violence against the Jews were also aimed against the Polish state.

[30] See the discussion about slaughterhouses in the 80th session of the Sejm, 25 Mar. 1938 (BS, Sejm 1919–1939, Stenogramy Sejmu, RPII/4/80, no. 000021956, pp. 139–42).

[31] The 10th session of the Sejm, 17 Feb. 1936 (BS, Sejm 1919–1939, Stenogramy Sejmu, RPII/4/10, no. 000021886, p. 100).

[32] The 11th Session of the Senate, 12 Mar. 1936 (BS, Sejm 1919–1939, Stenogramy Senatu, RPII/5/11, no. 000022995, p. 48). On the pogrom in Przytyk see Żyndul, 'If Not a Pogrom, Then What?'.

[33] See Mincberg's speech at the 18th session of the Sejm, 26 Feb. 1936 (BS, Sejm 1919–1939,

against the Jews 'poisons the souls of Jewish youth', who lacked the historical knowledge of better times. But younger Jews lacked the perspective of the elders who were able to see through the crisis:

> When the older generation encounters expressions of hostile attitude from certain circles of Polish society, it does not identify the Polish nation with Endeks [members and sympathizers of National Democracy] or members of ONR [Obóz Narodowo-Radykalny, The National Radical Camp]. We [the older generation] have witnessed different times and shared memories of the sad days we survived under the yoke of the tsar, and the beautiful days of regaining state sovereignty bind us together.[34]

A year earlier, in February 1937, Mincberg had admonished parliament that

> we have an entire legion of home-grown philosophers and economists and historical philosophers and sociologists, creating... some new myth of a Jewish danger and aiming at depriving us of historical and civic rights acquired in the course of centuries and won with blood. These rights of ours have too famous an affiliation and too great a genealogy, rooted in the legal acts of Kazimierz the Great, Zygmunt August, and Stefan Batory, for the ideology of ultra-Endeks, or crypto-Endeks to break this framework. We will defend our rights tooth and nail and no power will take them away from us.[35]

Ideas opposing these traditions of tolerance and hospitality were not only morally questionable, he suggested, but foreign.[36] Rubinstein echoed this argument, describing Poland as a country that found itself at a crossroads, choosing either to follow the idealistic heritage that had brought it prosperity and well-deserved glory, or to succumb to totalitarian influences from the Soviet Union and Nazi Germany. As in the past, he declared, Poland needed to serve as the bulwark of Christianity, and in the 1930s it became the bulwark of European culture.[37]

Parliament provided an important stage for Jewish representatives, whose appeals nonetheless increasingly fell on deaf ears. Yet no less importantly, the representatives also addressed their constituencies. While their appeals failed to strike a chord with the country's politicians, they circulated widely in the Jewish

Stenogramy Sejmu, RPII/4/18, no. 000021894, p. 42). See also Rubinstein's speech at the 14th session of the Sejm, 21 Feb. 1936, in which he indicated that anti-Jewish violence in Poland tainted the country and the memory of Piłsudski (BS, Sejm 1919–1939, Stenogramy Sejmu, RPII/4/14, no. 000021890, pp. 58, 61–3).

[34] The 67th session of the Sejm, 11 Feb. 1938 (BS, Sejm 1919–1939, Stenogramy Sejmu, RPII/4/67, no. 000021943, p. 60).

[35] The 46th Session of the Sejm, 24 Feb. 1937 (BS, Sejm 1919–1939, Stenogramy Sejmu, RPII/4/46, no. 000021922, p. 19).

[36] See Mincberg's speech at the 80th session of the Sejm, 25 Mar. 1938 (BS, Sejm 1919–1939, Stenogramy Sejmu, RPII/4/80, no. 000021956, p. 139).

[37] The 66th Session of the Sejm, 10 Feb. 1938 (BS, Sejm 1919–1939, Stenogramy Sejmu, RPII/4/66, no. 000021942, p. 84).

press, in Polish as well as in Yiddish and Hebrew translations. By referring to history as a tool for defending Jewish rights, Jewish representatives addressed, educated, and mobilized a wide audience. Jewish political representatives issued special brochures which framed the struggles of Jewish parliamentarians for equal rights of Jewish citizens in the country in historical terms. In the introduction to one such brochure, published in Warsaw in 1922, Apolinary Hartglas—a lawyer and Zionist representative in the Polish parliament—explained contemporary political discourse about the status of the Jews in Poland as a continuation of the reforms discussed in 1791, on the eve of the last partition of the Polish–Lithuanian Commonwealth, and a noble effort to banish the legacy of the Russian domination during the partitions.[38] Moreover, the Jewish press followed the activities of the Jewish caucus closely and cited extensively speeches delivered in the Polish parliament.

## History Lessons in the Jewish Press

In the interwar period, local and national Jewish newspapers in Polish, Yiddish, and Hebrew served as a means through which Polish Jewish historians writing about Jewish history could reach a wide audience.[39] Despite economic challenges and censorship, the Jewish press flourished.[40] In 1932 there were 1,831 newspapers and journals published in Poland officially: 1,544 in Polish, including Polish Jewish press, 84 in Yiddish, and 9 in Hebrew.[41] Not only in the capital but also in other urban centres or even smaller towns, Jewish dailies and journals were widely read. There were also local publications,[42] and in 1936 the daily circulation of the Yiddish press reached 450,000 copies.[43]

The editors of some Jewish journals saw the discussion of the Polish Jewish past as part of their educational and political agenda. These publications provided Jewish readers with the historical context for understanding their current political and economic battles. Professional historians and journalists responded to allegations in the Polish press and in parliament by recounting the close relationship that had existed in the past between Polish Jewry and the Polish land and state, or

---

[38] See Hartglas, 'Żółta lata (zamiast wstępu)'.

[39] Chone Shmeruk describes these newspapers as a crucial component of the trilingual 'Jewish cultural polysystem in which language is the major vehicle of expression'. Shmeruk, 'Hebrew–Yiddish–Polish', 296. For a theoretical discussion of cultural polysystems see Even-Zohar, *Polysystem Studies*. For a discussion of the Jewish press in Warsaw, see Fuks, *Prasa żydowska w Warszawie*. On the Jewish press in Polish see White, 'Jewish Lives in the Polish Language' and Steffen, 'Polska—to także my!'     [40] See Nalewajko-Kulikov, 'Prasa żydowska na ziemiach polskich', 16–19.

[41] *Statystyka druków, 1932*, 21.

[42] Fuks, 'Prasa żydowska w Lublinie'. See also Kopciowski's exemplary study of a provincial Jewish daily, *Wos hert zich in der prowinc*.     [43] Jamiński, *Prasa żydowska w Polsce*, 5.

by enumerating Jewish economic contributions and acts of patriotism. The discussion of the Jewish contribution to Poland's economic development and the country's political interests had clear contemporary overtones. By describing Jewish autonomy in the Polish–Lithuanian Commonwealth, they presented their readers with a viable model for Jewish national autonomy in the newly established Polish Republic, arguing that the Jewish community had earned its place in Poland and that the Polish political leadership in the past had appreciated the close connection between the fate of the state and the security of its Jewry. Ironically, the argument that the Jews had proved themselves useful or loyal to Poland was rooted in an assumption that they needed to earn their place, that they were still alien and not entitled to the same rights as other Poles. It showed how fragile the sense of being at home in Poland was even to those who used the press to argue for it. The Jewish daily press thus saw history not just as appealing content, but as a subject of significant relevance to its readership.

From the beginning of their academic careers, Schorr, Bałaban, and Schiper wrote in Polish-language journals such as *Wschód* and *Moriah*, addressing the young Jewish intelligentsia in Galicia. In the 1920s and 1930s, they continued publishing their work in Polish-, Yiddish-, and Hebrew-language journals such as *Tel-Awiw*, *Tygodnik Nowy*, *Życie Żydowskie*, *Tygodnik Żydowski*, *Nowe Życie*, *Opinia*, *Miesięcznik Żydowski*, *Baderekh*, and *Literarishe bleter*. Articles on the history of Polish Jewry also appeared in the journals of Jewish communities: *Kronik fun der yidisher kehile* in Łódź, *Głos Gminy Żydowskiej* in Warsaw, and *Urzędowa Gazeta Gminy Izraelickiej* in Katowice. Last but not least, Jewish historians addressed readers of the daily press in the popular Yiddish *Der moment* and *Haynt*, and the local *Łodzer togblat*, *Nayer folksblat*, and *Lubliner togblat*, as well as in the Polish-language *Nowy Dziennik*, *Chwila*, and *Nasz Przegląd*. Historical articles in the dailies appeared in special Sunday sections, such as *Chwila*'s 'Literatura – Nauka – Sztuka', or in connection with anniversaries of current events that made historical context particularly relevant to the readers. Leading Jewish dailies in Warsaw—*Haynt*, *Der moment*, *Folks-tsaytung*, *Dos yidishe togblat* and *Nasz Przegląd*—had their regional sections and local correspondents, which made them relevant for a wide Jewish audience beyond the capital, for example in Lublin, where Jews read such Polish Jewish newspapers as *Nasz Przegląd*, *Chwila*, and *Nowy Dziennik*.[44] But Jewish newspapers continued to appear locally even in smaller towns.[45] The provincial press took an interest in local history in parti-

---

[44] For articles about the Yiddish and Polish Jewish press see Nalewajko-Kulikov, '"Hajnt" (1908–1939)'; Weiser, '"Der moment" (1910–1939)'; Kozłowska, '"Folkscajtung" (1921–1939)'; Fuks, 'Prasa żydowska w Lublinie'.

[45] *Statystyka druków wydanych w Rzeczypospolitej Polskiej na rok 1937*, 20.

cular. Among the founders of *Lubliner togblat*, for example, and its first editor, was Shlomo Nusenbaum, a local merchant but also a journalist and historian of the local community.[46]

The Polish-language Jewish press faced unique challenges and offered unique opportunities of its own. By employing the same language as the surrounding Polish nation, the Polish-language Jewish press was able to speak to that nation; a Polish Jewish newspaper was therefore involved in Polish culture as no Yiddish paper could be or wanted to be. It provided Polish Jews with insights into general culture and a window onto the Jewish world for non-Jewish Poles, in an endeavour to give Polish society, 'with whom we live on one land'—as the first issue of *Opinia* put it—'a mirror in which it can see a faithful image of Jewish society'. In the words of Jakób Appenszlak in the founding issue of *Nasz Przegląd*, the object was to render 'accessible to Polish society an understanding of our national self, its laws and ideals'.[47] Katrin Steffen has termed the collective identity promoted in the Polish-language Jewish press 'Jewish Polishness', a project in which history played a key role.[48]

The Polish-language Jewish journals reached a wide swath of the Jewish intelligentsia who were fluent in Polish and familiar with Polish and European culture: 'The development of the Polish-Jewish press must continue', declared the editors of *Tygodnik Nowy* in the summer of 1919, 'in light of the fact that Polish weeklies ignore Jewish matters'.[49] To fill this void, Jewish journals in Polish became a forum for discussions of Jewish history and culture in the diaspora.[50] For the most part, the journal *Miesięcznik Żydowski* sought to reach the Jewish intelligentsia who read Polish.[51] In keeping with the journal's pledge 'to rescue from oblivion and to illuminate the thoughts, deeds, merits, and works of Polish Jewry in the past',[52] almost every issue included a discussion of the history of Jewish life in Poland. The journal strove to evoke the Jewish past for the sake of the present and future or, as Bałaban put it, 'to inform the Jewish intelligentsia about current problems

---

[46] Kopciowski, *Wos hert zich in der prowinc*, 213–14. The first issue appeared while Lublin was still under Austrian occupation, on 15 Jan. 1918, and it must have been approved by Majer Bałaban, who was responsible for Jewish publications (ibid. 42–3, 211, 213).

[47] 'Cele i zadania', *Opinia*, 1933. no. 1, as cited in Fuks, *Prasa żydowska w Warszawie*, 279; *Na posterunku*, no. 1, 25 Mar. 1923, as cited in Appenszlak, 'Piętnastolenie "Naszego Przeglądu"'. See Steinlauf, 'The Polish-Jewish Daily Press', 229.

[48] Steffen, *Jüdische Polonität*, 92–9.     [49] See 'Prospekt' in *Tygodnik Nowy*, 27 June 1919, 2.

[50] See e.g. 'Od wydawnictwa', *Tel-Awiw*, 1/1 (June 1919), 1–2, and Bałaban, 'Chazarowie'. See also the introduction from the editors recommending Bałaban's article as a counter-polemic to the assimilationists, who pointed to the alleged shared roots between east European Jews and the Khazars (ibid. 74).     [51] See Chapter 3. See also Aleksiun, 'Molding the Liberal Jewish Intelligentsia'.

[52] *Miesięcznik Żydowski*, 'Prospekt', undated, 2, as cited in Borzymińska, '*Miesięcznik Żydowski*: w 50 rocznicę wydania pierwszego numeru', 63–4.

from a certain historical perspective'.⁵³ In the very first issue of *Miesięcznik Żydowski*, Bałaban published an article entitled 'When and Whence Did the Jews Come to Poland'.⁵⁴ He argued that the question was important 'for [Jews] in Poland, for Polish science and for an understanding of the issue that we generally call "the Jewish question"', a question that 'did not interest the founders of a general Jewish history in the first (or even in the second) half of the nineteenth century, namely Jost, Geiger, and Grätz'.⁵⁵ Bałaban stressed the parallel between the antiquity of Jewish history in the Polish lands and the early stages of the formation of the Polish state. He also acknowledged that the questions of both timing and direction of the Jewish immigration to Poland were political and as such had often been treated with bias by historians. He supported the theory of two directions of Jewish migration to Poland: from the west and from the east, although he admitted to the lack of solid material pertaining to the latter.⁵⁶

The question of the antiquity of Jewish settlement in the Polish lands was of particular importance. In 1937 recent statements made in the Polish parliament and the general 'anti-Jewish psychosis' motivated Bałaban to publish a series of articles arguing that Jews had been settled in Poland for hundreds of years.⁵⁷ He presented the consecutive waves of Jewish immigration in Poland and insisted that 'Jewish scholarship must not be silent but must elucidate the general problem and especially the sacramental question: When did the Jews arrive in Poland?'⁵⁸ Going beyond the argument about the ancient origin of the Jewish community in the Polish lands, dating back to the dawn of the Polish state, Bałaban insisted that the masses of Jewish immigrants in the middle of the thirteenth century had not been powerless exiles. Rather, they brought with them the privileges they had

> won in Germany in the period of Crusades and [were] granted and confirmed for the first time in [the charter of] 1264 by the Kalisz prince Bolesław the Pious for the Jews in Great Poland. . . . The very fact of granting the immigrants their rights [that] they had enjoyed, namely the privileges, and even expanding them, teaches us that Jewish immigrants in Poland were a desirable element, with an important economic mission to fulfil.⁵⁹

---

⁵³ Bałaban, '"Miesięcznik Żydowski": Na marginesie dwóch roczników', quoted in Prokop-Janiec, *Polish-Jewish Literature in the Interwar Years*, 11. See *Miesięcznik Żydowski*, 'Prospekt', undated, 4. See also Steinlauf, 'The Polish-Jewish Daily Press', 229.

⁵⁴ Bałaban, 'Kiedy i skąd przybyli Żydzi do Polski'.

⁵⁵ Ibid. 1–2. For Bałaban 'the reason for this phenomenon can be easily understood: it results from the line of thought of these men, who established the foundations of the edifice of a universal Jewish history'. ⁵⁶ Ibid. 1, 6.

⁵⁷ Bałaban, 'Od kiedy my, Żydzi, mieszkamy na ziemiach polskich?' ⁵⁸ Ibid., 7 Feb. 1937, p. 11.

⁵⁹ Ibid. Moreover, he argued, the fact that Polish rulers continued confirming the first privilege further proved that it was not a coincidence.

Concluding his account of Jewish migrations, Bałaban linked history and contemporary politics once more and condemned Polish politicians who questioned the status of Jews in the eastern borderlands of the Second Polish Republic. Even if Jewish communities who had lived there experienced a degree of Russification in the nineteenth century, argued Bałaban, they still were Polish Jews, with deep roots in the land.[60]

In the pages of Jewish journals and dailies readers found historical evidence that Jews of the diaspora, including Polish Jews, had benefited their countries 'in all fields of life and thought, working together with the rest of the society'.[61] Some of the central topics pertained to perceptions of the Jews' economic role in the nation. Historians and journalists asked whether, in the past, Polish Jewry had been a productive element of society.[62] Many authors reminded their readers of the multifaceted contribution of Polish Jewry to the Polish economy and culture over the course of centuries. In his article 'Ten Centuries of Coexistence', in *Miesięcznik Żydowski*, Galician Zionist Ludwik Oberlaender noted that Jews did not come to Poland as an 'inert group of refugees' or 'undesired strangers', but because the country needed them to develop a monetary economy.[63] Jews had been invited to Poland 'to counterbalance the German influx and to develop the economy and to provide capital necessary for the development of the country, which proved the organizational genius of Kazimierz the Great'.[64] Oberlaender argued that Jews brought their talents and repaid the country for its hospitality:

What we managed to rescue from the burning stakes of the Spanish Inquisition, from the hands of the raving crowd of the German Crusaders, we brought here. It was not only gold and precious stones; it was also bright thought, pointing to new paths in economic development with the accumulated experience, the hand of the artisan trained in skills unknown to the inhabitants of this land and a stubborn energy, which crystallized like a stone in the constant struggle for existence.[65]

Later waves of Jewish immigration from the west brought a 'high level of culture and . . . capital' and 'creative co-operation with the burghers in the fields of treasury and trade'. Jewish economic activities promoted the interests of the Polish state on the Baltic coast and linked the eastern borderlands with the Crown.[66] Jews participated in the economic development of the Polish–Lithuanian Commonwealth from the fourteenth to the seventeenth centuries, playing an important role in the country's economic life. The Polish nobility bore full responsibility

---

[60] Ibid., 21 Feb. 1937, p. 9.      [61] Sternbach, 'O antysemityźmie', 106–7.
[62] Eisenstein, 'Prawda o lichwie żydowskiej w Polsce w XIV w.'; Eisenstein, 'Jeszcze raz "Prawda o lichwie żydowskiej w Polsce w XIV w."'; Feldman, 'Jeszcze "Prawda o lichwie żydowskiej w XIV w."'.
[63] Oberlaender, 'Dziewięć wieków współżycia', 98–9.
[64] Ibid. 100.      [65] Ibid. 101–2.      [66] Ibid. 102–3.

for shaping the country's economy in such a way as to give the Jews their status.⁶⁷ These were historical claims with contemporary overtones. But Oberlaender also responded directly to contemporary accusations: 'We often come across the thesis that we contributed to the collapse of towns in Poland, that in the weakened body of the state the Jews multiplied in excess and led Poland to her decline, eating the marrow out of her bones.' He compared conditions in Poland with the more advantageous situation in western Europe, concluding: 'In our [country] reasons and results got mixed up . . . We have not been eating the marrow out of her bones, since there was none there.' Oberlaender argued that Jews continued to contribute to Poland's economic development after the partitions, whenever conditions enabled them to show initiative and to work. In the second half of the nineteenth century, in Congress Poland, 'Jewish energy, labour, frugality, and capital greatly helped in the magnificent development of industry and trade of the Kingdom [of Poland]'.⁶⁸ This co-operation, lasting until the last decade of the nineteenth century, also had important political implications. Not only did economic and commercial institutions founded by Jews create employment opportunities for Poles, but the Jews' activities prevented 'foreign, i.e. German, French, Belgian, and Russian capital from taking over many more economic outposts'.⁶⁹ Numerous articles in the Jewish press echoed Oberlaender's argument. Historians such as Bałaban reminded Jewish readers that the positive attitudes of such Polish rulers as Kazimierz the Great towards Jews resulted from their having understood the Jews' important role in Poland.⁷⁰

In 1932 *Miesięcznik Żydowski* published the first in a series of articles by Aron Eisenstein discussing usury.⁷¹ The author questioned the dominant hypothesis that Jews in fourteenth-century Poland were predominantly moneylenders, pointing to Jewish involvement in trade and agriculture. Though he admitted that Jewish creditors played an important role, Eisenstein stressed that 'seventy-three Jewish creditors [from the city books of Kraków, Lwów, and the province of Great Poland] do not constitute the entire Jewish society in Poland'.⁷² In his study of the Warsaw Jewish community in 1840, one S. Warszawski concluded that despite their concentration in commerce, 'the majority of the Jewish population is busy in productive professions'.⁷³ He pointed to the difficulties Jews faced when trying to find employment in other professions, such as the civil service.⁷⁴ Wilhelm Berkel-

---

⁶⁷ Oberlaender, 'Dziewięć wieków współżycia', 105.
⁶⁸ Ibid. 108–10. See also Friedman, 'Rola Żydów w rozwoju łódzkiego przemysłu włókienniczego'.
⁶⁹ Oberlaender, 'Dziewięć wieków współżycia', 110.
⁷⁰ Bałaban, 'Kazimierz Wielki a Żydzi polscy'.
⁷¹ Eisenstein, 'Prawda o lichwie żydowskiej w Polsce w XIV w.'. ⁷² Ibid. 163.
⁷³ Warszawski, 'Struktura społeczna i gospodarcza żydostwa warszawskiego w 1840 r.', 261–2.
⁷⁴ Ibid. 260.

hammer argued that Poland benefited from allowing Jewish settlement in the country as much as the Jews did, a fact often obscured by Polish historians. Poles and Jews, he noted, had coexisted in the past due to mutual interests, not selfless tolerance.[75]

In the Jewish press, historians portrayed the fate and fortune of the Polish state and its Jewish community as intimately linked, above all in the economy.[76] Oberlaender argued that 'the period of development in international trade was a period of Poland flourishing and Polish affluence. It was also a period of prosperity and strength for Polish Jewry, which thrived economically and culturally, despite difficult struggles for rights in commerce and rights of existence in the cities.'[77] In the second half of the seventeenth century, he reminded his readers, after Poland's economy collapsed following the Cossack and Swedish wars, the prosperity and security of the Jewish community ended as well.[78] Jewish autonomy began to break down, and it had disappeared by the mid-eighteenth century, a phenomenon seen in the context of the general crisis of the country, which failed to mobilize all its inhabitants, and the society of which proved 'incapable of creative effort'.[79] Due to their vulnerable position, Bałaban argued as well, Jews shared the misfortunes of the country and at times fared worse than the Gentile population.[80]

Oberlaender pointed to Polish politicians and reformers at the time of the Four Year Diet who realized that 'the Jewish question is linked with the whole of Polish affairs . . . They understood that the fate and development of the Jewish population cannot be ignored by the state. They understood that there are creative powers in the Jews, which should be uncovered and utilized.' This realization, he said, led to the idea of making them citizens of Poland.[81] Warszawski reminded his readers that his choice of the date of 1840 for analysing the economic and social structure of Jewish society in Warsaw was 'not accidental. The Jewish economy cannot be treated apart from the general economy of the country.'[82] He pointed out that, for two decades beginning in 1831, the whole country had struggled with poverty, the loss of the Russian market, and Russian persecutions.

This discussion, as well as the analyses of changing economic patterns among European Jewry during the Middle Ages, carried strong political overtones in the Polish Jewish context of the early 1930s. While reviewing Jewish economic history

---

[75] Berkelhammer, 'Istota problemu polsko-żydowskiego', 56–7.

[76] See Schall, 'Najdawniesze osadnictwo żydowskie w Przemyślu'; Halpern, 'Przyczynek do dziejów osadnictwa Żydów na Mazowszu'; Feldman, 'Dzieje Żydów w Warszawie'; Gelber, 'Żydzi a zagadnienie reformy Żydów na Sejmie Czteroletnim'; Lewin, 'Udział Żydów w wyborach sejmowych w dawnej Polsce'; Bałaban, 'Stan kahału krakowskiego'.

[77] Oberlaender, 'Dziewięć wieków współżycia', 104.

[78] Ibid. 107.    [79] Ibid. 108.    [80] See Bałaban, 'Walka o rządy w kahale krakowskim'.

[81] Oberlaender, 'Dziewięć wieków współżycia', 109.

[82] Warszawski, 'Struktura społeczna i gospodarcza żydostwa warszawskiego w 1840 r.', 245.

in Poland, Bałaban made this point clear by comparing past and present:

> Today in the resurrected and independent Poland, the old aspirations of townsmen, interrupted for the first time during the Renaissance and then again in the period of struggles for Poland's existence, have resurfaced. The struggle for the nationalization of commerce and industry rages similarly to the struggle in the west during the Middle Ages. This battle has not yet finished, with both sides on the ramparts![83]

Similarly, in writing about the history of public discourse concerning the status of Jews, Polish Jewish historians addressed contemporary concerns by referring to the attitudes of Stanisław Staszic, the revered Polish enlightened intellectual of the late eighteenth century. Popular articles published in the Jewish press in the 1930s addressed the attitudes and ambivalence towards the Jews among the Polish elites who had toyed with political, social, and economic reforms.[84] Moreover, Jewish authors raised questions about Jewish attitudes to the reforms. According to Nathan Gelber, in the last decades of the Polish–Lithuanian Commonwealth, Jews had tried to improve their situation through interventions with the king, before and after the Third of May Constitution (1791).[85] Under the influence of the Haskalah, Jewish leaders implored the king to improve the situation of the Jews and continued their struggle for the change in the status of the Jews. Their efforts were important even if they did not represent the entire Jewish community.[86] Thus, historical examples gave the readers of the Jewish press a historical context for the polemics of contemporary Poland and impressed upon them that Jews had always been central to the discussions about the country's future.

In addition to recognizing the history of the Jews' service to Poland and their role in developing trade and expanding the country's urban centres, the press brought up their role in Poland's international diplomacy.[87] Probing the relationship between the Polish state and Polish Jews, historians explored Jewish history in the Polish lands during the partitions, including the Jews' part in the struggles for independence. The Jewish press provided examples of Jewish participation in moments of Polish national triumph and mourning. In Warsaw and other cities,

---

[83] Bałaban, 'Zagadnienia historjozofji żydowskiej', 379. He pointed to the same link between historical and contemporary practices in another article, where he discussed the 'maturing of the Gentile tradesmen [or] what we call today nationalization of the commerce and craftsmanship [*unarodowienie handlu i rzemiosła*] which pushes Jews away from these posts and forces them to look for other sources of livelihood'. See Bałaban, 'Kiedy i skąd przybyli Żydzi do Polski', 9.

[84] See Lewin, 'Staszic a Żydzi', *Chwila*, 20 Jan. 1926 and id., 'Staszic a Żydzi', *Nowy Dziennik*, 18 Jan. 1926. See also, on the early history of hasidism, Feinkind, 'Dysputa żydowska za czasów Stanisława Staszyca'.      [85] Gelber, 'Żydzi a zagadnienie reformy Żydów na Sejmie Czteroletnim'.

[86] Ibid. 1/11 (1931), 440.

[87] See Mieses, 'Żyd w polskiej służbie dyplomatycznej w XVI wieku', and 'Żydzi w służbie dyplomatycznej w średniowieczu'.

Jews participated in celebrations of the first anniversary of the Third of May Constitution: 'in order to show their attachment, there were services in the synagogues, they sang songs of thanks that were translated into Polish, German, and French and sent to the king and the state dignitaries.'[88]

Historians pointed to the involvement of Jews in the struggle for Poland's independence, and to the cold welcome they received from Poles. In one example, Bałaban discussed the situation of Berek Joselewicz's son, Józef Berkowicz, who met with hostility when holding positions in Congress Poland before the uprising of November 1830.[89] Bałaban examined the correspondence between Joachim Lelewel (1786–1861) an eminent figure in Polish emigration following the November uprising of 1830, and Ozjasz Ludwig Lubliner, a Jew who was a similarly prominent member of Polish political exile circles. He pointed to the mistrust the Polish insurgent army had towards the Jews in Warsaw in 1831. Consequently 'only after many efforts and a failed attempt to create separate Jewish units, were [Jews] allowed in. Now, in exile ... Jews were seen as interlopers, imposing themselves on strangers and interfering in matters that had nothing to do with them. This was the basis of numerous complaints by Józef Berkowicz ... and Lubliner.'[90] Warszawski discussed Jewish participation in the Warsaw City Guard (Gwardia Miejska) during the uprising of November 1830.[91] He painted the picture of the whole country pervaded with enthusiasm at the outbreak of the uprising. Importantly, the leading circles of Jewish society in Warsaw had become enraptured by the general ardour and charged with enthusiasm for the endeavours of the Polish nation. This enthusiasm quickly cooled, however, when the new dictator, Józef Chłopicki, excluded Jews from the right to serve in the newly created City Guard. This was a painful and unexpected blow to the intelligentsia and the progressive section of Jewish society.[92] Following a Jewish petition, 'qualifying Jews' were allowed to join the Guard. For the youth, it was mostly an opportunity 'to get rid of the beard', according to Warszawski, but for 'the progressive section of the Jewish population' conceptions of citizenship must have been at stake.[93] Warszawski assured his readers that Jewish guards served faithfully, although they encountered hostility and ridicule.[94]

Schiper, Bałaban, and others published extensively on various aspects of

---

[88] Gelber, 'Żydzi a zagadnienie reformy Żydów na Sejmie Czteroletnim', 1/11 (1931), 436. See Bałaban, 'Fragmenty historyczne: Konstytucja 3-go maja a żydzi'.

[89] Bałaban, 'Syn Berka Joselewicza'. Despite his experiences, Bałaban notes, Berkowicz hurried to Warsaw, leaving behind his family as soon as the uprising broke out in order 'to complete his father's work, namely to organize a Jewish regiment'.

[90] Bałaban, 'Korespondencja Lublinera z Lelewelem (1832–1848)', 289.

[91] Warszawski, 'Gwardja Miejska miasta stołecznego Warszawy'.

[92] Ibid. 56.     [93] Ibid. 57.     [94] Ibid. 62–3.

Polish–Jewish relations before and during the January 1863 uprising.[95] Explaining Polish–Jewish rapprochement prior to the uprising, Schiper pointed to the Polish 'change of heart' in the practical search for allies for future struggle. Jews, including those in both hasidic and mitnagdic circles, supported the Polish cause with forgiving and generous hearts. Around 200 Jews were arrested or fell in battle, and many more worked for the underground government in propaganda and military intelligence, as well as providing food and ammunition.[96] Bałaban detailed the participation of the Jews in Congress Poland, Kraków, and Lwów in patriotic activities and as supporters of the Polish national cause, especially the acculturated Jewish intelligentsia, but even in more traditional circles, symbolized by Rabbi Dov Ber Meisels.[97] He pointed to new research demonstrating that involvement with the uprising surmounted religious, social, and geographical barriers and was not limited to the intelligentsia in the major cities of Congress Poland. He included insurgents from Jewish families who had converted to Catholicism, but whom contemporaries continued to view as Jews.[98]

Bałaban explained that hundreds, if not thousands, of Jewish youths demonstrated their patriotism by participating in Polish patriotic manifestations before the 1863 insurrection, then fought in the uprising, with many ultimately being exiled to Siberia. Some met death on the gallows and in the taigas of Siberia. Admittedly, not all of Polish Jewry supported and participated in the uprising. But Bałaban asked: 'Did all of native Polish [*rdzennie polskie*] society answer the appeal? What percentage of Polish youth joined the ranks of the uprising on 22 January 1863 and what were the attitudes of Polish lords and peasants towards the uprising?'[99] Historical facts about the participation of Jewish youth in the uprising, confirmed by sentences passed in Russian military courts, were evidence to put to rest contemporary doubts about Jews' loyalty to the country and put a stop to the idea that Jewish soldiers were of no value in the Second Polish Republic.[100]

Notably, on the eve of the Second World War, Jewish historians used the history of Jewish participation and sacrifices during the uprising of 1863 as an example

---

[95] See Bałaban, 'Żydzi a Powstanie Styczniowe (1863)', and Schiper, 'Żydzi w Powstaniu Styczniowym'. See also Brandstaetter, 'Za naszą i waszą wolność'.

[96] Schiper, 'Żydzi w Powstaniu Styczniowym'.

[97] Bałaban, 'Żydzi a Powstanie Styczniowe (1863)'; Bałaban published articles on Rabbi Dov Ber Meisels in both *Haynt* and *Nowy Dziennik*, stressing that thousands of Jews and Poles participated in Meisels's funeral. See Bałaban, 'R. Berish Mayzelsh' (Yid.), and 'Rabin Beer Meisels'.

[98] Bałaban, 'Udział Żydów w Powstaniu Styczniowym'.

[99] Bałaban, 'Żydzi a Powstanie Styczniowe (1863)', 24 Jan. 1937, p. 9.

[100] Ibid. The history of the Jewish military involvement was also discussed by other historians in the Jewish press. See Mieses, 'Żydzi w armiach średniowiecznej Europy'. Bałaban also brought to his readers' attention Piłsudski's acknowledgement of the Jewish contribution and sacrifice. See Bałaban, 'Udział Żydów w Powstaniu Styczniowym'.

of the democratic and liberal tradition of a past government that did not differentiate among insurgents from different ethnic and religious backgrounds. Accounts of Jewish patriotic deeds on battlefields in more recent times, such as during the First World War, were used in the same way.[101] Discussions of Jewish patriotism in the Jewish press not only provided Jews with historical counter-arguments to insinuations that they were indifferent foreign elements in the state, but also mobilized them in the face of threats and accusations in the Second Polish Republic. Just a few months before the outbreak of the Second World War, Mieses discussed the history of the Jews' participation in and contribution to the military efforts of Poland: 'Whenever an enemy endangered the safety of the Polish state, [Jews] contributed to the best of their abilities to organize proper resistance.' He used examples from the time of the Chmielnicki uprising, the time of the Four Year Diet, and the Kościuszko uprising in 1794.[102] Michael Steinlauf correctly attributed the more frequent discussions of Jewish patriotism in the Polish-language journals, compared to the Yiddish and Hebrew publications, to the higher '"visibility" in the Polish world' of the former.[103] The Yiddish press, however, also published articles on some of the same events and persons in the long history of Polish Jewry's patriotism.[104]

In the pages of the press, Jewish authors discussed the history of autonomous Jewish institutions as the hallmark of Jewish history in Poland.[105] According to Arie Tartakower, until the mid-eighteenth century autonomous Jewish communities in Poland resembled miniature state structures, and could be a source of inspiration for contemporary attempts to revive communal institutions and widen their scope of interest.[106] Although critical of the elite of the Kraków Jewish community, Bałaban praised its officials for their daring and faithful attempts to protect their community.[107] In his interpretation, the communal leadership's task was not easy even in times of peace. Leaders exercised great responsibility, serving their communities despite hardships and dangers.[108] These articles reflected a sense of continuity between the past and contemporary challenges faced by Jews in the Second Polish Republic. Discussing the periodization of Polish Jewish history, Bałaban suggested the following categories: the loss of rights, literary periods, economic conditions, and changing means of defence.

---

[101] See Konic, 'Żydzi w Legjonach w okresie 1914–1917'; Mieses, 'Ofiarność Żydów dla armii w czasach wojennych w dziejach Polski', 14 May 1939.
[102] Mieses, 'Ofiarność Żydów dla armii w czasach wojennych w dziejach Polski'.
[103] Steinlauf, 'The Polish-Jewish Daily Press', 229.
[104] See e.g. Mieses, 'A Jewish Battalion Defends Praga' (Yid.).
[105] Bałaban, 'Stan kahału krakowskiego'; Schiper, 'Samorząd żydowski w Polsce'.
[106] Tartakower, 'Organizacja gmin żydowskich', 389.
[107] See Bałaban, 'Stan kahału krakowskiego', 413.
[108] Ibid. 417–18.

In the latter two categories, the link between past and present became especially apparent. Bałaban likened the defensive mechanisms of the *kehilah* and the system of Jewish autonomy in the past to the Religious Council (Rada Religijna), which the Polish government promised to establish, but did not follow through on.[109]

As hopes for creating institutions of Jewish national autonomy in the Second Polish Republic failed, Jewish authors turned their attention to local Jewish communities and their histories, legends, and personalities. Their hybrid style of history-writing blended local legends, personal memories, and archival research.[110] Among the topics treated in *Miesięcznik Żydowski*, anti-Jewish propaganda and violence seemed exceptionally important to the liberal Polish Jewish intelligentsia in the 1930s.[111] Roman Brandstaetter, a Polish Jewish writer and poet from Tarnów in Galicia, complained about the antisemitism of university students in nineteenth-century Wilno:

> Unfortunately, a certain section of university youth of that time in Wilno did not appreciate these liberal ideas, and ethical feelings did not run very strong. Luckily, it was a small group, which did not influence the rest of Wilno youth. The excesses of street thugs, of a small part of the youth should not be generalized; at most they proved that, even in the shadow of a high culture, irresponsible and dark elements ... may come to the forefront, escaping the need to be law-abiding [subjects].[112]

In 1933, a few days after the burnings of 'un-German' books across Nazi Germany, Bałaban compared cases from Montpellier in 1233, Paris in 1242, Italy in 1533, Kamieniec Podolski in 1757, and finally Berlin on 10 May 1933, conveying to his readers a sense of imminent danger and raised a question about the future of the Jews:

> The French Revolution and the aspirations of rationalists broke through the barriers of ignorance and completely changed the attitudes of humanity ... But what we have lived to see in Berlin ... and in other cities of the Third Reich is incomprehensible and such

---

[109] Bałaban, 'Zagadnienia historjozofji żydowskiej', 377.

[110] Bałaban, for example, published extensively on topics related to the history of the Jews in Galicia in Jewish dailies in Kraków and Lwów. See Bałaban, 'Drukarnie hebrajskie w Żółkwi i Lwowie'. See also his work on the history of Jewish community of Kraków dedicated to the memory of Dembitzer and Wetstein, 'Rok zbawienia i lata niedoli'.

[111] See Sternbach, 'O antysemityźmie'. In April 1939, Bałaban published an article with explicitly contemporary overtones about Luigi Chiarini's attempts to fight against the Talmud. See Bałaban, 'Walka z Talmudem na przestrzeni dziejów'. Bałaban's interest in the activities of the Catholic theologian and orientalist was hardly new. In 1937, Bałaban's student Dwojra Raskin graduated from Warsaw University with an MA thesis devoted to Chiarini. The thesis was published in Warsaw in 2012, with an introductory essay by Paweł Fijałkowski ('Dwojra Raskin i jej praca o księdzu Alojzym Chiarinim', in Raskin, *Ks. Profesor Ludwik Alojzy Chiarini w Warszawie ze szczególnym uwzględnieniem jego stosunku do Żydów*, 7–15).

[112] Brandstaetter, 'Wybryki antyżydowskie studentów Uniwersytetu Wileńskiego w r. 1815', 481.

a new phenomenon, that we cannot pass judgement about it just yet. We leave it to a future historian!¹¹³

The popular press addressed the issues of Jewish national autonomy in the 1920s and Jewish civic rights in the 1930s from a historical perspective. What lessons could the Jewish community in the Second Polish Republic learn from 900 years of Polish Jewish history? This history 'created an obligation for both sides', requiring a 'heightened sense of responsibility from contemporaries'.¹¹⁴ Oberlaender concluded his article by saying: 'Desiring to create a strong state, Poland must endeavour to develop the strength of its population on the basis of a thorough analysis of today's conditions of life, i.e. interdependence of all groups and social agents in Poland and in the entire world. The strength of over three million of the Jewish people belongs to Poland's assets.'¹¹⁵

To what extent did historical articles in the Jewish press shape the identity of Polish Jews? These journals had limited circulation: *Miesięcznik Żydowski* boasted only 800 subscribers in 1931, over half of whom were centred in two cities—Warsaw and Łódź.¹¹⁶ However, anecdotal information indicates that these journals circulated more widely among various circles of the Jewish reading public. Leon Pomorski relayed the following anecdote about becoming an ardent reader of *Tel-Awiw*:

I would read *Tel-Awiw* when I still lived in Słomniki, at the age of 16. I was the only subscriber there. When I came to Łódź, I went to the magazine's editorial office at Piotrowska 23. I entered. There was some lady there. I told her I was from Słomniki, but she said nothing. She revealed no enthusiasm whatsoever. She just took the money for the subscription. I was very disappointed.¹¹⁷

Given that historical articles were also published in Jewish dailies such as *Nasz Przegląd*, which had a circulation of 40,000 to 50,000 and *Haynt* and *Moment* with 100,000 subscribers, the Jewish press seems to have succeeded in presenting the local and national history of Polish Jewry to readers far beyond the milieu of professional historians.¹¹⁸ Jewish historians also published popular brochures about Jewish and Polish Jewish history and culture for a wide circle of readers.¹¹⁹ Within historical narratives, the multilingual Jewish press emphasized economic

¹¹³ Bałaban, 'Palenie ksiąg hebrajskich'.
¹¹⁴ Oberlaender, 'Dziewięć wieków współżycia', 105. ¹¹⁵ Ibid.
¹¹⁶ Of the 800 subscribers, 300 lived in Warsaw, 150 in Łódź, and the rest in 135 localities in Poland (AAN, B'nai B'rith, file 3, p. 133: 'Protokół posiedzenia pod przewodnictwem Mayzla', 23 Mar. 1931).
¹¹⁷ Spodenkiewicz, *The Missing District*, 107.
¹¹⁸ See Fuks, *Prasa żydowska w Warszawie*, 180, 263.
¹¹⁹ For example Mateusz Mieses, a member of the 'Humanitas' branch of B'nai B'rith in Przemyśl, published with the organization a brochure entitled *Hellenizm a Judaizim*, 'the first serious and scholarly response against the work of Zieliński'.

conditions. Such an emphasis in this context seems to indicate what readers were particularly interested in, especially in a period of economic and political crisis across Europe. By disseminating knowledge about issues crucial to Jewish identity and the goal of Jewish national self-preservation, editors and contributors to the Jewish press helped to foster a sense of collective Polish Jewish identity, and in so doing they played a role in the creation of a national Jewish culture in Poland.

## Polish Jewish History in the Schools and Beyond

Jewish historians believed that knowledge of Jewish and Polish Jewish history affected the ways young Polish Jews defined their place in Poland. By building a compelling curriculum and co-ordinating instruction in history, Jewish educators hoped to strengthen the identity of young Jews. Jewish educators did not leave this task to the children themselves or their immediate families, but tried to address it in their work and in the training of Jewish teachers. Although the way history was taught and incorporated in the curriculum varied, all schools included the subject as an essential part of shaping their students' identity as Polish Jews.

The Jewish school system in interwar Poland was a complex maze of independent private institutions as well as those linked to various religious, cultural, and political movements.[120] Private Jewish schools were divided into several educational movements, with and without government recognition: Tsisho (Central Jewish School Organization), committed to secular Yiddish education, created at a 1921 conference in Warsaw; the Hebrew-language Tarbut schools; bilingual Polish–Hebrew schools (or 'Braude schools'); and Yiddish–Hebrew (*shul-kult*) schools. Last but not least, Mizrachi created its own school organization, Yavne, while Agudah developed a chain of Khoyrev schools for boys and Bais Yaakov establishments for girls.[121] In addition, Jewish students attended private schools supported by entrepreneurs that had no clear ideological direction.[122] All private Jewish schools struggled with financial difficulties and administrative challenges. Without financial assistance from the Ministry of Religion and Education (Ministerstwo Wyznań Religijnych i Oświecenia Publicznego), they operated with the support of the Jewish community. Thus, Jews paid twice for the education of their children: directly and through state taxes. Schools often faced the ambivalent or unfriendly attitudes of state officials and struggled to retain official recognition, with a demoralizing effect on these schools and on Jewish society at large.[123]

[120] See Tartakower, 'Problem szkolnictwa żydowskiego w Polsce'.

[121] See Zineman (ed.), *Almanach szkolnictwa żydowskiego w Polsce*; Eisenstein, *Jewish Schools in Poland, 1919–39*; Aleksiun, 'Marcus Braude and the Making of the Future Jewish Elite in Poland'.

[122] Tartakower, 'Problem szkolnictwa żydowskiego w Polsce', 9–10. See also Kazdan, *The History of Jewish Schools in Independent Poland* (Yid.), 550–1.

[123] Tartakower, 'Problem szkolnictwa żydowskiego w Polsce', 7–11. For an example of the Jewish

Despite the variety of ideological choices, the majority of Jewish pupils—between 60 and 80 per cent of those attending primary schools—enrolled at state institutions, including schools set up for Jewish children, the so called *szabasówki*. These latter closed on Saturdays in observance of sabbath, while schools in Poland observed a six-day week.[124] Most Jewish families were unable to afford the tuition in the privately operated schools and believed that state schools offered their children more opportunities upon graduation. Persuading schools that had not included Polish Jewish history to introduce it into the curriculum presented the Jewish intelligentsia with both an opportunity and a challenge. Contemporary Jewish observers feared that in state schools the majority of children would lose all connection to their own community and even their own religion, since the number of the so-called *szabasówki* kept declining, as did the number of Jews authorized to teach in the public school system.[125]

Between the two world wars, concerned activists rallied to create institutions to train Jewish pedagogues, especially teachers of Jewish religion, which both public schools and Jewish private institutions needed badly. In the Second Polish Republic, several seminaries trained Jewish teachers for Jewish and public schools. In 1918, with the support of Samuel Poznański, the rabbi of the Tłomackie Synagogue, Warsaw Jewish intellectuals opened the State Seminary for Teachers of the Mosaic Faith (Państwowe Seminarium dla Nauczycieli Religii Mojżeszowej). As discussed in the previous chapter, Warsaw also boasted the Institute of Jewish Studies (Instytut Nauk Judaistycznych), which trained Jewish teachers in addition to liberal rabbis and administrators of Jewish institutions, and the Yiddishist Tsisho Seminary for Teachers. Another Tsisho Seminary for teachers operated in Wilno. Also in Wilno, Tarbut organized a Hebrew Seminary for Teachers, run by Dr Szalom Jona Czarno. In Kraków, a seminary for teachers in the Bais Yaakov Orthodox schools for girls opened in 1933, run by Jehuda Leib Orlean.[126] Last but not least, an Institute for Training Teachers of the Mosaic Faith (Zakład dla Kształcenia Nauczycieli Religii Mojżeszowej) operated in Lwów. In addition to formal training, numerous additional courses gave Jewish teachers a chance to improve their skills. The Bais Yaakov movement of Orthodox schools for

schools' struggles with securing the state authorization, see Krieg, 'Prywatne Koedukacyjne Gimnazjum'.

[124] See Heller, *On the Edge of Destruction*, 223; Shmeruk, 'Hebrew–Yiddish–Polish', 291–2.

[125] Tartakower, 'Problem szkolnictwa żydowskiego w Polsce', 8. The situation of Jewish students in secondary schools was reportedly even more challenging because 'there, nobody takes cultural Jewish needs into consideration and Jews have no access to these institutions' (ibid.).

[126] Frydman, 'Wyższe Kursy Nauczycielskie "Bajs Jakow" (Seminarium) w Krakowie', 138–42. On Jehuda Leib Orlean, see ibid. 142–3. See also Naomi Seidman, *Sarah Schenirer and the Bais Yaakov Movement*, 98–9, 189–90.

Jewish girls organized courses for teachers and conferences discussing pedagogical issues, and inspected the schools.[127] Teachers who taught at the Khoyrev schools participated in courses for religious educators organized at a special institute founded in 1933 to train teachers in all fields of Jewish studies including Hebrew, pedagogy, Jewish history, and literary history.[128] In addition, Czarno organized a two-year pedagogical course and a seminary for teachers who would become the staff in kindergartens and primary schools.[129] These communal initiatives strove to prepare a cadre of Jewish teachers who would be expected to include Jewish and specifically Polish Jewish history in the curriculum, and to educate Jewish children despite hardships such as lack of textbooks and school supplies—all on a meagre salary.[130]

Leading historians of Polish Jewish history were involved in training teachers of Jewish religion. Already at the beginning of the twentieth century, Schorr and Bałaban taught at the Institute for Training Teachers of the Mosaic Faith, organized by the Jewish community in Lwów in 1902. At the Teachers' Seminary (Seminarium Nauczycielskie) in Lwów they offered lectures for future teachers and participated in organizing their association in Galicia.[131] During the First World War, Bałaban taught at courses for teachers of the Mosaic faith organized in Vienna, and in 1916 he became responsible for Jewish affairs in Lublin under the Austrian occupation. In that capacity, he inspected Jewish schools, assisted in founding new ones, and organized courses for *melamedim*.[132] In 1919 Schorr became the first chairman of the Jewish Association for Primary and Secondary Schools (Żydowskie Towarzystwo Szkoły Ludowej i Średniej), and he was named its honorary chairman in 1923. He founded schools for Jewish children with Polish as a language of instruction and a rich programme in Jewish studies and Hebrew.[133] In the 1920s and 1930s, Schorr served as a representative of the Polish Ministry of Education for qualifying exams at the previously mentioned State

---

[127] 'Ruch religijno-wychowawczy "Bajs Jakow" (szkic monograficzny)', in Zineman (ed.), *Almanach szkolnictwa żydowskiego w Polsce*, 133–7.

[128] Wechsler, 'Kursy dla wychowawców religijnych (Z sieci szkół "Chorew" w Polsce)'.

[129] See Unger, 'Błp Dr. Szałom Jona Czarno (zarys monograficzny)'.

[130] Tartakower, 'Problem szkolnictwa żydowskiego w Polsce', 11–12. On some Jewish teachers and educators in interwar Poland, see Stendig, 'Pedagogowie żydowscy w Polsce współczesnej'.

[131] Bałaban, 'Profesor Dr. Mojżesz Schorr', in *Księga jubileuszowa Schorra*, 17–19, and id., *Historia lwowskiej synagogi postępowej*, 156. Schorr's involvement in teacher training was extensive. See Żebrowski, *Mojżesz Schorr*, 31.

[132] F[alik] H[affner], 'Majer Bałaban (Fragment z monografii)', in Jolles (ed.), *Księga jubileuszowa Bałabana*, 7–12: 10–11. See Sonia Wisznia's account of Bałaban's inspection of the Jewish primary school in Kazimierz during the First World War (Yad Vashem Archives, O 3/3010, pp. 1–2). For an account of Bałaban's policies as a director in Częstochowa, see Salomon Wirstel, 'The Jewish Gymnasium' (Yid.), in Mahler (ed.), *The Jews of Częstochowa* (Yid.), 78–9.

[133] Freund, 'Gimnazja żydowskie we Lwowie'; Żebrowski, *Mojżesz Schorr*, 34.

Seminary for Teachers of the Mosaic Faith in Warsaw.[134] In 1924 he became a member of the State Council of Education (Państwowa Rada Oświaty i Wychowania), and from 1928 he participated in the commission examining teachers of the Mosaic faith. He also worked in the commission evaluating textbooks in the Ministry of Education. Last but not least, Schorr authored three volumes of excerpts of source material for the study of history.[135] Many Jewish intellectuals and communal leaders also worked at improving the Institute of Jewish Studies in Warsaw, which trained Jewish teachers.[136] And Ozjasz Thon was involved in developing the Hebrew-language Tarbut schools and presided over the commission overseeing final exams in Jewish subjects at the Jewish gymnasium in Kraków.[137] Many of these leaders began their careers teaching in public and Jewish schools. Furthermore, the YIVO Institute and Tsisho schools co-operated closely in preparing future Jewish teachers.[138]

Unable to secure academic appointments, Jewish historians turned to careers in Jewish secondary schools, as they could rarely get positions in state or non-Jewish institutions. Upon his return to Poland from his university studies in Vienna, Friedman took up a position as a history teacher at the Jewish Boys Gymnasium (II Gimnazjum Męskie Towarzystwa Żydowskich Szkół Średnich) in Łódź. There, he organized a study group for students interested in Polish and Jewish history. Friedman also edited a student journal, *Nasze Życie* (Our Life), where students published their work; and he organized a study group devoted to history, where students met to discuss such topics as the origins of the Jews in Poland, the Jewish role in the November 1830 uprising, and the history of the Jewish community in Łódź.[139] Dawid Wurm graduated from Warsaw University in 1934 and taught at a gymnasium in Brody.[140] Having received his university diploma in Warsaw, Biderman returned to Włocławek in 1935, where he taught Hebrew at a local Jewish gymnasium.[141] Among graduates of Warsaw University's History Department, Bela Mandelsberg returned to her home town of Lublin and taught in a local Jewish gymnasium. Like Friedman, she encouraged her students to explore local Jewish history.[142] Jewish schools served as important venues for teaching Polish Jewish history to Jewish youth. With a cohort of university-trained teachers, the study of Jewish history often involved extracurricular activities such as study groups, evening classes, and celebrations. Testimonies left by their former students suggest that these teachers stirred interest in intellectual

[134] Żebrowski, *Mojżesz Schorr*, 31.
[135] Ibid. 47. [136] See Zineman (ed.), *Almanach szkolnictwa żydowskiego w Polsce*, 22.
[137] See ibid. [138] Kuznitz, *YIVO and the Making of Modern Jewish Culture*, 258–9.
[139] 'Koło Historyczne', 9. [140] See Dawid Wurm's file (AUW, RP 31018).
[141] See Korzen, 'The Jewish Gymnasium' (Heb.). I would like to thank Israel Biderman's widow Rachela, his daughter Ruth Rootenberg, and his granddaughter Sharon Rootenberg for generously sharing their family history with me. [142] Blumental, 'A Profile of Bela' (Heb.).

pursuits, above all in the subject of Jewish history in the Polish lands. For example, Aleksander Kozłowski, born in 1918, recalled classes on Jewish history at the Kadima Gymnasium in Zamość.[143] In her memoir, Shulamit Soloveitchik-Meiselman affectionately remembered Ringelblum's inspiring influence on every student at the gymnasium in Warsaw. She owed him her 'understanding of world history' and her 'whole attitude towards education'.[144] Jewish schools also spread knowledge about Jewish history outside the regular curriculum, as study groups supervised by teachers visited Jewish monuments and archives and discussed scholarly literature. The Jewish gymnasium in Międzyrzec Podlaski (Mezrich), founded in 1918 as one of the first such schools in Poland, may serve as an example. In 1931 Dr Michael Handel accepted the position of director and teacher. An experienced educator, he grew up in Bolechów, attended ḥeder and Polish elementary school and gymnasium in Stryj, and studied at universities in Prague and Vienna. He worked in secondary schools and seminars for teachers in Łuck and Białystok, and in a Tarbut seminar for Hebrew teachers in Wilno. In Międzyrzec Podlaski, Handel initiated study groups for students interested in history and in literature. He took his students to the old Jewish and Christian cemeteries in the area, to the old synagogues and churches, and to various local archives; and he helped them collect material on the history of the local community.[145]

Yet the situation of Jewish teachers, even those who found employment in private Jewish gymnasia, was dire, especially in the 1930s. A Warsaw-born historian of the Polish Reformation, Marek Wajsblum, described his despair in trying to secure a teaching position at a Jewish gymnasium. He discovered that not only was he among many unemployed qualified Jews, and Jewish teachers would not be recommended for positions in Polish gymnasia, but that the struggling Jewish gymnasia would pay too little to support him and his family.[146] In a letter to Abraham Duker, Friedman complained of constant financial woes, as the salaries of teachers in the Braude Secondary School were cut by 30 per cent.[147] No wonder

[143] DRI, A 7, file 5: interview with Aleksander Kozłowski.

[144] Meiselman, *The Soloveitchik Heritage*, 220. Kassow notes, however, that there were students who remembered Ringelblum as less inspiring. See Kassow, *Who Will Write Our History?*, 26.

[145] See Rylski (Rubinstein), 'To the Memory of my Teacher and Mentor' (Heb.). See also Krieg, 'Prywatne Koedukacyjne Gimnazjum'.

[146] Wajsblum hoped to continue carrying out research. He met with Schorr and showed him his seminar paper on Polish Jewish history; see his letter dated from Warsaw, 4 July 1929, in Wajsblum, 'Zawsze byłem Żydem dla Polaków i Polakiem dla Żydów', 21. In his letter of 10 Oct. 1929, he said that there was a 'state extermination' of Jewish teachers through Educational Department (Kuratorium) recommendations, and complained of having to take up a position of business representative (ibid. 22–3). On 24 Sept. 1931 he complained again that Jewish gymnasia paid so little that one had to write for newspapers to earn extra money (ibid. 29–30).

[147] DRI, P 65, file 149: handwritten Hebrew letter dated 23 Oct. 1933.

Tartakower praised the commitment of Jewish teachers and the parents. He stressed that 'a large number of the Jewish schools in Poland, especially the primary schools, depended on the willpower and determination of the teacher', who 'despite hunger and cold perseveres at his post', and also on 'the resolve of the Jewish fathers, who spend their last pennies on the Jewish upbringing of their children'.[148]

Jewish schools framed Jewish history as part of a general or Judaica curriculum. The 'Tachkemoni' school in Kraków combined teaching general and Jewish subjects, with special attention paid to Hebrew language, Bible, Talmud, and Jewish history.[149] This institution, which included a primary school and a gymnasium, united the 'two worlds of the humanities and of the Torah', as its history lessons blended together general issues, contemporary issues, and religion.[150] Its stated goal was 'to take into consideration the official state programme, and to apply an exhaustive and intensive programme in Jewish studies based on religious principles: the school [strove] to educate a Jew—a good son of its nation and a good citizen, aware of his obligations with regard to the state in which he lives'.[151] Graduates of the gymnasium went on to study at the Institute of Jewish Studies in Warsaw; larger cities in Galicia expressed interest in setting up similar schools.[152] Private Jewish gymnasia also followed the official curriculum, but augmented it with the study of additional Jewish subjects, especially Jewish history and literature. For example, the co-educational gymnasium of Ludwika Wejntraub, in Radomsko, incorporated Jewish history and Hebrew into its regular curriculum.[153] Likewise, girls studied Jewish history at the Bais Yaakov gymnasium in Warsaw, founded during the 1936–7 school year.[154] In the programme of the 'Herzeliah' Tarbut school in Wilno, Polish Jewish history was incorporated into the long survey of Jewish history, while students delved into contemporary Polish geography and society separately. Beginning in the eighth grade, students discussed in class the period from the beginning of the Jewish settlement in Poland up to the Chmielnicki massacres, and such subjects as practical kabbalah, Rabbi Joseph Karo, and Shabetai Tsevi.[155] Similarly, in the guidelines for teachers of the

[148] Tartakower, 'Problem szkolnictwa żydowskiego w Polsce', 11. It is noteworthy that in this article Tartakower assumed fathers to be key to children's education.
[149] Korzennik, 'Gimnazjum Męskie "Tachkemoni" stow. "Cheder Iwri" w Krakowie'.
[150] Ibid. 104–5.    [151] Ibid. 103.    [152] Ibid. 104.
[153] See 'Gimnazjum Koedukacyjne L. Wejntraubówny w Radomsku', in Zineman (ed.), *Almanach szkolnictwa żydowskiego w Polsce*, 119–20. Apart from the obligatory state curriculum, its programme also included Hebrew and Jewish history.
[154] See 'Trzyklasowe żeńskie gimnazjum kupieckie "Bajs Jakow" w Warszawie, Zamenhofa 7', in Zineman (ed.), *Almanach szkolnictwa żydowskiego w Polsce*, 120–1. Among Judaic studies it taught 'Bible, prophets, Hebrew and Yiddish, Jewish history, prayer and commentaries to the prayers and the general instruction of religion'.
[155] The curriculum was published in Hebrew and Polish as *The Curriculum of the Eight-Grade*

Tarbut schools, published in 1932, Polish Jewish history was to be taught as part of general Jewish history and therefore made its first appearance in the fifth grade, as students became acquainted with the beginnings of Jewish community in Poland, Kazimierz the Great, the charters, and the institutions of Jewish autonomy. This education continued through the discussion of the Jewish community in the Polish–Lithuanian Commonwealth, the 3 May 1791 Constitution, and the policies of the three partitioning powers. The programme specifically mentioned such staples of Polish and Polish Jewish historical narrative as Berek Joselewicz and the November 1830 and January 1863 uprisings.[156]

Jewish primary schools and gymnasia, as well as state schools employing teachers of the Mosaic faith, incorporated Jewish studies into their programmes. But other types of educational institutions also offered insights into Jewish history and culture. At the Jewish vocational school, founded in Łódź in 1934 and attended by Jewish women from the provinces, students worked in the sewing workshop while at the same time attending classes in Hebrew, Jewish history, and literature. The institution wanted to give girls both professional training and a religious-social upbringing.[157] Jewish history became part of the curriculum of some vocational schools, such as the Professional Secondary School for Girls in Warsaw, founded in 1916. The school's goal was to prepare Jewish girls for future work and give them training in subjects such as accounting and correspondence. The students also studied Jewish history and literature, however, in addition to Hebrew, geography, and history. Similarly, in the Jewish co-ed trade schools in Kraków, run by Samuel Stendig, Jewish history and Hebrew culture became part of the curriculum in addition to professional and general courses.[158] Other Jewish educational facilities experimented with their teaching agendas as well, at times due to the pressure from the Polish authorities. Such was the case of the Mesivta yeshiva in Warsaw, founded in 1917 at the initiative of Agudat Israel, where young men studied for five years, focusing on the Talmud. In addition, they also took classes in Polish language, literature, and history as required by the state.[159]

Szalom Jona Czarno published a volume for teachers of Jewish history to help

*Gymnasium with Introductory Course 'Herzlia' in Wilno* (Heb.) / *Program nauczania Hebrajskiego Gimnazjum Herclija w Wilnie* (Wilno, 1927).

[156] 'Programme for the Study of Judaism, Hebrew, Bible, History' (Heb.) (Warsaw, Aug. 1934), 26–7. See Kijek, *Dzieci modernizmu*, 165–73. I am grateful to Dr Kamil Kijek for sharing this material with me.

[157] Unger, '"Ohel Sara" (Namiot Sary) Dom wychowawczo-zawodowy im błp Sary Szenirer przy "Agudas Isroel" w Polsce, Łódź ul. Kilińskiego 50', 159.

[158] J.Z., 'Prywatna Żydowska Koedukacyjna Średnia Szkoła Handlowa Stow. Żyd. Abs. W. S. H. w Krakowie'.

[159] 'Wyższa uczelnia rabinów Ortodoksyjnych, Warszawa, Św. Jerska 18', in Zineman (ed.), *Almanach szkolnictwa żydowskiego w Polsce*, 147–8.

them organize and discuss material with their students.[160] Jerachmiel Wajngarten, the organizer and chairman of the Association of Teachers of the Mosaic Faith, and Dr Majer Tauber co-wrote another textbook for Jewish students, published in Polish and Hebrew.[161] Books of Jewish history were also written for Orthodox schools. Mordechai Baumberg, for example, published a history of the Jews in three volumes, with an abbreviated version in one volume, and worked on a course book in Hebrew for religious schools.[162] Several history textbooks for Jewish students in Polish schools were published in the 1920s and 1930s. Among the most popular was Majer Bałaban's *Historja i literatura żydowska ze szczególnem uwzględnieniem historii Żydów w Polsce* (Jewish History and Literature with Particular Stress on the History of Jews in Poland), designed as a course book for the upper grades in secondary schools. Divided into three volumes, the book went through several editions in the Second Polish Republic.[163] Discussing ancient Jewish history, the first volume, *Od najdawniejszych czasów do upadku świata starożytnego* (From the Oldest Times until the Decline of the Ancient World), appeared during the First World War, in 1916, and was republished many times, almost exclusively with the prestigious publisher Zakład Narodowy im. Ossolińskich in Lwów. Focusing on the Middle Ages, the second volume, *Od upadku świata starożytnego do końca wieków średnich* (From the Decline of the Ancient World until the End of the Middle Ages), appeared in multiple editions, while the third volume, dealing with the history of Jews in the early modern period, appeared in 1925. One S. Winkler, a teacher in the Jewish gymnasium 'Ascola' in Warsaw, praised the pioneering work done by Bałaban in writing material useful for teachers of Jewish history and important in keeping youth interested in the history of its nation. Winkler rejoiced that Jewish students in Poland could at long last read about their history in Polish.[164] Clara Minskberg-Ma'ayan, a student at the Institute of Jewish Studies and Warsaw University, had read Bałaban's book at a public school in Rzeszów and recalled being moved by the encounter, saying that Bałaban, 'was very close to us because we studied from his book in school'.[165] Shortly before the war, Friedman worked on a broad survey comparing

---

[160] See Stendig, 'Pedagogowie żydowscy w Polsce współczesnej'.

[161] In 1930 Wajngarten began working for the publishing house Central, overseeing the publication of the new Hebrew edition of Graetz's *Geschichte der Juden*: see Unger, 'Jerachmiel Wajngarten (szkic biograficzny)'.

[162] See 'Mordechai Baumberg (szkic biograficzny)', in Zineman (ed.), *Almanach szkolnictwa żydowskiego w Polsce*, 90–1.

[163] See N[achman] Majzel, 'Prof. Majer Bałaban', *Haynt*, 7 Mar. 1937. Polish translation published in Jolles (ed.), *Księga jubileuszowa Bałabana*, 69–71.

[164] See Winkler, 'W imieniu grona nauczycielskiego gimn. "Ascola"', in Jolles (ed.), *Księga jubileuszowa Bałabana*, 22–3.

[165] Oral history interview with Clara Ma'ayan (USHMM, RG-50.120*0096, tape 1: 1.00.59).

pedagogical approaches to teaching Jewish history as the subject of instruction on a college level, in Jewish schools, and afternoon classes, comparing textbooks, syllabi in use by such organizations as B'nai B'rith Hillel Foundation, the Anti-Defamation League, the Youth Council of Agudat Israel, Hadassah, and others.[166]

Celebrating the newly established Poland's national holiday on 11 November served to strengthen the narrative linking Polish Jewry to Poland in the educational context.[167] In Kraków in November 1931 there was a special prayer for schoolchildren in the Tempel synagogue where 'Rabbi Dr. Schmelkes delivered an uplifting sermon'. In addition to representatives of the local administration and board members of the Jewish community, the 'Jewish gymnasium with its banner and orchestra took part, and afterwards it paraded on the streets of the Jewish neighbourhood'.[168] Aside from the celebration in the synagogue of the progressive Jewish community, another one was organized in the Old Shul where local government was in attendance and Rabbi Kornitzer delivered the sermon. Last but not least, there was a ceremony in the synagogue in Podgórze with a sermon by Rabbi Ojzasz Feiwel Frenkel.[169] Teachers took students for a special prayer on Poland's national holiday in Warsaw, Lwów, Łódź, and other cities.[170] In 1932, at the Jewish gymnasium in Łódź, Friedman delivered a lecture to students at a special celebration of 11 November.[171] The guidelines of the Tarbut gymnasia also incorporated celebrating Poland's national holiday. On the national holiday in the synagogue in Łysobyki, there was always a special prayer for Poland's welfare. Representatives of the local administration, police, the local priest, and the director of the local school participated in the services.[172] And Rabbi Jechiel Meir Blumenfeld, who ran the rabbinical seminary Tachkemoni, delivered a speech at the Nożyk Synagogue in Warsaw on the tenth anniversary of Poland's independence, for which he received a letter of thanks from Marshal Józef Piłsudski.[173] Dwelling on more recent history, local chapters of the Union of Jewish Participants in the Struggles for Poland's Independence (Związek Żydów Uczestników Walk o Niepodległość Polski) organized memorial services for Jews who had perished as soldiers during the war.[174] Stressing Polish Jews' heroism on

---

[166] DRI, P 65, file 149: correspondence with Abraham Duker, who wrote to various institutions on Friedman's behalf in the years 1937–8. [167] Biskupski, *Independence Day*.

[168] 'Uroczysty obchód Święta Niepodległości w Krakowie'. [169] Ibid.

[170] In a private letter to her brother Moniek, in Palestine, Mania mentioned her husband taking pupils to the synagogue on Poland's national holiday, 11 Nov. 1929. See Kula, *Autoportret rodziny X*, 431.

[171] 'Uroczystość 11 listopada'. [172] Rudawski, *Mój obcy kraj?*, 43.

[173] Rabbi Jechiel Meir Blumenfeld ran the yeshiva in Ostrów Siedlecki in 1913, and during the First World War served as a rabbi in Rostov upon Don. In 1920 he returned to Warsaw, where he ran the Mesivta yeshiva. In 1922 he founded Tomche Tmimim, and in 1927 Torat Israel Yeshiva. See 'Rabin Jechiel Meir Blumenfeld (Szkic biograficzny)', in Zineman (ed.), *Almanach szkolnictwa żydowskiego w Polsce*, 89.

[174] AŻIH 107, folder 613, Kraków, 1 Oct. 1935: an invitation from the chapter in Kraków of the Asso-

battlefields made the public aware of Jewish contributions on the local and national levels and exemplified Jewish participation in all of Polish history. The impact of the lessons, sermons, and discussions remains uncertain. While these public events focused on the Polish account of national revival, they offered an opportunity to inscribe Polish Jews into that narrative.

In addition to schools, the general Jewish public familiarized themselves with stories from the Jewish past in Polish lands through public history. Popular speakers and Jewish historians lectured often about Polish Jewish history to wide and diverse audiences, from youth groups to members of Jewish institutions. One such organization, B'nai B'rith, emerged as an important actor in and source of funding for educational activities.[175] Schorr joined the 'Leopolis' chapter of B'nai B'rith in Lwów as early as 1901, and in 1921, shortly before moving to Warsaw, he became its chairman.[176] He continued his involvement with the organization, joining the Warsaw chapter, 'Braterstwo', in December 1923. The latter included several historians, most notably Bałaban, who was a founding member, Menachem (Edmund) Stein, Abraham Weiss, and Israel Ostersetzer. Mateusz Mieses joined the 'Humanitas' chapter in Przemyśl, while Schiper was considered as a candidate in Warsaw.[177] According to the bylaws of B'nai B'rith, the association strove to spread education among Jews, and especially to elevate the intellectual and ethical level of its members. It planned to achieve these lofty goals by organizing lectures, conferences, exhibitions, and meetings, founding libraries, and publishing brochures and journals.[178] B'nai B'rith's mission was to reach out to Jewish youth, asserting that 'the most valuable work of the Jewish spirit, namely the treasures of its culture and making it available to the young generation is one of the most important duties of our generation'.[179] At a meeting of B'nai B'rith in Warsaw in May 1929, Bałaban reported on his trip to Berlin and to the exhibition 'Das Judentum in Schlesien in der Vergangenheit', and he suggested that they organize a similar exhibition. Schorr supported the idea of an exhibition that would have a political meaning, 'proving most clearly that we are not foreigners in

---

ciation of the Jews of the Fight for Poland's Independence to the Jewish community in Kraków to the mourning services for Jewish soldiers who fell in the war, held at the Jewish cemetery at Miodowa Street, on 6 Oct. 1935.

[175] The library of B'nai B'rith serves as one of indications of its interest in history. The library included works on Jewish history in Polish, German, Russian, French, Hebrew, and Yiddish, and a considerable collection of works by Friedman, Bałaban, Schiper, and Schall. See AAN, B'nai B'rith, file 19, pp. 1–38.   [176] Żebrowski, *Mojżesz Schorr*, 31.

[177] See AAN, B'nai B'rith, file 13. Schiper was recommended for Warsaw's 'Braterstwo' chapter of B'nai B'rith in November 1937. For the early members of B'nai B'rith in Poland, see *Książka adresowa członków Żyd. Stow. Humanitarnego 'B'ne B'rith' w Polsce*.   [178] AAN, B'nai B'rith, file 1, Statut 1.

[179] AAN, B'nai B'rith, file 14, p. 6: 'Stan obecny i przyszłe zadania Naszej Organizacji (Sprawozdanie bra Dra Rudolfa Beresa z objazdu Stowarzyszeń w charakterze delegata Związku)'.

Poland but that we have lived in this land since its dawn and that we have shared for many centuries the fate of this country'.[180] Bałaban regularly lectured on both general subjects and Polish Jewish history at the events organized by B'nai B'rith. For example, in November 1928 he delivered a lecture when the Warsaw branch met to celebrate the tenth anniversary of Poland's independence.[181] He also spoke at other Jewish venues. In 1934 he held a series of lectures 'about the history, organization and the importance of Jewish communities in Poland' for the Union of Jewish Participants in the Struggles for Poland's Independence. Vice chairman of the Jewish community in Warsaw Herman Schwartz assured Bałaban that his classes were not in vain, and that he himself 'strove to implement the knowledge he had gained in his work at the Jewish *kehilah* in Warsaw'.[182] Jewish historians spoke at other venues as well. At the First Convention of the Jewish Merchants in Poland, which met in October 1919 in Warsaw, Schatzky spoke about the role of the Jews in Polish commerce.[183] As part of cultural activities carried out by the Central Merchants' Association (Centrala Związku Kupców), Bałaban gave several lectures on the history of Polish Jewry.[184] Cultural and political activists in local Jewish communities included lectures in Jewish history in curricula of evening courses.[185] As part of the cultural activities of the left-wing Zionist party Po'alei Zion Left branch in Częstochowa, the association Ovent-Kursn far Arbeter organized lectures with speakers from Warsaw and Kraków, such as Ringelblum and Mahler.[186] Jewish historians also published guidebooks describing places of interest and histories of local Jewish communities.[187]

## The New Rabbinate and Its Institutions

Poland's leading Jewish historians took on the ambitious project of reforming the institution of the rabbinate and using newly appointed community rabbis to pro-

[180] AAN, B'nai B'rith, file 3, pp. 38–9: protocol of a closed meeting on 13 May 1929.

[181] See AAN, B'nai B'rith, file 3, p. 8: protocol of the meeting on 10 Nov. 1928.

[182] Herman Schwartz, 'Przemówienie w imieniu Gminy Żydowskiej w Warszawie', in Jolles (ed.), *Księga jubileuszowa Bałabana*, 24–5: 25.

[183] Pierwszy Zjazd Kupiectwa Żydowskiego (First Convention of Jewish Merchants), 21–22 Oct. 1919. See Schiper, *Dzieje handlu żydowskiego*, 683.     [184] See Schiper, *Dzieje handlu żydowskiego*, 693.

[185] See Elkana Chrobolowski, 'Evening Courses' (Yid.), in Mahler (ed.), *The Jews of Częstochowa* (Yid.), 79–80: 79.

[186] Yakov Kener, 'Left Poale Zion' (Yid.), in Mahler (ed.), *The Jews of Częstochowa* (Yid.), 144–50: 148.

[187] See Bałaban, *Przewodnik po żydowskich zabytkach Krakowa*; *Dzielnica żydowska, jej dzieje i zabytki*; and *Die Judenstadt von Lublin*; Schall, *Przewodnik po zabytkach żydowskich m. Lwowa*. See also Blumental, 'A Profile of Bela' (Heb.), 24–5. On the Jewish tourist movement, see Roskies, 'Landkentenish', in Hundert (ed.), *The YIVO Encyclopedia of Jews in Eastern Europe*, i. 968–70; Kassow, 'Travel and Local History as a National Mission'.

mote Jewish history to a wide audience.[188] There were two aspects to this project: the 'making' of rabbis—their education and accreditation—and reversing the perceived ongoing decline in the position and influence of rabbis in larger social circles. While they did not expect to change the views of rabbis already serving Jewish communities, the scholars envisioned a new kind of training that would result in a new kind of rabbinate. Jewish historians insisted on incorporating Jewish and Polish Jewish history into the religious curriculum of future rabbis. Already in the early years of the resurrected Polish republic, several members of the Jewish intelligentsia, including some of the leading historians, expressed their conviction that the large, diverse, and changing Jewish community needed 'modern rabbis' to stimulate their congregants intellectually and exert moral influence. Their vision of rabbinical education departed from the customary model in combining rigorous traditional learning with the academic study of Jewish history and literature. Thus, the training of both new rabbis and future teachers of Jewish studies emphasized the importance of history, specifically Polish Jewish history, as a source for understanding and responding to the problems that Polish Jews faced in the 1920s and 1930s.

In the newly independent Polish state, opportunities arose for redefining the legal status of Jewish religious communities and their rabbis. Both Jewish religious and communal leaders and Polish authorities sought to shape the future of the rabbinate. In 1919, within the span of a few months, two events occurred regarding future rabbis: one internal to the Jewish community and one external from the Polish government. In February 1919 Józef Piłsudski signed a decree with regard to Jewish religious communities in the former territories of Congress Poland. It stipulated that rabbis needed to speak and write both Polish and Hebrew.[189] Moreover, the Polish Ministry of Religion and Education created a blueprint for future rabbinical seminaries as a condition for their approval. As early as June 1919 the Ministry passed the 'Directive Concerning the Establishment and Maintenance of Private Religious Jewish Seminaries'.[190] Community boards (*gminy wyznaniowe żydowskie*), associations, institutions, and private persons who held Polish citizenship could apply for the Ministry's authorization to open

---

[188] Portions of this section are drawn from Aleksiun, 'Jewish Historians and the Vision of a New Rabbinate' (Heb.).

[189] See 'Dekret o zmianie organizacji gmin wyznaniowych żydowskich na terenie byłego Królestwa Kongresowego', in *Dziennik Ustaw* 1919, no. 14, document 175, Art. 9, p. 254. The decree was signed by Józef Piłsudski on 7 Feb. 1919.

[190] 'Rozporządzenie Ministra Wyznań Religijnych i Oświecenia Publicznego w przedmiocie zakładania i utrzymywania prywatnych "Seminarjów Religijnych Żydowskich"', 21 June 1919, in *Dekrety, Statuty, Rozporządzenia, Okólniki i.t.p., dotyczące spraw Wyznania Mojżeszowego (Odbitka z Dziennika Urzędowego Ministerstwa Wyznań Religijnych i Oświecenia Publicznego Rzeczypospolitej Polskiej*, 212–13 (AAN, MWRiOP).

and maintain 'Jewish Religious Seminaries' ('Seminarja Religijne Żydowskie').[191] The director had to be approved by the Minister of Religion and Education. Government regulations obliged the seminaries to introduce secular subjects and the study of the Polish language. According to the Ministry's directives, Jewish religious seminaries should educate rabbinical candidates to be 'enlightened and useful for the country and for their co-religionists'.[192] To ensure that rabbinical candidates graduated with a satisfactory level of secular knowledge, the Ministry insisted that the curriculum include a sufficient number of hours in both Judaic and secular subjects. During the eight years of study, at least one third of the courses taken by students at a Jewish seminary had to be in secular subjects.[193] The Ministry also stipulated that rabbinical candidates should have some background in secular studies before entering the seminary. All entry and final examinations in secular subjects had to be taken in the presence of a delegate from the Ministry, whose evaluation was binding. Secular subjects were to be taught in Polish; the diploma was to be issued in both Polish and Hebrew. Insistence on including knowledge of Polish as a prerequisite for future rabbis was strengthened by the requirement that candidates, 'apart from religious-scientific and moral qualifications', be fluent in Polish, spoken and written.[194]

Even before the passing of this new law, prominent members of the Jewish community in Warsaw had voiced ideas that to some extent mirrored the hopes for broadening the education of future rabbis. In the early spring of 1919 Rabbi Poznański expressed the gist of this new approach to rabbinical training in a public address in Warsaw:

The rabbi must also be a leader of his community, stand before it, speak in its name, influence the education of the younger generation and so on and so forth, and with the way he [has] studied so far, the education he has received so far, he is not going to be able to perform his duty appropriately . . . I believe there is no one, even amongst the more devoted, who does not recognize the necessity of secular studies in the training of rabbis . . . But secular education must be introduced not outside the yeshiva but within it, not in secret but as a necessary addition to the study of the lore, without which the student will not be fit to serve as a rabbi in our community.[195]

---

[191] For the procedure of issuing concessions, see Art. 18 in 'Rozporządzenie Ministra Wyznań Religijnych i Oświecenia Publicznego w przedmiocie zakładania i utrzymywania prywatnych "Seminarjów Religijnych Żydowskich"' (AAN, MWRiOP). [192] Ibid.

[193] According to ministerial guidelines, in general the number of school hours was not to be more than forty-eight hours per week, and these should include at least fifteen hours of study devoted to secular subjects. See ibid., Art. 5. [194] Ibid.

[195] Quoted in *Hamizraḥi*, 26 Mar. 1919, 4–5. According to Yitzhak Mishael, Poznański and Nissenbaum were already discussing the possibility of creating a new rabbinical seminary as early as 1917. See Mishael, 'The Takhkemoni Rabbinical Seminary in Warsaw' (Heb.), 586.

Poznański, who had served as rabbi of the liberal community (Adat Hane'orim) and chief preacher at the Tłomackie Street Synagogue since 1908, envisioned a rabbinate steeped in Jewish tradition, but also knowledgeable in Jewish history, philosophy, and religion. He followed this vision while building the library of the Great Synagogue, of which historical books constituted an integral part.[196] He envisioned a twofold transformation of the rabbinate: on the one hand, he believed that Poland required 'modern rabbinical seminaries if not identical than very similar to those already in existence in western Europe and in North America'. On the other hand, he predicted that more traditional yeshivas would also undergo 'modernization' through the inclusion of secular subjects and 'the study of Talmud fitting contemporary notions', and as a result would produce 'enlightened rabbis'. Future Polish seminaries would become centres of Judaic studies because 'students [would] come equipped with rich knowledge of the Hebrew language and literature . . . A rabbinical seminary in Poland will be in a position to set much higher standards for its candidates, and to set a much bigger programme of special studies than its sisters in the west.' The study of 'all phenomena spiritual and historical' would be part of the transformation of the minds of Polish Jewry in the new era.[197] According to Poznański, Jewish history should be part of religious studies, and general history a part of secular studies.[198]

The precise relationship between the government initiatives and Poznański's call for reform is unclear. Surely the actions of the Jewish community were in part an effort to maintain control of their own rabbinate in the face of government moves to interfere. However, the direct influence of Polish legislation should not be overemphasized, nor should the internal reforms within the Jewish community be interpreted as purely pragmatic. The relationship between the two was complex. But the efforts of members of the Jewish community to change the rabbinate was inspired at least as much by their own vision as by any external interference.

Bałaban took a balanced position when discussing traditional religious training and the functioning of the Polish rabbinate in the past. While critical of some aspects of the traditional model, he did not condemn it or suggest abandoning it

---

[196] Bałaban, 'Doktor Samuel Poznański (1864–1921)'; IRRZ, Oral Testimonies 20, p. 13, 11 June 1973.

[197] Poznański, 'Widoki nauki judaistycznej w nowotworzącej się Polsce'.

[198] Quoted in *Hamizraḥi*, 26 Mar. 1919, 5. Poznański's position was questioned by more conservative members of the Warsaw rabbinate and Jewish community in general. The tension found its expression in the so called 'Poznański affair' of 1921, in which members of the Tłomackie Synagogue petitioned 'the executive to use all the means at its disposal to achieve the official appointment of their spiritual leader Dr Samuel Poznański, as a recognized member of the Warsaw rabbinate. . . . In their petition his congregants stressed the need for a rabbi with academic credentials who could properly represent Judaism to the outside world. They further claimed that elementary fairness required that all trends within traditional Judaism be represented within the ranks of the rabbinate' (Bacon, 'The Poznański Affair of 1921', 138).

completely, finding virtue in the traditional model of training in the Polish–Lithuanian Commonwealth. He argued that 'a sensible youth was coming of age, maybe only too much trained in dialectics and logic'.[199] He also pointed to periods in Polish Jewish history when Jewish knowledge had been combined with European culture. Looking into the Polish Jewish past, Bałaban picked and chose religious leaders worthy of particular respect for their combination of expertise in the Talmud with history and other disciplines, such as Rabbi Moses Isserles, or their commitment to the Polish national cause, such as Ber Meisels.[200] In Bałaban's eyes, Poznański offered an example of the enlightened rabbi: deeply involved in the political and social affairs of his community, ready to give advice on matters concerning a wedding, a circumcision, or a funeral, capable of answering questions and solving dilemmas both in the private and the scientific spheres, and 'everywhere delivering wise and fitting speeches in Polish, Yiddish, and the Holy Tongue'.[201] In contrast, Bałaban criticized both mitnagdic and hasidic Jews as 'generous with bans in defence of allegedly endangered Jewry'. In particular, he condemned hasidim for their attitude towards secular studies in rabbinical education, and the *kehalim* for hiring rabbis who had no 'secular knowledge of the culture and needs of their country and [who] stood attentive guards so that no ray of light enters'. Bałaban took an interest in programmes and initiatives concerning the establishment of theological seminaries in Lwów and in Warsaw, writing approvingly about the 1825 curriculum of the Rabbinical School in Warsaw, as it included secular studies such as Polish, general history, and geography. However, he criticized the school's dependence on government policies and its graduates' detachment from the Jewish community. Government rabbis could not influence their communities 'in the direction of progress and enlightenment'.[202]

Bałaban argued that already in the last decades of the eighteenth century Polish Jewry had begun to experience an acute need for enlightened rabbis. He analysed the initiatives of the Jewish intelligentsia in Galicia to create a rabbinical school and train future teachers of the Jewish religion. The establishment of a rabbinical seminary in Vienna in 1894 mitigated the situation, and efforts to create a

---

[199] Bałaban, *Historya projektu szkoły rabinów i nauki religii mojż.*, 7. He took pride in the period when 'Polish talmudic schools . . . supplied rabbis for all of Europe and whoever looks at indexes of rabbis in Amsterdam, Hamburg, Wormacja, Frankfurt, will recognize his old acquaintances from Lida, Pinczow, Lublin, Lwów, Kraków and others' (ibid. 7–8).

[200] Bałaban, 'Sabataizm w Polsce', in *Księga jubileuszowa Schorra*, 49; id., 'Rabin Beer Meisels', 7.

[201] Bałaban, *Rabbi Dr Shmuel Poznanski of Blessed Memory (1864–1921)* (Yid.), 5.

[202] Bałaban, *Historya projektu szkoły rabinów i nauki religii mojż*, esp. 18–22. He further examined the model of the rabbinate in his book on the history of Lwów Progressive Synagogue. See Bałaban, *Historia lwowskiej synagogi postępowej*. Bałaban's student Aron Sawicki wrote his MA thesis on the Rabbinical School in Warsaw, and this was the basis for his article 'Szkoła Rabinów w Warszawie (1826–1863)'.

school in Galicia resurfaced in Lwów and Stanisławów.²⁰³ Bałaban's interest in nineteenth-century initiatives to establish rabbinical seminaries were closely connected to his contemporary concerns. In 1907 he argued that 'today there is a need to found such a school, from which enlightened people could graduate'. These would be 'learned in the scripture, progressive but also pious, carrying the torch of light to the people but also setting an example for the community with their pious and virtuous lives'.²⁰⁴ He believed that a future rabbinical school would meet the needs of an ever-growing Jewish intelligentsia and produce graduates to work with young people.²⁰⁵ Moreover, he argued that Jewish youth educated in the public schools of Galicia, and estranged from the traditional Jewish community due to 'the neglect of their religious education in the public school and the lack of enlightened rabbis', acutely needed enlightened rabbis to bridge European culture with that 'of their fathers'.²⁰⁶ Rabbinical students from eastern Europe could provide the type of education offered at rabbinical seminaries in western Europe, because they 'retained remnants of Judaic and rabbinical knowledge and the tradition of their fathers'.²⁰⁷ Among fields of expertise one would gain in such a school, Bałaban listed 'an extensive knowledge of Judaica, especially of the Talmud and Jewish history, because this—apart from a pious life—is the only element that humbles every Jew'.²⁰⁸

When Schorr discussed the rabbinate of the Association of Rabbis with Higher Education (Zrzeszenie Rabinów o Wyższem Wykształceniu) he elaborated on the roles of the organization and its views on the rabbinate. The association had both internal and external goals. One of the most important of these was '[to educate] youth in the spirit of faithfulness and devotion to the faith along with the wider love for the nation—both on the basis of a deepened knowledge and estimation of the ... ethics of Judaism, and thorough familiarity with history and national writings'. The purpose of the association, and of the education the rabbis would champion, was 'to harmonize national and religious upbringing'. The rabbis, with the help of teachers, should influence not only schoolchildren of both sexes, but also working-class youth, artisans, merchants, and the wide circles of the Jewish intelligentsia, bringing them back to Jewish ideals and the traditional way of life. The association strove to create cultural centres for organizing youth activities with lectures and reading rooms.

---

²⁰³ Bałaban, *Historya projektu szkoły rabinów i nauki religii mojż.*, 20–32.
²⁰⁴ Ibid. 45.          ²⁰⁵ Ibid. 47.          ²⁰⁶ Ibid. 29–31.
²⁰⁷ Bałaban, *Dziesięciolecie 'Braterstwa'*, 8. Bałaban's family background exemplified the combination of tradition with secular knowledge. In the introduction to the history of the progressive synagogue in Lwów, Bałaban described his childhood memories connected with the Temple, a place where he and his father had come to listen to the sermons, while they prayed in more traditional settings. In the years of his youth the Temple became 'his second home'. See Bałaban, *Historia lwowskiej synagogi postępowej*, pp. ix–x.          ²⁰⁸ Bałaban, *Historya projektu szkoły rabinów i nauki religii mojż.*, 47.

It is possible that in no other country does such indifference for religious matters reign as among Polish Jewry, all the more striking because religious problems, the so-called 'search for God', torments the soul of humanity, which longs for inner spiritual stability in the midst of waves of stormy life in the aftermath of the war . . . And what can be said about these circles of intelligentsia who do not recognize either national or religious bonds and remain Jewish by the power of inertia—euphemistically speaking pietism? The association saw its goal as:

organizing synagogues in which the working intelligentsia and merchants group themselves under the banner of revitalizing religious life as a creative element of the national life in general, both in the family and in social activity, and above all in the House of God which should become—in the modern spirit—one of the main spiritual centres for the educated Jew, who has stood so far from the synagogue in his false concept of Jewishness.

In all, Schorr maintained that with the support of the Jewish intelligentsia, the association was to help restore the traditional Jewish way of life 'in harmony with the spirit of contemporary general culture'.[209]

## Institutions to Train New Rabbis

Polish Jewish historians had an opportunity to implement Poznański's vision of a rabbinate that combined Jewish tradition with a broader education by shaping the curricula of two new Warsaw institutions: the Rabbinical Seminary 'Tahkemoni' (Seminarium Religijno-Żydowskie 'Tachkemoni'; Beit Hamidrash Lerabanim Tahkemoni), established in 1920, and the Institute of Jewish Studies (Instytut Nauk Judaistycznych; Hamakhon Lehokhmat Yisra'el, and after 1936 Hamakhon Lemada'ei Hayahadut), established in 1927.[210] Both institutions adopted to a large extent the new model of training as elaborated by Poznański, Bałaban, and Schorr.

At the Second Convention of Mizrachi, the Religious Zionist organization, which took place in Warsaw in 1919, Heszel Farbstein, leader of Mizrachi, argued that 'it is also necessary to establish a large modern yeshiva, to train rabbis commanding respect and reverence from every side. The rabbi's authority must be enhanced, the rabbi should be acknowledged as a true *mara de'atra* [literally 'head of the local community', whose rulings are binding].'[211] Similar calls for the creation of a modern yeshiva came from Poznański.[212] At the Mizrachi convention he

[209] Schorr, 'Zrzeszenie Rabinów o Wyższem Wykształceniu (jego zadania i cele)'. This vision of a new rabbinate seems to have been a pressing issue for members of the Jewish intelligentsia. See Taubeles, *Żydowska gmina wyznaniowa i rabinat w naszej dobie*.

[210] See Eden, 'The Institute of Jewish Studies' (Heb.), 326; Bałaban, *Księga pamiątkowa ku czci dra Samuela Poznańskiego*, p. xxviii.

[211] Quoted in 'Address by Mr Farbstein' (Heb.), *Hamizraḥi*, 14 May 1919, 6.

[212] See *Hamizraḥi*, 26 Mar. 1919, 4–5.

specifically called for the creation of a seminary for rabbis and teachers. Tachkemoni was founded half a year later.[213] Having secured governmental recognition in December 1919, the school opened in 1920 at 19 Grzybowska Street, in the heart of the Jewish district in Warsaw. In the autumn of 1920 Farbstein invited Rabbi Moshe Soloveitchik to head the Talmud Department of the recently organized Tachkemoni, embarking on a new programme that incorporated both talmudic and secular education.[214] Bałaban served as head of the school from 1920 to 1928, and was responsible for both secular studies and administration.[215] Students described Bałaban not only as the head of the seminary, but also as a highly influential figure, despite the fact that he was not associated with Mizrachi. Krone remembered Bałaban's lecture on Hanukah, in which he 'opened with a series of questions to the students about the historical image of Yohanan the high priest', leading his students to enthusiastic applause. He developed close relationships with his students, inviting them home during the first convention of Hashomer Hadati in Warsaw.[216]

The Institute of Jewish Studies aspired to be academically comparable to a university, and it was particularly well equipped to become a centre of Jewish studies, having a faculty of leading scholars in the field.[217] Founders and faculty of the Institute declared their interest in developing a centre of scholarship for young Jews in the context of the national Jewish revival.[218] At the opening of the Institute, in 1928, Schorr claimed it would become a centre of Jewish studies 'in honour of the whole of Polish Jewry', and would penetrate 'wide sections of the intelligentsia'.[219] Israel Ostersetzer, who lectured on Talmud, argued that the Institute 'should become a focus which brings together all the forces working in the field of Jewish knowledge in Poland. From there [it should] permeate through and through the largest Jewish community in the world—Jewish society in Poland—with the revitalizing beams of science, national culture, self-discovery.'[220]

The Institute's programme for rabbis opened in the academic year 1929–30, at the initiative of Markus Braude. A 1929 report signed by Braude, Bałaban, and

[213] Bałaban, 'Doktor Samuel Poznański (1864–1921)', p. xx. See IRRZ, Oral Testimonies 20, p. 13, 9 Nov. 1973.    [214] Meiselman, *The Soloveitchik Heritage*, 203–4.

[215] In his curriculum vitae submitted for the purpose of the tenure procedure, Bałaban mentioned that he 'took over . . . the leadership of the newly established rabbinical seminary in Warsaw (Tachkemoni) in November 1920 at the demand of the Ministry of Religion and Education'. See AAN, MWRiOP 1614: Majer Bałaban, curriculum vitae, 16 Dec. 1935, p. 1.

[216] Krone, *My Teachers and Rabbis* (Heb.), 17. See also IRRZ, Oral Testimonies 45, p. 2, 9 Nov. 1973.

[217] See Eden, 'The Institute of Jewish Studies' (Heb.), 327; Dold, 'A Matter of National and Civic Honor', 56. See Chapter 3 for discussion of its role as an academic institution.

[218] Eden, 'The Institute of Jewish Studies' (Heb.), 330.

[219] *Sprawozdanie Instytutu Nauk Judaistycznych w Warszawie*, pp. xxi and xvii. See also Bałaban, *Dziesięciolecie 'Braterstwa'*, 12.    [220] Ostersetzer, 'Instytut Nauk Judaistycznych w Warszawie', 273.

Schorr had argued for such an institution, stating that 'Jewish society in Poland lacks an institution for educating academically trained rabbis, which would enable progressive circles of Jewish society to appoint to rabbinical posts people with deep religious and secular knowledge'.[221] And the Institute's constitution, approved by the Ministry of Education and Religion in 1925, and confirmed in 1929, had included the training of rabbis in its mission: 'The rabbinical faculty has a goal to educate and qualify on the basis of exams . . . rabbis and teachers of Jewish religion in secondary schools.'[222] As Shevach Eden pointed out, the founders wished to distance themselves from the theological character of similar institutions in western Europe, aspiring instead to 'become a place of work for all ideologies, for every kind of scientific work as long as it is based on scientific investigation'. It trained both teachers of Hebrew language and Judaic subjects and rabbis, using critical methods for both. Future teachers concentrated on modern Hebrew literature, while rabbinical students concentrated on the Talmud.[223]

There was no formal division between secular and religious studies at the Institute. Rabbinical candidates were required to take classes in ancient, medieval, and early modern Jewish history.[224] Future rabbis were expected to be familiar with 'the outline of all of Jewish history with special attention to the history of Jews in Poland [and to acquire] orientation in historical sources'.[225] Lectures by Bałaban, who moved from Tachkemoni to the Institute in 1928, and classes given by other historians such as Schiper and Friedman, constituted a central part of the Institute's curriculum, including the training of rabbis.[226] Attention to history was manifested not only in these lectures, but also in the Institute's approach to other fields of Jewish studies, taught from a critical point of view. Among many other subjects, future rabbis heard lectures and participated in historical seminars on the history of the Jews in the biblical period, the Bible, and Hebrew philology.[227]

The Institute and Tachkemoni differed in their approaches to balancing the

[221] See Eden, 'The Institute of Jewish Studies' (Heb.), 326. See also *Sprawozdanie Instytutu Nauk Judaistycznych w Warszawie*, p. xxiv. The report was dated July 1929.

[222] 'Statut Instytutu Nauk Judaistycznych w Warszawie', in *Sprawozdanie Instytutu Nauk Judaistycznych w Warszawie*, p. xxxix.

[223] Kaplan and Dresner, *Abraham Joshua Heschel*, 280.

[224] See 'Wykaz obowiązkowych wykładów i ćwiczeń seminaryjnych', in *Sprawozdanie Instytutu Nauk Judaistycznych w Warszawie*, pp. lxiii–lxiv.

[225] 'Porządek studiów w Instytucie Nauk Judaistycznych w Warszawie', in *Sprawozdanie Instytutu Nauk Judaistycznych w Warszawie*, p. lix.

[226] On the curriculum, see 'Skład osobowy Instytutu w roku akad. 1929/30, 1930/31', in *Księga jubileuszowa Braudego*, 13–16; and 'Skład osobowy Instytutu w roku akad. 1933/34' and 'Skład osobowy Instytutu w roku akad. 1934/35', in *Księga jubileuszowa Schorra*, pp. xi–xiii. See also Eden, 'The Institute of Jewish Studies' (Heb.), 329.

[227] See 'Spis wykładów i ćwiczeń seminaryjnych na rok akad. 1931/32, 1932/33, 1933/34', in *Księga jubileuszowa Schorra*, pp. xv–xvi.

methods and critical analysis of Wissenschaft des Judentums with traditional textual study; but this very balancing act itself set the two schools apart from other Polish Jewish educational institutions, such as the YIVO Institute of Jewish Studies and the Hakhmei Lublin Yeshiva.[228] From the outset, the agendas of Tachkemoni and the Institute of Jewish Studies were formed by historians. Moreover, the two institutions shared a national mission, defined in Zionist terms, of preparing a new generation of rabbis. These institutions, and the efforts to create and maintain them, reveal the ways in which Jewish historians and intellectuals tried to formulate and implement a new vision of the rabbinate and the rabbi in interwar Poland. The Institute trained future historians and teachers, as well as rabbis. The inclusion of all three reflected the constraints placed on Jewish professionals, but it also signalled the wider perceptions of the founders, who were historians, teachers, and rabbis themselves, and who wished to create graduates in their own image.

Neither the Institute nor Tachkemoni were intended by their founders to continue in the path of earlier attempts to establish rabbinical training. Over the course of the nineteenth century, and in line with the emerging western European model of rabbinical seminaries in Padua, Breslau, Berlin, and Budapest, the Jewish intelligentsia in Galicia and Congress Poland had put forward a postulate for a new type of rabbinate. Repeated attempts to establish an institution to train enlightened rabbis in Lwów had failed due to the resistance of Orthodox circles and the lack of consistent government support. The Rabbinical School in Warsaw, existing from 1826 to 1862, lacked credibility in the Jewish community and had failed to produce a single acting rabbi. Established in the independent Polish state, the Institute and Tachkemoni were thus a fresh start in many ways. However, the founders did recognize the Institute's close affinity with rabbinical seminaries in western Europe, where 'Jewish scholarship, understood in the spirit of the time and the historiographical conception of its creators, as Jewish theology, found refuge'.[229] Numerous students from eastern Europe, especially from Galicia, studied at the rabbinical seminaries in Vienna, Berlin, and Breslau, and some of these later taught at the Institute.[230]

Leaders of both institutions stressed that their founding originated from internal Jewish developments. Nevertheless, training rabbis to represent Jewish communities with the Polish authorities played an important role in their agendas. Indeed, both Tachkemoni and the Institute of Jewish Studies complied with the decrees of the new Polish regime to intensify the modernization and Poloniza-

---

[228] See Eden, 'The Institute of Jewish Studies' (Heb.), 325. Eden lists three important institutions of Jewish learning: the Institute, YIVO, and Yeshivat Hochmei Lublin.
[229] Ostersetzer, 'Instytut Nauk Judaistycznych w Warszawie', 263.
[230] See the list of graduates of the seminary in Vienna: *Memorial Volume of the Viennese Rabbinical Seminary* (Heb.), 72–82.

tion of the rabbinate; and they accepted the government's control over the future rabbis' education.²³¹ Having responded positively to the official requirements, broadening their curriculum to include secular subjects, both Tachkemoni and the Institute of Jewish Studies secured accreditation from the Polish Ministry. However, for both institutions, combining secular and traditional education was a matter of conviction and vision rather than a pragmatic decision to conform to external demands.²³²

Both institutions received money from the Polish Ministry of Religion and Education, and the Institute also enjoyed financial support from the city council of Warsaw.²³³ In addition to governmental subsidies, both institutes received donations from Jewish communities, organizations, and individuals. Private scholarships were granted to excellent outstanding students and for special purposes such as publishing. Wealthier parents paid tuition. Tachkemoni also received donations from Jewish institutions abroad, especially from France and the United States.²³⁴

Although both institutions tried to avoid the impression that they were closely tied to a political party, their Zionist agenda was clear. Tachkemoni strove 'to enable a future rabbi after receiving a rabbinical diploma, duly to fulfil [his] duties in one of the Jewish communities in Poland', and also instilled national values.²³⁵ Tachkemoni's establishment was part of the educational agenda of Mizrachi just after the First World War.²³⁶ According to Moshe Krone, who enrolled as a student in Tachkemoni in the late 1920s,

---

[231] Bacon, 'The Poznański Affair of 1921', 136. Bacon points to the tactics of the Polish officials 'looking toward full independence and anxious to prevent a Jewish nationalist takeover of the kehillot' (p. 137).

[232] Tartakower, 'The Institute of Jewish Studies in Warsaw' (Heb.); Dold, 'A Matter of National and Civic Honor'. See also Biderman, *Mayer Balaban*, 76.

[233] Report to the Ministry of Religions and Education (MWRiOP), Warsaw, 20 Dec. 1926, from Majer Bałaban and Rady Nadzorczej, director and president respectively of the Tachkemoni Seminary (AAN, MWRiOP, 1460, p. 84). They received 27,000 zł in five instalments over the course of 1925. Apart from Tachkemoni and the Institute of Judaic Studies, the Ministry of Religions and Education also supported the State Seminary for Teachers of Mosaic Religion in Warsaw. See AAN, MWRiOP, 1460, p. 119: 'Z rejestru uchybień stwierdzonych przy kontroli rachunkowości dokumentalnej w pozycjach rozchodowych działu 2-go budżetu Ministerstwa Wyznań Relijnych i Oświecenia Publicznego za rok budżetowy 1927/28'. For the Hebrew version of the budget, see ibid., pp. xxii–xxv.

[234] See the budget for the academic year 1924/25 (31 Aug. 1924–23 Aug. 1925) at Tachkemoni, recorded 2 Sept. 1925 (AAN, MWRiOP, 1460, pp. 85–6). See also Alter, 'Uczelnia "Tachkemoni" w Warszawie', 271. On private scholarships see 'Sprawozdanie za lata akademickie 1931/32, 1932/33, 1933/34', in *Księga jubileuszowa Schorra*, pp. vi–vii. On funding from Jewish institutions abroad see Alter, 'Uczelnia "Tachkemoni" w Warszawie', 271.

[235] Alter, 'Uczelnia "Tachkemoni" w Warszawie', 268. Krone speaks of brainwashing (*shetifat mo'aḥ*) that the students at Tachkemoni willingly accepted, Krone, *My Teachers and Rabbis* (Heb.), 18.

[236] Krone, *My Teachers and Rabbis* (Heb.), 15.

Mizrachi sought to establish a large yeshiva institution in the centre of the country and at the same time to introduce a new spirit to the world of rabbinics. The aim was to train learned rabbis, with a national Zionist worldview; to raise young rabbis with rabbinic talents, with an understanding of current trends and the needs of the younger generation.[237]

Nevertheless, Tachkemoni was not a party institution, and the relationship to the Zionist movement was not evident on a daily basis. According to Mordechai Szulman, who studied at Tachkemoni between 1928 and 1936, Farbstein was the only connection with Mizrachi until the founding of a branch of Hashomer Hadati among the students.[238] Moshe Alter, the director from 1929, personified the synthesis Tachkemoni strove to achieve. He was a member of Mizrachi, a religious Jew, and a scholar with a particular interest in Jewish history and critical research, who believed that history indeed belonged to *limudei kodesh* (religious studies) and taught it accordingly.[239]

History played an important part in rabbinical training at Tachkemoni. According to a contemporary report, the seminary combined 'religious-moral, spiritual, and secular education'. It 'look[ed] after raising up and keeping its students on a high ethical level, implanting in them love for God and the people, of their motherland [*kraj rodzinny*] and all its inhabitants'.[240] Religious education followed the traditional format of rabbinical training, focusing on the comprehensive study of the Talmud, *Shulḥan arukh* (the code of Jewish law compiled by Joseph Karo), and Tanakh (the Hebrew Bible) 'in traditional interpretation'.[241] Religious studies included classes in Jewish history, especially the history of the Jews in Poland, Hebrew literature, both medieval and contemporary, philosophy of religion, and Hebrew grammar. While the Talmud was taught in Yiddish, the remaining Judaic topics were studied in Hebrew. The programme attempted to harmonize religious and secular studies: twenty hours a week out of forty-eight were devoted to secular studies.[242] Rabbis of the Warsaw district examined and approved the candidates for new rabbis, who received an official diploma signed by a delegate of the Ministry.[243]

Tachkemoni struggled—it seems—to balance the traditional and secular aspects of the programme. According to Yitzhak Mishael, Soloveitchik was brought to Tachkemoni in 1920 after several failed attempts to engage rabbis who would examine future students.[244] Moreover, the seminary faced internal

---

[237] Ibid.   [238] IRRZ, Oral Testimonies 45, p. 2, 9 Nov. 1973.
[239] Seidman, 'Moshe Alter', in id., *People I Used to Know* (Heb.), 395–7. Seidman stressed that Alter brought to the seminary a harmony that had been lacking, due to the conflict of approaches between Rabbi Soloveitchik and Majer Bałaban.
[240] Quoted in Alter, 'Uczelnia "Tachkemoni" w Warszawie', 268.   [241] Ibid. 268–9.   [242] Ibid. 269.
[243] Ibid. 270.   [244] See Mishael, 'The Takhkemoni Rabbinical Seminary in Warsaw' (Heb.).

tensions when bringing together scholarship and Orthodox learning, in particular between Bałaban and Soloveitchik. The conflict was only resolved after Soloveitchik left Warsaw for New York and Alter replaced Bałaban.[245] Krone blamed the inclusion of secular studies in the school's curriculum, and the role of Bałaban as its director for the perception of Tachkemoni as *pasul* or invalid, in the eyes of the Orthodox community.[246] In his history lectures, Bałaban questioned the reliability of the tannaitic and amoraic traditions; his lectures were full of blasphemies. His approach to textual study brought Bałaban into direct conflict with Rabbi Soloveitchik, who had joined Tachkemoni with a very different vision of what would be expected of its students. Upon arriving at the seminary, Soloveitchik heard disturbing accounts of rabbinical students' halakhic transgressions, and of Bałaban's argument that 'freedom of expression had to prevail in classroom discussions and could not be curtailed even if something contrary to biblical and talmudic teachings was being said'.[247] Bałaban also supported the idea of examinations supervised by an external non-Jewish authority—the Warsaw Board of Education—while Soloveitchik insisted on thorough examination of students in 'Yoreh de'ah'. These were two dramatically different visions of Jewish education that could not be reconciled. Soloveitchik left Tachkemoni, having refused to sign rabbinical diplomas.[248] After Bałaban left Tachkemoni, in 1928, his place was taken by his brother-in-law, Moshe Alter, who had taught Jewish and general history there since 1925.[249]

Rabbinical tracks at Tachkemoni and the Institute of Jewish Studies both attracted young men who were interested in pursuing both secular and religious education and open to the Zionist undertones in both schools' agendas. Nevertheless, the students differed in age and in the degree to which they were willing to depart from the traditional model. According to Alter, 'Tachkemoni became an institution for training of Orthodox youth hungry for knowledge, wanting to prepare for the profession of an Orthodox rabbi in the modern sense of the word'.[250] Therefore, 'sons of rabbis and other community officials constituted a large proportion of the students; the rest came from Orthodox homes'. The seminary attracted young males from the provinces and the far-off borderlands, which Alter saw as a potential for influencing the future generation of rabbis, making it what he called 'uniform'. This probably meant clearing away regional differences and bringing all closer to his preferred model of a rabbi.[251] Also, students at Tachkemoni were generally younger than those at the Institute. Students ranged between the ages of seventeen and twenty-nine, but younger students (fourteen to

---

[245] Seidman, 'Moshe Alter', in id., *People I Used to Know* (Heb.), 396–7.
[246] Krone, *My Teachers and Rabbis* (Heb.), 16.   [247] Meiselman, *The Soloveitchik Heritage*, 232–3.
[248] Ibid. 233–5.   [249] Seidman, 'Moshe Alter', in id., *People I Used to Know* (Heb.), 394–9.
[250] Alter, 'Uczelnia "Tachkemoni" w Warszawie', 272.   [251] Ibid. 270.

nineteen) were admitted to introductory classes.[252] The programme also hoped to appeal to poor families, many of whom lacked financial resources.[253] Tachkemoni offered young Jews from Orthodox families the opportunity to study secular topics and possibly to qualify for university education.[254] Alter described how 'with unheard-of enthusiasm [youth] hungers after learning . . . These students must struggle with the most primitive conditions of daily life. They spend seven to eight hours at the lectures, and must earn a living with private lessons in the afternoon. In the evenings and nights, they study and read their assignments.'[255]

Only a small number of young men enrolled to train as rabbis at the Institute of Jewish Studies.[256] In the academic year 1929–30 there were nine full-time students and two auditors; in the following year, 16 more students enrolled for rabbinical studies.[257] During the academic year 1931–2, the rabbinical school had 31 students, less than half of the overall enrolment. Two years later, the rabbinical track had 42 men—more than half of all Jewish students, male and female, enrolled at the Institute.[258] The number of students at Tachkemoni was considerably higher. During the first academic year, 1920–1, it had 48 students; two years later their number rose to 137; and in 1928–9 it reached a peak of 232. But not all of those who studied at Tachkemoni graduated with a rabbinical diploma. Indeed, up to 1937, only 177 students were ordained as rabbis.[259]

However few in number, the graduates of both Tachkemoni and the Institute struggled to secure positions as rabbis. Some of those who attended or supported both Tachkemoni and the Institute of Jewish Studies expressed disappointment

[252] Ibid. 269. In cases of younger or older students, acceptance required the approval of the Ministry of Religion and Education.    [253] Ibid. 271–2. IRRZ, Oral Testimonies 45, pp. 3–4, 9 Nov. 1973.
[254] However, many paths to further education remained blocked, even with Tachkemoni's preparation. After studying at Tachkemoni, Moshe Krone, from Kraków, went on to enrol at the Department of Law, arguing that 'other options were closed to the Jews'. He alluded to *numerus clausus* policies at Polish universities which also, however, affected admissions to the Department of Law. Moshe Krone, *My Teachers and Rabbis* (Heb.), 20.    [255] Alter, 'Uczelnia "Tachkemoni" w Warszawie', 271–2.
[256] Eden, 'The Institute of Jewish Studies' (Heb.), 328–9. According to Eden, the rabbinical school also had older students from Galicia who had studied at yeshivas and obtained their gymnasium diplomas as externs. See for example the curriculum vitae of Chaim Simche Babad, who studied at the Institute: 'I was born in Lwów on May 22, 1907. . . . I did not attend school because I devoted myself to talmudic studies. In 1931, I passed my gymnasium exam with a speciality in humanities as an extern at the Second State Gymnasium in Tarnopol. The same year I enrolled at the Department of Humanities of the University of Warsaw, and in June 1935 I took my final exam with Prof. Dr. Majer Bałaban' (Chaim Simche Babad's student file, AUW, RP 39301). His handwritten and signed curriculum vitae is dated 9 Sept. 1935.
[257] There were 52 altogether, including 8 auditors; 30 of the 52 were women. See 'Wykaz słuchaczy w r. akad. 1929/30', in *Księga jubileuszowa Braudego*.
[258] 'Statystyka słuchaczy w latach akad. 1931/32–1933/34', in *Księga jubileuszowa Schorra*.
[259] Alter, 'Uczelnia "Tachkemoni" w Warszawie', 269–70.

in the students' training. Braude complained that the response to 'our appeal to other Jewish communities in Poland was utterly disappointing', ascribing it to the apparent 'lack of understanding of the significant mission which the Institute fulfils vis-à-vis Jewish science and Polish Jewry'.[260] Similar disappointment was voiced in the Institute's report for the academic years 1931–4: 'Jewish society in Poland responded to seven years of persistent academic and pedagogical work, although not to the extent it deserves.'[261] According to Krone, when he began his studies at Tachkemoni in the late 1920s, he understood that

> this will not be an institution producing great rabbinical luminaries, that the institution will not serve as a conservatory for prodigies, but merely a *beit midrash* [Jewish study hall] for the study of the lore and the rulings on a very serious level, that its students will be required to obtain extensive secular education, pass examinations and be properly trained in homiletics.[262]

An activist of the religious Zionist Mizrachi movement in Poland—Zerach Wahrhaftig—claimed that Tachkemoni was seen as a great institution that would educate a new generation of rabbis to serve Poland,[263] but that it failed to train them properly. Perhaps not surprisingly, Tachkemoni's graduates faced difficulties in finding communities willing to hire them. These problems were closely linked to the ideological struggle between Mizrachi and Agudat Israel in interwar Poland, with both parties claiming to represent traditional Polish Jews. The resistance of 'some Orthodox circles' to accept rabbis with secular education increased the problems faced by young graduates.[264]

Upon their graduation, a number of former students taught Judaic studies in secondary schools, and others led Jewish religious schools in the provinces while continuing their theological studies. The majority left Poland to study abroad; some travelled to the great Lithuanian yeshivas, while others continued their education in Berlin.[265] And others continued their preparations for taking rabbinical posts, but with difficulty due to their young age and the requirement that they marry.

In the new vision of the rabbinate formulated by scholars such as Bałaban, Poznański, and Schorr, history was an indispensable element of rabbinical education. This conviction shaped the curricula of the two rabbinical schools they had helped to build. The influence of intellectuals who taught at Tachkemoni and the

---

[260] M. Braude and M. Bałaban, 'Sprawozdanie kuratorium', in *Księga jubileuszowa Braudego*, 8(v).
[261] See 'Sprawozdanie za lata akademickie 1931/32, 1932/33, 1933/34', in *Księga jubileuszowa Schorra*, p. vi.      [262] Krone, *My Teachers and Rabbis* (Heb.), 15.
[263] IRRZ, Oral Testimonies 20, p. 12, 11 June 1973. Wahrhaftig argued that Bałaban was not the right person to train rabbis and that Tachkemoni's graduates knew a little bit of this and of that but nothing in depth.      [264] Alter, 'Uczelnia "Tachkemoni" w Warszawie', 269–70.
[265] Krone, *My Teachers and Rabbis* (Heb.), 16.

Institute cannot be measured simply in the number of rabbis who graduated from the two institutions. With their knowledge of general Jewish history, but also of Jewish history in Poland, these future rabbis felt better suited to serve contemporary Jewish communities, especially the youth. This new intellectual training for rabbis also gave them better tools to combat assimilation. In fact, Bałaban, who shaped the curriculum of both Tachkemoni and the Institute of Jewish Studies, described studying Jewish history as a matter of national emergency: 'No plans for Jewish literature, no praising hymns for Jewish history will be of help, unless we enable our youth to learn and deepen these branches of knowledge.'[266]

While historians, teachers, and other intellectuals and professionals of Galician origin took advantage of opportunities and openings in the new Polish state, a group of rabbis did so as well. As noted above, two leading historians who came to Warsaw had also served as rabbis. Bałaban served as a military rabbi on the Austrian front of Lublin during the First World War, and Schorr took the position of rabbi and preacher at the Tłomackie Synagogue in Warsaw after the death of Poznański, serving therefore as one of the rabbis of the Warsaw *kehilah*.[267] Schorr's nomination to this post was expected to attract members of the Jewish intelligentsia to the synagogue.[268] He considered supporting modern scholarship in Jewish studies part of his call as a rabbi.[269] Galicia offered a model of a new rabbi, rare in the other provinces of Poland: a scholar rabbi, with academic education and broad secular knowledge, and, in many cases, university trained in history and fluent in Polish language and culture.

## Military Service

The creation of the Polish state and the establishment of compulsory military service for all Polish citizens, included in the March 1921 Constitution, took Polish Jews down the path taken by Galician Jews decades earlier. Although the Ministry of War of the Second Polish Republic sought to avoid drafting soldiers from among national minorities, citing their political unreliability, Jews still constituted approximately 4.9 per cent of the soldiers in the armed forces of the Second Polish Republic. Altogether, 174,000–180,000 young Jews served in the Polish army.[270] To tend to the religious needs of thousands of Jewish draftees, the Ministry of

---

[266] Bałaban, 'Rabin Dr Samuel Poznański'. See also Bałaban, 'Zagadnienia historjozofji żydowskiej'.

[267] See Schorr, *Kazanie inauguracyjne wygłoszone w Wielkiej Synagodze na Tłomackiem*.

[268] See Biblioteka Uniwersytecka w Warszawie, Papiery osobiste prof. Mojżesza Schorra, (personal papers of Mojżesz Schorr), inv. no. 721, p. 49.   [269] See Schorr, *Przemówienie inauguracyjne*, 8.

[270] For a biased account of the Jews' service, see Rezmer, 'Służba wojskowa Żydów'. For statistical data see Kowalski, *Mniejszości narodowe w siłach zbrojnych Drugiej Rzeczypospolitej Polskiej (1918–1939)*, 120, table 17. See also the study of the meaning of Jewish military service, Henschel, *Jeder Bürger Soldat*.

War created the Chief Rabbinate and incorporated a number of rabbis as chaplains. Military rabbis cared for Jewish soldiers in military districts such as Warsaw, Brześć, and Grodno, taking their military oath, giving sermons, and ensuring they had access to kosher food and a *minyan* (a prayer quorum of adult Jewish men). Moreover, local rabbis in communities in which large garrisons were located also tended to the religious needs of soldiers in the lower ranks. The path to becoming a military chaplain led through civilian nomination to drafting the rabbi into military service.[271]

The difficulties in nominating official military rabbis arose from the complex cultural and political expectations of the Polish military authorities and those already nominated to the position of chief military rabbi. The Ministry of War sought rabbis to fit a particular intellectual and political profile. Candidates were required to show proof of secular education in addition to traditional rabbinical training, and they needed to appear politically reliable.[272] All three chief military rabbis came from Galicia: Józef Mieses, Chaim Eliezer Fränkel, and Baruch Steinberg. When describing his background, Józef Mieses stressed that he had studied Talmud with private tutors while attending the Polish gymnasium in his native Przemyśl and had then studied at the Rabbinical Seminary and the University of Vienna.[273] In his curriculum vitae, Steinberg described his family as 'the oldest rabbinical family, going back to the eleventh century', with 'considerable influence on the life of Jews since the fourteenth century'. Moreover, as Steinberg assured his military superiors, 'for centuries, members of the family propagated Polish thought among wide circles of Jewry, as attested by several royal decrees favouring the members of the family. These decrees are held in the Main Archives of Old Records (Główne Archiwum Akt Dawnych) in Warsaw.'[274] Steinberg received a traditional education, and he passed his exams to become a rabbi in Vienna in 1917. Upon his return to Poland he took a position as a communal rabbi in Dunajów, near Lwów. He pursued a career as a military rabbi as early as 1925, but he was initially turned down with the suggestion that he needed more secular education. In 1926 he passed the gymnasium final exams as an extern, and in 1927 enrolled in oriental studies at Jan Kazimierz University in Lwów and later at Stefan Batory University in Wilno, graduating in 1932. Steinberg received a nomination as a military rabbi to serve in the Grodno Military District. He believed it was his

---

[271] See the article about Rabbi Baruch Steinberg, 'Rabin Baruch Steinberg—rabin wojskowy przy tut. DOK [Dowództwo Okręgu Korpusu]' (CAW, I.300.20.133, p. 57). This is a Polish translation of an article that originally appeared in Yiddish.

[272] For example, around 1928 Baruch Steinberg was described as 'a good Polish patriot' and a supporter of Marshal Piłsudski's ideas. See CAW, I.300.20.125, p. 24, 'Pro domo'.

[273] See the handwritten curriculum vitae, written in 1920 (CAW, I.300.20.124, p. 6).

[274] See the typescript of Steinberg's curriculum vitae, dated in Dunajów, November 1927 (CAW, I.300.20.125, p. 111).

role to not only fulfil the religious needs of Jewish soldiers, but also to educate them and elevate their spiritual level. He also wished to serve as a liaison between the Polish government and Jewish society.[275]

Military chaplains encouraged Jewish soldiers' sense of patriotic duty towards Poland and assisted at military ceremonies in which Jewish soldiers participated. Jewish soldiers took an oath swearing their loyalty to the motherland and promising to 'defend the honour of the Polish soldier'.[276] From 1922, on the Saturday following completion of their initial military training, Jewish soldiers took an oath, in the presence of a rabbi, 'promising to live and die as a loyal Polish soldier'; this was followed by a religious service with special sermons.[277] Military rabbis were expected to 'awaken the feelings of organic ties with the Motherland and faithfulness to her' by referring to the history of the Polish army and to the most prominent personalities and heroes who had participated in the struggle for the country's independence.[278] As part of this mission, sermons were delivered to Jewish soldiers on Polish national holidays. Filled with historical references, these talks stressed the connection between Polish Jewry and the Polish state over the centuries. On 3 May 1930 Rabbi Chaim Pozner, who served as a military rabbi in Warsaw, delivered a sermon stressing the importance of this festive celebration, evoking the constitutions of 3 May 1791, which supported the values of equality and liberty. In recognition of this noble attempt, argued the rabbi, God blessed Poland and brought it back to life so it could fulfil these ideals. Moreover, this Polish national holiday reminded Pozner of the patriarchs Abraham, Isaac, and Jacob, who embodied with their deeds the same ideals of equality and freedom. Thus, a deep connection united 'the Jews and the country in which they lived forever and who participated in its struggles for independence and gave our lives for gaining independence back'. Reminding his audience about the deeds of patriotic Jews such as Berek Joselewicz and Rabbi Meisels, Pozner spoke directly to Jewish soldiers:

[275] See Steinberg's curriculum vitae (CAW, I.300.20.125, p. 7). See also the article about Steinberg (CAW, I.300.20.133, p. 57), and the negative response to his 1925 application by the chief military rabbi, Józef Mieses, pointing to Steinberg's inadequate secular education ('odpowiedni cenzus naukowyświecki'), signed by Rab. Dr Józef Mieses, Naczelny Rabin WP, 6 Aug. 1925, Warsaw (CAW, I.300.20.125, p. 17).

[276] See the typed draft of the oath, with the stamp dated 8 Nov. 1922 (CAW, I.300.20.133, p. 3).

[277] See a copy of the circular from the Ministry of War to the Department of Non-Catholic Denominations, [day unclear] Oct. 1922 (CAW, I.300.20.130, p. 260). The circular was signed by Marian Kukiel, chief of the 3rd Department in the military headquarters, and by General Władysław Sosnkowski. See also CAW, I.300.20.130, p. 100: 'Przysięga wojskowa szer. wyznania mojżeszowego', signed by General A. Galica.

[278] See the instructions in 'Główny Wojskowy Urząd Duszpasterski Wyznania Mojżeszowego, Instrukcja w przedmiocie wygłaszania nauk etyczno-religijnych przez duchownych wojskowych' (CAW, I.300.20.133).

You soldiers of the Polish army ought to show special generosity, sacrifice yourself for the country, and fight for Poland's prosperity to the last drop of blood. You carry on your shoulders a double burden as citizens and as soldiers. You resemble priests who had to guard the Temple and who were punished with death for the smallest infringement in their service.[279]

The military rabbinate also participated in patriotic commemorations of soldiers who had fallen in Polish wars of independence. Their presence demonstrated the Jews' recognition of and participation in the struggles and sacrifices of these soldiers.[280]

Military rabbis referred to history in their sermons and in classes organized for the soldiers. Steinberg considered 'the cultural education of the Jewish soldier-citizen' the most important part of his rabbinate, and he 'very often organized talks about the history of the Jews and especially the history of the Jews in Poland'.[281] On the initiative of the local military leadership at the Grodno garrison, Steinberg organized special lectures for both officers and non-commissioned officers 'in order for them to get to know Jewish history. In this way a corner stone for the harmonious coexistence of Poles and Jews can be laid.'[282] In addition to their obligations to the Jewish soldiers, military rabbis visited local Jewish schools and organized patriotic initiatives among and on behalf of the Jewish population.[283] For example, Steinberg collected donations in Grodno for the Ministry of Internal Affairs, referring to the example of Berek Joselewicz.[284] Rabbis held talks for Jewish soldiers addressing religious issues and Jewish history, especially Polish Jewish history, in individual garrisons and at local synagogues.[285] Rabbi-scholars involved in curriculum development and teaching Jewish children, such as Kalman Chameides and Efraim Sonnenschein, also worked with Jewish soldiers.[286]

---

[279] Rabbi Pozner's sermon is preserved in CAW, I.300.20.133, p. 61: 'Przemówienie Rabina Poznera w dniu 3 maja 1930 r'.

[280] See the letter dated 7 Sept. 1931 from the board in Kraków of the Association of Organizations of Jewish Invalids and Military Orphans (Zjednoczenie Związków Żydowskich Inwalidów Wdów i Sierot Wojennych Rzeczypospolitej Polskiej), to the Chief Military Rabbinate of the Polish Army, about sending a representative to the unveiling of a memorial to the fallen soldiers in Dąbrowa, near Tarnów (CAW, I.300.20.133, p. 70).

[281] CAW, I.300.20.125, p. 39: 'W sprawie działalności Rabina wojskowego DOK Grodna', translation into Polish of an article in *Unzer Grodner Expres*, 107, 9 May 1929.

[282] Ibid. 40. [283] See Steinberg's curriculum vitae (CAW, I.300.20.125, p. 111).

[284] See his peers' recommendation for Steinberg: Dowództwo Okręgu Korpusu Nr III, Grodno, 19 Feb. 1930 (CAW, I.300.20.125, p. 67). See also a copy of the article 'Ludność żydowska na fundusz dyspoz. Marszałka Piłsudskiego', *Głos Prawdy Ziemi Grodzieńskiej*, 19 June 1929 (CAW, I.300.20.125, p. 59).

[285] See a letter to Steinberg from Stanisławów, dated 16 Feb. 1936 (CAW, I.300.20.133, p. 19).

[286] See the article describing lectures delivered to Jewish soldiers (CAW, I.300.20.133, p. 137). The article, translated from Yiddish into Polish as 'Wykłady dla żołnierzy—żydów', originally appeared in

Likewise, local teachers of the Mosaic faith organized lectures and courses in Jewish history, especially Polish Jewish history. In 1936, in his application to the Department of Jewish Affairs in the Ministry of War, Pinkas Zgał, a local teacher of the Mosaic faith in two state primary schools in Ostrołęka, offered to hold classes for soldiers in Jewish and Polish Jewish history to teach them about the Jewish religion, preparing them to participate in services and religious practices.[287]

Commemorating the anniversary of Berek Joselewicz's birthday, in May 1933, Captain Raab, a military rabbi at the garrison in Lublin, organized a special service in the Maharshal synagogue. There, he delivered a sermon in Polish and Yiddish to the general public and Jewish soldiers about Joselewicz's courage. In addition, Raab organized a ceremony for Jews and Christians in front of the city's headquarters and a demonstration by the grave of the legendary hero, during which Polish officers and representatives of the Jewish community in Lublin and the city of Kock addressed the crowd.[288] Likewise, Hanukah celebrations offered an opportunity for delivering patriotic speeches to Jewish soldiers.[289] Upon issuance of the order of mobilization, in August 1939, the Chief Rabbinate called on Jewish soldiers to volunteer for the defence of Poland against German aggression, and to read about the continuous participation of Polish Jews in the struggle for Poland's independence from the Kościuszko uprising of 1794, through the uprisings of 1831 and 1863, linking the generations with Jews in the army of the Second Polish Republic.[290]

## Conclusion

In interwar Poland, history served as a useful tool for educating young Polish Jews and shaping their identity as Polish citizens. Jewish historians saw their discipline as relevant in training teachers, rabbis, and chaplains to write for and lecture to wide and diverse Jewish and non-Jewish audiences. They insisted on incorporating history into the curricula of the training programmes for both teachers and

the local Yiddish newspaper, *Zagłebier Cajtung*, 9 Apr. 1937. See also the report by Dr E. Sonnenschein for Steinberg (CAW, I.300.20.133, p. 114).

[287] See the application of Pinkas Zgał to the Bureau of Non-Catholic Denominations in the Ministry of War, dated 29 Oct. 1936 in Ostrołęka (CAW, I.300.20.133, p. 144).

[288] See the translation of a Yiddish newspaper article into Polish as 'Uroczystość Berka Joselewicza w Lublinie i Kocku' (CAW, I.300.20.133, p. 110). The original Yiddish article was published in *Unzer ekspres*, 117 A, 22 May 1933. Rabbi Raab referred to these commemorations for 'an opportunity for civic enlightenment and strengthening of the patriotic spirit'. See his letter to the head of the Bureau for Non-Catholic Denominations at the Ministry of War, Nr 052/DM, 28 June 1933, Lublin (CAW, I.300.20.133, p. 111).

[289] See the report by Dr E. Sonnenschein for Steinberg (CAW, I.300.20.133, p. 114).

[290] CAW, I.300.20.133, p. 125: 'Obywatele Żydzi!'

rabbis. Thus, the press, parliament, schools, military and religious services, and adult education all became channels for ideas about Polish Jewish history. Historians honed specific historical arguments for the political arena. In the political culture of interwar Poland, which held historical arguments and academic credentials in high regard, eminent Jewish historians could both voice their arguments directly, as representatives of the Jewish public, and supply other public figures with arguments and refutations. Jewish political representatives also used historical references in their speeches, to call on the liberal and tolerant traditions of the multi-ethnic Polish–Lithuanian Commonwealth, and to raise questions of ethics and basic decency in daily coexistence.[291] Curricula developed for Jewish schools made Jewish history, including Polish Jewish history, an essential part of their programme. Teachers graduating from Jewish institutions, responsible for training pedagogues, focused on Jewish history in addition to Jewish religion and literature. Jewish historians worked in Jewish schools and chaired organizations championing the cause of Jewish education. They also wrote course books for Jewish school children on Jewish and Polish Jewish history. While teaching in the Jewish gymnasia, Bałaban, Friedman, and Schall advised and recruited students with an interest in Polish Jewish history. Students also discussed these subjects in their extracurricular activities in Jewish gymnasia and primary schools. Jewish historians worked on preparing a new generation of rabbis and teachers. In accordance with this vision, Polish Jews attending celebratory synagogue services or Jewish soldiers drafted into the Polish army, encountered military chaplains and heard sermons referring prominently to Polish and Polish Jewish history. Polish Jews also had the opportunity to attend lectures on Jewish history at Jewish institutions and organizations and to read about it in the Jewish press. These sermons, lectures, and popular publications corrected misrepresentations about Jews and Jewish history in Polish historiography and the popular public discourse, instilling pride and a well-deserved sense of entitlement to equal status and fair treatment for Jews in the Second Polish Republic. Reaching out to the Polish non-Jewish audience remained the most difficult part of the project, more a hope for generating change in the future than a reality. Schorr, Bałaban, Schiper, Ringelblum, Mahler, and Friedman served as public figures in their capacity as teachers, rabbis, communal activists, and political leaders. Their work outside academia resulted not only from limited opportunities for full-fledged academic careers, but also from their sense of mission and agenda. They envisioned a wide audience for their work, hoping to educate both Polish and Jewish audiences and to strengthen the identity of Jewish citizens of Poland. These widely disseminated ideas did not differ greatly from the subjects and arguments they put forward in scholarly publications.

[291] Żebrowski, *Mojżesz Schorr i jego Listy do Ludwika Gumplowicza*, 49–50.

FIVE

# THEMES AND TRENDS OF HISTORICAL ENQUIRY

IN THE SECOND POLISH REPUBLIC, university and research seminars trained a cohort of Jewish historians to study the history of Polish Jewry using critical analysis of a wide variety of sources for the benefit of both Jewish and general audiences in the country. Meeting the standards of professional scholarship made the field of Polish Jewish history respectable and worthy of inclusion in the general historical discourse. Despite financial difficulties and ideological differences, Majer Bałaban, Mojżesz Schorr, Ignacy Schiper, Emanuel Ringelblum, Filip Friedman, Raphael Mahler, Bela Mandelsberg, and other Jewish historians hoped gradually to build an institutional base with modern archives, museums, the cataloguing of existing material, and publishing houses for primary sources, monographs, and surveys. They not only discussed research priorities and agendas but also sketched the stages of research necessary to create a full body of knowledge about the Polish Jewish past.[1]

Discussing the role of their field and profession, Jewish historians stressed the usefulness of history beyond the Polish and Jewish scholarly communities. They saw their work as inherently relevant for both Polish and Jewish general audiences, since it drew on examples from the past both to provide a sense of belonging for Jews and to address pressing political and social problems. Polish Jewish history also promised to build a better future for peaceful Polish–Jewish coexistence by correcting misconceptions and giving 'people of good will' historical arguments to use in the battle for recognition of the Jews' right to be at home in Poland. This sense of carrying out both an intellectual project and a political mission on behalf of the Jewish community united scholars who were divided by training, background, and ideological agenda. Combining their intellectual pursuit of academic excellence with the national mission, Polish Jewish historians strove to find a balance between the professional ideal of academic objectivity and the pressing needs of the Polish Jewish community.

[1] See Chapter 3 for discussion of the building of academic networks in the field of Polish Jewish history. For a general analysis of Jewish historiography in interwar Poland see Friedman, 'Polish Jewish Historiography between the Two Wars (1918–1939)'; Eisenbach, 'Jewish Historiography in Interwar Poland'; Trunk, 'On the History of Polish Historiography' (Heb.).

Harmonizing these two aspects of their profession to ensure a reception for Polish Jewish history in contemporary Jewish and non-Jewish society in Poland became the core issue in envisioning and defining the field. Both in scholarly writings and popular historical ones, three intertwined subjects emerged as central to Polish Jewish historiography: the history of local Jewish communities, Jewish–Gentile relations, and the history of Jewish communal institutions. These subjects both addressed the scholarly needs and the political agenda of Polish Jewish historians and allowed for the integration of the external and internal aspects of the history of Polish Jewry. They also provided the Polish Jewish community with historical narratives on both local and national levels. They constructed a past, supporting Polish Jews' claim for the moral right to equal civic status and to consider Poland their home.[2]

## The Reasons for Writing Polish Jewish History

Despite their generational, ideological, and stylistic differences, Polish Jewish historians shared an academic quest: to contribute to the general body of historical knowledge and to Polish historiography. This was an urgent imperative, because the existing historical literature omitted, obscured, or misrepresented the role of the Jews. In a decorous and subtle manner, Polish Jewish historians made their point about the partiality of Polish historiography abundantly clear. They argued that omissions and biases appeared most striking in discussions of the Jews' role in Poland's economy and their attitudes towards the country.[3] In 1911 Schiper discussed Jewish trade from the mid-fourteenth century to the late fifteenth in Poland, stressing the Jews' role in trade with the Far East. He argued that Polish scholars failed to acknowledge this, whether out of ignorance of Jewish history or by deliberately misrepresenting it. Discussing the work of Stanisław Kutrzeba, for example, Schiper noted: 'Despite all the respect we have for such scholarly works of Kutrzeba as his research on medieval trade in Poland—we cannot resist the impression that he is biased when he discusses the issue of Jewish trade, trying to put the Jews—at any cost—to the category of moneylenders only.'[4] Commenting on the need for 'a proper history of Jews in Poland', Antoni Marylski rebuffed the work of Polish Jewish historians as dishonest. But he also concluded that as a Pole he was unable to explore Jewish spiritual and religious life. Therefore, he doubted that Jewish history in Poland could ever be truly studied.[5]

[2] See Roskies, *The Jewish Search for a Usable Past*.
[3] In discussions at the Fourth Congress of Polish Historians in 1925, Bałaban reminded his colleagues that urban history written solely on the basis of city records would be skewed unless scholars also studied Jewish communal records (*Pamiętnik IV*, ii. 111).
[4] Schiper, *Studya nad stosunkami gospodarczymi Żydów w Polsce*, 171 n. 13. See also Uruszczak, 'Stanisław Kutrzeba (1876–1946)', 297.   [5] Marylski, *Dzieje sprawy żydowskiej w Polsce*, 2.

Bałaban pointed to additional leading Polish historians such as Jan Ptaśnik, Antoni Prochaska, and Fryderyk Papée who, unable to overcome their prejudices, ignored or misinterpreted the role of Jews in Polish towns and the Polish economy.[6] He charged scholars who omitted Jewish history with 'falsify[ing] the picture of the past and skew[ing] it beyond recognition'.[7] On another occasion, in order to avoid alienating his non-Jewish colleagues, Bałaban attributed omissions and misrepresentation to ignorance of Jewish sources, rather than anti-Jewish bias. In 1935 Bałaban reviewed three recent city monographs published by Polish historians and concluded that most urban historians sympathized with the townsmen of the seventeenth and eighteenth centuries in their competition and struggle with the Jews.[8] Since 'only very few urban historians were capable of a measure of objectivity in portraying Jewish history', he argued, the Jewish perspective was indispensable in reconstructing the Jewish past. Bałaban concluded that 'one should and must explore Jewish history in our towns on one's own'.[9] Indeed, the omission or misrepresentation of Jews in Polish history books became a driving force behind several research projects in urban history taken up by Jewish historians. Mojżesz Steinberg looked for information about his home town of Jarosław, but concluded that 'it is hard even to get a general sense of the Jewish past in our town'.[10] Bela Mandelsberg decided to research the history of the Jewish community in her native Lublin when she found it absent from the history books she read at the university.[11]

In his thesis on the Jewish community in Przemyśl at the turn of the seventeenth and eighteenth centuries, Mojżesz Krämer described in detail two distinct 'strangely extreme' historiographies. Without explicitly disclosing the national identities of each of these two 'opinions about the situation of the Jews in Przemyśl in the period under our consideration', he made the distinction clear: historians of the general chronicle of the town, and 'ours, discussed in part by Schorr'. The first account blamed the Jews for the downfall of the town while they flourished, looking only at rich individual Jews. It 'zealously reads the materials and protests of the burghers, entering into their spirit [*wżywa się w nie*] and nothing else concerns

---

[6] Bałaban, 'Przedmowa', in Wurm, *Z dziejów żydostwa brodzkiego za czasów dawnej Rzeczypospolitej Polskiej*, p. iii.

[7] Bałaban, 'Zadania i potrzeby historjografji Żydów w Polsce', ii. 225.

[8] See Bałaban, 'Żydzi w monografjach historycznych miast polskich'.

[9] Bałaban, 'Przedmowa', in Wurm, *Z dziejów żydostwa brodzkiego za czasów dawnej Rzeczypospolitej Polskiej*, p. iii.

[10] Steinberg, *Żydzi w Jarosławiu od czasów najdawniejszych do połowy XIX wieku*, 3.

[11] Blumental, 'A Profile of Bela' (Heb.), 25. Similarly, Józef Bursztyn wrote his thesis on the history of the Jews in Opatów to fill a gap in the scholarship on that town. See the introduction to Bursztyn's thesis, which was written for Bałaban's seminar: Józef Bursztyn, 'Żydzi opatowscy na przełomie XVII i XVIII w.' (AŻIH 117, folder 8, 1–2).

it'. Polish chroniclers recorded anti-Jewish assaults and disturbances casually and described the competition with the same attitude.[12]

The other historiography—represented by Schorr, Krämer, and, by extension, other Jewish historians—understood that

> the ruin of the city resulted from a whole variety of events . . . and for the Jews of Przemyśl, just like for all Jews living in Poland at the time, this was a period of the hardest struggle for the right to live . . . a time of painful historical disappointments and of utter economic ruin, in short, a peak followed by fast downfall in a spiral to material bankruptcy.[13]

Seeing beyond a few wealthy Jews, this historical school recognized the suffering of the majority of the Jewish community, ordinary Jews victimized by the town's Christian populace. Jewish historians argued that the situation resulted from decisions made by the nobility and the clergy, who preferred to hide behind scapegoats. Rather than overlook or undervalue anti-Jewish violence, they treated it seriously and put it into its proper context. They also realized that competition in commerce was 'a struggle for daily bread', a struggle in which 'the one more resourceful and inured to struggle had a better chance to stay afloat'. Before drawing any conclusions, they listened to both sides of the story, investigated a variety of primary materials, including the statistics on anti-Jewish violence, the fast-growing debts of the Jewish community, and the taxes paid by Jews. They also strolled down 'the Jewish street', and visited houses occupied by Jews to explore their living conditions. Krämer implied that Jewish scholars' empathetic, open-minded, and thorough approach to the situation of the Jewish community in Przemyśl and Jewish–Gentile relations in the town ultimately allowed them to write a better, more objective history.[14]

How involved should the historian of Jews in Poland be with the problems of the national minority to which he or she belonged? Some Jewish historians explicitly condemned detached scholarship in the ivory tower of the academy. As early as 1917 Schiper argued that 'if we submerge ourselves in the waves of our history, it is not in order to emerge to the surface with a handful of news, good or bad, interesting or of little consequence. Our aim is always before us. It is the understanding of the present that we seek in our history. One must want something from the past.'[15] The leaders of the Young Historians Circle, Mahler and Ringelblum, also insisted on explicitly linking the past and the present.[16] Likewise,

---

[12] Moses Krämer, 'Dzieje Żydów w Przemyślu na przełomie XVII i XVIII w', Master's thesis held in AŻIH 117, folder 24, pp. 5–6.    [13] Ibid.    [14] Ibid.

[15] Schiper, 'Dr. Majer Bałaban: Dzieje Żydów w Galicyi i w Rzeczypospolitej krakowskiej 1772–1868', review, 434, cited in Litman, *The Economic Role of Jews in Medieval Poland*, 232.

[16] Mahler, 'History and People' (Yid.), 17. Mahler ascertained that studying Jewish history would

the leadership of the YIVO Institute often contrasted such work to the disengaged attitude of German Jewish scholars.[17] Although Schiper criticized Bałaban for his lack of clear-cut involvement in contemporary issues, Bałaban continually expressed his conviction of the crucial importance, for the Jewish community and its future, of studying the Jewish past in Poland. Moreover, at the time Bałaban was seen as performing a service in his role as author and public persona at Warsaw University, bearing a striking resemblance to the ideal described by Schiper. In 1937 Falik Hafner praised Bałaban not only as his mentor but also as a scholar on the front line: 'Precisely now, when various unfit experts and brazen-faced falsifiers want to delude us into the belief that we are strangers on this soil, we should celebrate the jubilee of the person who contributed the most to reconstructing our centuries-old history on this soil.'[18]

In fact, the line between an innocent omission as a result of available sources and ideologically motivated bias could be narrow. Since scholars such as Franciszek Bujak denied the very existence of a historical and cultural entity known as 'Polish Jewry', the very act of studying Polish Jewish history constituted a scholarly response to a contemporary crisis.[19] By providing accurate and otherwise-missing details about of the history of the Jews in Poland, including the dynamics of local Jewish communities and their relations with their Gentile neighbours, Jewish historians engaged in political activism on behalf of Polish Jewry in the 1920s and 1930s. The publishers of the monumental *Żydzi w Polsce Odrodzonej* (Jews in Resurrected Poland) assured readers that historians who contributed to the volumes—including Schorr, Bałaban, Schiper, Ringelblum, and Friedman—provided 'the facts and the numbers' essential for understanding the Jews' past in Poland and for improving the present.[20] Beyond correcting mistakes in the academic historiography, Jewish historians had access to reliable historical data, and they provided material for a discussion in wide intellectual circles. Friedman

have 'real value [*Lebensvert*] for contemporary Jewish society'. See also Ringelblum, 'Three Years of a Jewish History Seminar' (Yid.), 10. See Chapter 3 for discussion of the Yunger Historiker Krayz.

[17] See Kuznitz, *YIVO and the Making of Modern Jewish Culture*, 64.

[18] Hafner, 'Przemawia w imieniu uczniów', in Jolles (ed.), *Księga jubileuszowa Bałabana*, 30–1. In January 1938 the publishers of a volume about Jewish participation in the struggles for Poland's independence also wrote about the 'attacks, slander, and calumny against the honour and dignity of Polish Jews and Jewish soldiers', noting bitterly that they were denigrated 'now more than ever'. See Urbach, *Udział Żydów w walce o niepodległość Polski*, p. vi.

[19] While writing about 'foreign elements', 'Jews of Poland', and 'our Jews', Bujak refused to use the term 'Polish Jews': 'Contrary to the West-European Jews, those in Poland do not try even superficially to assimilate in a cultural way with the Polish population, so that, to define this difference, they were lately called "Eastern Jews" (*Ostjuden*) instead [of] as heretofore "Polish Jews"'. See Bujak, *The Jewish Question in Poland*, 20–1, 45, 47.

[20] See Schiper, Tartakower, and Hafftka (eds.), *Żydzi w Polsce Odrodzonej*, i. 5.

explained that, apart from scholarly interest, his work was motivated by his social-political concerns:

Our time abounds in attacks against Polish Jewry, its role in economic and social life, for the most part coming from the incompetent side. In the polemical swordplay [*szermierka polemiczna*] on the subject, often both sides—the antagonists and the apologists of Jewry—reach for historical arguments, drawing them from sources not always reliable and trustworthy. Thus, it seemed to me that the historian's assignment is to provide the people of goodwill, who want to investigate this problem seriously, with reliable material and a picture reflecting as faithfully as possible the economic activities of the Jews in the recent past, in the extremely important period of emergence and development of the forms of capitalist economy in Polish lands, and to shed light on it as free as possible of the atmosphere of turmoil of political strife, in a study as objective as possible, *sine ira et studio*.[21]

These two distinct motivations behind historians' work were hard to separate in practice. 'Dry facts' mattered, but they never quite remained dry; or, as one reviewer noted of Schiper's *On the History and Economic Conditions of the Jews* (*Yidishe geshikhte: Virtshaftsgeshikhte*), 'objective, sober, matter of fact and strictly scholarly discussion of facts and problems' was by virtue of these qualities an indictment—a powerful '*J'accuse*'—for the persecution inflicted on medieval Jewry.[22] In his *Dzieje handlu żydowskiego na ziemiach polskich* (1937), Schiper ended the historical part of his opus by referring to 'the events of the last months and weeks' that undermined the Jewish position in commerce in the country.[23] In 1938 Schiper argued that European Jewry were 'living in a boiler' where constant persecution left them no time to take stock of their predicament. By providing sober, academic analysis YIVO could give the Jewish public the means to assess its situation rationally, 'a kind of pause for the Jewish community, a chance to reflect'.[24]

In the 1930s more Polish Jewish historians and communal leaders shared that sense of urgency expressed by Friedman, Schiper, and Hafner about the importance of historians' work.[25] Indeed, the 1930s witnessed a heated debate about the status of Polish Jewry in the Polish state and in society, as ideas about the essentially ethnic and Catholic character of the resurrected Polish commonwealth

---

[21] Friedman, *Dzieje Żydów w Łodzi*, 8.
[22] Friedman, 'Dzieło na czasie', 557.    [23] Schiper, *Dzieje handlu żydowskiego*, 648.
[24] Minutes of a scholarly meeting, 18 Apr. 1938, as quoted in Kuznitz, *YIVO and the Making of Modern Jewish Culture*, 174.
[25] See for example the introduction signed by the Union of Jewish Participants in the Struggles for Poland's Independence (Związek Żydów Uczestników Walk o Niepodległość Polski), which alluded to the dire situation of the Jews in the country and the abuse of history ('Przedmowa', in Urbach, *Udział Żydów w walce o niepodległość Polski*).

gained popularity.²⁶ Responding to the escalation of antisemitism in Germany after Hitler's rise to power, and to the deteriorating situation of the Jews in Poland, Jewish intellectuals resorted to history both in their internal debates and in discussions in the public arena. Schiper referred to history to console his readers: 'If we look back, however, at the history of Jewish trade in Polish lands . . . we conclude that Jewish merchants emerged victorious from many occasions of being between Scylla and Charybdis thanks to their experience, the spirit of initiative, persistence and talent for sensing the economy's booms and slumps [*konjunktury*].' Schiper suggested that 'the depth of historical experience' allowed Jewish merchants to hope to survive through difficult times, just as generations of their brethren had done before in Polish lands.²⁷ Friedman referred to history, especially economic history, not only as a tool for understanding the dire economic situation of the Jews but also as a source of useful admonition, a lesson, and a 'signpost for the future'. As Polish Jewry experienced the results of harsh economic competition and pauperization in the 1930s, the link between the past and the present rendered writing economic history particularly worthy of scholarly pursuit.²⁸ For this reason, he argued, historians' work served as a source of hope and solace.

The community's economic vulnerability and political marginalization raised the question of the roots of biased government policies and antisemitic popular attitudes. At a time when Polish Jews struggled to understand Polish–Jewish relations, history gave them a perspective and an intellectual platform to deal with the rise of antisemitism. After the first assault on Bałaban at Warsaw University, he explained to his students that one could look at the current deterioration of Polish–Jewish relations and draw from it hope for the future:

We are learning the history of Polish Jewry. We are familiar with the waves of antisemitism that Jews have experienced in this country. Sometimes various limitations were imposed on them in certain cities: here a prohibition on trade or settling on various streets, there a prohibition on taking certain professions or a prohibition on showing up on the streets at the time of a Christian religious procession. Did the Jews decide

---

²⁶ For a view from the period, see treatises by Koneczny, *Cywilizacja żydowska* and *Państwo i prawo w cywilizacji łacińskiej*. Among later scholars who have analysed these currents in the Polish intellectual and political debate, see Domagalska, *Antysemityzm dla inteligencji?*; Bergmann, *Narodowa Demokracja wobec problematyki żydowskiej w latach 1918–1929*; Hertz, *Żydzi w kulturze polskiej*; Landau-Czajka, 'Żydzi w oczach prasy katolickiej okresu II Rzeczypospolitej'; Landau-Czajka, *W jednym stali domu*; Rudnicki, *Obóz Narodowo-Radykalny*; Żyndul, 'Cele akcji antyżydowskiej w Polsce w latach 1935–1937'; Melzer, 'Antisemitism in the Last Years of the Second Polish Republic'; Natkowska, '*Numerus clausus*', getto ławkowe, '*numerus nullus*', '*paragraf aryjski*'.

²⁷ Schiper, *Dzieje handlu żydowskiego*, 648.     ²⁸ Friedman, 'Dzieło na czasie', 555.

to leave these towns because of such prohibitions? Nowadays we experience history on our own flesh just as previous generations did. Life has somehow continued.[29]

During his fundraising visit to Poland in February 1936 Gelber noted in his diary that he strove to survey the situation from the 'historical objective point of view' and that he had correctly assessed the Poles' attitude towards the Jews in his previous research.[30] Jewish intellectuals believed that the findings from historical research could improve the future of Polish–Jewish relations, laying the foundations for 'the national and social liberation of Jewish society in Poland'.[31] As discussed in the previous chapter, Ringelblum envisioned future Polish teachers learning 'objective history' about the Jews from their Jewish colleagues at the university.[32] The editors of *Żydzi w Polsce Odrodzonej* hoped that presenting a historical 'summary of achievements' would motivate the contemporary Jewish community in its 'creative co-operation with Polish society for the glory of the Reborn Commonwealth'.[33] The publishers of Urbach's popular survey of Jewish participation in Poland's struggles for independence hoped that 'recreating historical truth' would establish paths for peaceful coexistence among all citizens of the Polish Republic: 'We hand it over to the society convinced that the guiding principles of the author will meet with a response from all people of goodwill and his work will achieve its intended goal.'[34]

Learning Polish Jewish history provided context for what it meant to be a Polish Jew on both the national and local levels. Dawid Wurm praised the leaders of the Jewish community in Brody, whose financial support made possible the publication of his *Z dziejów żydostwa brodzkiego*, and he dedicated his book to 'this section of the society, which . . . has not ceased to worship . . . the past of Our Nation'.[35] In this respect, Jewish historians closely resembled their Polish colleagues who 'had helped nurture Polish national identity and had encouraged sober and searching examination of the national past in order to solve the serious problems of the present'.[36] Thus, in the autumn of 1918, Ozjasz Thon argued, Jews welcomed the birth of Poland with hopes based on a knowledge of history, which indicated that the reborn state would become a democratic country.[37] Knowledge

[29] Quoted in Bosak, *Shadows of the City* (Heb.), 31–2. See a very similar thought expressed by Schiper in his summary of Bałaban's work in Jolles (ed.), *Księga jubileuszowa Bałabana*, 29.

[30] CAHJP, P 83, A/23: Gelber's journal from his travels to Poland, 24 Feb. 1936.

[31] See Ringelblum's reflections discussed in Kassow, 'Polish–Jewish Relations in the Writings of Emmanuel Ringelblum', 143.

[32] Ringelblum, 'Three Years of a Jewish History Seminar' (Yid.), cited in Zimmerman, *Contested Memories*, 145.

[33] See 'Od wydawnictwa', in Schiper, Tartakower, and Hafftka (eds.), *Żydzi w Polsce Odrodzonej*, i. 6.

[34] Urbach, *Udział Żydów w walce o niepodległość Polski*, p. v.

[35] Wurm, *Z dziejów żydostwa brodzkiego*, 8.     [36] Kassow, *Who Will Write Our History?*, 57.

[37] Thon, 'Wstęp', in Schiper, Tartakower, and Hafftka (eds.), *Żydzi w Polsce Odrodzonej*, i. 7.

of history was essential because, as Ludwig Oberlaender put it, the Jew who is 'unable to see himself in Polish history and his truth connected to the history of this land will only have political claims; the Jew who is aware of his political role will give new expression to it and will create for himself political rights. Our rights must be well set in the new historical and political consciousnesses.'[38]

In comparison with the Polish Jewish daily press, which provided general news coverage, historians—without being directly involved with Jewish self-defence—communicated a strong sense of Polish Jews' entitlement to civic and national rights. Local history offered perspective on the dynamic of Polish–Jewish relations. Polish Jews had lived among their non-Jewish neighbours, contributed to their cities' economic prosperity, and suffered during periods of national decline.

## The Ways of Writing Polish Jewish History

In the last two decades of the nineteenth century leading Polish historians expressed their desire gradually to build a national historiography. They repeatedly spoke about the necessary step in this process of creating a Polish urban history focused on social and economic developments. As early as 1890, at the Second Congress of Polish Historians assembled in Lwów, Aleksander Semkowicz called for the publication of sources documenting the history of Polish towns, particularly Lwów.[39] Ten years later, at the Third Congress of Polish Historians in Kraków, Stanisław Kutrzeba issued a passionate call for a new historiography of Polish small towns, stating that the first stage should be devoted to publishing annotated collections of sources for as many individual communities as possible.[40]

Like their Polish colleagues, Schorr and Bałaban complained about the lack of local studies, agreeing that individual communities must be studied before a synthetic view of the past could be formulated.[41] At the Third Congress of Polish historians, in 1900, Schorr made several recommendations for the future of Polish Jewish historiography: 'publishing archival materials on the history of Jews *in individual towns*', 'locating Hebrew manuscripts, particularly *pinkasim* [record books]', and research on 'the history of Jews in larger cities, particularly in [the regions of] Red Russia and Little Poland in connection . . . with the role played by

---

[38] Oberlaender, 'Dziewięć wieków współżycia', 97.
[39] See Semkowicz, 'O potrzebie i sposobie wydania ważniejszych źródeł znajdujących się w miejskiem Archiwum we Lwowie'.
[40] Kutrzeba, 'W sprawie historyi miast w Polsce'. See also Charewiczowa, 'Stan badań nad dziejami miast polskich'.
[41] See Bałaban, 'Praca mojego życia', in Jolles (ed.), *Księga jubileuszowa Bałabana*, 35–40: 38.

nobility and townsmen'.[42] Schorr argued that historical records of Jewish urban life in Poland needed to be edited and published as the first stage of building a comprehensive and professional field of research.[43] In 1902 Schorr voiced these same ideas in the introduction to his *Żydzi w Przemyślu do końca XVIII wieku* (Jews in Przemyśl to the End of the Eighteenth Century), demonstrating his commitment to the research agenda of the Third Congress:

> So far, the main weakness of the method for developing Jewish history in Poland is that the general issues have been treated before the detailed ones have been solved. One wanted to present the history of the Jews in *the whole of* Poland before [even] learning about the history of individual towns; the whole of history was considered before single periods were illuminated.[44]

This methodological mistake was responsible for the sorry state of Polish Jewish historiography. The lack of sources had obscured any sophisticated understanding of Polish Jewish history 'either in the political-economic or the cultural spheres'. Schorr concluded: '[A] thorough and scientific presentation of the grand history [of Poland] will only be possible when ... the economic and cultural history in individual cities is presented comprehensively on the basis of archival sources.'[45] Individual Jewish communities should thus be studied because the general history of Polish Jews could only emerge from the sum total of microhistories.[46] Studies of local Jewish history by professionally trained Jewish historians before 1918 include Schorr's work on Przemyśl and Bałaban's studies of Jewish communities in Kraków, Lwów, and Lublin.[47]

Jewish historians with university training in Galicia, Vienna, and interwar Poland saw archival research as the unquestionable and indispensable basis for historical work. They stressed the necessity of carrying out archival research as a basis for any conclusions about the Jewish past, taking into consideration a wide variety of both Jewish and non-Jewish sources in communal, municipal, and church archives.[48] As early as 1903 Bałaban called for writing the history of Jews in Polish lands using proper tools and drawing on an array of materials from the

---

[42] Schorr, 'Historya żydów w Polsce', 3.

[43] Schorr, *Żydzi w Przemyślu do końca XVIII wieku*, p. vii.     [44] Ibid.     [45] Ibid.

[46] As Bałaban put it in the introduction to his study of the history of Jews in Lwów, 'although they deal with one town, they enlighten many an issue that has to do with the Jews of all of Poland and throw light on the history of the Jews in this country at that time' (Bałaban, *Żydzi lwowscy na przełomie XVI i XVII wieku*, p. xxiii).

[47] Schorr, *Żydzi w Przemyślu do końca XVIII wieku*; Bałaban, *Dzielnica żydowska, jej dzieje i zabytki*; id., *Historja Żydzi w Krakowie i na Kazimierzu*; *Żydzi lwowscy na przełomie XVI i XVII wieku*; and *Die Judenstadt von Lublin*. See also Bałaban, *Przewodnik po żydowskich zabytkach Krakowa*.

[48] See, for example, the praise of broad archival research in Schall, 'Friedman Filip: Dzieje Żydów w Łodzi'.

archives and Polish chronicles as well as Hebrew sources.[49] A few years later, in 1908, Schiper laid out the general blueprint for writing Jewish history: 'Our principal rule was to accumulate as many primary materials as possible to illustrate ... more general conceptions.'[50] The scholars aspired to objectivity, bringing in all perspectives and weighing competing and conflicting accounts. Bałaban argued that Jewish historians in the past had relied only on Hebrew sources, while their Polish colleagues utilized skewed sources produced by townsmen who had competed with the Jews. Historians able to access both sets of sources would thus be able 'to create here and there a more or less objective picture of the past'.[51]

Jewish communal sources remained vitally important for the reconstruction of Jewish institutional and cultural history, as well as for providing an understanding of daily lives. Discussing the content of the Jewish communal archives in Wilno, Pinchas Kon criticized all historians who had written about the history of Wilno Jews—Bershadski, Samuel Joseph Finn, Hillel Noe Sztajnsznajder, J. T. Kraszewski, Juliusz Gessen, and Dawid Magid (of Leningrad)—whose writing was not based on material from the *kahal*.[52] According to Zygmunt Ellenberg, research on the history of Łódź and the Jewish community there began only in the Second Polish Republic. Although they provided a plethora of details about the Jews, the existing sources were not sufficient for understanding the city's Jewish society in the nineteenth century.[53]

Non-Jewish archives also played a vitally important role. The lack of relevant Jewish material meant that Jewish historians had to rely on Polish sources, particularly in local studies.[54] Ringelblum stressed the use of archival material from a variety of Polish archives in Warsaw and its surrounding communities, given the lack of relevant Jewish sources for his research on the earliest Jewish community in Warsaw.[55] Similarly, in his work on the nineteenth-century history of the Jews in Łódź, Friedman had no Jewish communal records at his disposal apart from *ḥevrot*.[56] Non-Jewish archives were not only useful in cases where Jewish material was missing, they also offered a balanced perspective on the Jewish past. Interested in pursuing research on Jewish economic history of the nineteenth century, Friedman complained,

Our scholars who work on these issues did not always reach as far as the archives—especially when the economic history of Polish Jews is concerned—and for the lack of

---

[49] Bałaban, *Przegląd literatury historyi Żydów*, 5–6.
[50] Introduction (dated 1908) to Schiper, *Studya nad stosunkami gospodarczymi Żydów w Polsce*, 1.
[51] Bałaban, 'Zadania i potrzeby historjografji Żydów w Polsce', ii. 226.
[52] Kon, 'Odnaleziona część Archiwum dawnego Kahału Wileńskiego', 152.
[53] Ellenberg, *Żydzi i początki szkolnictwa powszechnego w Łodzi (1806–1864)*, 4.
[54] See Aleksiun, 'Setting the Record Straight'.
[55] See Ringelblum, *Żydzi w Warszawie*, 5–7.   [56] See Friedman, *Dzieje Żydów w Łodzi*, 10–12.

archival material they operated with generalizations that said very little and formulated risky hypotheses, without a basis in source material. Investigating the economic history of the Jews in the nineteenth century, I came across works that drew on secondhand materials, with biases and assumptions that seemed to me not completely reliable, which, among other things prompted me to think about seeking source materials to elucidate these issues.[57]

These building blocks of local history were necessary steps towards a synthesized Polish Jewish history. Surveying the early academic publication on Polish Jewish history, in 1903, Bałaban had advocated utilizing the vast sources of Polish Jewish history first, and only 'when these springs dry out at least partially [would it] be possible to create a synthesis and get to present the entirety [*całokształt*] of the history of Jews in this land; otherwise no constructive work will be useful for anything'.[58] The microhistorical research carried out by Polish historians during the Second Republic stemmed from these earlier initiatives and methodological discussions.

For Polish Jewish historians reaching the peak of their careers in the 1920s and 1930s, far more was at stake than filling in gaps in historical research; they were attempting to fashion a comprehensive Polish historiography in order to buttress Polish national interests. Envisioning the further development of the field, authors as different in their ideological approaches as Bałaban, Schorr, Ringelblum, and Jakub Berman called for a co-ordinated creative enterprise. Scholars struggled with methodological issues and debated new directions in research. Although questions surrounding the partitions of Poland continued to draw some attention, the general trend was away from political history and towards social and economic history. But the basic unit continued to be local history— individual cities and towns. Leading Polish scholars such as Stanisław Kutrzeba, Franciszek Bujak, and Stanisław Arnold also advocated organizing and co-ordinating microhistorical research, including detailed studies of Polish towns.[59] Gathered in Poznań in 1925 for their first congress in the new political circumstances, historians discussed the role of their profession and directions for writing Polish history. Historian and archivist Kazimierz Kaczmarczyk reiterated previous appeals, stressing the urgent need for thorough editions of sources documenting the history of major Polish urban cities such as Warsaw, Toruń, Wilno, Lublin, and Przemyśl, as well as smaller towns and hamlets.[60] In a resolution sponsored by Kaczmarczyk, the congress 'recognized the need for publishing documents and books relating to the history of our towns and hamlets as one of the most important scientific postulates, because of the necessity to learn about their past more

---

[57] See Friedman, *Dzieje Żydów w Łodzi*, 7.   [58] Bałaban, *Przegląd literatury historyi Żydów*, 5.
[59] See Gieysztor, Maternicki, and Samsonowicz (eds.), *Historycy warszawscy ostatnich dwóch stuleci*.
[60] Kaczmarczyk, 'Wydawnictwa do historji miast polskich'.

closely'.[61] Several leading Polish historians repeated these calls in subsequent publications, making concrete suggestions for research in Polish urban history. And as early as 1918 Franciszek Bujak outlined priorities in Polish economic history and proposed a series of projects on urban history.[62] Polish historians agreed that such publications required the support of universities and historical associations. Writing local urban and regional history became an important feature of Polish historiography between the two world wars. The major centres for this research included university towns such as Warsaw, Kraków, Poznań, and Lwów, but interest in local history spread throughout Poland, cultivated by local and regional historical associations and by academic and popular journals that published sources and studies in local history.[63]

The imperative to develop a comprehensive scholarly literature on the history of Polish towns stemmed from both academic and contemporary national considerations. Polish historians blamed the shortcomings of urban history on Poland's partitions and 'the lack of funds and lack of interest in our past by the elements foreign to us from the national point of view, which held power in the majority of our cities (in the Prussian and Russian parts [of partitioned Poland]), and by the lack of people who had been trained for research'. They asserted that 'now the time has come to even it out and mend our neglect in this direction'.[64] Polish historians who advocated research in urban history not only ascribed to it great academic importance, but also argued that it served Poland's national interests. Łucja Charewiczowa, a historian based in Lwów, believed that such research had profound contemporary relevance for the resurrected Polish state. Publication of sources and monographs of individual towns constituted the basis for future synthetic work on Polish urban history. Such research, Charewiczowa argued, had 'to show clearly and thoroughly all and true reasons for the underdevelopment of Polish towns. . . . The awareness of the mistakes of the past can guard one from making them in the present and in the future'.[65] Thus Polish historians saw a better understanding of past social and economic dynamics of Polish towns and townships as essential to developing economic, social, and political policies in the Second Polish Republic. In addition, urban histories indicated a new facet of Polish historiography: greater interest in the social and economic aspects of the past. Many prominent historians criticized previous Polish historiography for, as Charewiczowa put it, a 'tendency towards one-sidedness

---

[61] *Pamiętnik IV*, ii. 112.    [62] Bujak, 'Uwagi o potrzebach historii gospodarczej'.
[63] These local publications included *Biblioteka i Rocznik Krakowski*, *Biblioteka imienia T. Korzona*, *Biblioteka Lwowska*, *Ziemia Czerwieńska*, *Kwartalnik Litewski*, *Litwa i Ruś*, *Ateneum Wileńskie*, and *Roczniki i Zapiski Towarzystwa Naukowego Śląskiego*. See Konopczyński, 'Rozwój badań nad dziejami Polski Nowożytnej 1506–1795', 298.    [64] Kaczmarczyk, 'Wydawnictwa do historji miast polskich', 3.
[65] Charewiczowa, 'Stan badań nad dziejami miast polskich', 152.

and shallowness in the way it addresses the issues and the lack of new subjects'. She called for historical writing to treat a town as 'a phenomenon created in the centuries of work, as a layered sedimentation of the culture of past generations'.[66] She hoped towns would cease to be viewed only in terms of their political structure, and would be considered in all their social and economic complexity.

Jewish historians used similar arguments in assessing Polish Jewish historiography. According to Schorr, the relatively late—in comparison with west European Jewries—awakening of interest in Jewish history among Polish Jews resulted mainly from the partitions of Poland.[67] In the introduction to his *Żydzi w Warszawie* (Jews in Warsaw), Emanuel Ringelblum blamed the lack of serious research on the Russian occupation during the partitions:

The policy of the tsarist government during the partitions, which slowed down the normal cultural development of Poland, created difficulties in the study of the historiography of Jews in the former Congress Poland. This is why, while in the West almost each and every larger or even smaller Jewish community already has its monograph, the history of the largest Jewish community in Europe—Warsaw—has been unknown to us so far.[68]

In 1928 Bałaban complained about the state of research, especially the lack of published editions of archival sources and monographs about the main Jewish communities such as Wilno, Grodno, Kalisz, and Warsaw.[69] In Bałaban's opinion, the challenging task of writing the general history of a given town over the course of centuries required a great deal of work.[70] Analysing the state of research on Polish Jewish history at the 1930 Congress of Polish Historians, Bałaban listed the stages that would lead to the broadening of knowledge about the past of Polish Jews: 'constructive work' could only follow the preservation and registration of available sources and research in archives, libraries, and cemeteries, and this constructive work would entail researching individual Jewish communities. Finally, this knowledge should be incorporated into general Polish as well as Jewish history.[71] Bałaban suggested that the congress call for 'preserving, researching, and publishing sources on the history of Jews in Poland as a significant postulate of Polish [historical] science'.[72]

This subject of the stages in building the field was similarly expressed by the Young Historians Circle in Warsaw. A member of the seminar, Jakub Berman,

[66] Charewiczowa, 'Stan badań nad dziejami miast polskich', 150.
[67] Schorr, 'Historya żydów w Polsce', 1.
[68] Ringelblum, *Żydzi w Warszawie*, 5.   [69] Bałaban, 'Przedmowa', in Alperin, *Żydzi w Łodzi*, 3.
[70] See Bałaban's remarks about Schorr's monograph on the Jewish community in Przemyśl, in Bałaban, *Przegląd literatury historyi Żydów*, 14.
[71] Bałaban, 'Zadania i potrzeby historjografji Żydów w Polsce', i. 120.   [72] Ibid. ii. 228.

argued that the Historical Section of YIVO should prepare monographs based on archival materials and critical publications of those materials. Synthesis would come later.[73] He proposed a very similar programme for the Young Historians Circle.[74] Ringelblum praised Jewish communities in Germany for establishing historical museums and preparing monographs devoted to their history: 'We have a few monographs of Jewish history in Poland', he complained, 'we do not however have any complete history [*gantse geshikhte*].' As long as research on all aspects and all periods of Jewish history in Poland was still lacking, no synthetic narrative could be constructed.[75] Eliezer Feldman criticized 'our historians' for not paying sufficient attention to archival materials essential for understanding internal Jewish migrations in the Middle Ages and the emergence of Jewish communities in Eastern Poland.[76] The young Warsaw Jewish historians also proposed a series of monographs on individual Jewish communities in Poland to be funded by the communities themselves.[77]

With the increasing emphasis on local history in the new Polish Republic, the variety and scope of historical work on Jewish communities in Poland gained momentum. Local history became a dominant genre among young Jewish historians in interwar Poland. Although contemporary Polish Jewish historians differed in their mapping of the centres of local historiography, the idea of writing about individual local communities resonated with numerous Jewish scholars precisely because it answered both the academic and the socio-political needs of Jewish historiography.[78] Bałaban transformed his seminars at the Institute of Jewish Studies and Warsaw University into 'reservoirs of materials for monographs on Jewish *kehalim* in Poland'.[79] He encouraged his students to carry out archival research and to base their theses on primary sources, anticipating that 'putting together [these

[73] Berman, 'The Tasks of the Historical Section' (Yid.), 19.
[74] Ibid. See also Kuznitz, *YIVO and the Making of Modern Jewish Culture*, 72–3.
[75] Ringelblum, 'Three Years of a Jewish History Seminar', 8–9.
[76] Feldman, 'The Earliest Data about Jews in Polish Towns in the 14th–16th Centuries' (Yid.).
[77] See the minutes of meeting of the Warsaw Historical Commission, 8 Nov. 1929, YIVO Archives, RG 82, folder 2243.
[78] Bałaban stressed his own influence while also praising the publications of the *Bleter far geshikhte*, which he described as 'independent' work (Bałaban, 'Najnowsze rozprawy z historii Żydów w Polsce', 7).
[79] Ostersetzer, 'Majer Bałaban—historiograf żydostwa Polskiego', in Jolles (ed.), *Księga jubileuszowa Bałabana*, 62. In the introduction to Majer Bałaban's Festschrift, his students appealed to the Jewish public for support in publishing a second volume, celebrating Bałaban's scholarship, which would include a selection of studies prepared at his seminar. They asked their readers to pay special attention to the part that would include about ten contributions to local history by Brody, Drohobycz, Kołomyja, Łuck, Przemyśl, Opatów, Sandomierz, Tykocin, and Zamość. See 'Od redakcji', in Jolles (ed.), *Księga jubileuszowa Bałabana*, 6. This second volume never appeared. See Chapter 3 for discussion of the difficulties Jewish historians faced when getting their work published.

studies] will be an important contribution to the history of the Jews in Poland.'[80] For example, in 1936 he assigned them topics on the history of Jews in Sanok, Żurawno, and Częstochowa.[81] Bałaban asked Clara Minskberg to prepare a family tree as her graduation assignment at the Institute of Jewish Studies; in preparation, she explored Jewish cemeteries.[82] Another report mentioned four regional works in progress: on Sandomierz, Opatów, Słonim, and Pińsk.[83] Students wrote histories of Kraków Jewry (Ezechiel Rosenbaum and Marek Bosak), Łuck (Fani Kraszyńska), Kołomyja (Samuel Gottlieb), Sandomierz (Abraham Getter), Brody (Dawid Wurm), Lwów (Abraham Fenster), Opatów (Józef Bursztyn), Przemyśl (Mojżesz Krämer), Tykocin (Abraham Gawurin), Wilno (Hirsz Gerszater), and Zamość (Lejzor Estrin). Other towns researched by Bałaban's students included Łęczyca, Lublin, Słonim, Pińsk, and Tarnopol. In fact, many students wrote about their own home towns. The 1938 Festschrift devoted to Bałaban listed sixty dissertations written by his students, including twelve local studies.[84]

In the introduction to his thesis, Bałaban's student Jakób Wikler recorded his decision to write about the town where he lived and studied, Drohobycz: 'While reading and entering into the spirit of [wczytując się] the history of Jews in Poland, I noticed the lack of a monograph on Drohobycz—one of the biggest and most prominent Jewish centres in Small Poland [Małopolska]. Having the opportunity, I decided to fill this gap.' Taking the monographs of Bałaban and Schorr as examples and aiming at presenting a full picture of the town's Jewish community from 1648 until Poland's partitions, Wikler had to settle for a study of more limited scope due to the lack of sources.[85]

Schorr, Bałaban, Ringelblum, and Friedman shared the vision of a concerted effort in studying the most important Jewish communities as representative of various aspects of Jewish life in Polish lands, wherever the sources allowed. Researching their history gave local Jewish communities a sense of belonging, by connecting them with general Polish Jewish history, as well as affirming their right to their particular locus. As Mojżesz Steinberg argued in his work on

---

[80] Hafner, 'Przemawia w imieniu uczniów', in Jolles (ed.), *Księga jubileuszowa Bałabana*, 34.

[81] For a list of topics, see 'Ćwiczenia seminaryjne: z historji Żydów w Polsce', in *Sprawozdanie z działalności Wydziału Humanistycznego Uniwersytetu Warszawskiego za rok akadem. 1934–1935*, p. 66.

[82] Oral history interview with Clara Ma'ayan (USHMM, RG-50.120*0096, tape 1: 1.00.59).

[83] 'Ćwiczenia seminaryjne: z historji Żydów w Polsce', in *Sprawozdanie z działalności Wydziału Humanistycznego Uniwersytetu Warszawskiego za rok akadem. 1930–1931*, 59.

[84] See 'Prace Magisterskie pisane w seminarium hist. żyd. Profesora Bałabana, które będą drukowane w części drugiej Księgi Jubileuszowej', in Jolles (ed.), *Księga jubileuszowa Bałabana*, 102–4. See Chapter 3 for discussion of Bałaban's seminar.

[85] Jakób Wikler, 'Przedmowa', in *Z dziejów Żydów w Drohobyczu (od r. 1648 do upadku Rzeczypospolitej)* (AŻIH 117, folder 36, p. 5).

the history of Jewish community in Jarosław, the preservation of *pinkasim* (community registers) from various Jewish communities was important because these records could shed light on the establishment of an individual Jewish settlement and its development over the centuries.[86]

Several monographs on local Jewish communities were published before 1918, and many more appeared in the 1920s and 1930s, documenting the past of the authors' home towns: Schorr wrote on Przemyśl, Bałaban on Lwów, Steinberg on Jarosław, Sonnenschein on Czortków, and Trunk on Kutno, to cite just a few examples.[87] Bałaban often required that his students work first on individual Jewish communities, especially their home towns.[88] He assigned five students from Kraków to carry out research on the history of the rabbinate in Kraków from the earliest times until the contemporary period.[89] Hillel Seidman recalled that during the first class Bałaban routinely asked new students about their family names and home towns, and then began his lecture with anecdotes about related historical figures or communities.[90] In addition to having the obvious benefit of making access to archival materials easier, working on one's own home town and family history invested historical research with a personal element that could then serve as a basis for making claims for inclusion in Polish nationhood. For example, Steinberg declared that he 'decided to serve the Jewish community in Jarosław, where I was raised and where I spent my youth and I wrote this book. In the faded pages of the documents and dusty books I searched for and found the past of Jarosław Jewry and I immortalized it for future generations.'[91]

Local studies featured prominently in the four volumes of the journal published by the Young Historians Circle. For example, the second volume of *Yunger historiker* included articles on the social and economic aspects of the history of the Jewish community in Lublin.[92] Trunk's study of the Jewish community in Kutno appeared in the 1934 volume of *Bleter far geshikhte*.[93] Trunk portrayed the community of Kutno as a model of the social and economic structure of a community in a private town in the eighteenth century. In the second volume of the journal,

---

[86] Steinberg, *Żydzi w Jarosławiu od czasów najdawniejszych do połowy XIX wieku*, 5.

[87] See Trunk, 'The Jewish Community in Poland' (Yid.), and Sonnenschein, *Chapters from Jewish History in Tchortkov* (Heb.). See also Feinkind, *Dzieje Żydów w Piotrkowie i okolicy*.

[88] See 'Ćwiczenia seminaryjne: z historji Żydów w Polsce', in *Sprawozdanie z działalności Wydziału Humanistycznego Uniwersytetu Warszawskiego za rok akadem. 1929–1930*, 54. Bałaban, 'Najnowsze rozprawy z historii Żydów w Polsce', 7.

[89] *Sprawozdanie z działalności Wydziału Humanistycznego Uniwersytetu Warszawskiego za rok akadem. 1931–1932*, 82.     [90] Seidman, 'Meir Bałaban' (Heb.), 243–5.

[91] Steinberg, *Żydzi w Jarosławiu od czasów najdawniejszych do połowy XIX wieku*, 3.

[92] See Mandelsberg, 'Jewish Artisans in Lublin and the City Guilds' (Yid.); Mahler, 'Statistical Information about Jews in the Lublin Voivodship' (Yid.).

[93] Trunk, 'The Jewish Community in Poland' (Yid.).

Trunk analysed the legal status of the Jews in Płock in the sixteenth century.[94] Together, Bałaban's seminar and the Young Historians Circle constituted the two most vibrant centres of research on local and regional Jewish history.

Despite differing research agendas, these Jewish historians shared an interest in and dedication to researching and writing on regional Polish Jewish history, with a particular focus on social and economic history.[95] The choice of which Jewish community to study was guided by the desire to fill all lacunae, while making historical scholarship relevant to the local Jewish communities; but local studies also provided valuable insights into the Jews' struggle against the burghers for the right to carry out commerce and crafts. Thus Friedman considered working on the history of the Jewish community in Warsaw, the political capital of the country, and Łódź, the industrial capital; he decided to continue with the latter, as other scholars began archival research on Warsaw.[96] Friedman argued that the study of the relatively young and prominent Jewish community of Łódź had particular interest for scholars because it offered a unique case study of socio-economic history in the nineteenth century, due to the 'immensely intensive and fast process of economic and social transition [that] has been taking place in the midst of the Jewish community' there.[97] Friedman saw potential in this study because 'in the course of only a hundred years, in the midst of the Jewish community such powerful development processes and structural changes took place that [in] this—I would say classic example—one can observe in a condensed form the economic and social evolution of the entire Polish Jewry'.[98]

## From Political to Social, Cultural, and Economic History

Jewish historians began researching the history of Polish Jewry in the modern period, especially the last decades of the Polish–Lithuanian Commonwealth.[99] In the first issue of *Yunger historiker* (1926) Ringelblum chastized Jewish society in Poland for not doing more to promote historical research on the history of Polish Jewry, since 'Jewish society in Poland at large has done nothing to organize research about the history of Polish Jews, nor has it created an administrative body to publish a journal or scholarly work devoted to the history of Jews in Poland'. Indeed, he noted that little work that had been done depended on 'the initiatives of the few individuals who through their haphazard work had elucidated episodes and periods from the rich and colourful life of the Jews in old

[94] Trunk, 'The Legal Status of Jews in Plock in the 16th Century' (Yid.).
[95] Mahler, *Historians and Guides* (Yid.), 304. Their research agendas differed, since Ringelblum was devoted 'heart and soul to the mission of furthering Yiddish culture in general and scholarship in Yiddish in particular'.   [96] Friedman, *Dzieje Żydów w Łodzi*, 7.   [97] Ibid.   [98] Ibid. 7–8.
[99] See Abraham Roth's positive review of two books by Gelber in 'Dr. N. M. Gelber: *Aus zwei Jahrhunderten*'.

Poland'.¹⁰⁰ But Ringelblum believed that all periods of Jewish history in Poland deserved scholarly attention.

Jewish historians criticized Jewish historiography for focusing on the political and religious aspects of Jewish life, and thereby inhibiting a more integrated picture of the social and economic issues in Jewish urban communities. According to Bałaban, Jewish historical research had been 'accidental and with few exceptions dilettante'. He described previously published Hebrew monographs on the Jewish communities in Kraków, Wilno, Grodno, Żółkiew, Lwów, and Ostróg as 'pitiable dictionaries of biographies with a random selection of people' that lacked historical objectivity.¹⁰¹ The focus on local studies differed from the subjects of the nineteenth- and early twentieth-century orthodox compendia. Local studies now served as building blocks in the ambitious project of the scholarly study of the Polish Jewish past, reflecting the shift in the vision of Jewish history embraced by professional Polish Jewish historians.

Bałaban, Schiper, and the historians who debuted in the Second Polish Republic shared a conviction about the importance of expanding the intellectual horizons of the field beyond political and cultural history. Their interest shifted decidedly from the study of the legal status of the Jews that had formed the focus of nineteenth-century integrationist Polish and Polish Jewish authors, or the focus on rabbinical elites found in traditional communal monographs, to broader issues of economy and culture. Study of the legal status of the Jews in Polish lands was now seen as an introduction to broader questions. In addition to monographs on communities, Bałaban stressed the importance of subject-based work in the areas of commerce, industry, customs, and intellectual history, especially on subjects such as kabbalah, the Shabatean, Frankist, and hasidic movements, and the Jewish Enlightenment (Haskalah). All these subjects, he argued, belonged to both Jewish and Polish history.¹⁰² He listed the stages in the historiography of the Jews in Poland as conservation, registration, archival research, constructive work, and publishing.¹⁰³

Bałaban criticized Hebrew communal monographs for lacking information on private life, commerce, and crafts. The study of leading rabbis no longer sufficed.¹⁰⁴ Without dismissing what he called 'the external picture of Jewish life',

---

¹⁰⁰ Ringelblum, 'Three Years of a Jewish History Seminar' (Yid.), 9. Ringelblum himself shifted his focus from the medieval period to the late eighteenth century. He shared this diverse interest in both medieval and modern history with his mentor at Warsaw University, Marceli Handelsman.

¹⁰¹ Bałaban, 'Zadania i potrzeby historjografji Żydów w Polsce', i. 117.    ¹⁰² Ibid. i. 118–21.

¹⁰³ Ibid., *passim*; see also the review of Bałaban's article by 'A.G.', 'Bałaban Majer: Zadania i potrzeby historjografji Żydów w Polsce'.

¹⁰⁴ See Bałaban's short review of Buber's work on Żółkiew in Bałaban, *Przegląd literatury historyi Żydów*, 8. See Buber, *The Exalted Town of Żółkiew* (Heb.). See Chapter 2 for discussion of the Hebrew monographs.

based on privileges, court files, and administrative documents from state and church archives, Bałaban called for supplementing it with 'the internal picture, namely the private life and cultural life of Jewish communities and individuals' based on communal records.[105] As Schiper saw it, the change in writing about Jewish life required exploration of 'life praxis instead of the dry paragraphs of Jewish privileges about which one could not say to what degree they entered life'.[106] Schiper envisioned the writing of the history of 'hundreds of thousands of Jews who carried the memory about themselves not based on spiritual treasures but on the work of their hands and speculative talents'. 'We know', he wrote, 'the Saturday Jew with his festive soul; the time has come to get to know his everyday life, his everyday thoughts, and to illuminate the history of Jewish labour.'[107] Moreover, for Schiper, analysing their legal status offered an opportunity to explore the character of the Jews' economic activities.[108]

Schorr, Bałaban, and Schiper opposed organizing historical material according to the reigns of Polish kings, because that arrangement did not reflect turning points important for Jewish history.[109] Abandoning this practice indicated a different focus for Jewish history, though it was still closely connected to what happened to Gentiles in the same town, province, or land. Polish Jewish historiography continued to stress the influence of Poles and Jews on each other in the past. Bałaban researched Jewish history in the context of general history, exploring the links between the two while emphasizing what was particular to the Jews, especially aspects of Jewish history in which religious elements played a crucial role. He formulated his position on the relationship between the history of Polish Jewry and general Polish and Jewish histories in an inaugural lecture given at the Institute of Jewish Studies on 15 November 1931 and published in *Miesięcznik Żydowski* in 1932. Bałaban stressed the critical importance of studying Polish Jewish history both as an integral part of world Jewish history and as a critical component of Polish history. He represented the inherent link between Polish and Polish Jewish history with an image of a cross: 'The short, thick stripe stands for the history of Poland. The long, narrow one symbolizes the history of the Jews. The intersection—the rectangle in the middle—is the history of Polish Jews. This rectangle . . . belongs to both courses of history.'[110] On the other hand, Jewish

---

[105] See Bałaban, *Zabytki historyczne Żydów w Polsce*, 44. For this purpose, he argued, creating the Central Archives of the Polish Jews in Warsaw was necessary.

[106] Schiper, *Studya nad stosunkami gospodarczymi Żydów w Polsce*, 3–4.

[107] Ibid. 1: 'Słowem znamy Żyda sobotniego z świąteczną duszą, czas poznać dzieje jego dni powszechnich i myśli powszednich, czas sięgnąć po światło do historyi pracy żydowskiej'. [108] Ibid. 45.

[109] Bałaban, *Przegląd literatury historyi Żydów*, 15. However, Schorr returned to this staple of nineteenth-century historiography in his *Żydzi w Przemyślu do końca XVIII wieku*.

[110] Bałaban, 'Zagadnienia historjozofji żydowskiej', 369, quoted in Dold, 'A Matter of National and Civic Honor', 55.

history was also an independent and self-contained subject of academic enquiry. According to Bałaban, 'We must look at the Jews' development in connection with Poland's evolution. . . . However, in doing so, time and again we will encounter phenomena that cannot be explained by Polish history alone but are linked to Jewish history in general. We will therefore always look at what is beyond the borders of the Polish state.'[111]

Schiper and Friedman also saw historical accounts of Jewish society in various centres as building blocks of what would eventually become a complete analysis of Jewish history.[112] On the basis of archival material, Friedman sketched the 'general background against which [he] constructed the development of Jewish society'. He considered the inclusion of this general background as essential to avoiding the mistake of some scholars of Jewish history who presented Jewish history as a process detached from the general surroundings and separated from the historical background. Friedman warned his fellow scholars against creating in the reader's mind a kind of 'optical illusion [*złudzenie optyczne*]' leading to underestimating or overestimating the role of the Jews: 'Only a description based on the general development of the non-Jewish surroundings, taking into consideration as much as possible the comparative moment, allows for an assessment of the role of the Jews in a given economic and social organism precisely reflecting the historical reality.'[113]

Throughout the interwar period Schiper and Bałaban remained interested in various aspects of Jewish cultural history and in the everyday history of Jewish communities. Both had long been interested in the subject. Bałaban published a serialized essay on the importance of preserving historical artefacts, and both were invited by the Historians' Circle to lecture at its course on conservation.[114] Thus the Warsaw Historical Commission's concern for the preservation of artefacts, and its campaign to collect them and expeditions to document synagogues, cemeteries, and 'Jewish antiquities', did not necessarily result from ideas imported from Wilno.[115]

Bałaban's own research indicated his preference for social history. Introducing a study of the early Jewish community in Łódź, he stated that he wanted to discover

---

[111] Ibid.

[112] See Schiper, 'Introduction', in *On the History and Economic Conditions of the Jews* (Yid.), i, pp. i–ii.     [113] Friedman, *Dzieje Żydów w Łodzi*, 12.

[114] Minutes of the meeting of the Historical Section, 25 Jan. 1929 (YIVO Archives, RG 1.1, Lithuanian addendum, folder 603); Minutes of the meeting of the Warsaw Historical Commission, 18 Nov. 1929 (YIVO Archives, RG 82, folder 2243). Kuznitz, *YIVO and the Making of Modern Jewish Culture*, 90.

[115] Although, as Kuznitz points out, there was a sense of the urgency of preserving 'an endangered legacy' (Kuznitz, *YIVO and the Making of Modern Jewish Culture*, 80).

how they [the Jews in Łódź] lived, how they raised their children, if and how they responded to contemporary political currents, to the fall of the [Polish–Lithuanian] Commonwealth. We would love to also know if they visited the tsadik in Lublin or Kozienice or one of the smaller tsadiks, if they participated in the collective enterprises of Polish Jews, as far as a tax cut or release from the obligatory military service.[116]

He was not interested exclusively in the heads of the communities, religious functionaries, or rabbis, but rather in the community in its entirety (*kol hakahal al hamonav*), in its habits and spiritual and material culture, as well as conflicts that sometimes led to violence.[117] His students set out to reconstruct the daily lives of Jewish communities, describing their internal life, bylaws, and rabbinical authorities, and exploring their organization, education, learning, charities, and professional structure.[118] Bałaban also encouraged his students to take an interest in Jewish cultural history, especially the history of Jewish printing press and theatre. He advocated protecting, collecting, and researching Jewish monuments and Jewish art, otherwise 'everything that our forefathers created for nine centuries . . . [everything] that was holy and dear to them would be lost forever'.[119]

Although building on the experiences and programmes laid out before the First World War, Jewish historians in interwar Poland also called for a radical change in approaches to writing Jewish history. Schiper pointed out this generational shift of paradigms: the young, he noted in 1930, were no longer satisfied with the way Jewish history was studied and presented.[120] Indeed, young Jewish historians in Warsaw discussed the way historical work should be carried out. Mahler, Friedman, Mandelsberg, and several of the members of the Historians Circle called for a shift of interest to economic history from a particular ideological point of view. Stressing the importance of showing the ongoing struggle of the Jewish community, especially working-class Jews in local settings, Mandelsberg presented a case study on the history of Lublin.[121] While Friedman discussed the solidarity of the wealthy against the poor, crossing ethnic and religious boundaries, he also referred to 'antagonisms germinating within Jewish society'. As a result, 'probably patriarchal relations between Jewish entrepreneurs and workers and pupils began to deteriorate' and serious cases of class struggle began to take

[116] Bałaban, 'Przedmowa', in Alperin, *Żydzi w Łodzi*, 5.
[117] Seidman, 'Meir Bałaban' (Heb.), 258.
[118] See, for example, the thesis by Motel Siemiatycki, 'Prawo obywatelstwa w gminach żydowskich w Polsce (w XVI–XVIII w.)' (AUW, KEM 6358). Another student at Warsaw University, Herz Glejzer, wrote a thesis on the life of Polish Jews in the sixteenth and seventeenth centuries based on rabbinical responsa. See Herz Glejzer, 'Życie Żydów w Polsce w XVI i XVII wieku na podstawie responsów'. (AŻIH 117, folder 51). See also Dawid Wurm, *Z dziejów żydostwa brodzkiego*.
[119] Bałaban, *Zabytki historyczne Żydów w Polsce*, 3–4.
[120] Schiper, 'Introduction', in *On the History and Economic Conditions of the Jews* (Yid.), i, p. iv.
[121] Blumental, 'A Profile of Bela' (Heb.), 26.

place, beginning with the tailors in Łódź.[122] Jewish elites, both religious and enlightened, showed no understanding of the worsening economic situation of the Jews.[123] The differences in the way historians viewed writing Polish Jewish history 'stemmed from closely intertwined ideological and methodological questions', as Friedman noted, 'both important and burning'.[124]

While their colleagues and scholars of Jewish historiography underlined the differences between Bałaban's and Schiper's approaches to Jewish history, the two scholars may have had similar views on the shifting paradigms and their limits. Schiper considered economic history an independent and autonomous field of enquiry and a necessary approach for understanding the development of Jewish national history.[125] At the same time, he refused to dismiss the ideological aspects of Jewish history, arguing that historical materialism, an important research method, should not be elevated to a worldview.[126] Both Schiper and Bałaban published extensively on Jewish autonomy in Poland, presenting the conflicts and competitions between communities, especially in the seventeenth century, in which Polish nobility and town owners played a role.[127] Both scholars criticized the adoption of a materialist approach to historical research that would dismiss other questions. Bałaban recognized the importance of economic factors in Jewish history, but he distanced himself from historical materialism.[128] Following Mahler's lecture at the International Congress of Historical Studies, Bałaban dissented with Mahler's demand that Jewish historiography exclusively adopt the materialist approach. Mahler's lecture sparked a long discussion involving 'almost all those present', who expressed concern that 'if we take the path of the lecturer we will receive several historical monographs separate for each country, since the economic background is different in almost every country, but these loose groups will share precisely the sum of the factors stressed by the Geiger-Graetz [school] (religion, awareness of the shared roots, history and the hopes [for] the future)'.[129]

Yet Schiper and Bałaban both praised research in the field of economic history. Like Polish historians such as Bujak and Charewiczowa in Lwów, Rutkowski in Poznań, and Gąsiorowska and Arnold in Warsaw, Jewish historians introduced analysis of statistical data and the study of changing prices and markets, without necessarily embracing historical materialism. Despite the consensus on shifting

---

[122] Friedman, *Dzieje Żydów w Łodzi*, 348.   [123] Ibid. 363.

[124] See CAHJP, P 9, file 94: Friedman's letter to Shatzky, dated in Łódź, 8 Sept. 1934, handwritten in Yiddish.

[125] For this reason, Schiper agreed to prepare a study to accompany a new edition of Graetz; see Schiper, 'Introduction', in *On the History and Economic Conditions of the Jews* (Yid.), i, p. iii.

[126] Ibid., p. vi.   [127] See Bałaban, 'Z zagadnień ustrojowych żydostwa polskiego'.

[128] Bałaban wrote disparagingly that 'looking for an answer in the teachings of Marx and his students became too much of a fashion with us' (Bałaban, 'Zagadnienia historjozofji żydowskiej', 375–6).

[129] Bałaban, 'Po 7 kongresie historyków w Warszawie'.

scholarly focus from the political to the socioeconomic, for historians like Bałaban, Schiper, Arnold, and Gąsiorowska the degree to which historical analysis should be shaped by Marxism remained in question.

Bałaban's students took up this theme as well. They described Jewish professions and the economic success of individual Jewish merchants and industrialists, as well as the periods of success and decline of an entire community, but their accounts remained descriptive rather than analytical. They did not overlook class conflicts within the Jewish community, but neither did they focus on them. In one study, Wurm stressed that the Jews' position resulted from the work of the entire community, although he praised members of the leading families of the communal oligarchy in Brody, whose wealth and position benefited the entire community.[130] Another student, Herz Glejzer, discussed 'the wilfulness [*samowola*] of the *kahal* oligarchy, which did not take the will of the rest of the people into account', judging this 'one of the most serious troubles of the Jewish community', in his thesis.[131] Economic issues played a role in the portrayal of local Jewish communities, especially in the context of Jewish contributions to the town's development and relations with non-Jewish inhabitants. Wurm, whose published work on Brody serves as an example, discussed the professions of local Jews, dwelling on the competition between Jewish merchants and artisans of the town and their Scottish, Armenian, and Greek counterparts.[132] This research addressed questions of economic competition, religious hostility, and occasional violence, but with very little focus on specific instances of conflict.[133]

## The Jews' Place in the Economy

Two aspects of the economic role of the Jews occupied historians' attention: understanding the impact of the Jewish occupational structure on the country's economic development and presenting the context for the competition between Jewish and Christian burghers and the non-Jewish bourgeoisie in the nineteenth century. The economic role of the Jews proved to be a central element in the discussion of Polish–Jewish relations and the possible roots of anti-Jewish antagonism. Jewish historians faced a particularly heavy burden of bias in the Polish historical literature that addressed Jewish occupational structure.

[130] Wurm, *Z dziejów żydostwa brodzkiego*, 39.
[131] Glejzer, 'Życie Żydów w Polsce' (AŻIH 117, folder 51), 16. See also S. Babad, 'Walka gminy żydowskiej ze zbytkiem ze szczególnym uwzględnieniem gmin na ziemiach polskich' (AUW, KEM 4587).
[132] Interestingly, in this context Jews are presented as the locals (*tubylec*) in contrast to the influx of strangers. See Wurm, *Z dziejów żydostwa brodzkiego*, 7–9.
[133] See Glejzer, 'Życie Żydów w Polsce' (AŻIH 117, folder 51), 91–8; Wurm, *Z dziejów żydostwa brodzkiego*, 22.

Most of the respected Polish historians who trained a young generation of economic and social historians at Lwów, Jagiellonian, and Warsaw Universities held an ambivalent view at best of the role of Polish Jews in the country's economy. Pointing to the Jews' exceptional organizational and trading talents, Ptaśnik accused them of breaking up the townspeople and their organization.[134] In 1918 Kutrzeba ascribed the small percentage of Jews in industries such as mines and brickyards to the 'Jews' aversion to hard work'.[135] In the same year Bujak depicted Jews in terms resembling parasites:

The Jews do not represent a full and independent social and economic body, but depend entirely upon the still more numerous Christian population surrounding them, and chiefly upon whether this population is producing and consuming enough to give so numerous a trading people a chance to earn their living, and lastly upon whether this population is not adverse to economic relations with them.[136]

As strangers in Polish society, Bujak argued, Jews employed 'so much easier all unscrupulous means of dealing in relations with the economically weaker population', leading—and rightly so he argued—to contention and animosity. Driven by their 'unbounded and unrestricted covetousness for money', the Jews in Poland engaged 'mainly in undertakings in which invention and cunning have a fairer play then capital and physical work'.[137] It came as no surprise that, as Roman Rybarski put it, 'Jews in Poland were not the yeast on which the economic life only flourished, but rather a leaven which destroyed the old economic organization without replacing it with anything that would increase the economic strength of the country'.[138]

Within this challenging context Jewish historians examined Jewish trade with special thoroughness. Some articles in the Jewish press bemoaned the occupational structure formed over the course of Jewish history—Polish Jewish history included. In a 1939 article Mojżesz Schorr explained:

It is not our fault that we—an agricultural nation, who, on our own soil and by the toil of our own hands—were searching for an ideal, and in time not only did we lose the feeling

---

[134] Ptaśnik, *Miasta Polskie w Polsce*, 139.

[135] Kutrzeba, *Sprawa żydowska w Polsce*, 54. Kutrzeba argued that, for the same reason, Jews had rushed to become landowners in Galicia but stayed away from purchasing small portions of land that they would need to work themselves (ibid. 72). [136] Bujak, *The Jewish Question in Poland*, 20.

[137] Ibid. 23. More often, Bujak claimed, Jews committed a whole variety of offences: 'usury, imposture, concealment of stolen goods, horse stealing, fraud in alimentary provisions, false coinage, bribery of functionaries, false bankruptcy' (ibid. 24).

[138] Rybarski, *Handel i polityka handlowa Polski w XVI stuleciu*, i. 227. On Roman Rybarski see Szymon Rudnicki, 'Wstęp', in id., *Roman Rybarski o narodzie, ustroju i gospodarce*, 5–19; Jakubowska, 'Rybarski Roman Franciszek', 290; Rutkowski, 'Roman Rybarski (1887–1942)', 596.

for the blessed effort of our own hands, but we began to look down on craftsmen who see sense in their lives. We placed craftsmen almost at the very bottom of the social ladder. This tragedy of our *golah* [Yid. diaspora] and the blame for it should be laid rather on the consciousness of the Middle Ages.[139]

But more positive assessments of the influence of Jewish trade prevailed among other Jewish historians of the Second Polish Republic. They pointed to the contributions of Jewish merchants since the dawn of the Polish state in the early Middle Ages, and argued that Jews deserved credit for the revival of international trade and had continued to play a decisively positive role in domestic and international trade in the medieval and early modern periods. Engaging in explicit polemics over Polish economic history, Schiper sharply criticized Roman Rybarski's claim regarding the negative impact of the domination of Jewish trade on the development and status of Polish towns:

What we have determined differs from the 'facts' that Prof. [Roman] Rybarski had 'formulated' in his opus about Polish trade in the sixteenth century. According to Rybarski these are 'facts beyond any doubt', that 'when Polish trade flourished in the middle of sixteenth century, Jewish participation in such trade was on the whole "very weak"'—and that 'their participation systematically increased in this time period when the economic status of the town people deteriorated, when towns fell into decay'.[140]

Polish Jewish historians argued that because the kings and the nobility bestowed the privileges that allowed Jewish trade to flourish in the Polish Kingdom and the Polish–Lithuanian Commonwealth,[141] Polish Jews bore no responsibility for this state of affairs:

Polish commerce was weakened by the process of absorption into the nobility [*warstwa szlachecka*] of the most prominent individuals from among the patriciate. Every prominent Polish merchant, having accumulated wealth, cast away the ell and the scales and tried very hard to rise to the rank of nobility, in order to become a part of the gentry. . . . Polish commerce fell into decay because of this infiltration; its wealth melted away and its social standing deteriorated in strength as competition with the Jews weakened.[142]

In numerous monographs Jewish historians showed how crucial the Jewish presence was to the functioning of Polish towns from the Middle Ages to the modern period. Moreover, as Józef Bursztyn argued, despite the differences

[139] Schorr, 'Ku pracy', 185. Among scholars who wrote about the professional restructuring of Polish Jewry were Arje Tartakower and Majer Bałaban. See also the articles in *Głos Gminy Żydowskiej*, 1939 no. 5–6. Mateusz Mieses, Ignacy Schiper, and Majer Bałaban, among others, published studies on the history of Jewish crafts. Jewish historians paid much attention to the history of Jewish agriculture and peasantry in Poland as well. See Schiper, 'Dzieje gospodarcze Żydów Korony i Litwy w czasach przedrozbiorowych', 186–90, and 'Żydzi w rolnictwie na terenie Małopolski'.

[140] See Schiper, *Dzieje handlu żydowskiego*, 58.  [141] Ibid. 13.  [142] Ibid. 24.

'between the Jewish and Christians neighbourhoods in character, specific conditions of cultural life, as far as economic relations were concerned, were shared'.[143] Some writers considered defensive historical arguments unnecessary. Friedman argued that the whole idea of making the Jews gainfully employed (productivization of the Jewish masses) was based 'on false premises' since the division into productive and unproductive occupations should be abandoned, with the exception of occupations that harmed society.[144] According to Friedman,

> productivization is understood too mechanically and in the mercantilist spirit: productivization is described as every process in which Jews moved from commerce to crafts and industry. But this kind of employment does not always mean moving from unproductive to productive occupations. For example, moving from commerce to the overcrowded Jewish crafts such as tailoring has nothing to do with productivization. On the other hand, the Jews' participation in the new branches of trade (or industry) in which they contributed to the country's economy and created for themselves a solid source of livelihood should be considered a process of productivization.[145]

Finally, Jewish trade served as a tool in the struggle of the nobility with the German—in the national and linguistic sense—patriciate of the towns.[146]

Friedman emphasized that Jews played a 'very serious role in the economic life of Łódź', pointing to their contribution to trade, the role of Jewish capital, the small textile industry and exports to the East, and the food and clothing industries.[147] In Congress Poland, he noted, Warsaw Jews took an active part in the mining, metal, and sugar industries, as well as in the paper and tobacco industries, and worked in building rail track and flour milling.[148] In the context of the lack of capital in Congress Poland, Jewish merchants provided essential capital for the development of the textile industry in general and in Łódź in particular, allowing the city to become Poland's main industrial centre. The positive impact of Jewish economic activities went unappreciated. On the contrary, Friedman argued, Jews were accused of dishonest business practices and never enjoyed the governmental assistance available to others; instead, the government took measures against Jewish merchants.[149] On the basis of the data from research on Łódź, Friedman concluded that in the nineteenth century attempts intensified to oust the Jews not only from various branches of commerce, but also from crafts and industry, leading to their pauperization.[150] Jewish merchants who wanted to shift to industry encountered multiple difficulties, including the hostility of Christian guilds and

---

[143] Bursztyn, 'Żydzi opatowscy na przełomie XVII i XVIII w.', 6.

[144] Friedman, *Dzieje Żydów w Łodzi*, 358, n. 1. See also Aleksander Hafftka, 'Żydzi w przemyśle polskim', in Schiper, Tartakower, and Hafftka (eds.), *Żydzi w Polsce Odrodzonej*, ii. 479–502.

[145] Ibid. 358–9.   [146] Schiper, *Dzieje handlu żydowskiego*, 16.

[147] Friedman, *Dzieje Żydów w Łodzi*, 320.

[148] Ibid. 367.   [149] See ibid. 353–5.   [150] See ibid. 19, 195–7, 268–9, 359–61.

entrepreneurs who would not accept Jews as members.[151] With clear references to contemporary attacks against Jewish businesses, Schiper argued that attempts to boycott Jewish business before the First World War were 'naïve and unsuccessful' since Jews could not easily be separated from the Polish economy.[152]

## Degrees of Separation

As part of their nationalistic vision of history, Polish historians stressed the lack of social interaction between Jews and the rest of Polish society. Unlike other immigrants, they said, Jews remained foreigners and lived separately from the rest of the society, failing to assimilate. As Bujak saw it,

While a considerable number of Germans settled in the Polish towns and villages and became entirely Polonized in the fifteenth and sixteenth centuries, the Jews remained there as a vanguard of Germanism with respect to the language as well as to economic relations. They contributed greatly to the development of German industry and commerce by traveling in masses from Poland to fetch German goods from Breslau, Leipzig, Frankfurt, and other towns.[153]

After the partitions, Bujak argued, the Jews in Polish lands became dangerous anti-Polish elements, acting first as cultural agents of Russia and Germany and then spreading their innate radicalism and revolutionary tendencies, resulting from 'their heated temperament and their inclination towards analysis and criticism', as part of an international conspiracy.[154] Bujak argued that this inclination towards oppressive government was a cultural trait of the Jews. He painted a picture of an international Jewish conspiracy, since Jews were not only responsible for creating and propagating socialism and bolshevism, but also spread 'international and revolutionary propaganda among other societies, in order to weaken by internal dissension the nations who shelter them'.[155]

Bujak, Rybarski, Kutrzeba, and others rehearsed a historical narrative in which Jews received a generous and tolerant welcome in Poland after they escaped oppression and violence in western and central Europe in the fourteenth and fifteenth centuries. Poland provided a refuge for the Jews, granted them unprecedented privileges and autonomy, and never expelled them or confiscated their wealth.[156] Bujak admitted that violence against the Jews existed, but only in the seventeenth and eighteenth centuries when 'it was exclusively the work of the Cossack and Ukrainian peasants, who massacred [the Jews] as much as [the Poles] and destroyed their estates'.[157] Even Łucja Charewiczowa, who was well respected

[151] Friedman, *Dzieje Żydów w Łodzi*, 371–2.
[152] Schiper, *Dzieje handlu żydowskiego*, 542.   [153] Bujak, *The Jewish Question in Poland*, 5.
[154] Ibid.   [155] Ibid. 27.   [156] See ibid. 6–7, and Papée, *Historya miasta Lwowa w zarysie*, 69–71.
[157] Bujak, *The Jewish Question in Poland*, 6.

by Jewish historians, stressed the complete division between Christian society and Jews in the past. Though stopping far short of recommending removal of Jews from Poland's economic life, she nevertheless described Jewish merchants as strangers, not part of the city's native commercial life.[158]

The narrative of the foreignness and uselessness of the Jews, and of the harm they had allegedly done to Poland and its economy in past centuries, was a dangerous weapon for those arguing that Jews had no rights to Polish citizenship or to Poland's continued hospitality. Rybarski and Bujak championed a programme of forced emigration of Jews from Poland in the name of building the country's economy and strengthening its middle class.[159] As Bujak put it, there were simply 'too many Jews in Poland'. Their monopoly in trade harmed the interests of the country, making the Poles dependent on a foreign element and crippling them economically and politically. The struggle against the Jewish role in the economy was 'an inevitable feature of a healthy social evolution', and Jews should not enjoy the same political rights in the country as the truly indigenous population of ethnic Poles.[160] Referring to historical precedents for a solution to 'the Jewish question' in the Second Polish Republic, Rybarski called for separating the Jews 'from the Polish political organism', on the basis of the 'true' tradition of the Polish–Lithuanian Commonwealth.[161] As early as 1918 he suggested that both in the Middle Ages and at present Jews in fact chose and wanted to live separately in a ghetto. On the subject of a ghetto, Bujak stated that

In bygone times, in Western Europe, the Jews were ordered by the State authorities to dwell in a separate Jewish quarter, the so-called Ghetto; however, nowadays they themselves do not want to leave the ghettos; they even organize new ones, as for example in New York. This proves that the creation of concentrated quarters of religious and social life emanates from a deeply rooted need of the Jews and is not a consequence of oppression.[162]

Against the background of this body of literature, Schiper, Bałaban, Ringelblum, and other Jewish historians presented a vision of past Polish–Jewish relations as a mutually beneficial coexistence, despite occasional conflicts. Jewish historical narratives underscored the bond between Jews and the Polish state; the Jews had always been loyal citizens with close links to the rest of the population. They pointed to social interactions between Jews and Christians despite

---

[158] When describing Lwów's commercial circles in the fifteenth and sixteenth centuries, Charewiczowa contrasted 'the average Lwów merchant who was strangely attracted to land and in this way disappeared' with the investments made by Jews and Italians in financial enterprises such as tax leasing and mines (Charewiczowa, *Handel średniowiecznego Lwowa*, 25; see also id., 'Ograniczenia gospodarcze nacyj schizmatyckich i Żydów we Lwowie XV i XVI wieku').

[159] See Rybarski, *Roman Rybarski*, 190–1. [160] Bujak, *The Jewish Question in Poland*, 44–5.
[161] See Rybarski, *Roman Rybarski*, 190–1. [162] Bujak, *The Jewish Question in Poland*, 16.

condemnations, prohibitions, and complaints by the clergy and communal prohibitions well into the eighteenth century.[163] According to Schiper, only the presence of German-speaking townspeople prevented the fuller cultural integration of Jews in the towns of the Polish commonwealth, making the adoption of 'Slavic' as the Jewish daily language impossible.[164]

Bałaban insisted on the complexity of Polish–Jewish relations in the Middle Ages. On the one hand, distinguishing Jews from non-Jews was not enforced as strictly as in the West. Jewish and Christian musicians competed with each other, and Christians strove to limit the activities of their Jewish competitors. However, in Lwów in 1629 both sides agreed that Christian musicians could play on Jewish holidays and Friday nights, while Jews could play at Christian weddings. Bałaban discussed the proclivity of 'a medieval man' to seek colourful clothes and expensive jewellery, and to invite scores of guests to happy and sad family celebrations, and concluded that 'Jews were not an exception to this medieval "order" . . . although pushed into the crowded and dark streets of the Jewish quarters, they surrounded themselves with articles of luxury no less than the rest of the urban population'. He berated women for their passion for luxury without concern for the dangerous envy and hatred they caused among Christians, or for the financial ruin of their husbands. Bałaban compared Jewish and Christian customs relating to life-cycle events, and found many similarities. For example, the spiritual vulnerability of a Jewish mother and her newborn son before circumcision reminded Bałaban of the fear surrounding a Christian newborn before its baptism. In Bałaban's interpretation, the same desires and weaknesses drove Jews and Christians. They expressed them differently, depending on their religious customs. Jewish preachers resembled Catholic clergy in their complaints about the excessive luxury and licentiousness of their respective religious communities.[165]

In his history of the Jews of Warsaw, Ringelblum also argued that Jewish–Christian relations were closer than previously believed: 'More recent research about the . . . life of Jews dispels the prevalent legend about the Chinese wall that allegedly separated Jewish and Christian societies. However, research on Jewish culture and the life of Warsaw Jews indicates that the two worlds permeated each other. The signs of mutual influence mark almost every field of life.'[166] Ringelblum gave examples of 'Jewish familiarity with the Polish population' as business partners or neighbours, including a case of a Jew and a nobleman drinking wine and

---

[163] Bałaban, 'Zbytek u Żydów polskich i jego zwalczanie'.

[164] See Schiper, 'Język potoczny Żydów polskich i ich ludowa literatura w dawnej Rzeczypospolitej', in Schiper, Tartakower, and Hafftka (eds.) *Żydzi w Polsce Odrodzonej*, i. 228.

[165] Bałaban, 'Zbytek u Żydów polskich i jego zwalczanie', esp. 165 for quotation.

[166] Ringelblum, *Żydzi w Warszawie*, 129. Ringelblum argued further that such coexistence was a feature of the Jewish diaspora.

playing dice together. He believed that historical sources revealed mutual openness, despite religious prohibitions: 'Not only is the Chinese wall allegedly dividing Jews and Christians the figment of the imagination of old-style historians, but one should consider the proverbial religiosity of Polish Jews in the Middle Ages a legend.'[167] Business transactions, social interaction, and common daily practices and concerns linked Poles and Jews over the course of Jewish history in Poland, argued Jewish historians. Poles and Jews also fought together to defend their towns against enemies. Fortified synagogues built in the Polish–Lithuanian Commonwealth's borderlands attested to the financial effort and participation of the Jewish inhabitants.[168] This story of the Jews' contribution to the defence of Poland's cities contrasted with the less-positive portrait emerging from the works of Polish historians.[169]

Ellenberg pointed to the change in the nineteenth century when cultural contacts between Jews and Gentiles intensified. Although Jews lacked secular education, they were not uneducated, and some began to study European languages, mathematics, and other sciences; some became scholars and contributed to general European scholarship.[170] Although conflicts continued, the relationship between Jews and Gentiles in Polish lands also showed peaceful coexistence. According to Friedman, 'It would be naive to maintain that frictions and conflicts . . . dominated daily economic life, trade and industrial dealings between the Jews and the Germans. These conflicts were rather interruptions in the daily, quiet work, short clashes, in which deeply hidden antagonisms came to the surface.'[171]

Writings on the theme of social interaction between Jews and Gentiles in Old Poland–Lithuania and during the partitions continued some of the ideas formulated by integrationist Jewish historians. Gumplowicz, Nussbaum, and other 'assimilationist' historians contributed to the discussion about Jews becoming part of Polish society before and during their legal emancipation. When Bałaban, Schiper, Ringelblum, and others sought expressions of the interconnectedness of

---

[167] Ibid. 130–1. The existence of Jewish physicians practising medicine among both Jews and non-Jews also allowed Jewish historians to address the issue of relations between the two groups. See Bałaban, 'Italienische und spanische Aerzte und Apotheker'; Friedman, 'Pierwsi lekarze i felczerzy żydowscy w Łodzi'; see also Kassow, *Who Will Write Our History?*, 68–9.

[168] See Bałaban, 'Bóżnice obronne na wschodnich kresach Rzeczypospolitej z siedmiu rycinami', in id., *Studja historyczne*, 93–9; Urbach, *Udział Żydów w walce o niepodległość Polski*, 6–11.

[169] In 1918 Kutrzeba argued that 'the number of Jews in Poland grew faster than the Christian population of the country partly because of the fact that throughout the Polish state's existence Jews were freed from military service and therefore did not pay the tax in blood, which in the course of so many wars decimated the Christian population' (Kutrzeba, *Sprawa żydowska w Polsce*, 74).

[170] Ellenberg, *Żydzi i początki szkolnictwa powszechnego w Łodzi (1806–1864)*, 8.

[171] Friedman, *Dzieje Żydów w Łodzi*, 345.

Gentile and Jewish societies and cultures in Polish lands, they did so against the background of a public discourse in which history served as an argument for those demanding reversal of Jewish emancipation.

However, not all Jewish historians agreed with such a characterization of Jewish–Gentile relations. Feldman questioned Ringelblum's interpretation of a case in which a nobleman and a Jew drank wine together and played dice. 'It is hard to imagine', wrote Feldman in his review of the study, 'that in fact such coexistence [*spółżycie*] took place, given the religious and economic antagonism and the Church prohibitions and Jewish canons.'[172] Moreover, the picture of Polish–Jewish relations that Jewish historians painted was far from idyllic. They argued that economic competition among various groups within the urban population affected Christian–Jewish relations the most. Townspeople constituted the main antagonists of Polish Jews; the nobility tended to assist the Jews in these confrontations.[173] Ringelblum dated the first pogrom of Jews in Warsaw to 1454 or 1455:

> Although . . . staged by the Bernardines, we consider it to be a result of competition between the townspeople and the Jews. . . . It would be naïve to explain away the pogrom as caused only by religious hatred. There were other hidden motivations, usually behind the guise of religion, which were in the majority of cases of a material nature.[174]

Ultimately the townspeople's hatred of Jewish competition failed to subvert the advantageous conditions of Jewish existence in old Poland. Although the townspeople gradually managed to achieve 'edicts and royal prescripts which limited the commercial freedom of the Jews . . . The reality was never as bad for the Jews as one might infer from the edicts and agreements. Limitations on Jewish trade, established by the pacts and court decisions were enforced only temporarily or in reality never enforced at all.'[175] Thus, despite economic competition and the struggle of the townspeople against Jewish traders, Ringelblum argued that relations on the ground were often better than the legal sources suggest.[176] Despite 'a tangle of social, economic, national and other antagonisms . . . relations between the Jews and Christians were peaceful and agreeable.'[177]

In the 1930s Polish Jewish historians also wrote about such topics as the period of Catholic reaction in Poland during the seventeenth and eighteenth centuries, anti-Jewish propaganda, the Chmielnicki pogroms (1648–1649), blood libel accusations, allegations of Jews spying for Poland's enemies, and forced conversions.[178] Although downplaying their significance in the grand scheme of things, Ringelblum admitted that 'many times economic antagonisms, incited by a religious

---

[172] Feldman, 'Dzieje Żydów w Warszawie', 528.
[173] See Schiper, *Dzieje handlu żydowskiego*, 23.   [174] Ringelblum, *Żydzi w Warszawie*, 12–13.
[175] Ibid. 24, 26–9.   [176] Ibid. 60.   [177] Ibid. 131.
[178] See Ringelblum's articles in Schiper, Tartakower, and Hafftka (eds.), *Żydzi w Polsce Odrodzonej*.

moment, exploded in the form of pogroms, disturbances, etc.'.[179] Without overlooking religious differences, then, local studies pointed to economic competition as the essential factor generating conflicts and tensions between Jews and Gentiles in the multi-ethnic context of the Polish–Lithuanian Commonwealth.[180] That economic competition was the most important contributor to periodic conflicts, and anti-Jewish violence remained, for the most part, unquestioned.

## Polish Struggles for Independence

Jewish historians faced a historiography of the majority culture that emphasized Jews' indifference to the cause of Polish independence during the partitions.[181] Kutrzeba claimed: 'Jews did not participate in the 1831 uprising; they were indifferent to the struggle of the Polish nation against the tsar for freedom. Just as they had no love for the Duchy of Warsaw, neither did they feel love for Congress Poland.' Even in the case of the 1863 uprising, he argued, Jews remained for the most part 'platonically sympathetic'.[182] The subject of the partitions as a formative period in the creation of modern national identity, and Polish romantic mythology surrounding this subject, proved a leading element in the historical tale of Polish–Jewish relations. Discussing the events of the late eighteenth and nineteenth centuries, Jewish historians extended and consolidated the familiar theme of Polish–Jewish brotherhood through exemplary figures who became symbols of the harmonious coexistence of Poles and Jews and of their joint struggle for Poland's freedom and independence. Zdzisław Zmigryder-Konopka observed:

The history and cultural traditions of Polish Jewry link it to the spiritual culture that flourished in the land where they lived. The aspiration to sustain and broaden this tradition harmonizes with the ideological testament of the Polish democrats of the nineteenth and twentieth centuries and with the lives of such personalities as Berek Joselewicz, Henryk Wohl, or Feliks Perl.[183]

The life and work of artist Maurycy Gottlieb also attracted considerable attention, since he was deemed suitable for 'a Polish Jewish manifestation in the field of spiritual coexistence and cultural rapprochement of the two nations', as a reviewer of his 1932 exhibition in the National Museum of Kraków noted.[184] The

---

[179] Ringelblum, Żydzi w Warszawie, 131.
[180] See Charewiczowa, Handel średniowiecznego Lwowa, 48–9.
[181] Kutrzeba, Sprawa żydowska w Polsce, 50.     [182] Ibid. 53.
[183] Zmigryder-Konopka, 'O równowagę duchową', 139–40. The argument fell on deaf ears with historians such as Rybarski, who referred to 'historical falsifications' in ascribing to the Jews an exceptional role in rebuilding Poland. As Rybarski put it, 'Berek Joselewicz cannot serve as an argument' (Rybarski, Roman Rybarski, 194).     [184] Berkelhammer, 'Manifestacja, której nie było', 281.

reviewer described Gottlieb as

> the first Jewish creator in Poland in whose soul these two vibrant streams came together —his Jewishness and Polishness. . . . Despite this tragic duality, he affirmed in himself both currents that had been placed in his soul by life and by history. He did not cover up his Jewishness or blur his Polishness. Lovingly, he embraced both elements struggling within him.[185]

A similar tone can be discerned in Adam Czerniaków's article devoted to the life of Maksymilian Heilpern, who from 1891 to 1924 served as director of the school for artisans named after Natanson. Czerniaków stressed that 'everybody recognized his chemically pure Polishness. He presided over the Polish organization of school teachers, was somewhat right-wing, and the ethnically Polish society organized a jubilee and created a foundation that bore his name.'[186] Joselewicz, Wohl, Perl, Gottlieb, and other nineteenth-century Jewish personalities served not only as examples of a difficult, painful dual national identity but also of the integration of two national identities. Czerniaków argued that they had to 'digest and assimilate both elements, creating a conglomerate after it had melted into a precious combination'. Such Jews loved Poland 'not out of selfishness, but felt [it] with all the fibres of [their] soul'. They stayed faithful to their Jewishness and never 'disgraced [themselves] by running away from the people out of which [they] grew'.[187]

The struggle for Polish independence attracted significant attention among Jewish historians, allowing them to discuss Jewish patriotism. They stressed Jewish participation in military struggles and uprisings, but also noted other types of assistance extended to the Polish national cause by Polish Jews. For example, one historian noted that during the Kościuszko uprising of 1794, 'Warsaw Jews: tailors [and] hat makers did a great deal of work, providing thousands of pairs of trousers, coats . . . hats for the army.'[188] Berek Joselewicz became one of the most popular national heroes of this type, with numerous articles devoted to his life.[189] Historians also dealt with Poland's struggle for independence during the First World War, stressing that Jews had taken an active part. Bronisław Mansperl, who died in 1915 fighting for Poland's independence under Józef Piłsudski, embodied such selfless patriotism and heroism.[190]

[185] Berkelhammer, 'Manifestacja, której nie było', 281.
[186] Czerniaków, 'Tym, co odeszli', 151.    [187] Ibid.
[188] Mieses, 'Rzemiosło w dziejach Żydów', 231. In the pages of the same organ, Józef Kermisz stressed the military commitment of the Jewish proletariat in Warsaw to the insurrection (Kermisz, 'Żydzi warszawscy w Insurekcji Kościuszkowskiej'). See Ringelblum, *Żydzi w powstaniu kościuszkowskiem*, 72–87. See also Halpern, 'Żydzi w powstaniach polskich 1831 i 1863 r'; Kermisz, 'Nieznany list patriotyczny rabina do Kościuszki z roku 1792'.
[189] Bałaban, *Album Pamiątkowy ku czci Berka Joselewicza*. See Ringelblum, *Żydzi w powstaniu kościuszkowskiem*, 55–69; Urbach, *Udział Żydów w walce o niepodległość Polski*, 5–21.
[190] On Jews in Poland's struggle for independence, see Mieses, 'Żydzi w akcji wyzwolenia Polski';

In the debates of the 1930s, articles about such personalities mattered to the Jewish intelligentsia. At the end of 1937 Samuel Stendig asserted: 'When our very right to life is being questioned today, our right to bread, air, and sun, we must remind the world who made a deity [*bożyszcze*] out of demagogy that we deserve a better reward than the one that is being served to us daily by our enemies.'[191] A small but important group of theses prepared by members of Bałaban's seminar examined Jewish participation in the struggles for independence, a theme central to Polish historiography.[192] Closely following in the traditions of Shatzky's writing, these authors wrote to prove the extent to which Jews were involved on the right side of the Polish national cause.[193] Other studies implicitly proved Jewish contributions and loyalty. Researching Jewish communities in Polish urban centres and Jewish social and economic life, Bałaban's students amassed historical examples and data on Jewish contributions to the history of these towns. They collectively portrayed national history, including the long-standing Jewish presence in various Polish towns and the establishment of venerable Jewish institutions. The Jewish history emerging from these studies offered important examples of Jewish life in Poland without idealizing it. The articles also represented a particularly positive aspect of Polish traditions, undermined in the political debates of the 1930s. Zmigryder-Konopka called on the Polish and Jewish public to continue these liberal traditions.[194]

## The Polish Tradition and Antisemitism

Praising Poland's 'good and noble tradition', Jewish historians argued that hatred of the Jews in Poland was the result of foreign influences that sometimes caused grievances and crises in Polish–Jewish relations.[195] In order to support the narrative of an age-old Polish benevolence towards Jews, historians pointed to a variety of direct and indirect cultural, religious, and political factors which originated abroad. In a popular 1932 article, Bałaban noted the 'totally exclusionist' attitude of Polish society towards the Jews in Poland since the beginning of Jewish settlement in Polish lands from the ninth to the twelfth centuries. But he attributed this exclusionism to the 'external' influence of the Justinian Code:

Konic, 'Żydzi w Legionach Józefa Piłsudskiego'; Konic, 'Z galerii zasłużonych Żydów polskich: Dr Ludwik Natanson (1822–1896)', no. 5, p. 113.

[191] Stendig, 'Legendy i fakty'.

[192] These include Mejer Rozenblat, 'Żydzi Warszawy w przededniu Powstawnia Styczniowego (od procesu Lesznowskiego do wybuchu powstania)' (AUW, KEM 3916), and L. Lewinson, 'Ozeasz Ludwik Lubliner i jego działalność na emigracji' (AUW, KEM 3235).

[193] Urbach, *Udział Żydów w walce o niepodległość Polski*.

[194] Zmigryder-Konopka, 'O równowagę duchową', 139–40.

[195] This portion of the chapter is drawn from Aleksiun, 'Narratives under Siege'.

From the sixth century on the Christian societies took over; thus with the baptism of Mieczysław, Polish society also adopted Western attitudes towards the Jews as being unfaithful [and] existing beyond the pale of other estates. The more the currents from the West blew [over Poland] the more Polish society separated itself (nobility and the townspeople) from the Jews: with a wall, a trench, a fence, and hatred.[196]

Similarly, describing the life of Kraków Jews in the fifteenth century, Bałaban bemoaned influences and ideas from the West as 'redemptive for Poland, but catastrophic for Polish Jewry. Western Europe displayed enmity towards the Jews . . . and the fruits of anti-Jewish literature found their way to Poland in various ways'.[197]

Ringelblum turned attention to Russia, noting the hatred of 'the Jewish masses for Russia, which was known for its policy of intolerance towards the Jews, and for the Russian army, particularly the Cossacks, recalled from earlier eras (the Chmielnicki pogroms), and the . . . 1768 Confederation at Bar'.[198] Anti-Jewish violence in the late nineteenth century and the pogroms of 1900–4 were planned, directed, and provoked by the Russian authorities. In 1900 Schiper pointed out: 'the worst instincts [were] unleashed against the Wilno Jews by the staging of a blood libel trial'.[199] Describing a wave of pogroms that devastated the northern and eastern borderlands of the Polish lands at the end of the nineteenth and the beginning of the twentieth centuries, Schiper stressed that responsibility for their organization and implementation rested with the Russian authorities. Similarly, when writing about the anti-Jewish violence of 1905–14, Schiper described it as a crime perpetrated by 'dark reactionary forces' or as having been 'arranged by the army'.[200]

This characterization of antisemitism as essentially foreign to Polish culture and tradition led Czerniaków to make a sarcastic remark about the wave of antisemitism and the resulting rupture of the 'radiant thread binding the sons of one land'. Moreover, 'patriots, often of foreign and inimical origin, who have been living in Poland in some cases for two or three centuries, fuel the flames. The blood calls these wolves back to the forest.'[201] In 1932 Szalom Asz drew early attention to the role of Germany in contemporary radical Polish antisemitism:

However absurd this might sound, we have to state clearly that the current wave of 'Jewish excesses' in Poland is not a purely Polish creation, but an imported one—from

---

[196] Bałaban, 'Zagadnienia historjozofji żydowskiej'. See also Schiper, *Dzieje handlu żydowskiego*, 15. See Ringelblum, *Żydzi w Warszawie*, 13–16; Bałaban, *Historia Żydów w Krakowie i na Kazimierzu 1304–1868*, 40–54.   [197] Bałaban, *Historia Żydów w Krakowie i na Kazimierzu 1304–1868*, 41.

[198] Ringelblum, *Żydzi w powstaniu kościuszkowskiem*, 121.

[199] Schiper, 'Żydzi na Kresach Północnych i Wschodnich w czasach porozbiorowych', in Schiper, Tartakower, and Hafftka (eds.), *Żydzi w Polsce Odrodzonej*, ii. 5–12, esp. 10.

[200] See ibid. 5–16.   [201] Czerniaków, 'Szkodliwe zaniedbanie', 133.

Germany. The leaders of Polish hooligans do not let Adolf Hitler rest on his laurels. ... Altars to Adolf Hitler are being constructed not only in Germany, but also in this country for which he has a sword hidden in store. Look at the incense that is being burned for him in this country.[202]

Jewish historians argued that 'the essence of Polishness', in the sense of an open and democratic society, was embodied in and best expressed by spiritual and political leaders such as Tadeusz Kościuszko; romantic writers such as Adam Mickiewicz; and national leaders, particularly Józef Piłsudski.[203] In the past, tolerance towards Jews had been an expression of an open society, drawing on the resources of all the inhabitants of various nationalities and creeds who lived in Polish lands.[204] This vision was personified by the Jews who contributed significantly to the cultural and political life of the country, fought for its independence, and yet remained Jewish. History served as a source of consolation and hope for the restoration of Polish–Jewish relations true to that legacy. Commenting on the decision of the rectors of Polish institutions of higher education to establish 'ghetto benches' for Jewish students, Pinchas Wasserman expressed the overly optimistic belief that 'the nation of Mickiewicz, Lelewel, Kościuszko, and Puławski will not allow itself to impose imported slogans that are incompatible with Polish culture, and the spirit of true and egalitarian [*zglajchszaltowany*] Christianity'.[205]

Comparing the tradition of Polish–Jewish coexistence with the gradual marginalization of Jews in the public, social, and professional arenas in the Second Polish Republic, Zmigryder-Konopka admitted in the summer of 1938: 'This very moment can take away any hope for sustaining this tradition.' Yet he still professed faith that the deterioration was an aberration, in contrast to 'the great historical processes', suggesting that Jews should respond to it with what he called 'the heroism of honesty', producing 'attractive values that will make the demagogy of some groupings about the alleged worthlessness of Jewish citizens in the eyes of future generations [far] from the truth'.[206]

---

[202] Asz, 'Nie mogę dłużej milczeć', 508–9.

[203] Ringelblum, *Żydzi w powstaniu kościuszkowskiem*, 31–3.

[204] Ringelblum characterized the policy of the insurrection leadership and its ability to attract Jews to the uprising as part of a 'wise policy ... of attracting people of all nationalities and religions to the insurrection' (ibid. 30).

[205] Wasserman, 'W obronie godności człowieka'. According to Wasserman, the 'bench ghetto' 'struck against the traditions of the struggle for liberation in the Polish Commonwealth, which used to be in the care of the great national poets and the great marshal Józef Piłsudski'. Thus 'fighting the above-mentioned discrimination constitutes not only a defence of our national and human dignity but also a struggle in defence of the splendid and glorious and many-centuries-old Polish tradition' (ibid.). [206] Zmigryder-Konopka, 'O równowagę duchową', 139–40.

In the autumn of 1938, celebrating the twentieth anniversary of Poland's independence, Schorr declared:

Together with the entire public of the citizens of the state, Polish Jewry, which for centuries has been settled on Polish lands, participates with all its heart and soul in the joy aroused by this special moment of the twentieth century since the resurrection of the most Enlightened Commonwealth [*Najjaśniejsza Rzeczypospolita*]. The Jewish community has a moral right to it because during the period of 150 years of bondage it participated in the uprisings and struggles for [Poland's] liberation as well as the battles of the Great World War. It took part in the first years of shaping the framework of the Polish commonwealth. In the following years [Polish Jewry] participated in creative work in all sectors of economic, cultural, and social life—sacrificing a share of their means and their blood—together with all the Polish nation.[207]

Although Jewish historians were wary of such a one-sided politicized picture, they used it to argue that Jews deserved their rights in the Second Polish Republic.[208]

The editors of a 1939 collection tellingly titled *Żydzi bojownicy o niepodległość Polski* (Jews—Fighters for Poland's Independence) included a list of Polish political leaders and intellectuals who championed civic equality in Poland, with portraits of Tadeusz Kościuszko, Tadeusz Czacki, Joachim Lelewel, Adam Mickiewicz, Franciszek Smolka, Eliza Orzeszkowa, Maria Konopnicka, and Józef Piłsudski.[209] Writing in July of that year, the editors summarized the history of the Jews in Poland as a story of loyal service with 'merchant talents, artisan skills, and contacts abroad increasing [their] wealth and therefore [their] position in Europe'. Jews also contributed in other fields such as medicine and state finance, defended Polish towns, and fought for Poland's independence under Kościuszko in the 1830 and especially the 1864 uprisings, the 1905 revolution, in Polish underground patriotic organizations before the First World War, and in Piłsudski's Legions. They fell in battles for the new borders of Poland. The publication of this work was intended to record the names of heroic Jewish patriots whose memory served to strengthen the connection between past, present, and future generations.[210] But with the outbreak of the Second World War and the reality of the Nazi occupation, Jewish historians would be forced to re-evaluate their understanding of Polish–Jewish relations and the notions of conflict and coexistence in the Polish–Lithuanian Commonwealth in the period of the partitions.[211]

[207] Schorr, 'Nasze życzenia', 231.     [208] Friedman, 'Dzieło na czasie', 557.
[209] See 'Orędownicy równości obywatelskiej w Polsce', in Getter, Schall, and Schipper (eds.), *Żydzi bojownicy o niepodległość Polski*, 3–9.
[210] 'Od redakcji', in Getter, Schall, and Schipper (eds.), *Żydzi bojownicy o niepodległość Polski*, 10–11.
[211] See Kassow, 'Polish–Jewish Relations in the Writings of Emmanuel Ringelblum'. On historians and their construction of the past see Myers and Ruderman (eds.), *The Jewish Past Revisited*; see also Schorsch, *From Text to Context*, 373–88, on Baron's 'lachrymose conception of Jewish history'.

## Between Objectivity and Apologetics

Striking the right balance between scholarship, apologetics, and politics proved an ongoing challenge in the writing of Polish Jewish history. For some historians, political affiliation played an important role in their public activities and overshadowed their scholarly personae to some extent. Ringelblum functioned simultaneously as a professional historian and an active member of Po'alei Zion.[212] Mandelsberg's socialism turned her interest to working-class Jews, who had to fight not only the upper classes but also their fellow working-class members on the issue of Jews.[213] Jewish historians agreed on the need for objectivity, but they also hoped to reach Polish readers. Likewise, the fact that historians wrote at the request of Jewish institutions and organizations presented a challenge. For example, Bałaban described the agenda of his book on the Lwów synagogue as 'eternalizing for the future generations and for the glory of these men who were [the synagogue's] initiators and those who in full understanding of this mission for over 100 years contributed to the development of our synagogue with their self-sacrificing and selfless work'.[214] Moreover, Jewish historians knew some of the subjects of their study personally. Bałaban recognized this and left the task of objective evaluation of his generation to future historians:

It was not always possible to treat all subject matter with the same objectivity. The more remote people and times, I tried to elucidate as objectively as possible. . . . In more recent times that I have lived through myself, [I could not discuss] the history and activities of men of the newer epoch in such a way since I lacked the historical perspective necessary for an objective evaluation. It is hard to judge objectively a person with whom one fought together, whom one loved and supported in his aspirations, and whose support one enjoyed. It is also difficult to judge the facts in which one played a bigger or smaller role objectively.[215]

Assuming the role of implicit, and at times explicit, defenders of the Jewish minority in Poland, Jewish historians placed themselves in a difficult position, aware of the danger of having Jewish history in Poland serve merely as an instrument in the struggle for ingratiating Jews with contemporary Polish society.[216] Describing the patriotic fervour of Polish Jewry upon Poland's resurrection as an independent political entity, Ozjasz Thon assured the readers of the two-volume prestigious collection of studies *Żydzi w Polsce Odrodzonej* that, 'I do not say this in

---

[212] Kassow, *Who Will Write Our History?*, 27–48.  [213] Blumental, 'A Profile of Bela' (Heb.), 25–6.
[214] Wasser, 'Słowo wstępne', in Bałaban, *Historia lwowskiej synagogi postępowej*, p. iii.
[215] Bałaban, *Historia lwowskiej synagogi postępowej*, pp. xi–xii.
[216] In Polish professional historical writing a similar tension and a shift from political to socio-economic history was reflected in the founding of seminars organized by Bujak, Arnold, and Rutkowski.

order to prove my patriotism before this or that group, this or that social circle . . . to gain a little bit of favour and merit with anybody'.²¹⁷ Accounts of the positive attitude of Jews towards the rebirth of Poland were necessary to counter the claims expressed in public discourse by leading Polish intellectuals, including historians. Bujak claimed that

> the majority of Jews took a cool, passive and indifferent attitude; a small part of them declared their satisfaction and readiness for participation in public affairs, while a very considerable part, exceedingly radical in their social views, active in politics and well organized (this means the most important part, composed of the Bund, Poale-Zion, the Social-Democracy of the Kingdom and Lithuania, the People's Party), did not refrain from showing their animosity, and even their hatred in newspapers and at meetings, shouting and demonstrating against the Polish army, the Polish white eagle, the symbol of the State, and even against the State itself. There were even cases where they attacked the Polish soldiers and tried to disarm them by force.²¹⁸

Historical writing on the participation of Jews in the Polish struggle during the partitions sought to disprove claims of this kind. But this counter-argument was particularly vulnerable to apologetics, which Ringelblum described as 'looking [at historical sources] through a magnifying glass'.²¹⁹ In the introduction to his book on Jewish participation in the Kościuszko uprising, Ringelblum criticized the state of research on the topic as overtly ideological:

> The authors often came to radically contradictory conclusions. Some overestimated the role of Jews in the insurrection, ascribing an exaggerated importance to Berek Joselewicz's Jewish unit, while others negated Jewish participation in the uprising altogether, ascribing to them a decidedly negative attitude towards it. Without a doubt, issues that had nothing to do with research were at work in both cases.²²⁰

Rafał Gerber criticized the work of Ringelblum on the Jews' role in the Kościuszko uprising:

> The grasping of the issue of the Jews' participation in the uprisings constitutes a very difficult task. Being a group that was completely eliminated from political life, leading its life on the margins of the gravest events taking place in the country, they did not en masse take part in insurrections. . . . One cannot investigate the participation of the Jews in uprisings (apart from the January one); instead, one ought to discuss the changes taking place in the Polish society's attitude to the Jews at the time of the uprising on the one hand, and the struggle for Polish independence on the other hand.²²¹

---

²¹⁷ Thon, 'Wstęp', in Schiper, Tartakower, and Hafftka (eds.), *Żydzi w Polsce Odrodzonej*, i. 17.

²¹⁸ Bujak, *The Jewish Question in Poland*, 29–30.

²¹⁹ Ringelblum, *Żydzi w powstaniu kościuszkowskiem*, 5.

²²⁰ Ibid. Compare Ringelblum's cautions remarks in his introduction to those of Friedman, *Dzieje Żydów w Łodzi*, 12.   ²²¹ Gerber, 'Ringelblum Emanuel: Żydzi w powstaniu kościuszkowskiem', 105.

Gerber pointed to such exaggerated interpretations as including Jews who were providing for the army as participants in the insurgency, complaining: 'Dr Ringelblum . . . tries to prove as numerous of the Jews' participation in the insurgency as possible, despite the fact that the material cited by him does not point to it at all.'[222] Gerber suggested that 'the author took his conception of the active participation of the Jews in the insurrection to absurdity'.[223] And he concluded that

it is clear that there was a group of Jews who actively supported the insurrection. In part, they stemmed from the people [*sfery ludowe*], the masses were however indifferent towards the cause of the uprising. If Dr Ringelblum tried to find an explanation of their attitude, he would not have found himself in the blind alley of inconsistencies stemming from the apologetic disposition.[224]

Ringelblum accused other writers of 'being tendentious in their interpretation of the sources', arguing that the only correct approach was to understand the context for Jewish attitudes to the uprising.[225] Thus he claimed that the Jewish intelligentsia and plutocracy showed no great interest in the cause of the Kościuszko insurgents, linking their position to a lack of Polish education and thus difficulty in 'merging with the local society',[226] and to the failure of projects for reforming Polish Jewry. Ringelblum contrasted this limited understanding and support for the uprising with the situations in 1830 and 1863 when 'the Jewish intelligentsia, educated in part in Polish schools took a lively part in the struggle for freedom, simultaneously mobilizing Jewish society to fight the invader'.[227]

Jewish historians of two generations—those who began their academic careers before 1918 and those who attended universities in interwar Poland—paid close attention to past instances of conflict and co-operation in Polish–Jewish relations.[228] Writing extensively on the Jewish past in the Polish and Polish–Lithuanian Commonwealth, they focused on relations between the crown and the nobility with the Jews. The historians examined the processes leading to political and economic alliances and discussed groups that were antagonistic towards Jews. Analysing the period of the partitions, they pointed to Jewish contributions to the economy and culture of the Polish lands and particularly to Polish national culture, stressing examples of Jewish patriotism as positivist work 'at the foundations' (*u podstaw*), but also emphasizing the role of the Jews in the armed struggles for Poland's independence in the nineteenth and twentieth centuries.[229]

---

[222] Ibid. [223] Ibid. 106. [224] Ibid. 107.
[225] Ringelblum, *Żydzi w powstaniu kościuszkowskiem*, 5. [226] Ibid. 35. [227] Ibid. 37–9.
[228] See Dold, 'Die Wahrnehmung Majer Bałabans im polnischen Kontext'. See also Aleksiun, 'Polish Jewish Historians before 1918'.
[229] On the main themes of the Polish historiography of this period see Grabski, *Zarys historii historiografii polskiej*, 165–97.

## Conclusion

With a host of institutional initiatives, a considerable change was possible in the project of the academic writing of Polish Jewish history. The possibility of co-ordinated research allowed for a considerable change in the field. A cohort of university-trained historians engaged in discussions about the nature of their profession. Despite their ideological and methodological differences with the earlier generation, scholars of Polish Jewish history in the 1920s and 1930s continued to address the same research agenda that Bałaban, Schorr, and Schiper had advocated since the turn of the century.[230] As the cohort of professional Jewish historians expanded, their model of mapping Polish Jewish communal life, writing cultural history, and experimenting with identity and integration continued to play an important role, adjusted and modified to fit the new national and political circumstances. In the nation state of interwar Poland, Jewish historians told a tale of a multi-ethnic Polish commonwealth, of a large Jewish community, and of Polish–Jewish coexistence.

With calls for the broad use of both Polish and Jewish archives, for taking into consideration the non-Jewish context for a better understanding of Jewish history, and, most important, for a focus on its social and economic aspects, the question of Polish–Jewish relations attracted the attention of most Jewish historians. In analysing the interaction between Jewish and non-Jewish inhabitants, historians pointed to the importance of Jewish trade, crafts, and industry. Jewish historians believed that local Jewish history had an inherent value for Jews themselves, providing them with knowledge about their past and strengthening their national identity. In the interwar period Jewish historians perceived such research as a legitimate part of the development of Polish historiography. Answering the calls of Polish historians, they applied their research agenda to Jewish urban historiography. In this way, they made a claim to be included within the mainstream of the profession, and by extension the Polish nation defined by shared historical past.

Calls for socio-economic and local histories also resonated powerfully with Jewish historians as they attempted to redefine the ways in which the history of Polish Jews should be researched and written. The professional agendas of Polish Jewish historians, and Jewish historians' complex relationship with mainstream Polish historiography, resulted in a wealth of local studies. Local history—in particular—seemed to offer new avenues for rethinking Polish–Jewish relations, past and present, and it also provided an opportunity to argue that Polish history could not be complete without the history of its Jewry. Jewish historians had long claimed that the Jewish past in Poland was often misrepresented or omitted

---

[230] Kassow, *Who Will Write Our History?*; Aleksiun, 'Polish Jewish Historians before 1918'; Seidman, 'Meir Bałaban' (Heb.), 272–3.

entirely from the general Polish narrative. They hoped that research on local history could provide a much-needed corrective, offering a balanced picture of social and economic relations in towns where Jews and Gentiles lived together. In researching and writing these histories, Jewish historians not only participated in a discourse on Poles' and Jews' perceptions about each other in the past and present, but also created a unique intellectual space in which Jews were part of Poland's landscape.

Historians strove to mould this new historical and political consciousness by discussing the Jewish relationship with the Polish land and state, and Jewish contributions to the country's prosperity. They proved to their readers that the Jewish community in Poland had earned its place, and that Polish political leadership in the past had appreciated the close connection between the fate of the state and the security of its Jewry. The discussion of the Jewish past in Poland also considered instances of conflict and showed how Jews built a thriving Jewish community on Polish soil.

History served as a repository for positive examples of Polish–Jewish coexistence, thus also becoming a tool in the struggle against antisemitism. Jewish historians writing in Poland in the 1930s found it necessary to impart group identity in an atmosphere of prevalent antisemitic rhetoric, while combining a separate Jewish identity with immersion in general Polish history.[231] In the introduction to the third volume published by the Warsaw Young Historians Circle, the editors presented the group as part of the modern culture of the Jewish masses. Their goal was 'to elucidate the dynamics of the Jewish social-economic and cultural development in order to solve on this basis the actual problems of the Jewish masses for their social and national liberation'.[232] Indeed, their books and articles devoted to the history of Polish Jewry constituted a highly politicized body of literature. Troubled by contemporary issues, these historians attempted to prove the success of Jewish integration in the past.

The historians' work was relevant beyond the immediate academic milieu: it served as a source of hope and solace, and it offered the Jewish community in Poland solutions to their contemporary struggle against marginalization. The interwar years created new challenges for historians in Poland as they strove to define their roles and duties in the newly resurrected Polish republic. Jewish historians tried to refute historical narratives portraying Jews as a foreign and harmful element in the past and, by implication, in the present. A positive assessment of the history of Polish–Jewish relations constituted evidence against contemporary adversaries' claim that Jews lacked the ability to become good Polish citizens. Such

---

[231] On the impact of the Polish cultural context see Dold, 'Die Wahrnehmung Majer Bałabans im polnischen Kontext'. See also Thon, 'Wstęp', in Schiper, Tartakower, and Aleksander Hafftka (eds.), *Żydzi w Polsce Odrodzonej*, i. 17.   [232] 'From the Editors' (Yid.), *Bleter far geshikhte*, 1 (1934), 3.

a narrative attested to the possibility of Polish–Jewish coexistence and described the mutual benefits of Jews' integration into Polish social, cultural, and economic life. History thus became an intellectual refuge in which integration remained a viable option in a political climate strongly influenced and at times dominated by demands for the emigration of Jews from Poland, or for their marginalization within the country. By writing about Jewish history in Poland scholars like Bałaban, Schorr, and Krämer brought an understanding of Jewish contributions and the Jewish plight in all their complexities to both Jewish and Polish audiences.

The discussion about the nature of Polish–Jewish relations in the past served as an important commentary on the crisis of the second half of the 1930s, with the emergence of radical antisemitic ideology and Hitler's rise to power in Germany.[233] 'Polish Jews know that this country is also theirs and that they have nowhere to go', declared Szalom Asz, noting that their rights were rooted deeply in history. Pointing to the historical coexistence of Poles and Jews, Asz stated: 'For over one thousand years both streams, Poles and Jews, had been flowing in the same riverbed that is called the Polish land.' He argued that 'since the Jews were allowed to join in the defence, they fought for their motherland [*w obronie tej swojej ziemi rodzinnej*], from the Kościuszko uprising to Napoleon, to the uprisings of 1830 and 1863, to the last war, which fulfilled Poland's hopes'.[234] Thus Jews over the centuries, in the Polish–Lithuanian Commonwealth and during the period of the partitions, had earned full civil rights in Poland. Therefore, Asz concluded, 'the Poles must make the Jews part of their state programme [*program państwowy*]', and 'a brotherly coexistence of both nations . . . is a necessity for our dear and tear-stained land'.[235]

This sense of contemporary crisis, especially in the second half of the 1930s, shaped and influenced the interpretations of earlier Polish Jewish history, particularly the issue of the place of the Jews in Poland and the nature of Polish Jewish identity. Analysing the texts that constituted the bulk of the discussion allows us to understand the internal discourses among the intelligentsia of this highly diversified, politicized, and divided community, permitting reconstruction of the narrative they wanted to present to non-Jewish audiences. In the interwar period Jewish historians' perception of Polish–Jewish relations in the past seemed to have hardly changed in comparison to their work on the eve of the First World War. It appears highly unlikely that they did not take note of the crisis.

Historical accounts of Polish–Jewish relations barely reflected the sense of threat experienced by Polish Jews in Poland during the 1930s. The impact of this

---

[233] In the summer of 1938 Zdzisław Zmigryder-Konopka discussed the 'serious nature of the situation in which Jews of various European countries found themselves at this very moment' (Zmigryder-Konopka, 'O równowagę duchową', 137).

[234] Asz, 'Nie mogę dłużej milczeć', 511.    [235] Ibid. 512, 513.

menace was greatly heightened by the close presence and influence of Nazi Germany. However, the vision of antisemitism emerging from Jewish historical writing in 1930s Poland does not portray hatred of the Jews as endemic. To borrow the term coined by Daniel Blatman for the attitudes of the left-wing underground Jewish press in the Warsaw ghetto, interwar historical writing expressed 'nostalgia for the future'.[236] While Jewish historians presented Poland as a safe refuge for Jews, they also discussed instances of violence and pogroms. This picture contrasted starkly with the image of Polish–Jewish relations presented by the leading Polish historians. For example, Kutrzeba repeated the story about Polish tolerance with only a few pogroms and no expulsion from the country except for a short expulsion from Lithuania; Poland, according to him, thus became 'a safe oasis'.[237] In the immediate aftermath of the First World War, there seem to have been opportunities to shape the social, cultural, and political life of the Jewish community in Poland. Thus, when writing about Polish Jewish history, Jewish historians still sought lessons and useful paradigms for Polish–Jewish relations and Jewish national autonomy. In the last decade of the Second Polish Republic little hope was left for immediate change, but history remained one of the few tools for defending Jewish rights in Poland and giving the community a sense of dignity under siege.

[236] Blatman, Introduction to id. (ed.), *Reportage from the Ghetto*, 32.

[237] See Kutrzeba, *Sprawa żydowska w Polsce*, 11–12. Only for the nobility, Kutrzeba claimed, was Poland truly a paradise, but in comparison to other countries Poland could still be described as a paradise for the Jews (ibid. 30–2). In his discussion Kutrzeba referred to the writings of Polish and Polish Jewish historians. He contrasted the policies of the Polish state, which did not interfere with internal Jewish affairs, and the policies of the three partitioning powers (ibid. 74–5).

# EPILOGUE

ALMOST A DECADE AGO an elderly woman approached me after a talk I had given at the YIVO Institute for Jewish Research in New York. She introduced herself as Ignacy Schiper's niece, a native of Vienna who was fortunate to have left the city of her childhood after the *Anschluss* in the spring of 1938. She fondly remembered her uncle, who would visit his brother's family and bring delicious chocolate. I thanked her for the warm-hearted story but did not ask for her telephone number. The image of Schiper visiting Vienna with a box of chocolates for his young niece accompanied me as I worked on this book. While I considered his role as a historian of Polish Jewry, I also wondered about the missed insights into his private life entangled with the public accomplishments accessible to us mostly through his writings. The challenge of composing this collective biography was linking the intellectual work of leading Polish Jewish historians to their public and private lives, while revealing the ways in which a much larger cohort of their disciples engaged with their work.[1] The paper trail that might have led us to a better understanding is barely traceable due to the destruction of personal libraries and institutional archives, as well as the loss of memoirs and personal correspondence. Given the scarcity of surviving archival sources, only Schiper's intellectual toil remains available for our examination—surviving in his published books and articles. Yet these limited sources can still shed light on Schiper's understanding of his own role within the community and the ways in which he and his colleagues envisioned the purpose and methodology behind writing Polish Jewish history. Beyond his interpretation of Jewish history, they offer a window onto his practices as a public intellectual.

This book has examined the emergence and dissemination of academic and popular writing of Polish Jewish history by university-trained Jewish historians in interwar Poland, tracing the development of the field from its early beginnings in the nineteenth century to the outbreak of the Second World War and the Holocaust. The emergent field of Polish Jewish history was influenced by changing ideas about writing Jewish history, Polish historiography, and the ethnic politics of Habsburg Galicia and, later, the Second Polish Republic. On the eve of the Holocaust, Polish Jewish historians like Schiper, Majer Bałaban, Mojżesz Schorr, Emanuel Ringelblum, Raphael Mahler, Filip Friedman, Bela Mandelsberg, and many others had at their disposal a number of training institutions, scholarly

---

[1] Samuel Kassow's magisterial book on Emanuel Ringelblum, *Who Will Write Our History?*, is exceptional in bringing to life both the public and private contexts of Ringelblum's work.

and popular journals, and bibliographical enterprises. They directed their efforts towards collecting historical documents at the YIVO Institute in Wilno, the Institute of Jewish Studies in Warsaw, and the existing communal archives and museums, all of which were being prepared for expansion and reorganization. Relying on their academic credentials and familiarity with the literature, these scholars created a blueprint for a historiography of Polish Jewry, encompassing an increasing number of monographs as well as a few comprehensive surveys, synthesizing the earlier archival research. While many worked as teachers in Jewish schools, the women and men trained by Bałaban, Schiper, and Friedman, as well as those mentored by Ringelblum and Mahler, continued to collect material, carry out research, and seek opportunities to publish their work. Thinking of themselves as part of the larger academic community, Jewish historians directed their work to an audience of fellow historians, both Polish and Jewish. Moreover, they saw their work as relevant for contemporary Jewish life rather than taking place in an academic vacuum. Jewish historiography thus reacted to two seemingly irreconcilable factors: scholarly standards and political engagement on behalf of a national minority under siege.

The sense of participating in a national struggle through the writing of Jewish history permeated the efforts of Jewish historians before the Holocaust.[2] In the introduction to his historical essays published in 1947, Jacob Shatzky mourned the Jewish community in Poland, which 'for hundreds of years carried out a struggle for bread and rights'. Employing the imagery of battle, he went on to emphasize the critical role of historians who 'created historical weapons for that great heroic struggle. The Jewish historian in Poland carried ammunition to the front lines of the Jewish masses.'[3] He reminded his readers that historians had used their scholarship unabashedly to debunk antisemitic stereotypes and promote contemporary Jewish culture. The notion of an inherent connection between the Jewish past, present, and future in Poland greatly influenced Polish Jewish historians in their choice of subjects, their desire to get involved with political and cultural initiatives on behalf of their community, and the ways in which they disseminated their work.

[2] Litman quoted Schiper's definition of the role of the historian as to 'forge a sword for battle out of knowledge'. However, Litman's translation from Schiper's speech and its interpretation appear inaccurate. In the speech, delivered at the celebration in honour of Bałaban's sixtieth birthday, Schiper was ambiguous, describing two styles of writing Jewish history: one by 'a man fighting against the elements of life and creating weapons [*oręż*] out of knowledge', and the other the baroque, emotional style characteristic of Bałaban's work. The latter was not necessarily detached from the historian's contemporary political and social reality. For the quotation from Schiper, see Litman, *The Economic Role of Jews in Medieval Poland*, 233. For the speech, see Jolles (ed.), *Księga jubileuszowa Bałabana*, 29. This passage in Litman's translation has been quoted by other historians. See Rosman, 'Hybrid with What?', 149. Michael Brenner uses the same quotation from Litman's translation, in *Prophets of the Past*, 112.

[3] Shatzky, Introduction to *In the Shadow of the Past* (Yid.), 7.

Polish Jewish historians were also driven by the hope that their work would have political implications beyond the Jewish community, by influencing Polish historical scholarship and Polish intellectual elites. In explaining the Jews and the so-called Jewish question to a Polish audience, national Jewish historians followed—without acknowledging it—in the footsteps of nineteenth-century integrationist authors. They emphasized the Jewish connection to the country and the flourishing of Jewish culture in the periods of Poland's prosperity, and they underlined the Jews' contribution to the country's economic development. For the same reasons, they highlighted Jewish participation in Poland's struggles for independence from the late eighteenth century until the establishment of the Second Polish Republic in 1918.

Yet interwar Jewish historiography surpassed these familiar claims, making the case for the close and complex connection between Poland and its Jewry. It argued that despite the conflicts, competition, anti-Jewish legislation, and violence, Jews did not live in complete separation from their non-Jewish neighbours. Social interaction took place beyond financial transactions, and this cultural cross-fertilization affected both groups. Rather than merely poring over legislative acts affecting the status of Jews culled from volumes of legal codes, these historians addressed all aspects of Polish Jewish history: social, economic, and cultural. Whether studying individual Jewish communities, Jewish autonomous cultural and religious institutions, or the Jewish economy in the Polish–Lithuanian Commonwealth and during the partitions, Jewish historians aspired both to present an objective analysis and to provide their readers with historical arguments for the existence of a Jewish presence in the Polish landscape for hundreds of years, contributing to Poland's glory and suffering in its downfalls. Jewish historians wrote about the Jews' fierce competition with Gentile burghers, inconsistent protection provided by Polish kings and nobles, and instances of coexistence along with those of persecution and violence. These discussions resonated with the contemporary battles of Jewish shopkeepers and artisans.

Seeing in history not only *magistra vitae* but also a source of national pride and hope, these historians disseminated their research beyond the confines of academic discourse through their roles as teachers, preachers, journalists, and politicians on behalf of the Jewish community in the Second Polish Republic. They believed that Polish Jewish history was relevant to Polish Jewry, whether Yiddish- or Polish-speaking, religious or secular, educated or working-class. With their involvement in educational projects, popular writing, and lectures, these historians played an active role in shaping the self-understanding of Jewish citizens of the Second Polish Republic into a decidedly Polish Jewish identity. At the beginning of the Second World War, many Jews identified themselves as 'Polish Jews' despite their embittered ambivalence towards the country in which they experienced persecution and marginalization.[4]

The outbreak of war irrevocably interrupted the project of writing Polish Jewish history for fellow academics and their broader audience in the Second Polish Republic. During the war, some of the historians continued their research in the ghettos and in hiding. In the Warsaw ghetto, for instance, Bałaban headed the Archives Department of the Judenrat and continued to work on his bibliography of Polish Jewry.[5] On the orders of the Nazi authorities, he was forced to write, 'Die Zivilstandesgesetzgebung für die jüdische Bevölkerung im einstmaligen Polen (Heute GG) in ihrer historischen Entwicklung' (The Civil Status Legislation for the Jewish Population in the Former Poland (today GG) in its Historical Development).[6] For a limited period, thanks to his renown as a historian of Polish Jews, Bałaban enjoyed privileges such as access to state archives in order to enable him to complete such studies.[7] Continuing to work as a scholar, he sought to secure his personal survival as well as securing the survival of the Jewish staff at the archive and the Jewish archival heritage in Warsaw. Although his efforts proved futile, the ongoing research, writing, and teaching at the underground university in the Warsaw ghetto and elsewhere attest to these historians' lasting commitment to a national mission, as well as to the needs of the present, offering ever newer

---

[4] For example, Herman Kruk wrote, in 1940: 'The recently extinguished fires are still smoking. Corpses are regularly dragged out from under the ruins. Bombed-out houses collapse, covering passers-by. Who knows how many years, perhaps decades, it will take to heal the wounds of the destruction of Jewish Poland. For two decades Poland has built, and the annihilation took only three weeks' (Kruk, 'On the Ruins of Poland', in id., *The Last Days of the Jerusalem of Lithuania*, 40). On 9 July 1942, Czerniaków noted in his diary: 'In the afternoon Polish urchins [keep] throwing stones over the little wall to Chlodna Street. Ever since we removed the bricks and stones from the middle of Chlodna Street, they have not got much ammunition left. I have often asked myself the question whether Poland is Mickiewicz and Slowacki or whether it is that urchin. The truth lies in the middle' (Czerniaków, *The Warsaw Diary of Adam Czerniakow*, 377). For a discussion of the Jewish image of Poland in the first years of the Holocaust, see Dreifuss (Ben Sasson), *'We Are the Jews of Poland'?* (Heb.), and 'Chcemy wierzyć w inną Polskę'.

[5] See Adler, *In the Warsaw Ghetto 1940–1943*, p. 101. See also Adam Lewak's testimony for the Central Jewish Historical Commission, dated 4 Feb. 1947 (Yad Vashem Archives, M 49.E/3471). Lewak knew Bałaban before the war, serving as his liaison with the bibliographical project, and he continued working in the library during and after the war.

[6] See the memoirs of Bałaban's secretary in the ghetto, Krystyna Nowakowska (born Zigler), Nowakowska, *Tak było w Niemczech*, 186. See also her testimony in the Yad Vashem Archives, O 3/737. See also AAN, Rząd GG 434/7. I would like to thank Giles Bennett for sharing this document with me. The Nazis took a keen interest in Jewish birth and other registers and sought expert opinion on how to interpret the seized registries, because they wished to find the last *Judenstämmling*, or descendant of Jews, in Poland.

[7] See his expert opinion in AAN, Rząd GG 434/7, fos. 38–49. I would like to thank Giles Bennett for sharing this insight with me.

interpretations and understandings of current events. In October 1942, after the deportation of the vast majority of Jews from the Warsaw ghetto to the death camp in Treblinka, Schiper noted in the introduction to his study of hasidism in Poland,

> We wrote this study during a stormy time, in the face of a catastrophe, which befell Polish Jewry and whose end is not yet in sight. With a burning wound in our heart, with difficulty, we brought ourselves to carry out the discussions connected with the subject chosen here. What is this subject after all in comparison with the tragedy which has taken place and is still happening in front of our eyes?! Nevertheless, we told ourselves: *navigare necesse est!* One ought to write so that the pen does not rust.[8]

Continuing to work as historians engaged with contemporary life increasingly meant shifting their focus to the events taking place around them: the destruction of Polish Jewry. Ringelblum's Oyneg Shabes serves as the most sophisticated example of an elaborate communal effort to study and record aspects of Jewish life under Nazi occupation and document Nazi crimes.[9] Jakub Schall and Filip Friedman collected documents about the fate of the Jews in Lwów.[10] In the autumn of 1942 Bałaban handed over several lists of Jews from the Warsaw ghetto buried in the Jewish cemetery to the personnel of the Warsaw University Library.[11] Following the great deportation from the Warsaw ghetto in 1942, Schiper tried to safeguard the books of deported Jews, and Bałaban and Hillel Seidman searched for the most valuable Jewish books and attempted to hide them from the Nazis.[12]

Few of the Jewish historians who created and contributed to the historiography of Polish Jewry survived the Holocaust. Bałaban died in the Warsaw ghetto. At his modest funeral in December 1942 at the Jewish cemetery at Okopowa Street, Seidman paid his last respects in the name of all the students of this pre-eminent historian of Polish Jewry.[13] Bałaban's other students who became professional historians and educators shared his fate. Schiper and Bela Mandelsberg perished in the Majdanek death camp; Jakub Schall and Falik Hafner in the Lwów ghetto. Dawid Wurm was executed in his home town of Brody, Ringelblum was shot in the ruins of the Warsaw ghetto, and Mojżesz Schorr died in a Soviet camp in Uzbekistan. With the majority of the historians killed and many of the survivors pressed to emigrate from Poland, and with the communities whose histories they sought to study destroyed or dispersed, the vision

---

[8] Schiper, *Przyczynki do dziejów chasydyzmu w Polsce*, 13. On other studies written by Schiper in the Warsaw ghetto, see Ringelblum, *Kronika getta warszawskiego*, 548.

[9] See Kassow, *Who Will Write Our History?*

[10] See an anonymous testimony concerning Filip Friedman's activities during the Holocaust (Yad Vashem Archives, O 6/419, pp. 1–2).

[11] See Lewak's testimony (Yad Vashem Archives, M 49 E/3471).

[12] See Adler, *In the Warsaw Ghetto 1940–1943*, 296.

[13] See Seidman, *Diary of the Warsaw Ghetto* (Heb.), 280.

of a flourishing historical project could not materialize. Together with these historians, their libraries, manuscripts, lifelong research projects, recent work, and records created during the Holocaust were lost or scattered.

For those east European Jewish historians who survived or who emigrated before the war, the period of interest dramatically changed as they began to work on the modern period and on the destruction of Jewish communities during the Holocaust rather than on the medieval and early modern periods of Jewish history. Nevertheless, these scholars understood their work as following up on their pre-war and wartime historical projects. The handful of Polish Jewish historians who survived focused on the Holocaust, playing an active role in the early stages of documenting, researching, teaching, and laying the foundations for Holocaust historiography. Turning their attention to the Holocaust, these historians continued to carry out research that served the needs of their now devastated communities. Friedman and Artur Eisenbach published full-length monographs on the destruction of Polish Jewish communities; Mahler assisted with the publication of many communal *yizkor* (memorial) books, offering his historiographical expertise by editing and writing chapters of local history; Joseph Kermish helped to create the archives of Yad Vashem in Israel and served as the director from 1953 until 1979; and Seidman documented his personal experiences in the Warsaw ghetto and commemorated many of his former teachers and colleagues. Most of the historians eventually also published in their original fields of study. While Friedman—who died prematurely—hoped to return to the study of Polish Jewish history before the Holocaust, Eisenbach and Gerber continued their pre-war interest in the nineteenth century.[14]

In the aftermath of the Holocaust, few research institutions devoted to the study of Polish Jewish history remained in Poland, and the centre of academic study of east European Jewish history moved to Israel and the United States. Some scholars such as Mahler and Shatzky had left Poland before the war.[15] Mahler's colleague Friedman moved to New York to work at Columbia University and the YIVO Institute, supported by Salo Baron.[16] Trunk graduated from the University of Warsaw and belonged to the Young Historians Circle in Warsaw. Having

[14] See Mahler, 'The Circle of Young Historians in Warsaw' (Yid.), 307. Rafał Gerber published primarily on the history of education in the nineteenth century and the revolutionary movement. See e.g. Gerber, *Historia ruchów robotniczych* and 'Szkolnictwo Królestwa'. See also Eisenbach, 'Le Problème des Juifs polonais en 1861'; id., 'Hotel Lambert wobec sprawy żydowskiej w przede dniu Wiosny Ludów'; and id., 'Próby uregulowania statusu Żydów w dobie konstytucyjnej Królestwa Polskiego'. See also Polonsky, 'Prace Artura Eisenbacha: Bibliografia'.

[15] Mahler left for the United States in 1937. In 1950 he immigrated to Israel. See Shapiro, 'Mahler, Raphael', in Hundert (ed.), *The YIVO Encyclopedia of Jews in Eastern Europe*, i. 1115–16. Shatzky moved to New York as early as 1929. See Shapiro, 'Shatzky Yankev', ibid. ii. 1704–5.

[16] See Stauber, *Laying the Foundations for Holocaust Research*.

escaped to the Soviet Union during the war, he emigrated from Poland to Israel, and eventually arrived in New York in 1954. He found his academic home at YIVO and published a pioneering book on the *Judenräte*.[17]

The historiographical tradition that developed in independent Poland—with its particular national features—inspired these historians' later academic and popular endeavours. This influence was particularly strong in the activities of the Central Jewish Historical Commission in post-war Poland, headed by Filip Friedman.[18] With its wide popular appeal to Polish Jews, the historiographical enterprise of the interwar period proved pertinent in the teaching of history in the first decades of the newly established State of Israel, as well as in the collection of documents about the destruction of Polish Jewish communities during the Holocaust.

Survivors and refugees who had been students at the Institute of Jewish Studies and at Warsaw University, had been members of the Young Historians Circle, or those who had otherwise been exposed to the leading historical concepts and training in Poland, made important contributions to the development of the disciplines of pedagogy and teacher training in the nascent State of Israel. Many of them became teachers, and the experiences of and attitudes formed in interwar Poland were brought to bear on the tasks and challenges of the new national project in Israel. Having received a certificate to continue her university education at the Hebrew University in Jerusalem, Franciszka Wiesenfeld emigrated to Palestine in 1937. Under her Hebraized name Tzafrira Azrieli she taught Hebrew and Jewish history for many years. While it would be difficult to point to specific ways in which her Polish experiences and attitudes informed her work as a teacher in Israel, her commitment to Jewish history had its roots in her youth in Kraków and Warsaw. Her classes were remembered as a formative experience by generations of pupils.[19] Shevach Eden, Eliezer Feldman, and others worked in the Israeli Ministry of Education and helped prepare national teaching programmes. Raphael Mahler, Michael Handel, and Michael Ziv—who had been active in the Braude network of schools in Łódź—wrote textbooks widely used in Israeli schools. They emphasized the centrality of history in shaping Jewish national consciousness in the pedagogy and curricula in Israel's formative years.[20] Israel M. Biderman, who

[17] Trunk, *Judenrat*; see also Mahler, 'The Circle of Young Historians in Warsaw' (Yid.), 307–8, and Trunk's obituary: 'Isaiah Trunk, Author of A History of Jews during the Nazi Era', *New York Times*, 1 Apr. 1981.

[18] Jockusch, *Collect and Record!*, 84–120; Cohen, *Israeli Holocaust Research*, 503; Stauber, *Laying the Foundations for Holocaust Research*; Aleksiun, 'Philip Friedman and the Emergence of Holocaust Scholarship'.

[19] According to an obituary by Oded Akiva, 'Tzafrira Azrieli of Blessed Memory—the Teacher for Life' (Heb.), in the private collection of Rachel Garber. The clipping has neither the source nor the date. I would like to thank Rachel Garber for sharing with me details of her mother's life.

[20] For detailed lists see Eden, 'The Institute of Jewish Studies' (Heb.), and Weiss and Kremer-Weiss, 'The Institute of Jewish Studies in Warsaw' (Heb.).

emigrated to the United States in 1950, headed the Youth and Education Department of the Jewish National Fund of America.[21] Having worked in the Israeli Ministry of Education, Aron Sawicki (Soviv) directed the Bureau of Jewish Education of Providence, Rhode Island, and was a district chairman of the National Bible Contest. He remained connected with the academic discourse on Polish Jewish history, reviewing Artur Eisenbach's work published in Poland.[22] The work of Polish Jewish historians from before the war appeared on university syllabi, for example, when Abraham Duker taught a course on east European Jewish history at the Graduate Faculty, Columbia University, in the 1955/6 academic year. A course he taught as Visiting Associate Professor in Jewish History in Columbia University's Graduate School during 1966/7, included the work of Majer Bałaban, Filip Friedman, Raphael Mahler, and Mateusz Mieses.[23]

Many of the historians who contributed to the body of Polish Jewish historiography before the Holocaust continued to be remembered and memorialized by their former students and associates. Memorial books and articles dedicated to the work of Schorr and Mandelsberg appeared in United States and Israel. In the prologue to the volume published in Schorr's memory in 1944, Rabbi Louis Ginzberg and Abraham Weiss linked together the impossible tasks of commemorating the destruction of European Jewry in general, and Polish Jewry in particular, with the call to continue Schorr's commitment to scholarship in Jewish history.[24] Bela Mandelsberg's family fund created an award for students working on Polish Jewish history, which is currently based at Bar-Ilan University.[25] In 2009, in a symbolic gesture, the prize for the best master's theses and doctoral dissertations awarded biannually by the Jewish Historical Institute in Warsaw was named after Majer Bałaban, and the Institute itself took on the name of Emanuel Ringelblum.[26]

What is left of the historiographical tradition that flourished in Poland before the Holocaust? To what extent and in what forms did surviving historians and their disciples carry ideas about scholarly involvement in social and national

---

[21] See his obituary: 'Israel M. Biderman, Jewish Leader, 60', *New York Times*, 20 Apr. 1973.

[22] Soviv, '*Kwestia Równouprawnienia Żydów w Królestwie Polskim* by Artur Eisenbach'. See also Soviv, *Louis D. Brandeis*.

[23] See DRI P 65, file 3: Dr Abraham G. Duker, Chicago, Career and Publications, Education and Research, and DRI, P 65, file 271: A. Duker, 'History of the Jews in East Central Europe (Bibliographical Guide)'. See also Gartner, 'In Memoriam: Abraham G. Duker, 1907–1987'.

[24] See Ginzberg and Weiss, *Studies in Memory of Moses Schorr* (Heb.), [p. vi]. The volume included articles by such scholars as Salo Baron, Louis Finkelstein, Umberto Cassuto, and Abraham Heschel, but no article was devoted to the history of Jews in Polish lands.

[25] See Żytomirski-Avidar, 'Historian Bela Mandelsberg-Schildkraut'.

[26] The Institute has continued the traditions of both the Institute of Jewish Studies and YIVO. See Bergman, 'Pamięć o JIWO w Warszawie'.

enterprises into their new lives and new countries? Several initiatives continued to raise the same questions that drove the research of the scholars who had created the school of Polish Jewish historiography. Their experiences in rebuilding Polish Jewish historiography, and in keeping it relevant for the community whose past they studied, offered a perspective on the role of Jewish historians and historiography after the Holocaust in the new centres of historical scholarship—the United States and Israel. Within a few years of the Holocaust, studies and articles exploring the works and views of Bałaban, Schiper, Ringelblum, and others began to appear in Yiddish, Hebrew, and English. These mark a process of interpretation and reformulation in which surviving historians, and later a new generation of scholars, sought to explore interwar historiographical ideas. A series of short overviews of the historiographical activity in the interwar years also appeared during the first decade after the Holocaust, introducing to English and Hebrew readers the main themes and projects, and laying the foundations for new scholarly work.[27]

To what extent, then, did ideas about the place of the Jews in Polish history formulated in interwar Poland become integrated into the study of Jewish history? Salo Baron, a historian from Galicia who moved to the United States before the war, advocated that historians write Jews into local European narratives. His call for a 'non-lachrymose' history before the Holocaust, reinstated in its aftermath, was widely understood as an appeal not to overstate isolated cases of violence during longer periods of Jewish coexistence in their respective home countries.[28] This notion primarily resonated with his fellow Galician historians, and the life of Jewish communities became their primary topic. It echoed Bałaban's reaction to violence at the university: isolated cases should not count, it was the bigger picture that mattered.[29] There certainly seems to be an affinity between later concepts of history-writing and the interwar model, but how other elements of the historiographical practice developed in Poland fared in the post-Holocaust world remains to be studied. This Polish Jewish historiographical tradition offers a window onto the writing of history from a minority perspective.

Apart from the influence of the Polish Jewish historiographical model on Holocaust research and documentation—both during the war and in its aftermath—the continued resonance of the interwar Polish Jewish historiographical school can be traced through the explicit attempts to revive institutions crucial to Polish Jewish historiography and the further training of historians of Polish and

[27] See Ginzburg and Weiss, *Studies in Memory of Moses Schorr*; Seidman, *People I Used to Know*; Smith, *The Yiddish Historians*.

[28] On the interpretation of this call, see Engel, 'Crisis and Lachrymosity'.

[29] Interestingly, Baron did not study the Holocaust as part of his scholarly agenda. He was, however, called on as an expert witness at the Eichmann trial.

eastern European Jewry. Clearly, these institutions left a lasting imprint on scholars who looked up to them as a model of how Jewish studies have been pursued. In 1958 Gershon Taffet wrote to Filip Friedman expressing hope that he would come to Buenos Aires and help in building an institute modelled on the Institute of Jewish Studies in Warsaw.[30] In 1974 history students in New York 'expressed the need for an ongoing seminar which would augment formal course study and would provide a forum for students to discuss problems in their discipline',[31] and the Max Weinreich Center for Advanced Jewish Studies developed a proposal for the formation of a new Historiker Krayz (Historians Circle). The seminar, launched in 1975, covered a variety of subjects and proved successful and the core group began to meet regularly every month; the plans for 1976 were to be 'concerned specifically with eastern European Jewish history, the focus of the students' studies. It is hoped that contact between present and future scholars will further stimulate the development of the historical research of YIVO.'[32] The Krayz functioned under the chairmanship of Isaiah Kuperstein, a fellow of the centre, and under the guidance of Isaiah Trunk, a member of the original group in Poland, and Lucjan Dobroszycki.[33] To some extent, the Jewish Historical Institute in Warsaw also continued the tradition of the Institute of Jewish Studies, occupying the building of the former library of the Tłomackie Synagogue. Other lines of continuity included libraries and archival collections, such as Jacob Shatzky's extensive library collection, which he bequeathed to the Hebrew University.[34]

Geographical displacement affected the scholars personally, of course, but it also disrupted their access to archives, their audiences, and their choice of subjects. Friedman and Bernard D. Weinryb both lamented the difficulties of scholarship after the sources had been irrevocably lost in the Holocaust.[35] Much of the research carried out in interwar Poland—in Polish and in Yiddish—became effectively 'lost' through language barriers. This is particularly true for the theses of Warsaw University students: only a small number were ever published before

[30] YIVO Archives, RG 1258, folder 468: handwritten letter, 4 Sept. 1958, Buenos Aires.
[31] 'Students organize Krayzn at Max Weinreich Center', News of the YIVO/Yedies fun YIVO, no. 137 (June 1976), 5. As the YIVO newsletter summarized it, 'Among the topics discussed were the Folkist Party in interwar Poland; Bernard Weinryb's book The Jews of Poland; the uses of oral history in Holocaust studies; contemporary Eastern European communities (accompanied by a slide presentation); two Lithuanian Jewish communities in the interwar period; and Polish Jewry in the time of Chmielnicki. Also, a number of sessions were devoted to presentations by such visiting scholars as Dr Ezra Mendelsohn, Dr Jacob Tolpin and Dr Mordechai Altshuler. Last year's success has ensured the continuation of the krayz and more sessions are being planned.' I am grateful to Veronique Mickisch for sharing her research with me.   [32] 'Students organize Krayzn at Max Weinreich Center'.
[33] Ibid.   [34] See Stampfer, A Catalog of the Jacob Shatky Collection of 'Polonica Judaica', 1–2.
[35] See Weinryb, Introduction to The Jews of Poland. I would like to thank Ofer Dynes for directing me to Weinryb's essay. See also Friedman, 'The Fate of the Jewish Book in the Nazi Era'.

or after the war, and most remain in the archives of Warsaw University and the Jewish Historical Institute. A Hebrew edition of Bałaban's monumental *Historja Żydów w Krakowie i na Kazimierzu 1304–1868* appeared in 2002. The geographical and linguistic shifts in the aftermath of the Holocaust brought other tensions: while many scholars sought to document and research east European Jewish life, they also struggled with the need to commemorate and even eulogize it.

At the same time, the work written by Jewish historians in the 1920s and 1930s is increasingly utilized by specialists, especially in the case of local studies.[36] Former colleagues and family members strove to commemorate and publish the work of the scholars who had perished in the Holocaust. Bela Mandelsberg's study of Lublin appeared in Hebrew translation in 1965.[37] In New York, Shatzky undertook to write the history of Warsaw Jews, using diverse Jewish and non-Jewish sources, reconstructing the rich fabric of the community. His ambitious project remained unfinished at his death.[38] Based first in New York, and later at Tel Aviv University, Mahler published works in Yiddish, Polish, German, Hebrew, and English focusing on the Haskalah, hasidism, and the Jewish community in the Second Polish Republic. He also prepared critical editions of sources pertaining to the history of Jews in the Polish lands in the medieval, early modern, and modern periods.[39]

In Poland, among the scholars who took up research on the history of Polish Jewry were such eminent historians as Jerzy Tomaszewski and Józef A. Gierowski. In Israel, Jakub Goldberg played a seminal role in opening new avenues for discussion and exploring new topics in the history of Jews in the Polish lands. In the 1980s, dialogue became increasingly open in Poland, and contact with Jewish scholars abroad allowed for a radical re-evaluation of Holocaust research. International conferences took place at Columbia University in 1983, Oxford University in 1984, Brandeis University in 1986, and the Hebrew University in Jerusalem in 1988.[40] And the scholarly annual *Polin: A Journal of Polish-Jewish Studies* (later renamed *Polin: Studies in Polish Jewry*) created an important platform for the development of an international cohort of scholars in Polish and east European Jewish history.[41] In the early 1990s, following the democratic transformation in Poland and the collapse of the Soviet Union, Jewish history in eastern Europe attracted the attention of young researchers. Local initiatives to study, preserve, and commemorate the Jewish past became common in Poland, not only in large

---

[36] For example Gershon Hundert in his work on Opatów (Hundert, *Jews in a Polish Private Town*).

[37] Mandelsberg-Schilkraut, *Meḥkarim letoledot yehudei Lublin*.

[38] Shatzky, *History of the Jews in Warsaw* (Yid.).

[39] See Shapiro, 'Mahler Raphael'. For a full list of his writings, see Segal-Moldavi, 'Bibliography of Professor Raphael Mahler's Writings' (Yid.).

[40] See Polonsky, 'Polish–Jewish Relations since 1984: Reflections of a Participant'.

[41] See Hundert and Bacon, *The Jews in Poland and Russia*.

cities but also in provincial settings. While this scholarship largely focused on the Holocaust, it increasingly integrated other periods of Jewish history into east European historiography.[42] No longer isolated from the scholarship carried out abroad, and eager to participate in the discussions about Jewish experiences in the Polish lands, numerous Polish historians found themselves increasingly involved in collective research initiatives in western Europe, Israel, and the United States. In his introduction to the printed edition of the *YIVO Encyclopedia of Jews in Eastern Europe* in 2008, Gershon D. Hundert argued that its goal was 'to recover and represent the civilization of the ancestors of the majority of Jews in the world on the basis of the most up-to-date and objective scholarly research available'.[43] Reflecting a diverse and transnational community of scholars interested in the subject, the encyclopaedia brought together '450 contributors, living in 16 countries, [writing] on their own fields of expertise and collectively represent[ing] the leading experts in the various divisions of East European Jewish Studies'.[44]

Moreover, Jewish scholars in Israel, the United States, and western Europe have initiated surveys of Polish Jewish history that are in direct continuity with the traditions of scholarly work carried out before the war. In the 1950s, Abraham Duker tried to bring together authors, including his former teacher Salo Baron, to publish a volume on the history of Polish Jewry.[45] A similar initiative was the two-volume work edited by Israel Bartal and Israel Gutman, *Kiyum veshever: yehudei polin ledoroteihem* (*The Broken Chain: Polish Jewry through the Ages*), which explored various aspects of political, social, cultural, and economic history.[46] In order to address the scholarly lacunae in the field of Polish Jewish history, several edited volumes brought together Jewish and non-Jewish scholars of various generations from Israel, the United States, and Poland. Recognizing that no single scholar would be capable of writing such a comprehensive study, the editors hoped this collaborative work could capture the richness of Jewish religious, cultural, and political life in eastern Europe from the beginning of the Jewish settlement in the Polish lands to the Holocaust and its aftermath.[47] Nevertheless, for the first time in many years Antony Polonsky took up the interwar idea of writing a new grand synthesis of Polish Jewish history based on detailed local studies. The result is a sweeping single work interpreting the history of the Jews in the Polish lands.[48]

---

[42] See Tomaszewski, 'Polish Historiography and the Jewish Historical Institute'; 'Centrum Badania i Nauczania Dziejów i Kultury Żydów w Polsce'; and 'The History of the Jews as an Integral Part of the History of Poland'. See also Wodziński, 'Jewish Studies in Poland'.

[43] Hundert, Preface to id. (ed.), *The YIVO Encyclopedia of Jews in Eastern Europe*, i, p. ix.   [44] Ibid.

[45] See DRI, P 65, file 3: principal publications in Polish History published by Dr Abraham G. Duker, Professor Emeritus, Brooklyn College.   [46] Bartal and Gutman (eds.), *The Broken Chain*.

[47] Bartal and Gutman, 'Foreword', ibid. i. 9.   [48] Polonsky, *The Jews in Poland and Russia*.

The growing number of collaborative projects bringing together scholars from various countries points to unprecedented communication and access to material, not only to formerly closed archives and libraries, but also to surviving community records and other historical documentation. Inevitably, the sensitive question of where to preserve these precious historical documents, artefacts, and libraries has been repeatedly raised by scholars and communal activists. Before the war, the Association of the Friends of the Hebrew University sought to acquire or copy valuable manuscripts and publications to be sent to Palestine. After the Holocaust, eastern Europe seemed neither a safe nor an appropriate place to keep the remaining records of the vanished Jewish communities. In recent years, joint research projects, edited volumes, and encyclopedias reflect a more positive attitude by contemporary scholars from abroad towards eastern Europe, not only as a site of the Jewish past and of Jewish catastrophe but also as one of continued engagement and scholarship. Without a doubt, the digitization projects sponsored by such leading institutions as the Jewish Historical Institute in Warsaw, YIVO, the United States Holocaust Memorial Museum in Washington DC, the Central Archives of the History of the Jewish People in Jerusalem, and the American Jewish Joint Distribution Committee have made sources for Jewish history in eastern Europe increasingly accessible to scholars throughout the world.

The work of Polish Jewish historians of the interwar period continues to inform and influence scholarship. Their intellectual project inspires interest in such topics as local history, relations between Jews and non-Jews, and the history of Jewish autonomous institutions. Study of the history of Jews in Polish lands continues to grapple with many of the questions that drove the scholars working in the Second Polish Republic, and modern researchers face many of the same challenges, both ideological and practical: the tension between the communal and the academic, the push to rethink periodization, and the problem of access to sources. But despite the shifts in the geography of the academic study of Jewish history and the many ruptures that have challenged the continuities in writing Polish Jewish history, the field thrives. And it is important, not only, as Michael Marrus wrote, because 'Tragedy clings to the subject because the reader knows that the historical path was leading ultimately to the Nazi extermination of the Jews',[49] but because of its new approaches, its outreach to wider audiences, and, perhaps most of all, its legacy of historians deeply committed to writing the history of their community.

[49] Marrus, *The Politics of Assimilation*, 1.

# Bibliography

## Archival Collections

*Jerusalem*
Central Archives for the History of the Jewish People (CAHJP)
Central Zionist Archives (CZA)
Yad Vashem Archives

*Kraków*
Archiwum Uniwersytetu Jagiellońskiego (AUJ)

*Lviv*
Derzhavnyi arkhiv L'vivs'koyi oblasti (DALO) (State Archives of Lviv Oblast)
Tsentalnyi derzhavnyi istorychnyi akkhiv Ukraiiny m. L'viv (Central State Historical Archives in L'viv)

*New York*
YIVO Archives and Library Collections

*Ramat Gan*
Bar Ilan University, Dr Zerah Warhaftig Institute for the Research on Religious Zionism (IRRZ)

*Stanford, Calif.*
Stanford University, Green Library

*Tel Aviv*
Tel Aviv University, Diaspora Research Institute Archive (DRI)

*Warsaw*
Archiwum Akt Nowych (AAN)
    Ministerstwo Spraw Zagranicznych (MSZ)
    Ministerstwo Wyznań Religijnych i Oświecenia Publicznego (MWRiOP)
    Stowarzyszenie Humanitarne 'Braterstwo B'nai B'rith' w Warszawie (Braterstwo B'nai B'rith)
Archiwum Główne Akt Dawnych (AGAD)
Archiwum Polskiej Akademii Nauk (APAN)
    Polskie Towarzystwo Historyczne (PTH)
Archiwum Uniwersytetu Warszawskiego (AUW)
Archiwum Żydowskiego Instytutu Historycznego (AŻIH)
Bibliotecka Sejmowa (BS)

Biblioteka Uniwersytecka w Warszawie
Centralne Archiwum Wojskowe (CAW)

*Washington DC*
United States Holocaust Memorial Museum (USHMM)

## Secondary Sources

A.G., 'Bałaban Majer: Zadania i potrzeby historjografji Żydów w Polsce', *Roczniki Dziejów Społecznych i Gospodarczych*, 1 (1931), 183–4.

ADAMSKI, ŁUKASZ, *Nacjonalista postępowy: Mychajło Hruszewski i jego poglądy na Polskę i Polaków* (Warsaw, 2011).

ADAMUS, JAN, 'Ringelblum Dr. E.: Projekty i próby przewarstwowienia Żydów w epoce stanisławowskiej', *Ateneum Wileńskie*, 11 (1936), 529–30.

ADLER, STANISŁAW, *In the Warsaw Ghetto 1940–1943: An Account of a Witness* (Jerusalem, 1982).

'Akt darowizny bóżnicy przez Berka', *KPBPŻwP*, 1/3 (1913), 180–2.

ALEKSIUN, NATALIA, 'Female, Jewish, Educated, and Writing Polish Jewish History', in Natalia Aleksiun, Brian Horowitz, and Antony Polonsky (eds.), *Writing Jewish History in Eastern Europe*, Polin 29 (Oxford, 2017), 195–216.

—— 'From Galicia to Warsaw: Interwar Historians of Polish Jewry', in Glenn Dynner and François Guesnet (eds.), *Warsaw. The Jewish Metropolis. Essays in Honor of the 75th Birthday of Professor Antony Polonsky* (Leiden, 2015), 370-89.

—— 'Jewish Historians and the Vision of a New Rabbinate: The Takhkemoni Rabbinical Seminary and the Institute of Jewish Studies in Warsaw between the World Wars' (Heb.), in Guy Miron (ed.), *From Breslau to Jerusalem: Rabbinical Seminaries Past, Present and Future* [Mibreslau liyrushalayim: batei midrash lerabanim kire'i lehithadshut yehudit] (Jerusalem, 2009), 165–202.

—— 'Marcus Braude and the Making of the Future Jewish Elite in Poland', in Michał Galas and Shoshana Ronen (eds.), *Polish Jew: Rabbi Ozjasz Thon from Various Perspectives* (Kraków, 2015), 151–67.

—— 'Molding the Liberal Jewish Intelligentsia in Interwar Poland: *Miesięcznik Żydowski* ("The Jewish Monthly") and its Audience', in Michael A. Shmidman (ed.), *TURIM: Studies in Jewish History and Literature Presented to Dr. Bernard Lander*, vol. ii (New York, 2008), 25–47.

—— 'Narratives under Siege: Polish–Jewish Relations and the Writings of Jewish Historians in Postwar Poland', *Anti-Semitism Worldwide 2003–2004* (Tel Aviv, 2005), 29–50.

—— 'Philip Friedman and the Emergence of Holocaust Scholarship', *Simon Dubnow Institute Yearbook*, 11 (2012), 333–46.

—— 'Polish Jewish Historians before 1918: Configuring the Liberal East European Jewish Intelligentsia', *East European Jewish Affairs*, 34/2 (2004), 41–54.

—— 'Setting the Record Straight: Polish Jewish Historians and Local History in Interwar Poland', *Simon Dubnow Institute Yearbook*, 7 (2008), 127–41.

—— 'Training a New Generation of Jewish Historians: Majer Bałaban's Seminar on the History of Polish Jews', in François Guesnet (ed.), *Zwischen Graetz und Dubnow: Jüdische Historiographie in Ostmitteleuropa im 19. und 20. Jahrhundert* (Leipzig, 2009), 147–76.

ALPERIN, ARON, *Żydzi w Łodzi: Początki gminy żydowskiej 1780–1822* (Łódź, 1928).

ALTER, MOJŻESZ, 'Uczelnia "Tachkemoni" w Warszawie', *Miesięcznik Żydowski*, 2/3 (1932), 268–72.

ANDERSON, BENEDICT, *Imagined Communities: Reflections on the Origin and Spread of Nationalism*, rev. edn. (London, 1991).

APPENSZLAK, JAKÓB, 'Piętnastolenie "Naszego Przeglądu"', *Nasz Przegląd*, 18 Sept. 1938.

ARMBORST, KERSTIN, 'Wegbereiter der Geschichtsforschung—Über den Vorstand der Jüdischen Historisch-Ethnographischen Gesellschaft in St. Petersburg', *Simon Dubnow Institute Yearbook*, 6 (2007), 411–40.

ASKENAZY, SZYMON, 'O Berku', *KPBPŻwP*, 1/2 (1912), 104–6.

—— 'Pierwszy "syonista" polski', *Biblioteka Warszawska*, 1908, vol. 4, 454–69.

—— *Przymierze polsko-pruskie* (Lwów, 1900).

—— *Szkice i portrety* (Warsaw, 1937).

—— 'U grobu Żyda-Polaka', *Tygodnik Ilustrowany*, 1909, no. 45 (6 Nov.), 921–2.

—— *Uniwersytet Warszawski* (Warsaw, 1905).

—— 'Z dziejów Żydów polskich w dobie Księstwa Warszawskiego', *KPBPŻwP*, 1/1 (1912), 1–14.

—— 'Ze spraw żydowskich w dobie kongresowej', *KPBPŻwP*, 1/3 (1913), 1–36.

ASZ, NACHUM, *W obronie uboju rytualnego* (Częstochowa, 1935).

ASZ, SZALOM, 'Nie mogę dłużej milczeć', *Miesięcznik Żydowski*, 2/11–12 (1932), 508–13.

AVRON, DOV, *Education and Its Struggles: Jewish Religious Zionist Education in Poland in the Interwar Years* [Ḥinukh bema'avako: lidemuto shel haḥinukh hayehudi dadati-le'umi bepolin bein shetei milḥamot ha'olam] (Jerusalem, 1988).

—— *The Religious Zionist Youth Movement in Poland between the Two World Wars (Hashomer Hadati and Bnei Akiva)* [Tenuat hano'ar hatsiyonit-datit bepolin bein shetei milḥamot olam (Hashomer hadati uvenei akiva)] (Tel Aviv, 2001).

BACON, GERSHON C., 'The Missing 52 Percent: Research on Jewish Women in Interwar Poland and Its Implications for Holocaust Studies', in Dalia Ofer and Lenore J. Weitzman (eds.), *Women in the Holocaust* (New Haven, 1998), 55–67.

—— 'The New Jewish Politics and the Rabbinate in Poland: New Directions in the Interwar Period', in Jack Wertheimer (ed.), *Jewish Religious Leadership: Image and Reality* (New York, 2004), ii. 447–77.

—— 'The Poznański Affair of 1921: Kehillah Politics and the Internal Political Realignment of Polish Jewry', in Jonathan Frankel, Peter Y. Medding, and Ezra Mendelsohn (eds.), *The Jews and the European Crisis, 1914–1921*, Studies in Contemporary Jewry 4 (New York, 1988), 135–43.

BACON, GERSHON C., 'Reluctant Partners, Ideological Opponents: Reflections on the Relations between Agudat Yisrael and the Zionist and Religions Zionist Movements in Interwar Poland', *Gal Ed*, 14 (1995), 67–90.

—— 'Warsaw–Radom–Vilna: Three Disputes over Rabbinical Posts in Interwar Poland and Their Implications for the Change in Jewish Public Discourse', *Jewish History*, 13 (Spring 1999), 103–26.

BAŁABAN, MAJER, *Album Pamiątkowy ku czci Berka Joselewicza pułkownika wojsk polskich w 125-letnią rocznicę Jego bohaterskiej śmierci 1809–1934* (Warsaw, 1934).

—— 'Chazarowie', *Tel-Awiw*, 1/2 (July 1919), 74–8.

—— 'Doktor Samuel Poznański (1864–1921): Szkic biograficzny', in *Księga pamiątkowa ku czci dra Samuela Poznańskiego (1864–1921) ofiarowana przez przyjaciół i towarzyszy pracy naukowej* (Warsaw, 1927), pp. xviii–xx.

—— 'Drukarnie hebrajskie w Żółkwi i Lwowie (Do dziejów drukarstwa w Polsce)', *Chwila*, 11 Apr. 1920, 5–9.

—— *Dzieje Żydów w Galicyi i w Rzeczypospolitej Krakowskiej 1772–1868* (Lwów, 1916).

—— *Dzieje Żydów w Krakowie i na Kazimierzu (1304–1868)*, vol. i: *(1304–1655)* (Kraków, 1913).

—— *Dzielnica żydowska, jej dzieje i zabytki* (Lwów, 1909).

—— *Dziesięciolecie 'Braterstwa': Przemówienie wygłoszone na uroczystem zebraniu stowarzyszenia humanitarnego 'Braterstwo—B'nei-B'rith' w Warszawie dnia 18 grudnia 1932 roku* (Warsaw, 1933).

—— 'Fragmenty historyczne: Konstytucja 3-go maja a żydzi', *Nasz Przegląd*, 6 May 1923, 3–4.

—— *Historia lwowskiej synagogi postępowej* (Lwów, 1937).

—— *Historja i literatura żydowska ze szczególnem uwzględnieniem historji Żydów w Polsce dla klas wyższych szkół średnich*, 3 vols. Vol. i: *Od najdawniejszych czasów do upadku świata starożytnego*; vol. ii: *Od upadku świata starożytnego do końca wieków średnich*; vol. iii: *Od wygnania Żydów z Hiszpanji do rewolucji francuskiej (od Zygmunta Starego do trzeciego rozbioru Polski)* (Lwów, 1916–25).

—— *Historja Żydów w Krakowie i na Kazimierzu 1304–1868*, 2 vols. (Kraków, 1931, 1936).

—— *Historya projektu szkoły rabinów i nauki religii mojż.: na ziemiach polskich* (Lwów, 1907).

—— 'Historycy Żydzi i historycy żydowscy na Wszechświatowym Kongresie Historycznym w Warszawie (21–28 sierpnia 1933)', *Nasz Przegląd*, 26 Feb. 1933, [p. 11].

—— 'Italienische und spanische Aerzte und Apotheker im XVI. und XVII. Jahrhundert in Krakau', in *Heimkehr: Essays Juedischer Denker* (Czernowitz, 1912), 173–86.

—— *Die Judenstadt von Lublin* (Berlin, 1919); trans. from the German by Jan Doktór as *Żydowskie miasto w Lublinie* (Lublin, 1991).

—— 'Kazimierz Wielki a Żydzi polscy. 600 lat od dnia koronacji wielkiego władcy', *Chwila*, 10 July 1933, 7–8 and 12 July 1933, 7–8.

—— 'Kiedy i skąd przybyli Żydzi do Polski', *Miesięcznik Żydowski*, 1/1 (Dec. 1930), 1–12.

—— 'Korespondencja Lublinera z Lelewelem (1832–1848)', *Miesięcznik Żydowski*, 3/4 (1933), 289–321.
—— 'Kronika: O uniwersytet żydowski', *Nowe Życie*, 1/1–3 (June–Aug. 1924), 119–21.
—— *Makabeusze: Studyum historyczne* (Lwów, 1905).
—— '"Miesięcznik Żydowski": Na marginesie dwóch roczników', *Nasz Przegląd*, 7 June 1933.
—— 'Najnowsze rozprawy z historii Żydów w Polsce (Przegląd bibliograficzny)', *Chwila*, 1 Jan. 1938, 9–10; 2 Jan. 1938, 7–8.
—— 'Obzor literatury po istorii evreev v Pol'she (1907–1909)', *Evreiskaya starina*, no. 1 (1910) 141–7; no. 2 (1910), 305–17; and no. 3 (1910), 442–53.
—— 'Od kiedy my, Żydzi, mieszkamy na ziemiach polskich? Osiadli czy przybłędy?', *Nasz Przegląd*, 7 Feb. 1937, 11; 14 Feb. 1937, 9; 21 Feb. 1937, 9.
—— 'Palenie ksiąg hebrajskich', *Nasz Przegląd*, 21 May 1933.
—— 'Po 7 kongresie historyków w Warszawie (pokłosie historji żydowskiej)', *Nasz Przegląd*, 3 Sept. 1933, 10.
—— 'Profesor Szymon Askenazy (1867–1935)', *Nasz Przegląd*, 24 June 1935, 4.
—— 'Przedmowa', in Dawid Wurm, *Z dziejów żydostwa brodzkiego za czasów dawnej Rzeczypospolitej Polskiej (do r. 1772)* (Brody, 1935), pp. iii–vi.
—— *Przegląd literatury historyi Żydów w Polsce 1899–1903* (Lwów, 1903).
—— *Przewodnik po żydowskich zabytkach Krakowa: Z 13 rycinami w tekście, z 24 rotograwjurami na oddzielnych tablicach, z 2 planami* (Kraków, 1935).
—— 'R. Berish Mayzelsh: Upon the 60th Anniversary of his Passing, 1870–1930' (Yid.), *Haynt*, 14 Mar. 1930, p. 9.
—— *Rabbi Dr Shmuel Poznański of Blessed Memory (1864–1921): His Life and Works* [Harov dr shemuel avraham poznanski z"l (1864–1921): zayn leben un zayne verk] (Warsaw, 1922).
—— 'Rabin Beer Meisels (Z powodu 60-lecia zgonu)', *Nowy Dziennik*, 6 Apr. 1930.
—— *Rabin Dr Samuel Abraham Poznański (1864–1921): Szkic biograficzny* (Warsaw, 1922).
—— 'Rabin Dr Samuel Poznański', *Nowiny Codzienne*, 24 Nov. 1922, 4.
—— 'Rok zbawienia i lata niedoli (Do dziejów Żydów krakowskich w latach 1666–1670)', *Nowy Dziennik*, 16 July 1928, 15–17.
—— 'Stan kahału krakowskiego na przełomie XVII i XVIII wieku', *Miesięcznik Żydowski*, 1/11 (1931), 413–28.
—— *Studja historyczne* (Warsaw, 1927).
—— 'Syn Berka Joselewicza: Józef Berkowicz 1789–1846', *Nowy Dziennik*, 12 Apr. 1933, 8–9.
—— 'Szymon Dubnow: Z powodu jego siedemdziesiątych urodzin', *Miesięcznik Żydowski*, 1/1 (1930), 78–84, repr. as monograph (Warsaw, 1931).
—— 'Ustrój kahału w Polsce XVI–XVIII wieku', *KPBPŻwP*, 1/2 (1912), 17–54.
—— 'Udział Żydów w Powstaniu Styczniowym (Nowe badania)', *Nasz Przegląd*, 15, 22, 29 Jan. 1939.

BAŁABAN, MAJER, 'Umysłowość i moralność żydostwa polskiego XVI w.', in *Kultura staropolska* (Kraków, 1932), 606–39.

—— 'Walka o rządy w kahale krakowskim w okresie Konfederacji Barskiej (1768–1772)', *Chwila*, 28 May 1931, 7.

—— 'Walka z Talmudem na przestrzeni dziejów (sprawa dziś na czasie)', *Nasz Przegląd*, 9 Apr. 1939.

—— 'Wiedza żydowska i jej uczelnie w Polsce', in *Instytut Nauk Judaistycznych w Warszawie* (Warsaw, 1927), 19–33.

—— 'Z zagadnień ustrojowych żydostwa polskiego', in Karol Badecki et al. (eds.), *Studja lwowskie* (Lwów, 1932), 41–66.

—— *Zabytki historyczne Żydów w Polsce* (Warsaw, 1929).

—— 'Zadania i potrzeby historjografji Żydów w Polsce', in *Pamiętnik V: Powszechnego Zjazdu Historyków Polskich w Warszawie 28 listopada do 4 grudnia 1930 r.* (Lwów, 1930–1), vol. i: *Referaty*, 115–21, vol. ii: *Protokoły*, 225–7.

—— 'Zagadnienia historjozofji żydowskiej w stosunku do historji Żydów w Polsce', *Miesięcznik Żydowski*, 2/11–12 (1932), 369–82.

—— 'Zbytek u Żydów polskich i jego zwalczanie (Urywek z większej pracy o życiu prywatnem Żydów polskich)', in W. Kucharski (ed.), *Księga pamiątkowa 50-lecia Gimnazjum im. Jana Długosza we Lwowie* (Lwów, 1928), 165–75.

—— 'Ze studjów nad ustrojem prawnym Żydów w Polsce: Sędzia żydowski i jego kompetencja', in *Pamiętnik trzydziestolecia pracy naukowej prof. dr. Przemysława Dąbkowskiego* (Lwów, 1927), 245–80.

—— *Życie prywatne Żydów lwowskich na przełomie XVI i XVII wieku: Studyum historyczne* (Lwów, 1905).

—— 'Żydzi a Powstanie Styczniowe (1863) (Rozważania historyczne)', *Nasz Przegląd*, 24 Jan. 1937 and 31 Jan 1937.

—— *Żydzi lwowscy na przełomie XVI i XVII wieku* (Lwów, 1906).

—— 'Żydzi w monografjach historycznych miast polskich (Krotoszyn, Złoczów, Stryj)', *Chwila*, 12 Feb. 1933, 9.

—— 'Żydzi w powstaniu 1863 r. (Próba bibliografii rozumowanej)', *Przegląd Historyczny*, 34/2 (1937–8), 564–99.

BAR-YITSHAK, CHAYA, 'Meir Bałaban's Contribution to the Field of Jewish Ethnography and Folklore' (Heb.), *Huliot*, 7 (Autumn 2002), 339–45.

BARDACH, JULIUSZ, *Wacław Aleksander Maciejowski i jego współcześni* (Wrocław, 1971).

BARON, SALO WITTMAYER, *A Social and Religious History of the Jews* (New York, 1937).

BARTAL, ISRAEL, and ISRAEL GUTMAN (eds.), *The Broken Chain: Polish Jewry through the Ages* [Kiyum veshever: yehudei polin ledoroteihem] (Jerusalem, 1997).

BARYCZ, HENRYK, *Na przełomie dwóch stuleci: Z dziejów polskiej humanistyki w dobie Młodej Polski* (Wrocław, 1977).

BAUER, ELA, *Between Poles and Jews: The Development of Nahum Sokolow's Political Thought* (Jerusalem, 2005).

—— 'The Ideological Roots of the Polish Jewish Intelligentsia', in Israel Bartal, Antony Polonsky, and Scott Ury (eds.), *Jews and Their Neighbours in Eastern Europe since 1750*, Polin 24 (Oxford, 2012), 95–109.

BELKIN, SAMUEL, *The Abraham Weiss Jubilee Volume: Studies in His Honor Presented by His Colleagues and Disciples on the Occasion of his Completing Four Decades of Pioneering Scholarship* (New York, 1964).

BEMPORAD, ELISSA, *Becoming Soviet Jews: The Bolshevik Experiment in Minsk* (Bloomington, 2013).

BERGMAN, ELEONORA, 'Pamięć o JIWO w Warszawie', in Ewa Geller and Monika Polit (eds.), *Jidyszland—polskie przestrzenie* (Warsaw, 2008), 197–203.

BERGMANN, OLAF, *Narodowa Demokracja wobec problematyki żydowskiej w latach 1918–1929* (Poznań, 1998).

BERKELHAMMER, WILHELM, 'Istota problemu polsko-żydowskiego', *Tel-Awiw*, 3/2 (Feb. 1921), 56–9.

—— 'Manifestacja, której nie było', *Miesięcznik Żydowski*, 2/3 (1932), 280–3.

—— 'Pierwszy tom Miesięcznika Żydowskiego', *Nowy Dziennik*, 14 June 1931, 5–6.

BERMAN, JAKUB, 'The Tasks of the Historical Section of the Jewish Historical Institute' (Yid.), *Yunger historiker*, 1 (1926), 18–20.

BERNFELD, IZYDOR, *Nauka języka polskiego dla Izraelitów* (Lwów, 1885).

—— *Zupełny słownik języka hebrajskiego i polskiego* (Berlin, 1926).

BERSHADSKI, SERGEI A., 'Pierwsze Jeszyboty w Polsce (Szkic historyczny)', *Izraelita*, 1899, no. 33, 357–8, no. 34, 370–1, and no. 36, 393.

BERSOHN, MATHIAS, *Dyplomataryusz dotyczący Żydów w dawnej Polsce na źródłach archiwalnych osnuty (1388–1782)* (Warsaw, 1910).

—— *Kilka słów o dawnych dawniejszych bóżnicach drewnianych w Polsce*, 3 parts (Kraków, 1895–1900; Warsaw, 1903).

—— *Słownik biograficzny uczonych Żydów Polskich XVI, XVII i XVIII wieku* (Warsaw, 1905).

BIDERMAN, ISRAEL M., 'The Jewish Press', in id. (ed.), *Włocławek and Kujawy: Memorial Book* (New York, 1969), 93–102.

—— *Mayer Balaban, Historian of Polish Jewry: His Influence on the Younger Generation of Jewish Historians* (New York, 1976).

BIEŃKOWSKI, WIESŁAW, 'Gumplowicz Ludwik', *Polski Słownik Biograficzny*, 9 (1960), 150–3.

*Biographical Dictionary of Modern Yiddish Literature* [Leksikon fun der nayer yidisher literatur], 8 vols. (New York, 1956–81).

BISKUPSKI, MIECZYSŁAW B., *Independence Day: Myth, Symbol, and the Creation of Modern Poland* (Oxford, 2012).

BISKUPSKI, MIECZYSŁAW B., 'Marceli Handelsman (1882–1945)', in Peter Brock, John D. Stanley, and Piotr J. Wróbel (eds.), *Nation and History: Polish Historians from the Enlightenment to the Second World War* (Toronto, 2006), 352–85.

BŁACHOWSKA, KATARZYNA, 'Ludwik Finkel (1858–1930)', in Jerzy Maternicki and Leonid Zaszkilniak (eds.), *Złota księga historiografii lwowskiej XIX i XX wieku* (Rzeszów, 2007), 285–308.

BLATMAN, DANIEL (ed.), *Reportage from the Ghetto: A Selection from the Jewish Underground Press in Warsaw, 1940–1943* [Geto varshah: sipur itonai: mivḥar me'itonut hamaḥteret] (Jerusalem, 2002).

BLOCH, PHILIPP, 'Die General-Privelegien der polnischen Judenschaft', *Zeitschrift der historischen: Gesellschaft für die Provinz Posen*, 6 (1891), 69–105.

BLUMENTAL, NACHMAN, 'A Profile of Bela' (Heb.), in Bela Mandelsberg-Schildkraut, *Studies in the History of Lublin Jewry* [Meḥkarim letoledot yehudei lublin] (Tel Aviv, 1965), 15–28.

BLUTINGER, JEFFREY CHARLES, 'Writing for the Masses: Heinrich Graetz, the Popularization of Jewish History, and the Reception of National Judaism', Ph.D. diss., University of California, Los Angeles, 2003.

BOROWSKI, STANISŁAW, *Maciejowskiana: Materiały do biografii Wacława Aleksandra Maciejowskiego* (Wrocław, 1959).

BORZYMIŃSKA, ZOFIA, 'Miesięcznik Żydowski: w 50 rocznicę wydania pierwszego numeru', *Biuletyn ŻIH*, 119 (1981), 63–75.

BOSAK, MEIR, *Shadows of the City* [Bein tselalei ir] (Tel Aviv, 1986).

BRANDSTAETTER, ROMAN, 'Ignis Ardens, Rozmowa z d-rem Ignacym Schiperem z powodu 50-lecia Jego urodzin', *Opinia*, 1934, no. 45, 3.

—— 'Wybryki antyżydowskie studentów Uniwersytetu Wileńskiego w r. 1815', *Miesięcznik Żydowski*, 2/6 (1932), 481–8.

—— 'Za naszą i waszą wolność: Żydzi – nieznani, uczestnicy powstania styczniowego (Na podstawie badań archiwalnych)', *Chwila*, 15 Apr. 1939, 11.

BRAUDO, ALEKSANDR, MARK VISHNITSER, YULII GESSEN, et al. (eds.), *Istoriya evreiskogo naroda*, vols. i and xi (Moscow, 1914).

BRENNER, MICHAEL, *Prophets of the Past: Interpreters of Jewish History* (Princeton, 2010).

BROCK, PETER, JOHN D. STANLEY, and PIOTR J. WRÓBEL (eds.), *Nation and History: Polish Historians from the Enlightenment to the Second World War* (Toronto, 2006).

BRONSZTEJN, SZYJA. *Ludność żydowska w Polsce w okresie międzywojennym: Studium statystyczne* (Wrocław, 1963).

BUBER, SALOMON, *The Exalted Town of Żółkiew: Rabbis, Scholars, and Their Books* [Kiryah nisgabah hi ha'ir zolkva: rabaneiha, ge'oneiha, ḥakhameiha, shemot hasefarim asher ḥibru] (Kraków, 1903).

—— *Men of Renown* [Anshei shem] (Kraków, 1895).

BUDZYŃSKI, ZDZISŁAW, 'Franciszek Bujak (1875–1953)', in Jerzy Maternicki and Leonid Zaszkilniak (eds.), *Złota księga historiografii lwowskiej XIX i XX wieku* (Rzeszów, 2007), 421–40.

—— 'Szkoła historii społeczno-gospodarczej Franciszka Bujaka na Uniwersytecie Jana Kazimierza we Lwowie', in Jerzy Maternicki and Leonid Zaszkilniak (eds.), *Wielokulturowe środowisko historyczne Lwowa w XIX i XX w.*, vol. ii (Rzeszów, 2004), 309–28.

BUJAK, FRANCISZEK, *The Jewish Question in Poland* (Paris, 1919).

—— 'Kilka uwag w sprawie dalszego rozwoju Polskiego Towarzystwa Historycznego', *Kwartalnik Historyczny*, 47 (1933), 1–16.

—— 'Uwagi o potrzebach historii gospodarczej', *Nauka Polska, Jej Potrzeby, Organizacja i Rozwój*, 1 (1918), 275–86.

B.W.S., 'Nauka na obstalunek', *Izraelita*, 1902, no. 24, 277–9.

CAHNMAN, WERNER JACOB, 'Scholar and Visionary: The Correspondence between Herzl and Ludwig Gumplowicz', *Herzl Year Book* 1 (1958), 165–80; repr. in Joseph B. Maier, Judith Marcus, and Zoltán Tarr (eds.), *German Jewry, Its History and Sociology: Selected Essays of Werner J. Cahnman* (New Brunswick, NJ, 1989), 161–74.

CAŁA, ALINA, *Asymilacja Żydów w Królestwie Polskim (1864–1897): Postawy, konflikty, stereotypy* (Warsaw, 1989).

—— *Ostatnie pokolenie: Autobiografie polskiej młodzieży żydowskiej okresu międzywojennego ze zbiorów YIVO Institute for Jewish Research* (Warsaw, 2003).

—— 'The Social Consciousness of Young Jews in Interwar Poland', in Antony Polonsky, Ezra Mendelsohn, and Jerzy Tomaszewski (eds.), *Jews in Independent Poland, 1918–1939*, Polin 8 (London, 1994), 42–65.

CARO, JECHESKIEL, *Geschichte der Juden in Lemberg von den ältesten Zeiten bis zur Theilung Polens im Jahre 1792* (Lwów, 1894).

CHAJES, WIKTOR, *Semper fidelis: Pamiętnik Polaka wyznania mojżeszowego z lat 1926–1939* (Kraków, 1997).

CHAREWICZOWA, ŁUCJA, *Dzieje miasta Złoczowa* (Złoczów, 1929).

—— *Handel średniowiecznego Lwowa*, Studja nad Historją Kultury w Polsce 1 (Lwów, 1925).

—— 'Ograniczenia gospodarcze nacyj schizmatyckich i Żydów we Lwowie XV i XVI wieku', *Kwartalnik Historyczny*, 39 (1925), 193–227.

—— 'Stan badań nad dziejami miast polskich', *Przegląd Historyczny*, 27/1 (1928), 139–52.

—— 'Towarzystwo Miłośników Przeszłości Lwowa: Z powodu dwudziestopięciolecia istnienia', in Karol Badecki et al. (eds.), *Studja lwowskie*, Biblioteka Lwowska 31–32 (Lwów, 1932), pp. ix–xvi.

CHONIGSMAN, JAKUB, and WACŁAW WIERZBIENIEC, 'Z badań nad lwowskim okresem działalności naukowej, dydaktycznej i społecznej Mojżesza Schorra', in Jerzy Maternicki and Leonid Zaszkilniak (eds.), *Wielokulturowe środowisko historyczne Lwowa w XIX i XX w.*, vol. ii (Rzeszów, 2004), 218–39.

COHEN, BOAZ, *Israeli Holocaust Research: Birth and Evolution*, trans. Agnes Vazsonyi (New York, 2013).

COHEN, JULIA PHILLIPS, *Becoming Ottomans: Sephardi Jews and Imperial Citizenship in the Modern Era* (New York, 2014).

COHN, ADOLF JAKUB, 'Nasz dorobek literacki', *Izraelita*, 1901, no. 10, 110–12.

—— 'Prawa żydów', *Izraelita*, 1867, no. 21, 59–60.

—— *Rzut oka na prawo i prawodawstwo mojżeszowe podług źródeł najnowszych* (Kraków, 1865).

—— 'Wstęp: Wiadomości historyczne o szkołach dla żydów w Polsce', in *Z dziejów gminy starozakonnych w Warszawie w XIX stuleciu*, vol. i: *Szkolnictwo* (Warsaw, 1907), 1–2.

CRAIG, JOHN E., *Scholarship and Nation Building: The Universities of Strasbourg and Alsatian Society, 1870–1939* (Chicago, 1984).

CYWIŃSKI, BOHDAN, *Rodowody niepokornych* (Warsaw, 1971).

CZACKI, TADEUSZ, *Dzieła*, ed. Edward Raczyński, 3 vols. (Poznań, 1843–5).

—— *Rosprawa o Żydach* (Wilno, 1807). Rev. as *Rozprawa o Żydach i Karaitach: Z dodatkiem wiadomości o życiu i pismach autora* (Kraków, 1860), and as *Rozprawa o Żydach i Karaitach* (Lwów, 1885).

CZEPULIS-RASTENIS, RYSZARDA, *'Klassa umysłowa': Inteligencja Królestwa Polskiego, 1832–1862* (Warsaw, 1973).

CZERNIAKÓW, ADAM, 'Szkodliwe zaniedbanie', *Głos Gminy Żydowskiej*, 1938, nos. 6–7, 133.

—— 'Tym, co odeszli', *Głos Gminy Żydowskiej*, 1939, nos. 7–8, 148–51.

—— *The Warsaw Diary of Adam Czerniakow: Prelude to Doom*, ed. Raul Hilberg, Stanislaw Staron, and Josef Kermisz, trans. Stanislaw Staron (New York, 1979).

DĄBKOWSKI, PRZEMYSŁAW, 'Tadeusz Czacki jako prawnik: W setną rocznicę zgonu (1813–1913)', *Przegląd Prawa i Administracyi*, 38 (1913), 337–67.

DANIŁOWICZ, BARBARA, *'Jutrzenka*—tygodnik Izraelitów polskich', in Stefania Walasek (ed.), *Studia o szkolnictwie i oświacie mniejszości narodowych w XIX i XX wieku* (Wrocław, 1994), 23–62.

DANOWSKA, EWA, 'Poglądy Tadeusza Czackiego na kwestię żydowską', in Feliks Kiryk (ed.), *Żydzi w Małopolsce: Studia z dziejów osadnictwa i życia społecznego* (Przemyśl, 1991), 159–64.

DATNER, HELENA, *Ta i tamta strona: Żydowska inteligencja Warszawy drugiej połowy XIX wieku* (Warsaw, 2007).

DAWIDOWICZ, LUCY S., *From That Place and Time: A Memoir, 1938–1947*, introd. Nancy Sinkoff (1989; New Brunswick, NJ, 2008).

—— (ed.) *The Golden Tradition: Jewish Life and Thought in Eastern Europe* (New York, 1984).

—— *The Holocaust and the Historians* (New York, 1981).

—— 'Zakhor: Jewish History and Jewish Memory by Yosef Hayim Yerushalmi', review, *American Jewish History*, 73/1 (1983), 112–16.

DEMBITZER, CHAYM NATHAN, *The Perfection of Beauty* [Kelilat yofi], 2 vols. (Kraków, 1888–93).

DEREVIANSKI, YOSEF-DOVID, 'The Attitude of the Society and the Government Circles to the Rabbinical School' (Yid.), *YIVO Bleter*, 10 (1936), 14–19.

DOBROSZYCKI, LUCJAN, 'YIVO in Interwar Poland: Work in the Historical Sciences', in Yisrael Gutman, Ezra Mendelsohn, Jehuda Reinharz, and Chone Shmeruk (eds.), *The Jews of Poland Between Two World Wars* (Hanover, NH, 1989), 494–518.

DOLD, MARIA, '"A Matter of National and Civic Honor": Majer Bałaban and the Institute of Jewish Studies in Warsaw', *East European Jewish Affairs*, 34/2 (2004), 55–72.

—— 'Die Wahrnehmung Majer Bałabans im polnischen Kontext', *Kwartalnik Historii Żydów*, 4 (2004), 558–70.

DOMAGALSKA, MAŁGORZATA, *Antysemityzm dla inteligencji? Kwestia żydowska w publicystyce Adolfa Nowaczyńskiego na łamach 'Myśli Narodowej' (1921–1934) i 'Prosto z mostu' (1935–1939) (na tle porównawczym)* (Warsaw, 2004).

DREIFUSS (BEN SASSON), HAVI, '"Chcemy wierzyć w inną Polskę": Stosunki żydowsko-polskie w podziemnej prasie żydowskiej getta warszawskiego', *Zagłada Żydów*, 1 (2005), 96–113.

—— 'We Are the Jews of Poland'? Relations between Jews and Poles in the Holocaust Era from a Jewish Perspective ['Anu yehudei polin'? Hayeḥasim bein yehudim lepolanim bitkufat hasho'ah min hahebet hayehudi] (Jerusalem, 2010).

DUBNOW, SIMON, *Kniga zhizni: Vospominaniia i razmyshleniia: Materialy dlia istorii moego vremeni*, vol. i (Riga, 1934).

—— 'Let Us Seek and Investigate', trans. from the Hebrew by Avner Greenberg, *Simon Dubnow Institute Yearbook*, 7 (2008), 353–82.

—— *Ob izuchenii istorii russkikh evreev i ob uchrezhdenii russko-evreiskogo istoricheskogo obshchestva* (St Petersburg, 1891).

—— 'Społeczne i duchowe życie Żydów w Polsce w pierwszej połowie XVIII wieku', *Izraelita*, 1900, no. 27.

—— 'Szkice historyczno-obyczajowe z wewnętrznego życia polskich i litewskich żydów w XVI-ym wieku', *Izraelita*, 1901, nos. 35–36, 38–40, 42.

DUTKIEWICZ, JÓZEF, 'Seminarium Marcelego Handelsmana w świetle jego papierów', *Zeszyty Naukowe Uniwersytetu Łódzkiego: Nauki Humanistyczno-Społeczne*, 34 (1964), 133–61.

DZWONKOWSKI, WŁODZIMIERZ, 'Szymon Askenazy 1866–1935', *Wiadomości Literackie*, 28 July 1935, 1–2.

ECK, NATHAN, 'The Educational Institutions of Polish Jewry (1921–1939)', *Jewish Social Studies*, 9/1 (1947), 3–32.

EDEN, SHEVACH, 'The Institute of Jewish Studies' (Heb.), in Y. Grunbaum (ed.), *Encyclopedia of the Diaspora: In Memory of the Lands of Exile and Their Jewish Communities* [Entsiklopedyah shel galuyot: zikaron le'artsot hagolah ve'edoteiha, Sidrat Polin, vol vi: Varshah], part B (Jerusalem, 1959), 323–30.

EDEN, SHEVACH, 'The Institute of Jewish Studies in Warsaw' (Heb.), in Shmuel K. Mirski (ed.), *The Emergence and Destruction of Torah Institutions in Europe* [Mosedot torah be'eiropah bevinyanam uveḥurbanam] (New York, 1957), 561–84.

EFRON, JOHN M., *German Jewry and the Allure of the Sephardic* (Princeton, 2016).

EISENBACH, ARTUR, 'Hotel Lambert wobec sprawy żydowskiej w przededniu Wiosny Ludów', *Przegląd Historyczny*, 67/3 (1976), 369–98.

—— 'Jewish Historiography in Interwar Poland', in Yisrael Gutman, Ezra Mendelsohn, Jehuda Reinharz, and Chone Shmeruk (eds.), *The Jews of Poland Between Two World Wars* (Hanover, NH, 1989), 453–93.

—— 'Le Problème des Juifs polonais en 1861 et les projets de réforme du marquis Aleksander Wielopolski', *Acta Poloniae Historica*, 20 (1969), 138–62.

—— 'Próby uregulowania statusu Żydów w dobie konstytucyjnej Królestwa Polskiego', *Biuletyn ŻIH*, 147–8 (1988), 57–77.

—— *Z dziejów ludności żydowskiej w Polsce w XVIII i XIX wieku: Studia i szkice* (Warsaw, 1983).

EISENBERG, ELIAHU, *Plock: The History of an Old Jewish Community in Poland* [Plock: toledot kehilah atikat yamim bepolin] (Tel Aviv, 1967).

EISENSTEIN, A., 'Jeszcze raz "Prawda o lichwie żydowskiej w Polsce w XIV w."', *Miesięcznik Żydowski*, 3/1–2 (1933), 153–5.

—— 'Prawda o lichwie żydowskiej w Polsce w XIV w.', *Miesięcznik Żydowski*, 2/7–8 (1932), 161–4.

EISENSTEIN, MIRIAM, *Jewish Schools in Poland, 1919–39: Their Philosophy and Development* (New York, 1950).

ELLENBERG, ZYGMUNT, *Żydzi i początki szkolnictwa powszechnego w Łodzi (1806–1864): Przyczynek do dziejów szkolnictwa oraz ludności żydowskiej m. Łodzi* (Łódź, 1930).

ENGEL, DAVID, 'A Book Is Born: From the Correspondence between Filip Friedman and Shalom (Salo) Baron, 1927–1928' (Heb.), *Gal Ed*, 21 (2008), 141–56.

—— 'Crisis and Lachrymosity: On Salo Baron, Neobaronianism, and the Study of Modern European Jewish History', *Jewish History*, 20 (2006), 243–64.

—— '"Damaging Traditions": Observations on Political Processes and the Political Culture of Polish Jewry in the Interwar Period' (Heb.), in Israel Bartal and Israel Gutman (eds.), *The Broken Chain: Polish Jewry through the Ages* [Kiyum veshever: yehudei polin ledoroteihem], vol. ii (Jerusalem, 2001), 649–65.

—— 'On Reconciling the Histories of Two Chosen Peoples', *American Historical Review*, 114 (2009), 914–29.

ESTRAIKH, GENNADY, 'Jacob Lestschinsky: A Yiddishist Dreamer and Social Scientist', *Science in Context*, 20/2 (2007), 215–37.

EVEN-ZOHAR, ITAMAR, *Polysystem Studies*. Special issue of *Poetics Today*, 11/1 (1990).

FALLEK, WILHELM, 'Twórczość Żydów na polu literatury polskiej do 1918 r.', in Ignacy Schiper, Arje Tartakower, and Aleksander Hafftka (eds.), *Żydzi w Polsce Odrodzonej*:

*Działalność społeczna, gospodarcza, oświatowa i kulturalna*, 2 vols. (Warsaw, 1932, 1933), ii. 74–90.

FEINER, SHMUEL, *Haskalah and History: The Emergence of a Modern Jewish Historical Consciousness* (Oxford, 2002).

—— *The Jewish Enlightenment*, trans. Chaya Naor (Philadelphia, 2004).

—— 'Nineteenth-Century Jewish Historiography: The Second Track', in Jonathan Frankel (ed.), *Reshaping the Past: Jewish History and the Historians*, Studies in Contemporary Jewry 10 (New York, 1994), 17–44.

FEINKIND, MOJŻESZ, 'Dysputa żydowska za czasów Stanisława Staszyca', *Nasz Przegląd*, 9 Feb. 1926.

—— *Dzieje Żydów w Piotrkowie i okolicy: Od najdawniejszych czasów do chwili obecnej* (Piotrków, 1930).

FEINSTEIN, ARIE LEIB, *City of Praise* [Ir tehilah] (Warsaw, 1886).

FELDMAN, ELEAZAR, 'Dzieje Żydów w Warszawie', *Miesięcznik Żydowski*, 2/11–12 (1932), 521–8.

—— 'The Earliest Data about Jews in Polish Towns in the 14th–16th Centuries' (Yid.), *Bleter far geshikhte*, 1 (1934), 59–73.

—— 'Jeszcze "Prawda o lichwie żydowskiej w XIV w."', *Miesięcznik Żydowski*, 2/11–12 (1932), 554–6.

FIAL, HERMAN, 'Alma Mater Judaica—Instytut Nauk Judaistycznych w W-wie (z okazji dziesięciolecia)', *Trybuna Akademicka*, 149/3–4 (May–June 1939), 10–11.

FINK, CAROLE, *Defending the Rights of Others: The Great Powers, the Jews, and International Minority Protection, 1878–1938* (Cambridge, 2004).

FINKEL, LUDWIK, *Bibliografia historii polskiej*, 3 vols. (Kraków, 1891, 1895, and 1906).

FINKELSTEIN, ZYGMUNT F. (ed.), *Almanach Żydowski na rok 5678 (1917/1918)* (Vienna, 1918).

FINN, SAMUEL JOSEPH, *Faithful City: History of the Wilno Jewish Community and Memorials to Its Sages, Writers, and Benefactors* [Kiryah ne'emanah: korot adat yisra'el ba'ir vilna vetsiyunim linefashot ge'oneiha, ḥakhameiha, sofreiha unedive iha] (Wilno, 1860; 2nd edn. 1915).

FISHMAN, DAVID E., *The Rise of Modern Yiddish Culture* (Pittsburgh, 2005).

FRANKEL, JONATHAN, 'S. M. Dubnow: Historian and Ideologist', introduction to Sophie Dubnov-Erlich, *The Life and Work of S. M. Dubnow* (Bloomington, 1991), 1–33.

FREUND, JAKÓB, 'Gimnazja żydowskie we Lwowie', *Tygodnik Nowy*, 7 Nov. 1919, 11–12.

FREYLICHÓWNA, JUDYTA, 'Zagadnienie likwidacji długów Kahału Kazimierskiego po III rozbiorze Polski (1795–1809) i w okresie Rzeczypospolitej Krakowej (1817–1829)', *Miesięcznik Żydowski*, 3/5–6 (1933), 467–78.

FRIEDMAN, FILIP [PHILIP], *Dzieje Żydów w Łodzi: Od początków osadnictwa Żydów do r. 1863. Stosunki ludnościowe, życie gospodarcze, stosunki społeczne* (Łódź, 1935).

—— 'Dzieło na czasie', *Miesięcznik Żydowski*, 1/6 (1931), 555–9.

FRIEDMAN, FILIP [PHILIP], 'The Fate of the Jewish Book during the Nazi Era', *Jewish Book Annual*, 15 (1955–8), 3–13.

—— *Die galizischen Juden im Kampfe um ihre Gleichberechtigung (1848–1868)* (Frankfurt am Main, 1929).

—— 'Ludność żydowska w Łodzi do roku 1863 w świetle liczb', *Kwartalnik Statystyczny*, 10/4 (1933), 461–95.

—— 'O zjazd historyków żydowskich i wszechświatową organizację żydowskiej nauki historycznej', *Miesięcznik Żydowski*, 3/3 (1933), 275–84.

—— 'Pierwsi lekarze i felczerzy żydowscy w Łodzi', *Nasz Przegląd*, 22 Feb. 1935.

—— 'Polish Jewish Historiography between the Two Wars (1918–1939)', *Jewish Social Studies*, 11/4 (1949), 373–408; repr. in id., *Roads to Extinction*, 467–99.

—— 'Prof. Majer Bałaban (W 30-lecie pracy naukowej)', *Miesięcznik Żydowski*, 3/4 (1933), 340–6.

—— *Roads to Extinction: Essays on the Holocaust*, ed. Ada June Friedman (Philadelphia, 1980).

—— 'Rola Żydów w rozwoju łódzkiego przemysłu włókienniczego', *Miesięcznik Żydowski*, 1/5 (1931), 431–50.

—— 'Rzemiosło żydowskie w dawnej Polsce', *Głos Gminy Żydowskiej*, 1939, nos. 7–8, 234–42.

—— *Writings of Philip Friedman: A Bibliography* (New York, 1955).

—— (ed.), *Stary cmentarz żydowski w Łodzi*, Bibljoteka Prac Historycznych 1, ed. J. Szper (Łódź, 1938).

FRIEDMAN, MICHAL, 'Reconstructing "Jewish Spain": The Politics and Institutionalization of Jewish History in Spain, 1845–1940', *Hamsa: Journal of Judaic and Islamic Studies*, 1 (2014), 55–67.

FROST, SHIMON, *Schooling as a Socio-Political Expression* (Jerusalem, 1998).

FRYDMAN, B., 'Wyższe Kursy Nauczycielskie "Bajs Jakow" (Seminarium) w Krakowie', in Jakub Zineman (ed.), *Almanach szkolnictwa żydowskiego w Polsce. Trzeci zeszyt okazowy* (Warsaw, 1937), 138–43.

FUKS, MARIAN, 'Prasa żydowska w Lublinie', in Tadeusz Radzik (ed.), *Żydzi w Lublinie*, vol. ii: *Materiały do dziejów społeczności żydowskiej Lublina* (Lublin, 1998), 349–65.

—— *Prasa żydowska w Warszawie 1823–1939* (Warsaw, 1979).

—— 'Schorr, Mojżesz', *Polski Słownik Biograficzny*, 35 (1994), 602–4.

—— 'Warszawska prasa żydowska w języku polskim (1918–1939)', *Biuletyn ŻIH*, 102 (1977), 55–75.

GALAS, MICHAŁ, *Rabbi Marcus Jastrow and His Vision for the Reform of Judaism: A Study in the History of Judaism in the Nineteenth Century*, trans. Anna Tilles (Boston, 2013).

—— (ed.), *Synagoga Tempel i środowisko krakowskich Żydów postępowych* (Kraków, 2012).

GARLICKI, ANDRZEJ (ed.), *Dzieje Uniwersytetu Warszawskiego 1915–1939* (Warsaw, 1982).

GARTNER, LLOYD P., 'In Memoriam: Abraham G. Duker, 1907–1987', *Jewish Social Studies*, 49/3–4 (1987), 189–94.

GĄSIOROWSKA, NATALIA, 'Cenzura żydowska w Królestwie Kongresowem', *KPBPŻwP*, 1/2 (1912), 55–64.

—— 'Mieszczaństwo w powstaniu styczniowym', *Przegląd Historyczny*, 34/2 (1937–8), 526–43.

GEARY, PATRICK J., *The Myth of Nations: The Medieval Origins of Europe* (Princeton, 2002).

GELBER, NATAN M., *History of the Zionist Movement in Galicia* [Toledot hatenuah hatsiyonit begalitsyah], 2 vols. (Jerusalem, 1958).

—— 'Żydzi a zagadnienie reformy Żydów na Sejmie Czteroletnim', *Miesięcznik Żydowski*, 1/10 (1931), 326–44, and 1/11 (1931), 429–40.

GERBER, RAFAŁ, *Historia ruchów robotniczych* (Warsaw, c.1948).

—— 'Ringelblum Emanuel: Żydzi w powstaniu kościuszkowskim', *Kwartalnik Historyczny*, 53/1 (1939), 105–7.

—— 'Szkolnictwo Królestwa Polskiego w pierwszym dziesięcioleciu rządów Paskiewicza', *Rozprawy z dziejów oświaty*, 2 (1959), 167–97.

GETTER, NORBERT, JAKUB SCHALL, and ZYGMUNT SCHIPPER (eds.), *Żydzi bojownicy o niepodległość Polski: Ilustrowana monografia w opracowaniu zbiorowym* (Lwów, 1939; repr. Warsaw, 2002).

GIEYSZTOR, ALEKSANDER, 'Środowisko historyczne Warszawy w okresie międzywojennym', in Józef Kazimierski (ed.), *Nauka i szkolnictwo wyższe w Warszawie* (Warsaw, 1987), 88–106.

——JERZY MATERNICKI, and HENRYK SAMSONOWICZ (eds.), *Historycy warszawscy ostatnich dwóch stuleci* (Warsaw, 1986).

GINZBERG, LOUIS, AND ABRAHAM WEISS, *Studies in Memory of Moses Schorr* [Kovets mada'i lezekher mosheh shor] (New York, 1944).

'Głośni a nieznani: Szkic historyczny', *Izraelita*, 1877, no. 13, 101–3.

GOLDBERG, JAKUB, 'Artur Eisenbach—der letzte Historiker der polnischen Juden aus der alten Schule', *Judaica*, 52/3 (1996), 190–5.

—— 'Majer Bałaban—czołowy historyk polskich Żydów', *Kwartalnik Historyczny*, 3 (1991), 85–97.

—— 'Mojżesz Schorr—pionier badań dziejów Żydów polskich', in Mojżesz Schorr, *Żydzi w Przemyślu do końca XVIII wieku* (Jerusalem, 1991), 9–22.

GOLDMANN, NAHUM, 'Naród żydowski w dobie kryzysu światowego', *Miesięcznik Żydowski*, 2/7–8 (1932), 170–6.

GOTTESMAN, ITZIK NAHKMEN, *Defining the Yiddish Nation: The Jewish Folklorists of Poland* (Detroit, 2003).

GOTZEN-DOLD, MARIA, *Mojżesz Schorr und Majer Bałaban: Polnisch-jüdische Historiker der Zwischenkriegszeit* (Göttingen, 2014).

GRABSKI, ANDRZEJ F., *Zarys historii historiografii polskiej* (Poznań, 2000).

GRAETZ, HEINRICH, *Geschichte der Juden: Von den ältesten Zeiten bis auf die Gegenwart*, 11 vols. (Leipzig, 1856–78). Hebrew translations: Shaul Pinhas Rabinovich (Shefer): *Sefer divrei yemei yisra'el miyom heyot yisra'el le'am ad yemei hador ha'aḥaron* (Warsaw, 1907–8); Nachum Sokołów, *Toledot hayehudim min ha'et hakadmoniyah* (Warsaw, [1905]). Polish translation: Stanisław Szenhak, *Historia Żydów (mniejsza)* (Warsaw, 1902–13, 1929, 1936–9).

GUMPLOWICZ, LUDWIK, *Prawodawstwo polskie względem Żydów* (Kraków, 1867).

GUŚCIORA-SZELOCH, EWA, 'Żydzi i ich rola w dziejach Polski w pracach Szymona Askenazego', Jerzy Maternicki (ed.), *Wielokulturowe środowisko historyczne Lwowa w XIX i XX w.*, vol. i (Rzeszów, 2004), 253–63.

GUTERMAN, ALEXANDER, *Chapters in the History of Polish Jews in the Modern Era* [Perakim betoledot yehudei polin ba'et ḥahadashah] (Jerusalem, 1999).

—— *From Assimilation to Nationalism: Chapters in the History of the Great Synagogue in Warsaw 1806–1843* [Mehitbolelut lile'umiyut: perakim betoledot beit hakeneset hagadol hasinagoga bevarshah, 1806–1943] (Jerusalem, 1993).

GUTMAN, ISRAEL (ed.), *Emanuel Ringelblum: The Man and the Historian* (Jerusalem, 2006).

HAFFTKA, ALEXANDER, 'Życie i twórczość dr. Jakóba Szackiego', in Philip Friedman, Aleksander Hertz, and Joseph L. Lichten (eds.), *Jakób Szacki: In Memoriam / Yacov Shatzky: Tzum Ondenk* (New York, 1957), 13–23.

HAFNER, FALIK, 'Księga ku czci prof. dr. Majera Bałabana', *Trybuna Akademicka*, 145–6/4–5 (Nov.–Dec. 1938), 11.

HALAMISH (FLINT), MORDECHAI, 'Rabbinical School "Tahkemoni"', *Encyclopaedia of the Diasporas* [Entsiklopedyah shel galuyot], vol. vi: *Warsaw* [*Varshah*], part A (Jerusalem, 1953), 351–6.

HALPERN, ABRAHAM, 'Żydzi w powstaniach polskich 1831 i 1863 r', *Głos Gminy Żydowskiej*, 1937, no. 5, 110–12.

HALPERN, IZRAEL, 'Przyczynek do dziejów osadnictwa Żydów na Mazowszu', *Miesięcznik Żydowski*, 2/1–2 (1933), 135–9.

HANDELSMAN, MARCELI, 'O nauce i nauczaniu historji nowożytnej w szkole wyższej', *Przegląd Historyczny*, 26/1 (1926–7), 107–23.

—— 'Problem narodowości współczesnej', in *Pamiętnik IV: Powszechnego Zjazdu Historyków Polskich w Poznaniu 6–8 grudnia 1925*, vol. i: *Referaty* (Lwów, 1925).

HARKAVY, ABRAHAM ELIYAHU (ALBERT), *Compendium of Rare Sources* [Me'asef nidaḥim], reprint (Jerusalem, 1970).

—— *Jews and the Language of the Slavs: Explorations and Enquiries in the History of Jews in the Land of Russia* [Hayehudim usefat haslavim: midrishot veḥakirot bekorot benei yisra'el be'erets rusyah] (Vilna, 1867).

HARTGLAS, APOLINARY, *Na pograniczu dwóch światów*, ed. Jolanta Żyndul (Warsaw, 1996).

—— 'Żółta łata (zamiast wstępu)', in Izaak Grünbaum (ed.), *Żółta łata (Sprawa ograniczeń prawnych)*, Materiały w sprawie żydowskiej w Polsce 5–6 (Warsaw, 1922).

HEFTMAN, YOSEF, DAVID TSEVI PINKES, and AVRAHAM ZAMIR (eds.), *An Exemplary Official: Jubilee Volume in Honour of R. Joshua Heshl Farbstein* [Askan lemofet: sefer hayovel likhvod reb yehoshua heshel farbstein] (Tel Aviv, 1945).

HELLER, CELIA S., *On the Edge of Destruction: Jews of Poland between the Two World Wars* (New York, 1977).

HENSCHEL, CHRISTHARDT, *Jeder Bürger Soldat: Juden und das polnische Militär (1918–1939)* (Göttingen, 2017).

HERTZ, ALEKSANDER, *Żydzi w kulturze polskiej* (Paris, 1961). Translated by Richard Lourie as *The Jews in Polish Culture* (Evanston, 1988).

HILBERG, RAUL, STANISLAW STARON, and JOSEF KERMISZ (eds.), *The Warsaw Diary of Adam Czerniakow: Prelude to Doom* (Chicago, 1999).

HIRSCHAUT, YEKHIEL, 'Dr I. Schiper—His Life and Work (1884–1943)' (Yid.), *Fun noentn ovar*, 1 (1955), 185–256.

HIRSCHBERG, ADOLF, 'Kulturalny ruch żydowski w Wilnie', *Kurjer Wileński*, no. 226 (2168) (1 Oct. 1931), 2.

—— 'Schall Jakób: Historja Żydów w Polsce, na Litwie i Rusi', *Roczniki Dziejów Społecznych i Gospodarczych*, 4 (1935), 448–51.

—— 'Schipper Ignacy: Żydzi Królestwa Polskiego w dobie Powstania Listopadowego', *Roczniki Dziejów Społecznych i Gospodarczych*, 3 (1934), 583–5.

'"Historja Żydów" prof. H. Graetza', *Izraelita*, 1903, no. 42, 503.

HOFFMANN, CHRISTHARD, 'Jüdische Geschichtswissenschaft in Deutschland, 1918–1938: Konzepte, Schwerpunkte, Ergebnisse', in Julius Carlebach (ed.), *Wissenschaft des Judentums: Anfänge der Judaistik in Europa* (Darmstadt, 1992), 132–52.

HOŃDO, LESZEK, 'Das Verhältnis der Juden in Westgalizien zur polnischen und deutschen Kultur an der Wende vom 19. zum 20. Jahrhundert', in Hans Hecker and Walterh Engel (eds.), *Zwischen Symbiose und Traditionsbruch: deutsch-jüdische Wechselbeziehungen in Ostmittel- und Südosteuropa (19. und 20. Jahrhundert)* (Essen, 2003), 81–93.

HOROWICZ, K. and R. KEMPNER, 'Podatek gminny w Warszawie, 1903–1912', *KPBPŻwP*, 1/3 (1913), 160–5.

HOROWITZ, BRIAN, *Jewish Philanthropy and Enlightenment in Late-Tsarist Russia* (Seattle, 2009).

—— *Russian Idea–Jewish Presence: Essays on Russian-Jewish Intellectual Life* (Boston, 2013).

HOSZOWSKA, MARIOLA, *Szymon Askenazy i jego korespondencja z Ludwikiem Finklem* (Rzeszów, 2013).

HUNDERT, GERSHON, *Jews in a Polish Private Town: The Case of Opatów in the Eighteenth Century* (Baltimore, 1992).

—— (ed.), *The YIVO Encyclopedia of Jews in Eastern Europe*, 2 vols. (New Haven, 2008). Online at <www.yivoencyclopedia.org>.

HUNDERT, GERSHON, and GERSHON C. BACON, *The Jews in Poland and Russia: Bibliographical Essays* (Bloomington, 1984).

INGLOT, STEFAN, 'Rozwój historii społecznej i gospodarczej', *Kwartalnik Historyczny*, 51 (1937), 377–411.

JAGODZIŃSKA, AGNIESZKA, *Pomiędzy: Akulturacja Żydów Warszawy w drugiej połowie XIX wieku* (Wrocław, 2008).

—— and MARCIN WODZIŃSKI (eds.), *'Izraelita' 1866–1915: Wybór źródeł* (Kraków, 2015).

JAKUBOWSKA, U. 'Rybarski Roman Franciszek', *Polski Słownik Biograficzny*, 33 (1991–2), 289–93.

JAMIŃSKI, ZYGMUNT, *Prasa żydowska w Polsce* (Lwów, 1936).

JANOWSKI, MACIEJ, *Narodziny inteligencji, 1750–1831*, Dzieje inteligencji polskiej do roku 1918 1 (Warsaw, 2008).

JEDLICKI, JERZY, *Błędne koło, 1832–1864*, Dzieje inteligencji polskiej do roku 1918 2 (Warsaw, 2008).

—— 'Intelektualiści oporni wobec fali antysemityzmu (Królestwo Polskie w latach 1912–1914)', *Czasy Nowożytne*, 15 (2003), 177–93, repr. in Grażyna Borkowska and Magdalena Rudkowska (eds.), *Kwestia żydowska w XIX wieku: Spory o tożsamość Polaków* (Warsaw, 2004), 463–76.

—— *Jakiej cywilizacji Polacy potrzebują: Studia z dziejów idei i wyobraźni XIX wieku* (Warsaw, 2002).

JERKIEWICZ, LIDIA, '"Kwestia żydowska"' w Królestwie Polskim w latach 1815–1830', Ph.D. diss., Wrocław University, 2014.

JOCKUSCH, LAURA, *Collect and Record! Jewish Holocaust Documentation in Early Postwar Europe* (New York, 2012).

—— 'Introductory Remarks on Simon Dubnow's "Let Us Seek and Investigate"', *Simon Dubnow Institute Yearbook*, 7 (2008), 343–53.

JOLLES, S. (ed.), *Księga jubileuszowa dla uczczenia sześćdziesięciolecia profesora Majera Bałabana* (Warsaw, 1938).

J.Z., 'Prywatna Żydowska Koedukacyjna Średnia Szkoła Handlowa Stow. Żyd. Abs. W. S. H. w Krakowie', in Jakub Zineman (ed.), *Almanach szkolnictwa żydowskiego w Polsce. Trzeci zeszyt okazowy* (Warsaw, 1937), 72–8.

KACZMARCZYK, KAZIMIERZ, 'Wydawnictwa do historji miast polskich', in *Pamiętnik IV: Powszechnego Zjazdu Historyków Polskich w Poznaniu 6–8 grudnia 1925*, vol. i: *Referaty* (Lwów, 1925).

KANDEL, DAWID, 'Berek Joselewicz', *Przegląd Historyczny* 9/3 (1909), 290–8.

—— 'Bóżnica w Pinczowie', *KPBPŻwP*, 1/2 (1912), 28–35.

—— 'Bóżnica w Sandomierzu', *KPBPŻwP*, 1/1 (1912), 10–26.

—— 'Bóżnica w Stepaniu', *KPBPŻwP*, 1/3 (1913), 37–46.

—— 'Elegia na śmierć księcia Józefa', *KPBPŻwP*, 1/2 (1912), 127–31.

—— 'Hymn przy obchodzie uroczystości dnia 3 Maja 1792 roku', *KPBPŻwP*, 1/3 (1913), 166–74.

—— 'Komitet starozakonnych', *KPBPŻwP*, 1/2 (1912), 85–103.

—— 'Montefiore w Warszawie', *KPBPŻwP*, 1/1 (1912), 74–84.

—— 'Z korespondencyi rabina Meiselsa', *KPBPŻwP*, 1/1 (1912), 114–15 and 1/3 (1913), 185–8.

—— 'Z papierów Jakóba Tugendholda', *KPBPŻwP*, 1/3 (1913), 184–5.

—— 'Żydzi w dobie utworzenia Królestwa Kongresowego', *KPBPŻwP*, 1/1 (1912), 95–113.

—— 'Żydzi w roku 1812', *Biblioteka Warszawska*, 1910, vol. 2, 157–75.

—— 'Żydzi w wojsku polskiem w r. 1831', *KPBPŻwP*, 1/3 (1913), 183–4.

KAPLAN, EDWARD K., and SAMUEL H. DRESNER, *Abraham Joshua Heschel: Prophetic Witness* (New Haven, 1998).

KARWASIŃSKA, JADWIGA, 'Ringelblum Emanuel: Żydzi w Warszawie. I. Od czasów najdawniejszych do ostatniego wygnania w r. 1527', review, *Roczniki Dziejów Społecznych i Gospodarczych*, 3 (1934), 577–81.

KASSOW, SAMUEL D., 'Polish–Jewish Relations in the Writings of Emmanuel Ringelblum', in Joshua D. Zimmerman (ed.), *Contested Memories: Poles and Jews during the Holocaust and in Its Aftermath* (New Brunswick, NJ, 2003), 142–57.

—— 'Travel and Local History as a National Mission: Polish Jews and the Landkentenish Movement in the 1920s and 1930s', in Julia Brauch, Anna Lipphardt, and Alexandra Nocke (eds.), *Jewish Topographies: Visions of Space, Traditions of Place* (Aldershot, 2008).

—— *Who Will Write Our History? Emanuel Ringelblum, the Warsaw Ghetto, and the Oyneg Shabes Archive* (Bloomington, 2007).

KATZ, JACOB, *From Prejudice to Destruction: Anti-Semitism, 1700–1933* (Cambridge, Mass., 1980).

KAZDAN, HAYYIM SOLOMON, *The History of Jewish Schools in Independent Poland* [Di geshikhte fun yidishn shulvezn in umophengikn poyln. meksiko: Gezelshaft 'Kultur un hilf'] (Meksike, 1947).

KEMPNER, RAFAŁ, 'Agonia Kahału', *KPBPŻwP*, 1/1 (1912), 67–73.

KENAN, ORNA, 'Between History and Memory. Israeli Historiography of the Holocaust: The Period of "Gestation", from the Mid-1940s to the Eichmann Trial in 1961', Ph.D. diss., University of California, Los Angeles, 2000.

KERMISZ, JÓZEF, 'Nieznany list patriotyczny rabina do Kościuszki z roku 1792', *Głos Gminy Żydowskiej*, 1937, no. 4, 87–8.

—— 'Żydzi warszawscy w Insurekcji Kościuszkowskiej (W 145 rocznicę powstania 1794 r.)', *Głos Gminy Żydowskiej*, 1939, nos. 5–6, 121–3.

KIENIEWICZ, STEFAN, *Joachim Lelewel* (Warsaw, 1990).

KIJEK, KAMIL, *Dzieci modernizmu: Świadomość, kultura i socjalizacja polityczna młodzieży żydowskiej w II Rzeczypospolitej* (Wrocław, 2017).

KIPA, EMIL, 'Berka Joselewicza projekt legionu ochotniczego dla Austryi w r. 1796', *Przewodnik Naukowy i Literacki*, 42/3 (1914), 537–48.

—— 'Prawda o Askenazym', in id., *Studia i szkice historyczne* (Wrocław, 1959), 183–97.

—— 'Z r. 1848', *KPBPŻwP*, 1/2 (1912), 139–40.

KIRSZENBAUM, H., 'Bractwo Pogrzebowe na Pradze', *KPBPŻwP*, 1/3 (1913), 133–46.

KIRSZROT, JAKÓB, *Prawa Żydów w Królestwie Polskiem: Zarys historyczny* (Warsaw, 1917).

—— [as Jakób K-t], 'Żydzi w Warszawie', *Izraelita*, 1866, nos. 24–26.

KLIŚ, ANDRZEJ, and CZESŁAW MAJOREK, 'Doktoraty historyczne w Uniwersytecie Jagiellońskim w latach 1918–1939', in Jerzy Maternicki (ed.), *Środowiska historyczne II Rzeczypospolitej* (Warsaw, 1989), iii. 154–73.

KNOT, ANTONI, 'Tadeusz Czacki', *Polski Słownik Biograficzny*, 4 (1938), 144–6.

KOCZY, LEON, *Handel Poznania do połowy wieku XVI*, Prace Komisji Historycznej Poznańskiego Towarzystwa Przyjaciół Nauk 6 (Poznań, 1930).

—— 'Studja nad dziejami gospodarczemi Żydów poznańskich przed połową wieku XVII', *Kronika Miasta Poznania*, 3 (1934), 257–99; 4 (1934), 333–62; 1 (1935), 47–63; 2–3 (1935), 171–231.

KOFLER, OSKAR, *Żydowskie dwory: Wspomnienia z Galicji Wschodniej od początku XIX wieku do wybuchu I wojny światowej* (Warsaw, 1999).

'Koło Historyczne', *Nasze Życie*, 3/1–2 (1932), 9.

KOŁODZIEJSKA, ZUZANNA, *'Izraelita' (1866–1915): Znaczenie kulturowe i literackie czasopisma* (Kraków, 2014).

KON, PINCHAS, 'Odnaleziona część Archiwum dawnego Kahału Wileńskiego', *Ateneum Wileńskie*, 5 (1928), 151–66.

—— 'Przyczynki do historji Żydów w Lubczy', *YIVO Bleter*, Jan.–May 1932: 468–72.

—— 'The Recently Found Portions of the Wilno Kehilah Archives' (Yid.), *Historishe shriftn*, 2 (1937), 538–48.

KONECZNY, FELIKS, *Cywilizacja żydowska* (Komorów, 1997).

—— *Państwo i prawo w cywilizacji łacińskiej* (Warsaw, 2001).

KONIC, WŁADYSŁAW, 'Z galerii zasłużonych Żydów polskich: Dr Ludwik Natanson (1822–1896)', *Głos Gminy Żydowskiej*, 1937, no. 4, 91–2 and no. 5, 113.

—— 'Żydzi w Legionach Józefa Piłsudskiego', *Głos Gminy Żydowskiej*, 1938, nos. 10–11, 239–41.

—— 'Żydzi w Legjonach w okresie 1914–1917', *Nasz Przegląd*, 11 Aug. 1932, no 222, 6.

'Konkurs naukowy z ofiary p. Hipolita Wawelberga', *Izraelita*, 1900, no. 29, 347.

KONOPCZYŃSKI, WŁADYSŁAW, 'Rozwój badań nad dziejami Polski Nowożytnej 1506–1795', *Kwartalnik Historyczny*, 51 (1937), 289–302.

KOPCIOWSKI, ADAM, *Wos hert zich in der prowinc: Prasa żydowska na Lubelszczyźnie i jej największy dziennik 'Lubliner Tugblat'* (Lublin, 2015).

KORZEN, MEIR, 'The Jewish Gymnasium' (Heb.), in Kathariel F. Thursh and Meir Korzen (eds.), *Vloclaveck and Its Environs: Memorial Book* [Vloclaveck vehasevivah: sefer zikaron] (Tel Aviv, 1967), 381–402.

KORZENNIK, MEIR, 'Gimnazjum Męskie "Tachkemoni" stow. "Cheder Iwri" w Krakowie', in Jakub Zineman (ed.), *Almanach Szkolnictwa Żydowskiego w Polsce. Trzeci zeszyt okazowy* (Warsaw, 1937), 102–5.

KORZON, TADEUSZ, 'Kraushar Aleksander: Frank i Frankiści polscy 1726–1816. Monografia historyczna osnuta na źródłach archiwalnych i rękopiśmiennych', review, *Kwartalnik Historyczny*, 12 (1898), 415–30.

KOWALSKI, TADEUSZ ANTONI, *Mniejszości narodowe w siłach zbrojnych Drugiej Rzeczypospolitej Polskiej (1918–1939)* (Toruń, 1997).

KOZIŃSKA-WITT, HANNA, 'Ludwig Gumplowicz's Programme for the Improvement of the Jewish Situation', in Israel Bartal and Antony Polonsky (eds.), *Focusing on Galicia: Jews, Poles, and Ukrainians, 1772–1918*, Polin 12 (1999), 73–8.

KOZŁOWSKA, MAGDALENA, '"Folkscajtung" (1921–1939)', in Joanna Nalewajko-Kulikov (ed.), *Studia z dziejów trójjęzycznej prasy żydowskiej na ziemiach polskich (XIX–XX w.)* (Warsaw, 2012), 89–99.

KRÄMER, MOJŻESZ, 'Prof. M. Bałaban—Jubilatem', in S. Jolles (ed.), *Księga jubileuszowa dla uczczenia sześćdziesięciolecia profesora Majera Bałabana* (Warsaw, 1938), 87.

KRAUSHAR, ALEKSANDER, *Echa przeszłości: Szkice, wizerunki i wspomnienia historyczne* (Warsaw, 1917).

—— *Frank i Frankiści polscy 1726–1816: Monografia historyczna osnuta na źródłach archiwalnych i rękopiśmiennych*, 2 vols. (Kraków, 1895).

—— *Historya Żydów w Polsce*, 2 vols. (Warsaw, 1865–6).

—— 'Ludwik Gumplowicz (nieco wspomnień osobistych)', in *Echa przeszłości: szkice, wizerunki i wspomnienia historyczne* (Warsaw, 1917).

KRIEG, 'Prywatne Koedukacyjne Gimnazjum', in Jakub Zineman (ed.), *Almanach szkolnictwa żydowskiego w Polsce. Trzeci zeszyt okazowy* (Warsaw, 1937), 113–18.

KRONE, MOSHE, *My Teachers and Rabbis, Brothers and Friends: Memoirs* [Morai verabotai, ahai vere'ai: pirkei zikhronot] (Tel Aviv, 1987).

KRUK, HERMAN, *The Last Days of the Jerusalem of Lithuania: Chronicles from the Vilna Ghetto and the Camps, 1939–1944*, trans. Barbara Harshav, ed. Benjamin Hashav (New Haven, 2002).

*Książka adresowa członków Żyd. Stow. Humanitarnego 'B'ne B'rith' w Polsce* (Kraków, 1926).

*Księga jubileuszowa ku czci d-ra Markusa Braudego* (Warsaw, 1931).

*Księga jubileuszowa ku czci prof. d-ra Mojżesza Schorra* (Warsaw, 1935).

*Księga pamiątkowa ku czci dra Samuela Poznańskiego (1864–1921) ofiarowana przez przyjaciół i towarzyszy pracy naukowej* (Warsaw, 1927).

*Księga pamiątkowa ku uczczeniu dwudziestopięcioletniej działalności naukowej prof. Marcelego Handelsmana* (Warsaw, 1929).

KULA, MARCIN, *Autoportret rodziny X: Fragment żydowskiej Warszawy lat międzywojennych* (Warsaw, 2007).

KULCZYKOWSKI, MARIUSZ, Żydzi—studenci Uniwersytetu Jagiellońskiego w Drugiej Rzeczypospolitej, 1918–1939 (Kraków, 2004).

KUTRZEBA, STANISŁAW, Sprawa żydowska w Polsce (Lwów, 1918).

—— 'W sprawie historyi miast w Polsce', in Pamiętnik III. Zjazdu Historyków Polskich w Krakowie, urządzonego przez Towarzystwo Historyczne Lwowskie w dniach 4, 5 i 6 czerwca 1900, i (Kraków, 1900).

KUZNITZ, CECILE ESTHER, 'An-sky's Legacy: The Vilna Historic-Ethnographic Society and the Shaping of Modern Jewish Culture', in Gabriella Safran and Steven J. Zipperstein (eds.), The Worlds of S. An-sky: A Russian Jewish Intellectual at the Turn of the Century (Stanford, 2006), 320–45.

KUZNITZ, CECILE ESTHER, YIVO and the Making of Modern Jewish Culture: Scholarship for the Yiddish Nation (New York, 2014).

L.H., 'Kronika: O uniwersytet żydowski', Nowe Życie, 1/4–6 (September–December 1924), 271–4.

L-T, 'Z piśmiennictwa: "O dawniejszych bóżnicach drewnianych w Polsce"', Izraelita, 1899, no. 46, 512.

LANDAU, MOSHE, 'Neufeld Daniel', in Michael Berenbaum and Fred Skolnik (eds.), Encyclopaedia Judaica, 2nd edn. (Detroit, 2007), xv. 117–18.

LANDAU-CZAJKA, ANNA, Syn będzie Lech... Asymilacja Żydów w Polsce międzywojennej (Warsaw, 2006).

—— W jednym stali domu... Koncepcje rozwiązania kwestii żydowskiej w publicystyce polskiej lat 1933–1939 (Warsaw, 1998).

—— 'Żydzi w oczach prasy katolickiej okresu II Rzeczypospolitej', Przegląd Polonijny, 4 (1992), 97–113.

LANDY, HENRYK, 'Zapiska o Michale Landym', KPBPŻwP, 1/3 (1913), 188–90.

LAUER, BERNARD, 'Przyczynek do historyi żydów krakowskich', KPBPŻwP, 1/2 (1912), 117–21.

—— 'Zum Polnisch–Jüdischen Problem (vom Standpunkt eines polnischen Juden)', Preussische Jahrbücher, 162/2 (1915), 281–301.

LEFF, LISA M., The Archive Thief: The Man Who Salvaged French Jewish History in the Wake of the Holocaust (New York, 2015).

LEWIN, IZAK, 'Staszic a Żydzi', Chwila, 20 Jan. 1926, 5.

—— 'Staszic a Żydzi', Nowy Dziennik, 18 Jan. 1926, 5–6.

—— 'Staszic a Żydzi: Dokończenie,' Nowy Dziennik, 20 Jan. 1926, p. 5.

—— 'Udział Żydów w wyborach sejmowych w dawnej Polsce', Miesięcznik Żydowski, 2/1 (1932), 46–65.

—— 'Wyższa Uczelnia Talmudyczna w Lublinie', Miesięcznik Żydowski, 1/11 (1931), 455–61.

LIBERLES, ROBERT, Salo Wittmayer Baron: Architect of Jewish History (New York, 1995).

LITMAN, JACOB, The Economic Role of Jews in Medieval Poland: The Contribution of Yitzhak Schipper (Lanham, 1984).

LÖWENSOHN, YITZHAK BAER, *A Call in Israel* [Te'udah beyisra'el] (Wilno, 1828).

LUTMAN, TADEUSZ, 'Marek Wischnitzer's *Die Stellung der Brodyer Juden im internationalen Handel der zweiten Hälfte des XVIII Jahrhunderts*', review, *Roczniki Dziejów Społecznych i Gospodarczych*, 1 (1931), 308–10.

—— 'Schiper Ignacy: Dzieje handlu żydowskiego w Polsce', review, *Roczniki Dziejów Społecznych i Gospodarczych*, 8 (1939), 189–91.

—— *Studja nad dziejami handlu Brodów w latach 1773–1880* (Lwów, 1937).

—— 'Wurm Dawid: Z dziejów żydostwa brodzkiego za czasów dawnej Rzeczypospolitej Polskiej', review, *Roczniki Dziejów Społecznych i Gospodarczych*, 6 (1937), 418–24.

MACIEJOWSKI, WACŁAW ALEKSANDER, *Żydzi w Polsce, na Rusi i Litwie: czyli opowieść historyczna o przybyciu do pomienionych krajów dziatwy Izraela—i o powodzeniu jej tamże w przestworze VIII–XVIII wieku* (Warsaw, 1878).

MAHLER, RAPHAEL, 'The Circle of Young Historians in Warsaw' (Heb.), in Bela Mandelsberg-Schildkraut, *Studies in the History of Lublin Jewry* [Meḥkarim letoledot yehudei lublin [me'et] bela mandelsberg-schildkroit] (Tel Aviv, 1965).

—— 'The Circle of Young Historians in Warsaw' (Yid.), in *Historians and Guides* [Historiker un vegvayzer] (Tel Aviv, 1967), 302–15.

—— *Historians and Guides* [Historiker un vegvayzer] (Tel Aviv, 1967).

—— 'History and People' (Yid.), *Yunger historiker*, 1 (1926), 12–17.

—— *Jews in Poland Between the Two World Wars: A Socio-Economic History on a Statistical Basis* [Yehudei polin bein shetei milḥamot olam: historyah kalkalit-sotsyalit le'or hastatistikah] (Tel Aviv, 1968).

—— 'Jews in Public Service and the Liberal Professions in Poland, 1918–39', *Jewish Social Studies*, 6/4 (1944), 291–350.

—— 'Statistical Information about Jews in the Lublin Voivodship in the Years 1764–65' (Yid.), *Yunger historiker*, 2 (1929), 67–108.

—— (ed.), *The Jews of Częstochowa* [Tshenstokhover yidn] (New York, 1947).

MAKOWSKI, KRZYSZTOF, *Siła mitu: Żydzi w Poznańskiem w dobie zaborów w piśmiennictwie historycznym* (Poznań, 2004).

MANDELSBERG, BELA, 'Jewish Artisans in Lublin and the City Guilds' (Yid.), *Yunger historiker*, 2 (1929), 54–66.

MANDELSBERG-SHILKRAUT, BELA, *Studies in the History of Lublin Jewry* [Meḥkarim letoledot yehudei lublin] (Tel Aviv, 1965).

MANEKIN, RACHEL, 'Constructing Polish Jewry's "Shrine of History": Galician Beginnings', in Natalia Aleksiun, Brian Horowitz, and Antony Polonsky (eds.), *Writing Jewish History in Eastern Europe*, Polin 29 (Oxford, 2017), 77–87.

—— 'The Galician Roots of the Historiography of Polish Jewry' (Heb.), in Daniel Blatman (ed.), *Conflicting Histories and Coexistence: New Perspectives on the Jewish–Polish Encounter* [Historyah mitnageshet vekiyum meshutaf: perspektivot ḥadashot al hamifgash hayehudi–polani] (Jerusalem, 2014), 319–31.

MANTEUFFEL, TADEUSZ, 'Marceli Handelsman jako nauczyciel', *Przegląd Historyczny*, 36 (1946), 9–11.

—— *Uniwersytet Warszawski w latach 1915/16–1934/35: Kronika* (Warsaw, 1936).

MARCINKOWSKI, ROMAN, 'Luigi Chiarini (1789–1832): An Anti-Judaistic Reformer of Judaism', *Studia Judaica*, 7/2 (14) (2004), 237–48.

MARRUS, MICHAEL R., *The Politics of Assimilation: A Study of the French Jewish Community at the Time of the Dreyfus Affair* (Oxford, 1971).

MARYLSKI, ANTONI, *Dzieje sprawy żydowskiej w Polsce* (Warsaw, 1912).

MAŚLAK-MACIEJEWSKA, ALICJA, *Rabin Szymon Dankowicz (1834–1910)—życie i działalność* (Kraków, 2013).

MATERNICKI, JERZY, 'Historia nowożytna w latach 1869–1918', in Jerzy Maternicki, Joanna Pisulińska, and Leonid Zaszkilniak (eds.), *Historia w Uniwersytecie Lwowskim: Badania i nauczanie do 1939 roku* (Rzeszów, 2016), 255–300.

—— *Historiografia polska XX wieku: Część I: Lata 1900–1918* (Wrocław, 1982).

—— '"Historyk sługą narodu": Poglądy Adama Naruszewicza, Joachima Lelewela, Tadeusza Korzona i Szymona Askenazego', in Joanna Pisulińska, Paweł Sierżęga, and Leonid Zaszkilniak (eds.), *Historia, mentalność, tożsamość: Miejsce i rola historii oraz historyków w życiu narodu polskiego i ukraińskiego w XIX i XX wieku* (Rzeszów, 2008), 44–77.

—— 'Kraushar Aleksander, pseud. Alkar', *Polski Słownik Biograficzny*, 15 (1970), 241–4.

—— JOANNA PISULIŃSKA, and LEONID ZASZKILNIAK (eds.), *Historia w Uniwersytecie Lwowskim: badania i nauczanie do 1939 roku* (Rzeszów, 2016).

—— and LEONID ZASZKILNIAK (eds.), *Złota księga historiografii lwowskiej XIX i XX wieku* (Rzeszów, 2007).

MEISELMAN, SHULAMIT SOLOVEITCHIK, *The Soloveitchik Heritage: A Daughter's Memoir* (Hoboken, NJ, 1995).

MELZER, EMANUEL, 'Antisemitism in the Last Years of the Second Polish Republic', in Yisrael Gutman, Ezra Mendelsohn, Jehuda Reinharz, and Chone Shmeruk (eds.), *The Jews of Poland Between Two World Wars* (Hanover, NH, 1989), 126–37.

—— *No Way Out: The Politics of Polish Jewry 1935–1939* (Cincinnati, 1997).

*Memorial Volume of the Viennese Rabbinical Seminary: Recollections and Scholarly Studies* [Sefer hazikaron leveit hamidrash lerabanim bevina: divrei zikhronot vedivrei mada] (Jerusalem, 1946).

MENDELSOHN, EZRA, 'Jewish Assimilation in L'viv: The Case of Wilhelm Feldman', in Andrei S. Markovits and Frank E. Sysyn (eds.), *Nationbuilding and the Politics of Nationalism: Essays on Austrian Galicia* (Cambridge, 1982), 94–110.

—— *The Jews of East Central Europe Between the World Wars* (Bloomington, 1983).

—— 'A Note on Jewish Assimilation in the Polish Lands', in Bela Vago (ed.), *Jewish Assimilation in Modern Times* (Boulder, 1981), 141–9.

—— *Zionism in Poland: The Formative Years 1915–1926* (New Haven, 1981).

M[ERMELSTEIN], W. 'Klauzner, Izrael Mgr. "Dzieje starego cmentarza żydowskiego w Wilnie", Wilno 1935', *Ateneum Wileńskie*, 11 (1936), 630–1.

MEYER, MICHAEL A., 'Jewish Religious Reform and Wissenschaft des Judentums: The Positions of Zunz, Geiger and Frankel', *Leo Baeck Institute Yearbook*, 16 (1971), 19–41.

—— *Response to Modernity: A History of the Reform Movement in Judaism* (Detroit, 1988), 75–99.

—— 'Two Persistent Tensions within Wissenschaft des Judentums', *Modern Judaism*, 24/2 (2004), 105–19.

MICHALSKI, JERZY, 'Smoleński Władysław', *Polski Słownik Biograficzny*, 39 (1999), 276–85.

MICHLIC, JOANNA B., *Poland's Threatening Other: The Image of the Jew from 1880 to the Present* (Lincoln, 2006).

MICIŃSKA, MAGDALENA, *Gołąb i Orzeł: Obchody rocznic kościuszkowskich w latach 1894 i 1917* (Warsaw, 1997).

—— *Inteligencja na rozdrożach, 1864–1918*, Dzieje inteligencji polskiej do roku 1918 3 (Warsaw, 2008).

MIESES, MATEUSZ, *Hellenizm a Judaizim (Uwagi na marginesie książki Tadeusza Zielińskiego pod powyższym tytułem)* (Przemyśl, 1928).

—— 'A Jewish Battalion Defends Praga (on the Anniversary of the Praga Massacres on 4 November 1794)' (Yid.), *Der moment*, 30 Oct. 1936, 7.

—— 'Ofiarność Żydów dla armii w czasach wojennych w dziejach Polski', *Nasz Przegląd*, 7 and 14 May 1939.

—— Rzemiosło w dziejach Żydów, *Głos Gminy Żydowskiej*, 1939, nos 7–8, 217–33.

—— 'Udział Żydów Polskich w nauce (wiek XIX i początek XX w. do 1918 r.)', in Schiper, Tartakower, and Hafftka (eds.), *Żydzi w Polsce Odrodzonej*, ii. 24–59.

—— 'Żyd w polskiej służbie dyplomatycznej w XVI wieku', *Chwila*, 2 Feb. 1935, 8.

—— 'Żydzi jako rolnicy w dawnej Polsce', *Głos Gminy Żydowskiej*, 1937, no. 5, 106–7.

—— 'Żydzi w akcji wyzwolenia Polski', *Głos Gminy Żydowskiej*, 1938, nos. 10–11, 235–8.

—— 'Żydzi w armiach średniowiecznej Europy', *Nasz Przegląd*, 14 Feb. 1937.

—— 'Żydzi w służbie dyplomatycznej w średniowieczu', *Chwila*, 27 Jan. 1935, 7.

MIKULSKI, ZDZISŁAW (ed.), *200-lecie Towarzystwa Królewskiego Warszawskiego Przyjaciół Nauk* (Warsaw, 2001).

MIŁOSZ, CZESŁAW, *Milosz's ABC's*, trans. Madeline G. Levine (New York, 2001).

MIRON, DAN, 'Between Science and Faith: Sixty Years of the YIVO Institute', *YIVO Annual of Jewish Social Science*, 19 (1990), 1–15.

MIRSKI, SHMUEL (ed.), *Personalities and Figures in Wissenschaft des Judentums in Eastern Europe before Its Decline* [Ishim udemuyot beḥokhmat yisra'el be'eiropah hamizraḥit lifnei shekiatah] (New York, 1959).

MISHAEL, YITZHAK, 'The Takhkemoni Rabbinical Seminary in Warsaw' (Heb.), in Shmuel K. Mirski (ed.), *Jewish Institutions of Higher Learning in Europe: Their Development and Destruction* [Mosedot torah be'eiropah bevinyanam uveḥurbanam] (New York, 1957), 585–603.

MOHRER, FRUMA, and MAREK WEB (eds.), *Guide to the YIVO Archives* (New York, 1998).

MOŚCICKI, HENRYK, 'Historiografia powstania styczniowego ostatnich lat piętnastu', *Przegląd Historyczny*, 34/2 (1937–8), 389–407.

—— 'Żydzi polscy pod berłem Katarzyny II', *KPBPŻwP*, 1/1 (1912), 54–66.

MOSS, KENNETH B., *Jewish Renaissance in the Russian Revolution* (Cambridge, Mass., 2009).

MÜLLER, MICHAEL G., 'Majer Bałaban (1877–1942) und das Konzept einer polnisch-jüdischen Geschichte', *Simon Dubnow Institute Yearbook*, 2 (2003), 387–406.

MYERS, DAVID N., 'The Ideology of *Wissenschaft des Judentums*', in Daniel H. Frank and Oliver Leaman (eds.), *History of Jewish Philosophy* (London, 1997), 706–20.

—— *Reinventing the Jewish Past: European Jewish Intellectuals and the Zionist Return to History* (New York, 1995).

—— and ALEXANDER KAYE (eds.), *The Faith of Fallen Jews: Yosef Hayim Yerushalmi and the Writing of Jewish History* (Waltham, 2014).

—— and DAVID B. RUDERMAN (eds.), *The Jewish Past Revisited: Reflections on Modern Jewish Historians* (New Haven, 1998).

NALEWAJKO-KULIKOV, JOANNA, '"Hajnt" (1908–1939)', in ead. (ed.), *Studia z dziejów trójjęzycznej prasy żydowskiej na ziemiach polskich (XIX–XX w.)* (Warsaw, 2012), 61–75.

—— 'Prasa żydowska na ziemiach polskich: historia, stan badań, perspektywy badawcze', in ead. (ed.), *Studia z dziejów trójjęzycznej prasy żydowskiej na ziemiach polskich (XIX–XX w.)* (Warsaw, 2012), 7–30.

—— 'Three Colors: Grey. Study for a Portrait of Bernard Mark', *Holocaust: Studies and Materials*, 2 (2010), 205–26.

NAMYSŁO, ALEKSANDRA, 'The Religious Life of Katowice Jews in the Inter-War Period', in Marcin Wodziński and Janusz Spyra (eds.), *Jews in Silesia* (Kraków, 2001), 125–38.

NATHANS, BENJAMIN, *Beyond the Pale: The Jewish Encounter with Late Imperial Russia* (Berkeley, 2002).

—— 'On Russian-Jewish Historiography', in Thomas Sanders (ed.), *Historiography of Imperial Russia: The Profession and Writing of History in a Multinational State* (Armonk, NY, 1999), 397–432.

NATKOWSKA, MONIKA, *'Numerus clausus', getto ławkowe, 'numerus nullus', 'paragraf aryjski': Antysemityzm na Uniwersytecie Warszawskim 1931–1939* (Warsaw, 1999).

NEUFELD, DANIEL, *Pięcioksiąg Mojżesza dla Żydów-Polaków* (Warsaw, 1863).

—— *Pirke Aboth: Gnomologia Ojców Synagogi. Zbiór zdań, zasad i maksym stanowiących osobny traktat w Misznach. Tekst hebrajski, z tłómaczeniem polskiem i uwagami* (Warsaw, 1865).

—— *Syfse Jeszenim, czyli Modły starożytne Izraelitów na cały rok, tekst hebrajski z nowym przekładem polskim z komentarzem Moreh Derech, czyli wykładem i objaśnieniem znaczenia historycznego i społecznego tych modlitw i obrządków religijnych, do których się odnoszą* (Warsaw, 1865).

—— *Urządzenie konsystorza żydowskiego w Polsce* (Warsaw, 1863).

NISSENBAUM, SHLOMO BARUCH, *History of the Jews of Lublin* [Lekorot hayehudim belublin] (Lublin, 1899).

NOWAKOWSKA, KRYSTYNA, *Tak było w Niemczech* (Warsaw, 1950).

NUROWSKI, MARCIN, *Szymon Askenazy: Wielki Polak wyznania mojżeszowego* (Warsaw, 2005).

NUSSBAUM, HILARY, *Historyja Żydów od Mojżesza do epoki obecnej*, 5 vols. (Warsaw, 1888–90).

—— *Szkice historyczne z życia Żydów w Warszawie od pierwszych śladów pobytu ich w tem mieście do chwili obecnej* (Warsaw, 1881).

OBERLAENDER, LUDWIK 'Dziewięć wieków współżycia', *Miesięcznik Żydowski*, 1/2 (1931), 97–111.

OCHYŃSKA, JANINA, 'Gumplowicz Maksymilian Ernest', *Polski Słownik Biograficzny*, 9 (1960), 153.

'Od wydawnictwa', *Tel-Awiw*, 1/1 (June 1919), 1–2.

'Odezwa Komitetu Synagogi', *Izraelita*, 1899, no. 27, 298–9.

OPALSKI, MAGDALENA, and ISRAEL BARTAL, *Poles and Jews: A Failed Brotherhood* (Hanover, NH, 1992).

ORENSTEIN, BENJAMIN, *The Life and Work of Dr Filip Friedman: A Short Biography and Bibliographic Overview* [Dos lebn un shafn fun dr philip friedman: kurtser bio-bibliografisher iberblik] (Montreal, 1962).

OSTERSETZER, IZRAEL, 'Instytut Nauk Judaistycznych w Warszawie', *Miesięcznik Żydowski*, 1/9 (1931), 262–73.

—— 'Majer Bałaban—historiograf żydostwa polskiego', in S. Jolles (ed.), *Księga jubileuszowa dla uczczenia sześćdziesięciolecia profesora Majera Bałabana* (Warsaw, 1938).

PACZKOWSKI, ANDRZEJ, *Prasa codzienna Warszawy w latach 1918–1939* (Warsaw, 1983).

*Pamiętnik III: Zjazdu Historyków Polskich w Krakowie urządzonego przez Towarzystwo Historyczne Lwowskie w dniach 4, 5 i 6 czerwca 1900*, 2 vols. (Kraków, 1900–1).

*Pamiętnik IV: Powszechnego Zjazdu Historyków Polskich w Poznaniu 6–8 grudnia 1925*, 2 vols. (Lwów, 1925–7).

*Pamiętnik V: Powszechnego Zjazdu Historyków Polskich w Warszawie 28 listopada do 4 grudnia 1930 r.*, 2 vols. (Lwów, 1930–1).

*Pamiętnik VI: Powszechnego Zjazdu Historyków Polskich w Wilnie 17–20 września 1935 r.*, 2 vols. (Lwów, 1935–6).

*Pamiętnik Drugiego Zjazdu Historyków Polskich we Lwowie*, 2 vols. (Lwów 1890–1).

PAPÉE, FRYDERYK, *Historya miasta Lwowa w zarysie* (Lwów, 1894).

PATKANIOWSKI, MICHAŁ, 'Mojżesz Schorr (1874–1940)', *Kwartalnik Historyczny*, 53/3–4 (1946), 598–600.

PAWELEC, TOMASZ, 'Bronisław Dembiński (1858–1939)', in Jerzy Maternicki and Leonid Zaszkilniak (eds.), *Złota księga historiografii lwowskiej XIX i XX wieku* (Rzeszów, 2007), 269–84.

PAWLAK, GRAŻYNA (ed.), *Księgi życia profesora Mojżesza Schorra* (Warsaw, 2005).

PAZDRO, ZBIGNIEW, *Organizacya i praktyka żydowskich sądów podwojewodzińskich w okresie 1740–1772 r.: na podstawie lwowskich materyałów archiwalnych* (Lwów, 1903).

—— *Przyczynek do historyi morderstw rytualnych* (Lwów, 1899).

PEDYCZ, WASYL, 'Myron Korduba (1876–1947)', in Jerzy Maternicki and Leonid Zaszkilniak (eds.), *Złota księga historiografii lwowskiej XIX i XX wieku* (Rzeszów, 2007), 453–66.

PELTYN, SAMUEL, 'Żydzi ze stanowiska ekonomii publicznej uważani (Dokończenie)', *Izraelita*, 1867, no. 10, 81–3.

PETERSEN, HEIDEMARIE, '"We see our History not as a Historical Fossil": The Historical Section of the YIVO and the Jewish History-Writing in Interwar Poland' (Yid.), in Marina Dmitrieva and Heidemarie Petersen (eds.), *Jüdische Kultur(en) im Neuen Europa: Wilna 1918–1939* (Wiesbaden, 2004), 163–79.

PIERADZKA, KRYSTYNA, 'Majer Bałaban (1877–1943)', *Kwartalnik Historyczny*, 53/3–4 (1946), 414–15.

PILCH, ANDRZEJ, *'Rzeczpospolita Akademicka': Studenci i polityka 1918–1933* (Kraków, 1997).

PINSON, KOPPEL S., 'Simon Dubnow: Historian and Political Philosopher', in id. (ed.), *Simon Dubnow, Nationalism and History: Essays on Old and New Judaism* (Philadelphia, 1958), 3–65.

PISULIŃSKA, JOANNA, 'Doktoraty historyczne na Uniwersytecie Jana Kazimierza 1918–1939', in Jerzy Maternicki (ed.), *Wielokulturowe środowisko historyczne Lwowa w XIX i XX w.*, vol. i (Rzeszów, 2004), 233–49.

—— 'Obraz społeczności żydowskiej w pracach historyków szkoły lelewelowskiej', in Monika Adamczyk-Garbowska and Konrad Zieliński (eds.), *Ortodoksja, emancypacja, asymilacja: Studia z dziejów ludności żydowskiej na ziemiach polskich w okresie rozbiorów* (Lublin, 2003), 13–24.

—— 'Problematyka żydowska w pracach historyków tzw. lwowskiej szkoły historycznej', in Jerzy Maternicki and Leonid Zaszkilniak (eds.), *Wielokulturowe środowisko historyczne Lwowa w XIX i XX w.*, vol. ii (Rzeszów, 2004), 192–200.

—— *Żydzi w polskiej myśli historycznej doby porozbiorowej (1795–1914): Syntezy, parasyntezy i podręczniki dziejów ojczystych* (Rzeszów, 2004).

POLONSKY, ANTONY, *The Jews in Poland and Russia*, 3 vols.: i: *1350 to 1881*; ii: *1881 to 1914*; iii: *1914 to 2008* (Oxford, 2010–12).

—— 'Polish–Jewish Relations since 1984: Reflections of a Participant', in Robert Cherry and Annamaria Orla-Bukowska (eds.), *Rethinking Poles and Jews: Troubled Past, Brighter Future* (Lanham, Md., 2007), 121–36.

—— 'Prace Artura Eisenbacha: Bibliografia', *Biuletyn ŻIH*, 164 (1992), 13–18.

—— 'Warszawska Szkoła Rabinów: Orędowniczka narodowej integracji w Królestwie Polskim, in M. Galas (ed.), *Duchowość żydowska w Polsce* (Kraków, 2000), 287–307.

PORTER, BRIAN, *When Nationalism Began to Hate: Imagining Modern Politics in Nineteenth-Century Poland* (New York, 2000).

POZNAŃSKI, SAMUEL, 'Widoki nauki judaistycznej w nowotworzącej się Polsce (Warszawa)', in Z. F. Finkelstein (ed.), *Almanach Żydowski na rok 5678 (1917/1918)* (Vienna, 1918), 225–9.

PROKOP-JANIEC, EUGENIA, *Polish-Jewish Literature in the Interwar Years* (Syracuse, NY, 2003).

PTAŚNIK, JAN, *Miasta Polskie w Polsce* (Lwów, 1922).

RABSKA, ZUZANNA, 'Bersohn Mathias', *Polski Słownik Biograficzny*, 1 (1935), 469–70.

RACHUBA, ANDRZEJ, and HENRYK RUTKOWSKI (eds.), *Towarzystwo Miłośników Historii: Stulecie 1906–2006* (Warsaw, 2006).

RASKIN, DWOJRA, *Ks. Profesor Ludwik Alojzy Chiarini w Warszawie ze szczególnym uwzględnieniem jego stosunku do Żydów* (Warsaw, 2012).

RASSIN, ARJE, 'Umysłowość i moralność żydostwa polskiego w XVII i XVIII wieku świetle literatury religijno-ludowej', *Miesięcznik Żydowski*, 2/11–12 (1932), 434–65.

RAWICZ, MELECH, untitled article, in I. Kahan (ed.), *The Book of Buczacz: Memorial Stone for a Holy Community* [Sefer butsats: matsevet zikaron likehilah kedoshah] (Tel Aviv, 1956), 227–8.

RECHTER, DAVID, *Becoming Habsburg: The Jews of Austrian Bukovina 1774–1918* (Oxford, 2013).

REIN, ARIELLE, 'The Historian as a Nation-Builder: Ben Zion Dinur's Evolution and Enterprise (1884–1948)', Ph.D. diss., Hebrew University, Jerusalem, 2000.

REZMER, WALDEMAR, 'Służba wojskowa Żydów w siłach zbrojnych Drugiej Rzeczypospolitej', in Zbigniew Karpus and Waldemar Rezmer (eds.), *Mniejszości narodowe i wyznaniowe w siłach zbrojnych Drugiej Rzeczypospolitej 1918–1939* (Toruń, 2001), 97–110.

RINGELBLUM, EMANUEL, 'Historja Żydów na VII Międzynarodowym Zjeździe Nauk Historycznych w Warszawie', *Miesięcznik Żydowski*, 3/11–12 (1933), 258–60.

—— *Kronika getta warszawskiego: wrzesień 1939—styczeń 1943*, ed. Artur Eisenbach, trans. from the Yiddish by Adam Rutkowski (Warsaw, 1983).

—— *Notes from the Warsaw Ghetto: The Journal of Emmanuel Ringelblum*, ed. and trans. Jacob Sloan (New York, 1974).

RINGELBLUM, EMANUEL, 'Projekty i próby przewarstwowienia Żydów w epoce stanisławowskiej', *Sprawy Narodowościowe*, 8 (1934), 1–30, 181–224. Published as a monograph, Warsaw, 1934.
—— 'Profesor Marceli Handelsman', in id., *Kronika getta warszawskiego: wrzesień 1939–styczeń 1943*, ed. Artur Eisenbach, trans. from the Yiddish by Adam Rutkowski (Warsaw, 1983), 541–2.
—— 'Three Years of a Jewish History Seminar (1923–1926)' (Yid.), *Yunger historiker*, 1 (1926), 7–11.
—— 'Ze studjów nad dziejami Żydów na Mazowszu', *Przegląd Historyczny* 26/3 (1926–7), 299–339.
—— *Żydzi w powstaniu kościuszkowskim* (Warsaw, 1938).
—— *Żydzi w Warszawie: Od czasów najdawniejszych do ostatniego wygnania w roku 1527* (Warsaw, 1932).
—— and JACOB SHATZKY (eds.), *Chapters of the History of Bygone Jewish Life in Poland* [Kapitlen geshikhte fun amolikn yidishn lebn in poyl] (Buenos Aires, 1953).
ROBACK, A. A., 'A History of Yiddish Literature in the United States, 1879–1900 by Elias Schulman', review, *Jewish Social Studies*, 5/3 (1943), 311–13.
ROSENBLATT, IZAAK, 'Dokument prawodawczy Czterech Ziemstw kraju Polskiego', *Jutrzenka: Tygodnik dla Izraelitów Polskich*, 2 Aug. 1861, 35–7 and 9 August 1861, 42–4.
ROSENHECK, SHMUEL, 'The Jewish Education System in Interwar Poland' (Heb.), in Israel Heilperin (ed.), *The Jews in Poland from the Earliest Times to the Days of Destruction* [Beit yisra'el bepolin miyamim rishonim ve'ad liyemot haḥurban] (Jerusalem, 1948), 142–55.
ROSIAK, STEFAN, 'Rzekomy przywilej Kazimierza Jana Sapiehy dla Żydów w Lubczu z 1690 r.', *Ateneum Wileńskie*, 13 (1938), 32–44.
ROSKIES, DAVID G., *The Jewish Search for a Usable Past* (Bloomington, 1999).
ROSMAN, MOSHE, 'Hybrid with What? The Variable Contexts of Polish Jewish Culture: Their Implications for Jewish Cultural History and Jewish Studies', in Anita Norich and Yaron Z. Eliav (eds.), *Jewish Literatures and Cultures: Context and Intertext* (Ann Arbor, 2008), 129–54.
ROTH, ABRAHAM, 'Dr. N. M. Gelber: Aus zwei Jahrhunderten: Beiträge zur neueren Geschichte der Juden . . . Die Juden und der polnische Aufstand 1863', *Kwartalnik Historyczny*, 38 (1924), 133–5.
ROZEN, SHLOMO, 'A Bunch of Memories from the Days of the Past', in *Plock: The History of an Old Jewish Community in Poland* [Plock: toledot kehilah atikat yamim bepolin] (Tel Aviv, 1967).
ROZENBLIT, MARSHA L., *Reconstructing a National Identity: The Jews of Habsburg Austria during World War I* (New York, 2001).
RUDAWSKI, MICHAŁ, *Mój obcy kraj?* (Warsaw, 1996).
RUDNICKI, SZYMON, *Obóz Narodowo-Radykalny: Geneza i działalność* (Warsaw, 1985).
—— *Żydzi w parlamencie II Rzeczypospolitej* (Warsaw, 2004).

RUTKOWSKI, JAN, 'Roman Rybarski (1887–1942)', *Kwartalnik Historyczny*, 53/3–4 (1946), 592–7.
RYBARSKI, ROMAN, *Handel i polityka handlowa Polski w XVI stuleciu*, vol. i: *Rozwój handlu i polityki handlowej* (Warsaw, 1958).
—— *Roman Rybarski o narodzie, ustroju i gospodarce*, ed. Szymon Rudnicki (Warsaw, 1997).
RYLSKI (RUBINSTEIN), HENRYK, 'To the Memory of My Teacher and Mentor, the Great Educator Dr Michael Handel' (Heb.), *Mezritcher Tribune* (Tel Aviv), 46 (Sept. 2006), 17–19.
RZEPECKI, TADEUSZ, and WITOLD RZEPECKI, *Sejm i Senat 1922–1927: Podręcznik dla wyborców zawierający wyniki wyborów w powiatach, okręgach, województwach, podobizny senatorów i posłów sejmowych oraz mapy poglądowe* (Poznań, 1923).
RZYMKOWSKI, ROMAN, 'Siedziba Kempnerów', *Sygnały Płocka: Pismo Urzędu Miasta Płocka*, 18 (114) (15 Oct. 2004), 11.
SAKOWSKA, RUTA, 'Archiwum Ringelbluma—ogniwem konspiracji warszawskiego getta', *Biuletyn ŻIH*, 152 (1989), 91–102; 153 (1990), 79–95; 155–6 (1990), 153–60.
—— 'Biuro Informacji i Propagandy KG Armii Krajowej a Archiwum Ringelbluma (luty-lipiec 1942)', *Biuletyn ŻIH*, 162–3 (1992), 19–34.
—— 'Conspirational Archives of the Warsaw Ghetto—Oneg Shabat', in Daniel Grinberg (ed.), *The Holocaust Fifty Years After: 50th Anniversary of the Warsaw Ghetto Uprising: Papers from the Conference Organized by the Jewish Historical Institute of Warsaw, March 29–31, 1993* (Warsaw, 1993), 181–7.
—— 'Ringelblum Archive', *Biuletyn ŻIH*, 107–8 (1978), 115–19.
—— 'Two Forms of Resistance in the Warsaw Ghetto: Two Functions of the Ringelblum Archives', *Yad Vashem Studies*, 21 (1991), 189–219.
SAPERSTEIN, MARC, *'Your Voice Like a Ram's Horn': Themes and Texts in Traditional Jewish Preaching* (Cincinnati, 1996).
SAWICKI, ARON, 'Szkoła Rabinów w Warszawie (1826–1863)', *Miesięcznik Żydowski*, 3/3 (1933), 244–74.
SCHALL, JAKUB, *Dawna Żółkiew i jej Żydzi* (Lwów, 1939).
—— 'Friedman Filip: Dzieje Żydów w Łodzi od początków osadnictwa Żydów do r. 1863.', *Kwartalnik Historyczny*, 49 (1935), 684–6.
—— 'Najdawniesze osadnictwo żydowskie w Przemyślu', *Miesięcznik Żydowski*, 2/7–8 (1932), 159–61.
—— *Przewodnik po zabytkach żydowskich m. Lwowa i historja Żydów lwowskich w zarysie* (Lwów, 1935).
SCHEDRIN, VASSILI, *Jewish Souls, Bureaucratic Minds: Jewish Bureaucracy and Policymaking in Late Imperial Russia, 1850–1917* (Detroit, 2016).
SCHIPER [SCHIPPER], IGNACY [IGNAZ], *Anfänge des Kapitalismus bei den abendländischen Juden im früheren Mittelalter (bis zum Ausgang des XII Jahrhunderts)* (Vienna, 1907).

SCHIPER [SCHIPPER], IGNACY [IGNAZ], 'Dr. Josef Meisl: Heinrich Graetz. Eine Würdigung des Historikers und Juden', review, *Moriah*, 13 (1917/18), 73–5.

—— 'Dr. Majer Bałaban: Dzieje Żydów w Galicyi i w Rzeczypospolitej krakowskiej 1772–1868', review, *Moriah*, 12/9–10 (1917), 434–5.

—— 'Dzieje gospodarcze Żydów Korony i Litwy w czasach przedrozbiorowych' in Schiper, Tartakower, and Hafftka (eds.), *Żydzi w Polsce Odrodzonej*, i. 111–90.

—— *Dzieje handlu żydowskiego na ziemiach polskich* (Warsaw, 1937).

—— 'The Earliest History of the Warsaw Jews: An Important Monograph by Dr E. Ringelblum' (Yid.), *Haynt*, 9 Sept. 1932, p. 9.

—— 'Graetz and his Monumental Work' (Yid.), in Heinrich Graetz, *History of the Jews*, vol. i: *From the Earliest Times to the Babylonian Exile* [Yidishe geshikhte, ershter band: fun uralter tsayt biz goles bavel] (Warsaw, n.d.), pp. xxxiv–xliii.

—— 'Graetz "W setną rocznicę urodzin historyka żydowskiego"', *Moriah*, 13/2 (1917), 52–6.

—— 'Prof. Szymon Askenazy z"l (Thoughts After the Passing of a great Polish Historian)' (Yid.), *Haynt*, 28 June 1935, 4.

—— *Przyczynki do dziejów chasydyzmu w Polsce*, ed. Zbigniew Targielski (Warsaw, 1992).

—— 'Samorząd żydowski w Polsce na przełomie wieku 18 i 19-go (1764–1831)', *Miesięcznik Żydowski*, 1/6 (1931), 513–29.

—— *Studya nad stosunkami gospodarczymi Żydów w Polsce podczas średniowiecza* (Lwów, 1911).

—— *On the History and Economic Conditions of the Jews* [Yidishe geshikhte: virtshafts-geshikhte], 4 vols. (Warsaw, 1930).

—— 'Żydzi neofici i prozelici w Polsce do r. 1569', *KPBPŻwP*, 1/2 (1912), 65–77.

—— 'Żydzi w Powstaniu Styczniowym (w 70-letnią rocznicę powstania)', *Opinia*, 1933, no. 5.

—— 'Żydzi w rolnictwie na terenie Małopolski', in Schiper, Tartakower, and Hafftka (eds.), *Żydzi w Polsce Odrodzonej*, ii. 424–31.

—— ARJE TARTAKOWER, and ALEKSANDER HAFFTKA (eds.), *Żydzi w Polsce Odrodzonej: Działalność społeczna, gospodarcza, oświatowa i kulturalna*, 2 vols. (Warsaw, 1932, 1933).

SCHORR, MOJŻESZ, 'Bałaban Majer: Żydzi lwowscy na przełomie XVI i XVII w.', *Kwartalnik Historyczny*, 21 (1907), 545–53.

—— 'Buber Salomon: Anshe-Schem' *Kwartalnik Historyczny*, 11 (1897), 584–90.

—— 'Historya żydów w Polsce', in *Pamiętnik III: Zjazdu Historyków Polskich w Krakowie*, i (Kraków, 1900).

—— 'Jewish Scholarship and the Jewish Book in Poland' (Yid.), in *Haynt yubiley bukh 1908–1928* (Warsaw, 1928), 96.

—— *Kazanie inauguracyjne wygłoszone w Wielkiej Synagodze na Tłomackiem, dnia 7 grudnia 1923* (Warsaw, 1924).

—— 'Ku pracy', *Głos Gminy Żydowskiej*, 1939, nos. 7–8, 184–5.

—— 'Nasze życzenia', *Głos Gminy Żydowskiej*, 1938, nos. 10–11, 231.

—— *Organizacya Żydów w Polsce (od najdawniejszych czasów aż do r. 1772)* (Lwów, 1899).

—— *Przemówienie inauguracyjne na uroczystości otwarcia gmachu Głównej Biblioteki Judaistycznej przy Wielkie Synagodze w Warszawie dnia 22 kwienia 1936* (Warsaw, 1936).

—— 'Przemówienie Prof. Uniw. dra Mojżesza Schorra', in *W sprawie polsko-żydowskiej: Przebieg ankiety odbytej w dniach 2,3,4, 9 i 16 lutego 1919 we Lwowie* (Lwów, 1919), 91–103.

—— 'Stan i potrzeby wiedzy żydowskiej w dobie dzisiejszej', in *Sprawozdanie Instytutu Nauk Judaistycznych w Warszawie za lata akademickie 1927/28–1928/29* (Warsaw, 1929), pp. xvii–xxi.

—— 'Wettstein P.H.: Diwre chefec. Dokumenta hebrajskie z pinaksów gminnych w Krakowie', *Kwartalnik Historyczny*, 17 (1903), 487–90.

—— 'Zrzeszenie Rabinów o Wyższem Wykształceniu (jego zadania i cele)', *Opinia*, 1933, no. 2, p. 6.

—— *Żydzi w Przemyślu do końca XVIII wieku* (Lwów, 1903; repr. Jerusalem, 1991).

SCHORSCH, ISMAR, *From Text to Context: The Turn to History in Modern Judaism* (Hanover, NH, 1994).

SEGAL-MOLDAVI, MOSHE, 'Bibliography of Professor Raphael Mahler's Writings', in Samuel Yeivin (ed.), *Studies in Jewish History: Presented to Professor Raphael Mahler on his Seventy-Fifth Birthday* [Sefer refa'el maler: kovets meḥkarim betoledot yisra'el] (Merhaviah, 1974), 219–70.

SEIDMAN, HILLEL, 'Archiwum Gminy Żydowskiej w Warszawie', in Jakub Zineman (ed.), *Almanach gmin żydowskich w Polsce*, vol. i (Warsaw, 1939), 70–5.

—— *Diary of the Warsaw Ghetto* [Yoman geto varshah] (New York, 1957).

—— 'Meir Bałaban' (Heb.), in S. Mirski (ed.), *Personalities and Figures in Wissenschaft des Judentums in Eastern Europe before Its Decline* [Ishim udemuyot beḥokhmat yisra'el be'eiropah hamizraḥit lifnei shekiatah] (New York, 1959), 223–74.

—— *People I Used to Know: Portraits from the Recent Past in Eastern Europe* [Ishim shehikarti: demuyot me'avar karov bemizraḥ eiropah] (Jerusalem, 1970).

SEIDMAN, NAOMI, *Sarah Schenirer and the Bais Yaakov Movement: A Revolution in the Name of Tradition* (London, 2019).

SEMKOWICZ, ALEKSANDER, 'O potrzebie i sposobie wydania ważniejszych źródeł znajdujących się w miejskiem Archiwum we Lwowie', in *Pamiętnik Drugiego Zjazdu Historyków Polskich we Lwowie*, 2 vols. (Lwów, 1890–1), i. 2–12.

SHANES, JOSHUA, *Diaspora Nationalism and Jewish Identity in Habsburg Galicia* (Cambridge, 2012).

SHAPIRO, ROBERT M., 'Jacob Shatzky, Historian of Warsaw Jewry', in Antony Polonsky (ed.), *The Jews of Warsaw*, Polin 3 (Oxford, 1988), 200–13.

SHATZKY, JACOB, 'Alexander Kraushar and His Road to Total Assimilation', *YIVO Annual of Jewish Social Studies*, 7 (1952), 146–74.

—— 'Balance Sheet of a Jewish Historian', in Lucy S. Dawidowicz (ed.), *The Golden Tradition: Jewish Life and Thought in Eastern Europe* (New York, 1984), 263–9.

SHATZKY, JACOB, 'A Contribution to the Biography of Daniel Neufeld' (Yid.), *YIVO Bleter*, 7 (1934), 110–16.
—— *History of the Jews in Warsaw* [Geshikhte fun yidn in varshe], 3 vols. (New York, 1947–53).
—— *In the Shadow of the Past* [In shotn fun over] (Buenos Aires, 1947).
—— [JAKÓB SZACKI] *Kościuszko a Żydzi (notatki historyczne)* (Warsaw, 1917).
—— 'My Memories' (Yid.), in E. Lifschutz (ed.), *The Shatzky Book: Impressions of Jacob Shatsky and Memoirs, Letters, Talks and Essays by Shatzky* [Shatski-bukh: opshatsungen vegn yankev shatski un shatskis zikhroynes, briv, referatn un eseyen] (New York, 1958).
SHEDEL, JAMES, 'Austria and Its Polish Subjects, 1866–1914: A Relationship of Interests', *Austrian History Yearbook*, 19–20, pt. 2 (1983–4), 23–42.
SHELTON, ANITA K., *The Democratic Idea in Polish History and Historiography: Franciszek Bujak 1875–1953* (Boulder, Colo., 1989).
—— 'Franciszek Bujak (1875–1953)', in Peter Brock, John D. Stanley, and Piotr J. Wróbel (eds.), *Nation and History: Polish Historians from the Enlightenment to the Second World War* (Toronto, 2006), 280–96.
SHMERUK, CHONE, 'Hebrew–Yiddish–Polish: A Tri-Lingual Jewish Culture', in Yisrael Gutman, Ezra Mendelsohn, Jehuda Reinharz, and Chone Shmeruk (eds.), *The Jews of Poland Between Two World Wars* (Hanover, NH, 1989), 285–311.
SIEMIEŃSKI, JÓZEF JAN, 'Ringelblum Emanuel: Żydzi w Warszawie. I. Od czasów najdawniejszych do ostatniego wygnania w r. 1527', review, *Kwartalnik Historyczny*, 47 (1933), 646–50.
SILBER, MARCOS, 'The Development of a Joint Political Program for the Jews of Poland during World War I—Success and Failure', *Jewish History*, 19 (2005), 211–26.
—— 'Meir Bałaban and his Civic-Political Activity in Poland during the First World War' (Heb.), *Shevut*, 11 (27) (2002–3), 139–57.
SILVERMAN, LISA, *Becoming Austrians: Jews and Culture between the World Wars* (New York, 2012).
SINKOFF, NANCY, *Out of the Shtetl: Making Jews Modern in the Polish Borderlands* (Providence, 2004).
ŚLIWIŃSKI, ARTUR, *Joachim Lelewel: Zarys biograficzny, lata 1786–1831* (Warsaw, 1932).
*Słownik geograficzny Królestwa Polskiego i innych krajów słowiańskich*, 15 vols. (Warsaw, 1880–1902).
SMITH, MARK L., *The Yiddish Historians and the Struggle for a Jewish History of the Holocaust* (Detroit, 2019).
SMOLEŃSKI, WŁADYSŁAW, *Stan i sprawa Żydów polskich w XVIII wieku* (Warsaw, 1876).
SMUSZKOWICZÓWNA, CHANA, 'Historyše Šriftn fun Jiwo: Prace historyczne JIWO, pod redakcją E. Tscherikowera', review, *Ateneum Wileńskie*, 12 (1937), 647–51.
SOIFER, PAUL E., 'The Bespectacled Cossack: S. A. Bershadskii (1850–1896) and the Development of Russo-Jewish Historiography', Ph.D. diss., Pennsylvania State University, 1975.

SOKOŁÓW, NACHUM, 'Dla postępu wiedzy judaistycznej', *Izraelita*, 1899, no. 23, 247.
SONNENSCHEIN, EFRAIM, *Chapters from Jewish History in Tchortkov* [Perakim mitoledot hayehudim bechortkov] (Warsaw, 1939).
SORKIN, DAVID, *The Berlin Haskalah and German Jewish Religious Thought: Orphans of Knowledge* (London, 2000).
SOVIV, AARON, 'Kwestia Równouprawnienia Żydów w Królestwie Polskim by Artur Eisenbach', review, *Jewish Social Studies*, 34/4 (1972), 369–70.
—— *Louis D. Brandeis: The Champion for Justice* (New York, 1969).
SPODENKIEWICZ, PAWEŁ, *The Missing District: People and Places of Jewish Łódź*, trans. Dorota Wiśniewska and John Crust (Łódź, 2007).
*Sprawozdanie Instytutu Nauk Judaistycznych w Warszawie za lata akademickie 1927/28–1928/29*, Pisma Instytutu Nauk Judaistycznych w Warszawie 1 (Warsaw, 1929).
*Sprawozdanie z działalności Towarzystwa Przyjaciół Uniwersytetu Hebrajskiego w Jerozolimie w roku 1927* (Warsaw, 1928).
*Sprawozdanie z działalności Wydziału Humanistycznego Uniwersytetu J. Piłsudskiego za rok akademicki 1935–1936* (Warsaw, 1937).
*Sprawozdanie z działalności Wydziału Humanistycznego Uniwersytetu Warszawskiego za rok akadem. 1929–1930* (Warsaw, 1930).
*Sprawozdanie z działalności Wydziału Humanistycznego Uniwersytetu Warszawskiego za rok akadem. 1930–1931* (Warsaw, 1931).
*Sprawozdanie z działalności Wydziału Humanistycznego Uniwersytetu Warszawskiego za rok akadem. 1931–1932* (Warsaw, 1932).
*Sprawozdanie z działalności Wydziału Humanistycznego Uniwersytetu Warszawskiego za rok akadem. 1934–1935* (Warsaw, 1936).
'Sprawozdanie z V Posiedzenia Komitetu Generalnego Związku Żydowskich Stowarzyszeń Humanitarnych B'nai B'rith w Rzeczypospolitej Polskiej w Krakowie, odbytego w Warszawie dnia 6 maja 1929 r.', *B'nai B'rith: Organ Związku Stowarzyszeń Humanitarnych 'B'nai B'rith' w Rzeczypospolitej Polskiej*, July 1929, no. 5.
STACH, STEPHAN, 'The Institute for Nationality Research (1921–1939)—A Think Tank for Minority Politics in Poland?', in Yvonne Kleinmann, Stephan Stach, and Tracie L. Wilson (eds.), *Religion in the Mirror of Law: Eastern European Perspectives from the Early Modern Period to 1939* (Frankfurt am Main, 2016), 149–84.
STAMPFER, SHAUL, *A Catalog of the Jacob Shatky Collection of 'Polonica Judaica'* (Jerusalem, 1989).
STANLEY, JOHN, 'The Politics of the Jewish Question in the Duchy of Warsaw, 1807–1813', *Jewish Social Studies*, 44/1 (1982), 47–62.
*Statut Towarzystwa Miłośników Przeszłości Lwowa* (Lwów, 1928).
*Statystyka druków 1932, Główny Urząd Statystyczny* (Warsaw, 1933).
*Statystyka druków wydanych w Rzeczypospolitej Polskiej na rok 1937* (Warsaw, 1938).
STAUBER, RONI, *Laying the Foundations for Holocaust Research: The Impact of the Historian Philip Friedman* (Jerusalem, 2009).

STAUBER, RONI, 'Philip Friedman and the Beginning of Holocaust Studies', in David Bankier and Dan Michman (eds.), *Holocaust Historiography in Context: Emergence, Challenges, Polemics and Achievements* (Jerusalem, 2008), 83–102.

STEFFEN, KATRIN, *Jüdische Polonität: Ethnizität und Nation im Spiegel der polnischsprachigen jüdischen Presse, 1918–1939* (Göttingen, 2004).

—— '"Polska—to także my!": Prasa polsko-żydowska (1918–1939)', in Joanna Nalewajko-Kulikov (ed.), *Studia z dziejów trójjęzycznej prasy żydowskiej na ziemiach polskich (XIX–XX w.)* (Warsaw, 2012), 129–46.

STEINBERG, MOJŻESZ, *Żydzi w Jarosławiu od czasów najdawniejszych do połowy XIX wieku* (Jarosław, 1933).

STEINLAUF, MICHAEL C., 'The Polish-Jewish Daily Press', in Antony Polonsky (ed.), *Jews and the Emerging Polish State*, Polin 2 (Oxford, 1987), 219–45.

STENDIG, SAMUEL, 'Legendy i fakty', *Głos Gminy Żydowskiej*, 1937, no. 6, 138.

—— 'Pedagogowie żydowscy w Polsce współczesnej', in Jakub Zineman (ed.), *Almanach szkolnictwa żydowskiego w Polsce. Trzeci zeszyt okazowy* (Warsaw, 1937), 13–43.

STERNBACH, HERMAN, 'O antysemityźmie (Uwagi)', *Miesięcznik Żydowski*, 2/2 (1932), 97–111.

STREIT, LEON, *Dzieje Wielkiej Miejskiej Synagogi w Stanisławowie* (Stanisławów, 1936).

SUCHYSTAW, GABRYEL, *Sacred Monument* [Matsevet kodesh], 4 vols. (Lwów, 1860–9).

SURMAN, JAN, and GERALD MOZETIČ (eds.), *Dwa życia Ludwika Gumplowicza: Wybór tekstów* (Warsaw, 2010).

SZCZERBAKIEWICZ, RAFAŁ, '"Sprytny dostawca optymizmu narodowego"(?): Ostatnie lata Szymona Askenazego na uboczu historii, Polski i Europy', in Grażyna Borkowska and Magdalena Rudkowska (eds.), *Kwestia żydowska w XIX wieku: Spory o tożsamość Polaków* (Warsaw, 2004), 331–42.

SZULKIN, MICHAŁ, 'Dr. Emanuel Ringelblum—historyk i organizator podziemnego archiwum getta warszawskiego', *Biuletyn ŻIH*, 86–7 (1973), 111–25.

—— 'Projekt utworzenia Katedry Historii Żydów w Polsce na Uniwersytecie Hebrajskim w Jerozolimie w latach 1934–1935', *Biuletyn ŻIH*, 106 (1978), 27–32.

TARTAKOWER, ARJE, 'The Institute of Jewish Studies in Warsaw' (Heb.), in Louis Ginzberg and Abraham Weiss (eds.), *Studies in Memory of Moses Schorr* [Kovets mada'i lezekher mosheh shor] (New York, 1944), 163–76.

—— 'Organizacja gmin żydowskich', *Miesięcznik Żydowski*, 2/5 (1932), 389–98.

—— 'Problem szkolnictwa żydowskiego w Polsce', in Jakub Zineman (ed.), *Almanach szkolnictwa żydowskiego w Polsce. Trzeci zeszyt okazowy* (Warsaw, 1937), 7–12.

TAUBELES, SAMUEL ARON, *Żydowska gmina wyznaniowa i rabinat w naszej dobie: Referat aktualny* (Tarnopol, [1936]).

TOCZEK, ALFRED, 'Środowisko historyków lwowskich w latach 1860–1918', *Prace Komisji Historii Nauk Polskiej Akademii Umiejętności*, 6 (2004), 123–58.

TOMASZEWSKI, JERZY, 'Centrum Badania i Nauczania Dziejów i Kultury Żydów w Polsce im. Mordechaja Anielewicza w Uniwersytecie Warszawskim', in Krzysztof

Pilarczyk (ed.) *Żydzi i judaizm we współczesnych badaniach polskich*, vol. 1: *Materiały z konferencji, Kraków 21–23 XI 1995* (Kraków, 1997), 29–33.

—— 'The History of the Jews as an Integral Part of the History of Poland and Other Central-European Societies: Theory and Reality', in Michael Heyd and Oded Heilbronner (eds.), *Varieties of Multiculturalism in Modern European History: The Case of Jews* (Jerusalem, 1998), 41–62.

—— 'Polish Historiography and the Jewish Historical Institute', in Eleonora Bergman (ed.), *Jewish Historical Institute: The First Fifty Years 1947–1997* (Warsaw, 1996), 14–20.

TORSTENDAHL, ROLF, *The Rise and Propagation of Historical Professionalism* (New York, 2015).

TRACHTENBERG, BARRY, *The Revolutionary Roots of Modern Yiddish, 1903–1917* (Syracuse, NY, 2008).

TRUNK, ISAIAH, 'The Jewish Community in Poland at the End of the 18th Century: Kutno (Monographic Study)' (Yid.), *Bleter far geshikhte*, 1 (1934), 87–140.

—— *Judenrat: The Jewish Councils in Eastern Europe under Nazi Occupation* (New York, 1972).

—— 'The Legal Status of Jews in Plock in 16th Century' (Yid.), *Bleter far geshikhte*, 2 (1938), 89–103.

—— 'On the History of Polish Historiography in Recent Years' (Heb.), *Gal Ed*, 3 (1976), 245–68.

TUROWSKI, STANISŁAW. 'Polska rajem dla żydów', *KPBPŻwP*, 1/3 (1913), 73–100.

UNGER, MORDECHAI, 'Błp Dr. Szałom Jona Czarno (zarys monograficzny)', in Jakub Zineman (ed.), *Almanach szkolnictwa żydowskiego w Polsce. Trzeci zeszyt okazowy* (Warsaw, 1937), 48–9.

—— 'Jerachmiel Wajngarten (szkic biograficzny)', in Jakub Zineman (ed.), *Almanach szkolnictwa żydowskiego w Polsce. Trzeci zeszyt okazowy* (Warsaw, 1937), 79–83.

—— '"Ohel Sara" (Namiot Sary) Dom wychowawczo-zawodowy im błp Sary Szenirer przy "Agudas Isroel" w Polsce, Łódź ul. Kilińskiego 50', in Jakub Zineman (ed.), *Almanach szkolnictwa żydowskiego w Polsce. Trzeci zeszyt okazowy* (Warsaw, 1937), 159.

URBACH, JANUSZ KONRAD, *Udział Żydów w walce o niepodległość Polski* (Warsaw, 1938).

'Uroczystość 11 listopada', *Nasze Życie*, 3/1–2 (1932), 10.

'Uroczysty obchód Święta Niepodległości w Krakowie', *Nowy Dziennik*, 13 Nov. 1931, 9.

URUSZCZAK, WACŁAW, 'Stanisław Kutrzeba (1876–1946)', trans. Peter Brock, in Peter Brock, John D. Stanley, and Piotr J. Wróbel (eds.), *Nation and History: Polish Historians from the Enlightenment to the Second World War* (Toronto, 2006), 297–306.

VEIDLINGER, JEFFREY, *Jewish Public Culture in the Late Russian Empire* (Bloomington, 2009).

*W sprawie polsko-żydowskiej: Przebieg ankiety odbytej w dniach 2, 3, 4, 9 i 16 lutego 1919 we Lwowie, tudzież wnioski Komisyi wydelegowanej przez Tymczasowy Komitet Rządzący uchwałą z 1. stycznia 1919* (Lwów, 1919).

W-W, L., 'Słów kilka o rzemieślnikach żydach', *Izraelita*, 1900, no. 2, 18–19.
WAGNER, ARTUR, 'Steinberg Mojżesz: Żydzi w Jarosławiu od czasów najdawniejszych do połowy XIX wieku', review, *Roczniki Dziejów Społecznych i Gospodarczych*, 4 (1935), 451–4.
WAJSBLUM, MAREK, '*Zawsze byłem Żydem dla Polaków i Polakiem dla Żydów*': Listy Marka Wajsbluma do Stanisława Kota z lat 1927–1961, ed. Zdzisław Pietrzak and Zbigniew Koziński (Kraków, 1996).
WARCHAŁ, KS. JAN, 'Żydzi polscy na Uniwersytecie padewskim', *KPBPŻwP*, 1/3 (1913), 37–72.
WARĘŻAK, JAN, 'Friedman Filip: Dzieje Żydów w Łodzi od początków osadnictwa do roku 1863', review, *Roczniki Dziejów Społecznych i Gospodarczych*, 5 (1936), 280–3.
—— 'Friedman Filip: Rozwój gospodarczy Łodzi do roku 1914', *Roczniki Dziejów Społecznych i Gospodarczych*, 8 (1939), 172–3.
WARSZAWSKI, S. 'Gwardja Miejska miasta stołecznego Warszawy podczas powstania listopadowego (1830–1831)', *Miesięcznik Żydowski*, 1/1 (1930), 55–67.
—— 'Struktura społeczna i gospodarcza żydostwa warszawskiego w 1840 r.', *Miesięcznik Żydowski*, 2/9 (1931), 245–62.
WASSERMAN, PINCHAS, 'W obronie godności człowieka', *Głos Gminy Żydowskiej*, 1937, no. 4, 79.
WEB, MAREK, 'Dubnov and Jewish Archives: An Introduction to his Papers at the YIVO Institute', in Kristi Groberg and Avraham Greenbaum (eds.), *A Missionary for History: Essays in Honor of Simon Dubnov* (Minneapolis, 1998), 87–92.
WECHSLER, L., 'Kursy dla wychowawców religijnych (Z sieci szkół "Chorew" w Polsce)', in Jakub Zineman (ed.), *Almanach Szkolnictwa żydowskiego w Polsce. Trzeci zeszyt okazowy* (Warsaw, 1937), 149–50.
WEEKS, THEODORE R., *From Assimilation to Antisemitism: The 'Jewish Question' in Poland, 1850–1914* (DeKalb, Ill., 2006).
WEINRYB, BERNARD D., *The Jews of Poland: A Social and Economic History of the Jewish Community in Poland from 1100 to 1800* (Philadelphia, 1973).
WEISER, KALMAN, 'The Jewel in the Yiddish Crown: Who Will Occupy the Chair in Yiddish at the University of Vilnius?', in Israel Bartal, Antony Polonsky, and Scott Ury (eds.), *Jews and Their Neighbours in Eastern Europe since 1750*, Polin 24 (Oxford, 2012), 223–55.
—— *Jewish People, Yiddish Nation: Noah Prylucki and the Folkists in Poland* (Toronto, 2011).
—— '"Der moment" (1910–1939)', in Joanna Nalewajko-Kulikov (ed.), *Studia z dziejów trójjęzycznej prasy żydowskiej na ziemiach polskich (XIX–XX w.)* (Warsaw, 2012), 77–88.
WEISS, ABRAHAM, 'Moses Schorr' (Heb.), in Louis Ginzberg and Abraham Weiss (eds.), *Studies in Memory of Moses Schorr* (New York, 1944), pp. ix–x.
—— and PNINA KREMER-WEISS, 'The Institute of Jewish Studies in Warsaw' (Heb.), in Arie Tartakower (ed.), *Year Book* [Sefer hashanah/yorbukh], vol. ii (New York, 1967), 359–80.

WEISSBERG, M. [MEIR, MAKSYMILIAN, MAX], 'Literatura nowohebrajska w Galicyi (1786–1850)', *KPBPŻwP*, 1/1 (1912), 35–53.

—— *Die Neuhebräische Aufklärungsliteratur in Galizien* (Leipzig, 1898).

—— 'Język literacki Żydów w Galicyi', *KPBPŻwP*, 1/2 (1912), 1–16; 1/3 (1913), 101–32.

WENDLAND, WOJCIECH, *'Trzy czoła proroków z matki obcej': Myśl historyczna Tatarów polskich w II Rzeczypospolitej* (Kraków, 2013).

WHITE, ANGELA, 'Jewish Lives in the Polish Language: The Polish-Jewish Press, 1918–1939', Ph.D. diss., Indiana University, 2007.

WIĘCKOWSKA, HELENA, *Joachim Lelewel: Uczony, polityk, człowiek* (Warsaw, 1980).

WIERZBICKA, MARIA, *Władysław Smoleński* (Warsaw, 1980).

WIERZBICKI, ANDRZEJ, 'Oswald Balzer (1858–1933)', in Jerzy Maternicki and Leonid Zaszkilniak (eds.), *Złota księga historiografii lwowskiej XIX i XX wieku* (Rzeszów, 2007), 253–68.

WIERZBIENIEC, WACŁAW, 'Mojżesz Schorr (1874–1941)', in Jerzy Maternicki and Leonid Zaszkilniak (eds.), *Złota księga historiografii lwowskiej XIX i XX wieku* (Rzeszów, 2007), 399–420.

—— 'Z badań nad lwowskim okresem życia i działalności Majera Bałabana', in Jerzy Maternicki and Leonid Zaszkilniak (eds.), *Wielokulturowe środowisko historyczne Lwowa w XIX i XX w.*, vol. iii (Rzeszów, 2005), 296–316.

WIESE, CHRISTIAN, 'Struggling for Normality: The Apologetics of "Wissenschaft des Judentums" in Wilhelmine Germany as an Anti-Colonial Intellectual Revolt against the Protestant Construction of Judaism', in Rainer Liedtke and David Rechter (eds.), *Towards Normality? Acculturation and Modern German Jewry* (Tübingen, 2003), 77–101.

WODZIŃSKI, MARCIN, *Haskalah and Hasidism in the Kingdom of Poland: A History of Conflict* (Oxford, 2005).

—— 'Jewish Studies in Poland', *Journal of Modern Jewish Studies*, 10/1 (2011), 101–18.

WOLFF, LARRY, *The Idea of Galicia: History and Fantasy in Habsburg Political Culture* (Stanford, 2010).

WRÓBEL, PIOTR J., 'Szymon Askenazy (1865–1935)', in Peter Brock, John D. Stanley, and Piotr J. Wróbel (eds.), *Nation and History: Polish Historians from the Enlightenment to the Second World War* (Toronto, 2006), 221–45.

WRONA, STANISŁAW TADEUSZ, 'Chłopi w powstaniu styczniowym', *Przegląd Historyczny*, 34/2 (1937–8), 544–63.

'Wspomnienia o pracownikach naukowych i członkach PTH zmarłych w latach 1939–1945', *Kwartalnik Historyczny*, 53/3–4 (1946), 405–659.

WUNDER, MEIR, *Galician Luminaries: Encyclopaedia of the Galician Sages* [Me'orei galitsyah: entsiklopedyah leḥakhmei galitsyah] (Jerusalem, 1978).

WURM, DAWID, *Z dziejów żydostwa brodzkiego za czasów dawnej Rzeczypospolitej Polskiej do r. 1772* (Brody, 1935).

YERUSHALMI, YOSEF HAYIM, *The Lisbon Massacre of 1506 and the Royal Image in the Shebet Yehudah* (Cincinnati, 1976).

YERUSHALMI, YOSEF HAYIM, *Zakhor: Jewish History and Jewish Memory* (Seattle, 1996).
'Z historji żydów w Polsce: Epizod dziejowy z wieku XVI (1566–1600)', *Izraelita*, 1877, no. 6, 44–5.
ZARROW, SARAH ELLEN, 'Object Lessons: Art Collection and Display as Historical Practice in Inter-War Lwów', in Natalia Aleksiun, Brian Horowitz, and Antony Polonsky (eds.), *Writing Jewish History in Eastern Europe*, Polin 29 (Oxford, 2017), 157–75.
ZARZYCKI, W., *Biskup Adam Naruszewicz, luminarz polskiego Oświecenia* (Lublin, 1999).
ZASZKILNIAK, LEONID, 'Historia Ukrainy', in Jerzy Maternicki, Joanna Pisulińska, and Leonid Zaszkilniak (eds.), *Historia w Uniwersytecie Lwowskim: badania i nauczanie do 1939 roku* (Rzeszów, 2016), 347–72.
'Ze sprawozdania Stow. "Humanitas" w Przemyślu', *B'nai B'rith: Organ Związku Stowarzyszeń Humanitarnych 'B'nai B'rith' w Rzeczypospolitej Polskiej*, January 1929, no. 1.
'Ze sprawozdania Stowarzyszenia "Leopolis" B'nai B'rith we Lwowie', *B'nai B'rith: Organ Związku Stowarzyszeń Humanitarnych 'B'nai B'rith' w Rzeczypospolitej Polskiej*, January 1929, no. 1.
ŻEBROWSKI, RAFAŁ, 'Budowa domu akademickiego w Warszawie i jej miejsce w dziejach warszawskiej gminy wyznaniowej', *Kwartalnik Historii Żydów*, 4 (2005), 467–80.
—— 'Jakuba Szackiego żywot paradoksalny', *Kwartalnik Historii Żydów*, 2 (2002), 171–94.
—— *Mojżesz Schorr i jego listy do Ludwika Gumplowicza* (Warsaw, 1994).
ZIELIŃSKI, KONRAD, and NINA ZIELIŃSKA, *Jeszywas Chachmej Lublin: Uczelnia mędrców Lublina* (Lublin, 2003).
ZIMMERMAN, JOSHUA D., *Contested Memories: Poles and Jews during the Holocaust and its Aftermath* (New Brunswick, NJ, 2003).
ZINEMAN, JAKUB (ed.), *Almanach gmin żydowskich w Polsce*, vol. i (Warsaw, 1939).
—— (ed.), *Almanach szkolnictwa żydowskiego w Polsce. Trzeci zeszyt okazowy* (Warsaw, 1937).
ZMIGRYDER-KONOPKA, ZDZISŁAW, 'O równowagę duchową', *Głos Gminy Żydowskiej*, 1938, nos. 6–7, 137–40.
*Żydowski Dom Akademicki w Warszawie 1924–1926: monografia* (Warsaw, 1928).
ŻYNDUL, JOLANTA, 'Cele akcji antyżydowskiej w Polsce w latach 1935–1937', *Biuletyn ŻIH*, 161 (1992), 53–63.
—— 'If Not a Pogrom, Then What?', in Antony Polonsky (ed.), *The Shtetl: Myth and Reality*, Polin 17 (Oxford, 2004), 385–91.
—— *Państwo w państwie? Autonomia narodowo-kulturalna w Europie Środkowowschodniej w XX wieku* (Warsaw, 2000).
—— *Zajścia antyżydowskie w Polsce w latach 1935–1937* (Warsaw, 1994).
ŻYTOMIRSKI-AVIDAR, NETA, 'Historian Bela Mandelsberg-Schildkraut' (Heb.), in *Kol Lublin 'Lubliner shtime'*, 45 (2009), 44–50.
ŻYWCZYŃSKI, MIECZYSŁAW, 'Kościół i duchowieństwo w powstaniu styczniowym (stan badań w zarysie)', *Przegląd Historyczny*, 34/2 (1937–8), 512–25.

# Index

**A**
Abraham, Władysław 67–8
Adalberg, Samuel 66, 75
Adamus, Jan 151
Adler, Cyrus 132
Agudat Israel:
  founders 166
  Mesivta yeshiva 190
  representation in parliament 125, 141, 163
  struggle with Mizrachi 208
  Youth Council 192
Alter, Moshe 205, 206–7
Ameisen, Zofia 142
An-sky, S. (Solomon Zainwil Rappoport) 59, 93
Appenszlak, Jakób 173
Arnold, Stanisław 117 n.39, 159, 226, 237–8, 253 n.216
Askenazy, Szymon:
  attitude to writing Polish Jewish history 78–80, 84, 86–8, 90, 93, 99
  career 65–6, 93, 113, 115
  establishment of Wawelberg competition 66–8, 70, 78
  foundation of *KPBPŻwP* 76, 78
  funeral 65 n.6
  relationship with Bałaban, Schiper, and Schorr 70, 73 n.49, 90–1
  relationship with Shatzky 74–5, 115
  students 80–1, 82–3, 85, 90–1, 115
Association of History Lovers (TMH) 18 n.23, 145, 148, 153
Association of Rabbis with Higher Education 199
Association of Scholars of Jewish History in Russia 58
Asz, Szalom 250–1, 258
*Ateneum Wileńskie* 149–50
Austria 104–5, 186, 209
Austro-Hungarian empire:
  educational opportunities 9, 73
  Jewish national rights 97
  last decades 64
  liberal values 108
  partitioning power 4, 13, 63; *see also* Galicia
  political reforms 110

**B**
*Baderekh* 172
Bałaban, Majer:
  academic training 70, 72–3
  approach to economic history 237–8
  assaulted at university 156–7, 221, 268
  attitude to writing Polish Jewish history 6, 9–10
  background 72, 73
  B'nai B'rith membership 193–4
  career 1–2, 72, 94, 109, 110–11, 122–3, 144, 156, 160, 201, 209, 214, 260–1
  Congresses of Polish Historians 146, 216 n.3
  current reputation 8, 267
  death 2, 264
  fate of students in the Holocaust 264–5
  Festschrift 125, 143
  funding for publications 141–3
  history of Jewish community in Kraków 1, 150, 224
  history of Jewish community in Lublin 224
  history of Jewish community in Lwów 94, 140, 150, 224, 231
  history of the Jews in Galicia 100–1, 106–7
  history of Lwów liberal synagogue 140, 253
  history textbook for Jewish students in Polish schools 191
  Institute of Jewish Studies role 202, 209
  Institute of National Studies 156, 164
  Jewish archive planning 135, 215
  Jewish Historical-Ethnographic Society 93, 94

Bałaban, Majer (cont.):
  Jewish university plans 120–1, 131, 215
  lectures 91, 92, 117 n.38, 147, 158, 194, 201
  membership of national and local Polish historical associations 145–6
  on antiquity of Jewish settlement in the Polish lands 174–8, 219
  on Dubnow 92, 93–4
  on functions and needs of Jewish historiography in Poland 151
  on history of Jarosław Jews 152
  on importance of Jewish cultural history 236
  on importance of Jewish urban history 217
  on importance of local studies 94, 223
  on importance of social history 235–6
  on importance of sources 225, 226, 228
  on internal government of Polish Jews 99–100, 181–2
  on Jewish emancipation 104–5
  on Jewish identity 90, 96, 104–5
  on Jewish–non-Jewish relations 102, 103, 149, 153
  on Jewish separateness 103–4
  on link between Polish history and Polish Jewish history 234–5
  on local history 94, 228, 229, 233–4
  on Poland's partitions 101
  on Polish Jewish patriotism 101–2, 179–81, 249
  on Polish–Jewish relations 153, 177–9, 243–4, 245–6, 249–50, 258
  on Polish Jewish scholarship 93, 98, 107, 124
  on political borders before partitions 96–7
  on preservation of artefacts 235, 236
  on rabbinical training 198–9, 200, 201–2, 208
  on traditional religious training 197–8
  political and communal activism 161, 163, 164, 194
  popularizing history 163
  publications 91, 106, 140, 141–3, 144, 147–8, 160
  relationship with Askenazy 65 n.6, 70
  relationship with Polish historians 155, 156–7, 158–9
  relationship with Schorr 72
  research agenda 215, 256
  role in Hebrew University in Jerusalem 131, 132
  role as teacher and educator 160, 186
  romantic historiography 97
  scholarly journals in Polish 136–7, 138–9
  sense of mission towards Jewish and Polish audiences 100–1, 107, 161, 214
  Seventh International Congress of Historical Studies (1933) 134
  students working on local history 229–31, 249
  study of Jewish historical monuments 144
  survival of work 268, 270
  Tachkemoni seminary role 201, 202, 205–6, 209
  training teachers of Jewish religion 186
  Warsaw ghetto work 263, 264
  Warsaw Institute of Jewish Studies 121–3, 124, 125, 126
  Warsaw seminar in Polish Jewish history 112, 119, 123, 124, 159, 232
  Warsaw University role 123, 124–6, 219
  wartime role as military rabbi 209
  Wawelberg Prize 70, 139, 140
  work compared with Schiper's 237, 261 n.2
  World Congress of Jewish Studies plan 132–3
  writing in Jewish press 172–5
  Zionism 89, 95
Balzer, Oswald 68
Baron, Salo 73, 102, 140, 265, 268, 271
Bartal, Israel 271
Baumberg, Mordechai 191
Berkelhammer, Wilhelm (Ze'ev) 138, 176–7
Berkowicz, Józef 179
Berman, Jakub 118, 226, 228–9
Bernfeld, Izydor 55, 60
Bershadski, Sergei 49, 53, 225
Bersohn, Mathias 20–1, 23, 26, 61, 74, 146
*Biblioteka Warszawska* 87
Biderman, Israel M. 162, 187, 266–7
Blatman, Daniel 259
*Bleter far geshikhte* 117–18, 120, 137, 229 n.78, 231
Blumenfeld, Rabbi Jechiel Meir 192
Blumental, Nachman 111

Blutinger, Jeffrey 50, 97
B'nai B'rith:
  Bałaban's membership 141, 142, 193–4, 157, 163
  financial backing 121, 138, 141, 142
  funding for educational activities 193
  Hillel Foundation 192
  library 193 n.175
  Schorr's membership 163, 193
  support for *Miesięcznik Żydowski* 138–9
  Warsaw branch 123, 135, 138, 142
Bolesław V, Prince 27 n.76, 28
Bosak, Marek 123, 230
Brandstaetter, Roman 182
Brann, Marcus 71
Braude, Markus 122, 168, 184, 201, 208, 266
Brody 141, 152, 222, 230, 238, 264
Brüh, Seweryn 158
Brześć (Brisk) 45, 210
Buber, Salomon 47–8, 73, 98
Bujak, Franciszek:
  attitude to Jewish history 113–14, 156, 219
  career 113–14, 145
  depiction of Jews 239, 242–3, 254
  economic history 151, 227, 237
  local history 226–7
  journal of economic history 151
  programme of forced emigration of Jews from Poland 243
Bund 7, 118, 254
Bursztyn, Józef 217 n.11, 230, 240–1

**C**

Central Jewish Historical Commission 263 n.5, 266
Central Merchants' Association 142, 194
Chameides, Kalman 212
Charewiczowa, Łucja 151, 156, 227–8, 237, 242–3
Charter of Privileges (1264) 28, 31–2, 41, 174
Chiarini, Reverend Luigi 86, 182 n.111
Chmielnicki uprising (1648) 36, 84, 90, 181, 189, 246, 250
Church, the 29–31, 34–5, 39, 99, 103, 246
*Chwila* 172
Cohn, Adolf Jakub 42, 44, 53
Comber, Lipman 118, 129
Congress Poland, *see* Poland, Congress

Congresses of Polish Historians 149
  1890 223
  1900 98, 146, 223
  1925 146, 216 n.3, 226
  1930 124, 146, 228
Council of Four Lands (Va'ad Arba Aratsot) 38, 41, 47
Czacki, Tadeusz:
  approach to Jewish history 9, 13–14, 21
  documentary sources 21
  influence 14
  on Jewish–non-Jewish relations 33
  on rights of Jews 27, 252
  on role of Jews 26–7, 43, 252
  *Rosprawa o Żydach* (Treatise on the Jews) 13–14, 17, 21–3, 25
Czarno, Szalom Jona 185–6, 190–1
Czarnowski, Stefan 157
Częstochowa 110, 134, 186 n.132, 194, 230

**D**

Dąbkowski, Przemysław 156, 158
Dawidowicz, Lucy 12 n.21, 127
Dembiński, Bronisław 67–8, 71, 112, 145, 147 n.194
Dembitzer, Chaym Nathan 46–7, 48 n.222
Derevianski, Yosef-Dovid 128
Dmowski, Roman 3
Dobroszycki, Lucjan 269
Doktorowicz, Henryk 131
Drohobycz 143, 230
Dubnow, Simon:
  approach to writing Jewish history 49, 55–8, 60, 65, 68, 92, 96
  Bałaban's view of 94
  defining Jewish history 18 n.20
  influence 53, 58–9, 61, 64, 92, 93–4, 155
  publications 53, 55, 93
  Schiper's view of 95
  view of *KPBPŻwP* 78
  view of Schorr's thesis 71, 93
Duker, Abraham 118, 137, 139, 188, 267, 271

**E**

Eden, Shevach 202, 266
Eisenbach, Artur 111, 129, 265, 267
Eisenstein, Aron 176
Ellenberg, Zygmunt 137, 225
Estrin, Lejzor 230

*Evreiskaya starina* 53–4, 75, 76, 91, 93, 97

**F**
Farbstein, Heszel 200–1, 205
Feiner, Shmuel 16
Feinstein, Arie Leib 45–6
Feldman, Eliezer:
  Association of History Lovers 145
  career 266
  languages 118, 137
  on archival research 229
  on Polish–Jewish relations 246
  on publishing difficulties 139–40, 143–4
  publications 137, 143
  Young Historians Circle 137, 143
Fenster, Abraham 230
Finkel, Ludwik:
  career 113
  publications 97–8
  seminars 71
  support for Bałaban and Schorr 73 n.49, 98
  Wawelberg competition committee 66, 67–8
Finn, Samuel Joseph 44–5, 73, 225
First World War:
  aftermath 4–5, 9, 86, 163, 259
  Austrian occupation of Lublin 186, 209
  German occupation of Warsaw 112 n.13
  Jewish patriotic deeds 181, 248, 252
  Poland's struggle for independence 248
  Shatzky's career 75
Folkist Party 7, 163, 269 n.31
*Folks-tsaytung* 172
Frank, Jacob 35, 40, 42, 84 n.123, 90
Fränkel, Chaim Eliezer 210
Frankist movement:
  Bałaban's approach 233
  Graetz's presentation of 51
  Kraushar's study 20, 26 n.72, 30 n.94, 35, 36, 40
  Smoleński's view 42–3
Frenkel, Rabbi Osjasz Feiwel 192
Friedman, Filip:
  approach to writing Jewish history 6, 163, 191–2, 219–21, 230, 235, 260–1
  career 111, 117 n.39, 187, 188, 214, 265, 266, 269
  death 265
  documenting fate of Jews in Lwów 264
  economic history perspective 236–7, 241, 245
  history of Jewish community in Łódź 141, 144, 150, 154–5, 156, 225, 232
  influence 261, 267
  Institute of Jewish Studies 122, 202
  London conference plan 133
  on *Miesięcznik Żydowski* 139
  on Ringelblum's work 153 n.233
  on sources lost in Holocaust 269
  plan for international organization of Jewish studies 134
  PTH membership 145
  publications 140, 141, 144, 265
  relationship with YIVO Institute 131
  research agenda 215, 225–6, 261
  reviews 152, 154–5
  sense of mission towards Jewish and Polish audiences 214, 220
  Seventh International Congress of Historical Studies 134
  Zionism 131

**G**
Galicia:
  Agudas Achim association 55
  Askenazy and the academic training of Polish Jewish historians 65–70, 90–1
  Bałaban and Schorr: Galician academic historians 70–3
  collecting circles 127 n.91
  historians 49, 52, 62, 63 n.1, 90–1, 268
  importance of Jewish history 54–5
  Jewish education 186, 189, 198–9
  Jewish intelligentsia 61, 64, 86, 88–9, 110, 172, 198, 203
  Jewish landowners 239 n.135
  model of historical scholarship 7, 64–5, 92–108, 161
  modernizing Jewish circles 15, 64
  political developments 9, 66
  rabbis 209, 210
  research agenda 90, 224
  Shatzky's career 74–5, 115
  Vienna influence 110, 111

Warsaw influence 110, 111–12
Zionist movement 89
Gąsiorowska, Natalia 152, 237, 238
Gawurin, Abraham 230
Geiger, Abraham 93, 174, 237
Gelber, Nathan Michael 73, 147, 178, 222
Gerber, Rafał 254–5, 265
German:
  burghers 30
  empire 4
  Jewish–German relations 34, 43, 86, 241, 245
  Jewish historians 93, 219
  Jewish historiography 8, 12, 94
  Jewish journals 50
  Jewish writing 44
  Jewry 5, 6, 27, 74, 79, 88, 104
  language 4, 49, 106, 139, 179, 193 n.175, 241, 242, 244, 270
  population in Poland 27, 30, 34, 99–100, 167, 175, 241, 242
  scholarly network 61 n.290
Gerszater, Hirz 230
Gertner, Haim 48
Gessen, Iulii (Juliusz) 93, 225
Getter, Abraham 230
Gierowski, Józef A. 270
Ginzberg, Rabbi Louis 267
Glejzer, Herz 236 n.118, 238
Głos Gminy Żydowskiej 172, 240 n.139
Głos Związkowy 75
Głowacki, Bartosz 81
Goldberg, Jakub 270
Goldmann, Nahum 5
Goliger, Mojżesz 122
Golinkin, Rachel 127
Gottlieb, Maurycy 247–8
Gottlieb, Samuel 230
Graetz, Heinrich:
  account of hasidism 51–2, 92
  approach to writing Jewish history 97, 174, 237
  criticisms of 51, 92, 93, 95
  *Geschichte der Juden* (History of the Jews) 49–51
  influence 49–51, 56, 61, 91–2, 99
Grodno 49 n.224, 210, 212, 228, 233
Gumplowicz, Ignacy 82

Gumplowicz, Ludwik:
  approach to Jewish history 9, 23–4, 26–7, 61, 245
  career 16 n.14, 24 n.56
  legal history 23–4, 29–30, 31–2, 40–1, 245
  on German treatment of Jews 34
  on Jewish–non-Jewish relations 28–30, 31–2, 35, 41
  publications 24
  relationship with Schorr 70–1, 89, 91, 94 n.201
  research 93
Gumplowicz, Maksymilian 27 n.74, 70
Gutman, Israel 271

**H**
Hafner, Falik 118, 126, 129, 219, 220, 264
*Hamazkir* 55
Handel, Michael 188, 266
Handelsman, Marceli:
  approach to Polish Jewish history 1, 115, 116, 123, 134, 156, 159
  career 1, 114–16, 148
  Fifth Congress of Polish Historians 146
  International Congress of Historical Studies 134, 147
  students 2, 115–16, 148, 159
  support for Bałaban 156
  threatened at Warsaw University 157
  Warsaw University role 114–15, 123
*Hapardes* 55
Harkavy, Avraham 49, 50, 53 n.245, 91, 95, 105
Hartglas, Apolinary 171
Hashomer Hadati 201, 205
hasidism:
  Askenazy's view of 79
  Bałaban's approach 198, 233
  Czacki's work 43 n.185
  Galician historians' view of 95
  Graetz's critical history 51, 92
  *Izraelita*'s coverage 51
  Kandel's view of 84, 85
  Maciejowski's view of 25, 42
  Mahler's work 270
  Neufeld's view of 38 n.151, 39
  Nussbaum's interpretation 51–2
  Schiper's work 180, 264

318                                  *Index*

hasidism (*cont.*):
  Smoleński's view of 42
  Weissberg's work 104
Haskalah (Jewish Enlightenment) 14, 74, 104, 105, 178, 233, 270
*Hatsefirah* 50, 51, 60
*Haynt* 172, 183
Hebrew language:
  chroniclers 54, 62
  collecting Hebrew manuscripts 59, 223
  dates 74 n.57
  Dubnow's work 55, 57
  education 111, 121, 122, 184, 186–91, 197, 202, 205
  grammar 15, 122, 205
  ignorance of 69
  interpretation of unknown documents 66, 69–70
  Jewish citizens of Poland reading 4
  literature 77, 105, 202, 205
  living language 105, 118
  local studies 63, 233
  popular writing on Jewish history 10
  press 55, 59, 60, 171, 172
  publications on Jewish history 15, 47, 48, 49, 54, 65, 73, 139, 149–50, 181, 233, 268, 270
  rabbis 195–6
  Schorr's work 98–9
  Shatzky's work 74 n.57, 81 n.100
  sources 57, 98, 155, 225
  translation from 17 n.15
  translation into 1 n.1, 50, 171, 270
Hebrew University, Jerusalem:
  Association of the Friends of the 131, 272
  foundation 121, 131
  Institute of Jewish Studies 124, 131, 132
  Shatzky's library collection 269
  suggestion of Polish chair 147
  support for 131
Heilpern, Maksymilian 248
Herzl, Theodor 89
Heschel, Abraham Joshua 122
Hirschberg, Adolf 152
Historical-Ethnographic Commission 53
Hitler, Adolf 221, 251, 258
Holocaust:
  deaths of Polish Jewish historians 2, 6, 264, 270
  destruction of Polish Jewish communities 2, 265, 266, 272
  destruction of sources 269
  memorials of historians 267
  preservation of community records 272
  research and documentation 268, 270–1
  survival of Jewish historians 2, 264–6
Hundert, Gershon D. 271

I

Iłowajski (Ilovaysky), Dmitrij 154
Inglot, Stefan 114 n.22, 156
Institute of Jewish Studies, Jerusalem 124, 131, 132
Institute of Jewish Studies, Warsaw:
  Bałaban's role 112, 121–2, 123, 126, 229, 234
  Central Archives of Polish Jewry project 135
  collection of historical documents 261
  criticisms of 124
  finances 139, 204
  foundation 121–2, 201
  graduates 207–8, 209
  influence postwar 269
  link to Warsaw University 121, 123
  patrons 7
  publishing 139, 144
  rabbinical training 122, 185, 200, 201–4, 206–7
  relationship with YIVO Institute 131
  Seventh International Congress of Historical Studies (1933) 134
  staff 111, 118, 122, 208–9
  students 118, 124–5, 189, 191, 206–7, 229–30, 266
  training for Jewish teachers 122, 185, 187
Institute of National Studies 156, 164
International Congress of Historical Studies 134, 147, 237
Israel Ben Shabbetai (the Kozienice Maggid) 84
Isserles, Rabbi Moses 48 n.222, 198
*Izraelita* 15, 36, 44, 51, 53, 54 n.251, 58, 59, 60, 67, 68–70, 75

J

Jagiełło, Eugeniusz 77
Jan de Capistrano 34
Jarosław 152, 217, 231

Jewish Association for Primary and
  Secondary Schools 186
Jewish Historical-Ethnographic Society 53,
  75, 93, 96, 97
Jewish Tourist Association 141
Jolles, Samuel 143
Joselewicz, Berek:
  anniversary of birthday 213
  commemorative album 143
  example of Jewish patriotism 80–1, 90, 96,
    190, 211, 212, 247
  grave 213
  national identity 248
  reformer role 80
  role in Kościuszko uprising 77, 80, 248,
    254
  son 179
Jost, Isaac 19, 53 n.249, 93, 95, 99, 174
*Jutrzenka* 15, 17, 19, 20, 24, 51

**K**

Kaczmarczyk, Kazimierz 226
*kahal (kehalim)* 38, 40–1, 57–8, 99, 104, 238
Kalina, Antoni 151
Kalisz 143, 228
Kalmanowicz, Zelig 128, 129 n.97
Kandel, Dawid 74, 76, 78 n.77, 80, 82–7, 90
Karo, Joseph 189, 205
Karwasińska, Jadwiga 153–4
Kassow, Samuel 88, 157
Kayserling, Meyer 95
Kazimierz the Great, King:
  death 27
  Jewish judicial system 40
  Jewish policies 28–9, 166, 169, 170, 175–6
  privileges for Jews 24, 28–9, 40, 190
*kehilah* 104, 168, 182
  Jewish nationalist takeover of, feared by
    Polish officials 204 n.231
Kempner, Rafał 74, 76, 84–5
Kermish, Joseph 265
Kipa, Emil 80 n.93, 148
Klauzner, Izrael 150
Kochanowski, Jan Karol 112, 116
Koczy, Leon 155
Kołodziejska, Zuzanna 33 n.118, 36, 54 n.251
Kon, Pinchas 127, 148, 149, 150 n.213, 225
Konopczyński, Władysław 145

Konopnicka, Maria 252
Korduba, Myron 123, 147
Kornitzer, Rabbi 192
Kościuszko, Tadeusz:
  'essence of Polishness' 251
  Jewish attitudes to uprising 248, 254, 255,
    258
  relationship with Jews 81, 96, 252
  uprising 77, 80, 82, 181, 213, 248
Kozłowski, Aleksander 188
*KPBPŻwP* (A Quarterly Devoted to the
  Jewish Past in Poland) 76–8, 81, 91
Kraków:
  Association of Organizations of Jewish
    Invalids and Military Orphans 212
    n.280
  blood libel accusations 35 n.126
  city's relationship with Jews of Kazimierz
    86
  Commonwealth 101
  Dembitzer's work 48 n.222
  elite of Jewish community 181
  history of rabbinate 231
  Institute of History 113
  Jewish creditors 176
  Jewish historical studies 26
  Jewish–non-Jewish relations 33 n.115, 34
    n.123
  Jewish schools 189, 190, 192
  Jewish support for Polish national cause
    180
  local urban and regional history 227
  National Museum 247
  Polish Academy of Letters 156
  Polish historical tradition 16
  press 75, 182 n.110
  publishing 14, 24, 98
  records of Jewish community 71
  school of Polish history 78
  seminary for teachers 185
  services for Jewish soldiers 193 n.174
  studies of Jewish community 1, 49 n.224,
    98, 142, 150, 224, 230, 233, 250
  synagogues 192
  Tachkemoni school 189
  Third Congress of Polish Historians
    (1900) 98, 146, 223

Kraków (cont.):
  university (Jagiellonian) 9, 24, 25, 66, 73, 75, 112, 113
Krämer, Mojżesz 137, 217–18, 230, 258
Kraszewski, J. T. 225
Kraszyńska, Fani 230
Kraushar, Aleksander:
  approach to Jewish history 9, 17–18, 23, 26, 29–30, 61, 98
  career 17, 82
  Congresses of Polish Historians 146
  criticisms of Graetz 51
  on archival materials 20, 25 n.68
  on Jewish education 39–40, 41–2
  on Jewish institutions 39
  on Jewish–non-Jewish relations 31, 33 n.115, 34–6
  on legal status of Jews 29–30
  publications 17–18, 20, 39, 44
  relationship with Schorr 71
  relationship with Shatzky 74
  writing in Polish 73
Krone, Moshe 201, 204–5, 206, 207 n.254, 208
*Kronik fun der yidisher kehile* 172
Kruk, Herman 139 n.155, 263 n.4
*Krytyka* 75
Kukiel, Marian 145, 148, 211 n.277
Kuperstein, Isaiah 269
Kutno 137, 231
Kutrzeba, Stanisław:
  attitude to Jews 156, 216, 239
  call for local studies 223, 226
  on Polish–Jewish relations 242, 245 n.169, 247, 259
*Kwartalnik Historyczny* 68 n.20, 71, 98, 140, 145 n.187, 147, 156, 159

**L**

Landy, Michał 77, 82
languages 4, 105–6
  *see also* German; Hebrew; Polish; Russian; Yiddish
Lauer, Bernard 74–5, 86
Lelewel, Joachim 179, 251, 252
Lerner, Daniel 128
Levinzohn, Yitshak Ber 45
Lieben, Koppelman 45

Liliental, Regina 149
Linder, Menachem 129
*Literarishe bleter* (*Literarish bleter*) 172
Litman, Jacob 88 n.153, 261 n.2
Łódź:
  archives 225
  historical seminar 133
  Jewish schools 111, 187, 190, 192, 266
  *kehilah* 166
  press 172, 183
  PTH 145
  studies of Jewish community 141, 144, 150, 154–5, 187, 225, 232, 235–7, 241
  synagogues 168
*Łodzer togblat* 172
Lor, Alfred 53
Lublin:
  anniversary of Berek Joselewicz's birthday 213
  Austrian occupation 173 n.46, 186
  Bałaban's role 173 n.46, 186, 209
  documentary history 226
  Hakhmei Lublin Yeshiva 203
  Jewish newspapers 172
  studies of Jewish community 143, 144, 217, 224, 230, 231, 236, 270
  Union of (1569) 166
Lubliner, Ozjasz Ludwig 179
*Lubliner togblat* 172, 173
Łuck 188, 230
Łuniński, Ernest 148
Lutman, Tadeusz 151–3
Luzzatto, Samuel David 45
Lwów:
  Association of the Lovers of Lwów's History 146
  B'nai B'rith 193
  documentation of fate of Jewish community 264
  ghetto 264
  histories of rabbis 46–7
  Institute for Training Teachers of the Mosaic Faith 185, 186
  local urban and regional history 227
  Polish Historical Association (PTH) 145
  Polish–Jewish relations 95 n.209, 244
  press 55, 147, 151, 182 n.110
  publishing 14, 191

Second Congress of Polish Historians
 (1890) 223
studies of Jewish community 94, 101, 140,
 224, 231, 233
synagogues 140, 199 n.207, 253
Temporary Governing Committee 95
university (Jan Kazimierz University) 9,
 65–6, 68, 71, 72–3, 75, 89, 110, 112, 113–14,
 115, 139, 156, 158, 210, 239

**M**
Ma'ayan, Clara Minskberg 191
Maciejowski, Wacław Aleksander:
 approach to Jewish history 9, 25
 career 25
 on legal status of Jews 26–8, 31
 on Polish–Jewish relations 27–8, 31, 34, 35
  n.128, 37, 42
 publications 25, 61
Magid, Dawid 225
Mahler, Raphael:
 approach to Jewish history 6, 9, 134, 236,
  237, 260–1
 archival research 116
 Association of History Lovers 145
 career 111–12, 214, 265
 influence 267
 lectures 194, 237
 on Ringelblum's work 117
 publications 266, 270
 relationship with Handelsman 116
 relationship with YIVO Institute 131
 research agenda 215
 Young Historians Circle 218
 Zionism 131
Mandelsberg, Bela:
 approach to Jewish history 253
 career 6, 112, 187, 260–1
 death 6, 264
 memorials 267
 popularizing history 163
 research agenda 215
 study of Jewish community in Lublin 144,
  217, 236, 270
Manekin, Rachel 73
Mansperl, Bronisław 248
Margulies, Samuel 158
Marrus, Michael 272

Marylski, Antoni 216
Meiselman, Shulamit Soloveitchik 188
Meisels, Dov Ber:
 Polish–Jewish relations 77, 180
 support for Polish independence 81, 86,
  198, 211
Meisl, Josef 155
Mickiewicz, Adam 87, 169, 251, 252
Mieses, Józef 210
Mieses, Mateusz 141 n.170, 181, 183 n.119, 193,
 267
*Miesięcznik Żydowski* 137–8, 143, 172, 173–4,
 175, 176, 182, 183, 234
Miłosz, Czesław 6
Mincberg, Jakub Lejb 141, 166, 169–70
Minskberg, Clara 125, 191, 230
Mishael, Yitzhak 205
Mizrachi movement:
 membership 7, 166, 208
 Second Convention (1919) 200–1
 Tachkemoni seminary 110, 201, 204–5, 208
 Yavne school organization 184
*Moment* 51, 183
*Der moment* 172
Montefiore, Moses 83
*Moriah* 172
Munitz, Chaim 127

**N**
Napoleon 13, 38, 78–9, 81, 101, 258
*Nasz Kraj* 75
*Nasz Kurier* 75
*Nasz Przegląd* 172, 173, 183
*Nasze życie* 131
*Nasze Życie* 187
Nathans, Benjamin 52, 57, 58 n.272
*Nayer folksblat* 172
Neufeld, Daniel:
 approach to Jewish history 17, 22, 61
 career 17
 on Jewish autonomy 38–9
 on Jewish legal status 30
 on Polish–Jewish relations 22, 23, 27, 34
 publications 17 n.15, 61, 73
Nicholas I, Tsar 83
Nissenbaum, Shlomo Baruch 49
Novosiltzev, Nikolay 79, 88
*Nowa Gazeta* 75

*Nowe Życie* 136, 172
*Nowy Dziennik* 121, 138, 172
Nusenbaum, Shlomo 173
Nussbaum, Hilary:
  approach to Jewish history 19–20, 22–3, 61
  career 18–19
  on hasidism 51–2
  on Jewish autonomy 40–1, 43
  on Jewish–non-Jewish relations 30, 34, 36, 43–4, 245
  on legal status of Jews 30–1
  publications 19, 44, 61, 98
  research 20

O
Oberlaender, Ludwik 175–7, 183, 223
*Ojczyzna* 55
Opatów 217 n.11, 230
*Opinia* 172, 173
Orlean, Jehuda Leib 185
Orzeszkowa, Eliza 252
Ostersetzer, Israel 118, 122, 125, 193, 201
Ovent-Kursn far Arbeter 194
Oyneg Shabes Archives 144, 157, 264

P
Pale of Settlement 49, 52, 55, 74
Papée, Fryderyk 217
Paskiewicz, Ivan 83, 116
Pazdro, Zbigniew 70
Peltyn, Samuel 51
*Perezhitoe* 76
Perl, Feliks 247, 248
Piłsudski, Józef:
  champion of civic equality 169, 252
  decree on rabbinic education 195
  'essence of Polishness' 251
  Handelsman's view of 114
  Legions 75, 248, 252
  patronage of publications 148
  treatment of Jewish citizens 166, 180 n.100, 192
  vision of Poland 3
Pińsk 230
*Pisma Instytutu Nauk Judaistycznych* 139
Płock 85 n.132, 232
Płoński, Salomon 88
Po'alei Zion (Workers of Zion) 7, 95, 110, 118, 194, 253–4

Poland:
  economic development after partitions 176, 255
  Jewish communal institutions after partitions 90
  Jewish history after partitions 96, 101–2, 105, 107, 178, 228
  legal status of Jews during partitions 258
  partitions 4–5
  Polish–Jewish relations before and during partitions 77, 78–9, 165–6, 169, 242, 245, 252, 255
  struggle for independence during partitions 7, 11, 247, 254, 255
  urban history after partitions 227
Poland, Congress:
  creation 84
  former territories 195
  hasidism 85
  historians 49, 52, 62, 91, 161
  Jewish communal organizations 84, 110
  Jewish economic activities 241
  Jewish educational institutions 110
  Jewish historical records 59
  Jewish history 4–5, 76
  Jewish intelligentsia 61, 86, 203
  Jewish 'reactionary heritage' 43
  modernizing Jewish circles 15
  Polish–Jewish relations 23, 34, 86, 176, 179, 180, 247
  Russian policies 83, 116, 228
  Schiper's work 152 n.223
  Shatzky's work 116
  status of Jews 85–6
  study of Polish history 62
  urban centres 111
Poland, Kingdom of:
  Jewish history publications 49
  Jewish–non-Jewish relations 33, 35, 87, 102, 176
  Jewish privileges 28–9, 31–2, 40–1, 174, 240
  Jewish self-government 38
  legal status of Jews 29–32
  Russian perspective 68
Polish Academy of Letters 148, 156
Polish Commission for the History of Social Movements 145

Polish Historical Association (PTH) 133, 145, 146, 147 n.194
Polish language:
  education 42, 63, 74, 147, 190, 196
  Jewish citizens of Poland reading and speaking 4, 6
  Jewish historians 63, 108
  Jewish integration into Polish society 19, 44, 55
  Jewish–non-Jewish relations 39
  Jews in Galicia 104, 105–6, 110
  press 15, 55, 121, 172–3
  publications of Jewish history 14, 15, 16, 51
  rabbis 209
Polish–Lithuanian Commonwealth:
  Bałaban's tales of daily life 1
  Galicia 7
  Jewish autonomy 11, 16, 104, 172
  Jewish economic activities 175, 240, 247, 262
  Jewish education 41, 84
  Jewish institutions 15, 16, 38, 57, 84–5, 90, 101, 104
  Jewish–non-Jewish relations 33, 35, 36, 67, 68, 78, 82, 243, 245, 247, 252
  Jewish participation 13–14
  Jewish settlement patterns 40
  legal status of Jews 29, 30–1, 53, 97, 258
  multi-ethnic traditions 115, 214
  partitions 3, 5, 61 n.290, 255
  rabbinical training 198
  reform projects 25, 151, 171, 178
  studies of communities 44
  studies of Jewish history 49, 53, 54, 76, 101, 148, 190, 232, 255
Polish Ministry of Education 186–7
Polish Ministry of Religion and Education:
  funding 184, 204
  Institute of Jewish Studies 202, 204
  Jewish private schools 184
  rabbinical seminaries 195–6, 201 n.215, 204
  Schorr's role 186–7
  Tachkemoni 201 n.215, 204, 207 n.252
Polish Republic, Second (1918–39):
  academic community 109
  exclusionary nationalism 2
  importance of Jewish history 3–6, 11, 159–61, 183, 213–14, 222, 240–2, 262–3

Jewish autonomy issue 172, 181–3
Jewish–non-Jewish relations 115, 145, 157, 243, 251–2
Jewish patriotism 180–1, 262
Jewish political representation 163–71
Jews in armed forces 209–10
local history research 225–9
military rabbis 210–13
rabbinical seminaries 185
role of historians 145
role of Jewish historians 8, 9–10, 12, 70, 108, 113, 157, 162–4, 222, 233
status of Jews in eastern borderlands 175
Polonsky, Antony 271
Pomorski, Leon 183
Poniatowski, Prince Józef 81
Posen region 49, 96
Poznań:
  archives 71
  Fourth Congress of Polish Historians (1925) 146, 216 n.3, 226
  Jewish–non-Jewish relations 35 n.126, 36 n.134
  local urban and regional history 227
  publishing 14
  studies of Jewish community 49 n.224, 143
  university 151, 155
Poznański, Samuel:
  call for a modern yeshiva 196–7, 200–1
  career 59, 197, 198
  collecting historical records 59
  death 120, 209
  Judaic University project 120–1
  rabbinical training concerns 59, 185, 196–7, 200, 208
  relationship with Shatzky 75
Pozner, Rabbi Chaim 211–12
Prochaska, Antoni 217
Prokop-Janiec, Eugenia 137
Prussia:
  partitioning power 4, 13, 227
  Posen region 96
  studies of Prussian partition 61 n.290, 63, 99
  treatment of Jews 28 n.79
*Przegląd Historyczny* 98, 147, 148, 158

Przemyśl:
  B'nai B'rith  141 n.170, 183 n.119, 193
  Institute of Judaic Studies  141 n.170
  studies of Jewish community  217–18, 224,
    226, 228 n.70, 230, 231
*Przyszłość*  89
Ptaśnik, Jan  153, 156, 217, 239
PTH, *see* Polish Historical Association

**R**
Raab, Rabbi  213
Reichzeig, Azriel  129
Reisen, Zalman  128
Ringelblum, Emanuel:
  approach to writing Polish Jewish history
    6, 9–10, 119–20, 126, 134, 163, 215, 226,
    232–3, 260
  article on reform projects  151
  Aspirantur programme  129
  Association of History Lovers (TMH)
    145, 153–4
  background  111
  career  111, 115, 116–17
  death  264
  funding issues  137, 143–4, 148
  history of Warsaw Jewish community
    143–4, 148, 150, 153–4, 228
  influence  188, 261
  Institute  267
  lectures  194
  on *Bleter far geshikhte*  137
  on importance of archival material  225,
    229
  on Jewish participation in the Kościuszko
    uprising  254–5
  on local history  228, 229, 230
  on Polish–Jewish relations  243, 244–7
  on Russian government during partitions
    228
  on Russian–Jewish relations  250
  on Warsaw Institute  124
  Oyneg Shabes Archives  157, 264
  Polish Commission for the History of
    Social Movements  145
  political affiliation  253
  publications  143–4, 151, 153–4, 164, 219, 232
  relationship with Handelsman  115, 116
  relationship with YIVO Institute  119, 131
  research agenda  119, 215
  reviews of work  153–4, 155, 254–5
  sense of mission towards Jewish and Polish
    audiences  214, 222
  studies of  8, 157, 268
  Warsaw Seminar  112, 116–19
  work in Warsaw ghetto  8, 157, 264
  Young Historians Circle  218, 232
  Zionism  131, 253
*Roczniki dziejów społecznych i gospodarczych*
  151
*Roczniki Łódzkie*  149
Rosenbaum, Ezechiel  230
Rosenblatt, Isaak  137
Rotwand, Jakób  82
Rubinstein, Izaak  165–6, 168, 170
Rutkowski, Jan  151, 237, 253 n.216
Russia:
  historians  154, 155
  Jewish historiography  52–4, 55–8
  Jewish intelligentsia  52
  legal status of Jews  27 n.74, 52–3, 74–5
  partitioning power  4, 13, 63, 68, 166, 171,
    177, 227
  Russian Jewish historians  93–4, 96–7
  Russian–Jewish relations  74–5, 78–9,
    82–3, 242, 250
  secret police  88
  tsarist government policies  228
  uprising against (1794)  43, 181, 213, 248
  uprising against (1863)  1, 16, 19, 80, 81, 82,
    86, 101, 158, 180, 247
  Warsaw administration  79
Russian language  4, 42 n.177, 45, 49–50, 105,
  106
Rybarski, Roman  239, 240, 242–3, 247 n.183

**S**
Sawicki, Aron (Soviv)  162, 198 n.202, 267
Schall, Jakub  73, 141, 142, 152, 214, 264
Schiper, Ignacy:
  approach to writing Polish Jewish history
    6, 9–10, 94–5, 99, 218–21, 225, 233–7, 260
  background  73
  career  73, 109, 110, 111, 164, 214
  current reputation  8
  death  264
  funding for publications  142–4

history of Jewish community in
    Drohobycz 143
ideological position 237, 238
Institute of Jewish Studies 122, 202
Institute of National Studies 164
Jewish Historical-Ethnographic Society
    93
local studies 94
niece 260
on anti-Jewish violence 250
on Dubnow 92
on Graetz 91–2, 95
on Jewish–non-Jewish relations 102
on Jewish role in trade 216, 221, 234, 240,
    242
on Polish–Jewish relations 168–9, 179–80,
    243–4, 245–6
on political borders before partitions
    96–7
popularizing history 163
publications 91, 106, 139, 142, 147, 219, 220,
    260
relationship with Askenazy 65 n.6, 70
relationship with B'nai B'rith 193
relationship with Hebrew University in
    Jerusalem 131, 134
relationship with Polish historians 155, 156
relationship with YIVO Institute 131, 134
research agenda 215, 256
reviews of his work 151
sense of mission towards Jewish and Polish
    audiences 107, 161, 214
students 160, 261
studies of his works 268
studies of Jewish economic history and
    statistics 95, 99, 100, 237
Warsaw seminar in Polish Jewish history
    112, 119
Wawelberg Prize 70, 139
work during Holocaust 264
work for National Library in Jerusalem 131
writing in Jewish press 172
Zionism 89, 131
Schorr, Mojżesz:
    approach to writing Polish Jewish history
        6, 9–10, 94–5, 99, 226, 234, 260, 267
    argument for chairs in Jewish history 120
    background 73

B'nai B'rith membership 163, 193
career 71–2, 73, 109, 110, 144, 164, 167, 214
Congresses of Polish Historians 98, 146
current reputation 8
death 264
exhibition of Jewish antiquities plan 135
influence of Graetz on 91
Institute of Jewish Studies 121–2, 208
Institute of National Studies 164
local studies 94, 230–1
membership of national and local Polish
    historical associations 145
on Bałaban's Warsaw appointments 123
on importance of Hebrew sources 98–9
on Institute of Jewish Studies 201–2
on internal Jewish history 98
on Jewish collective 95–6
on Jewish community in Przemyśl 217–18,
    231
on Jewish–non-Jewish relations 98, 102–3
on Jewish occupational structure 239–40
on Jewish patriotism 252
on local studies 223–4
on Polish Jewish historiography 99
on Polish–Jewish relations 169, 252
on political borders and partitions 96–7,
    228
on rabbinate of the Association of Rabbis
    with Higher Education 199–200
popularizing history 163
publications 91, 106, 111, 140, 147, 219
rabbi at Tłomackie Synagogue 209
relationship with Askenazy 70
relationship with Bałaban 72
relationship with Polish historians 156
research agenda 215, 256
role in Hebrew University in Jerusalem
    131, 132, 134
sense of mission towards Jewish and Polish
    audiences 100–1, 107, 161, 214, 258
students 160
Warsaw seminar in Polish Jewish history
    119
Wawelberg Prize 70, 139
work in Jewish education 186–7
World Congress of Jewish Studies
    initiative 132–3

Schorr, Mojżesz (*cont.*):
  writing in Jewish press 172
  Zionism 89–90
Schulman, Elias 129
Schwartz, Herman 194
Schwarzbart, Ignacy 121, 131 n.107
Second World War 4, 181, 252, 262–3
Seidman, Hillel 125, 135–6, 231, 264, 265
Semkowicz, Aleksander 223
Shabatean movement 93, 233
Shabetai Tsevi 84 n.123, 90, 189
Shatzky, Jacob:
  approach to writing Jewish history 261
  background 74
  career 73, 74–5, 115–16, 134 n.120, 265
  history of Warsaw Jews 270
  influence 249
  library collection 269
  on importance of archives 162
  on Polish–Jewish relations 81–2
  on tsarist treatment of Jews 83
  publications 75, 81–3, 261
  relationship with Askenazy 74–5
  relationship with Handelsman 116, 156 n.252
  relationship with Kraushar 74
  relationship with Lauer 74–5
  war service 75
Shneur Zalman of Lyady 83 n.114, 85
Shulman, Kalman 50
Siemieński, Jan Józef 148, 153–4
Słonim 230
Słonimski, Chaim Zelig 74
Smoleński, Władysław:
  approach to Jewish history 9, 24–5, 26, 61
  on Frankist movement 42–3
  on hasidism 42
  on Jewish autonomy 41
  on Jewish privileges 27–8
  on Jewish separatism 31
  on Polish–Jewish relations 31–2, 37–8, 41
  on religious tolerance 31
  publications 24–5
Smolka, Franciszek 252
Smuczkewicz, Chana, *see* Szmuszkowiczówna
Society for the Advancement of Judaic Studies in Poland 121

Society for Jewish Scholarly Publications 54
Sokołów, Nachum 50, 59–60
Soloveitchik, Rabbi Moshe 201, 205–6
Sommerstein, Emil 165–9
Sonnenschein, Efraim 212, 231
*Sprawy Narodowościowe* 164
Stand, Adolf 95
Stanisław August, King 36, 38
Staszic, Stanisław 178
Stawski, Borys 131
Steffen, Katrin 173
Stein, Menachem (Edmund) 122, 193
Steinberg, Baruch 210–11, 212
Steinberg, Mojżesz 152, 217, 230–1
Steinschneider, Hillel Noah, *see* Sztajnsznajder
Steinschneider, Moritz 95
Stendig, Samuel 190, 249
Straszun, Matitiahu 45
Święcicki, Hilarion 134, 147
Szaraniewicz, Izydor 71
Szenhak, Stanisław 50
Szlagowski, Antoni 123
Szmuszkowiczówna, Chana 127, 150
Sztajnsznajder, Hillel Noe 225
Szulman, Mordechai 205

T
Tachkemoni:
  Kraków secondary school 189
  Warsaw rabbinical seminary 110, 192, 200–9
Taffet, Gershon (Gerszon) 269
Tarnopol 135, 230
Tartakower, Arie 122, 164, 181, 189
Tauber, Majer 122, 191
Tcherikower, Elias 117, 119 n.50, 128
*Tel-Awiw* 172, 183
Tenenbaum, Ester (Emilia) 118
Tenenbaum, Leon 143
Thon, Abraham Ozjasz 5, 107 n.279, 187, 222, 253–4
Tikoczinski, Pinchas 127
TMH, *see* Association of History Lovers
Tomaszewski, Jerzy 270
Toruń 226
Trockenheim, Jakub 166–7
Trunk, Isaiah 127, 128, 129, 231–2, 265–6, 269

Tugenhold, Jakub 77
*Tygodnik Nowy* 172, 173
*Tygodnik Żydowski* 172
Tykociński, Pinchas, *see* Tikoczinski

U
Union of Jewish Participants in the Struggles for Poland's Independence 164, 192, 194, 220 n.25
Urbach, Janusz Konrad 222
*Urzędowa Gazeta Gminy Izraelickiej* 172

V
Veidlinger, Jeffrey 94, 97
Vienna:
  Galician historians 110, 111
  Imperial Ministry of Religion and Education 72 n.44
  Rabbinical Seminary 71, 198, 203, 210
  training teachers of Jewish religion 186
  university 9, 71, 73, 111, 188, 210
Vinaver, Maksim 93
*Voskhod* 55, 76, 93

W
Wagner, Artur 152
Wajngarten, Jerachmiel 191
Wajsblum, Marek 188
Warężak, Jan 154–5
Warsaw:
  archives 20, 59, 71, 75, 135–6, 148, 210, 225, 263, 270
  Association of History Lovers (TMH) 145, 148, 153
  B'nai B'rith 123, 135, 142, 157, 193–4
  Board of Education 206
  burghers 36, 41
  Duchy 13, 67 n.17, 78–9, 82, 84, 247
  Fifth Congress of Polish Historians (1930) 124, 146, 228
  First Convention of the Jewish Merchants in Poland 194
  Galician historians 110, 111–12
  German occupation 112 n.13
  ghetto 2, 8, 144, 157, 259, 263–4, 265
  Historical Commission 112, 117, 126, 127, 129, 130, 235
  History Seminar 116–17, 119, 133
  Institute of History 114

Institute of Jewish Studies, *see* Institute of Jewish Studies
Jewish Academic Centre 116
Jewish historians from Galicia 107–8, 110
Jewish Historical Institute 267, 269–70, 272
Jewish historical studies 26
Jewish integrationist group 18
Jewish intelligentsia 17, 66, 85
Jewish–non-Jewish relations 36, 41, 154, 178–9, 221
Jewish population 32 n.113, 36
Jewish schools 42, 189–91, 192
Judaica Library 59–60
*kehilah* 85 n.130, 166, 194, 209
Learned Society (TNW) 114, 148
local urban and regional history 227
pogrom (1454 or 1455) 154, 246
Polish historians 97
Polish Historical Association (PTH) 145
Polish historical tradition 16
press 15, 17, 60, 75, 76, 98, 147, 172, 183
progressive Jewish circles 42, 43
publishing 50, 171
Rabbinical School 15, 43, 198, 203
Russian Imperial University 112 n.13, 114
'school' of Jewish historians 108
Second Convention of Mizrachi 200
secretaries of Jewish community 74 n.53, 82
Seventh International Congress of Historical Studies 134
State Seminary for Teachers of the Mosaic Faith 185, 187
studies of Jewish community 19, 23, 44, 143–4, 150, 153–4, 176–7, 232, 241, 244, 270
synagogues 59, 140, 192, 209
Tachkemoni rabbinical school 110, 192, 200–8
Theological Seminary 25
Tsisho Seminary for Teachers 185
university 25, 65, 86, 109, 112 n.13, 114, 123–5, 159, 266; History Department 7, 116, 123, 159, 187
Young Historians Circle 117, 119–20, 137, 228–9, 236, 257, 265, 266
Warszawska, Hava-Joheved 118

Warszawski, S. 176, 177, 179
Wasiutyński, Wojciech 156
Wasserman, Pinchas 251
Wawelberg, Hipolit 66, 70
    prize competition 66–70, 76, 78, 139, 140
Weinreich, Max 128
Weinryb, Bernard D. 269
Weiss, Abraham 89, 122, 193, 267
Weissberg, Maksymilian 104, 105–6
Wettstein, P. H. 98
Wielopolski, Aleksander 83
Wiesenfeld, Franciszka (Tzafrira Azrieli) 266
Wikler, Jakób 230
Wilno:
    An-ski Historical-Ethnographic Association 149
    antisemitism 182, 250
    archives 149, 225
    Aspirantur programme 126–9
    chief rabbi 165
    Congress of Polish Historians (1935) 146
    Jewish schools 189
    Jewish teacher training 129 n.98, 185, 188
    *kahal* 127, 225
    pogrom (1919) 116
    press 75
    publishing 148
    Rabbinical School 128
    studies of Jewish community 44–5, 49 n.224, 150, 228, 230, 233
    university (Stefan Batory) 6, 113, 127, 149, 210
    YIVO 7, 117, 120, 126, 130, 261
Winkler, S. 191
Wischnitzer, Mark 73, 152
Wissenschaft des Judentums (study of Judaism):
    celebration of religious sages 58
    compared with maskilic literature 16 n.12
    compared with Polish Jewish scholarship 93
    compared with traditional textual study 203
    emergence 14
    Graetz's work 91
    influence 6, 15, 19
    Russian interest in 52

Witkowski, Stanisław Józef 89
Wohl, Henryk 80, 247, 248
Wojciechowski, Tadeusz 67, 71
*Wschód* 172
Wurm, Dawid:
    career 111, 187
    death 6, 264
    funding for his work 222
    history of Jewish community in Brody 141, 152–3, 187, 222, 230, 238
    Lutman's review of his work 151, 152–3

**Y**

Yerushalmi, Yosef Hayim 11–12
Yiddish:
    academic scholarship in 112
    B'nai B'rith library 193 n.175
    folk culture 95
    folklore 143 n.178
    hasidism and 95
    ignored by Warsaw Institute 124
    'jargon' 42 n.177, 81 n.100, 105
    Jewish citizens of Poland reading and speaking 4
    Jewish education 42, 129 n.98, 185
    Jewish historians 106, 262, 268
    importance of publishing in 118
    linguistic dissimilation 44
    linguistics, philology, and literature 128
    mission of furthering scholarship in Yiddish 117, 232 n.95
    modern historical scholarship 9
    popular historical articles 10
    press 117–18, 137, 139, 144, 162, 171–2, 181
    publications 8, 106, 137, 149, 270
    rabbinical education 205
    rabbis 198, 213
    research in interwar Poland 269
    schooling 184, 189 n.154
    traditional Jewish homes 6, 12, 74
    translation from 210 n.271, 212 n.286, 213 n.288
    translation into 50, 51 n.236, 92 n.183, 108, 171
    wartime military call-up 75
    YIVO's agenda 130
Yiddish Scientific Institute (YIVO):
    approach to Jewish history 219, 220

Aspirantur graduate programme 126–30, 158
Berlin Historical Section 117, 119, 120, 229
collecting and cataloguing 126
foundation 117, 130
information for Jewish politicians 164
Institute for Jewish Research in New York 260, 265, 266, 269, 272
Institute in Wilno 117, 120, 126, 103, 261
patrons 7
publishing 126, 139, 271
relationship with Institute of Jewish Studies 131, 134, 139
Seventh International Congress of Historical Studies (1933) 134
staff 111
training for Jewish teachers 187
Warsaw Historical Commission 112, 117, 126, 127, 129, 130, 235
Yiddish language 9, 130
*Dos yidishe togblat* 172
*YIVO Bleter* 128
*Yunger historiker* 117–18, 120, 137, 231, 232

Z

Zamość 188, 230
Zgał, Pinkas 213
Zionism:
  emergence 77
  historians' membership and activities 89–90, 95, 131–2
  range of perspectives 7–8, 87–8
  Tachkemoni and the Institute of Jewish Studies 203, 204–5, 206
Ziv, Michael 266
Zmigryder-Konopka, Zdzisław
  approach to Jewish history 168
  career 164
  on Jewish position in 1938 258 n.233
  on Polish–Jewish relations 165 n.13, 247, 249, 251
Żółkiew 47–8, 141, 142, 233
*Życie Żydowskie* 172

www.ingramcontent.com/pod-product-compliance
Lightning Source LLC
Chambersburg PA
CBHW061421300426
44114CB00015B/2021